A CHRONOLOGICAL HISTORY

OF THE

ORIGIN AND DEVELOPMENT

OF

STEAM NAVIGATION.

BY

GEO. HENRY PREBLE,
REAR-ADMIRAL U.S.N.

Copyright © 2018 Read Books Ltd.
This book is copyright and may not be
reproduced or copied in any way without
the express permission of the publisher in writing

British Library Cataloguing-in-Publication Data
A catalogue record for this book is available from
the British Library

PREFACE.

THIS volume is the outgrowth of a newspaper article on the origin, etc., of steam navigation, published in the Boston *Commercial Bulletin* in 1856 or 1857. My interest having been attracted to the subject, I have continued for twenty-five years to collect Notes for a History of Steam Navigation, most of which have been printed in the *United Service* during the last eighteen months.

Those Notes, revised and chronologically arranged, with many additions, are the substance of this volume, which is believed to contain more facts relating to the progress of steam navigation over the world than have ever been gathered together in one book. The large share which is shown that Americans have had in the invention of the steamboat will be gratifying to my countrymen.

To record all the improvements in the marine steam-engine from its inception to the present time would require many volumes. The abridgments or index of the specifications of patents in the English Patent-Office, relating to marine propulsion exclusive of sails, 1618 to 1866, fill two closely-printed 12mo volumes of 333 and 440 pages. The United States Patent-Office has published no such compendium.

GEO. HENRY PREBLE.

BROOKLINE, MASSACHUSETTS, February 1, 1883.

CONTENTS.

CHAPTER I.—1543–1800.
A HISTORY OF STEAM NAVIGATION.

Early Experimenters: Blasco de Garray, 1543.—David Ramseye, 1680.—Salomon de Carrs, 1641.—Marquis of Worcester, 1663.—Denis Papin, 1690–95.—Thomas Savary, 1698.—M. Duguet, 1699.—Jonathan Hulls, 1736.—M. Gautoir, 1752.—David Bournoulli, 1753.—Euler, 1753.—Mathonde la Cour, 1753.—M. Gautoir, 1756.—M. Genevois, 1759.—Comte de Auxiron, 1774.—Perrier, 1775.—M. Ducrest, 1777.—Guyon de la Plombiere, 1776.—Andrew Ellicott, 1775.—Marquis de Jouffroy, 1778 and 1783.—Thomas Paine, 1778.—Matthew Washbrough, 1779.—Abbé Darical, 1782.—Desblancs, 1782.—James Rumsey, 1784 and 1788.—William Bushnell, Inventor of the Screw, 1784.—Joseph Bramah, 1785.—John Fitch, 1785–91.—Oliver Evans, 1788.—Nathan Read, 1788.—Patrick Millar, James Taylor, William Symington, 1788.—William Longstreet, 1790.—John C. Stevens, 1791.—Baron Seguier, 1792.—Earl Stanhope, 1792–94.—Elijah Ormsbee, 1792–94.—William Littleton, 1794.—Samuel Morey, 1794–97.—Edward Thomson, 1796.—Livingston, Stevens, and Roosevelt, 1800.—Hunter and Dickinson, 1800.—Edward Shorter, 1800—Samuel Brown, 1800 9

CHAPTER II.—1800–1819.

Wm. Symington's Steam-Tug, 1802.—Robert Fulton's French Experiments, 1802–4.—Oliver Evans, 1802–4.—Stevens, 1804.—The Clermont, Fulton's first successful Steamboat, 1807.—Robert L. Stevens, 1808.—Jonathan Nichols, 1807–9.—Inland Steam Navigation, United States, 1809.—John Cox Stevens's Sea-Voyage, 1809.—Robert Fulton's Patent, 1811.—Rapid Traveling in Steamboats, 1811.—First Steamboat on the Western Waters of the United States, 1811.—Fulton's Steamboats, 1812.—Steamboat on the Delaware, 1812.—Steamboats between Philadelphia and New York, 1818.—Hezekiah Bliss, 1810–19.—The Comet, and Henry Bell, 1812.—The Elizabeth, 1813.—The Clyde, and Glasgow, each 1813.—First Steamboat on the St. Lawrence, 1813.—Robert Fulton's Patent, 1813.—First Steamboat in India, 1810, 1819, 1821.—Early English Steamboats, 1813–15.—Loss by Wreck of Steamers in War, 1812–14.—The Margery *et al.*, 1814.—The Demologos, or Fulton the First, the First War Steamship, 1814.—Steamers in England in 1814.—The Argyle, or Thames, 1815.—Steam Navigation adopted in Russia, 1815–16.—Trevatheniet's Patents on Screw-Propeller in England, 1815.—Roosevelt claims the Invention of Paddle-Wheels, 1814–16.—Liverpool Steam Ferry-Boat, 1816.—The Majestic first to cross the English Channel, 1816.—First Line of Steamboats, New York to New London, 1816.—Iona Morgan's Steamboat in Maine, 1816.—First Steamboat commanded by Cornelius Vanderbilt, 1817.—First Steam Tow-Boat, 1816.—The Firefly, 1817.—First Steamboat on the Rhine, 1817.—The Manifest of First Steamboat to Boston, 1817.—First Steamboat on

Lake Erie, 1818.—Baltimore and Philadelphia Steamboat, 1813-15.—The first English Steam-Tug, 1818.—Steamers between the Mersey and Clyde, 1819.—First Steamer, Liverpool and Ireland, 1819 44

CHAPTER III.—1819-1838.

The Savannah, the First Ocean Steamship, 1819.—David Napier's Enterprise, 1819-22.—First Steamboats on the Missouri, 1819.—The Robert Fulton Steamship between New Orleans and New York, 1819.—Walk-in-the-Water, First Steamboat on Lake Erie, 1819.—First Steamboat on Lake Michigan, 1827.—First Ramsgate Steamboat, 1820.—First Steam-Vessels in the Royal Navy, 1820-23.—French Officers sent to United States to inquire about Steam-Vessels, etc., 1820.—First Steamboat on the Indus, 1820.—First Sea-going Steamboat for Hull, England, 1821.—First Steamboat Excursion from New York to Providence, 1821.—First Steamboat Line between Providence and New York, 1822.—David Gordon's Patent for Boxing Paddle-Wheels, 1822.—Table of Comparative Voyages of Sailing- and Steam-Vessels, 1822.—Number of Steamboats on American Waters, 1823.—Captain de Lisle proposes Screws to be applied to French Ships of the Line, 1823.—Delangue, of Paris, patents a Screw, 1824.—Steamer Enterprise goes from London to Calcutta, 1825.—Jacob Perkins's Propeller, 1825.—Samuel Brown's Canal Towing Company's Propeller, 1825.—Steamboat Speed on the Hudson, 1826.—Woodcroft's Screw, 1826.—Winter Steamboats between Philadelphia and New York, 1827.—The Atlas launched at Rotterdam, 1828.—The Swift, First Steamer in Turkey, 1828.—The Curaçoa, 1828.—The Steam-Brig New York, 1826.—Patten's Screw; Copley's Screw; Pettier's Screw, 1830.—First Steamboats on the Danube, 1830.—Temperance Resolutions of the Livingston Steam-Packet Company, 1829.—The Meteor, the First Ship of the Royal Navy to carry the Mails, 1830.—The Hugh Lindsay, First Steamer to navigate the Red Sea, 1830.—Girard's Screw, 1831.—First Steamer to arrive at Chicago, 1831.—Woodcroft's Screw, 1832.—First Wrought-Iron Steamboat, 1832.—The Firebrand's Long Voyage, 1833.—First Vessel of the Royal Navy to West Indies, 1832.—Junius Smith, the Originator of Ocean Steam Navigation, 1832-38.—The Second Steamship to cross the Atlantic, 1832.—First Steamer on the Merrimac River, 1834.—Smith's Screw, 1835.—Fitzpatrick's, 1835.—French Steamboats, 1836.—First Steamer to China, 1832.—An American Ironclad, 1836.—Commodore Barron's Ram, 1836.—Steam Tow-Boats introduced on the Delaware, 1836.—Steam-Vessels of Great Britain, 1836-37.—The Francis B. Ogden, Ericsson's First Practical Screw Steamer, 1836.—The Enterprise, 1839.—The Robert F. Stockton Screw, 1838-39.—Crossing the Atlantic under Sail.—The Princeton, First Screw War Steamer.—Smith's Screw Steamer Archimedes, 1836-88.—The Rattler, First English Screw War Steamer, 1843.—Austrian, Russian, and Hungarian Steamers, 1837.—Dr. Lardner on Steam Navigation of the Atlantic, 1837.—Steam-Vessels of the United States, 1838.—The Germ of the United States Navy, 1887 109

CHAPTER IV.—1838-1858.

The Inauguration of Regular Transatlantic Steam Navigation.—Arrival of the City of Kingston at New York from Cork, April 2, 1838.—Arrival of the Sirius from Cork and the Great Western from Bristol at New York, April 23, 1838.—The President, 1839.—The British Queen, 1839.—Dimensions of the Earliest and Largest Transatlantic Steamships, 1840.—Miscellaneous Notes.—The Cyclops, Steam Frigate, 1840.—The Nemesis,

CONTENTS.

1840.—The Screw Steamer Archimedes, 1840.—The Argyle, Chili, and Peru, 1839.—The Cunard Line Inaugurated, 1840.—The Bangor, 1842. —The French Steam Navy, 1840.—Screw Steamers in Great Britain, 1842.—Steam Navigation on the Indus, Established 1842.—The Driver, the First Steamship to Circumnavigate the Globe, 1842.—United States Steamship Princeton, the First Screw Steam War-Vessel, 1843.—H. M. Ship Rattler, the Second Screw Steam War-Vessel, 1843.—The Great Britain, 1843.—First English Steam Collier, 1844.—The Midias and Edith, the First Steam Screw Vessels to China, 1844-45.—The Witch, 1845 — American Mail Steamships to Havre and Bremen, 1845-50.—The Propeller Massachusetts, 1845.—Thames Steamboats, 1845.—The North River Steamer Oregon, 1846.—The First French Atlantic Steamer, 1847.—First American Steamer to the Pacific, 1848.—The Gemini Iron Twin Steamer, 1850.—Screw Steamship Himalaya, 1851.—The Francis Skiddy, 1852.— The Australian, 1852.—The Argo, the Second Steamship and First Screw to Circumnavigate the Globe, 1854.—The Golden Age, 1854.—The Cunard Steamer Persia, 1855.—Steam Vessels of the Royal Navy, 1856 175

CHAPTER V.—1858–1882.

The Great Eastern, 1858; Description of the Vessel, etc.; Her First Voyage to New York and Arrival described.—The Emperor, a Steam Yacht, presented to the Japanese, 1859.—The Scotland and England purchased by the Prince of Satsuma, 1861.—The Monitor, First Turreted Steam War-Vessel, 1861.—The Faid Rabani Yacht of the Khedive, 1863.—Number of British Inventions patented in the Ten Years preceding 1866.—Steamers on Lake Memphremagog, 1867.—The Kate Corser, the First Steamer on the Great Salt Lake, 1869.—An Extraordinary Inland Voyage, 1869.— Coal-Saving Discovery, 1872.—The Cable Steamer Faraday, 1873.—A Chinese Steamboat Enterprise, 1874.—The Bessemer Anti-Sea-Sick Steamboat, 1875.—The Double-Hulled Castalia, 1875.—The Iona, 1876.—Steamboats in Corea, 1878.—The Solano, 1879.—The Remarkable Voyage of a Wrecked Steamer, 1880.—The Comet on Lake Bigler, 1880.—A Mountain Steamer on Twin Lakes, 1880.—The Three Brothers transferred to the British Flag, 1880.—A Canal-Boat propelled by Air, 1880.—The Hochung, the First Chinese Steamer to cross the Pacific, 1880.—The Chinese Steamer Meefoo arrives at London with a Cargo of Tea, 1881.—Taggart's Screws, 1880.—The Anthracite, the Smallest Steamer that has crossed the Atlantic, 1880.—The Harriet Lane, 1881.—The Dessoug, 1881.—A Hydraulic Ship, 1881.—A Novel Steam Yacht, 1881.—The Kittatinny, 1881.—Steamboat Disaster, 1881.—The Fall River Line, 1882.—A West India Steamship Enterprise, 1882.—The Colossus, 1882.—Recent Novel Inventions and Experiments.—Morse's Unsinkable Ship.—Lundborg's Twin-Screws.— Root's Side-Screw Steamship.—Coppin's Triplo Steamship.—Fryer's Buoyant Propeller.—Rosse's Catamaran Steam Tugs 221

CHAPTER VI.

The Great Ocean Steamship Companies.—General Remarks, Ocean Tramps, etc.—The Cunard, 1840.—The Peninsular and Oriental, 1840. —Pacific Steam Navigation, 1840.—Royal West India Mail, 1841.— Collins Line, 1847.—Pacific Mail Steamship Company, 1848.—Warren Line, 1850.—Inman Line, 1850.—The Messageries Maritimes, 1851.— Allan Line, 1854 —Hamburg American Packet Company, 1855.—Anchor Line, 1856.—North German Lloyds, 1857.—Leyland Line, 1860.—Compagnie Générale Transatlantique, 1862.—National Steamship Company,

1863.—Williams & Guion Line, 1866.—Old Dominion Line, 1867.—White Star Line, 1870.—American or Keystone Line, 1871.—City Line.—State Line, 1872.—Red Star Line, 1873.—The Monarch Line, 1874.—Harrison Line.—Ocean Steamship Company of Savannah.—The Mitsu-Bishi Steam Navigation Company, 1875.—The Atlas Steamship Company.—Roach's United States and Brazil Steamship Line, 1875.—The Mallory Line.—The Red "D" Line, 1879.—New York, Havana, and Mexican Mail Line.—Boston and Savannah Steamship Company, 1882.—Thingvalla Line, 1882.—West India Steamship Enterprise 305

HISTORY

OF

STEAM NAVIGATION.

CHAPTER I. 1543–1800.

A HISTORY OF STEAM NAVIGATION.

Early Experimenters: Blasco de Garray, 1543.—David Ramseye, 1630.—Salomon de Carrs, 1641.—Marquis of Worcester, 1663.—Denis Papin, 1690-95.—Thomas Savary, 1698.—M. Duguet, 1699.—Jonathan Hulls, 1736.—M. Gautoir, 1752.—David Bournoulli, 1753.—Euler, 1753.—Mathon de la Cour, 1753.—M. Gautoir, 1756.—M. Genevois, 1759.—Comte de Auxiron, 1774.—Perrier, 1775.—M. Ducrest, 1777.—Guyon de la Plombiere, 1776.—Andrew Ellicott, 1775.—Marquis de Jouffroy, 1778 and 1783.—Thomas Paine, 1778.—Matthew Washbrough, 1779.—Abbé Darical, 1782.—Desblancs, 1782.—James Rumsey, 1784 and 1788. —William Bushnell, Inventor of the Screw, 1784.—Joseph Bramah, 1785.—John Fitch, 1785-91.—Oliver Evans, 1788.—Nathan Read, 1788.—Patrick Millar, James Taylor, William Symington, 1788.—William Longstreet, 1790. —John C. Stevens, 1791.—Baron Seguier, 1792.—Earl Stanhope, 1792-94.—Elijah Ormsbee, 1792-94.—William Littleton, 1794.—Samuel Morey, 1794-97. —Edward Thomson, 1796.—Livingston, Stevens, and Roosevelt, 1800.—Hunter and Dickinson, 1800.—Edward Shorter, 1800.—Samuel Brown, 1800.

1543.—It has been asserted that Blasco de Garray, a native of Biscay, June 17, 1543, tried a vessel of two hundred and nine tons, called the "Trinity," with tolerable success, at Barcelona, in Spain, the motive-power of which consisted of a caldron of boiling water and a movable wheel suspended on each side of the vessel.

The story or legend of De Garray is this:

In 1543 a native mechanic of Marina, named Blasco de Garray, or, according to other accounts, a captain in the navy, the probability being he was made one for his invention, offered to exhibit in the presence of the Emperor Charles V. a machine by means of which a vessel might be impelled without the assistance of sailors or oars. The proposition appeared ridiculous, but De Garray was so convinced that the power of his machine would be adequate to the production of the effect announced, that he renewed his representations to the government, supplicating his majesty to command the execution of the project. The emperor, in consequence, appointed a commission to proceed to Barcelona to witness the experiment and to report upon the result. De Garray, secure now of making a proof of his invention, prepared a merchant ship called "La Trinidad," of two hundred tons burden, which came from Coubre to discharge a cargo of corn at Barcelona, of which Peter de Scary was captain (thus states the record), and the commissioners, Don Henry de Toledo, the Governor Don Pedro de Cordova, the Treasurer Ravago, and the vice-chancellor, having arrived, the experiment was made on the 17th of June, 1543. Immediately upon a given signal the vessel was put in motion; proceeding forward, it turned from one side to the other, according to the will of the steersman, and finally returned to the place whence it started, without the assistance of sails, oars, or any visible machinery, except an immense caldron of boiling water, a complicated number of wheels within, and paddles gyrating without. The multitude assembled on the sea-shore were filled with admiration at the sight of this prodigy, the port of Barcelona resounded with applause, and the commissioners, who witnessed the performance with the greatest enthusiasm, related to the emperor that De Garray had accomplished with his machine all he had undertaken to do. But the head of the commission, Ravago, who was the chief treasurer of the kingdom, through ignorance or some other of those unknown causes which influence the conduct of statesmen, showed himself little favorable either to the inventor or the machine. Confessing the success of the experiment, and expressing his approbation of the ingenuity of De Garray, he endeavored to persuade the emperor that the invention would be of little or no utility; that its complicated construction would require constant repairs, attended with immense expense; that the vessel would not proceed at the rate of much more than a league an hour, and more slowly when freighted; and finally, that the boiler, unable to resist the force of the steam for any extended period, would frequently burst and be productive of the most dreadful accidents. Such was the substance of the opinion given by this covetous or invidious minister. Though Charles V. was influenced by the representations of his treasurer, he was not insensible to the merits of the inventor, whom he promoted one grade to the rank of an officer, and in addition to paying him the expenses of the experiment, presented him with a reward of two hundred thousand *maravedis* from the royal treasury, equivalent to sixty-six thousand *reales de vellon*, a very considerable sum at that period, the munificence of which proves that the invention of De Garray equaled, if it did not surpass, the most extraordinary productions of that era.

This statement was first published in 1825, by Thomas Gonzales, who certified: "This account is derived from the documents and original registers kept in the royal archives of Simancas, among the commercial papers of Catalonia, and from those of the military and naval departments for the said 1543."

Mr. Woodroft, after a careful search among those papers, failed to discover the documents in question or any trace of De Garray's invention.

John MacGragor, Esq., in a paper read before the Society of Arts, April 14, 1858, stated:

"On the 23d of September last (1857) I visited the town of Simancas, near Valladolid, in Spain, with Captain John Ussher, to inspect some letters of Blasco de Garray, which are there preserved among the national archives.

"Having obtained the requisite royal permission, I was allowed, after much difficulty, to read (but not to copy) two letters signed by Blasco de Garray, written clearly in Spanish and well preserved. One of these was addressed from Malaga, the other from Barcèlona; and both were dated A.D. 1543. They described two separate experiments with different vessels, *both of them moved by paddle-wheels turned by men.*

"One vessel was stated to be of two hundred Spanish tons burden, propelled by a paddle-wheel on each side, worked by twenty-five men. The other vessel was moved in a similar manner by forty men. The speed attained is mentioned in the texts, and is stated in a side-note (written in a different hand) to have been one league, or about three and a half English miles, per hour. Various calculations as to the tonnage, the motive-power, the cost, and other matters are contained in the letters, and it is said the vessels thus moved were found to steer well, but could be propelled more easily for a long time by oars. Also that, like other inventions, this would probably be improved by the experience of further trials. We read the letters carefully through, and *neither of them contained any mention whatever of the use of steam*, or any expression to indicate that this was contemplated."

There were no other letters of De Garray, or documents relating to his experiment, in the archives, and no traces of the relics of the machinery could be found at the school of artillery. Since Mr. MacGragor's visit M. Bergenroth has been allowed to copy the documents relating to De Garray.

1. A notograph from him to the emperor dated Malaga, September 10, 1540, containing his report on the trial of one of his paddle-wheel ships.

2. The report of Captain Des Ugasura on the same trial trip.

3. The report of the Provedores of Malaga concerning the same trip, dated July 24, 1540.

4. The report of Blasco de Garray to the emperor, dated July 6, 1543, concerning the trial trip of another of his paddle-wheel ships, made at Barcelona in June, 1543.

5. A letter of Blasco de Garray to Carrs, dated June 20, 1543. In *none of these is any reference to steam-power to be found.*

Blasco de Garray's connection with the invention of boats moved by steam, notwithstanding the prominence and general belief it has attained, may hereafter be dropped as having no foundation in fact.

1630.—In Sanderson's edition of Rymer's "Fœdera," vol. xix., there is a copy of a patent granted by Charles I. to David Ramseye, a groom of the privy chamber, dated January 21, 1630. Among its specifications is one " to raise water from low pits by fire," and another " to make boats, shippes, and barges to go against strong wind and tide."

1641.—The following letter written by Marion Delorme, dated at Paris, February, 1641, suggested to Dumas one of the best scenes in one of his wonderful romances:

"PARIS, February, 1641.

"MY DEAR EFFIAT,—While you were forgetting me at Narbonne, and giving yourself up to the pleasures of the court and the delight of thwarting M. le Cardinal de Richelieu, I, according to your express desire, am doing the honors of Paris to your English lord, the Marquis of Worcester; and I carry him about, or rather he carries me, from curiosity to curiosity, choosing always the most grave and serious, speaking very little, listening with great attention, and fixing on those whom he interrogates two large blue eyes, which seem to pierce to the very centre of their thoughts. He is remarkable for never being satisfied with any explanations which are given him; and never sees things in the light in which they are shown to him. You may judge of this by a visit we made together to Bicêtre, where he *imagined he had discovered a genius in a madman.*

"If this madman had not been actually raving I verily believe your Marquis would actually have entreated his liberty, and have carried him off to London, in order to hear his extravagances from morning to night at his ease.

"We were crossing the court of the mad-house, and I, more dead than alive with fright, kept close to my companion's side, when a frightful face appeared behind some immense bars, and a hoarse voice exclaimed, '*I am not mad! I am not mad! I have made a discovery which would enrich the country that adopted it!*' 'What has he discovered?' I asked the guide. 'Oh,' he answered, shrugging his shoulders, 'something trifling enough,—you would never guess it: IT IS THE USE OF THE STEAM OF BOILING WATER.' I began to laugh. 'This man,' continued the speaker, 'is named SALOMON DE CARRS;

he came from Normandy four years ago, to present to the king a statement of the wonderful effects that might be produced from this invention. To listen to him you would imagine that with steam you COULD NAVIGATE SHIPS, move carriages,—in fact, there is no end to the miracles which, he insists upon it, could be performed. *The cardinal sent the madman away without listening to him.* SALOMON DE CARRS, far from being discouraged, followed the cardinal wherever he went, with the most determined perseverance, who, tired of finding him forever in his path, and annoyed to death with his folly, ordered him to be shut up in the Bicêtre, where he has now been for three years and a half, and where, as you hear, he calls out to every visitor that *he is not mad, but that he has made a valuable discovery.* He has even written a book upon the subject, which I have here.'

"Lord Worcester, who had listened to this account with much interest, after reflecting a time, asked for the book, of which, after reading several pages, he said, 'This man is not mad. In my country, *instead of shutting him up,* he would have been rewarded. Take me to him, for I should like to ask him some questions.'

"He was accordingly conducted to his cell, but after a time he came back sad and thoughtful. 'He is indeed mad now,' said he; 'misfortune and captivity have alienated his reason, but it is you who have to answer for his madness. When you cast him in that cell you confined THE GREATEST GENIUS OF THE AGE!' After this we went away, and since that time he has done nothing but talk of SALOMON DE CARRS. Adieu! my dear and faithful Henry. Make haste and come back, and pray do not be so happy where you are as not to keep a little love for me.

"MARION DELORME."

1651.—An anonymous pamphlet was published in London in 1651, entitled "Inventions of Engines of Motion lately brought to Perfection," etc. The author claims "to have erected one little engine or great model at Lambeth," which among its capabilities was intended "*to draw or haul ships, boates, etc.,* up river against the stream." Steam is not indicated in the pamphlet, but it is difficult to conceive any other agent, unless some explosive compound by which the pressure of the atmosphere was exerted.

1663.—The Marquis of Worcester published a little book in 1663, which he called "A Century of the Names and Scantlings of Inventions." In it he evidently describes an engine capable of raising water by the repellant power of steam. In this book one hundred inventions are enumerated, but the account of each is so short as often to be very obscure. Among his other boasts he says, "I can make a vessel, of as great a burden as the river can bear, to go against the stream, which the more rapid it is the faster it shall advance, and the movable part that works it may be by one man still guided to take advantage of the stream, and yet steer the boat to any point; and this engine is applicable to any vessel or boat whatsoever, without therefore being made on purpose; and it worketh these effects,—it moveth, it draweth, it driveth (if need be) to pass London Bridge against the stream at low water; and a boat lying at anchor, the engine may be used for loading and unloading." A recent investigation of his patent shows, as it is expressly so stated, that he had no idea of using steam, but "the force of the wind or stream caused its motion."

1690.—Denis Papin, a French engineer, who was forced, after the revocation of the Edict of Nantes, to quit his country, took refuge at the court of the landgrave of Hesse, and was a professor of mathemathics at the University of Marburg during several years. In 1690 he published a methodical and clear description of the fire-engine, now known as the atmospherical engine, and suggested the practicability of applying the power of steam to the navigation of rivers.

1695.—Papin, in another work dated 1695, says, "It would be too long to describe here in what manner this invention (the atmospherical engine) could be applied to drain rivers, throw bombs, and *row against wind.* I cannot abstain from remarking how much this power would be preferable to that of galley-slaves to navigate with rapidity the sea." Papin next criticises the use of men as agents, who, he says, occupy a larger space, and consume a great deal, even when they do no work, and observes that his tubes or pumps would be less cumbersome; "but," he adds, "as they cannot be conveniently adapted to ply common oars, it would be necessary to apply to them rotatory oars." He mentions having seen oars of that description fixed to an axle-tree in a boat belonging to Prince Robert of Hesse, which were turned by horses. He thought, however, that they might be put in motion by the *aid of a steam-engine.* To Denis Papin is attributed the invention of the safety-valve.

The "Encyclopædia Britannica" appears to think that Papin's suggestions for the application of steam to navigation must be considered as theory alone, never carried out. But his correspondence with Leibnitz, which has recently been brought to light, fully proves *that he actually constructed a steamboat which he navigated upon the river Fulda in* 1707, which boat may serve as a warning to men not to be too clever for their age. M. Fournier relates that Papin labored at his construction for some years at Hanau, and that at Cassel the boat was launched in presence of the landgrave. The experiment succeeded, but he derived from it only scorn, ridicule, and abuse. He was treated as a charlatan and a fool. Disgusted with the conduct of the Hessians, Papin attempted to go to London in his steam-vessel. He descended the Fulda as far as Münden, and was entering the Weser, formed by the union of the Fulda and Werra, when the boatmen of

Münden, envious or suspicious of what might arise from the invention, laid violent hands upon him and his boat. He escaped with difficulty, but his boat was destroyed. He tried in vain to obtain redress; and then came to reside in London, where he died three years afterwards (1710) without having built a new boat.

1698.—July 25, 1698, Captain Thomas Savary, an Englishman, took out a patent for raising water by the impellant force of fire. The same year he recommended the use of paddle-wheels similar to those now employed on steam-vessels, though without in the remotest degree alluding to his engine as a prime mover. It is probable he intended to employ the force of men or animals working a winch. In 1696 he obtained a patent for rowing ships with greater ease and expedition than had hitherto been done by any other. In 1698 *" he believed steam might be made useful to ships,"* but not daring to meddle with the matter, left it to the judgment of those who were better judges of maritime affairs.

1699.—M. Duguet appears to have tried revolving oars; and experiments were made with them on a large scale, both at Havre and Marseilles. This mode was soon given up as impracticable.

1736.—John Barrow, under-secretary of the admiralty, in his autobiography says, "Neither Lord Stanhope, nor Fulton, nor the American Livingston, nor Patrick Millar, nor his assistant Symington, have the least claims of priority to the application of steam and wheels for propelling vessels. There can be no doubt that Jonathan Hulls was the real inventor of the steamboat."

Jonathan Hulls was a man of no ordinary capacity, but we cannot admit that " he was the inventor of the steamboat;" that must be conceded to Papin, who actually moved a boat by the power of steam on the Fulda in 1707. He, undoubtedly, in a rough way, was the first Englishman to point out how steam might be employed in the propulsion of vessels. His scheme was clever, but speculative. It did not obtain any practical trial, and like many other efforts of genius, came to nothing. John Scott Russell, in the " Encyclopædia Britannica," however, asserts that Hulls not only made a model of his invention, but that a boat was actually constructed and usefully employed.

According to the tradition of the neighborhood in which Hulls was born, he was the son of a mechanic of Hanging-Aston, near Campden, Gloucestershire; his name being entered in the baptismal register December 17, 1699. Thomas Hull, or Hulls, the father, having removed from Aston to Campden, the boy was educated at the ancient grammar school there. With a natural turn for mechanics, Jonathan Hulls was brought up as a clock-maker, or rather clock-mender,—one of an humble class of artisans whose business it is to make a circuit through a district, cleaning and repairing cottage and farm-house clocks, and the clocks of churches. He married early, and settled in the hamlet of Broad Campden about 1729.

During the earlier years of manhood Hulls bore the reputation of being a thoughtful and studious man, and his neighbors regarded his superior mental powers with no small degree of respect. It is asserted that the idea which has given him claim to posthumous honor occurred to him while he was yet young, and was matured in his mind long before any channel was opened through which he could make it known to the world; for Hulls had a family to support, and no means beyond his precarious handicraft. A patron at last appeared in Mr. Freeman, of Batsford Park, whose seat (now that of Lord Redesdale) is about a mile from Aston, the native place of the inventor. With the funds provided by this gentleman Hulls was enabled to go to London to procure a patent and to publish the pamphlet in which his invention is described.

Hulls's patent is dated December 21, 1736, when he was thirty-seven years old, and bears the sign-manual of Queen Caroline as a witness. In this instrument the invention is described as a "machine for carrying ships and vessels out of or into any harbor or river against wind and tide;" and further, it sets forth that as the inventor could not at that time "safely discover the nature of his invention," he might afterwards enroll a description of the same in the High Court of Chancery.

The little pamphlet in which Hulls made his scheme known to the world was printed in London in 1737. It is entitled "A Description and Draught of a new-invented Machine for carrying Vessels or Ships out of or into any Harbour, Port, or River against Wind and Tide or in a Calm." In his preface he says, "There is one great hardship lies too commonly upon those who propose to advance some new though useful scheme for the public benefit. The world abounding more in rash censure than in a candid and unprejudiced estimation of things, if a person does not answer their expectations in every point, instead of friendly treatment for his good intentions, he too often meets with ridicule and contempt. But I hope this will not be my case, but that they will form a judgment of my present undertaking only from trial. If it should be said that I have filled this tract with things that are foreign to the matter proposed, I answer: There is nothing in it but what is necessary to be understood by those who desire to know the nature of that *machine* which I now offer to the world, and I hope that, through the blessing of God, it may prove serviceable to my country."

Mr. Hulls proposed to put his engine into a *tow-boat*, and in discussing its advantages says, "If this machine is put in a separate vessel, this vessel may lie in any port, etc., to be ready on all occasions. A vessel of small burden will be sufficient to carry the machine to take out a large one. A vessel will serve for this purpose for many years after she is not safe to be taken abroad." Alluding to the wheel being at the stern, "When the wind comes ahead of the tow-boat the fans will be protected by it; and when the wind comes sideways the wind will come edgeways of the fans, and therefore strike them with less force." Again he says, "The work to be done by this machine will be upon particular occasions, when all other means yet found out are wholly insufficient. How often does a merchant wish that his ship were on the ocean, when if she were there the wind would serve tolerably well to carry him on his intended voyage, but does not serve at the same time to carry him out of the river, etc., he happens to be in, which a few hours' work of this machine would do."

Hulls gives a full description of all the mechanism of this steamboat, and shows how steam is applied, and the comparative advantages of having the steam machinery in the ship itself, or in a separate tow-boat. He seems to have studied the matter very fully, even to the consideration of the relative expense, and there seems to be no doubt of his having been the first inventor of an ingenious and practicable mechanism for propelling vessels by a condensing steam-engine and by paddle-wheels.

This pamphlet seems to have attracted no attention, and Freeman, unwilling to risk further outlay, abandoned Hulls and his project. It is evident that the invention did not receive a practical trial, and whatever hopes the projector based upon its success were disappointed. Commercially, like all the ventures of Jonathan Hulls, it proved a complete failure. Incurring some derision from his want of success, he quitted the place where he was best known and hid himself among the crowds of London with what might be called a broken heart, and died in extreme poverty, the date of his decease being unknown.

The following doggerel is still the burden of a common street-ditty among the boys of Campden in Gloucestershire, Hulls's native place:

> "Jonathan Hulls,
> With his patent skulls,
> Invented a machine
> To go against wind and stream;
> But he, being an ass,
> Couldn't bring it to pass,
> And so was ashamed to be seen."[1]

1752.—Gautoir, a regular canon, and professor of mathematics, presented to the Royal Society of Nancy a memoir, in which, having shown the inconveniences of navigation by means of sails, he proposed to employ a fire-engine (*machine feu*) of his invention for navigating purposes.

In 1851 there was discovered in the archives of Venice a treatise

[1] *Notes and Queries*, vol. iii., first series.

on "Navigation by Fire," by M. Gautoir, member of the Royal Society of Paris, which shows that the professor's plans for steam navigation were exhibited by him to the Venetian republic in 1756.

1753.—Daniel Bournoulli wrote a memoir mathematically proving that a steam-engine might be advantageously used in vessels, which obtained a prize from the French Academy of Sciences.

His proposition was to propel vessels by wheels, with vanes set at "an angle of sixty degrees both with the arbor and keel of the vessel, to which the arbor is placed parallel. To sustain this arbor and the wheels two strong bars of iron, of between two and three inches thick, proceed from the sides of the vessel, at right angles to it, about two feet and a half below the surface of the water." The propellers for the stern he describes to be of similar construction, but shorter, and for driving them he says they "can be moved by men aboard the vessels, or *by steam-engines*, or on rivers by horses placed in the barges."

Bournoulli's plan is described, and several modifications proposed, in "Annales des Arts et Manufactures," tome xx. p. 329 (A.D. 1803). These represent, by drawings, shafts annexed at the sides, bow, and stern of the vessel. Each shaft carries eight wheels, each wheel having eight spokes, with inclined broad vanes at the ends. It is suggested that a shaft might go out at the stern, under water, through a stuffing-box, and means are described for raising the shaft which is under water. The steam-engine is proposed to be used to turn the shaft by having a T cross-head on the piston-rod, working vertically, with a crank or connecting-rod at each end, turning wheels, one of which works the shaft.

In 1753, Euler proposed to use a shaft with four floats at right angles. This was worked by a vertical shaft with a toothed wheel and pinion. Fincham's "History of Naval Architecture" has a drawing of this device.

The same year "Mathon de la Cour proposed floats on each axle, and the intervention of an endless cord passing over a drum at the end of the axle, which was fastened to the side of the ship, and over a corresponding drum annexed to the frame." [1]

1759.—M. Genevois, a Swiss clergyman of the canton of Berne, published at Geneva a book containing what he called the discovery of the "*Great Principle.*" This was to concentrate power, by whatever means obtained, into a series of springs, which might be applied to a variety of purposes, among which he suggested the application of the "Great Principle" to propel a vessel by oars, and also proposed the application of an atmospheric steam-engine to bend or empower the springs by which the oars were to be worked; but his favorite project appears to have been to accomplish that object by the expansive force of gunpowder. M. Genevois visited England in 1760 and submitted

[1] Fincham's History of Naval Architecture, London, 1851, p. 280, for drawing.

HISTORY OF STEAM NAVIGATION.

his plan to the Board of Admiralty, without receiving any encouragement. His apparatus resembled in principle the feet of aquatic birds, opening when moving through the water in one direction, and closing on its return.

1774.—The Comte de Auxiron made an experiment, but his boat moved so slowly and irregularly that those who had been at the expense of the trial at once abandoned all hopes of success.

1775.—The elder Perrier, for whom M. Arago claimed the honor of having constructed the first steamboat, and who was afterwards celebrated as the introducer of the manufacture of steam-engines into France, constructed in 1775 a vessel impelled by a steam-engine; but the power of the engine was so small—being scarcely that of one horse—that it could not impart sufficient velocity to the vessel to ascend the river Seine to advantage. Not discouraged, and ascribing his failure to the use of paddle-wheels, he applied himself for several years to the search for other substitutes for oars. It does not, however, appear that he made any valuable discovery. M. Ducrest published a work in 1777 which contains an account of various experiments made by Perrier in his presence.

In 1776, Guyon de la Plombiere suggested the use of the steam engine for propelling a vessel.[1]

Mr. Andrew Ellicott, an American, in 1775, states that he had a conversation on the subject of steam with Mr. William Henry, of Lancaster, who suggested the possibility of applying steam to vessels, as did also Mr. Thomas Paine, the author of "Common Sense," in 1778.

1778.—The Marquis de Jouffroy made his first experiments, in 1778, at Baumes les Dames, and in 1781 he built upon the Saône a steam-vessel one hundred and forty feet long by twenty feet wide. In 1783 his experiments became the subject of a favorable report made to the French Academy of Sciences by Borda and Perrier. M. de Jouffroy demanded a patent, but before it was granted the Revolution compelled him to emigrate. On his return to France, in 1796, he learned that M. de Blanc, an artist of Trévoux, had obtained a patent for the construction of a steamboat.

1779, March 10.—Matthew Washbrough took out a patent for machinery to be attached to a steam-engine, one use of which he mentions as follows: "Lastly, I intend to apply my engine, as described above, for the purpose of moving ships, boats, and lighters, or any vessel in water."

1782.—The Abbé Darical proposed several plans, which were not superior to Perrier's, and were speedily laid aside. In 1782, Desblancs sent a model to the Conservatoire des Arts et Métiers of a steamboat moved by a chain of floats carried by wheels at its side turned by a horizontal cylinder.

[1] Encyclopédie Moderne, Paris, 1855. Article "Vapeur," 171.

1783.—In the great Patent Office Library, England, there is a French print by Jamont, dated A.D. 1816, entitled "Plan et profil du Bateau à Vapeur exécuté par M. le Marquis de Jouffroy à Lyon, en 1783." It represents a steamboat one hundred and forty feet long, with paddle-wheels on a shaft turned by a single horizontal steam cylinder and piston, with a double rack work and pauls on the piston-rod.

"An experiment was tried in the river Thames on a coal-barge to work against the tide by means of an apparatus fixed to the sides; so contrived that when put in motion, which was done by a fire-engine, it rowed three pair of oars, and required only the assistance of one man to steer. It seems rather too complex a business in its present state, but the plan appears practicable, and should it succeed by some judicious constructing, it must prove of immense advantage to the [coal?] trade."[1]

1784.—Moses Hunter, May 19, 1788, certifies that November, 1784, being at Richmond, Virginia, attending the Assembly as a representative from Berkeley County, Mr. James Rumsey, a working bath-tender, informed him in confidence that "he intended to construct a boat which was to be wrought altogether by steam; that he had tried the principles, some of which he mentioned." From the tenor of the conversation, he understood Rumsey that his principal dependence for the operation of his boat was upon steam. A rude model was exhibited to a company of visitors at Berkeley Springs in the year 1784. George Washington was one of the favored few who witnessed the successful launch of the little boat and testified to the value of the discovery. Fearful of his invention being stolen, Rumsey appears to have sworn all who witnessed the experiment to secrecy, for the certificate given him by General Washington, and meant for publication, is so carefully worded as to avoid using the word steam. It reads:

"I have seen the model of Mr. Rumsey's boat, constructed to work against the stream; examined the powers upon which it acts; been eye-witness to an actual experiment in running waters of some rapidity; and give it as my opinion (although I had little faith before) that he has discovered the art of working boats by mechanism and small manual assistance against rapid currents; that the discovery is of vast importance, may be of the greatest usefulness in our inland navigation; and if it succeeds, of which I have no doubt, the value of it is greatly enhanced by the simplicity of the work, which, when explained, may be executed by the most common mechanic.

"Given under my hand and seal, in the town of Bath, county of Berkeley, in the State of Virginia, this 7th day of September, 1784.

"GEORGE WASHINGTON."

[1] *British Magazine and Review*, October 26, 1783.

HISTORY OF STEAM NAVIGATION.

In 1785 Rumsey gave a public exhibition on the Potomac, above Shepherdstown, Virginia, of his discovery that a boat could be propelled *by steam* up-stream against the current. The boiler and machinery for Rumsey's boat were made at the Catoctin Iron Furnace, in Frederick County, owned by Johnson and brothers. Afterwards, encouraged by his success, he sailed for England, but first destroyed his precious model. He hoped in that older and richer country to perfect his work and realize fame and fortune. Doomed to disappointment, after a long and harassing struggle, he died before completing and satisfactorily demonstrating the principles of a new model. Rumsey accused Fitch of "coming pottering around" his Virginia work-bench and carrying off his ideas, to be afterwards developed in Philadelphia. Rumsey died in England of apoplexy at a public lecture where he was explaining his inventions.

A gentleman not many years ago had in his possession letters written by Rumsey in London, which mentioned his receiving frequent visits there from a young American studying engineering, who showed a sympathetic and intelligent interest in Rumsey's labors. This young man was *Robert Fulton*, who, nineteen years *after* Rumsey's death, gave the world a successful steamboat.

1785.—Thomas Jefferson, writing from Paris in 1785, describes a vessel recently invented, which he examined while in operation. He says the inventor did not know the principle of his own invention. "It is a screw with a very broad or thin worm, or rather it is a thin plate, with its edge applied spirally round an axis. This being turned operates on the *air* as a screw does, and may be literally said to screw the vessel along. . . . The screw, I think, would be more effectual if placed below the surface of the water." Mr. Jefferson adds that he thinks Mr. Bushnell, of Connecticut, has a prior claim to the invention of the screw as a motive-power for vessels. During our Revolutionary War he invented a submarine torpedo-vessel, to be driven by screws. This torpedo was the original of Fulton's, and may have been the first instrument of its kind; but the screw had been suggested as a motive-power for vessels long before. Brande's Dictionary says that "the screw-propeller is probably as old as the windmill, and a windmill of the construction now usually employed is represented in the seventy-seventh proposition of Hero's 'Spiritalia,' a work written one hundred and thirty years before the Christian era."

For a century and a half efforts were made to introduce the screw as a propeller of vessels before Ericsson and Smith successfully demonstrated the utility of the screw, and its advantages over paddle-wheels.

The first attempt to connect a steam-engine with a screw-propeller was by Joseph Bramah, of Piccadilly, engine-maker, who on the 9th of May, 1785, took out a patent for improvements in machinery, including two new methods of propelling vessels through the water.

The first of these contrivances was the application of a paddle-wheel to the stern of the vessel, driven by a steam-engine, the rudder being placed in the *bow*, in order to facilitate this contrivance.

His other invention was the application to the stern of the vessel of "a wheel with inclined fans or wings, similar to the fly of the smoke-jack or the vertical sails of a windmill." This wheel was to be fixed on the spindle of the rotatory engine without intermediate gearing, and wholly under water, where, by being turned either way, it would force the ship backward or forward, as the inclination of the fans or wings would act as oars with equal force both ways, and their power be in proportion to the size and velocity of the wheel, allowing the fans to have a proper inclination. Where the engine-shaft passed through the vessel it was to be made tight with a *stuffing-box*.

This is considered to be the *first* attempt at coupling together a submerged screw-propeller and the steam-engine for the propulsion of vessels, but there is no evidence that Bramah ever made or tried a propeller, and his rotatory engine by which it was to be driven turned out a failure.

At a special meeting of the American Philosophical Society of Philadelphia, held on the 27th of September, 1785, John Fitch laid before it a drawing and description of a machine for working a boat against a stream by means of a steam-engine, and on the 2d of December following presented a copy of the model and drawing to the Society, as appears by the minutes of Samuel Magan, one of the secretaries.

In the latter part of the year Fitch set out from Philadelphia with a view of visiting Kentucky, but he turned aside from his purpose at Richmond, and petitioned the Legislature of Virginia for assistance for his steamboat. No formal report was made, but believing that the experiment would not be costly, he executed a bond to Patrick Henry, governor of Virginia, conditioned that if he should sell one thousand copies of his map of the Western country in that State at 6*s.* 8*d.* each, he would, in nine months thereafter, exhibit a steamboat in the waters of Virginia or forfeit the penalty of three hundred and fifty pounds.

In November of the same year he received from Patrick Henry, the governor of Virginia, the following certificate:[1]

"I certify that John Fitch has left in my hands a bond, payable to the Governor for the time being, for £350, conditioned for exhibiting his *steamboat* when he receives subscriptions for one thousand of his maps, 6*s.* 8*d.* each.

                                   (Signed)   "P. HENRY.

"November 16, 1785."

[1] United States Patent Reports, 1849-50.

HISTORY OF STEAM NAVIGATION. 23

This provision was never put in operation, because the sales of the maps were very small. On his return to Pennsylvania to print the maps he stopped at Philadelphia, and presented a petition for assistance to the Legislature of Pennsylvania, and immediately afterwards went to Annapolis and made a similar application to the Legislature of Maryland. These attempts were unsuccessful, and an effort to induce the State of New Jersey to appropriate one thousand pounds of loan certificates for the purpose of building a steamboat also failed. Shortly afterwards the Legislature of the latter State enacted a law giving to John Fitch the exclusive right for fourteen years of making and using all and every species of boats and water-crafts which might be urged or propelled by fire or steam in the waters of the State. He then returned to Philadelphia, and succeeded in forming a company. The stock was divided into forty shares. The original subscribers were Samuel Vaughn, Richard Wells, Benjamin W. Morris, John Morris, Joseph Budd, John and Chamless Hart, Thomas Say, Magnus Miller, Gideon Hill Wells, Thomas Palmer, Thomas Hutchins, Richard Wells, Jr., John Strother, Israel Israel, William Reubel, and Edward Brooks, Jr., each of whom had one share; Richard Stockton, of Princeton, three shares; Benjamin Say, two shares. Stacy Potts, of Trenton, was an early member of the company, but soon withdrew from it. In the beginning it was agreed that Fitch should have twenty shares for his interest and services in the experiment. The first difficulty of the company was about the making of a steam-engine. The assistance of Henry Voight, an ingenious clock- and watch-maker of Philadelphia, whom Fitch looked upon as a practical man of sound sense and experience, was obtained, and shares were gradually made over for his services, until in 1787 he held five.

1786.—The subscribers generally paid in twenty dollars each on their shares, and with this small sum the experiments were commenced. A model steam-engine, with a cylinder of one inch diameter, was made, but although it worked, it was too small to demonstrate anything. A new model, with a three-inch cylinder, was then made and applied to a small skiff. With this machinery trials were made on the Delaware, about the 20th of July, 1786, with "a screw of paddles," a screw-propeller, the endless chain, and the side wheels, without much success. The next night, while in bed, Fitch thought of a plan of rowing the boat by oars or paddles on the sides, to be moved by cranks worked by machinery. He immediately rose and drew a plan, and the next morning showed it to Voight, who approved of it with some modifications. This was afterwards tried on the skiff with the steam-engine, and the first boat successfully propelled by steam in America was moved in the Delaware on the *27th of July*, 1786, with flattering promises of the future usefulness of the invention.

The members of the company were so much pleased with its success that they determined to build a steamboat for practical use, as a passage and freight boat. But the original subscriptions were now exhausted, and the shareholders were tardy in the payment of new installments. Fitch induced a committee of the Assembly of Pennsylvania to report, in September, in favor of loaning him one hundred and fifty pounds; but the House rejected the report by a vote of twenty-eight yeas to thirty-two nays. Application was made to General Mifflin without success. Matters then languished for a while, during which a law was passed by the State of Delaware securing (1787) Fitch's right to the invention. A new deed was signed by the shareholders in February, 1787, and fresh advances were made. The engine was to be of twelve-inch cylinder, and the boat twelve feet beam and forty-five feet long. The engine was finished in May, 1787, but "the wooden caps" to the cylinder admitted air, and the piston was leaky. The works were all taken out to the foundation and set up again, when the condensation was found to be imperfect. New condensers and other machinery were made, and the boat moved at times as fast as three or four miles an hour. But something was continually going wrong. The work was very imperfect, the details of such machinery being unknown in America, and the workmen common blacksmiths. By entreaty the company was induced to persevere. On the 22d of August, 1787, this boat was propelled on the Delaware in the presence of nearly all the members of the convention to frame the Federal Constitution; but the rate of progress was too slow to satisfy the projector. Nevertheless, certificates of the perfect success of this attempt were given by Governor Randolph, of Virginia, Dr. Johnson of the same State, David Rittenhouse, the astronomer, Andrew Ellicott, professor in the Episcopal Academy, and Dr. John Ewing, of the University.

The following is the certificate of David Rittenhouse:

"This may certify that the subscriber has frequently seen Mr. Fitch's (John Fitch) steamboat, which with great labor and perseverance he has at length completed; and has likewise been on board when the boat was worked against both wind and tide, with considerable velocity, by *the force of steam only*. Mr. Fitch's merits in constructing a good steam-engine, and applying it to so useful a purpose, will no doubt meet with the encouragement he so richly deserves from the generosity of his countrymen, especially those who wish to promote every improvement of the useful arts in America.

     (Signed)   "DAVID RITTENHOUSE.
"PHILADELPHIA, December 12, 1787."

1786.—Fitch a year earlier communicated to the *Columbian Magazine* this description of his steamboat:

"PHILADELPHIA, December 8, 1786.

"TO THE EDITOR OF THE COLUMBIAN MAGAZINE:

"SIR,—The reason of my so long deferring to give you a description of the steamboat has been in some measure owing to the complication of the works, and an apprehension that a number of drafts would be necessary in order to show the powers of the machine as clearly as you would wish. But as I have not been able to hand you herewith such drafts, I can only give you the general principles. It is in several parts similar to the late improved steam-engines in Europe, though there are some alterations. Our cylinder is to be horizontal, and the steam to work with equal force at each end. The mode by which we obtain what I take the liberty of terming a vacuum is, we believe, entirely new, as is also the method of letting the water into it, and throwing it off against the atmosphere without any friction. It is expected that the engine, which is a twelve-inch cylinder, will move with a clear force of eleven or twelve hundred weight after the frictions are deducted; this force to act against a wheel of eighteen inches diameter. The piston is to move about three feet, and each vibration of the piston gives the axis about forty evolutions. Each evolution of the axis moves twelve oars or paddles, five and half feet, which work perpendicularly, and are represented by the stroke of the paddle of a canoe. As six of the paddles are raised from the water six more are entered, and the two sets of paddles make their strokes about eleven feet in each evolution. The cranks of the axis act upon the paddles about one-third of their length from the lever end, on which part of the oar the whole force of the axis is applied. Our engine is placed in the boat about one-third from the stern, and both the action and reaction turn the wheel the same way.

"With the most perfect respect, sir, I beg leave to subscribe myself,
"Your very humble servant,
"JOHN FITCH."

Oliver Evans, in 1814, affirmed before a justice of the peace in Washington, D. C., that when Fitch and his company were constructing their steamboat in Philadelphia he suggested the propelling of her by paddle-wheels at the sides. One of the company, Dr. William Thornton, had also urged the use of wheels at the sides, but Fitch objected to their use. He also affirmed that Fitch declared his intention to establish steamboats on Western waters, of the advantages of which he appeared to have formed the greatest expectations; further, about the year 1786–87 or 1788 Fitch informed him that he contemplated employing his steamboat on the lakes, and meant to construct it with two keels to answer as runners, and when the lakes should freeze over, he would raise his boat on the ice, and by a wheel on each side, with spikes in the rims to take hold of the ice, he calculated it would be possible to run thirty miles an hour; also, that he meant to tow boats and other floats by steamboats.

1787.—Mr. Patrick Millar, in 1787, published in English and French an account of his naval experiments, illustrated with plates, copies of which were presented to every sovereign in Europe, to the American States, and to the Royal Societies in London and Edinburgh. In this work, speaking of the use of wheels as the moving power of vessels, he says, " I have reason to believe *that the power of the steam-engine may be applied to work the wheels so as to give them a quicker motion,* and consequently to increase that of the ship. In the course of the summer I intend to make the experiment," etc.

The same year Millar took out a patent for propelling boats by means of paddle-wheels turned by men. His vessel had a double deck, was sixty feet long, and had two wheels turned by two men each.

During the summer Mr. James Taylor proposed to Millar the application of a steam-engine to the wheels of his boat in place of the men, who were soon fatigued by the labor necessary to force the boat to any speed through the water. Dr. Brewster, speaking of the invention, says, " That this gentleman was the inventor of the steamboat in the strictest sense of the word I will not venture to affirm, but I have no hesitation in stating it as my decided opinion that he is more entitled to this distinction than any other individual who has been named." Dr. Brewster was not aware of the successful experiment of Fitch a year earlier.

1787.—The next and third boat propelled by steam within the waters of the United States was built this year, by James Rumsey, of Virginia, who had a long controversy with Fitch as to the priority of the application of steam as a moving power for vessels. Rumsey tried his boat at Shepherdstown, Virginia, on the 3d of December, 1787, and the success of his experiment is certified to by Major-General Horatio Gates, Rev. Robert Stubbs, and others. This boat was propelled by sucking in water at the bow and ejecting it at the stern. It moved at the rate of four miles an hour, but made only one trip, and probably did not go half a mile in distance.

1788.—As early as 1788, Nathan Read, a graduate of Harvard and a resident of Salem, Massachusetts, devoted himself to the purpose of applying steam-power to navigation. Having learned of the unsuccessful experiments of Rumsey on the Potomac, and Fitch upon the Delaware the year previous, and believing their failure was owing to their ill-constructed machinery and modes of propulsion, he sought to overcome the difficulty by the invention and combination of machinery of a different and more perfect kind. He believed this could be done by a modification of "Watt's" improved engine, also that the modes of propulsion used by Rumsey and Fitch—setting poles, oars, paddles, or the ejection of water from the stern of the boat—were awk-

HISTORY OF STEAM NAVIGATION.

ward and unsuitable. He succeeded in inventing a new boiler. This boiler was constructed of seventy-eight vertical tubes placed within it, and he called it the Multi-tubular boiler.

1791.—In 1791 he obtained a United States patent for this boiler, and for the improvement of the steam cylinder, and for " a practical mode of driving or impelling boats or vessels of any kind in the water or against the current, by means of the chain-wheel, a rowing-machine, constructed and operating upon the general principles of the chain-pump, and moved by the force of steam or any other power, in the same manner as the chain-pump is moved."

1789.—Read constructed in 1789 a boat to which he attached paddle-wheels to an axis extending across the gunwales of the boat, turned by a crank, and designed to be moved by his high-pressure engine, with the continuous rotative principle of Watt. By means of the crank worked by hand Read propelled himself with great rapidity across an arm of the sea (called Porter's River) in Danvers. Satisfied from his experiment that paddle-wheels would drive a boat with great ease and speed when turned by the power of a steam-engine and controlled by its steady rotative principle, he determined to use *paddle-wheels,* and constructed a model of his steamboat accordingly, with a view to a patent. January, 1790, a committee of the American Academy of Arts and Sciences, and eleven of the most prominent citizens of Salem, certified to the importance of his improvements to the steam-engine.

1790.—He petitioned Congress February 8, 1790, to grant him a patent for his inventions, specifying he had "discovered an improved method of applying the power of steam to the purposes of navigation," and "The machinery for communicating motion to boats, vessels, etc., is very simple and takes up but little room." No patent laws or regulations had been established or patents granted by the general government, but soon after his petition to Congress the "Act to promote the progress of the useful arts" was passed, constituting the Secretaries of State and War and the Attorney-General a board of commissioners, to whom all matters of this character were to be referred, and his application came before the new board. He first asked for a patent for a boat consisting of paddle-wheels, his newly invented boiler and improved cylinder, but in looking over some of the old volumes of "The Transactions of the Royal Society," he chanced to notice an article relating to an experiment a long time previous in France, which related that paddle-wheels and oars had both been tried to control a ship of war in a calm. Erroneously supposing such an experiment interfered with his right to a patent for a boat with paddle-wheels, he withdrew so much of his petition as related to them, and, January 1, 1791, presented a new petition and substituted a new propelling agent, which he denominated a rowing-machine, to revolve like a chain-pump, which he believed would answer the next best purpose to paddle-wheels, which he still considered preferable. As Fulton obtained his patent for paddle-wheels in 1811, Read was surely entitled to a patent for similar wheels in 1791. The paddle-wheel had been rejected by Fitch and Perrier principally on account of the oblique resistance the paddles met with as they entered and emerged from the water, and which was greatly increased as the boat was laden.

To obviate this Read constructed his wheels to be raised or lowered as occasion might require.

The first patents issued under the authority of the United States were to Read, Fitch, Rumsey, and Stevens, under date August 26, 1791. Read's was for his portable-furnace tubular boiler; Fitch's, for applying steam to draw water in at the bow and force it out at the stern of a vessel; Rumsey's, for propelling boats by means of the reaction of a stream of water forced by the agency of steam through a cylinder parallel to the keel, out of the stern. Stevens's was for propelling his boat in a like way. The patents of Rumsey, Fitch, and Stevens clashed in several particulars, but neither interfered with the patent of Read.[1]

1788.—In 1788, Rumsey carried his invention to England and procured a patent for it. He then succeeded in inducing a wealthy American merchant to join him, and began building a steamboat. It was all but completed when Rumsey suddenly died. His partners got the vessel afloat in February, 1793, and sailed her many times on the Thames, against wind and tide, with a speed of four knots an hour.

The thought of drawing water in at the bow and pushing it out at the stern was not new, and it has been said to have originated with Dr. Franklin, or to have come originally from France. Mr. Arthur Donaldson proposed it, also, to the Assembly of Pennsylvania in 1776.

Rumsey published in 1788 a pamphlet entitled "A Short Treatise on the Application of Steam; whereby is clearly shown from *actual experiments* that steam may be applied to propel boats or vessels of any burden, against rapid currents, with velocity, etc. By James Rumsey, of Berkeley County, Virginia. Philadelphia, printed by Joseph James, Chestnut Street, 1788."

The Newport *Herald*, dated March 6, 1788, contains the following item: "Mr. Rumsey's steamboat, with more than half her loading (upwards of three tons) and a number of people on board, made a progress of *four miles in an hour against the current of Potomac River by the force of steam, without any external application whatever*, impelled by a machine that will not cost more than twenty guineas for a

---

[1] Nathan Read was born in 1759, and died in Belfast, Maine, January 20, 1849, in his ninetieth year. So he lived full ten years after the successful inauguration of ocean steam navigation. See Nathan Read, etc., by his friend and nephew, David Read, New York, Hurd & Houghton, 1870, 12mo, pp. xv. and 20.

ten-ton boat, and that will not consume more than four bushels of coal in twelve hours."

1788.—The *fourth* steamboat in the United States was built in 1788, by John Fitch, and proved eminently successful. This boat was sixty feet long, and had eight feet beam. The oars or paddles were placed at the *stern*, and pushed against the water. The engine had a twelve-inch cylinder. About the end of July, 1788, she was propelled by steam from Philadelphia to Burlington, some twenty miles, *being the longest trip ever made by any boat under steam up to that time.* On the 12th of October this boat took thirty passengers from Philadelphia to Burlington in three hours and ten minutes, a fact well authenticated by reliable certificates. Several other trips were made in 1788 and 1789.

Dr. Franklin writes to Dr. Ingenhauz, Philadelphia, October 24, 1788: " We have no philosophical news here at present, except that a boat moved by a steam-engine rows itself against tide in our river, and it is apprehended the construction may be so simplified and improved as to become generally useful."

1788.—About the middle of October, 1788, a boat, the joint production of Patrick Millar, James Taylor, and William Symington, propelled by steam, was put in motion on the Lake of Dalswinton, in Scotland. A successful and beautiful experiment. The vessel moved delightfully, and, notwithstanding the cylinders were only four inches in diameter, went at the rate of five miles an hour. The engine, in a strong oak frame, was placed in a pleasure-boat, the boiler being parallel to it on the opposite side of the vessel, and the paddles in the *centre* of the boat. The vessel continued to ply for some days for the amusement of the projector, and to the astonishment of the country people, who assembled from all quarters to see a boat driven by *reik* (smoke). After these experiments the engine was removed into the library of Dalswinton House, where it stood for a long time as an ornamental model. In 1870 it was on exhibition in London, and an engraving of it was published in the London *Illustrated News.*

Satisfactory as was the result of this experiment, it did not fulfill all the designs of the inventors. A model vessel even as large as theirs might succeed and still leave it doubtful whether a larger scale might not impair the efficiency of the contrivance. Their success determined them to make an expensive trial on a large scale. From this determination resulted their second steamboat, constructed in 1789.

1789.—The date of commencing this vessel is fixed by the following letter, the original of which is preserved in the Millar family:

" DUMFERLINE, 6th of June, 1789."

" GENTLEMEN,—The bearer, Mr. William Symington, is employed by me to erect a steam-engine for a double vessel, which he proposes to have made at Carron. I have therefore to beg that you will order the engine to be made according to his directions. As it is of importance that the experiment should be made soon, I beg also that you will assist him, by your orders to the proper workmen, in having it done expeditiously. I am ever, with great regard, gentlemen, your most obedient humble servant,

"PATRICK MILLAR.

"TO THE CARRON COMPANY, CARRON."

It was proposed to make the second experiment on the Forth or Clyde Canal. For this purpose Mr. Millar's large twin or double pleasure-boat, the same he had previously used with paddle-wheels, driven by men, was sent up from Leith to the Forth and Clyde Canal, at Grangemouth, on the Frith of Forth, to receive the new steam-engine.

This double or twin vessel was sixty feet in length, and had cylinders to her engines of eighteen inches diameter. Her engine was in all respects a larger machine than the first, but identical in construction, and of about twelve horse-power. At the first trial the boards of the paddle-wheels were broken by the concussion of the engine, which rendered the experiment incomplete, but on the 26th of December, 1789, the experiment was repeated, and the vessel propelled at the rate of *seven* knots an hour. The next day the voyage was repeated with the same success. The vessel being a light skiff with plank less than an inch thick, as soon as the experiments were over was replaced on her original station as a pleasure-boat, and the engine deposited at the Carron Works.

The following account of this experiment, drawn up by Lord Cullen, was published in three of the Edinburgh newspapers: " It is with great pleasure I inform you that the experiment which some time ago was made upon the Great Canal here by Mr. Millar, of Dalswinton, for ascertaining the power of the steam-engine when applied to sailing, has lately been repeated with great success. Although these experiments have been conducted under a variety of disadvantages, as having been made with a vessel built for a different purpose, yet the velocity acquired was no less than six and a half to seven miles an hour.

"This sufficiently shows that with vessels properly constructed a velocity of eight or nine, or even ten, miles an hour may be easily accomplished, and the advantages of so great a velocity in rivers, straits, etc., and in cases of emergency, will be sufficiently evident, as there can be few winds, tides, or currents which can easily impede or resist it, and it will be evident that even with slower motion the utmost advantage must result to inland navigation."

1790.—John Fitch, June 22, 1790, petitioned the Secretaries of State and War, and the Attorney-General of the United States, that in the year 1785 he conceived the idea of applying steam to propel vessels through the water; that the impossibility of procuring experienced workmen and his total ignorance of the construction of a steam-engine, etc., caused him to expend about eight thousand dollars in experiments; that having at length *fully succeeded*, he comes forward as a man who, contrary to popular expectation, has *really* accomplished a design which will evince the many important advantages which must result to the United States.

He adds to his petition:

"The introduction of a complete steam-engine formed upon the newest and best principles, into a country like America, where labor is high, would entitle him to public countenance by encouragement independent of its use in navigation; the great time and money he has expended in bringing his scheme to perfection have been occasioned by his ignorance of the improved state of the steam-engine, for not a person could be found who was acquainted with the minutia of Bolton & Watt's new engine.

"And *whether your petitioner's engine is similar or not to those in England he is this moment totally ignorant;* but is happy to say, that he is now able to make a complete steam-engine which in its effects, he believes, is equal to the best in Europe; the construction of which he has never kept secret.

"On his first undertaking the scheme he knew there were a great number of ways of applying the power of steam to the propelling of vessels through the water, perhaps all equally effective, but this formed no part of his consideration, knowing that if he could bring his steam-engine to work *in a boat,* he would be under no difficulty in applying its force; therefore he trusts no interference with him in propelling boats by steam, under any pretense of a different mode of application, will be permitted; for should that be the case, the employment of his time and the amazing expense attending the perfecting of his scheme would, while they gave the world a valuable discovery, and to America peculiar and important advantages, 'eventuate in the ruin of your petitioner; for a thousand different modes may be applied by subsequent navigators,' all benefited by the expense and persevering labor of your petitioner, and then sharing with him those profits which they never earned."

1789-90.—The *fourth* steamboat built in the United States not being considered fast enough, the steamboat company which had acquired an interest in John Fitch's invention built a *fifth,* which was first tried December, 1789, about the time Millar was making his second successful experiment in Scotland. Her speed not proving satisfactory, various alterations were made in her machinery, until April, 1790, when the most complete success was attained. In May, General Mifflin and the whole Supreme Executive Council of Pennsylvania were passengers in her. The following account of this experiment is given by William Thornton, Esq., who was one of the company interested, and a passenger on board:

"The day was appointed, and the experiment made in the following manner. A mile was measured in Front Street (or Water Street) Philadelphia, and the bound projected at right angles as exact as could be to the wharves, where a flag was placed at each end, and also a stop-watch. The boat was ordered under way at dead-water, or when the tide was found to be without movement; as the boat passed one flag it was struck, and at the same instant the watches were set off; as the boat reached the other flag it was also struck and the watches instantly stopped. Every precaution was taken before witnesses, the time was shown to all, the experiment declared to be fairly made, and the boat was found to go at the rate of eight miles an hour, or one mile within the eighth of an hour. The Governor and Council of Pennsylvania were so highly gratified that, without their intentions being previously known, Governor Mifflin, attended by the Council in procession, presented to the company, and placed in the boat, a superb silk flag, prepared expressly, which Mr. Fitch afterwards took to France and presented to the National Convention."

They were thus particular in ascertaining the exact speed of the boat, as on her going at the rate of *eight miles an hour* depended the assignment of her in shares to a company. It seems to be a little uncertain whether the silk flag presented contained the arms of Pennsylvania or was simply the flag of the United States.

The boat afterwards ran eighty miles in a day. She was placed upon the Delaware in the summer, and ran regularly as a packet, passenger, and freight boat for three or four months. Advertisements of her trips were published in the Philadelphia newspapers. Of these notices, twenty-three have been found, giving advice of thirty-one trips to Trenton, Burlington, Chester, Wilmington, and Gray's Ferry. One of these advertisements, taken from *The Federal Gazette and Philadelphia Daily Advertiser* of Monday, July 26, 1790, is as follows. It will be seen it *was thought* sufficiently distinctive to call her *the* steamboat, since there was none other in the world at that time:

"THE
STEAMBOAT

Sets out to morrow morning at ten o'clock, from Arch Street Ferry, in order to take passengers for Burlington, Bristol, Bordentown, and Trenton, and return next day.
PHILADELPHIA, July 26th, 1790."

It is estimated that during the summer this steamboat passed over between two and three thousand miles. In the autumn she was laid up and never used afterwards, there not being sufficient travel and transportation to pay the expense of running her.

HISTORY OF STEAM NAVIGATION.

Before this conclusion was arrived at the company had projected and commenced building another, intended for the navigation of the Mississippi, and called the "Perseverance." She was of twenty-five tons burden, and rigged schooner fashion. The boat was completed, and her engines nearly so, when she broke adrift from her fastenings at the wharf, in a storm, and was blown on shore at Petty's Island, in the Delaware. Before she could be gotten off, the company in their attempts to simplify the machine had ruined it, and, moreover, had got into debt, which obliged them to sacrifice both boats and all the machinery.

1790.—William Longstreet, an American inventor, born in New Jersey, and who died in 1814, removed to Georgia. In 1790 he wrote a letter to Thomas Tolfairs, of Savannah, asking him to assist him in raising means to construct a boat to be propelled by steam. This letter was published in the Savannah and Augusta, Georgia, newspapers, but the funds were not immediately obtained. He subsequently obtained the necessary means for experiment, and constructed a small model boat upon a plan very different from Fulton's, which went on the Savannah River against the stream five miles an hour.[1]

1790.—Earl Stanhope, May 7, 1790, patented a *Janus*-shaped vessel, which he styled an "Ambi-navigator," with a propeller in the form of a duck's foot, worked by a twelve-horse cross-head engine, with double connecting-rods. At the conclusion of the experiment it was laid up in Deptford Dock-Yard. This engine, at least such portion of it as could be made available, was in 1802 applied to the *first steam-dredge*, built for the Admiralty. The "Ambi-navigator" had a novel description of rudder, styled by the inventor an "equipollant rudder."

1791.—On the 26th of August, 1791, John Fitch obtained a United States patent for his invention, which is signed by George Washington, President, Thomas Jefferson, Secretary of State, who also certifies that the patent was delivered to him August 30. The patent recites "he having invented the following useful devices not before known or used, viz.: for applying the force of steam to a trunk or trunks for drawing water in at the bow of a boat or vessel, and forcing the same out at the stern, in order to propel the boat or vessel through the water, for forcing a column of air through a trunk or trunks filled with water by the force of steam, and for applying the force of steam to cranks, paddles, for propelling a boat or vessel through the water." The said John Fitch, his heirs, etc., were granted for the time of fourteen years the sole and exclusive right and liberty of making, using, and vending to others the said inventions.

At the request of Aaron Vail, Esq., the United States consul at L'Orient, John Fitch was sent in 1791 by the company to France for the purpose of building steamboats. A brevet of invention was granted

[1] Appleton's American Cyclopædia.

him on the 29th of November, 1791, for his invention, but in the "Description des Machines et Procédés specific dans les Brevets d'Inventions expires Paris, 1811," it is stated that Des Blancs had previously proposed a similar scheme, and that a model of his plan had been deposited in the "Conservatoire des Arts et Métiers."

Mr. Vail, unable to obtain workmen to build the boats, paid the expenses of Mr. Fitch, who returned to the United States. Mr. Vail afterwards subjected to the examination of Mr. Fulton, when in France, the papers and designs of the steamboat appertaining to the company.

Under date "Philadelphia, 29 June, 1792," Fitch wrote to David Rittenhouse, "I conceive that navigation by steam will be the second mode of navigation, but can never take the preference of a fair wind, as air is much cheaper than steam. It may also be boldly asserted that it would be much easier to carry a first-rate man-of-war by steam at an equal rate than a small boat; for in such a case we should not be so cramped for room, nor should we so sensibly feel a few pounds weight of machinery.

"This, sir, whether I bring it to perfection or not, will be the mode of crossing the Atlantic in time, for packets and armed vessels."

In his autobiography, Fitch uses this touching and prophetic language: "The day will come when some more powerful man will get fame and riches from MY invention; but nobody will believe that poor John Fitch can do anything worthy of attention."[1]

[1] JOHN FITCH.—The remains of John Fitch were interred in the village graveyard of Bardstown, Nelson County, Kentucky, in the rear of the court-house and county jail, in 1798. Not a pebble of all the fine stone in the land marks his last resting-place. But his last will and testament is on record, as copied by a correspondent of the Philadelphia *Evening Telegraph*,—viz.:

"I John Fitch of the County of Nelson do make this my last will and testament. To William Rowan Esq., my trusty friend my beaver hat shoe knee and stock buckles walking stick, and spectacles. To Doctor William Thornton of the City of Washington in District of Columbia. To Eliza Vail, daughter of Aaron Vail Consul of the United States at L'Orient. To John Rowan Esq. of Beards Town son of said William and to James Nourse of said town I bequeath all the rest of my estate real and personal to be divided amongst them share and share alike and I appoint the said John Rowan Esq. and James Nourse Esq: my executors and the legacies hereby bequeathed to them my said Executors is in consideration of their accepting the Executorship and bringing to a final close all suits at law and attending to the business of the estate hereby bequeathed. Hereby declaring this to be my last will and testament this the 20th day of June One Thousand Seven Hundred and ninety-eight—Witness my hand and seal,

"JOHN FITCH.

"Acknowledged, signed and sealed in presence of

"JAMES NOURSE
"MICHAEL RENCH
 Her
"SUSANNAH × McCOWN"
 mark

On the 10th of July following the will was proved by the executors, and ordered to be recorded.

1791.—Colonel John C. Stevens, of Hoboken, New Jersey, commenced his experiments in steam navigation in 1791, and by careful study succeeded in mastering the theory and practice of the steam-engine. With this knowledge as a basis he made further investigations, which resulted in inventions, the first practical tests of which proved so satisfactory that he at once set about developing his ideas in order to devote them to the public good. His first attempts were made with a rotatory engine, for which he substituted one of Watt's. His first engineer proved an incorrigible sot. His second became a consumptive, and died before his experiment was completed. He then resolved to depend upon his own resources, and built a workshop on his own estate, where he employed workmen under his own superintendence. It has been claimed that he invented the first tubular boiler about 1804, but Nathan Read took out a patent for one in 1790. With various forms of vessels and different modifications of propelling apparatus, he impelled boats at the rate of five or six miles per hour. They were in truth more perfect than any of his predecessors, but did not satisfy his own hopes and sanguine expectations.

1792.—Baron Seguier experimented with a submerged propeller.

1792.—The Historical Chronicle of the *Bee*, page 23, says, "Earl Stanhope's experiments for navigating vessels by the steam-engine, without masts or sails, have succeeded so much to his satisfaction on a small scale, that a vessel of two hundred tons burden on this principle is now building under his direction. The expense of this vessel is to be paid by the Navy Board in the first instance, on condition that if she do not answer after the first trial, she shall be returned to Earl Stanhope, and all the expense made good by him."

A similar account of the earl's steam-vessel appeared in the *Gentlemen's Magazine* for October, 1792 (page 956), where it is stated that it was then being built under his direction by Mr. Stalkart, the author of a very valuable work on naval architecture. About this time Robert Fulton, then living at Torbay, in Devonshire, held some correspondence with Earl Stanhope on the subject of moving ships by a steam-engine.

1793.—The Earl of Stanhope, in 1793, revived the project of Genevois, and this machine, in 1795, was placed in a boat furnished with a powerful engine, and tried by him in Greenland Dock. In this experiment the paddles were two gigantic duck's feet, suspended from either side of the vessel, and opening and shutting like huge umbrellas. He was unable to obtain for his boat a greater velocity than three miles an hour. While engaged in this experiment he received a letter from Robert Fulton, who proposed the use of paddle-wheels; and it is probable his neglect to listen to this suggestion caused a delay in the introduction of the steamboat of at least twelve years, for it cannot be doubted that the ingenuity of Fulton, backed by the wealth and influence of Lord Stanhope, would have been as successful then as it was years later.

It is not known at what date Fulton's intention was first directed to the application of steam to navigation, but among the papers of Mr. Fulton, after his death, was found a letter from the Earl of Stanhope, dated at Holdsworth, Devon, October 7, 1793, in which he says,—

"SIR,—I have received yours of the 30th of September, in which you propose to communicate to me the principles of an invention which you say you have discovered respecting the moving of ships by the means of steam. It is a subject on which I have made important discoveries. I shall be glad to receive the communication which you intend, as I have made the principles of mechanics my particular study," etc.

In 1792 or 1794, Elijah Ormsbee, a carpenter by trade and inventor by birth, and a native of Connecticut, is said to have moved a boat successfully by steam. He had noted the difficulties of navigation on the Hudson River, and when afterwards he saw steam used as a power for pumping water from mines, saw how those difficulties could be overcome. One day, David Wilkinson, of Pawtucket, another inventor, stopped at Cranston, Rhode Island, where Ormsbee was at work, when Ormsbee said he had been thinking about a steamboat, and added if Mr. Wilkinson would make the castings he would make the boat; to which Mr. Wilkinson agreed, and went home and cast and bored a cylinder, and made the necessary wrought-iron connections. Two kinds of paddles were proposed, one called a flutter-wheel (a sidewheel), the other termed a goose-foot, which they decided to try, as the power could be applied more cheaply. Mr. Ormsbee obtained from Messrs. Clark & Nightengale the loan of a long boat belonging to the ship "Abigail" for the experiment, and also borrowed from Captain Ephraim Bowen a copper still of about one hundred and fifty gallons capacity, and retreated to a place called Windsor Cave, where all of the wood and much of the iron-work was done by himself. At last one pleasant afternoon or evening in the autumn of 1792 he got into his boat, pulled the throttle-valve, and the boat glided out into the bay. He was yet fearful that his new-found power might fail him, and so sat silent and eager, watching the piston rise and fall and the paddles go to and fro. But it did not fail; the boat went steadily through the water, and arrived at Long Wharf in Providence. The next day Mr. Ormsbee left in the boat for Pawtucket to show Mr. Wilkinson the success which had attended his enterprise. After a day or two the boat came back to Providence, where it was received with astonishment. For several weeks the boat went up and down the river; Captain John H. Ormsbee, then a lad of twelve, going in her as steersman.

The steam was not applied to elevate and depress the piston, as was done by Watt, but applied to raise the piston, and then being condensed by cold water, the piston was turned by atmospheric pressure. In this way the goose-foot paddles of the boat were moved forward and aft. When they moved forward they closed, and when moved aft they expanded to a width of from eighteen to twenty-four inches. The progress of the boat was from three to four miles an hour, which would probably have been increased to five or six if wheels had been substituted for paddles. But Ormsbee had no Livingston with open purse to assist him, and so, after having demonstrated the possibility of steam navigation, his golden dreams faded, and he sorrowfully returned the still to the distillery and the boat to its owner.

When, in 1817, the "Firefly" arrived in Pawtucket, people remembered the steam long-boat, and said, "We have seen a boat go by steam before;" and Colonel John S. Eddy a few years since related that when fourteen years old he went with his father to Kettle Point and "saw Mr. Ormsbee in a canoe with a kettle in it raising steam to propel a boat." This was in 1794. He did not build it on Kettle Point, but went down there to get out of sight of people. He worked first on a canoe dug out of a log, and afterwards applied steam to a long-boat. He used to talk a great deal when steamboats first came into use about Elijah Ormsbee's getting up such a thing a great while before. Mr. Henry H. Ormsbee, of Providence, has a statement in the handwriting of his father, Captain John H. Ormsbee, in accordance with this statement, and there is corroborative evidence on record in the files of the Transactions of the Society for the Encouragement of Domestic Industry. It was stated by Mr. Wilkinson, who took the works after the boat was abandoned, that he exhibited and explained them to one Daniel French, who in turn made Robert Fulton acquainted with them.[1]

1793.—John Smith, in June, 1793, used a steamboat with paddle-wheels on the Duke of Bridgewater Canal, from Runcorn to Manchester. The vessel had on her an engine on the old atmospheric principle, was worked with a beam, connecting-rod, double cranks, in a horizontal line, with seven paddles on each side, which propelled her after the rates of two miles an hour.[2]

1794.—In 1794, Lord Stanhope addressed a letter to Wilberforce on the question of peace or war, likely, he thought, to be brought under discussion on the meeting of Parliament. In his letter he speculates on the possible resources of France, and hints that England is not invulnerable. He says,—

"This country, Great Britain, is vulnerable in so many ways, the

---

[1] History of Steam Navigation between Providence and New York, 1792–1877 by Charles H. Dow.

[2] *Nautical Magazine*, vol. i., 1832.

picture is horrid. By my letter I will say nothing on that subject. One instance I will, however, state, because it is information you cannot, as yet, receive from any other quarter; though in two or three months from the date of this letter the fact will be fully established, and you may then hear it from others. The thing I allude to is of peculiar importance. The fact is this. I know (and in a few weeks shall prove) that ships of any size, and for certain reasons the larger the better, may be navigated in any narrow or other sea without sails (though occasionally with), but so as to go without wind, and even directly against both wind and waves. The consequences I draw are as follows: First, that all the principal reasons against the French having the ports of Ostend, etc., cease, inasmuch as a French fleet composed of ships of the above-mentioned description would come out at all times from Cherbourg, Dunkirk, etc., as well as from Ostend, etc., and appear in the same seas. The water, even at Dunkirk, will be amply deep enough for the purpose of having them there. The French having Ostend, ought not, therefore, under this new revolution in naval affairs,—for it would be a complete revolution,—to be a bar to peace. Under the old nautical system, naval men might have reasoned differently upon that subject. But the most important consequence which I draw from this stupendous fact mentioned at the top of this page is this, namely, that *it will shortly render all the existing navies of the world (I mean military navies) no better than lumber.* For what can ships do that are dependent upon the wind and weather against fleets wholly independent of either? Therefore the boasted superiority of the English navy is no more. We must have a new one. The French and other nations will, for the same reasons, have their new ones."

This is a curious prediction as to the effect of the introduction of steam to navigation upon naval warfare and armaments, written, as the Earl's letter was, full thirteen years before Fulton's success with the "Clermont" on the Hudson.

1794.—William Lyttleton, July 15, 1794, took out a patent in England for a screw propeller of three blades, which was to be rotated by hand-power or a steam-engine, and experimented with a copper screw so formed as described by Colonel Beaufry.

The same year Samuel Morey, of Connecticut, who commenced his experiments on the Connecticut River in 1790, propelled his boat by a stern wheel from Hartford to New York City, at the rate of five miles an hour. Chancellor Livingston, Judge Livingston, Edward Livingston, John Stevens, and others, were on board this boat when she went from New York to Greenwich. This was the *sixth* steamboat built in the United States.

The most reliable account of Morey's experiments and claim to having made the first application of steam to navigation, and of having made the "first practical steamboat," was published in 1864, by the

Rev. Cyrus Mann, of Orford, New Hampshire. Mr. Mann, an educated man, of strict integrity, spent both time and research in the investigation of the claims of Fulton, Morey, and others, of a practical success in steam navigation. The following is an extract from his book:

"The credit of the invention of the steamboat is commonly awarded to Robert Fulton, but it belongs primarily and chiefly, it is believed, to a more obscure individual. So far as is known, the first steamboat ever seen on the waters of America was invented by Captain Samuel Morey, of Orford, New Hampshire. The astonishing sight of this man ascending Connecticut River, between Orford and Fairlee, in a little boat just large enough to contain himself and the rude machinery connected with the steam-boilers and a handful of wood for a fire, was witnessed by the writer in his boyhood, and by others who yet survive.[1] This was as early as 1793 or earlier, and before Fulton's name had been mentioned in connection with steam navigation."

The records of the Patent Office at Washington show that several patents for the *application of steam* were taken out by Morey for the application of steam " to boats" previous to Fulton's, as Morey's great aim had always been to invent a steamboat.

Captain Samuel Morey, a son of General Israel Morey, who moved to Orford from Connecticut in 1766, died in 1843, aged seventy-one years. He originally owned fifteen hundred acres of woodland about Fairlee Pond, and employed a large number of men and oxen during the winter months in clearing the lumber for market, the proceeds of which, forty thousand dollars, were consumed in scientific projects. He began in 1780 to give attention to subjects of light, heat, and steam, and invented several ingenious contrivances. He was a correspondent of Professor Silliman, and contributed to the pages of the *American Journal of Science and Arts*. He also corresponded with Fulton, and visited him twice in New York, and exhibited to him the model of his boat, receiving a return visit from Fulton.

After visiting Morey, Fulton commenced his boat on the Hudson, and Morey always held that he surreptitiously imitated his model. In 1820, Morey put on Fairlee Pond a boat named the "Aunt Sally." It was twenty feet long, and neatly painted. Some unprincipled person sunk it soon after its trial trip, and it now rests beneath the waters of the pond.

Writing to William A. Duer, Esq., October 31, 1818, Morey says, "As near as I can recollect it was as early as 1790 that I turned my attention to improving the steam-engine and in applying it to the purpose of propelling boats. . . . In June, 1797, I went to Bordentown, on the Delaware, and there constructed a steamboat, and devised

---

[1] Mrs. Nathaniel Mann was on board the steamboat of Morey, and "ordered it," as she said.

the plan of propelling by means of wheels, one on each side. The shafts ran across the boat with a crank in the middle, worked from the beam of the engine with a shackle bar. . . . The boat was openly exhibited in Philadelphia. . . . I took out patents for my improvements. . . . I never had any doubt but that I had a right to take out a patent for the application of two wheels to a steamboat, and often told Mr. Livingston and Mr. Fulton that I had. To the latter, I once asserted this right when on board his steamboat with him." Nothing but want of pecuniary means, as he asserted, seems to have been wanting for his inaugurating his methods of propelling boats by steam.

Morey's claim as the inventor of the first successful steamboat must give way before the superior claims of Fitch's steamboat already recounted, however.

Captain Morey continued his scientific pursuits to the time of his decease, and they were more or less honored and recognized, but he never recovered from the blow received through the alleged perfidy of Fulton.

1796.—The tenth volume of the "Repository of Arts" contains a description of the fire-ship of Edward Thomason, which was laid before the Lords of the Admiralty, in England, in 1796. It had vertical wheels at the sides, operated on by steam-engines, and was intended to possess the power of moving given distances in all directions according to the intentions of the director, so that, *without any person on board*, it would conduct itself into an enemy's port, and by *clock-work*, at the given moment, explode the combustible. This seems to have been the pioneer of the modern torpedo-boat, which is moved from the shore by electricity.

The *seventh* successful steamboat was tried in 1796, in the United States, the invention of John Fitch after his return from France. The experiment was tried under the patronage of Robert H. Livingston, as certified to by John R. Hutchings, General Anthony Lamb, and William H. Westlock. It was made with a *screw-propeller*, the vessel used was a yawl, about eighteen feet in length and having six feet beam, and steered at the bow with an oar. The boiler was a ten-gallon iron pot, with a thick plank lid firmly fastened to it by an iron bar placed transversely. The cylinders were of wood, barrel-shaped on the outside, straight on the inside, and strongly hooped. Steam was raised sufficiently high to send the boat once or twice around the pond, when more water was needed to generate steam for a new start. The time was the summer of 1796, and the scene of the experiment was "*The Collect*," a fresh-water pond in New York City, near what is now called Canal Street. The pond has been drained, and its site, covered with houses, is now in the heart of the city.

1797.—The *eighth* United States steamboat was built by Samuel

Morey, assisted by the Rev. Burgess Allison, of Bordentown, New Jersey. It was constructed with paddle-wheels at the sides, in the same manner as Fulton's steamboat subsequently, and was propelled from Bordentown to Philadelphia in the summer of 1797, and publicly exhibited. In this year, also, Chancellor Livingston built a boat on the Hudson River, and obtained exclusive privilege from the New York Legislature for one year, on condition that he produced a vessel impelled by steam *three miles an hour*, but which he was unable to effect. He was associated in this enterprise with a person of the name of Nisbett, a native of England. Brunel, afterwards distinguished as the engineer of the Thames Tunnel, acted as their engineer.

Morse, in his "Gazetteer," published in 1797, under the head of Territory, and referring to the Northwest Territory, says that he thinks "*it is probable steamboats will be found of infinite service in all our extensive river navigation.*"

In 1797 an experiment in canal steam navigation was made in the neighborhood of Liverpool, and the *Monthly Magazine* for July of that year says, "Lately the Newton-Common, in Lancashire, a vessel heavily laded with copper slag passed along the Sankey Canal without the aid of haulers or rowers, the oars performing eighteen strokes a minute by the application of *steam* only! After a course of ten miles the vessel returned the same evening by the same means to St. Helen's, whence she had set out. This ingenious discovery by the original form and motion of the oars may be ranked among the most useful or modern inventions, and in particular promises the highest benefits to inland navigation."

1798.—The next vessel moved by steam, in the United States, was a model boat, about three feet long, built by John Fitch, at Bardstown, in Kentucky, in the summer of 1798, and tried upon the creek near that town.

The success of the steamboat was assured by the adoption of vertical paddle-wheels over the sides, though later inventions have so modified the hulls and engines, that the screw placed at the stern has in a general measure supplanted the side wheels.

In 1815, Nicholas J. Roosevelt in a petition to the New Jersey Legislature asserts, with the modesty and manly firmness of honesty, that "he is the true and original inventor and discoverer of steamboats with vertical wheels."

In an affadavit attached to his petition he says,—

"In or about the year 1781 or 1782" he resided with Joseph Vostenhandt, about four miles above Esopus, on the North River, in New York, and that he did there make, rig, and put in operation on a small brook near Vostenhandt's house, "a small wooden model of a boat with vertical wheels over the sides," each wheel having four arms or paddles made of shingles, and that "these wheels being acted on by hickory or whalebone springs propelled the model boat through the water by the agency of a tight cord passed between the wheels, and being reacted on by the springs."

In 1798, in conjunction with Chancellor Livingston and John Stevens, he entered into an agreement to build a boat on joint account, for which the engines were to be constructed at Second River by Roosevelt, while the propelling power was to be on the plan of the chancellor's.

Steam was applied to the machinery about the middle of the year 1798 unsuccessfully. Improvements were made in it until in October Roosevelt wrote the chancellor an account of a trial trip on which the speed attained was equivalent to about three miles in still water, though with wind and tide, the Spanish minister, who was on board and highly elated, estimated the actual speed at double that amount.

The month previous to this trial, on the 6th of September, 1798, Roosevelt wrote the chancellor in this connection, after referring to a change in the plan, a letter in which he says, "I would recommend that we throw two wheels of wood over the sides, fastened to the axis of the flys [fly-wheels] with eight arms or paddles; that part which enters the water of sheet iron to shift according to the power they require either deeper in the water, or otherwise, and that we navigate the vessel with these until we can procure an engine of the proper size, which I think ought not to be less than 24-inch cylinder." On the 16th of the same month he again wrote the chancellor, "I hope to hear your opinion of throwing wheels over the sides," and the chancellor answers, "I say nothing on the subject of wheels over the sides, as I am perfectly convinced from variety of experiments of the superiority of those we have adopted."

Their apparatus was a system of paddles, resembling a horizontal chain-pump, set in motion by an engine of Watt's construction. We know that such a plan, if inferior to paddle-wheels, might answer the purpose; it, however, failed, in consequence of the weakness of the vessel, which, changing its figure, dislocated the parts of the engine. Their joint proceedings were interrupted by the appointment of Chancellor Livingston to represent the American government in France. Stevens, however, undiscouraged, continued his experiments at Hoboken, while Livingston carried to Europe the most sanguine expectations of success. Previous to these attempts, Mr. Nicholas R. Roosevelt and R. R. Livingston had made some experiments in steam navigation, the detailed account of which has not been preserved.[1]

1800.—Messrs. Hunter and Dickinson are said to have taken out a patent in England in 1800 for propelling vessels by steam, which

---

[1] A detailed account of these experiments can be found in a pamphlet entitled "A Lost Chapter in the History of the Steamboat," by J. H. B. Lathrop. Published by the Maryland Historical Society, Baltimore, March, 1871.

HISTORY OF STEAM NAVIGATION.   43

was tried on the Thames, in January, 1801. The English *Monthly Magazine* contains an account of this performance, " as very creditable to them, and as exceeding everything before accomplished ;" and says that "the vessel was moved at the rate of three miles an hour through the water."

The newspapers of 1801 announce that on the 1st of July "an experiment took place on the river Thames for the purpose of working a barge or any other heavy craft against the tide by means of a steam-engine on a very simple construction. The moment the engine was set to work the barge was brought about, answering her helm quickly, and she made way against a strong current, at the rate of two and a half miles an hour."

1800.—Edward Shorter patented a screw-propeller in 1800, which was successfully tried by *manual* power, to move vessels of war, in 1802.

Mr. Samuel Brown had a boat built expressly for being propelled by a gas vacuum-engine, of which he was the inventor, made to drive a two-bladed submerged propeller, in the bow of the boat, by which a speed of from six to seven miles an hour was obtained.

CHAPTER II.—1800–1819.

Wm. Symington's Steam-Tug, 1802.—Robert Fulton's French Experiments, 1802–4.—Oliver Evans, 1802–4.—Stevens, 1804.—The Clermont, Fulton's first successful Steamboat, 1807.—Robert L. Stevens, 1808.—Jonathan Nichols, 1807–9.—Inland Steam Navigation, United States, 1809.—John Cox Stevens's Sea-Voyage, 1809.—Robert Fulton's Patent, 1811.—Rapid Traveling in Steamboats, 1811.—First Steamboat on the Western Waters of the United States, 1811.—Fulton's Steamboats, 1812.—Steamboat on the Delaware, 1812.—Steamboats between Philadelphia and New York, 1813.—Hezekiah Bliss, 1810–19.—The Comet, and Henry Bell, 1812.—The Elizabeth, 1813.—The Clyde, and Glasgow, each 1813.—First Steamboat on the St. Lawrence, 1813.—Robert Fulton's Patent, 1813.—First Steamboat in India, 1810, 1819, 1821.—Early English Steamboats, 1813–15.—Loss by Wreck of Steamers in War, 1812–14.—The Margery *et al.*, 1814.—The Demologos, or Fulton the First, the First War Steamship, 1814.—Steamers in England in 1814.—The Argyle, or Thames, 1815.—Steam Navigation adopted in Russia, 1815–16.—Trevatheniet's Patents on Screw-Propeller in England, 1815.—Roosevelt claims the Invention of Paddle-Wheels, 1814–16.—Liverpool Steam Ferry-Boat, 1816.—The Majestic first to cross the English Channel, 1816.—First Line of Steamboats, New York to New London, 1816.—Iona Morgan's Steamboat in Maine, 1816.—First Steamboat commanded by Cornelius Vanderbilt, 1817.—First Steam Tow-Boat, 1816.—The Firefly, 1817.—First Steamboat on the Rhine, 1817.—The Manifest of First Steamboat to Boston, 1817.—First Steamboat on Lake Erie, 1818.—Baltimore and Philadelphia Steamboat, 1813–15.—The first English Steam-Tug, 1818.—Steamers between the Mersey and Clyde, 1819.—First Steamer, Liverpool and Ireland, 1819.

1802.—In 1802, William Symington, who had been associated with Millar and Taylor in the experiments at Dalswinton, under the patronage of Lord Dundas, of Kerse, an extensive proprietor in the Forth and Clyde Canal, constructed a steam-vessel for the purpose of superseding the use of horses in towing vessels along the canal. His narrative of the experiment, the truthfulness of which has been confirmed by others, is as follows:

"Having previously made various experiments, in March, 1802, at Lock Twenty-two, Lord Dundas, the great patron and steamboat promoter, along with Archibald Spiers, Esq., of Elderslee, and several gentlemen of their acquaintances being on board, the steamboat took in drag two loaded vessels, the 'Active' and 'Euphemia,' of Grangemouth, Gow and Elspine, masters, each upwards of *seventy tons* burden, and with great ease carried them through the long reach of the Forth and Clyde Canal at Port Dundas, a distance of nineteen and a half miles, in six hours, although the whole time it blew a very strong breeze right ahead of us; so much that no other vessel could move to windward in the canal that day but those we had in tow."

When unimpeded by having other boats in tow, this vessel went steadily at the rate of six miles an hour, and may be considered to have been a complete success. Her cylinder had a diameter of twenty-two inches, and her piston a stroke of four feet. She had her paddle-wheel astern, and steering apparatus in front. Mr. Symington proposed to apply side-wheels to this boat, but it was feared they would injure the banks of the canal, and he was induced to substitute a stern-wheel.

The "Charlotte Dundas," as this vessel was called, is said to have cost three thousand pounds. If not the first practical English steamboat, she was certainly the first tug- or tow-boat ever built, and her performance, says Scott Russell, writing in 1841, "appears to be about as great as any since accomplished by the many boats which on the same canal have attempted the same duty. So simple was the machinery that it might have been at work to this day with merely ordinary repairs."[1]

1802.—Robert Fulton, with whose name the history of steam navigation is inseparably connected, the son of a poor Irish laborer who emigrated to America, born in Pennsylvania in 1765, was in 1802 spending the winter at Paris, where he made a model, and wrote a description of a small steamboat with paddle-wheels. He also wrote the following letter to a friend, showing he was at that early day engaged in the attempt to move vessels by mechanical power.

"PARIS, the 20th of September, 1802.
"To MR. FULNER SKIPWITH:

"SIR,—The expense of a patent in France is 300 livres for three years, 800 ditto for ten years, and 1500 ditto for fifteen years; there can be no difficulty in obtaining a patent for the mode of propelling a boat which you have shown me; but if the author of the model wishes to be assured of the merits of his invention before he goes to the expense of a patent, I advise him to make the model of a boat in which he can place a clock spring which will give about eight revolutions; he can then combine the movements so as to try oars, paddles, and the leaves which he proposes; if he finds that the leaves drive the boat a greater distance in the same time than either oars or paddles, they consequently are a better application of power. About eight years ago the Earl of Stanhope tried an experiment on similar leaves in Greenland Dock, London, but without success. I have also tried experiments on similar leaves, wheels, oars, paddles, and flyers similar to those of a smoke-jack, and found oars to be the best. The velocity with which a boat moves is in proportion as the sum of the surfaces of the oars, paddles, leaves, or other machine is to the bow of the boat presented to the water, and in proportion to the power with which such machinery is put in motion; hence, if the sum of the surfaces of the oars is equal to the sum of the surfaces of the leaves, and they pass through similar curves in the same time, the effect must be the same; but oars have their advantage, they return through air to make a second stroke, and hence create very little resistance; whereas the leaves return through water, and add considerably to the resistance, which resistance is increased as the velocity of the boat is augmented: no kind of machinery can create power; all that can be done is to apply the manual or

---

[1] The machinery of this boat was exhibited at an exhibition in London a few years since.

other power to the best advantage. If the author of the model is fond of mechanics, he will be much amused, and not lose his time, by trying the experiments in the manner I propose, and this perhaps is the most prudent measure, before a patent is taken.

"I am, Sir, with much respect, yours,
"ROBERT FULTON."

1803.—About the same time, in connection with Chancellor Livingston, then the American minister at the French court, he commenced the construction of an experimental steamboat on a large scale, which was launched in the spring of 1803, on the Seine, below Paris, and the steam-engine and boilers put on board. He had, however, miscalculated the strength of his vessel, and when the weight of the machinery was placed in the centre she broke through the middle and sunk, and when raised was found to be unworthy of repairs. He therefore built a new hull to receive the machinery, which was but little injured, and in August, 1804, made a second trial. This new vessel was sixty-six feet long and eight feet wide; but she moved so slowly as to be altogether a failure. Soon after the experiment, Fulton visited England, where he sought out Mr. Symington, and made a trip with him in his steam-tug on the Forth and Clyde Canal. Mr. Symington says, "In compliance with Mr. Fulton's earnest request, I caused the engine fire to be lighted up, and in a short time thereafter put the steamboat in motion, and carried him from Lock Sixteen, where the boat then lay, four miles west in the canal, and returned to the place of starting, in one hour and twenty minutes, to the great astonishment of Mr. Fulton and several gentlemen, who at our outset chanced to come on board."

An act passed the Legislature of New York, April 5, 1803, by which the rights and exclusive privilege of navigating all the waters of that State, by vessels propelled by fire or steam, which had been granted to Livingston in 1798, were extended to Livingston and Fulton for twenty years from the date of the new act. By this act the producing proof of the practicability of propelling a boat by steam, of twenty tons capacity, at the rate of four miles an hour, with and against the ordinary current of the Hudson, was extended two years. Subsequently it was extended to April, 1807.

Fulton's experiments on the Seine in 1800–4, and his relations with Napoleon I., are thus graphically narrated by Mr. A. Ducasse. He says,—

"Between six and eight o'clock on the 8th of August, 1804, the two banks of the Seine, at Paris, at the foot of the heights of the 'Pompe à Feu' at Chaillot, were crowded with curious observers collected together to witness an experiment, the importance of which, unfortunately for the civilized world, was not recognized for a long time afterwards.

HISTORY OF STEAM NAVIGATION. 47

"Fulton was trying on the Seine the first steamboat, already invented by him some years before, and subsequently offered in vain first to France, then to England, and subsequently to his native country, the United States, which adopted the grand discovery.

"On that evening, then, vast numbers of curious gazers were assembled on the quay, and unfortunately the emperor, detained at the camp of Boulogne, was not in Paris. The trial took place without being witnessed by him, and, in spite of the scientific men delegated by his orders, this was not appreciated.

"A strange history is that of the short-lived relations of these two men of genius, Napoleon I. and Fulton, made to understand one another, and yet whom a fatal and jealous destiny seems to have perpetually kept apart.

"Towards the end of the year 1800, Fulton, then for some time residing in Paris, had been able to establish relations with several savans. He asked Volney, who was known to the First Consul, and who was a member of the Conservative Senate, to propose to the great man who governed France to make a trial of his system of navigation with steam as a motive-power.

"Volney naturally addressed himself to Forfait, the Ministre de la Marine, who laid the matter before the First Consul in the following terms:

"'The Ministre de la Marine submits to the First Consul the proposals concerning the "Nautilus,"—the name of Fulton's steamboat,—which Mr. Robert Fulton, citizen of the United States, has placed before him, through the citizen Volney, member of the Conservative Senate.'

"On the 4th of December, 1800, the First Consul wrote on the margin of this demand the following decision:

"'The Ministre will treat this affair with Fulton, Volney, and others.'

"Napoleon, occupied with the affairs of Germany, whither Moreau was then marching to fight the battle of Hohenlinden, occupied with the vast interests placed in his powerful and organizing hands, unceasingly tormented with projects and inventions, did not at first seize the importance of Fulton's discovery. Moreover, he thought it was the business of the Ministre de la Marine to examine the affair, and to make a report upon it to him if it were serious.

"For the present, then, he thought no more about it.

"In the month of March of 1801, Forfait returned to the charge and submitted to the Chief of the State the following:

"'The Ministre de la Marine proposes to allow Fulton a sum of 10,000f. to enable him to make a thorough trial of the "Nautilus" at Brest, and to give him certain sums by way of reward.'

"Napoleon wrote on the margin of this demand, 'The First Consul agrees to this arrangement.'

"Fulton's project was then, by order of the Chief of State, sent to the institute to be examined. But it was not till three years later, in 1804, that the trial of the steamboat took place on the Seine, as we shall presently show.

"This boat, built under the direction of Fulton, by Messrs. Brown, of New York, was fifty metres long; it was moved by a double steam-engine, which turned paddles on each side, and gave it a speed equal to about that of a carriage drawn by post-horses.

"One fine day Napoleon bethought him of Fulton's project. It was at the time when he was in the midst of his troops at Boulogne, preparing his grand expedition against England.

"With his gaze constantly fixed on the great rival of France, he sought every means likely to insure the success of his descent upon the bank of the Thames. The plan of the American engineer recurred to him. Great indeed would be the chances of success if Fulton had really discovered the means of moving ships by means of steam,—a power the use of which might be regulated and controlled in spite of tides and winds. What a wondrous and unequaled victory obtained over the elements!

"Napoleon then asked his minister for Fulton's project. The minister sent it, and on the 21st of July, 1804, the First Consul, two months ago hailed as emperor, wrote the following curious letter:

"'I have just read the project of Citizen Fulton, engineer, which you have sent me much too late, since it is one which may change the face of the world. Be that as it may, I desire that you "immediately" confide its examination to a commission of members chosen by you among the different classes of the Institute.

"'There it is that learned Europe would seek for judges to resolve the question under consideration. A great truth, a physical, palpable truth, is before my eyes. It will be for these gentlemen to try and see it and seize it. As soon as their report is made it will be sent to you, and you will forward it to me. Try and let the whole be terminated within eight days, as I am impatient.

"'FROM MY IMPERIAL CAMP AT BOULOGNE, this 21st July, 1804.'

"In the last two months the Parisians had seen with astonishment, off the quay of the Pompe à Feu, at Chaillot, a boat presenting a most strange appearance. It was armed, said the journals of the time, with two large wheels, placed on an axle like that of a cart. Behind these wheels, which were intended to be put in motion,—so ran the journals of 1804,—there was a sort of large stove with a pipe, a little fire-engine by means of which the wheels, and consequently the whole vessel, might be put in motion, turned, and made to go backward or forward.

"Some evil-minded persons had attempted, shortly after its arrival in the Seine, to sink it, and they had partially succeeded in their attempt. The relations of the period do not tell us who these persons were or what were their motives.

"When Fulton had repaired the injuries done the ship, the first trial of a steamboat in France, as has already been mentioned, took place on the Seine on the 8th of August, 1804. Fulton, assisted by three other men, put his boat in motion, taking in tow two vessels of less tonnage.

"During an hour and a half he afforded a curious crowd the strange spectacle of a ship moved, like a carriage, by wheels fitted with oars and set in motion by a fire-engine. The trial succeeded wonderfully, and appeared conclusive.

"The rate of progress up the Seine was from five to six kilometres per hour; in going down it was double.

"The ship was easily manœuvred in every direction, answered readily to the helm, was anchored without difficulty, and rapidly put again in motion. No well-broken horse was more easy to manage.

"At the present time all this excites no astonishment, but sixty years ago, when navigation was only comprehended by means of sails or oars, the wonder we have described was natural.

"What is really surprising is that the results of this trial were so unimportant; above all, when we remember that the emperor had ordered a serious examination of the discovery by the members of the Institute, and that several of them, among whom were such men as Bossout, Carnot, Prony, Perrier, and Volney, were on board the 'Nautilus' when the trial trip was made.

"And yet, four days afterwards, on the 12th of August, the *Journal des Débats* received an article communicated by the government on the subject of this trial, which terminates thus:

"'Doubtless they (the members of the Institute) will make a report which will give this discovery all the *éclat* it deserves, since this mechanism, applied to our rivers, would be fraught with the most advantageous results to our internal navigation,' etc.

"Thus it appears that the system was not considered applicable to maritime navigation, and thus Messieurs de l'Institute—ocular witnesses of a fact the consequences of which they were able to appreciate, and of which they had been ordered to find out the value and to explain the causes—thought it was consistent with their dignity to reject scornfully the most wonderful discovery that had ever been submitted to their lofty understanding.

"For the rest, this is no exception to the general rule. Have we not seen in our own time distinguished soldiers reject percussion powder for muskets? Do we not even now see breech-loaders rejected for the army? and has it not required the campaign of Sadowa to open the eyes of most of the chiefs of the armies of Europe?

"Be this as it may, the reports on Fulton's discovery were far from favorable. Scientific men rejected it. The emperor is said to have sighed on reading their report, exclaiming, 'It is a pity!'

"What must have been the regret of the great captain when, eleven years later, while being borne into exile on board the 'Bellerophon,' under the English flag, he saw a small steamer manœuvring with facility in British waters, and, on inquiring who was the inventor, was told that his name was Fulton!"

1803.—M. Dalleney, a French engineer, in October, 1803, secured a patent, the first of its kind, for an original idea of his own for applying the steam-engine to two screws, one of which was placed on the bow on a movable axis, and served as a rudder.

At Boulogne-sur-Mer, on Monday, October 12, 1881, was unveiled a statue of Frederic Sauvage, whom the French claim to be the inventor of the screw-propeller. A Scotchman named Swan, born at Coldingham, Berwickshire, in the year 1787, who claimed to be the original inventor of the screw-propeller, died in London in 1869, and a monument in Abney Park Cemetery there bears the following inscription: "Few men have been greater benefactors to their country than the late John Swan. He was the original inventor of the screw-propeller in the year 1824, as now used in Her Majesty's ships, and published by the late Dr. Birkbeck in the *Mechanic's Register* of the same date."

1802–4.—In 1802, Oliver Evans agreed with James McKeever, of Kentucky (father of the late Commodore Isaac McKeever, United States navy), and Louis Valcourt, to build a boat to run on the Mississippi between New Orleans and Natchez. Mr. Evans's high-pressure engine was built in Philadelphia, and the boat in Kentucky; both were sent to New Orleans, but when the engine arrived at New Orleans it was found that the boat had been destroyed by a hurricane. The engine was then set to sawing timber in New Orleans, and Mr. Stackhouse (one of the engineers), who remained with it twelve months and fifteen days, stated that during that period the mill was constantly at work, and that "nothing relating to the engine broke or got out of order so as to stop the mill one hour." This was the engine sent by Oliver Evans to drive a steamboat against the current of the Mississippi five years before Robert Fulton started the "Clermont" on the Hudson.

In 1804, Oliver Evans built a scow-steamboat at Philadelphia, for the purpose of clearing out the docks, which he called the "Eruktor Amphibolis."

To prove that wagons could be moved on land and vessels moved on water by the force of steam, Evans geared machinery to the wagon upon which the "Eruktor" was placed, and propelled his wagon by steam from the Centre Square, Philadelphia, to the Schuylkill River, at Market Street. The wagon-wheels were then taken off, the scow launched, and a paddle-wheel placed at its stern. It was then propelled down the Schuylkill to the Delaware, and up the latter river to Philadelphia, a distance of sixteen miles, passing several vessels bound to the same port.

Mr. Evans has left the following account of this experiment:

"In 1804 I constructed at my works, a mile and a half from the water, by order of the Board of Health of the City of Philadelphia, a machine for cleaning docks. It consisted of a large flat or lighter, with steam-engine of the power of five horses on board to work machinery to raise the mud into lighters. This was a fine opportunity to show the public that my engine could propel both land and water carriages, and I resolved to do it. When the work was finished I put wheels under it, and though it was equal in weight to two hundred barrels of flour, and the wheels were fixed on wooden axle-trees for this temporary purpose in a very rough manner, and attended with great friction of course, yet with this small engine I transported my great burden to the Schuylkill with ease; and when it was launched into the water I fixed a paddle-wheel at the stern, and drove it down the Schuylkill to the Delaware, and up the Delaware to the city; *leaving all the vessels going up behind me* at least half-way, the wind being ahead."

On the 26th of September, 1804, he closed an address to the Lancaster Turnpike Company as follows:

"It is too much for an individual to put in operation every improvement which he may invent. I have no doubt my engines will propel *boats against* the current of the Mississippi, and carriages on turnpike roads with great profit."

In 1805 he published a work describing the principle of his steam-engine, with directions for working it when applied to propel boats against the current of the Mississippi, and carriages on turnpike roads.

1804.—In May, 1804, John Stevens[1] constructed a steamboat which went from Hoboken to New York and returned; its propelling power being a wheel at the stern, formed in the manner of a windmill or smoke-jack, and driven by a rotatory engine.

The engine not proving successful, it was superseded by one of

---

[1] Colonel John Stevens, born in New York, 1749. Died at Hoboken, New Jersey, 1838. Colonel Stevens was the father of Edwin A. Stevens, founder of the Stevens Institute of Technology. During the war of the Revolution he served in a variety of civil and military capacities, and afterwards became the owner of large estates in New Jersey.

In 1787 he became interested in steamboats, from seeing that of John Fitch, and experimented for near thirty years. In 1789 he petitioned the New York Legislature for a grant of the exclusive navigation of the waters of that State, but without success.

Watt's engines, when the vessel attained an average speed of four miles an hour. For a short distance Stevens could make his boat go at a speed of seven or eight miles per hour; but was unable to maintain that speed for any length of time from a deficiency of steam.

Professor Renwick read a paper several years since before the New York Historical Society, in which he stated that the first he ever heard of an attempt to use steam for the propulsion of vessels was from a classmate who, in 1803, witnessed an experiment made upon the Passaic River by John Stevens, of Hoboken. According to his account, the propulsion was attempted by forcing water, by means of a pump, from an aperture in the stern of the vessel. In May, 1804, Mr. Renwick saw Robert L. Stevens and the late Commodore Stevens, as he was styled, cross from the Battery to Hoboken in a boat propelled by steam. This boat was a small one, and had tubular boilers, the first ever made. The machinery was made under his own directions, and in his own shop at Hoboken. It set in motion *two* propellers (the first double-screw) of five feet diameter each, and each furnished with four blades having the proper twist,—to obtain which he had the greatest difficulty with his workmen,—and set at an angle of thirty-five degrees. It is a proof of the remarkable accuracy and skill of the Hoboken workshop that the engine of this first small propeller, which is carefully preserved in the Stevens Institute of Technology at Hoboken, was set up again forty years afterwards (1844) in a new vessel, which was modeled on the lines of the first boat, and without altering a screw was worked successfully, and in the presence of a committee from the American Institute was propelled at the rate of eight miles an hour. The second vessel is also preserved in the Stevens Institute at Hoboken. Three years before Robert Fulton's steamer, the "Clermont," plowed its way up the Hudson, this engine and boiler, in the hands of Colonel John Stevens, had demonstrated the efficiency of the screw-propeller.

1806.—Encouraged by the success of his former experiments, Colonel Stevens repeated them in 1806 on a larger scale, and built a pirogue fifty feet long, twelve feet wide, and seven feet deep, which attained considerable speed. He named her the "Phœnix."

THE "CLERMONT."

1807.—In the spring of 1807 Robert Fulton launched from the building-yard of Charles Brown, on the East Hudson, a steam-vessel, one hundred and thirty feet long, having eighteen feet beam and six feet hold, which he named the "Clermont," after the residence of his friend, patron, and associate, Chancellor Livingston. The "Clermont" was provided with a single engine, built by Boulton & Watt, in England, which lay for many months on the wharf at New York, near where the city prison now stands, between Canal Street and the Battery, being held by the agent of the ship which brought it over for non-payment of freight. This engine was twenty-four inches diameter of cylinder, and three feet stroke. The boiler was of the low-pressure pattern, twenty feet long, seven feet deep, and eight feet broad. The side-wheels were fifteen feet in diameter, with buckets four feet wide, dipping two feet in the water. The "Clermont" started on her first trip from New York for Albany, at 1 P.M., on the 7th of August, 1807, just three years to a day after Fulton's experiments with the "Nautilus" on the Seine.

Robert Fulton, with a few friends and mechanics and six passengers, was on board. An incredulous and jeering crowd were gathered on the shore as she cast loose. She arrived at Clermont, a distance of one hundred and ten miles, on Tuesday at the same hour. Leaving Clermont on Wednesday, at 9 A.M., she arrived at Albany at 5 P.M. the same day, a distance of forty miles, in eight hours. "The run," says Fulton, "is one hundred and fifty miles in thirty-two hours,— nearly equal to five miles an hour. She kept up the same rate of speed on her return trip to New York, and made several trips during the summer with like results."[1]

Professor Renwick, describing the "Clermont" as she appeared on her first trip, says, "She was very unlike any of her successors, and very dissimilar from the shape in which she appeared a few months afterwards. With a model resembling a Long Island skiff, she was decked for a short distance at stem and stern. The engine was open to view, and from the engine aft a house like that of a canal-boat was raised to cover the boiler and the apartment for the officers. There were

[1] Marcus Richardson, of Bangor, the oldest Mason in Maine, who died in that city January 7, 1881, aged one hundred and six years and two months, witnessed this trial trip of the "Clermont." He was a privateersman in the war of 1812, and was a Mason seventy-seven years.

In August, 1882, Geo. Dexter, aged eighty-four years, of Albany, and Wm. Perry, of Exeter, New Hampshire, aged ninety years, who were passengers in the "Clermont" on her return trip from Albany to New York, were still living.

At the time of the great triumph, Peter Cooper was an apprentice boy, Thurlow Weed was a cabin-boy on a Hudson River sloop, and Charles O'Connor a prattling child of three years. This year (1882) a movement has been set on foot to erect a suitable monument to the memory of the great inventor, whose ashes lie neglected in an obscure vault at the southwest corner of Trinity Church.

The name of the chief engineer of the "Clermont" on her first trip up-river has not been preserved; but Mr. Fulton, having had some difficulty with him, promoted Mr. Charles Dyck to his place on the return trip. Mr. Dyck was born in 1787 and died in 1871. While at Albany, a gentleman, Mr. Dyck said, came on board and engaged passage to New York. Mr. Fulton, on receiving his money, shed tears, remarking that it was the first he had received for all his labor.

In 1813, Mr. Dyck was engineer on the "Car of Neptune," from New York to Albany, and also on the "Firefly," from New York to Poughkeepsie. He was on the first steamer on the Ohio and Mississippi Rivers; also on the first steamboat on the Fulton Ferry Line, and from New York to New Brunswick on the Philadelphia Line with Captain Vanderbilt. For five years before his death he was blind.

no wheel-guards. The rudder was of the shape used in sailing-vessels and moved by a tiller. The boiler was of the form then used in Watt's engines, and was set in masonry. The condenser was of the size used habitually in land engines, and stood, as was the practice in them, in a large cold-water cistern. The weight of the masonry and the great capacity of the cold-water cistern diminished very materially the buoyancy of the vessel. The rudder had so little power that she could hardly be managed. The skippers of the river craft, who at once saw that their business was doomed, took advantage of the unwieldiness of the vessel to run foul of her as often as they thought they had the law on their side. Thus in several instances the steamer reached one or the other termini of the route with but a single wheel."

Before the season closed, the wheels were surrounded by a frame of strong beams and the paddles were covered in; the rudder was changed to the pattern now used on all river boats and was worked by a wheel, the ropes from which were attached to the ends most distant from the pintles. This rudder rendered the vessel manageable, and the beams placed around the wheel were capable of inflicting instead of receiving harm in a collision with sailing-vessels.

During the winter of 1807–8 she was almost wholly rebuilt. The hull was considerably lengthened, and covered from stem to stern with a flush deck. Beneath this two cabins were formed, and surrounded by double ranges of berths, fitted up in a manner then unexampled for comfort, and the public taste was consulted in the application of numerous coats of rather gaudy paint. Thus improved, she commenced her trips for the season of 1808, and started regularly at the appointed hour, at first much to the discontent of travelers, who had previously been waited for by sloops and stages. At the end of the season she proved too small for the crowds who thronged to take passage.

The success of the "Clermont" led Fulton and Livingston to build two other vessels and add them to the line, viz., "The Car of Neptune" and the "Paragon," of three hundred and three hundred and fifty tons respectively. Fulton sent the following account of the first trip of the "Clermont" to the *American Citizen:*

"SIR,—I arrived this afternoon at four o'clock in the steamboat from Albany. As the success of my experiment gives me great hopes that such boats may be rendered of great importance to my country, to prevent erroneous opinions and to derive some satisfaction to the friends of useful improvements, you will have the goodness to publish the following statement of facts:

"I left New York on Monday at one o'clock, and arrived at Clermont, the seat of Chancellor Livingston, at one; time, twenty-four hours; distance, one hundred and ten miles. On Wednesday I left the Chancellor's at nine in the morning, and arrived at Albany at five in the afternoon; distance, forty miles; time, eight hours.

"The run is one hundred and fifty miles in thirty-two hours,—equal to nearly five miles an hour. On Thursday, at nine o'clock in the morning, I left Albany, and arrived at the Chancellor's at six in the evening. I started from thence at seven, and arrived at New York at four in the afternoon; time, thirty hours; space run through, one hundred and fifty miles,—equal to five miles an hour. Throughout my whole way, both going and returning, the wind was ahead. No advantage could be derived from my sail. The whole has therefore been performed by the power of the steam-engine, etc.

"ROBERT FULTON."

Fulton also wrote to a friend, "I overtook many sloops and schooners beating to windward, and parted with them as if they had been at anchor. The power of propelling boats by steam is now fully proved. The morning I left New York there were not thirty persons who believed that the boat would ever move one mile an hour or be of the least utility; and while we were passing off from the wharf, which was crowded with spectators, I heard a number of sarcastic remarks. This is the way in which ignorant men compliment what they call philosophers and projectors. Although the prospect of personal emolument has been some inducement to me, yet I feel infinitely more pleasure in reflecting on the immense advantages my country will derive from the invention."

The British *Naval Chronicle* for 1808 has an extract from a letter written by a gentleman of South Carolina, one of the favored few who were passengers on board the "Clermont" on her first trip. Under date *September* 8, 1807, he says, "I have now the pleasure to state to you the particulars of a late excursion to Albany in the steamboat made and completed under the directions of the Hon. Robert R. Livingston and Mr. Fulton, together with my remarks thereon. On the morning of the 19th of August, Edward P. Livingston, Esq., and myself were honored with an invitation from the Chancellor and Mr. Fulton to proceed with them to Albany in trying the first experiment up the river Hudson in the steamboat. She was then lying off Clermont, the seat of the Chancellor, where she had arrived in twenty-four hours from New York, being one hundred and ten miles. Precisely at thirteen minutes past nine o'clock A.M. the engine was put in motion, when we made head against the ebb-tide, and head wind blowing a pleasant breeze. We continued our course for about eight miles, when we took the flood, the wind still ahead. We arrived at Albany about 5 P.M., being a distance from Clermont of forty-five miles (as agreed upon by those best acquainted with the river), which was performed in eight hours without any accident or interruption whatever. This decidedly gave the boat upwards of five miles an hour, the tide sometimes against us, neither sails nor any other implement but steam used.

"The next morning we left Albany with several passengers on the return to New York, the tide in favor but the wind ahead. We left Albany at twenty-five minutes past nine o'clock A.M., and arrived at Clermont in nine hours precisely, which gave us five miles an hour. The current on returning was stronger than when going up. After landing us at Clermont, Mr. Fulton proceeded with the passengers to New York. The excursion to Albany was very pleasant, and represented a most interesting spectacle. As we passed the farms on the borders of the river every eye was intent, and from village to village the heights and conspicuous places were occupied by sentinels of curiosity,—not viewing a thing they could possibly anticipate any idea of, but conjecturing about the plausibility of the motion. As we passed and repassed the towns of Athens and Hudson, we were politely saluted by the inhabitants and several vessels, and at Albany we were visited by his excellency the governor and many citizens. Boats must be very cautious how they attempt to board her when under way, as several accidents had nearly happened when boarding her. To board ahead will endanger a boat being crushed by the wheels, and no boat can board astern. The difference between the wake of 'Neptune's Chariot' and that of a common water-carriage is very materially open for observation, as when you approach the first you will be told by anticipation to pay respect to a lady in the 'Chariot,' as you will be readily notified by the expansion of a fan, which forms the dimensions of her wake, but moving with great impetuosity from the warm repulsion. It is a curious fan; it only spreads by an aquatic latchet, being sprung by the kicking of the horses. I may now venture to multiply and give you the sum-total. The boat is one hundred and forty-six feet in length and twelve feet in width (merely an experimental thing), draws to the depth of her wheels two feet of water, one hundred feet deck for exercise, free of rigging or any incumbrances. She is unquestionably the most pleasant boat I ever went in. In her the mind is free from suspense. Perpetual motion authorizes you to calculate on a certain time to land; her works move with all the facility of a clock, and the noise when on board is not greater than that of a vessel sailing with a good breeze."

The Philadelphia *Times* published in 1878 a chat with a survivor of the party on board the "Clermont" on her return trip. This gentleman, the Rev. Frederick Reynolds Freeman, a Baptist clergyman of Illinois, was then on a visit to Philadelphia. He was carried in his mother's arms at the time, being but two years old. His personal remembrance, of course, does not amount to much, but he has, said the *Times*, a store of information concerning the trip not in the possession of anybody else, for as soon as he was old enough to realize the importance of the occasion, he sought with more assiduity than a person less directly interested would for all the facts concerning it.

His father, Elisha Freeman, before retiring to a farm, had been a sea-captain, and for that reason was invited, with a small number of other persons, including municipal officials of Albany, to go on board the "Clermont" upon its arrival. Captain Freeman went, taking with him his wife and little son, Freddy. "The event is like a dream

HISTORY OF STEAM NAVIGATION.

to me," says Mr. Freeman. "Probably my memory would now be unable to reach it but for the constant rehearsals of the scenes and incidents made to me in my youth.

"When Columbus walked the streets in Spain meditating upon his project, which had become generally known, men and small boys would point their fingers at their foreheads and exchange smiles. Just so Robert Fulton was treated before he turned the laugh upon a country of scoffers.

"The first steam-packet was trim and handsome enough, excepting the boilers, machinery, and smoke-stack, which were rude, cumbrous, and of extremely formidable appearance.

"The side-wheel was a clumsy affair, uncovered and with twelve huge paddles, held in their place by a ring half-way between their extremities and the hub, that sent water splashing upon the deck with every revolution. The top of the smoke-stack was about thirty feet above the deck,—nearly as high as the two masts, from the rear one of which floated the Stars and Stripes. Hours before she started a great multitude had assembled along the wharves to witness the expected inglorious ending of what was generally known as 'Fulton's folly.' Cries of 'God help you, Bobby!' 'Bring us back a chip of the North Pole!' 'A fool and his money are soon parted!' etc., were frequent, loud and annoying. Fulton, however, knew the crowd were sincere in their ridicule, and with a confident smile went on superintending preparations for the start, as if he knew that triumph would presently more than overbalance the sneers, jibes, and cat-calls of the vulgar and the pitying manners of the more refined. Smoke issues from the stack; the hawser is drawn in; the side-wheel quivers; it slowly revolves; Fulton's own hand at the helm turns out the bow; he is pale, but still confident and self-possessed; the 'Clermont' moves out into the stream, the ponderous machinery thumping and groaning, the wheel frantically splashing, and the stack belching like a volcano; the 'Clermont' steadily moves; all aboard swing their hats into the air and give a cheer that is immediately taken up by the entire multitude on land; the crowd remain cheering on the piers until the 'Clermont' is out of sight up the Hudson."

Mr. Freeman says that the boat arrived at Albany thirty-six hours after starting from New York. It had not been continually in motion, the party having stopped at the residence of Chancellor Livingston on the way up. The speed was at the rate of five miles an hour. The appearance of the strange vessel as she steamed up the river had a remarkable effect, even in daytime, upon the crews of craft passing by, for comparatively few of the skippers coming down could, in those days of slow mail and no telegraph, have been prepared to encounter such an oddity; but at night the "Clermont" spread consternation and terror on all sides. It was very dark, and the fires were fed with dry white-pine wood, which when stirred would send up columns of flame and sparks from the mouth of the tall stack. This apparent volcano, moving steadily through the darkness up the middle of the river, and accompanied by the rumbling and groaning of the hard-laboring machinery, was well calculated to strike terror into the hearts of sailors on the sloops and other craft coming down with grain and general farm produce, who had never heard of any motive-power for vessels except wind, and who, withal, were extremely superstitious.

"My father and others told me," says Mr. Freeman, "that whole crews prostrated themselves upon their knees and besought Divine Providence to protect them from the horrible monster that was marching on the tides and lighting up its pathway by its fires."

When the members of the Freeman family went aboard the "Clermont," upon its arrival at Albany, Mrs. Freeman observed a workman emerging from the engine-room—a place very suggestive to her of the infernal regions—carrying in his hands a ladle filled with molten lead. With this he proceeded to stop up holes whose presence here and there in the rude machinery was indicated by escaping steam. Captain Freeman then learned that the workman had been busily employed doing the same thing ever since the "Clermont" had left New York. The people of Albany had been apprised of the arrival in advance, and the whole town turned out to receive Fulton and his steamboat, giving them an enthusiastic reception.

The "Clermont" had not been long under way on its first trial when Fulton ordered the engine stopped. Having observed that the paddle-floats were too deeply immersed in the water, he shifted them nearer to the centre of the paddle, so that they did not enter so deeply into the water; and this alteration had the effect of increasing the speed of the vessel.[1]

A correspondent of the Cincinnati *Gazette* in 1880 says,—

"Fulton's first successful boat was called, not the 'Clermont,' but the '*Katharine* of Clermont,' after Fulton's wife, Katharine Livingston, of Clermont Manor. I read the name so painted, having been a passenger on the first regular trip made by her down the Hudson. As there are few survivors of that notable event, which occurred in *April,*

---

[1] David Dunham, whose eccentricities and enterprise were alike celebrated, the principal owner of the celebrated privateer "General Armstrong," was one of the foremost patrons of Robert Fulton in his experiments with steam navigation, and advanced large sums to further his projects. An accident prevented him from being the first to apply steam to ocean transit. He was knocked overboard or fell from the deck of one of his own vessels. When his body was recovered, among the papers in his pocket was a contract with the government for carrying the mails between this country and Great Britain, giving specifications as to the fleet of steamers he proposed to establish. Soon after his demise his eldest son emigrated to the South and established a plantation in Florida. His lineal grandsons entered the Confederate army.

Fulton died in London, England, February 24, 1815.

1808, an account of it may gratify your readers. I was a student at Union College, Schenectady, and arrived at Albany in charge of a maiden lady of mature years. The river was then navigated by sloops, and on reaching Albany there was no vessel in port. The lady accordingly went to a friend's house, while I took up my quarters at a tavern. During the night the 'Katharine' arrived from Kinderhook, a few miles down the river. She had made her *trial trip the previous* fall,[1] being then a mere skeleton. The winter was spent in fitting her up. She was about the size and shape of an ordinary canal-boat, painted a light color, and provided with a small upright engine. She was advertised to leave for New York at nine o'clock on the morning after her arrival. I at once determined to take passage. My fair charge, with the proverbial dilatoriness of her sex, was slow in getting ready, and when we reached the wharf the steamer was out in the stream. She stopped, however, in response to the signal made by ourselves and the other persons gathered on the bank, and we went out to her in a skiff. There did not seem to be much excitement in Albany, but at Hudson, where the engineer showed the capacity of the craft by turning her about and steaming a little way up the river, a great crowd was gathered. There were about fifty passengers on board, quite a large proportion being boys and young men. I was to land at Kingston, seventy-five miles below Albany. Before reaching that place the boat ran aground, and it took twelve hours of hard work to get her afloat again. Fulton was on board. He was plainly dressed, and wore a boot on one foot and a shoe on the other. He appeared buried in thought and spoke to no one. Shortly after the boat left Kingston, where I quitted her, her boiler burst, but, as it was a *sheet-iron affair*, no one was hurt. She was taken to New York for repairs, where I saw her about a week later, having made the remainder of my voyage in a sailing-vessel."

1808.—"It is a little curious," says Scott Russell, "that, although Fulton was the first in America, and Bell in Europe, to successfully avail themselves of the advantage of steam applied to navigation, it was in both cases *non longo intervello distanti*. Fulton was first in the race only a few days, and Bell by a few months."

"Robert L. Stevens is probably the man to whom, of all others, America owes the greatest share of its present highly-improved steam navigation. His father was associated with Livingston in his experiments previous to the connection of the latter with Fulton, and persevered in his experiments during Livingston's absence in France. Undisputedly he is the pioneer of steam navigation on the open sea."

At the age of twenty he built a steamboat with *concave* water-lines

---

[1] Her trial trip was made August 7, 1807, as already shown.

—the first application of the wave-line to ship-building—and adopted a new method of bracing and fastening steamboats.

In conjunction with his father, John Stevens, the inventor, in 1807, he constructed a paddle-wheel steamer, which was in motion on the Hudson only a few days later than Fulton's first successful voyage. He called her the "Phœnix." Precluded by the monopoly which Fulton's success had obtained for him in the waters of New York, Mr. Stevens first employed the "Phœnix" as a passage boat between New York and New Brunswick, and finally conceived the bold idea of carrying her under steam around Cape May to the Delaware, and so to Philadelphia,—a voyage which was successfully accomplished in June, 1809, he going in command of the boat. A storm overtook them; a schooner in company was driven to sea and absent many days, but the "Phœnix" made a harbor at Barnegat until the storm abated, and then continued her voyage to Philadelphia, where she plied for many years between that city and Trenton.[1] She was commanded by Captain DeGraw. Robert L. Stevens was her temporary engineer, and she was placed on the Delaware River for the purpose of carrying the New York passengers. She ran from Philadelphia to Bordentown, and made the passage thence, in 1812, in three hours when running with the tide, and in five hours against it. The boat had no wheel-house, and sometimes when in motion the water would be thrown as high as her smoke-stack. She belonged to what was called the Swiftsure Line, and attracted much interest. Her hour of departure was announced by the blowing of a long tin horn, and hundreds of persons would crown the wharves to see her embark on her voyage. Passengers on this boat were landed in New York in 1812 some time during the following night if no accident occurred.

About 1816, Robert L. Stevens commenced steam ferriage between New York and the Jersey shore; in 1818 he discovered the utility of employing steam expansively and using anthracite coal for fuel in steamers; in 1821 he substituted the skeleton wrought-iron for the heavy cast-iron walking-beam; and in 1824 applied an artificial blast to the boiler-furnace, and in 1827 the hog-frame to boats to prevent them from bending at the centre. In 1842 he was commissioned by the United States government to build an immense steam-battery for the defense of New York harbor, which was left unfinished at the time of his death, April 20, 1856.[2]

[1] The first English experiment in deep-sea navigation by steam was made by James Watt, ten years later, from Leith to London, in 1818.

[2] It was relinquished by the United States government, in 1862 or 1863, after a large sum of money had been expended upon its construction, and was willed by Mr. Stevens to the State of New Jersey, with an annual sum of money towards its completion. It has never been launched, the improvement in naval armament having rendered it useless for the purposes intended, and recently has been sold at auction by the State of New Jersey. The purchaser will probably break the vessel

1807–9.—A *screw* vessel was constructed at Providence, in 1807 to 1809, by Jonathan Nichols, a blacksmith, a native of Vermont, and David Griere, a tailor, from Nantucket; she was forty feet long, and was worked by four horses. A small model boat had been before successfully worked. On June 24, 1807–8 or 1809, this craft conveyed to Pawtuxet a happy couple to be married in that place, and a party to attend a Masonic gathering. The trip to Pawtuxet was made in two hours, but on the return the vessel, being destitute of a keel, drifted ashore in a thunder-squall, but was not much injured. A Boston mechanic afterwards bought her at a sheriff's sale, but while being towed to Boston by a sloop he was obliged to cut loose from her, and she went ashore and was totally lost in Buzzard's Bay.

1809.—"Steam," says the *Gentleman's Magazine* for December, 1809, under the head of AMERICA, "has been applied in America to the purpose of inland navigation with the greatest success. The passage boat between New York and Albany is one hundred and sixty feet long, and wide in proportion for accommodations, consisting of fifty-two berths, besides sofas, etc., for one hundred passengers; and the machine which moves her wheels is equal to the power of twenty-four horses, and is kept in motion by steam from a copper boiler eight or ten feet in length. Her route is a distance of one hundred and fifty miles, which she performs regularly twice a week, and sometimes in the short space of thirty-two hours."

Mr. Longstreet, of Augusta, Georgia,[1] is said this year to have invented a steamboat, on principles entirely different from any that had been constructed, for navigating the rivers of the Southern States.

This steamer was fifteen feet long by four broad, with a cylinder of four inches. It carried eight persons, and went at a uniform rate of six miles an hour.

STEAMBOATS ON THE HUDSON.

1806.—Prior to the practical working of any steamboat in Europe, Mr. Charles Brown had built for Fulton the following vessels:

Name.	When built.	Tonnage.	Length.	Breadth.	Depth.	Cylinder.	Stroke.	How employed.
			Feet.	Feet.	Feet.	Inch.	Feet.	
Clermont	1806	160	133	18	7	24	4	On the Hudson River.
Raritan	1807	120	...	...	...	...	...	On the Raritan River.
Car of Neptune	1807	295	175	24	8	33	4.4	On the Hudson River.
Paragon	1811	331	173	27	9	32	4	On the Hudson River.
Jersey Ferry-Boat	1812	118	78	39	7	20	4	By the Ferry Company.
Firefly	1812	118	100	19	7	20	3.9	From New York to Newburgh.

up and utilize its material and engines. Some account of this vessel will be given farther on.

[1] See notice of him under heading, 1790.

The following advertisement is from the New York *Evening Post* of June, 1813, five years after the advent of the "Clermont," with a copy of a cut of the steamboat at its head:

"HUDSON RIVER STEAMBOATS.

"FOR THE INFORMATION OF THE PUBLIC.

"The *Paragon*, Capt. Wiswell, will leave New York every Saturday afternoon at five o'clock. The *Car of Neptune*, Capt. Roorbach, do, every Tuesday afternoon at five o'clock. The *North River*,[1] Capt. Bartholomew, every Thursday afternoon at five o'clock.

"The *Paragon* will leave Albany every Thursday morning at nine o'clock.

"The *Car of Neptune*, do, every Saturday morning at nine o'clock. The *North River*, do, every Tuesday morning at nine o'clock.

"PRICES OF PASSAGE.

"From *New York* to Verplanck's Point, $2; West Point, $2.50; Newburgh, $3; Wappingers Creek, $3.25; Poughkeepsie, $3.50; Hyde Park, $4; Esopus, $4.25; Catskill, $5; Hudson, $5; Coxsachie, $5.50; Kinderhook, $5.75; Albany, $7.

"From *Albany* to Kinderhook, $1.50; Coxsachie, $2; Hudson, $2; Catskills, $2.25; Red Hook, $2.75; Esopus, $3; Hyde Park, $3.25; Poughkeepsie, $3.50; Wappingers Creek, $4; Newburgh, $4.25; West Point, $4.75; Verplanck's Point, $5.25; New York, $7.

"All other way passengers to pay at the rate of one dollar for every twenty miles. No one can be taken on board and put on shore, however short the distance, for less than one dollar.

"Young persons from two to ten years of age to pay half price. Children under two years one-fourth price. Servants who use a berth two-thirds price; half price if none."

In 1816, eight steamers had been built to run on the Hudson; besides the four above named were the "Hope," "Perseverance," "Richmond," and "Olive Branch," and the "Clermont," having been enlarged, was renamed the "North River."

In 1816, the "Chancellor Livingston," named for his friend and patron, was constructed under the superintendence of Robert Fulton in New York, to run on the Hudson, and was the largest boat that had been built in that city, being of four hundred and ninety-six tons,—one hundred and twenty-five tons larger than any of her predecessors on that river. She was not launched until after his death, and may

---

[1] The "North River" was the "Clermont," which had been lengthened.

HISTORY OF STEAM NAVIGATION. 63

therefore be considered the crowning effort of his life. Her keel was one hundred and fifty-four feet long, decks one hundred and sixty-five feet, beam thirty-two feet, draught of water seven feet three inches, principal cabin fifty-four feet long, ladies's cabin, above the other, thirty-six feet long, with closets, forward cabin thirty feet long and seven feet high, permanent sleeping-berths in principal cabin thirty-eight, in ladies' cabin twenty-four, forward cabin fifty-six, in captain's cabin on deck eight, engineer's and pilot's three, forecastle six, cook's six; total, one hundred and thirty-five. Her original engine was of seventy-five horse-power, diameter of cylinder forty inches, length five feet, length of piston-rod eight feet six inches, stroke five feet, boiler twenty-eight feet long and twelve feet broad, with two funnels, paddle-wheels seventeen feet in diameter, paddle-boards five feet ten inches long. She had two fly-wheels, each fourteen feet in diameter, connected by pinions to the crank-wheel. The machinery rose four feet above the deck. Her average speed was eight and a half miles per hour; with strong wind and tide in her favor she made twelve miles; with the same against her, not more than six. This was as she was originally; afterwards she was lengthened, and with a larger engine her speed was increased.

In 1832 she was bought by Mr. C. Vanderbilt and Amos H. Cross, of Portland, and put on the route between Boston and Portland, as an opposition boat. At that time she had in her *third* engine, which was what is called a square or cross-head engine. Working-beams had not then come into use. This engine had a fifty-six-inch cylinder and six-feet stroke. She had three smoke-stacks athwartships, and three masts, a bowsprit and jib-boom, with yards and topsails on the foremast. In 1834 the "Chancellor Livingston" was broken up in Portland, and her engines placed in a new boat named the "Portland," which was launched June, 1835.

The "Portland" was chartered to the United States government during the Mexican War, and finally lost somewhere, about 1848, on the gulf coast of Mexico, between Tampico and Matamoras. Captain J. B. Coyle, then the engineer of the "Portland," is credited with having invented a blower by which he was able to use anthracite coal on board the "Portland, in 1835, and she was the first steamer that burnt anthracite coal with success. Small blower-engines were soon after adopted in New York.[1]

The following table of the dimensions of nine steamers which were running on the Hudson prior to 1838, compared with the table of the pioneer steamers on that river in 1812, will show the rapid development of steam propulsion in a little over a quarter of a century from its introduction.

---

[1] Captain Coyle is now the president of the Portland Steam Packet Company, and we may say was the originator of that successful enterprise.

Name.	Length of Deck.	Breadth of Beam.	Draught.	Diameter of Wheel.	Length of Paddles.	Depth of Paddles.	Number of Engines.	Diameter of Cylinder.	Length of Stroke.	Number of Revolutions.	Part of Stroke at which Steam is cut off.
	Ft.	Ft.	Ft.	Ft.	Ft.	In.		In.	Ft.		
De Witt Clinton	230	28	5.5	21	18.7	36	1	65	10	29	¼–½
Champlain	180	27	5.5	22	15	84	2	44	10	27.5	¼–½
Erie	180	27	5.5	22	15	84	2	44	10	27.5	¼–½
North America	200	30	5	21	13	30	2	44.5	8	24	¼–½
Independence	148	26	..	..	..	..	1	44	10	..	
Albany	212	26	..	24.5	14	30	1	65	10	19	
Swallow	233	22.5	3.75	24	11	30	1	46	..	27	
Utica	200	21	3.5	22	9.5	24	1	39	10	..	
Rochester	200	25	3.75	23.5	10	24	1	48	10	28	

Again, the following table gives the dimensions of ten steamers, recently built, plying on the Hudson and collateral waters in 1854, not quite half a century after the advent of Fulton's experimental steamboat, the "Clermont."

Name.	Dimensions of Vessel.				Engines.			Paddle-Wheel.		
	Length.	Beam.	Depth of Hold.	Tonnage.	Diameter of Cylinder.	Length of Stroke.	Number of Strokes.	Diameter.	Length of Bucket.	Depth of Bucket.
	Ft.	Ft. In.	Ft. In.		In.	Ft.		Ft. In.	Ft. In.	In.
Isaac Newton	333	40 4	10 0	..	81	12	18½	39 0	12 4	32
Bay State	300	39 0	13 2	..	76	12	21½	38 0	10 3	32
Empire State	304	39 0	13 6	..	76	12	21½	38 0	10 3.	32
Oregon	375	35 0	..	1000	72	11	18	34 0	11 0	28
Hendrick Hudson	320	35 0	9 6	1050	72	11	22	33 0	11 0	33
C. Vanderbilt	300	35 0	11 0	1075	72	12	21	35 0	9 0	33
Connecticut	300	37 0	11 0	..	72	13	21	35 0	11 6	36
Commodore	280	33 0	10 6	..	65	11	22	31 6	9 0	33
New World	375	35 0	10 6	..	76	15	18	44 6	12 0	36
Alida	286	28 0	9 6	..	56	12	24½	32 0	10 0	32

The new and largest class of steamers on the Hudson are capable of running from twenty to twenty-five miles an hour, and make on an average eighteen miles an hour. These remarkable speeds are obtained usually by rendering the boilers capable of carrying steam up to fifty pounds pressure above the atmosphere, and by urging the fires with fans worked by an independent engine. This extreme of speed is also obtained at a disproportionate increased consumption of fuel.

Up to 1836 steamboats in the United States had burned wood only. The "Novelty" burnt forty cords on each trip from Albany to New York, and the same on her northern trip. Experiments were made with coal for fuel with success, but wood was principally used for several years after.

"To obtain an adequate notion of the form and structure of one of the first-class steamboats on the Hudson," says Doctor Lardner in his "Museum of Science and Art," "let it be supposed that a boat is constructed similar in form to a Thames wherry, but above three hundred feet long and twenty-five to thirty feet wide. Upon this let a platform of carpentry be laid, projecting several feet upon either side of the boat, and at the stem and stern. The appearance to the eye will then be that of an immense raft, from two hundred and fifty to three hundred and fifty feet long and some thirty or forty feet wide. Upon this flooring let us imagine an oblong rectangular wooden erection, two stories high, to be raised. In the lower part of the boat, and under the flooring, a long, narrow room is constructed, having a series of berths at either side, three or four tiers high. In the centre of this flooring usually, but not always, is inclosed an oblong, rectangular space, within which the steam machinery is placed, and this inclosed space is continued upward through the structures raised in the platform, and is intersected at a certain height above the platform by the shaft or axle of the paddle-wheel.

"These wheels are propelled generally by a single engine, but occasionally by two. The paddle-wheels are of great diameter, varying from thirty to forty feet, according to the magnitude of the boats. In the wooden building raised upon the platform already mentioned is a magnificent saloon, devoted to the ladies and those gentlemen who accompany them. Over this, in the upper story, is constructed a row of small bedrooms (state-rooms), each handsomely furnished, which passengers can have who desire seclusion by paying a small additional fare. The lower apartment is commonly used as a dining- and breakfast-room.

"In some boats the wheels are propelled by two engines, which are placed on the platform which overhangs the boat at either side, each wheel being propelled by an independent engine; the wheels in this case acting independently of each other and without a common shaft or axle. This leaves this entire space in the boat, from stem to stern, free of machinery. It is impossible to describe the magnificent *coup d'œil* which is presented by the immense apparent length when the communication between them is thrown open. Some of these boats are upwards of three hundred feet long, and the uninterrupted length of the saloons corresponds with this.

"This arrangement of machinery is attended with some practical advantages, one of which is a facility of turning, as the wheels, acting independently of each other, may be driven in opposite directions, one propelling forward and the other backward, so that the boat may be made to turn on its centre. Although from the great width of the Hudson no great difficulty is encountered in turning the longest boat, yet cases occur in which this power of revolution is found extremely advantageous. Another advantage of this system is that if one of the two engines becomes accidentally disabled, the boat can be propelled by the other.

"No spectacle can be more remarkable than that which the Hudson presents for several miles above New York. The skill with which these enormous vessels, measuring from three to four hundred feet in length, are made to thread their way through the crowd of shipping of every description moving over the face of this spacious river, and the rare occurrence of accidents, is truly admirable. In dark nights these boats run at the top of their speed through fleets of sailing-vessels. The bells, through which the steersman speaks to the engineer, scarcely ever cease. Of these bells there are several different tones, indicating the different operations which the engineer is commanded to make, such as stopping, starting, reversing, slackening, accelerating, etc. At the slightest tap of one of these bells the enormous engines are stopped, or started, or reversed, by the engineer, as though they were the playthings of a child. These vessels, proceeding at sixteen and eighteen miles an hour, are propelled among the crowded shipping with so much skill as almost to graze the sides, sterns, or bows of the vessels among which they pass."

This graphic description was written in 1854, twenty-eight years ago, but conveys a good general description of the boats now running upon the river, electric bells and electric lights being among the later improvements, and the cabins and saloons perhaps being more sumptuously upholstered.

"No spectacle," adds Doctor Lardner, "can be more remarkable than a large steam tow-boat dragging its enormous load up the Hudson. They may be seen in the middle of this vast stream surrounded by a cluster of twenty or thirty loaded craft of various magnitudes. Three or four tiers are lashed to each side, and as many more at the bow and at the stern. The steamer is almost lost to the eye in the midst of this crowd of vessels which cling around it, and the moving mass is seen to proceed up the river, no apparent agent of propulsion being visible. As this *water goods train*, for so it may be called, ascends the Hudson, it drops off its load vessel by vessel at the towns which it passes. One or two are left at Newburgh, another at Poughkeepsie, two or three more at Hudson, one or two at Fishkill, and in fine the tug arrives with a residuum of some half a dozen vessels at Albany."[1]

STEAMBOATS ON THE DELAWARE.

1809.—The seventh vessel which was propelled by steam upon the Delaware arrived in Philadelphia, from Hoboken, New Jersey, in June, 1809. This steamboat was called the "Phœnix," and was the same built by John Cox Stevens, at Hoboken, in 1806, and intended

[1] The Museum of Science and Arts, edited by Doctor Lardner, vol. ii., 1854.

HISTORY OF STEAM NAVIGATION. 67

as a passenger-boat between New Brunswick and New York. But Fulton and Livingston having obtained from the State of New York an assignment or transfer of the rights of John Fitch under the law of March 19, 1786, securing to Fitch a monopoly in the nature of a patent for all boats and vessels navigated by fire and steam, Colonel Stevens found that employment of his boat in the waters of New York was restricted so much that it could not be made profitable. He therefore formed the design of sending the vessel to Philadelphia, as an assistant to the line of packets and stages upon the line to New York. This was a bold and hazardous experiment. The ocean had never been navigated by steam, and the power of the engines being limited, the danger from storms seemed very great. But Robert L. Stevens, son of John Cox Stevens, the inventor, determined to risk the trial, and accordingly with a small crew he left New York. A fierce storm overtook them. A schooner in company was driven off to sea, and was kept out several days. The "Phœnix" made a harbor at Barnegat. After the storm subsided, Stevens succeeded in bringing the boat around into the Delaware, and thus earned the distinction of having been the first man who ever navigated the ocean by steam. The first trip on the Delaware was made between Philadelphia and Trenton, July 5, 1809, there being nearly forty passengers on board. The " Phœnix" had "twenty-five commodious berths in her cabin and twelve in her steerage, with other ample accommodations for passengers." She was constructed with masts, so as to be able to take advantage of favorable winds and thereby add to the facility of her passages, and at the same time effect a saving in that important article, fuel.

After the "Phœnix," the next steamboat that ran up the Delaware was named the "Philadelphia." It was put on by the Union Line, and was commanded by Captain Jenkins. She ran from Philadelphia to Bristol, and afterwards established a wharf about three miles above, called "Van Hart's." Passengers thence took stages for New Brunswick and to New York in the " William Gibbons." For some reason this boat always went by the name of " Old Sal," probably from a grotesque-looking female figure-head on her bow.

The next steamboat was the "Pennsylvania," and carried passengers for the Citizens' Line. The engine of this boat was subsequently placed in the old "Lehigh." Passengers by this line landed at Bordentown, and thence took coaches to Washington, New Jersey, where they were conveyed to New York on the steamer " Ætna," Captain Robinson. The following is one of the advertisements of this boat, dated March 23, 1818:

"THE STEAMBOAT ÆTNA

" Leaves the upper side of Market Street daily, at 6 o'clock (after to-morrow), for Bordentown, touching up and down at Burlington,

Bristol, and White Hill. *Passengers for New York, via Bristol*, will be conveyed thro' by sunset of same day, and by way of Bordentown, by noon next day."

The following advertisement is from *The True American and Commercial Advertiser*, Philadelphia, Wednesday, June 4, 1817:

"PHILADELPHIA AND BALTIMORE LINE OF STEAM-BOATS AND STAGES,

(Cut of steamboat.)

"By way of Wilmington and Elkton every Monday, Wednesday, and Friday.

"The new steamboat Superior, Capt. Wm. Milnor, will leave the first wharf above Market St., Phila., at 3 o'clock in the afternoon on the aforesaid days for Baltimore.

"The steamboat New Jersey, Capt. Rogers, will leave Light St. wharf for Phila. in the afternoon of the same days. These boats are connected by a line of stages on the new turnpike between Wilmington and Elkton.

"N.B.—The Superior will leave Phila. every day for Wilmington (Sundays excepted) at three in the afternoon, and Wilmington every morning for Philadelphia at seven o'clock.

"Passengers rec'd and deliv'ed at Chester and Marcus Hook."

"THE STEAMBOAT BRISTOL

(For Burlington and Bristol.)

"Leaves the first wharf above Market St. every day at three o'clk. in the afternoon, taking passengers for New York by the way of Bristol, Trenton, Brunswick, and Elizabethtown; also by the way of South Amboy. On her return to Philada. she leaves Bristol at half-past seven and Burlington at eight o'clock every morning (Sundays excepted)."

Another advertisement in 1818 announces

"THE STEAMBOAT BRISTOL, OF BURLINGTON,

"Has commenced running for the season, leaving Bristol daily at half-past seven A.M.; Burlington at eight A.M. (and in returning), Philadelphia at three P.M.

"N.B.—A Coach leaves Bristol for Trenton every day, immediately upon the arrival of this boat, and in the morning leaves Trenton in time for the passengers to proceed in her to Philadelphia. Fare to Trenton, $1.25."

And still another informs us that

"THE PHILADELPHIA & NEW YORK LINE

"Of steamboats, *via* Trenton and New Brunswick, connected by new carriages. 26 Miles by land. Fare, $4.50 through. Deck passengers, $3.50 through.

"Passengers leave the south side of Market Street wharf, in the Steamboat PHILADELPHIA, for Trenton, every day at 11 o'clock, lodge in New Brunswick, and arrive in New York in the Steamboat OLIVE BRANCH, the next day at 10 o'clock A.M. On her return the Philadelphia will leave Trenton at 6 o'clock A.M., and arrive at 10 A.M.

"The Hull and Engine of the Philadelphia have been thoroughly repaired. She will work under a very low pressure of steam, and will be managed by a careful and experienced Engineer."

The "Ætna" exploded her boiler in New York harbor in 1824, having on board the Philadelphia passengers, and several lives were lost. Her place on the line was supplied by the steamboat "New York." The Union Line then built the "New Philadelphia," to compete with the "New York," of the Citizens' Line, and then the "Trenton" came out to run against the "Pennsylvania," of the Citizens' Line. This line then built a new float, and named it the "Philadelphia," to beat the "Trenton."

There was a wonderful competition among these lines for several years, when Captain Whilldin and Cornelius Vanderbilt started an opposition to them all. This was called the Dispatch Line, and the fare at one time was reduced to one dollar. The boat on this end was named the "Emerald." The Dispatch Line was soon disposed of, and the Union and the Citizens', with some of the others, afterwards became merged in the Camden and Amboy Railroad Company. The next boat was the "John Stevens," built at Hoboken in 1846, and destroyed by fire at Bordentown on the night of the 16th of July, 1855. The next was the "Richard Stockton," which ran between South Amboy and New York.

1810–19.—Mr. Hezekiah Bliss, who died at Brooklyn in 1876, made the acquaintance of Robert Fulton in 1810, then in the height of his fame as the pioneer of steamship navigation. Young Bliss was a frequent visitor at Fulton's home, and in his later years often spoke of the instruction that Fulton gave him. With his brain full of steamboats, young Bliss came to Philadelphia in the fall of 1811, and in the following spring associated himself with Daniel French in the organization of a company to build a steamboat. They constructed a boat about sixty feet long by twelve feet wide, with an oscillating engine and stern wheel, which he judged the best adapted to avoid the drift-wood that had proved a serious impediment to navigation in Western waters. The boat was for some time employed on a ferry between Philadelphia and William Cooper's landing.

In 1816, Mr. Bliss went to Cincinnati, and there in the following year he engaged, with the eldest son of General William H. Harrison, in the construction of steamboats. They built one, which they named "General Pike," in honor of General Zebulon Montgomery Pike, the father-in-law of young Harrison. It was one hundred feet long by twenty-five wide, and was the first boat ever built in Cincinnati, and the sixth on Western waters. The boat was first run in 1819.

Returning to New York in 1827, Mr. Bliss considered a flattering proposition to go to Mexico as an agent of the Barings of London, and soon afterwards, with Dr. Eliphalet Nott, formerly president of Union College, he engaged, in 1827-28, in experiments in steam navigation. In 1851 he established the since widely-known Novelty Works, with the view of constructing ocean steamers.—*Philadelphia Press.*

STEAM FERRY-BOATS IN NEW YORK HARBOR—1810-14.

In 1810 arrangements were made with Robert Fulton to construct steam ferry-boats, and on the 2d of July, 1812, one named the "Jersey" was put in operation between Paulus Hook, Jersey City, and New York. The event was celebrated with a grand banquet given by the Jerseymen to the New York Common Council. A correspondent to a newspaper of the times says,—

"I crossed the North River yesterday in the steamboat with my family in my carriage, without alighting therefrom, in fourteen minutes, with an immense crowd of passengers. On both shores were thousands of people viewing the pleasant object. I cannot express to you how much the public mind appeared to be gratified at finding so large and so safe a machine going so well."

This "large machine" was eighty feet long and thirty feet wide.

A year later the "York" was put on with the "Jersey." They were supposed to run every half-hour from sunrise until sunset, but frequently an hour was consumed in making a trip. Fulton's description of one of the boats is as follows:

"She is built of two boats, each ten feet beam, eighty feet long, and five feet deep in the hold; which boats are distant from each other ten feet, confined by strong transverse beam-knees and diagonal traces, forming a deck thirty feet wide and eighty long. The propelling water-wheel is placed between the boats to prevent it from injury from ice and shocks on entering or approaching the dock. The whole of the machinery being placed between the two boats, leaves ten feet on the deck of each boat for carriages, horses, and cattle, etc.; the other, having neat benches and covered with an awning, is for passengers, and there is also a passage- and stair-way to a neat cabin, which is fifty feet long and five feet clear from the floor to the beams, furnished with benches, and provided with a stove in winter. Although the two boats and space between them give thirty feet beam, yet they present sharp bows to the water, and have only the resistance in the water of one boat of twenty feet beam. Both ends being alike, and each having a rudder, she never puts about."

The Legislature of New York passed an act March 4, 1814, allowing William Cutting and others to run a steam ferry with passengers at four cents each between Brooklyn and New York. The first trips were made in the beginning of May, 1814, and the name of the boat was the "Nassau." The *Columbian*, a newspaper of that time, contained an account of the new ferry, and stated that on one of the first trips of the "Nassau," from the Beekman slip to the lower ferry in Brooklyn, there were five hundred and forty-nine passengers, one wagon and a pair of horses, two horses and chaise, and one single horse. The trip occupied from four to eight minutes, and forty crossings were made every day.

The veteran artist Banvard, in an interview with a reporter, December, 1881, says, "I crossed this Fulton Ferry from Fair, now Fulton, Street on this first steam ferry-boat. At that time the boilers were placed on deck, and Fulton Street was a country road with old farmhouses on either side."

Surmounted by a picture of the steamboat, an advertisement of the ferry company of 1814 reads:

"NEW YORK AND BROOKLYN FERRY.

"Such persons as are inclined to compound agreeable to law, in the Steam Ferry Boat, Barges, or common Horse boats, will be pleased to apply to the subscribers, who are authorized to settle the same.

"GEORGE HICKS, Brooklyn.
"JOHN PINTARD, 52 Wall St.

"Commutation for a single person not transferable for 12 months $10 00
    do   do   8 months 6 67
"May 3, 1814.   6 m."

Fulton and Cutting formed a company, "The New York and Brooklyn Steamboat Ferry Association," with a capital of sixty-eight thousand dollars, in sixty shares, valued at one thousand three hundred and thirty-three dollars and thirty-three cents each. The first steamboat of this company was the "Nassau," and the Long Island *Star* of May 14, 1814, mentions her *first* trip. The boat must have been adapted for the work, as it is stated, "Her trips varied from five to twelve minutes; carriages and wagons, however crowded, pass on and off the boat with the same facility as in passing a bridge."

Some time after the steamboat, supplementary scows were run by horses. The scows had double hulls, and with the paddle in the middle, eight horses supplied the power.

In 1817 the advantages of the steamboat were so manifest that the public were clamorous for a second boat, which, according to the agreement, was to be placed on the route by May 1, 1819. The company demurred on the ground of expense, and alleged that team-boats were more easily navigated and much safer in winter than steamboats. They offered to substitute the horse for the steam on the boat, and to run it until 8 P.M. The New York authorities, with reluctance and in order to avoid legislative interference, agreed, and the price was raised to four cents for both team- and steamboats. In 1833, David Leavitt and Silas Butler, having bought forty-four of the sixty shares of the Fulton Ferry stock, obtained control of the ferry and put on two new boats.

Mr. Banvard has recorded his reminiscences of the old horse ferry-boat from New York to Brooklyn in verse:

> "How well I remember the horse-boat that paddled
>   'Cross the East River ere the advent of steam;
> Sometimes the old driver the horses would straddle,
>   And sometimes ride round on the circling beam.

> "The old wheel would creak, and the driver would whistle
>   To force the blind horses to pull the wheel round;
> And their backs were all scarr'd and stuck out in bristles,
>   For the driver's fierce stick their old bones would pound.

> "The man at the gate, in fair weather or rainy,
>   Stood out in the storm by the cold river-side,
> With pockets capacious, to hold all the pennies:
>   It took just four coppers to cross o'er the tide.

> "The pilot, he, too, took the wind and the weather,
>   Perched o'er the horses, with his tiller in hand;
> Sometimes would the wind and the tide fierce together
>   Delay him in getting his boat to the land.

> "Though four-horse was the power that plowed the fierce river,
>   Yet oft in his hurry would the passenger curse,
> Though no thought would come to make a man shiver
>   About the dread danger of a boiler to burst."

1811.—On the 29th of November, 1811, Daniel Dod, a citizen of the United States, was granted a United States patent, by which he claimed as his invention,—

  1. The construction of the boiler.

  2. The condenser, consisting . . .

  3. The exclusive right to place the steam cylinder and other parts of the steam-engine between two boilers in a steamboat as described.

  4. The disposition and arrangement of the several parts and combination of the whole machinery.

In an accompanying schedule, Dod says, "I make the steam-engine to work with a double impulse, on the general principles of Watt and Bolton's steam-engines. I form the condenser of a pipe, or a number of pipes condensed together, and condense the steam by immersing the pipes in cold water, either with or without an injection of water. For propelling a boat I make use of two wheels, one on each side, hung on an axis which lies across the boat. In the middle of this axis is a crank to which is attached the lower end of a pitman. The upper end of the pitman is attached to one end of a lever-beam; the main piston-rod is attached. The lever-beam is placed above the cylinder of the steam-engine, in the manner practiced by Watt and Bolton.

"The fly-wheels of the steam-engine I fix on the axis of the propelling wheels; I make the fly-wheels by weighting the propelling wheels with iron buckets or propelling boards, or with iron segments.

"For steam I use two boilers placed in the bottom of the boat, one on each side of the space allotted for machinery. I fix the cylinder and steam-engine between the boilers.

"The boilers I construct, viz.,—the outside to be a cylinder of a length and diameter to produce the required steam. The cylinder to be horizontal, with a fixed flue equal to its length; its form the segment of a semicircle or greater. This flue, placed within and near the lower side of the cylinder, allowed space for the water to pass under it. Within the flue, at one end, was the fire; at the opposite end a pipe for carrying off the smoke and producing a draft to carry off the smoke and make the fire burn briskly. The flat or upper side was strengthened and supported by perpendicular tubes, and by rods and braces extending from the upper side of the flue to the upper side of the cylinder. The axis of the propelling wheels pass over the top of the boilers."

1812.—May 12, 1812, Daniel Dod obtained another patent for his mode of applying the steam-engine to boats, mills, etc. After specifying his invention, Dod says, "My mode of applying this invention to the navigation of a boat is as follows:

"I place two propelling wheels as near the bow of the boat as convenience will admit. The arbors of these two wheels are placed in the same right line, and the inner ends of the arbors approach near together in the middle of the boat. One crank attached to the end of both arbors, and one pitman from the end of the lower beam, put both wheels in motion.

"Then two other propelling wheels are placed so far abaft of the forward wheels that the distance shall be equal to the sum of the length of the two lever-beams. The arbors of these two abaft wheels also are placed in a right line with each other, and the inner ends of the arbors approach near together, and a crank is connected with the ends of both arbors, similar to the forward wheels. Then a pitman from the end of the other lever-beam will drive both wheels together.

"In this way, without a cog-wheel or sector of any kind, I employ one steam-engine and a boat to drive *four propelling wheels*, by which means I am enabled to avail myself of a large proportion of propellers, without making my wheels so wide as to project out an inconvenient distance from the sides of the boat."

Dod claimed the driving of double sets of machinery with one steam-engine, and the applying of four propelling wheels to a boat, as his invention and exclusive right; but no profitable result seems to have been achieved from his invention.

February 9, 1811, Robert Fulton obtained a United States patent supplementary to his patent of February 11, 1809, for inventions and discoveries for constructing boats or vessels to be navigated by the power of steam. Among other specifications describing his invention he says, " I use coupling boxes, or any other means to throw the propelling wheels in or out of gear, or to work one wheel out and the other as required. This convenience I claim as my discovery and exclusive right. I also claim as my invention the guards which are around and outside the propelling wheels, which guards may support the outside gudgeons of the wheels and afford a deposit for fuel, etc., water-closets for the use of passengers, and steps to enter from row-boats and to protect the water-wheels from injury from vessels and wharves." He also claimed the exclusive right to cover the water-wheels with boards, netting, grating, canvas or leather, etc., to prevent them from throwing water on deck or entangling the ropes. He claimed also to have invented placing the forward tiller or steering wheel farther forward in steamboats then used, since the boat being long and the deck covered with passengers the pilots behind could not see far ahead; also the straight and diagonal traces being far extending from the boiler to forward of the machinery, which he placed on the sides to give them strength; also a frame set in the bottom of the boat to bear the weight of the machinery and working of the engine; also as his invention and exclusive right " the combination of sails with a steam-engine to drive a boat, I being the first who have done so, and proved by practice the utility of the union of the two powers of wind and steam." He claimed also in the patent his " particular mode of proportioning and placing a propelling wheel or wheels in the stern of a boat in a chamber formed by the two sides of the boat extending aft one or more feet farther than the extreme diameter of the propelling wheel, to each side of which projection there is a rudder, which two rudders connected by a cross-bar working on pivots cause them to move together and parallel to each other; from this cross-bar on the rudders the ropes or *steering chains* lead on to the pilot."

John C. Hamilton, a son of Alexander Hamilton, wrote to the Philadelphia *Times* in 1878 : " About the year 1809 I went from New York to Washington City with my mother. Robert Fulton was in the stage

HISTORY OF STEAM NAVIGATION. 75

with us, and we were all day getting to Princeton, where we were to stop. Behind the stage Fulton had a submarine torpedo hitched up, which he was taking to Washington. Fulton was a gentleman in mind and manners."

The first steamboat launched on Lake Champlain was in 1809; she was called the "Vermont." Between 1809 and 1870 thirty steamboats had been built and run upon the lake, the last of which, like the pioneer boat, was named the "Vermont."

1811.—The Boston *Weekly Messenger* of November 8, 1811, under the head of RAPID TRAVELING, prints a letter from New York, dated October 24, which says, "The steamboat 'Car of Neptune,' which left this city on Saturday evening last at five o'clock, arrived at Albany in twenty hours. She returned this morning in twenty-two hours,—equal to *three hundred and thirty miles in forty-three hours!* Let foreigners say we have no talent for improvement. Point out where there is a mode of conveyance equal to this! In what country are there so many enjoyments combined in one great polytechnic machine and mounted with wings as this which wafts passengers as by enchantment between the cities of New York and Albany? To our countrymen, then, and our arts let justice be honorably and honestly measured out."

In January of the same year Fulton had so little idea of the capacity and speed attainable by steam that, in a letter to Dr. Thornton,[1] he says, "I shall be happy to have some conversation with you on your steamboat inventions and experience. Although I do not see by what means a boat containing one hundred tons of merchandise can be driven *six* miles an hour in still water, yet when you assert perfect confidence in such success, there may be something more in your combinations than I am aware of. . . . If you succeed to run six miles an hour in still water with one hundred tons of merchandise, I will contract to reimburse the cost of the boat, and to give you one hundred and fifty thousand dollars for your patent; or, if you convince me of the success by drawings or demonstrations, I will join you in the expense and profits."

Within forty years five times the amount of merchandise was propelled by steam twenty miles an hour.

On the 17th of March, 1811, a steamboat built by Fulton and Livingston was launched at Pittsburg, Pennsylvania, under the superintendence of Mr. Roosevelt, as the agent of Messrs. Fulton, Livingston & Co., of New York. She was a stern-wheel boat, and was the first steamboat ever run upon the Western waters of the United States. She was painted with a bluish-colored paint, and passed New Madrid, Missouri, at the time of the earthquake in December of that year. Mr. Scowls, who in 1853 was a wealthy citizen of Covington, Kentucky, was a cabin-boy on board.

[1] Recently in the possession of Colonel Force, Washington.

In 1814 she carried General Coffee and Don Carol from Natchez, with troops, down to New Orleans to aid General Jackson in his defense of that city.

FIRST STEAMERS ON THE ST. LAWRENCE.

1809–13.—In 1809 the first steamboat was launched on the St. Lawrence. The Quebec *Mercury* of that date says concerning her,—

"On Saturday morning at eight o'clock arrived here from Montreal, being her first trip, the steamboat "Accommodation," with ten passengers. This is the first vessel of the kind that ever appeared in this harbor. She is continually crowded with visitants. She left Montreal on Wednesday at two o'clock; so that her passage was sixty-six hours, thirty of which she was at anchor. She arrived at Three Rivers in twenty-four hours. She has at present berths for twenty passengers, which next year will be considerably augmented. No wind or tide can stop her. She has seventy-five feet keel, and is eighty-five feet on deck. The price for a passage up is nine dollars, and eight down, the vessel supplying provisions. The great advantage attending a vessel so constructed is that a passage may be calculated on to a degree of certainty in point of time, which cannot be the case with any vessel propelled by sails alone. The steamboat receives her impulse from an open, double-spoked perpendicular wheel on each side, without any circular band or rim. To the end of each double spoke is fixed a square board, which enters the water, and by the rotary motion of the wheel acts like a paddle. The wheels are put and kept in motion by steam operating within the vessel. A mast is to be fixed in her for the purpose of using a sail when the wind is favorable, which will occasionally accelerate her headway."

In the spring of 1813 a second boat, of increased dimensions, called the "Swiftsure," was launched from the banks of the St. Lawrence. She was one hundred and thirty feet in length of keel, and one hundred and forty feet on deck, with twenty-four feet beam, and, according to the *Mercury*, made the passage from Montreal to Quebec in twenty-two hours, notwithstanding that the wind was easterly the whole time and blowing strong.

The "Swiftsure" beat the most famous of the sailing packets on the river fourteen hours in a race of thirty-six hours, but her owners seem not to have been very confident of her movements under all circumstances, or of the number of passengers who would patronize her, for she was advertised to "Sail as the wind and passengers may suit."

FIRST STEAMBOATS IN INDIA.

1810.—The "Van der Capellen," the first steamboat of which we have any record in connection with India, was built at Batavia soon after the conclusion of the Java war, in 1810–11, at the expense of English merchants. She was employed by the government for two years, at the rate of ten thousand dollars a month, which well repaid her original outlay. She proved very effective for the transport of troops and general service. After some years she came into the possession of Major Schalch, and was used by him, under the name of the "Pluto," in 1822, as a dredging-boat. Then she went to Arraken as a floating battery. Finally she was lost, in 1830, in a gale.

In 1819, W. Trickett built at the Butterley Works a small steamboat of eight horse-power, for the Nawab of Oude, to ply on the Jumna.[1]

In 1821 the "Diana" was sent out for a Mr. Roberts, intended for employment on the Canton River. She had a pair of sixteen horsepower engines. At Calcutta she was nearly reconstructed by Messrs. Kyd & Co., and launched again July 12, 1823, after which she was purchased by the Bengal government and dispatched to Amarapura, five hundred miles up the river Irrawaddy, with Mr. Crawford, then the Resident in Burmah. She sailed in September, when that river is at its fullest, and her progress, which did not exceed thirty miles a day, was a disappointment to the Indian government. The water having fallen when she returned in December, the navigation was intricate, and her passage down was also tedious.

INTRODUCTION OF STEAMBOATS ON THE WESTERN WATERS.

First Trip of the "New Orleans" from Pittsburg to New Orleans.[2]

1811.—Prior to the introduction of steamboats on the Western waters the means of transportation thereon consisted of keel-boats, barges, and flat-boats. The two former ascended as well as descended the stream. The flat-boat, or "broad horn," an unwieldy box, was broken up for its lumber on arrival at its place of destination. Whether steam could be employed on the Western rivers was a question its success between New York and Albany was not regarded as having entirely solved, and after the idea had been suggested of building a boat at Pittsburg to ply between Natchez and New Orleans, it was considered necessary investigations should be made as to the currents of the rivers to be navigated. These investigations were undertaken by Mr. Nicholas J. Roosevelt, with the understanding that if the report was favorable, Chancellor Livingston, Mr. Robert Fulton, and himself were to be equally interested in the undertaking. Livingston and Fulton were to supply the capital and Roosevelt was to superin-

[1] Early Steam Navigation to India, by G. A. Prinsep, Calcutta, 4to, 1830.

[2] This account of the "New Orleans'" first voyage is condensed from "The First Steamboat Voyage on the Western Waters," by J. H. B. Latrobe, Baltimore, October, 1871, 82 pp., 8vo, Fund Publication, No. 6, of the Maryland Historical Society. Mrs. Roosevelt was a sister of Mr. Latrobe, and alive when he wrote this narrative. This successful voyage of the "New Orleans" down the Ohio and Mississippi antedates the first voyage of the "Comet" on the Clyde, which commenced to ply between Glasgow and Helensburgh January, 1812, with only a speed of five miles an hour.

tend the building of the boat and engine. He accordingly repaired to Pittsburg in May, 1809, accompanied by his bride, where he built a flat-boat which was to contain all the necessary comforts to float himself and wife with the current from Pittsburg to New Orleans, and this boat was the home of the young couple for six months. He reached New Orleans about December 1, 1809, and returned thence to New York in the first vessel. Mr. Roosevelt had made up his mind that steam was to do the work, and his visit was to ascertain how best it could be done upon the Western streams. He gauged them and measured their velocity at different seasons, and obtained all the statistical information within his reach. Finding coal on the banks of the Ohio, he purchased and opened mines of that mineral, and so confident was he of the success of his steam project that he caused supplies of the fuel to be heaped up on the shore in anticipation of the wants of a steamboat whose keel had yet to be laid, and whose existence was dependent upon the impression of his report upon capitalists, without whose aid the plan would have, temporarily at least, to be abandoned. Mr. Roosevelt's report so impressed Fulton and Livingston that in the spring of 1810 he was sent to Pittsburg to superintend the building of the first steamboat that was launched on the Western waters. On the Alleghany side, close by the creek, and immediately under a bluff called Boyd's Hill, the keel of Mr. Roosevelt's vessel was laid. The depot of the Pittsburg and Connellsville Railroad now occupies the ground (1882). The size and plan of this steamboat was furnished by Robert Fulton. It was to be one hundred and sixteen feet in length, with twenty feet beam. The engine was to have a thirty-four-inch cylinder, and the boiler, etc., to be in proportion. To obtain the timber, men were sent into the forest to find the ribs, knees, and beams, transport them to the Monongahela, and raft them to the ship-yard. The ship-builders and mechanics for the machinery department had to be brought from New York. A rise in the waters of the Monongahela set all the buoyant materials afloat, and at one time it seemed probable that the vessel would be lifted from its ways and launched before its time. At length the boat was launched, at a cost of near thirty-eight thousand dollars, and was named "New Orleans," after the place of her ultimate destination.

As the "New Orleans" approached completion and it became known that Mrs. Roosevelt intended to accompany her husband, friends endeavored to dissuade her from the utter folly, if not absolute madness of the voyage. Her husband was told he had no right to *peril her life*, however reckless he *might be of his own*. The wife, however, believed in her husband, and after a short experimental trip late in September the "New Orleans" commenced her voyage. There were two cabins, one aft for ladies and a larger one forward for gentlemen. In the former were four berths. Mr. and Mrs. Roosevelt took possession of the cabin, as they were the only passengers. There was a captain, an engineer named Baker, Andrew Jack the pilot, six hands, two female servants, a man waiter, a cook, and an immense Newfoundland dog, named "Tiger." Thus equipped and manned, the "New Orleans" began the voyage which changed the relations of the West to the East, and which may almost be said to have changed its destiny.

The people of Pittsburg turned out *en masse* and lined the banks of the Monongahela to witness the departure of the steamboat, and shout after shout rent the air, and handkerchiefs were waved, and hats thrown up in "Godspeed" when the anchor was raised, and as she disappeared behind the first headlands on the right bank of the Ohio.

Too much excited to sleep, Mr. Roosevelt and his wife passed the greater part of the first night on deck, and watched the shore, covered then with an almost unbroken forest, as reach after reach and bend after bend were passed at a speed of from eight to ten miles an hour.

On the second night after leaving Pittsburg the "New Orleans" rounded to opposite Cincinnati, and cast anchor in the stream. Levees and wharf-boats were things unknown in 1811. Here as in Pittsburg the whole town seemed to have assembled on the bank, and many of the acquaintances of their former visit came off in small boats. "Well, you are as good as your word; you have visited us in a steamboat," they said; "but we see you for the last time: your boat may go *down* the river, but as to coming up it, the idea is an absurd one." The keel-boatmen shook their heads as they crowded around the strange visitor and bandied river wit with the crew that had been selected from their own calling for the first voyage. Some flat-boatmen, whose arks the steamboat had passed a short distance above the town, and who now floated by with the current, seemed to have a better opinion of the new-comer, and proposed a tow in case they were again overtaken. But as to the boat's returning, all agreed that *that* could never be.

The stay at Cincinnati was brief, only long enough to take in a supply of wood for the voyage to Louisville, which was reached on the night of the fourth day after leaving Pittsburg. It was midnight on the 1st of October, 1811, that the "New Orleans" dropped anchor opposite the town. There was a brilliant moon. It was almost as light as day, and no one on board had retired. The roar of the escaping steam, then heard for the first time, roused the population, and, late as it was, crowds came rushing to the bank of the river to learn the cause of the unwonted uproar. A letter written by one of those on board records the fact that there were people who insisted that the comet of 1811 had fallen into the Ohio and produced the hubbub!

A public dinner was given Mr. Roosevelt a few days after his arrival, complimentary toasts were drunk, and the usual amount of good feeling on such occasions manifested. The success of the steamboat in navigating down-stream was acknowledged, but her return up-stream was deemed impossible, and it was regretted that it was the first and last time a steamboat would be seen above the falls of the Ohio.

Not to be outdone in hospitality, Mr. Roosevelt invited his hosts to dine on board the "New Orleans," which still lay anchored opposite the town. The company met in the forward or gentlemen's cabin, and the feast was at its height when suddenly there was heard unwonted rumblings, accompanied by a very perceptible motion in the vessel. The company had but one idea: the "New Orleans" had escaped from her anchor, and was drifting towards the falls, to the certain destruction of all on board. There was an instant rush to the upper deck, where the company found that, instead of drifting towards the falls of the Ohio, the "New Orleans" was making good headway up the river, and would soon leave Louisville in the distance down-stream. As the engine warmed to its work and the steam blew off at the safety-valve the speed increased. Mr. Roosevelt had, of course, provided this mode of convincing his incredulous guests, and their surprise and delight may be readily imagined. After going up the river a few miles the "New Orleans" returned to her anchorage.

On leaving Pittsburg it was intended to proceed as rapidly as possible to New Orleans to place the boat on the route for which it was designed between that city and Natchez. It was found, however, on reaching Louisville there was not a sufficient depth of water on the falls of the Ohio to permit the vessel to pass over them in safety. The "New Orleans" therefore returned to Cincinnati, convincing the most incredulous of her power to stem the current of the river. The waters having risen, the "New Orleans" returned to Louisville, and safely passed through the rapids, crowds collecting to witness her departure. "Instinctively each one on board grasped the nearest object, and with bated breath awaited the result. Black ledges of rock appeared only to disappear as the 'New Orleans' flashed by them. The waters whirled and eddied and threw their spray upon the deck as a more rapid descent caused the vessel to pitch forward to what at times seemed certain destruction. Not a word was spoken. The pilots directed the men at the helm by motions of their hands. Even the great Newfoundland dog seemed affected by the apprehension of danger, and crouched at Mrs. Roosevelt's feet. The tension on the nervous system was too great to be long sustained. Fortunately, the passage was soon made, and with feelings of profound gratitude to the Almighty at the successful issue of the adventure on the part of both Mr. Roosevelt and his wife, the 'New Orleans' rounded to in safety below the falls."

Hitherto the voyage had been one of exclusive pleasure, but now were to come, in the words of the letter referred to, "those days of horror." The comet had disappeared, and was followed by the earthquake of that year which accompanied the "New Orleans" far on her way down the Mississippi, the first shock of which was felt while she lay at anchor after passing the falls. On one occasion a large canoe fully manned came out of the woods abreast of the steamboat and paddled after it. There was at once a race, but steam had the advantage of endurance, and the Indians with wild shouts soon gave up the pursuit. One night there was an alarm of fire. The servant had placed some green wood too close to the stove in the forward cabin, which caught fire and communicated to the joiner-work of the cabin, when the servant, half suffocated, rushed on deck and gave the alarm. By great exertion the fire was extinguished. At New Madrid, a greater portion of which had been engulfed, terror-stricken people begged to be taken on board, while others, dreading the steamboat more than the earthquake, hid themselves as she approached. Having an insufficient supply of provisions for any large increase of passengers, the requests to be taken on board had to be denied. The earthquake had so changed the channels of the river that the pilots became confused, and guided her course more by luck and judgment than knowledge. As the steamboat passed out of the region of the earthquake the principal inconvenience was the number of shoals, snags, and sawyers. These were safely passed, and the vessel came in sight of Natchez and rounded to opposite the landing-place. Expecting to remain here for a day or two, the engineer had allowed his fires to go down, so that when the boat turned its head up-stream it lost headway altogether, and was being carried down by the current far below the intended landing. Thousands were assembled on the bluff and at the foot of it, and for a moment it seemed that the "New Orleans" had achieved what she had done so far only that she might be overcome at last. Fresh fuel, however, was added; the engine was stopped that steam might accumulate; presently the safety-valve lifted, a few turns of the wheels steadied the boat, a few more gave her headway, and overcoming the Mississippi, she gained the shore amid shouts of exultation and applause.

The romance of the voyage ended at Natchez, where the same hospitalities were extended to Mr. and Mrs. Roosevelt that had been enjoyed at Louisville. From thence to New Orleans there was no occurrence worthy of note. "Although forming no part of the story of the voyage proper," says Mr. Latrobe, "yet as this has been called a romance, and all romances end, or should end, in a marriage, the incident was not wanting here, for the captain of the boat, falling in love with Mrs. Roosevelt's maid, prosecuted his suit so successfully as to find himself an accepted lover when the 'New Orleans' reached Natchez; and a clergyman being sent for, a wedding marked the arrival of the boat at the chief city of the Mississippi."

The "New Orleans" ran afterwards between that city and Natchez. The first steamboat that ever ascended the streams of the Mississippi and Ohio was the fourth one launched on the Ohio and the second built at Brownsville, and was named the "Enterprise." She was of only seventy-five tons burden. In 1814 she descended to New Orleans, and after serving General Jackson in his defense of that city in 1815, undertook and completed the return voyage to Pittsburg, reaching Louisville in twenty-five days. The waters of the Mississippi at the time were high, and she was enabled to avoid the current where any existed, and made her way through "cut-offs" and over inundated fields in still water. The voyage of the "Enterprise," as is usually the case with first experiments, failed to convince the public of the practicability of ascending the Mississippi when that river was confined within its banks, and its current sweeping downward at a rate due to a descent of four inches to the mile. It was reserved to the steamboat "Washington," Captain Henry M. Shreve, to demonstrate by a second voyage of twenty-five days from New Orleans to Louisville that steamboats could ascend this river in at least one-fourth the time required by the barges and keel-boats hitherto in exclusive use. At a public dinner given to Captain Shreve[1] at Louisville on his return, he predicted that the time would come when his twenty-five-day voyage would be made in *ten*,—a feat which his audience no doubt considered visionary, but which has since been performed in *four days* and *nine* hours.

In 1823 there were public rejoicings at Louisville, Kentucky, when a steamboat arrived there in fifteen days and six hours from New Orleans. The captain, answering a complimentary toast, gravely stated the upward passage might possibly be accomplished in fifteen days, or six hours less than the time he had just made. Within twenty years the passage was actually performed in a few hours over *four days!*

The oldest steamboat company in the United States or in the world in 1858 (and we believe it still exists) was the United States Mail Line between Cincinnati, Louisville, and St. Louis. It was organized in 1818, and kept improving and adding to its boats. This company built the first steamer designed *exclusively* for passengers. She was named the "General Pike," and made her trips between Louisville and Cincinnati in thirty-one hours,—a passage now made in nine hours.

In 1858 eighteen miles an hour was the maximum speed attained on Western waters. At that date eight hundred and sixteen steamboats were employed on the Mississippi and its tributaries, having a total tonnage of three hundred and twenty-six thousand four hundred and forty-three tons.

The traveler now on the Father of Waters is seldom if ever out of sight of the smoke or sound of a steamboat, and the boats have increased in size from seventy-five tons to between one and two thousand tons, with machinery powerful in proportion.

The following table shows the progressive improvement made in the speed of the boats from New Orleans to Louisville (distance fourteen hundred and eighty miles), 1815 to 1853:

---

[1] Captain Shreve died March 6, 1851. He invented the first snag-boat.

Date.	Name of Steamer.	Days.	Hours.	Minutes.	Date.	Name of Steamer.	Days.	Hours.	Minutes.
May, 1815	Enterprise	25	2	40	April, 1840	Edward Shippen	5	14	00
April, 1817	Washington	25	00	00	April, 1842	Belle of the West	6	14	00
Sept., 1817	Shelby	20	4	20	April, 1843	Duke of Orleans	5	23	00
May, 1891	Paragon	18	10	00	April, 1844	Sultana	5	12	00
Nov., 1828	Tecumseh	8	4	00	May, 1849	Bostona	5	8	00
April, 1834	Tuscarora	7	16	00	June, 1851	Belle Key	4	23	00
Nov., 1837	General Brown	6	22	00	May, 1852	Reindeer	4	20	45
Nov., 1837	Randolph	6	22	00	May, 1852	Eclipse	4	18	00
Nov., 1837	Empress	6	17	00	May, 1853	A. L. Shotwell	4	10	20
Dec., 1837	Sultana	6	15	00	May, 1853	Eclipse	4	9	30

The last was the quickest time on record up to that date. Her average speed was fourteen miles an hour against the stream.

STEAMBOATS IN ENGLAND.

1812.—The " Comet."—Stimulated, as he tells us, by the success of Mr. Fulton, with whom he was in correspondence,[1] Mr. Henry Bell, of Helensburgh, for many years a house carpenter in the city of Glasgow, Scotland, determined, in 1812, to try the power of steam on the Clyde, and produced the first trading steam-vessel in Europe.

Helensburgh is a watering-place on the river Clyde, and Mr. Bell, for several years preceding, had been the proprietor of a hotel and bathing-establishment there. It was to increase the facilities for reaching these baths that Mr. Bell first constructed his steamboat.

In those days there were no conveyances on the river except " flyboats," pulled by four oars or using sails when practicable; with these the voyage was sometimes made in five or six hours, but often the time was longer and uncertain. After various experiments with paddle-wheels driven by hand in place of oars, Mr. Bell was convinced, by the experiments of Millar and Symington and the success of Fulton, that steam-power alone would effect his object. In consequence, after making several models of a steam-vessel, he succeeded in one suited to his ideas, and contracted with Messrs. John Wood & Co., ship-builders, in Port Glasgow, to build a steam-vessel after his model, to be forty feet on the keel and have ten feet six inches beam. She was called the " Comet," because she was built and finished the same year that a comet appeared in the northwest part of Scotland.

The " Comet" had two paddle-wheels, or rather two radiating sets of paddles, on each side, resembling very much in their appearance four malt shovels, radiating from a revolving axis to which they were all fixed. This was soon changed to Mr. Bell's complete wheel, which

---

[1] Mr. Bell, in a letter dated March 1, 1824, says, " When I wrote to the American government on the great utility that steam navigation would be to them on their rivers, they appointed Mr. Fulton to correspond with me; so in that way the Americans got their insight from your humble servant."—*Memoir by Patrick Millar, Jr.*

has been in use ever since. The engine known as the bell-crank, on Mr. Watt's principle, was put up under Mr. Bell's superintendence. The boiler was every way inferior to the boilers of Millar, Taylor, and Symington, inasmuch as the fire was on the outside of the boiler, separated from the wood of the vessel only by the bricks in which it was set, while in theirs, as in all steam-vessels of the present day, the fire was wholly within the boiler, and surrounded by water, so as to prevent danger from accident by fire or loss of heat. The boiler, which was fed by a cistern of fresh water, was on one side of the engine, the funnel being bent to the centre of the boat, where it served the purpose of a mast to carry sail. The early constructors of steamboats endeavored to disguise the odious funnel under the designation of a mainmast, and some went so far as to raise up a topmast in the thick folds of the dense, black smoke.

The "Comet" began to ply from Glasgow to Helensburgh in January, 1812, making a speed of about five miles an hour. She was of about twenty-five tons burden, and her engine exerted a force of about *three* horse-power. She continued during the summer to ply successfully as a passenger-boat.

The following is a copy of the original advertisement:

"STEAM PASSAGE BOAT. THE COMET. Between Glasgow, Greenock, and Helensburgh, for passengers only. The subscriber having, at much expense, fitted up a handsome vessel to ply upon the RIVER CLYDE BETWEEN GLASGOW AND GREENOCK, to sail by the power of wind, air, and steam, he intends that the vessel shall leave the Broomielaw on Tuesdays, Thursdays, and Saturdays, about midday, or at such hour thereafter as may answer from the state of the tide; and to leave Greenock on Mondays, Wednesdays, and Fridays, in the morning, to suit the tide.

"The terms are for the present fixed at 4s. for the best cabin and 3s. for the second; but, beyond these rates, nothing is to be allowed to servants or any other person employed about the vessel.

"The subscriber continues his establishment at HELENSBURGH BATHS the same as for years past, and a vessel will be in readiness to convey passengers in the Comet, from Greenock to Helensburgh.

"Passengers by the Comet will receive information of the hours of sailing by applying at Mr. Housten's office, Broomielaw; or Mr. Thomas Blackney's, East Quay Head, Greenock.

"HENRY BELL.

"HELENSBURGH BATHS, Aug. 5, 1812."

The "Comet" was wrecked in 1825 in the Firth of Clyde on a return trip from the Western Highlands, and many of her passengers were drowned. Bell, her originator, became as great a wreck as his vessel, and the Clyde trustees, out of gratitude, settled on him an annuity of one hundred pounds, which he enjoyed until he died, in 1830. His widow died in 1856, aged eighty-six.[1]

1813.—THE "ELIZABETH."—The success of the "Comet" soon excited competition, and three months after she began to ply upon the Clyde, the keel of a rival was laid, and in March, 1813, the "Elizabeth," the second steamer on the Clyde, was started, and continued to ply successfully, eclipsing the "Comet" and bringing much profit to the owner. The "Elizabeth," says John Scott Russell, was probably the first *remunerating* steam-vessel in the world; but we think he is mistaken.

Mr. Bell had employed in his experiments on fly-boats an engineer named John Thomson, of Glasgow, who appears to have assisted in planning his first boat, and to have felt himself ill-treated by Bell in not being made a partner in that speculation. To avenge his wrong he got Mr. Wood, who built the "Comet," to build a vessel fifty-one feet keel, twelve feet beam, and five feet deep. The tonnage of this vessel was about thirty-three tons, and her power about ten horses. The correct proportion of power to tonnage seems to have been the secret of her success. The owner's description of this vessel is an interesting and characteristic memorial of early steam navigation, he says,—

"The 'Elizabeth' was started for passengers on the 9th of March, 1813, and has continued to run from Glasgow to Greenock daily, leaving Glasgow in the morning and returning the same evening. The passage, which is twenty-seven miles, has been made, with a hundred passengers on board, in something less than four hours, and in favorable circumstances in two and three-quarters. The 'Elizabeth' has sailed eighty-one miles in one day, at an average of *nine miles an hour.* The 'Elizabeth' measures aloft fifty-eight feet; the best cabin is twenty-one feet long, eleven feet three inches at amidships, and nine feet four inches aft, seated all round, and covered with handsome carpeting. A sofa, clothed with marone, is placed at one end of the cabin, and gives the whole a warm and cheerful appearance. There are twelve small windows, each finished with marone curtains with tassels, fringes, and velvet, cornices ornamented with gilt ornaments, having altogether a rich effect. Above the sofa there is a large mirror suspended, and on each side bookshelves are placed containing a collection of the best authors for the amusement and edification of those who may avail themselves of them during the passage; other amusements are likewise to be had on board.

"The engine stands amidships, and requires a considerable space in length and all the breadth of the vessel. The forecastle, which is rather small, is about eleven feet six inches by nine feet six inches, not

[1] *Notes and Queries*, vol. iv., second series.

quite so comfortable as the after one, but well calculated for a cold day, and by no means disagreeable on a warm; all the windows in both cabins are made in such a way as to shift up and down like those of a coach, admitting a very free circulation of fresh air. From the height of the roofs of both cabins, which are about seven feet four inches, they will be extremely pleasant and healthful in the summer months for those who may favor the boat in parties of pleasure.

"Already the public advantages of this mode of conveyance have been generally acknowledged; indeed, it may without exaggeration be said that the intercourse through the medium of steamboats between Glasgow and Greenock has, comparatively speaking, brought those places ten or twelve miles nearer each other. In most cases the passages are made *in the same time as by the coaches;* and they have been, in numerous instances, done with greater rapidity. In comparing the comfortableness of these conveyances, the preference will be given decidedly to the steamboat. Besides all this, a great saving in point of expense is produced; the fare in the best cabin being only four shillings, and in the inferior one two shillings and sixpence, whereas the inside of a coach costs not less than twelve shillings and the outside eight shillings."

The "CLYDE," a third vessel, was built by Mr. Wood the same year for Mr. Robertson, an engineer of Port Glasgow, and commenced her trips in July. She was seventy feet on the keel, seventy-six feet long on deck, thirteen to fourteen feet beam, of fourteen horse-power, and sixty-nine tons measurement. Her speed was six miles an hour.

The "GLASGOW," a fourth vessel, was also launched by Mr. Wood in 1813, seventy-two feet long, fifteen feet beam, seventy-four tons measurement, and sixteen horse-power. Her engines were constructed by Mr. Cook, of Glasgow. She was intended to carry goods as well as passengers, and was moderately sharp, but afterwards improved by lengthening the bow five feet, and giving it greater sharpness. This vessel belonged to the first joint stock company for steam navigation ever established.

The "DUMBARTON CASTLE," eighty-one tons, one hundred and seven and a half feet long, sixteen feet ten inches broad, and eight feet eleven inches deep, having two engines of thirty-two horse-power, was built in 1815, and the following year accomplished the first trip to Rothesay, considered a feat, as the sailing-packets formerly on the station occupied one day, and occasionally three days, in making the passage. The succeeding year she made the passage through the Kyles of Bute, and up Lochfyne to Inverary, having left Glasgow at 6 A.M., and reaching Inverary about 10 P.M., a most remarkable occurrence.

The "BRITANNIA," of seventy-three tons, ninety-four feet four inches long, by sixteen feet five inches broad, and eight feet eight inches deep, having two engines of fourteen horse-power, was built in 1815, and

HISTORY OF STEAM NAVIGATION.

some years thereafter made the trip to Campbeltown in about fourteen hours.

The "ROB ROY," fifty-six tons, eighty feet eleven inches long, fifteen feet eight inches broad, and eight feet deep, was built in 1818, and was the first steamer that plied to Belfast.

The "ROBERT BRUCE," of ninety tons, ninety-four feet long, eighteen feet seven inches broad, and eleven feet deep, was also built in 1818, and was the first steamer that proceeded to Liverpool as a regular trader from Glasgow.

In 1813 a steamer was launched at Manchester and another at Bristol. October, 1814, the first steamer was in operation on the Humber, and in December the first steamer on the Thames was put in motion on the canal at Limehouse. June 28, 1815, a steamboat, built on the Clyde, arrived and was placed on the Mersey. On her passage she called at Ramsey, Isle of Man. She is notable as the first steamer which plied on the Mersey, and also as the pioneer of that noble fleet of steamers which ply with regularity between Liverpool and the numerous ports of the English, Irish, and Scotch coasts, also from being the first steamer to encounter the passage of these coasts.

About 1814 two vessels, "The Princess Charlotte" and the "Princess of Orange," were built and experimented with on the Clyde by a man named Miller, and proved unsuccessful. Watt & Bolton were the engineers.

THE "INDUSTRY."—The *seventh* steamer built on the Clyde was launched by William Fyle, May, 1814. She was of only fifty-four tons register. After an honorable career she lay a long time sunk in the East India harbor at Greenock, but November, 1872, was floated, beached, and calked, and in 1876 was presented by Messrs. Steele & Co., Catskill, her owners, to the Glasgow Chamber of Commerce, to be preserved as a memento of the early days of steam navigation, being beyond doubt the oldest steamboat in the world.

In 1815 ten steamboats were plying from the Clyde for the conveyance of passengers. The success of the steam-vessels at Glasgow soon excited attention elsewhere, and several Clyde-built vessels were purchased as models. A Mr. Lawrence, of Bristol, established a steamboat on the Severn, and having carried her to ply on the Thames, the Company of Watermen made such opposition he was obliged to take her back to Somersetshire.[1]

June 11, 1813.—Robert Fulton filed in the Patent-Office at Washington a petition for a patent, in which he asserted that he was the proprietor of two patents which contemplated the propelling of one single boat by the steam-engine, and that in this prosecution of his experiments on the navigation by steam on a large scale he had made discoveries and produced inventions extending to an incalculable degree the

[1] Buchanan's Practical Treatise on Propelling Vessels by Steam.

benefits of his original discovery and invention of the practical method of navigation by steam. These inventions he goes on to state consist principally in the combination and connection of several boats, constructed and connected in a manner so as to be propelled or drawn forward by one boat containing a steam-engine with the machinery necessary for the propelling of such steamboats. This invention consisting essentially in the separation of the steam-engine and of the boat containing the same from the boat or boats which carry the passengers and cargo, without, however, its being necessary to exclude from the boat carrying the steam-engine some part of the passengers and cargo. By which invention, the weight being distributed over a surface of water, which may be indefinitely increased, the draft of water necessary to carry the same may be indefinitely diminished, while at the same time all the inconveniences, expense, and liability to warp which attend one boat of very large dimensions and great length are avoided.

1814.—Early in 1814 there were five steamboats on the Thames River. 1. The "Thames" (originally the "Argyle"), fourteen horse-power, plying between London and Margate; reckoned the best boat. The paddles alternated with each other, and were set at an angle of forty-five degrees. 2. The "Regent," ten horse-power, paddles set square, with rims like an overshot wheel; expected to ply between Chatham and Sheerness. She was first built for the wheel to work in the middle; but this, not having been found to answer, was altered. 3. The "Defiance," twelve horse-power, to Margate, with double horizontal cylinder engine. 4. A boat which plied between London and Gravesend was laid aside on account of a lawsuit, as she was not worked by a privileged person. She was soon to start again, with a new twelve or fourteen horse-power Scotch engine, being originally fitted with a high-pressure engine. The wheels had rims, and the paddles swung like top butt-hinges. 5. A boat with double keel, six horse-power, was building above Westminster Bridge; paddles upright; said to be for London and Richmond. 6. Mr. Maudslay built a small boat in 1813 for Ipswich and Harwich, sixteen miles done in two and a quarter hours, but against a strong wind in three hours. This had six frying-pan paddles set square, without rims. "There are two steam-vessels on the River St. Lawrence, one forty-eight the other thirty-six horse-power, which go at seven miles an hour, measure about one hundred and seventy feet long and thirty feet wide! Another forty-eight horse-power vessel will be launched next year on that river. So that one may go by steam from Quebec to New York in eight days, with a short land carriage."[1]

In October, 1814, the first steamboat on the Humber was started to run between Hull and Gainsborough. She was called the "Caledonia," and accomplished, with a favorable tide, fourteen miles an hour. She

[1] Buchanan's Treatise on Propelling Vessels.

made the voyage between the two ports, a distance of fifty miles, in eight hours.

The "Margary" was taken south in 1814, along the east coast of Scotland. When she reached the Thames she passed close along the English fleet at anchor. Her extraordinary apparition excited a commotion among officers and men; none of them had seen a steamer before; by some she was taken for a fire-ship. The nearest man-of-war hailed her, and on being answered that she was a steamer built at Dumbarton, on the Clyde, a seaman named John Richardson, from Dumbarton, who was alive in 1857, ran along the deck of the man-of-war shouting, "Hurrah for Scotland! Dumbarton forever!" The "Margary" was fifty-six feet long and nineteen feet in breadth over all. On leaving for London she was taken through the Forth and Clyde Canal, and coasted up to London.[1]

The claims of the "Margary" conflict somewhat with those of the "Caledonia," but the "Margary" was launched June, 1814, according to Cleland's "Annals of Glasgow," published in 1816, and went to London November, 1814, while the same Annals say the "Caledonia" was not launched until April, 1815, and did not go to London until May, 1816. According to Cleland, twenty steam-vessels of various dimensions were built at Port Glasgow, Greenock, and Dumbarton, with engines of Glasgow make, during the four years 1812–16. Of these, the "Elizabeth," launched November, 1812, went to Liverpool in 1814; "Argyle," launched in June, 1814, went to London in 1815; "Margary," launched June, 1814, went to London November, 1814; "Caledonia," launched April, 1815, went to London May, 1816; "Greenock," launched May, 1815, went to Ireland, and then to London, May, 1816.[2]

A Margate hoy of large dimensions, propelled by steam, was, in 1815, run constantly from London to Margate, and, says a letter-writer, "from its novelty, and the certainty of its arrival within a given time (about twelve hours), it is much crowded with passengers." This was probably the "Margary."

Mr. Martin, the harbor-master of Ramsgate, who commanded a sailing-packet from Margate to Ramsgate, says that in June, 1815, on one of his trips, his companions pointed out to him an object some distance ahead, which they supposed to be a vessel on fire, but as they neared it, it was found to be the steamboat "Margary," *alias* "Thames."[3] With a fresh breeze he sailed round her easily, as her engine was of only fourteen horse-power, and her model a clumsy one. Nothing could exceed the ridicule his passengers bestowed upon the unseemly vessel; some compared her to a jaded horse with a huge pair of pan-

---

[1] Dumbarton *Herald;* also the Greenock *Advertiser,* May 12, 1857.

[2] London *Notes and Queries,* vol. v., second series.

[3] Another gives the name of the "Argyle" to the "Thames."

niers, others to a smoke-jack. Yet this vessel had voyaged from Port Glasgow to Dublin, and from thence to London, and traversed fifteen hundred miles of sea, some part of it in tempestuous weather.

1815.—The *British Naval Chronicle* for July, 1815, says, "The 'Thames' steam-yacht is said lately to have accomplished a voyage of fifteen hundred miles. She twice crossed St. George's Channel and sailed round Land's End, and is the first *steam*-vessel that ever traversed these seas. The advantages of a vessel enabled to proceed either by sail or steam, or both united, must indeed be sufficiently obvious, and especially in the certainty of reaching its place of destination in a given time."

The Hampshire *Telegraph*, June, 1815, notices a steam-vessel which "suddenly made its appearance lately at Portsmouth, England, and, coming into the harbor immediately against the wind, produced a considerable degree of curiosity. She is a very neatly-fitted vessel, and goes through the water at the rate of seven or eight miles an hour, which is produced by the steam-from an engine of fourteen horse-power. One ton of coal is sufficient fuel to produce the necessary force of steam for propelling her one hundred miles. She came from Plymouth Sound in twenty-three hours. It was intended, had the wind not been fair, that she should have towed the 'Endymion' frigate out of the harbor ;" the "Endymion" being the vessel which was on the coast of the United States during the war of 1812–14, and had the credit of receiving the surrender of the United States frigate "President."

This notice undoubtedly refers to the "Argyle," launched on the Clyde, June, 1814, and renamed the "Thames," which is memorable from being the first steamboat to make an extended sea-voyage in British seas.

The "Argyle," or "Thames," was seventy tons register, seventy-nine feet long on the keel, had sixteen feet beam, and engines of fourteen horse-power. Her paddle-wheels were nine feet in diameter. She had two cabins,—one aft, the other forward of her engines. In her waist was the engine, the boiler on the starboard, the cylinder and flywheel on the port side. Her funnel did duty *as a mast*, and was rigged with a large square-sail. A gallery upon each side of the cabin formed a continuous deck. She had eighteen painted ports on each side, with two astern, which to a casual observer were very formidable. After plying a year between Glasgow and Greenock she was purchased by a London company, to be run between that city and Margate, and it became necessary to bring her by sea from the Clyde to the Thames.

There was then in London a man named Dodd, who had served in the navy, and had distinguished himself as an engineer and architect, but who finally, driven by misfortune to intemperance, almost literally died in the streets a beggar.

To this Dodd was intrusted the task of taking the "Argyle" from the Clyde to the Thames. He arrived in Glasgow April, 1815, with a crew consisting of a mate, an engineer, a stoker, four seamen, and a cabin-boy; and with these put boldly to sea in the "Argyle" about the middle of May, 1815. His voyage at first was far from auspicious. The weather was stormy, the sea ran high in the strait which separates Scotland from Ireland, and, through ignorance, negligence, or misunderstanding, the pilot during the night altered the course, and the vessel came near being wrecked. At break of day, a heavy gale blowing, it was discovered they were within half a mile of a rock-bound lee-shore, two miles north of Port Patrick. To beat off in the teeth of the gale by the united power of steam and sails Dodd found impossible. Depending, therefore, entirely on his engine, he laid the vessel's head directly to windward, and kept the log going. The vessel began slowly to clear the shore, about three knots an hour. Having acquired a sufficient offing, he bore away for Loch Ryan, gained the Irish coast, and May 24 entered the Liffey.[1]

A graphic and detailed account of her voyage, written by Mr. Weld, the secretary and historian of the Royal Society, who with his wife took passage on board at Dublin, can be found in *Chambers' Journal* for April 25, 1857.

Leaving the Liffey on Sunday noon, the 28th of May, 1815, many persons from curiosity crossed the bay in her and landed at Dunleary (now Kingstown), and the sea being rough, the passengers were violently sea-sick. Several naval officers on board declared it to be their firm opinion that the vessel could not live long in heavy seas, and that there would be much danger in venturing far from shore. At Dunleary all the passengers except Mr. Weld and his wife left the boat, and it is to their brave resolve to remain that such a complete account of this pioneer voyage around the British Islands has been preserved.

The voyagers soon left behind them all the vessels which had sailed from Dublin with the same tide, and the next morning, when off Wexford, the dense smoke which issued from the mast-chimney being observed from the heights over town, it was concluded the vessel was on fire, and all the pilots put off to her assistance. Putting in at several intermediate points, on the 6th of June the adventurers arrived at Plymouth. The harbor-master, who had never seen a steamboat, was as much struck with astonishment when he boarded the "Thames" as a child in the possession of a new plaything. The sailors ran in crowds to the sides of their vessels as she passed, and, mounting the rigging, gave vent to their observations in the most amusing manner.

On her arrival at Portsmouth thousands of spectators assembled to gaze upon her, and the number of boats that crowded around her was so great that it became necessary to request the port-admiral to assign the voyagers a guard to preserve order. A court-martial sitting on

[1] *Morning Chronicle*, June 15, 1815.

board the "Gladiator" adjourned its session to visit her, and on the 10th of June, Sir Edward Thornborough, the port-admiral, sent his band and a guard of marines on board, and soon after followed himself, accompanied by *three* admirals, *eighteen* post-captains, and a large number of ladies. The morning was spent very pleasantly in steaming among the fleet and running over to the Isle of Wight, the admiral and the naval officers expressing themselves delighted with the "Thames."

From Portsmouth the steamer proceeded to Margate, which was reached Sunday, July 11, 1815. The next day she arrived at Limehouse, and was moored. They passed everything on the Thames,—all the fast-sailing Gravesend boats, pleasure-boats, West Indiamen, etc.

The whole distance sailed from Dublin to Limehouse was seven hundred and fifty-eight nautical miles, which were accomplished in one hundred and twenty-one and a half hours, with an expenditure of one ton of coal for every one hundred miles.

Sir Rowland Hill, the Post-Office Reformer, whose life has recently been published, makes a note as to the commencement of steam traffic at Margate. He was there in the year 1815, with his brother, Matthew Davenport Hill. On the 3d of July they "went to see the steamboat come in from London, generally performing the voyage in about twelve hours." "It is surprising to see," says Sir Rowland, "how most people are prejudiced against this packet. Some say that it cannot sail against the wind, if it is high; but when it entered the harbor (at Margate), the wind and tide were both against it, and the former rather rough; yet I saw it stem them both. There was a great crowd, and much enthusiasm, though carpers predicted failure, and sneered at 'smokejacks.'"[1]

1815.—Richard Trevithick obtained a patent in England for "a screw-propeller, consisting of a worm or screw, on a number of leaves placed obliquely around an axis, which revolves in a cylinder, fixed or revolving, or without a cylinder, at the head, sides, or stern of a vessel. In some cases the screw is made buoyant and works on a universal joint." In a second specification he adds, "A stuffing-box, inclosing a ring of water," also "a boiler of a number of small perpendicular tubes,—each tube closed at the bottom, but all opening at the top with a common reservoir." This was the first English patent for a screw-propeller. It never was, however, made the subject of a practical experiment.

EMPLOYMENT OF STEAMERS IN THE WAR OF 1812-14.—The *Gentleman's Magazine*, April, 1814, in an article on "Steam-Engine Passage-Boats," says, "For the information of those who are unacquainted with the fact, it may be necessary to state that the principal rivers of North America are navigated by steamboats; one of them passed two

---

[1] New Castle *Weekly Chronicle*, August 21, 1881.

thousand miles on the great river Mississippi in twenty-one days at the rate of five miles an hour against the descending current, which is perpetually running down. This steamboat is one hundred and twenty-five feet in length, and carries four hundred and sixty tons at a very shallow draught of water,—only two feet six inches,—and conveys whole ships' cargoes into the interior of the country, as well as passengers.

"The city of New York alone possesses *seven* steamboats for commerce and passengers. To name only one or two of them, that from thence to Albany, on the North River, passes one hundred and thirty miles; then (after about forty-five miles of land-carriage to Lake Champlain) you enter another steamboat that will take you about two hundred miles to near Montreal, between which place and Quebec a British steamboat one hundred and forty feet in length[1] is constantly passing, and usually goes down in twenty-eight hours, but sometimes in only twenty-four, although the distance is one hundred and eighty miles, and returning she is seldom more than twelve or fifteen hours additional time, though the stream is almost constantly running against her with the great velocity so peculiar to the river St. Lawrence of North America. This boat in the last year was found of the greatest service to the British government in carrying troops and stores with greater ease and dispatch than can possibly be effected by land; and it is here worthy of remark that in the late expedition of Admiral Sir John Borlase Warren up the Potomac River, chasing the enemy, they, keeping their ships at a prudent distance from ours, *sent one of their steamboats* directly against the wind, so as to be just without gun-shot, and reconnoitred our fleet. This fact is mentioned *because it is presumed that it is the first instance where they have been applied to such purposes.*

"The steamboats used at present in our own island are a sufficient demonstration of their utility; it will be only necessary to mention those working on the river Braydon between Yarmouth and Norwich, and on the river Clyde between Glasgow and Greenock; which boats on this latter station often beat the mail between the two places, and are always certain to time, let the wind and tide be what they may.

"It would occupy too considerable a space in this paper to enter into the merits of those steamboats now building and preparing on the rivers Tyne, Thames, and Medway, particularly those with patent and simplified apparatus for the use of rivers, to pass coastwise, and for short runs of passages to the Continent; but it is necessary to state, from most mature and deliberate examination, that some of these steamboats with patent apparatus are so constructed that they can carry sail, and perform all the manœuvres of other vessels at sea, when the wind is in their favor, and when against them by furling their sails pass right

---

[1] The "Swiftsure." See *ante.*

in the wind's eye with velocity, thus continuing their passages in a straight line, while other vessels are obliged to tack to and fro."

It is interesting to note, as a measure of the steamboat's speed during the war of 1812–14, the captions of the newspaper articles of that day. Here is one:

"By the arrival of the fast sailing '*Car of Neptune*' in twenty-four hours from Albany, we have news from the army under General Scott to a very late date."

At that time the price of passage from Albany to New York was ten dollars.

THE FIRST WAR STEAMBOAT.

1814.—Near the close of the year 1813, Robert Fulton exhibited to the President of the United States the drawing of a proposed war steamer or floating battery, named by him the "Demologos."

He contemplated, in addition to the proposed armament on deck, she should be furnished with four submarine guns, two suspended at each bow, to discharge a hundred-pound ball into an enemy ten or twelve feet below her water-line, and that she should have an engine for throwing an immense column of hot water upon the decks or through the ports of an opponent. Her estimated cost was three hundred and twenty thousand dollars, which was about the cost of a first-class sailing-frigate.

Fulton's project was favorably received, and in March, 1814, a law authorized the President to cause to be equipped "one or more floating batteries for the defense of the waters of the United States."

The construction of the vessel was committed by the "Coast and Harbor Defense Association" to a sub-committee of five gentlemen, appointed by William Jones, Secretary of the Navy.

Robert Fulton, whose soul animated the enterprise, was appointed the engineer, and on the 20th of June, 1814, the *keels* of this novel steamer were laid at the ship-yard of Adam & Noah Brown, in the city of New York. The blockade of our coast by the enemy enhanced the price of timber, and rendered the importation of copper, lead, and iron, and the supply of coal from Richmond and Liverpool difficult; these obstacles were, however, surmounted, and the enemy's blockade only increased the expense of her construction. With respect to mechanics and laborers there was also difficulty; shipwrights had repaired to the lakes in such numbers that comparatively but few were left on the sea-board; besides, a large number had enlisted as soldiers. By an increase of wages, however, a sufficient number of laborers were obtained; and the vessel was launched on the 29th of October, 1814, amid the hurrahs of assembled thousands.

The river and bay were filled with steamers and vessels of war in compliment of the occasion. In the midst of these was the floating mass of the "Demologos," or "Fulton," as she was afterwards named, whose bulk and unwieldy form seemed to render her as unfit for motion as the land batteries which were saluting her.[1]

Captain David Porter, writing the Secretary of the Navy under date New York, October 18, 1814, says, "I have the pleasure to inform you that the 'Fulton the First' was this morning safely launched. No one has yet ventured to suggest any improvement that could be made in the vessel, and, *to use the words of the projector, 'I would not alter her if it were in my power to do so.'*

"She promises fair to meet our most sanguine expectations, and I do not despair in being able to navigate in her from one extreme of the coast to the other. Her buoyancy astonishes every one. She now draws only eight feet three inches of water, and her draught will be *ten* feet with all her guns, machinery, stores, and crew on board. The ease with which she can now be towed by a single steamboat renders it certain that her velocity will be sufficiently great to answer every purpose, and the manner it is intended to secure her machinery from the gunners' shot leaves no apprehension for its safety. I shall use every exertion to prepare her for immediate service. Her guns will soon be mounted, and I am assured by Mr. Fulton that her machinery will be in operation in about six weeks."

On the 21st of November, 1814, the "Fulton" was moved from the wharf of Messrs. Brown, on the East River, to the works of Robert Fulton, on the North River, to receive her machinery. The steamboat "Car of Neptune" made fast to her port and the "Fulton" to her starboard side, towed her to her destination at the rate of three and a half to four miles per hour.[2]

The dimensions of this, the *first war steamer*, were: Length, 150 feet; breadth, 56 feet; depth, 20 feet; water-wheel, 16 feet diameter; length of bucket, 14 feet; dip, 4 feet; engine, 48-inch cylinder, 5-feet stroke; boiler, length 22 feet, breadth 12 feet, and depth 8 feet. Tonnage, 2475. She was the largest steamer by many hundreds of tons that had been built at the date of her launch.

The commissioners appointed to examine her in their report say,—

"She is a structure resting upon two boats, keels separated from end to end by a canal fifteen feet wide and sixty-six feet long. One boat contains the caldrons of copper to prepare her steam. The vast

[1] I have seen a large copper-plate engraving of the launch of the "Fulton." It is entitled "Launch of the Steam-Frigate 'Fulton the First,' at New York, Oct. 29, 1814; one hundred and fifty feet long, fifty-seven feet wide, mounting thirty long 32-pounders and two 100-pounders (columbiads). Philadelphia: Published March 27, 1815, by B. Tanner, 74 South Street. Drawn by I. I. Baralet, from a sketch by Morgan, taken on the spot."

[2] "Rees's Encyclopedia" states she was towed on this occasion by the "Paragon," of three hundred and thirty-one tons burden, at the rate of four miles an hour. That she was towed by "Car of Neptune" and "Fulton" is, I believe, correct.

cylinder of iron, with its piston, levers, and wheels, occupies a part of its fellow; the great water-wheel revolves in the space between them; the main or gun-deck supporting her armament is protected by a bulwark *four feet ten inches thick, of solid timber*. This is pierced by thirty port-holes, to enable as many 32-pounders to fire red-hot balls; her upper or spar-deck, upon which several thousand men might parade, is encompassed by a bulwark which affords safe quarters. She is rigged with two short masts, each of which supports a large lateen yard and sails. She has two bowsprits and jibs and four rudders, two at each extremity of the boat; so that she can be steered with either end foremost. Her machinery is calculated for the addition of an engine which will discharge an immense column of water, which it is intended to throw upon the decks and all through the ports of an enemy. If, in addition to all this, we suppose her to be furnished, according to Mr. Fulton's intention, with 100-pounder columbiads, two suspended from each bow, so as to discharge a ball of that size into an enemy's ship ten or twelve feet below the water-line, it must be allowed that she has the appearance at least of being the most formidable engine of warfare that human ingenuity has contrived."

Such is a correct description of this sea-monster of 1814, but exaggerated and fabulous accounts of her got into circulation. Among others, the following was published in a Scotch newspaper, the writer stating that "he had taken great care to procure full and accurate information."[1]

"Her length," he writes, "on deck is *three hundred feet;* thickness of sides, *thirteen feet,* of alternate oak plank and cork-wood; carries 44 guns, four of which are 100-pounders; and further to annoy an enemy attempting to board can discharge one hundred gallons of boiling water in a minute, and by mechanism brandishes *three hundred cutlasses* with the utmost regularity over the gunwales; works also an equal number of heavy iron pikes of great length, darting them from her sides with prodigious force, and withdrawing them every quarter of a minute."

The stores of artillery at New York not furnishing the number and kind of cannon she was to carry, guns were transported from Philadelphia, a prize having placed some excellent pieces at the disposal of the Navy Department. To avoid the danger of their capture, twenty of these guns were sent over the miry roads of New Jersey dragged by horses.

In consequence of the exhaustion of the treasury and temporary depression of the public credit, the commissioners were instructed to pay the bills for the "Fulton" in treasury notes, but solely at par. These notes were often so long withheld that those who had advanced

---

[1] Stuart's "War and Mail Steamers" has accurate drawings of the "Fulton" from the originals.

materials and labor were importunate for payment, and the commissioners had frequently to pledge their private credit. Once the men discontinued work. From these causes her completion was retarded until winter, and also by the unexpected death of Mr. Fulton, on the 24th of February, 1815.

All difficulties at length being surmounted, the machinery was put in motion, and she made her first trial trip on the 1st of June, 1815, only nine months after her keels were laid. On this trial she was found capable of opposing the wind, of stemming the tide, of crossing currents, and of being steered among vessels riding at anchor, though the weather was boisterous and the water rough. Her performance demonstrated the success of Fulton's idea, and that a floating battery composed of heavy artillery could be moved by steam.

She left the wharf near the Brooklyn ferry, propelled by steam alone, against a stiff south breeze (which was directly ahead) and a strong ebb-tide, and steamed by the forts, saluting them with her guns, her speed equaling the most sanguine expectations.

After circumnavigating the bay and receiving a visit from the officers of a French ship-of-war, she came to anchor at Powles' Hook ferry about 2 P.M., nothing occurring to mar the pleasure or success of the trip. It was discovered, however, that alterations were necessary, some errors to be corrected, and some defects to be supplied, before she was prepared for a second trial.

On the 4th of July, 1815, she again made a trip to the ocean, eastward of Sandy Hook, and back again, a distance of fifty-three miles, in eight hours and twenty minutes, without the aid of sails, the wind and tide being partly favorable and partly against her, the balance rather in her favor. The gentlemen who witnessed this experiment without exception entertained no doubt as to her fitness for the intended purpose. Expedients were sought to increase her power, and devised and executed for quickening and directing her movements.

A third trial of her powers was attempted, on the 11th of September, with twenty-six of her long and ponderous guns and a considerable quantity of ammunition and stores on board. Her draught of water was less than eleven feet. She changed her course by reversing the motion of her wheels, without the necessity of putting about, like the ferry-boats of the present day. She saluted as she passed the forts, overcame the resistance of the wind and tide in her progress down the bay, and performed beautiful manœuvres around the United States ship "Java," then at anchor near the light-house. She moved with remarkable celerity, and was perfectly obedient to her double helm. The explosion of powder produced very little concussion on board, and her machinery was not affected by it in the slightest degree. Her progress during the firing was steady and uninterrupted. On the most accurate calculation, her velocity was four and a half miles an hour, and she made headway at the rate of two miles an hour against the ebb of the East River, running three and a half knots. The day's exercise was satisfactory to the company on board beyond their most sanguine expectation, and it was universally conceded that the United States possessed a new auxiliary against every maritime invader. The city of New York was considered as having the means of making itself invulnerable, and that every bay and harbor of the nation might be protected by the same tremendous power. Her performance more than equaled Fulton's expectations, and it exceeded what he had promised the government,—that she should be propelled by steam at the rate of from three to four miles an hour.

' The commissioners who superintended her construction congratulated the government and the nation on the event of this noble project, and said, "Honorable alike to its author and its patrons, it constitutes an era in warfare and the arts. The arrival of peace indeed has disappointed the expectations of conducting her to battle. That best and conclusive act of showing her superiority in combat has not been in the power of the commissioners to make.

"If a continuance of tranquillity should be our lot, and this steam-vessel of war be not required for the public defense, the nation may rejoice in the fact we have ascertained as of incalculably greater value than the expenditures, and that if the present structure should perish, we have the information, never to perish, how, in any future emergency, others may be built. The requisite variation will be directed by circumstances."

The war having terminated, "Fulton the First," after these trial trips, was taken to the navy-yard at Brooklyn and moored on the flats abreast of that station, where she was used as a receiving-ship until the 4th of June, 1829, fifteen years after the laying of her keels, when she was accidentally or purposely blown up.

Commodore Chauncey, reporting this catastrophe, says that he had been on board of her all the morning inspecting the ship and men, particularly the invalids, who had increased considerably from other ships, and whom he had intended asking the Department's permission to discharge, as of little use to the service. He had left the ship but a few moments before the explosion took place. The report did not appear to him louder than a 32-pounder, although the destruction of the ship was complete and entire, owing to her very decayed state. There was on board at the time no more than *two and a half barrels of damaged powder*, kept in the magazine, for the morning and evening gun. By this explosion, however, twenty-four men and a woman were killed, nineteen wounded, and five reported as missing and probably killed. Among the killed was Lieutenant S. M. Breckinbridge, and among the wounded Lieutenant C. F. Platt, who died a captain in the navy, Lieutenant A. M. Mull, and Sailing-Master Clough; Lieu-

HISTORY OF STEAM NAVIGATION. 99

tenant Platt was dangerously, the others severely, wounded. Four midshipmen were among the wounded.

Commodore Chauncey was of opinion that "the explosion could not have taken place from accident, as the magazine was as well or better secured than the magazines of most of our ships; yet it is difficult to assign a motive to those in the magazine for so horrible an act as voluntarily to destroy themselves and those on board, yet if the explosion was not the effect of design, I am at a loss to account for the catastrophe."

Master Commandant John T. Newton,[1] her commander, was on shore at the time of the explosion. Such was the beginning, end, and uneventful history of the first steam-vessel of war ever put afloat,—the pioneer, and to an extent the model also, of the floating batteries, double-hulled vessels, and "double-enders" which have succeeded her.

Captain E. C. Bowery, U.S.N., a surviving officer of the "Fulton," writing me under date December 13, 1881, says, "I say the destruction of the 'Fulton' was by carelessness. I believe in Divine Providence, but not in accident. I joined her in the early part of 1826 as an acting midshipman, Commander Budd then having command. Her magazine (if it could be called one) was nearly under the ship's coppers, and separated only by a light bulkhead was the 'bag-room,' in which the sergeant of marines had a writing-desk, on which was a naked oil lamp. Soon after reporting, I had occasion to go down there; the bulk-head had a sliding door, which was open, and his lamp shone on the kegs of powder, one of which was without a head. I remarked to the sergeant, 'If your light was only five feet nearer (all the space that separated it from the powder) there would be trouble.' 'Yis,' said he, turning his beery eyes on me, 'there would be a sensation.' After that I never turned in at night without thinking there might be a sensation before cock-crowing, and to this day I have not forgot the appearance of that powder with the light shining on it, and draw the inference that gross carelessness caused the sensation. Yet at the time there was a story that a gunner's mate had been disrated and punished with the cats the morning before the blowing up of the 'Fulton.'"

FIRST STEAM-VESSELS IN RUSSIA.

1815.—Steam navigation was adopted in Russia at an early date. Mr. Baird, superintendent of the mines, made the first experiments in 1815 with an open boat of his own construction, fitted with a four horse-power engine, with which he made his first trip from St. Petersburg to Cronstadt and back on the 15th of November. In 1816 he built a steam-vessel of larger dimensions, with an engine of twenty

---

[1] Captain Newton also commanded the "Missouri" when she was burned in Gibraltar Bay, 1844.

horse-power, for conveyance of passengers between the two places. For twenty years he had the exclusive privilege of furnishing the Russian metropolis with steamboats for mercantile purposes. The first government steam-vessel, the "Rapid," was constructed at the Ishora yard in 1816, and was of thirty-two horse-power. The first Russian steam-vessel armed with guns was built in 1826. The Neva was the first river in Russia on which steamboats were applied. The Caspian Sea, in 1844, was navigated by four steamboats, each of forty horse-power. The first steamboat introduced into Siberia was built in 1843, and employed on Lake Balkan. She was of thirty-two horse-power, and called the "Emperor Nicholas."

In the *American Daily Advertiser* of November 27, 1816, there appears the following notice of a new steamboat to run between New York and Baltimore, commanded by Captain Moses Rogers, who three years later further immortalized himself, in connection with steam navigation, by commanding the "Savannah," the first steam-vessel that ever crossed the Atlantic:

"NEW STEAMBOAT.—On Tuesday last the elegant steamboat 'New Jersey,' Moses Rogers master, sailed from this port for Baltimore. This boat is coppered completely, and furnished with powerful *copper boilers*. She is finished in a style superior to any ever built in this place; the workmanship of the main and ladies' cabins is executed with great taste and with every possible accommodation for passengers.

"Her engine was constructed by Mr. Daniel Large, of this city, engineer; it appears to be an improvement of the plan proposed by Mr. David Prentice, and exemplified in one of the ferry-boats on the Delaware. The cylinder is fixed upon an inclined plane, and the shafts of the two wheels are furnished with a crank common to both, which crank, by a connecting-rod, puts the fixtures of the cylinder and air-pump in motion without that tremor and noise which is so injurious to steamboats in general, and unpleasant to the passengers. Her speed, in the trials which have been made, exceeds that of the fastest boats at their commencement, and if she continues to improve she will be one of the most expeditious steamboats in the United States. No expenses have been withheld; every opportunity has been employed to fit her for the station in the line of steamboats for which she is intended, between *Baltimore* and *Elkton*. Captain Rogers was also the *first who went to sea in a steamboat;* he navigated the 'Phœnix,' in 1809, from New York to Philadelphia; in 1813 he navigated the 'Eagle' from this port (New York) to Baltimore, and now, towards the close of November, he proposes to conduct this steamboat to the capes of the Delaware, and from thence to Baltimore, by way of Norfolk, in Virginia."

1816.—Nicholas J. Roosevelt, in the following advertisement, claims the invention of vertical paddle-wheels for steamers, and for which he obtained a United States patent in 1814:

"STEAMBOAT NOTICE.

"ALL persons are hereby informed that I claim the right of Inventor of Vertical Wheels, as now generally used for Steam Boats throughout the United States, having been first used, after my invention, in the *North River* Steam Boat, by Messrs. Livingston & Fulton.

"I have obtained a *Patent* in due form of law, for my invention, which is dated the 1st day of Dec. 1814.

"No other person in the United States has any *Patent,* but myself, for the invention of *Vertical Wheels.* Having obtained a *legal* title to the sole use of steam boats *with such wheels,* I hereby forwarn all persons from using them hereafter without license from me. The patent and evidence of my right are in the hands of Wm. Griffith, Esq., of the City of Burlington, my Counsel-at-Law.

"On this subject, so very important to me (being the only real and efficient invention since Fitch's Boat), I do not by this notice challenge controversy, but am prepared to meet it in any form. My object is to *make known,* that I am the inventor, and have the *Patent* right. Individuals or companies who use such wheels without my license after this, will be prosecuted under the Law of Congress, for damages amounting to the profits of the boat. Licenses will be sold under me at moderate rates, and warranted.[1]

"Nicholas J. Roosevelt."

"Burlington, N. J., 4th March, 1816."

1816.—The first steamer specially built at Liverpool for the purpose of a ferry was the "Etna," which in April, 1816, began to ply between Liverpool and Traumere. She was sixty-three feet long, with a paddle-wheel *in the centre,*[2] her extremities being connected by beams, and her deck twenty-eight feet over all. This primitive vessel initiated the transit by the numerous ferry-boats which now bridge the Mersey.

March, 1816.—The "Majestic" was the first steamboat that crossed

[1] "Note.—Although my Patent assures me a legal right, any person may be further satisfied of my just claim by recurrence to the evidences in the hands of my Counsel-at-Law. They consist principally of *original* letters between Chancellor Livingston, Mr. Stevens and myself, on this very thing, at *the time of my invention,* accompanied with depositions of many persons witnesses of, and knowing to the fact.

"N. J. R."

"March 15, 1816."

—*Philadelphia Newspaper, March 16, 1816*

[2] This was like Fulton's ferry-boats in New York in 1810.

the English Channel from Brighton to Havre. She was built at Ramsgate, and had engines of twenty-five horse-power, and was considered a gigantic concern. Her crossing from Dover to Calais with two hundred passengers and return without accident was a highly appreciated feat. The "Majestic" established the superiority of steamboats over other means of water conveyance. The sailing-packet between Margate and Ramsgate was often detained two days by calms and tides. The steamboat passed and repassed the sailing-packet loaded with passengers. On one occasion, the third night out, the packet caught at anchor in a sudden northerly gale, lost much of her gear, and the next day, while the gale was stronger, had the mortification of seeing the "Majestic" pass and convey her passengers into Margate.

1816.—The first line of steamboats from New York to New London, Connecticut, was established in 1816. On the 28th of September, 1816, the "Connecticut," Captain Bunker, arrived from New York in twenty-one hours,—which was regarded as a signal triumph for steam, the wind and the tide being against her. In October a regular line commenced making two trips per week to New Haven; the "Fulton," Captain Law, at the same time running between New York and New Haven. The price of passage was five dollars to New Haven, and from thence to New York four dollars.

Jonathan Morgan, Esq., of Wiscasset, Maine, a well-known and eccentric citizen of Portland, Maine, in 1816 ascended the Kennebec River by steam. In June, 1818, this boat, the "Alpha," of fifteen tons, was sold at "public vendue" by a constable of Wiscasset for eighty-seven dollars. The boat was a long, narrow, flat boat, and the machinery being taken out she was converted into a fishing-vessel. The steam-power was applied to a screw-propeller in the stern. Her boiler was built of pine plank, and about the size of a common molasses hogshead, into which was fixed a fire-box of iron. An endless chain connected the engine with her propeller. The machinery was invented and designed by Jonathan Morgan, who anticipated a fortune from its invention.

The first trip of the "Alpha" up the Kennebec was as far as Augusta. At Hallowell the boat halted, when many visitors inspected the strange craft. Mr. Morgan came on shore, and Page & Bemant, to encourage the enterprise, made him a donation in money. Leaving the wharf, she was unable to stem the current, and was carried sidelong across the river and fell back to Clark's wharf, lower down. At last she gained sufficient headway to proceed up river to Augusta, where she was greeted with many cheers. Mr. Morgan, who removed to Portland in 1820, was so ashamed of his failure that he never wished to have it spoken of.

THE FIRST ENGLISH STEAM-TUGS.

1816.—It has been asserted that the first application of steam for the purpose of towing vessels was made in October, 1816, when the "Harlequin" was towed out of the Mersey by the "Charlotte," a steamer which, in the summer of the same year, had been placed as a ferry-boat to run between Liverpool and Eastham.[1]

In 1819, Mr. Rennie, who planned the breakwater at Plymouth, England, was the "advising engineer" to the Admiralty, and on every occasion urged the application of steam-power to vessels of war. He hired at his own cost the Margate steamboat "Eclipse," and successfully towed the "Hastings," 74, against the tide from Woolwich to Gravesend, June 14, 1819. In consequence of this feat, Lord Melville and Sir George Cockburn, R.N., urged the great value of steam-power for towing men-of-war.

In his "Local Records," 1857, Mr. Latimer perpetuates the memory of The Tynesides, who introduced steam-towing: "Died in Gateshead, September 27, 1852, aged 81, Mr. Joseph Price, glass manufacturer, who was the first to apply steam-vessels to the towing of ships to and from sea, in adverse winds, for which he received a handsome testimonial in 1818."[1]

In Gateshead the first English steamboat was built. It was launched from the South Shore in the month of February, 1814; and the glass manufacturer took an interest in the question of navigation by steam. In his retrospect, July, 1838, "To Merchants, Manufacturers, Shipowners, &c.," he tells us that, "In 1815 he became a shareholder in a steamboat speculation on the Tyne, which was continued for two years, when the boats, becoming out of repairs, were laid up." Fertile in resource, Mr. Price devised a new use for the boat with wheels,—a contrivance that was celebrated in song by his townsman, Wilson, author of "The Pitman's Pay."

> "Steam neist cam' puffin' into play,
>   And put an end to rowin';
> When Price said, in his schemin' way,
>   'Let's try the chep at towin'.'"

"July, 1818," Mr. Price "conceived good might be done by towing vessels to sea." "In furtherance of my idea," as may be read in his address of 1838, "I applied to the late Mr. Robson, wharfinger of Newcastle, for leave to try an experiment with one of his loaded vessels, which was granted. I gave notice to Captain Copeland, of the *Friends' Adventure*, Hull trader, to have all ready from an hour to an hour and a half before highwater. At the time appointed I requested

---

[1] The "Charlotte Dundas," it should be remembered, however, was built for a tow-boat, and we have already shown that Fulton's steam-battery was towed on one occasion by the "Car of Neptune" and "Fulton."

him to throw a line on board the steamer. The tide was against us the first three miles. Everything answered as well as I could wish, and the vessel was towed two miles over the bar in two hours and ten minutes—a distance of thirteen miles—the wind against us all the way. *This was the first time a sailing vessel was ever towed by a steamboat.* The public did not at first appreciate my endeavors for expediting the sailing of ships in adverse winds. On the contrary, I was told I had ruined the port. I continued my two steamboats, the *Eagle* and *Perseverance,* in this employ, with little benefit to myself, for my captains were so timorous they would not stir but in moderate weather. They once had an offer to tow two ships with one boat. They would on no account undertake so heavy a task."

The "Perseverance" was originally known as the "Tyne Packet," or "Tyne Steamboat," and afterwards called by a distinctive name when she was no longer alone on the river. Mr. Price's example led the way to general traction by steam. "After a considerable interval other owners of steamboats saw the advantage of the towing system, and employed theirs in a similar manner, receiving pay according to the depth of water the sailing vessels drew. The advantage to the ship-owner was great. Previously no vessel over 240 tons register ever attempted to come up to Newcastle. After the introduction of the towing system vessels of 400 tons register were brought up; and vessels that previously averaged only eight voyages in the year between the Tyne and the Thames were able to average thirteen voyages, thereby keeping the coal market regularly supplied, and preventing those great fluctuations in prices which formerly had such a serious effect in increasing the misery of the poor."

The towing system, Mr. Price says, was in 1821 adopted between Hull and Gainsbrough; in 1826 at Liverpool; "afterwards at Montreal, where a large steam-vessel towed from three to four ships at once from Quebec in less than forty-eight hours, then thought a heavy task, considering the strong current she had to contend against. Previously, ships going to Montreal required from two to three weeks to complete the distance."

Mr. Price's services were recognized on the Tyne by a banquet and the presentation of a silver tankard bearing the following inscription:

<blockquote>
Presented to Mr. Joseph Price
by the
Shippers and Manufacturers of Lead,
and the
Wharfingers of the Goods Trade between
Newcastle and London,
as a mark of their approbation for
his zeal and spirited exertions
in the Application of Steamboats to the Towing
of Vessels on the River Tyne.
1818.
</blockquote>

PROGRESS OF STEAM NAVIGATION IN ENGLAND.

1819.—The first steamers on the line between the Mersey and the Clyde were the "Robert Bruce" and the "United Kingdom," which began to ply regularly in 1819, between Liverpool and Glasgow. The following is the advertisement of the first return voyage from Liverpool to Glasgow of the pioneer vessel, "Robert Bruce":

"SAFE AND EXPEDITIOUS TRAVELING BETWEEN LIVERPOOL AND GLASGOW.

"The elegant new steam-packet 'Robert Bruce,' Captain John Paterson, will sail from Glasgow to-morrow (Tuesday), the 23d of August, at eight o'clock in the morning, from the George's Dock pier-head. The accommodation of passengers is most excellent, and she is expected to perform the passage within thirty hours. The fare in the cabin forty shillings, steerage twenty-one shillings; passengers *will be accommodated with provisions* at moderate terms. For passage apply to Captain Paterson, or to John Richardson.

"LIVERPOOL, 22d August, 1819."

The first steam-vessel employed in the Irish trade with Liverpool was the "Waterloo," built at Greenock, and launched on the 18th of June, 1819. Being fitted with engines and other requisites for a passenger steamer, she proceeded to Belfast to ply between that port and Glasgow. Her destination was soon changed, and she was placed on the line between Liverpool and Belfast. Her first arrival was thus announced in the Liverpool *Mercury* of July 23, 1819:

"Yesterday a beautiful steam-packet arrived at this port from Belfast, after a passage of only twenty-four hours. She is called the 'Waterloo,' and is a fine, well-built vessel, burden two hundred and one tons, length ninety-eight feet, breadth on deck thirty-seven feet, and has two highly-finished steam-engines of thirty horse-power each, which work without noise or vibration, and are on the low-pressure construction, perfectly safe from accident. They are attended by two experienced engineers. The vessel is provided with two masts, with sails and rigging. Her interior accommodations are as complete and elegant as skill and expense can make them. She has a handsome dining-room, capable of accommodating all the cabin passengers, a separate and neatly decorated cabin for ladies, and two apartments for private families; twenty-two well-furnished beds, each accommodated with light and air; and a comfortable place for steerage passengers. She cost nearly ten thousand pounds. She will sail for Belfast at tide time to-day, and will return on Monday. She will sail the same day, and regularly every Monday and Friday. Fares, cabin, £1 11s. 6d.; steerage, 10s. 6d. The cabin passengers *are not under the necessity of taking provisions*, as they are well accommodated on board with everything at the most moderate prices."

The "Waterloo" was soon transferred to the more important traffic between Liverpool and Dublin, where her success resulted in the employment of more powerful steamers.

This detailed account of so small a steamer may be pardoned when we consider that the "Waterloo" was the germ and pioneer of the magnificent steam fleet which now sails in and out of the port of Liverpool. It is no longer necessary to caution passengers they are not under the necessity of provisioning themselves.

1817.—Herbert Lawrence, who died in 1882, aged ninety-four, built in 1817 the "Bolona," the first steamboat commanded by Cornelius Vanderbilt. Her model is in the possession of his son, William H. Vanderbilt. Mr. Lawrence remembered the trial trip of the "Clermont," and was thus a connecting link with the origin, gradual growth, and present state of steam navigation.

1817.—THE "FIREFLY."—On Monday, the 26th of May, 1817, the "Firefly," Captain Smith, arrived at Newport from New York. The sea was very rough as she rounded Point Judith, and she was twenty-eight hours in making the passage. She was intended to ply between Providence and Newport, and made her first trip to Providence on the 28th, leaving Newport at 9 A.M. and reaching Providence about noon. A sloop brought news of the approaching steamboat, and long before noon the wharves were crowded with people awaiting the arrival of the strange craft. At last she came wheezing and puffing up the river to where the Crawford Street bridge now stands; then, turning about, ran up to her wharf and made fast. A gentleman doing business in the Arcade in 1877 remembered being held aloft in his father's arms to see the boat come in. He described the "Firefly" as an ugly little thing, full of machinery and awkward in her motions. The people cheered, however, and shouted and looked her over as we would now inspect a balloon just arrived from St. Petersburg.

June 28, the "Firefly," with Governor Knight, United States Marshal Dexter, and others on board, sailed at 7 A.M. for Newport, to meet and escort President Monroe to Providence. He went, however, in a revenue cutter to Bristol, where he embarked on the "Firefly," reaching Providence about 9 P.M. On landing he was received by a salute of cannon and the ringing of bells. The next day he proceeded to Boston. On the 26th of July the "Firefly" made a "cherry" excursion to Fall River, two dollars being the charge for the fare and dinner.

The packet-masters resorted to every lawful means to break down the new enterprise. The "Firefly" was no match for a fast sloop with a favorable wind. She hoisted a huge square-sail when the wind was fair, but the packets would often come into port ahead. The packet captains even carried their opposition so far that they would stand upon the "Firefly's" wharf just before her hour of starting and offer to carry passengers to Newport for twenty-five cents, or for nothing if

HISTORY OF STEAM NAVIGATION.

they did not get there in advance of the "Firefly." In this way in four months they succeeded in running her off.

Then the packetmen held a meeting on the packet wharf and denounced the interlopers in striking and powerful language, after which they adjourned to a convenient packet and drank confusion to steamboats. Packets in those days furnished the best means of transportation between Providence and New York. The sailing of a mail-packet for New York aroused more attention than is now paid to the departure of an ocean steamship. Passengers came to the boat accompanied by relatives and friends. The master of the boat would bring out his stately decanters, and place a whole row of glasses on the mahogany table in the cabin. Then a solemn health would be drunk to the prosperity of the voyage.

The packets were beautifully modeled, sloop-rigged vessels of from seventy-five to one hundred tons burden, built with a view to speed, carrying capacity, and comfort. The sides of some were adorned with bead-work; others had polished strips of hard pine let into the sides, and all were painted in gay and lively colors. The cabins were frequently finished and furnished with mahogany, and decorated in every imaginable way. These cabins averaged twelve feet square, and from them opened tiny state-rooms.

Packets sailed from Providence for New York every week; the trip was of varying length. The "Huntress" often came through in eighteen hours, but sometimes the voyage lasted a week. The fare was ten dollars, including meals. Over the cabin stairs hung a mahogany letter-box, and on arrival there would be a rush of people to the packet to get letters in advance of the slow mail plodding over the post-roads. As soon as the immediate business of landing was over the captain would pour the contents of the letter-box upon the mahogany table, and after the distribution of letters the decanters were produced and everybody drank the captain's health. "Captain Whipple Brown, one morning, unloaded from his sloop seven hundred and fifty thousand dollars in silver. There were five thousand dollars in a keg, and kegs enough to load fifteen baggage-wagons, which before sunrise set out for Boston with two well-armed guards in charge of each wagon."[1]

Seventeen large steamboats were, in 1817, in constant employment on American rivers besides ferry-boats.

FIRST STEAMBOATS IN BOSTON.

1817.—The steamboat "Massachusetts," in 1817, introduced steam navigation to Boston early in June. She was owned by Joseph and John H. Andrews, William Fettyplace, Hon. Stephen White, and Andrew Watkins, of Salem, and Andrew Bell, of Portsmouth, New Hampshire, and was intended to run between Salem and Boston. She

[1] Charles H. Dow's "History of Steam Navigation between New York and

was of two hundred and thirty tons register, and had an engine of thirty horse-power. She made a few trips between Salem and Boston, but not being well patronized, in the autumn, or early in the winter, was sent south to Charleston or Savannah, to be sold, and was lost on the passage on the coast of North Carolina. On her arrival in Salem she was called by the *Enterprise* the "Brilliant North Star." She made her first trip from Salem to Boston July 4, 1817, leaving Salem at 8 A.M.; she arrived at Boston at 11 A.M., her greatest rate of speed being eight miles an hour. In consequence of some damage to her machinery she did not return to Salem on that day, and her passengers were sent back in coaches. The next day she made a trip to Hingham and returned, making the trip in two hours each way. The enterprise proved more than a total loss to her proprietors. There was a distrust in the public mind in relation to her, and many who cried out against her were thought to be influenced by the stage companies.

The Boston *Daily Advertiser*, July 4, 1817, announced, "We understand that the elegant steamboat 'Massachusetts' will be here this day at ten o'clock, and will take a few gentlemen and ladies for a few hours to sail about the islands in this harbor." This was beyond a doubt the first Fourth of July steamboat excursion in Boston harbor.

She seems to have been supplanted, in 1818, by the "Eagle," which filled her place as an excursion boat. The "Eagle" ran from Nantucket to New Bedford for six months the same year.

1818.—From a return made to the comptroller of New York, it appears that the tax upon steamboat passengers produced to that State during the years 1817 and 1818 was a net aggregate of $37,620.18. The gross amount of the tax for these two years was $41,440. All passengers for over one hundred miles paid a tax of $1 each, and for under distances over thirty miles, half the sum; under thirty miles, nothing. For every dollar collected by the State it was estimated that seven was received by the proprietors of the New York steamboats.

1818.—One hundred and thirty-nine years after the launch of the first vessel, the "Griffin," of sixty tons, by La Salle, August 7, 1679, upon the Niagara River, between the Falls and Lake Erie, steam navigation commenced on Lake Erie. The pioneer steamboat, called "Walk-in-the-Water," was launched at Black Rock on the 28th of May, 1818.

In the *Federal Gazette and Baltimore Daily Advertiser* of April 27, 1818, I find two advertisements of steamboats running to Philadelphia,—one, of the Union Line of Steamboats *via* Frenchtown and New Castle, advertised by William McDonald & Son to start from the lower end of Bowly's wharf every evening at five o'clock; the other, advertised by Briscoe & Partridge, leaving the same wharf at the same hour; "the passengers, traveling over a good turnpike road from Elkton to Wilmington, will then take steamboats, and arrive in Philadel-

CHAPTER III.—1819-1838.

The Savannah, the First Ocean Steamship, 1819.—David Napier's Enterprise, 1819-22.—First Steamboats on the Missouri, 1819.—The Robert Fulton Steamship between New Orleans and New York, 1819. — Walk-in-the-Water, First Steamboat on Lake Erie, 1819.—First Steamboat on Lake Michigan, 1827.—First Ramsgate Steamboat, 1820.—First Steam-Vessels in the Royal Navy, 1820-23.—French Officers sent to United States to inquire about Steam-Vessels, etc., 1820.—First Steamboat on the Indus, 1820.—First Sea-going Steamboat for Hull, England, 1821.—First Steamboat Excursion from New York to Providence, 1821.—First Steamboat Line between Providence and New York, 1822.—David Gordon's Patent for Boxing Paddle-Wheels, 1822.—Table of Comparative Voyages of Sailing- and Steam-Vessels, 1822.—Number of Steamboats on American Waters, 1823.—Captain de Lisle proposes Screws to be applied to French Ships of the Line, 1823.—Delangue, of Paris, patents a Screw, 1824.—Steamer Enterprise goes from London to Calcutta, 1825.—Jacob Perkins's Propeller, 1825.—Samuel Brown's Canal Towing Company's Propeller, 1825.—Steamboat Speed on the Hudson, 1826.—Woodcroft's Screw, 1826.—Winter Steamboats between Philadelphia and New York, 1827.—The Atlas launched at Rotterdam, 1828.—The Swift, First Steamer in Turkey, 1828.—The Curaçoa, 1828.—The Steam-Brig New York, 1826.—Patten's Screw; Copley's Screw; Pettier's Screw, 1830.—First Steamboats on the Danube, 1830.—Temperance Resolutions of the Livingston Steam-Packet Company, 1829.—The Meteor, the First Ship of the Royal Navy to carry the Mails, 1830.—The Hugh Lindsay, First Steamer to navigate the Red Sea, 1830. Girard's Screw, 1831.—First Steamer to arrive at Chicago, 1831.—Woodcroft's Screw, 1832.—First Wrought-Iron Steamboat, 1832.—The Firebrand's Long Voyage, 1833.—First Vessel of the Royal Navy to West Indies, 1832.—Junius Smith, the Originator of Ocean Steam Navigation, 1832-38.—The Second Steamship to cross the Atlantic, 1832.—First Steamer on the Merrimac River, 1834.—Smith's Screw, 1835.—Fitzpatrick's, 1835.—French Steamboats, 1836.—First Steamer to China, 1832.—An American Ironclad, 1836.—Commodore Barron's Ram, 1836.—Steam Tow-Boats introduced on the Delaware, 1836.—Steam-Vessels of Great Britain, 1836-37.—The Francis B. Ogden, Ericsson's First Practical Screw Steamer, 1836.—The Enterprise, 1839.—The Robert F. Stockton Screw, 1838-89.—Crossing the Atlantic under Sail.—The Princeton, First Screw War Steamer.—Smith's Screw Steamer Archimedes, 1836-38.—The Rattler, First English Screw War Steamer, 1843.—Austrian, Russian, and Hungarian Steamers, 1837.—Dr. Lardner on Steam Navigation of the Atlantic, 1837.—Steam-Vessels of the United States, 1838.—The Germ of the United States Navy, 1837.

1819.—THE "SAVANNAH," THE FIRST OCEAN STEAMSHIP.

THIS vessel—pronounced a myth by Mr. Woodcroft in his work on "Steam Navigation," and of which the London *Illustrated Times* for January 16, 1858, says it "is forced into the belief was merely an after-thought of the Americans," claiming that the "Rob Roy," a British steam-packet, between Glasgow and Belfast, was the first sea-going steamer—it can be easily shown was no myth, but a sea-going steamer, which by the aid of sails and steam made the passage from New York to Liverpool in twenty-six days in 1819.

The "Savannah" was built at Corlear's Hook, New York, by Crocker & Fickett. She was three hundred and eighty tons burden, and was launched on the 22d of August, 1818, and built to ply between New York and Liverpool as a sailing-packet. About the time of her launch, Captain Moses Rogers, then of Savannah, Georgia, suggested to Messrs. Dunning, Scarborough, Sturges, Burroughs, Henry, McKinna, and others of that city, the idea of constructing a steamer for plying between Savannah and Liverpool. They accordingly purchased this ship, just launched at Corlear's Hook, and well adapted for the purpose, and named her the "Savannah." They allowed the rigging and other appurtenances for sailing to remain, and supplied her with steam-machinery, and *paddle-wheels,* the latter constructed to fold up like a fan and to be laid upon deck when not in use, her shaft having also a joint for that purpose. The wheel-house was made of canvas extended on an iron rim. She made a trial voyage to Savannah in April, 1819, and arrived there from New York in seven days, after a boisterous passage, during which she had to take in her wheels several times and rely upon her sails.

She left New York under canvas, and arrived at Savannah early in May, 1819. President Monroe was in Charleston, South Carolina, and Mr. Scarborough directed her to go there and give the President an invitation to come to Savannah on the steamship. The President declined, as the people of Charleston did not wish him to leave their State in a Georgia conveyance, but said he would meet her at Savannah. Therefore she returned to Savannah, and a few days after the President arrived and came on board with his suite, accompanied by several naval officers and citizens. The vessel was controlled by steam, and proceeded upon an excursion down the river. The President dined on board, and expressed himself greatly pleased with the vessel, and told Mr. Scarborough that when he returned from her trip across the Atlantic to bring the vessel to Washington, for he thought no doubt the government would purchase her, and employ her as a cruiser on the coast of Cuba.

After her trial trip there was no doubt that the "Savannah" would successfully accomplish the object for which she was purchased, and she sailed from Savannah for Liverpool May 26, 1819. The New York papers of the 2d of June notice her having been spoken at sea, all well. The log-book of the "Pluto," which arrived at Baltimore from Bremen, contains the following passage:

"*June* 2, 1819.—Clear weather, smooth sea, latitude 42°, longitude 50°. Spoke and passed the elegant steamship eight days out from Savannah to Petersburg, by way of Liverpool. She passed us at the rate of *nine or ten knots,* and the captain informed us she worked remarkably well, and the greatest compliment we could bestow was to give her three cheers as the happiest effort of mechanical genius that ever appeared on the Western ocean."

Niles's *New York Register* for the 21st of August contains this paragraph, italicized, at the head of its column of foreign news: " *The steamship 'Savannah,' Captain Moses Rogers, the first that ever crossed the Atlantic, arrived at Liverpool in twenty-five days from Savannah, all well, to the great astonishment of the people at that place. She worked her engine eighteen days.*"

It is stated that " on the 'Savannah's' approach to Liverpool, with sails furled and American colors flying, the piers were thronged by thousands, who greeted her arrival with vociferous cheers, and before she anchored her decks were so crowded it was with the greatest difficulty the crew could move about in the performance of their duty."

The next record of her movements is that she sailed in August for St. Petersburg, passing Elsinore on the 13th, and that the British " wisely supposed her visit to be somehow connected with the ambitious views of the United States."

She returned to Savannah early in November, 1819, after a passage of fifty-three days from St. Petersburg, *via* Copenhagen and Arendal, in Norway, in the language of Captain Rogers, " with neither a screw, nor bolt, nor rope-yarn parted, though she encountered a heavy gale in the North Sea." She left Savannah for Washington on the 4th of November, and lost her boats and anchors off Cape Hatteras.

But for the war of 1812 the " Savannah" would have been anticipated in her ocean voyage by a larger and superior vessel, built by a company for the Russian government. This vessel, the " Emperor Alexander," was nearly ready for sea when her departure was prevented by the declaration of war in June, 1812. Under the name of the " Connecticut" she was known upon the waters of Long Island Sound, and later in her history was a weekly packet between Portland, Maine, and Boston, Massachusetts.

If these statements do not satisfy the most doubting that the " Savannah" was no myth or an after-thought of the Americans, these extracts from a petition to Congress, in 1856, by Mrs. Taylor, the daughter of her constructor, fortified by the sworn testimony of Captain Rogers, must be conclusive.

Mrs. Taylor says, " Your petitioner is the only surviving child of the late William Scarborough, of Savannah, Georgia, who, being an energetic and enterprising man of great mechanical genius, caused to be constructed in the years 1818–19, with his own means, and those of every friend he could enlist in the effort, the first steamer that ever crossed the Atlantic, 'The Savannah,' of Savannah, Georgia, Captain Moses Rogers, of New London, Connecticut, commanding."

For the details of this voyage she refers to the sworn statement of

Captain Steven Rogers, the sailing-master, "and prays that they will grant her some pecuniary acknowledgment," etc.

Captain Steven Rogers,[1] under date New London, Connecticut,

[1] Captain Steven Rogers, the sailing-master, died at New London, Connecticut, September, 1868, aged seventy-four years. The log-book of the "Savannah," containing the daily record of her memorable voyage, is in possession of his descendants.

This valuable relic is made up of ninety-six pages of coarse paper, twelve inches wide and nineteen and a half long, browned with age, and with edges ragged from much handling. Only fifty-two pages are written on, the rest are blank. It is unbound, but the sheets are sewed into an enveloping piece of sail-cloth, which is rudely hemmed at the upper and lower edges. This cloth cover bears the inscription, "Steamship 'Savannah's' Log-Book," printed in bold characters. The handwriting is that of Steven Rogers, the sailing-master. Every word in the closely-written pages is legible, the ink being still black; only a small portion of the entries have any present interest, the larger part being remarks on the weather, on the disposition of the ship's sails, and the results of the observations of latitude and longitude.

The caption of the first page is as follows:

"*A Journal of a Voyage from New York towards Savannah on steamboat 'Savannah;' Moses Rogers, Master.*"

This is continued on four pages; the caption of the fifth is,—

"A Half-Hour Journal on board steamship 'Savannah,' Moses Rogers, Master."

And after a few pages this caption gives place to—

"A Journal of a Voyage from Savannah towards Liverpool on board steamship 'Savannah;' Moses Rogers, Master."

The caption afterwards changes several times, but the same formula is preserved.

The first entry in the log-book is—

Sunday, March 28, 1819.—These 24 hours begin with fresh breezes at N. W. At 10 A.M. got under way for Sea with the crew on board. At 1 P.M. the Pilot left the Ship off Sandy hook light."

After this entry the page is ruled on the left side into six narrow columns, headed respectively, "H, K, HK [hours, knots, half-knots], Course, Winds, LW [lee-way];" and then a longer space, headed, "Remarks on board," with the appropriate date.

The second entry is as follows:

"Remarks on board Monday, March 29, 1819. The 24 hours begin with fresh breezes and clear. At 4 P.M. the Highlands of Neversink bore N. b. W. 6 Leagues distant from which I take my departure. At 10 P.M. took in Topgallant Sails. At 6 A.M. Set Topgallant Sails. At 8 A.M. Tacked Ship to the Westward. Saw a brig and Schooner Steering to the Westward. At 11 A.M. took in the Mizzen and Fore Topgallant Sails. At 11 A.M. got the Steam up and it coming on to blow fresh we took the Wheels in on deck in 30 minutes. At meridian fresh breezes and Cloudy. Lat. by Obs. 39° 19′."

This is a fair sample of the daily records, extending over a period of nine months.

The statement, "we took the wheels in on deck in thirty minutes," refers to the fact that this steamer was so constructed that, in case of boisterous weather, her paddle-wheels could be brought on deck.

Land was sighted on June 16, being the coast of Ireland, and on the 17th the "Savannah" "was boarded by the King's Cutter 'Kite,' Lieutenant John Bowie."

The log-book here, as elsewhere, is sternly brief. Fortunately, we have in Steven Rogers's own words a fuller account of the amusing circumstances connected with this boarding of the "Savannah" by the king's cutter. In a communica-

May 2, 1856, swears that he is aged sixty-eight years; that he was the *sailing-master* of the steamship " Savannah" on her trial trip to Liverpool, Copenhagen, St. Petersburg, etc. " Said steamship was built at the city of New York, in the year 1818, the builders being Fickett & Crocker. She was designed for a Havre packet, and was purchased by William Scarborough, of Savannah, and was named at his suggestion 'The Savannah,' he having told me that in his opinion the ocean would be navigated by steam, and he intended his own State and city should have the credit of sending the first steamer across the Atlantic. Her castings were made in New York, and her boilers at Elizabethtown, New Jersey, by Daniel Dodge. She left New York under canvas, and arrived at Savannah in the early part of May, 1819. President Monroe was then in Charleston, South Carolina, and Mr. Scarborough directed us to go there and give the President an invitation to come to Savannah on the steamship. The President declined because the people of Charleston did not wish him to leave their State in a Georgia conveyance, but said that he would visit us at Savannah. So we returned. A few days after we got back the President arrived, and came on board the vessel with his suite and several naval officers and citizens. The vessel was navigated by steam, and we proceeded down the river on an

tion to the New London (Connecticut) *Gazette* he said, " She [the steamer] was seen from the telegraph-station at Cape Clear, on the southern coast of Ireland, and reported as a ship on fire. The admiral, who lay in the Cove of Cork, dispatched one of the king's cutters to her relief. But great was their wonder at their inability, with all sail in a fast vessel, to come up with a ship under bare poles. After several shots were fired from the cutter, the engine was stopped, and the surprise of her crew at the mistake they had made, as well as their curiosity to see the singular Yankee craft, can be easily imagined. They asked permission to go on board, and were much gratified by the inspection of this naval novelty."

Two days later (June 20) they "shipped the wheels, furled the sails, and ran into the River Mersey, and at 6 P.M. come to anchor off Liverpool with the small bower anchor."

The London *Times* of June 21, 1819, has the following paragraph, credited to *Marwade's Commercial Report* for that week:

" Among the arrivals yesterday at this port we were particularly gratified and astonished by the novel sight of a fine steamship, which came round at 7½ P.M. without the assistance of a single sheet, in a style which displayed the power and advantage of the application of steam to vessels of the largest size, being *three hundred and fifty tons* burden. She is called the 'Savannah,' Captain Rogers, and sailed from Savannah (Georgia, United States) the 26th of May, and arrived in the Channel five days since. During her passage she worked the engine eighteen days. Her model is beautiful, and the accommodations for passengers elegant and complete. She is THE FIRST SHIP on this construction that has undertaken a *voyage across the Atlantic.*"

The *Times* of June 30, 1819, says, " The 'Savannah' steam-vessel recently arrived at Liverpool *from America*—the *first vessel* of the kind that *ever crossed the Atlantic*—was CHASED A WHOLE DAY off the coast of Ireland by the ' Kite' revenue cruiser, on the Cork Station, which mistook her for a ship on fire."

Lloyd's List reports the arrival of the "Savannah" at Liverpool on the 20th of June, 1819, bound to St. Petersburg; and in Gore's " Annals of Liverpool" this American steamer's arrival is recorded among " remarkable events."

excursion. The President dined on board, and expressed himself greatly pleased with the vessel, and told Mr. Scarborough that when she came back from her trip across the Atlantic, to bring the vessel around to Washington, for he thought there was no doubt the government would purchase her, and employ her as a cruiser upon the coast of Cuba.

"We sailed from Savannah for Liverpool on the 26th of May, 1819. Moses Rogers, my brother-in-law, was master and engineer. I was sailing-master, and Mr. Blackman was third officer. We made the port of Liverpool in twenty-two days after leaving Savannah, fourteen of the twenty-two under steam. The only reason why the whole voyage was not performed by steam was the fear of the fuel giving out. Off Cape Clear, the admiral at Cork dispatched a ship to our relief, supposing we were *on fire*. At Liverpool we caused a great deal of excitement, and suspicion of having some design to release Napoleon from St. Helena. From Liverpool we proceeded to Copenhagen, and from thence to Stockholm. At both places the 'Savannah' excited great curiosity; at the latter place she was visited by the royal family, our Minister, Mr. Hughes, and Lord Lyndoch. Lord L. went with us to St. Petersburg. On the passage he desired us to bring the vessel from steam to canvas. He held his watch and noted the time, fifteen minutes. He was so delighted that he exclaimed, ' I blame no man born in the United States for being proud of his country; and were I a young man I'd go there myself.' The Emperor of Russia came on board at Cronstadt, and was much pleased with the vessel, and presented Captain Rogers with two iron chairs (one of which is now in the garden of Mr. Dunning at Savannah)."

Steven Rogers then states that he has in his possession a gold snuff-box presented to him by Lord Lyndoch, upon which is the following inscription:

"Presented by Sir Thomas Gresham, Lord Lyndoch, to Steven Rogers, sailing-master of the steamship 'Savannah,' at St. Petersburg, Oct. 10, 1819."

He adds, "We sailed from St. Petersburg to Arendal in Norway, and from thence to Savannah, in twenty-five days, steaming on the passage *nineteen days*. We went from Savannah to Washington at the suggestion of President Monroe, but the government did not buy her. She was there sold at auction and converted into a packet."

Captain Rogers says that Scarborough ruined himself by her, and died poor. While at St. Petersburg the "Savannah" was anchored opposite and six miles from the city. After being used for a time as a sailing-packet between New York and Savannah, the "Savannah" went ashore on Long Island and was broken up.

These notices of the "Savannah" are from the newspapers of the day:

HISTORY OF STEAM NAVIGATION.

"By an advertisement in this day's paper it will be seen that the new and elegant steamship 'Savannah' is to leave her harbor to-morrow. Who would have had the courage twenty years ago to hazard a prediction that in the year 1819 a ship of three hundred tons burden would be built in the port of New York to navigate the Atlantic propelled by steam? Such, however, is the fact. With admiring hundreds have we repeatedly viewed this prodigy, and can also bear witness to the wonderful celerity with which she is moved through the water. On Monday last a trial was made of her speed, and although there was at no time more than *an inch* of steam upon her, and for the greater part not *half an inch*, with a strong wind and tide ahead, she went within a mile of the anchoring ground at Staten Island, and returned to Fly-Market wharf in one hour and fifty minutes. When it is considered that she is calculated to bear twenty inches of steam, and that her machinery is entirely new, it must be evident that she will with ease pass any of the steamboats upon our rivers. Her cabin is finished in an elegant style, and is fitted up in the most tasty manner. There are thirty-two berths, all of which are state-rooms. The cabin for ladies is entirely distinct from that intended for gentlemen, and is admirably calculated to afford that perfect retirement which is so rarely found on board of passenger ships."[1]

"The elegant steamship 'Savannah' arrived here about five o'clock yesterday evening. The bank of the river was lined by a large concourse of citizens, who saluted her with shouts during her progress before the city. She was also saluted by a discharge from the revenue cutter 'Dallas.' Her appearance inspires instant confidence in her security. It is evident that her wheels can be unshipped in a few minutes, so as to place her precisely in the condition of any other vessel, in case of a storm and rough sea. Our city will be indebted to the enterprise of her owners for the honor of first crossing the Atlantic Ocean in a vessel propelled by steam."[2]

"We are requested to state that the steamship 'Savannah,' Captain Rogers, will without fail proceed to Liverpool direct to-morrow, 20th instant. Passengers, if any offer, can be well accommodated."[3]

"Captain Livingston, of the schooner 'Contract,' who arrived at Newburyport on the 5th instant, sighted on the 29th of May, latitude 27.30, longitude 70, a vessel ahead to eastward, from which he saw volumes of smoke issuing. Judging it to be a vessel on fire, stood for her, in order to afford relief; 'but' (observes Captain Livingston) 'found she went faster with fire and smoke than we possibly could with all sail set. It was then we discovered that what we supposed a vessel on fire was nothing less than a steamboat crossing the Western Ocean,

---

[1] New York *Mercantile Advertiser*, March 27, 1819.
[2] Savannah *Georgian*, Wednesday, April 7, 1819.
[3] *Georgian*, Wednesday, May 19, 1819.

laying her course, as we judge, for Europe; a proud monument of Yankee skill and enterprise. Success to her.'"[1]

"*Norfolk, August* 10.— . . . I have received no shipping list by this arrival, but an article of great importance in the steam world (if I may use the expression) is contained in the Cork paper of the 19th of June. It is no less than the arrival at Kinsale, in twenty-one days, of the steamship 'Savannah,' from Savannah, laden with cotton and passengers. She put in for supplies, would remain a day or two, and then proceed for Liverpool. Previous to her putting in she was chased by a cutter under the impression that she was a ship on fire. No further particulars are stated."[2]

1819.—The model of the first canal-boat on the Erie Canal exists at the Historical Society Rooms in Buffalo. It is about two feet long, sharp at either end, and is flat-bottomed. There are cabins at each end, between which are the gangways. It is a faithful and accurate copy of the "Chief Engineer of Rome," the first canal-boat that was built to navigate old Erie. The following card of explanation says the "Chief Engineer of Rome" was the first boat built for the Erie Canal, of which the trial trip was made October 23, 1819. Governor De Witt Clinton, the canal commissioners, and chief and assistant engineers, other State officers and guests, with ladies and gentlemen of Utica, Whitesboro', Oriskany, and Rome, in all about sixty or seventy persons, made up the party. The boat was named in compliment to Benjamin Wright, the chief engineer of the Erie Canal. The model, without the forward and middle cabins, was brought from England in the early part of 1817 by Canvass White, then assistant engineer to Mr. Wright, subsequently a distinguished engineer. The model was presented to the Society to which it now belongs, in February, 1867, by William C. Young, a rodman of the Erie surveys of 1816–17, a kinsman of the Whites of Whitesboro', in which family the original model-boat has been kept for years.

1819.—Great Britain owes to David Napier the establishment of deep-sea communications by steam-vessels, and of post-office steam-packets, at about the same date as the adventurous voyage of the "Savannah." Previous to his enterprise steam-vessels rarely ventured, and only in fine weather, beyond the precincts of rivers and coasts of firths. Soon after the introduction of steam on the river Clyde he entertained the idea of establishing steam communication on the open sea, and as a first step endeavored to ascertain the difficulties to be encountered. For this purpose he took passage, at a stormy period of the year, on a sailing-packet which formed one of a line and the only means of intercourse between Glasgow and Belfast, a passage which required a week to accomplish what is now done by steam in nine hours. The captain of the packet found a young man, whom he after-

---

[1] *Georgian,* Thursday, June 24, 1819.   [2] Charlotte City *Gazette.*

wards knew as Mr. Napier, during one of his winter passages to Belfast, constantly perched on the bow of the vessel, fixing an intent gaze on the sea when it broke on the side of the ship, quite heedless of the waves and spray that washed over him. He only ceased from this occupation at intervals as the breeze freshened to ask the captain whether the sea was such that might be considered a rough one, and when told that it was by no means unusually rough, he returned to the bow of the vessel and resumed his study of the waves breaking at her stem. When the breeze began to freshen into a gale, and the sea to rise considerably, he again inquired of the captain whether the sea might now be considered a rough one, and was told that as yet it could not be called very rough. Disappointed, he returned again to his station at the bow and resumed his employment. At last he was favored with a storm to his contentment, and when the seas, breaking over the vessel, swept her from stem to stern, he found his way back to the captain and repeated his inquiry, "Do you call it rough now?" The captain replied "he could not remember to have faced a worse night in the whole of his experience," which delighted young Napier, who muttering as he turned away, "I think I can manage, if that be all," went down to his cabin. Napier saw then the end of his difficulties, and soon satisfied himself as to the means of overcoming them.

His next inquiry was as to the means of getting through the water with least resistance. To determine this, he commenced a series of experiments with models of vessels in a small tank of water, and soon found that the round full bluff bow adopted for sailing-vessels was quite unsuited for speed with mechanical propulsion of a different nature. This led him to adopt the fine, wedge-like entrance by which the vessels built under his superintendence were afterwards so distinguished.

In 1818 he established a regular steam communication between Greenock and Belfast by means of the "Rob Roy," a vessel of about ninety tons burden and thirty horse-power. She plied two winters between those ports with regularity and success, and afterwards was transferred to the English Channel as a packet between Dover and Calais. Having thus acquired steam navigation dominion of the open sea, Mr. Napier was not slow to extend it.

In 1819 the Messrs. Wood built for him the "Talbot," of one hundred and fifty tons, with two of Mr. Napier's engines, each of thirty horse-power, the most perfect vessel of her day in all respects, and a model which was long in being surpassed. The "Talbot" plied between Holyhead and Dublin, and conferred on Ireland the advantage of a direct, certain, and rapid communication with England.

Napier, in 1822, introduced surface condensers on board the "Post Boy," a steam-vessel built by him. The condenser consisted of a series of small copper tubes, through which steam passed towards the air-pump. By a constant current of cold water encircling the pipes the steam was cooled and returned into water, which was again returned into the boiler for conversion into steam, without being mixed with the cold salt water, which in the ordinary plan was injected into the condenser. The rapidity of condensation was found insufficient, and he returned to the old system for condensation. Years afterwards he returned to this system, in circumstances which rendered it desirable, and, using flat plates instead of tubes, was more successful, and plied for years with no other condenser. In 1826 the first of the so-called leviathan class of steamers, the "United Kingdom," was built for the trade between London and Edinburgh. She was of one hundred and sixty feet long, with twenty-six and one-half feet beam, and engines of two hundred horse-power, built by David Napier. She was considered the wonder of the day, and people flocked from all quarters to inspect and admire her.

1819.—The first steamboats to ascend the Missouri were three little government boats in 1819. A party of engineers and naturalists kept along near them on shore. The Pawnees pilfered the horses, provisions, and apparatus of the unfortunate *savants*, and left them to wander, hungry and half naked, till they found refuge among the friendly Kaws. These steamers stemmed the current with difficulty, and were delayed by sand-bars; for this was before steamboats were educated up to walking off on their spars as a boy walks on his stilts; and on their return they dropped down river stern foremost, as they were more manageable in that position. One of the first boats to ascend the Missouri carried the figure-head of a serpent at her prow. Through this reptile's mouth steam escaped, and the savages when they saw it fled in alarm, fancying the spirit of evil was coming bodily to devour them.

FIRST STEAMER BETWEEN NEW YORK AND HAVANA.

In 1819 a vessel of seven hundred tons, named the "Robert Fulton," ship-rigged, but furnished with a steam-engine, was built at New York, to ply as a packet between New York, Charleston, Cuba, and New Orleans. She performed her voyage over that long route with great regularity in nine days, and continued running on it over three years. So far as safety and speed were concerned she was successful; but she did not defray expenses, and was sold to the Brazilian government, when her engine was removed, and she was converted into a cruiser. As late as 1838 she was in the Brazilian service.

The "Walk-in-the-Water," the only steamboat on Lake Erie in 1819, was considered sufficient to transact the commercial business of that lake. This boat, named after a Wyandotte chief, made her first trip to the island of Mackinaw in the summer of 1819. There was no one to furnish her with a cargo except the American Fur Company.

In 1827 the waters of Lake Michigan were first plowed by steam, a boat having made an excursion to Green Bay; and in 1832 another steamboat reached Chicago with troops, that site being in course of clearance and settlement. In 1840 forty-eight boats were trading between Buffalo, Chicago, and other ports west of Detroit, the trip occupying fifteen days.

In 1820 the first steam-vessel was prepared for Ramsgate, and was called the "Eagle." She had two of Bolton & Watt's engines, equal to forty horse-power. She was in existence in 1850, and used by the King of Denmark as his steam-yacht. If a sailing-packet prior to the advent of steam conveyed to or from London and Ramsgate eight hundred passengers a month it was something extraordinary. Yet in November, 1850, the "City of London," steam-packet, conveyed five thousand three hundred and fifty-six persons.

1820–23.—The "Comet," "Lightning," and "Meteor" were the first steam-vessels that ever appeared in the British navy, and the "Comet" was the first that ever carried a pennant.

These sister vessels were constructed by Oliver Lang, then an assistant surveyor of the navy, in the year 1820, *the three surveyors in office having refused to take the responsibility of constructing a steam-vessel for sea service!* They were built at Deptford, in about three years, from Mr. Lang's drawings and plans of fittings, without the interference of any one, and solely under his direction and personal superintendence.

The following was the Admiralty return of their dimensions to the House of Commons, in answer to the inquiry of Rear-Admiral Sir Charles Napier, in 1846:

Name.	Guns.	Length.	Breadth.	Depth.	Class.	Horse-Power.	Engine.
		Feet.	Ft. In.	Ft. In.			
Comet . . .	8	115	21 8	11 11	Paddle	80	Bolton & Watt's side lever.
Lightning . .	8	126	22 8	13 8	"	100	"
Meteor . . .	8	126	22 8	13 8	"	100	"

The first *iron* steamboat ever built was constructed in 1820 at the Horsley Iron-Works. She was called the "Aaron Manby," after her projector. She was built in sections and put together in London, and was the first vessel that ever went direct from London to Paris.

In 1820 there was only *one* small steamboat on Lake Erie. In 1831, *eleven* steamboats, with an aggregate capacity of two thousand two hundred and sixty tons. In 1836, forty-five steamboats, of nine thousand one hundred and nineteen tons. In 1847, sixty-seven side-wheel steamers and twenty-six screw steamers.

In 1822, Messrs. Wood built on the Clyde the "James Watt," to ply between Leith and London. She measured four hundred and forty-eight tons and carried two engines of fifty horse-power each made by Bolton & Watt, under the superintendence of Mr. Brown, one of the firm. The "James Watt" was remarkable for having its paddles moved through the interposition of toothed wheels, and not directly by the engine; so that the revolution of the axis of the engine was greater than that of the paddles. With the exception of the low proportion of power to tonnage, the "James Watt" possessed nearly all the qualities of the most improved vessels of a quarter of a century later.

FIRST STEAMBOATS ON THE INDUS.

1820.—A small steamboat christened the "Snake" was built in Bombay in 1820, and was the first steam-vessel on the Indus, and, in fact, on any river in India. Her engines were designed and built by a Parsee, and were the first ever manufactured in India. How well they were constructed is evidenced by their lasting powers. She was twice wrecked,—once in a hurricane in 1837, and again in a cyclone in 1854. She was employed during the first British Burmese war and on the expedition to the Persian Gulf from 1823 to 1826, in the Chinese war of 1841–42, Burmese war of 1852, Persian war of 1856, mutiny of 1857, Chinese expedition of 1859, etc. She in her day carried most of the notables that arrived in India *via* Bombay, and closed her eventful career of sixty years in 1880, when she was broken up.

The "Falcon" in 1820 used steam during part of her voyage from England to India.

A steamboat was launched at Potsdam in 1820, larger than any yet built in Europe. It was two hundred feet long and forty-four feet wide, had two engines of twenty horse-power each, and was named The "Blucher" with great ceremony.[1]

Impressed with the importance of having steam ships of war as early as 1820, the French government sent two officers to America, Captain Mongery, of the navy, and M. Marestier, of the corps of marine engineers, to ascertain and report upon the properties of the steam-vessels of the United States, and their report was printed.

In 1820–21 an unsuccessful attempt was made by Boston ship merchants to establish steam towage on the rivers of South Carolina. A company was formed with a capital of twenty-five thousand dollars, and afterwards increased. A steamboat called the "Patent" and towing-barges were built and sent out to ply on the Pedee and Santee Rivers, but, as appears by a letter to Thomas H. Perkins, Esq., from John L. Sullivan, dated Troy, January 1, 1823, the enterprise resulted in the loss of the capital invested and its abandonment. It is worthy of note only as showing that thus early an attempt was made to in-

[1] *Literary Gazette*, February, 1820.

augurate steam navigation on the rivers of the Southern Atlantic coast of the United States.

1821.—The first sea-going steamboat sent out from Hull, England, was in 1821, and is reputed to be the first sea-going steamboat on the east coast of England. In 1854 the sea-going steamers connected with Hull had an aggregate tonnage of nine thousand one hundred and thirty-nine, and the river-boats two thousand two hundred and eighteen tons; other steamboats coming to and departing from Hull had a burden of five thousand nine hundred and nine tons; altogether there were eighty steamers trading with Hull, fifteen of which were screws.

In 1821 there was an excursion from New York to Providence in the steamboat "Robert Fulton,"[1] the first of its kind. The *Manufacturers' and Farmers' Journal* of August 27, 1821, has the following notice of the event:

"The 'Robert Fulton' left New York Thursday afternoon at five o'clock, and arrived below at nine Saturday morning. As soon as the tide would permit she came up to town, where she was the admiration of crowds of visitors. She brought eighty passengers, among whom was the *Hon. John Quincy Adams, Secretary of State*, who immediately proceeded to Boston by land. At two o'clock the 'Fulton' departed on her return to New York."

The journal of one of the passengers supplies further particulars of this interesting trip. He says,—

"On Friday, at a quarter before 8 P.M., we ranged alongside of the dock at Newport, music playing as we entered the harbor and passed he fortified island. Such a scene of tumult as was here witnessed I never saw before. The wharves were lined with people of all ages and conditions, who pressed forward and immediately on our landing took complete possession of the ship. The band and many of the passengers went on shore, and Governor Gibbs and some of the principal families in town were serenaded. When the party returned to the ship they were scarcely able to get on board, and the tumult lasted until one o'clock in the morning.

"We started at 5 A.M. next day for Providence. As we approached the scene became truly interesting. The inhabitants had anticipated our arrival, and every hill was covered with an admiring assemblage. India Point wharf presented a spectacle singular and gratifying. The beauty and fashion of this charming town greeted us with cheers and welcoming. At 7.45 we came up to the dock and landed the company, and here again numerous parties of ladies and gentlemen crowded the ship. The masts and rigging of the vessels lying in the vicinity were covered with spectators, and nothing could exceed the interest and gratification with which all appeared to greet

---

[1] This was not the New York and Havana packet already mentioned, but a steam-vessel of the same name built exclusively to navigate Long Island Sound.

our arrival. At 3 P.M. the 'Fulton' left the wharf amid the shouts of thousands.

"We arrived at Bristol at half-past 5 P.M., where we were met with the same spirit of enthusiasm which had characterized our whole route. Mr. De Wolfe's elegant mansion was thrown open to the visits of the passengers, and was much admired. We arrived at Newport at 8 P.M. It was quite dark, but the interest appeared to have increased rather than diminished. I took a station at the gangway to assist the inhabitants, and particularly the ladies, on board the ship,—notice having been given that none but ladies would be allowed on board at first,—and in the short space of twenty minutes I handed in three hundred and thirty-seven. I found that this number did not appear to have thinned the crowd in the least degree, and by nine o'clock there must have been on board upward of six hundred ladies."

EARLY STEAMBOATS ON LONG ISLAND SOUND.

After the "Fulton" steamed away, no steamboats came from Providence until the 6th of June, 1822, when the "Connecticut," Captain Bunker, arrived from New York.

On the 12th of July, of this year, a company was formed, called the "Rhode Island and New York Steamboat Company," and regular trips, twice a week, were begun between the two cities by the "Fulton" and "Connecticut."

The New York Legislature had granted great privileges to the Livingston and Fulton Steam Navigation Company. No steam-vessel could navigate New York Bay, the North River, Long Island Sound, or any of the lakes and rivers of the State of New York without their license. The Connecticut Legislature antagonistically enacted "no vessel bearing such a license should enter any water within that State." The "Connecticut" was running at this time between New York and New Haven in opposition to the packet lines. Through the influence of the packet-owners the Legislature of Connecticut passed a prohibitory law, and the "Fulton" and "Connecticut," running between New York and New London, were driven from Connecticut ports.

The Providence *Journal*, June 3, 1822, copies from the New York *Mercantile Advertiser* the announcement that steam communication between New York and New Haven had ceased, and states that the "Fulton" and "Connecticut" had sailed for some point in Rhode Island. June 6 the arrival of the Connecticut was announced in the "marine news," and July 12 the "Fulton," Captain Law, arrived at Providence from Pawcatuck. The same day the "Connecticut," Captain Elihu S. Bunker, and "Fulton" began regular trips between Providence and New York, touching at Newport. The fare between Providence and New York was *ten* dollars; between Newport and New York nine dollars. The first advertisement of this company appeared under the cut of a *man-of-war with port-holes open and every sail set,*—in a few weeks a steamboat cut was procured, and then the advertisement announced that

"*From New York* a boat will depart on Wednesday and Saturday at 4 o'clock P.M., and

"*From Providence* a boat will depart on Wednesday and Saturday at 6 o'clock A.M."

The "Fulton" and "Connecticut" continued their weekly trips through the season, and thus was inaugurated the steamboat trade between Providence and New York. The log of the first trip of the "Connecticut" is in substance: "Left New York on the 4th at 4 P.M.; was detained at Sandy Point 8¼ hours by easterly winds; on the 5th continued our voyage, and arrived off Fisher's Island at 8 P.M. Lay to 3 hours; doubled Point Judith at 2 A.M.; touched at Newport, and arrived at Providence at 8 A.M. on the morning of the 6th of June." During the autumn of 1822 the amount of travel and rate of speed between New York and Newport were: September 13, "Fulton," 27 hours from New York, 40 passengers; October 4, "Connecticut," 32 hours, 40 passengers; October 6, "Fulton," 24 hours, 26 passengers; October 10, "Connecticut," 18 hours, 35 passengers. The "Fulton" withdrew for the winter November 16, but the "Connecticut" was continued on the line, making one trip per week until the navigation was closed by the ice. The following announcement reads queerly now:

"The 'Connecticut' will leave Providence every Tuesday evening to go down the river, in order to start from Newport at an early hour on Wednesday morning. *It will therefore be necessary for the passengers to be on board at Providence at ten in the evening.*"

The "Connecticut" and "Fulton" were owned in New York. The "Connecticut" was one hundred and fifty feet long, twenty-six feet wide, and of about two hundred tons burden. Her color was white, with green trimmings. She had a square engine, and cost eighty thousand dollars.[1] The "Fulton" was the first steamboat built expressly to navigate Long Island Sound. She was enormously strong, but had little less machinery than is now put in a cotton-mill. Her wheels were turned through a cog-wheel with teeth five inches long. She made a terrific noise when in motion, but moved so slowly that she was once five hours going from Providence to Newport. Her color was black, and she had sails to help the steam. Her captain once told with glee he had come all the way from New York without hoisting his sails.

Neither boat had upper saloon, state-rooms, or hurricane-deck. Both boats burned pine wood under large *copper* boilers, which were kept polished to the last degree of brightness. The wood necessary to keep the steam up during the trip between Providence and New York

[1] She afterwards ran between Portland, Maine, and Boston, Massachusetts.

was piled everywhere, fore and aft, and high above the guards. But little freight was carried, as the wood took up nearly all the room. When, years afterwards, coal was introduced, iron boilers were substituted, and the old copper boilers paid for the new iron ones.

In the spring of 1823 the "Connecticut" and "Fulton" resumed their trips. The "Fulton" had been overhauled and improved, so that she was nearly as fast as the "Connecticut." She made her first trip to Providence on the 12th of May, 1823, and brought fifty passengers. When near Field's Point one of her boilers was discovered to be "partially ruptured." The fires were hauled and the boat anchored all night. In the morning she was taken to Providence, and five days afterwards was again on the line.

No sooner was the line again in operation than the packetmen caused to be introduced in the General Assembly of Rhode Island a Prohibitory Bill, which restricted the landing of steamboat passengers on Rhode Island soil, and a bill imposing a tax of fifty cents upon each passenger by steamboat. The tax bill passed the Senate, but was rejected by the House, the measure being decided unconstitutional. Consideration of the other bill was indefinitely postponed.

During the season of 1823 the "Connecticut" and "Fulton" made regular trips between Providence and New York, leaving Providence Wednesdays and Saturdays at 6 A.M., and New York Wednesdays and Saturdays at 4 P.M. The advertisement announcing this programme concludes with the remark, "Travelers are requested to read the above notice right."

As the "Connecticut" approached Nyaot Point one June morning in 1823, two skiffs were observed making for the steamer. The occupants seemed to signal the vessel to stop, and such interest was aroused that Captain Bunker steered towards the foremost skiff and hailed her. There was returned no answer, but from the rear boat came oaths and shouts from which those on the steamer gathered that the occupants of the foremost boat were runaways in pursuit of some Gretna Green. As their boat came within a few yards of the steamer a young man looked up and said, "Will you take us on board, sir?" An enthusiastic response from the passengers, and a score of hands lent their aid. Captain Bunker seemed unconscious of what was going on, but tradition says that the instant the young man's feet touched the deck of the steamer the engineer received an order to "*go ahead*" with a suddenness that took away his breath; and in a very few seconds a wide stretch of water lay between the steamer and the empty boat.

The following table exhibits the average and comparative length of the voyages of steam- and sailing-vessels between British ports and those of surrounding seas, as reported to the British Parliament in June, 1822:

Ports.	Steam-Vessels. Hours.	Sailing-Vessels.	Distance. Miles.	Ports.	Steam-Vessels. Hours.	Sailing-Vessels.	Distance. Miles.
Holyhead to Dublin	8	70 hours	55	Brighton to Dieppe	9	30 hours	73
Pt. Patrick to Donaghadee	3	8 "	19½	Southampton to Havre	15	36 "	120
London to Leith	55	5 days	429	" " Guernsey	16	37 "	125
" " Dublin	84	16 "	610	Milford to Waterford	11	25 "	81
Dublin to Liverpool	14	36 hours	131	Greenock to Belfast	13	30 "	90
Greenock to Liverpool	24	13 days	224	" to Glasgow, up	3	12 "	} 24
London Bridge to Calais	12	36 hours	120	" " down	2½	6 "	
London to Margate	8	20 "	84	" " Dublin	25	52 "	200
" " Plymouth	38	10 days	315	" " Ayr	6	12 "	48
" " Belfast	110	18 "	725	" " Largo	2	4 "	18
" " Ostend	12	24 hours	90	" " Port Patrick	9	20 "	90
" " Texel	22	54 "	170	" " Isle of Man	18	40 "	135
" " Scarborough	25	68 "	225	" " Cambeltown	16	18 "	67
" " Portsmouth	29	8 days	255	Edinburgh to Aberdeen	12	25 "	90
" " Hull	23	50 hours	215	" " Sterling	4	8 "	36

1823.—In 1823 there were about three hundred steamboats on American waters.

Between 1813 and 1823 one hundred and sixty steam-vessels were launched in England, varying all the way from nine to five hundred and ten tons in size, and from three horse-power to one hundred and twenty. The largest of these, the "Soho," was of smaller dimensions than the American steamboat "Chancellor Livingston," of five hundred and twenty tons, plying on the Hudson River between New York and Albany, and she was surpassed by the "Lady Sherbrooke," of seven hundred and eighty-seven tons, the largest then plying upon the St. Lawrence.

In 1822, David Gordon, of London, obtained a patent for certain improvements and additions to steam-packets applicable to naval and marine purposes, which consisted in boxing the paddle-wheels, or inclosing them in a case, by which plan the vessel can be easily made proof against shot.

In 1823, Captain Delisle addressed a letter to the French Minister of Marine, in which he proposed applying to ships of the line four screws of five arms each, of which two were to be placed in the bow and two in the stern of the ship. He gave the proportions of the length of the furrow of the screw to its diameter at 1.85. He also gave plans for raising the screws out of water and unshipping them while immersed,—that it might not impede the vessel while under sail.

Wickoff in his "Reminiscences of an Idler" mentions in 1823 that "a steamboat nicknamed 'Old Sal' ran daily in summer from Philadelphia to Bristol, some twenty miles, a distance which was usually accomplished in three hours," and that "a sensation was created in Philadelphia when a steamboat appeared called the 'Trenton' that ran to Bordentown, some twenty-six miles, in two hours and a half." Passengers then took stages to New Brunswick, when another steamboat carried them to New York. "With luck the journey was performed in twelve hours, but terrible work it was in the heat of summer. In winter the only route to New York was by land, the rivers being closed with ice."

1822.—EARLY STEAMBOATS IN MAINE.—The first advertisement or notice of a steamboat in Maine is found in the Portland *Argus*, August 13, 1822, viz. :

"The steamboat 'KENNEBEC' will leave Union wharf at four o'clock for North Yarmouth to spend the day. Will return on Thursday to take passengers to the Island as usual. If required, will stop at Week's wharf to receive and land passengers. Will also, should sufficient number of passengers apply, go to Commencement the day preceding, and also on the day of Commencement. For tickets apply to Mr. A. W. TINKHAM'S store."

Lewis Pease, constable and bank messenger and local poet, records her advent thus :

> "A fig for all your clumsy craft,
> Your pleasure boats and packets,
> The *Steamboat* lands you safe and soon,
> At Mansfield's, Trott's, or Bracket's."

This pioneer boat was the old hull of a flat-bottomed craft, in which Captain Seward Porter, the father of steam navigation in Maine, had placed a small, imperfect engine for excursions in the bay. His enterprise was so successful that two years later we find the following notice in the Portland *Argus* of July 8, 1824 :

"The steamboat 'Patent,' Captain Seward Porter, arrived here yesterday, in four days from New York, having touched at a number of places to land passengers. She is intended to ply between this place and Boston, is strong and commodious, and elegantly fitted for passengers. Her engine has been proved, is of superior workmanship, and propels the boat about ten miles an hour. From the perseverance of Captain Porter we have no doubt but he will meet with good encouragement and find it profitable. We wish him success."

In a report made to the stockholders she is described as of two hundred tons and as costing twenty thousand dollars. She had one mast, and a staff at her stern, from which was displayed the stars and stripes, a flag which, in 1832, was in the possession of Hon. William Gould, of Windham, Maine, to whom it was presented by Captain Porter in 1831.

The "Patent" was low and without a hurricane-deck ; her boiler and engine were below, and she had a heavy balance-wheel half above the deck, and an arrangement by which the paddle-wheels could be disconnected. It was said her engine had been built for a vessel to go to Russia (?). Her cabins were all below. The ladies' cabin was at the stern, but had no skylights on deck ; the entrance to it was through the gentlemen's cabin. The stern broad quarter-deck was clear with seats all around it. In the Boston *Courier* of August 12, 1824, her arrival on the 8th is noticed from Portland in seventeen and a half hours against a head wind with seventeen passengers.

In 1824 a small boat was built at Bath called the "Waterville," to run on the Kennebec River.

In 1825 the "Maine," built of the hulls of two schooners, with beams across, was fitted out in Bath. She was of one hundred and five tons, and cost thirteen thousand dollars. The fare between Boston and Portland, with meals, was $5.00; to Bath, $6.00; Augusta, $7.00; and Eastport, $11.00.

1826.—The steam-brig "New York" was running on the coast in 1826, and was lost three years after. A short time previous to her loss she had been purchased by Mr. Bartlett, of Eastport, and fitted with new machinery, etc., running regularly between Boston, Portland, Bath, and other ports on the coast, and while on a trip, and near Owl's Head, came in collision with another steamboat and the next day took fire. We learn from the statement of a passenger:

"Nothing material occurred until she ran on shore going up the Kennebec. She was got off on the next tide, and proceeded to Bath, where passengers were landed and received. She then sailed for Belfast; in the evening, near Owl's Head, she met the steamer *Patent* from Belfast to Portland; both vessels came in contact, and the *Patent* receiving injury was taken in tow by the *New York*, and returned to Belfast. The *New York* then proceeded to Eastport, having about thirty-two souls in all on board. On the same evening, between nine and ten o'clock, about eight miles to the eastward of Petit Menan Light, a glimmering light was discovered around the port funnel. Only two men were on deck, viz., one at the helm and one at the bow. No engineer or fireman was at his post, and but one bucket could be found on deck. Before assistance could be had the fire had got the upper hand, and the engineer could not stop the machinery.

"No fire-engine, hose, or buckets could be found to throw a drop of water. The passengers escaped in the boats, and landed about midnight at the light-house, and from thence to the mainland."

The "New York" had full round lines, flush deck, long scroll-head, like the packet-ships of that day; her name painted on the paddle-boxes, with the addition "New York and Norfolk Packet."

Captain Churchill, her commander, was known as a first-class sailor and coaster, and by his familiars was called "Old Churchyard."

1824.—FRENCH PATENT.—In 1824, L. A. Delangue, of Paris, France, patented a mode for propelling vessels and boats on rivers, by means of Archimedes's screw, placed horizontally, and put in motion by a steam-engine.

A. A. Geerault, of Paris, patented a system of oars moving in a vertical direction, applicable to the navigation of steamboats and G

Heath, of Paris, a method of keeping a boiler always full of water by condensing the steam.

1825.—FIRST STEAMER TO CALCUTTA.—The steamship "Enterprise" made the passage from London to Calcutta, and inaugurated the communication of England with India by steam. The "Enterprise" was a vessel of four hundred and seventy tons burden, having engines of one hundred and twenty horse-power. Commanded by Lieutenant Johnson, R.N.,[1] she sailed from Falmouth, August 16, 1825, and arrived in Diamond Harbor, Bengal, on the 7th of December, having achieved a distance of thirteen thousand seven hundred miles in one hundred and thirteen days, of which she was sixty-four days under steam, thirty-nine under sail, and ten at anchor. The "Enterprise" was built by an association of gentlemen, and was sold to the government of Bengal for forty thousand pounds, which, together with the passage-money, nearly paid her first cost. She was employed in the Burmese war with advantage, and on the occasion of the treaty of Malowa saved the government six lacs of rupees by reaching Calcutta in time to prevent the march of troops from the upper provinces.

1825.—Jacob Perkins, February, 1825, applied a propeller eight feet in diameter at the side of the rudder of a canal-boat. It was built like a double set of windmill vanes, the solid axle of one set working the hollow axle of the other, and rotating in opposite directions.

1825.—A vessel was also built at Rochester the same year by the Canal Towing Company, fitted, on the plan of Samuel Brown, with a gas vacuum-engine of twelve horse-power, working by means of beveled gear a *two*-bladed propeller at the bow. The blades were at an angle of ninety degrees to each other, and forty-five degrees to the axis.

Another vessel, with similar engine and propeller, was soon after tried on the Thames, and attained a speed of seven miles per hour.

1826.—The following hand-bill, if compared with others of the present time, will show the improvement that has been made in the North River boats during the past half-century:

"HUDSON RIVER STEAMBOAT LINE.

" CONSTITUTION,	CONSTELLATION,
" Captain W. J. Wiswell.	Captain R. G. Crittenden.

" DAILY.

"These new and splendid Boats will be dispatched DAILY from New York and Albany, during the Summer months, commencing their regular trips, under this arrangement, on Monday, the 5th June: leaving

---

[1] Captain Johnson received ten thousand pounds for making the first steam voyage to India.

HISTORY OF STEAM NAVIGATION. 129

the wharf, foot of Cortland Street, New York, at 10 A.M., and the wharf, near the steamboat office, South Market Street, Albany, at 9 o'clock.

"When practicable, the Boats will come to at the wharves at Newburgh, Poughkeepsie, Catskill, and Hudson. At Rhinebeck and Kingston a convenient barge will constantly be in readiness to receive and land passengers.

"At the other intermediate places passengers will be received and landed whenever it can be effected with safety.

"These boats are of the first-class, and for extensive and airy accommodations, speed, and quiet motion of engines, and skilful management, are not surpassed by any boats navigating the Hudson River, and the proprietors assure the public that the most assiduous attention will be paid to the safety and comfort of passengers.

"Agents for this line:
  A. N. HOFFMAN, No. 71 Dey Street, New York.
  A. BARTHOLOMEW, South Market Street, Albany.

"☞ All freight and baggage at the risk of owners. Freight of light articles, one shilling per cubic foot.

"May 23d, 1826."

1826.—November 18, 1826, Bennett Woodcroft patented a screw-propeller in England.

1827.—The following advertisement of a steamboat winter line between Philadelphia and New York is from a Philadelphia newspaper dated February 8, 1827:

"STEAMBOAT WINTER LINE FOR NEW YORK,

And the only one now running between the two Cities. Through in one day. Two Citizens' Line Coaches leave their office, No. 32 North Third street, nearly opposite the City Hotel, every morning (Sundays excepted) at 4 o'clock; breakfast at Vencleu's City Hotel, Trenton; dine on board the steamboat, under way from Perth Amboy, and arrive in New York early the same afternoon. Fare through, $6.

"For seats, apply at the above Office, Citizens' Line office, No. 23 South Third street, sign of Robinson Crusoe, and at the office of the Reading and Bethlehem Mail Stages, A. M'Calla's, White Swan, Race street.

"☞ All baggage at its owner's risque."

1828.—The steamship "Atlas," launched at Rotterdam in the summer of 1828, had three engines of one hundred horse-power each, and four masts. Her decks were thirty-five feet longer than a first-rate man-of-war, and she was described as "a gigantic steam-vessel, the largest ever built."

1828.—FIRST STEAMER IN TURKEY.—The first steamer ever seen in Turkey, the "Swift," arrived at Stamboul May, 1828. This solitary boat was purchased by an American and two or three others for three hundred and fifty thousand piasters, and was presented by them to the Sultan Mahmoud.

1828.—THE "CURAÇOA."—It seems probable that the sight of the "Caledonia," which James Watt, Jr., brought early in 1817 from the Clyde to take up the Rhine, staying a little while at Rotterdam, stimulated the interest of the Dutch in steam navigation; at any rate, they soon after ordered several small steamers from Scotland, and in 1827 a company of the merchants of Amsterdam and Rotterdam united for the hazardous experiment of running steamships between the Netherlands and the West Indies. Accordingly, they had a steamer built on the Clyde, which they named the "Curaçoa," of three hundred and fifty tons and one hundred horse-power, and dispatched her, in the summer of 1829, from Amsterdam to the Dutch West Indies. Another account says she started from Antwerp on her first trip August 12, 1828. The voyage to Curaçoa and from Antwerp was repeated several times with great commercial success; nevertheless, the enterprise soon came to an end.

December 10, 1828, Charles Commerow patented a perfect one-turn screw propeller or spiral, fixed parallel to the keel, the outer bearing being held by a second sternpost, behind which was the rudder.

1829.—TEMPERANCE ON LONG ISLAND SOUND.—At a meeting of the directors of the Chancellor Livingston Steam-Packet Company, in 1829, a resolution was adopted prohibiting the steward from placing decanters of brandy and spirits upon the tables. This action created a tremendous stir. As previously stated, the cuisine on the "Chancellor" had always been superb. In these meals the decanters had played an important part; to banish them was atrocious. The indignation was strong, and a letter in defense of the action was published. That letter said "the directors were not influenced by petty motives of economy or gain, but hoped to do a little to aid the cause of reform," and concluded as follows:

"The tables are now supplied with red wines of good quality and pleasant flavor, as well as a good tendency in its effects upon those who may be affected by the motion of the boat. In addition to all this, whenever any person may choose to order brandy or spirits from a belief of their necessity, it will be immediately and cheerfully supplied from the bar, and the gentleman will hear no more about it unless he pleases."

This sensible and moderate movement in favor of reform finally received the approval of all persons of true discernment.

1829.—November 29, 1829, Benjamin Smith, of Rochester, New York, obtained a patent "for propelling boats on the water by the application of sculling wheels, or a screw propelling wheel, formed like the wheel of a smoke-jack, and fixed at the *stem* or bow of the boat by means of a shaft running through the centre, and worked by any suitable power." July 10, 1830, a Mr. Doolittle, being at Syracuse, saw a steamer with wheels of this description arrive on the canal from the West.

1830.—February 4, 1830, John M. Patten, of Milton, Pennsylvania, patented "a spiral or screw-wheel" (described by him as an old invention).

May 22, Josiah Copley, of Warner Mark, Pennsylvania, patented "a shaft having affixed to it eight or any other number of vanes or fans, forming segments of spirals. These to be placed under water, parallel with the keel, and a rapid rotatory motion to be given to them.

October 1, Felix Peltier, of New York, patented "a screw placed in a horizontal position, and wholly uncovered or naked, whether formed of a single spiral wound round a solid arbor and cutting at constantly equal angles, or whether its inclination vary, and whether the spiral be of one or the same breadth throughout, measured from the arbor."

1830.—EARLY STEAMSHIPS OF THE FRENCH NAVY.—The Minister of the French Marines in 1830 announced that the arrangements for the transformation of the cannon foundry of the island of Indret, on the Loire, into an establishment for the supply of engines for the use of the steamship dock-yard at that place, commenced at the close of 1828, were then sufficiently advanced to be in active operation.

This steam dock-yard had already fitted out "Le Pelican." She had *four* wheels and four engines of sixty horse-power. The machine was made at Indret. Two steam-frigates, viz., the "Castor," and "Crocodile," were building, calculated to draw twelve feet of water. Their length on deck was one hundred and sixty-one English feet, keel one hundred and fifty feet, extreme breadth thirty-six feet four inches, breadth amidships twenty-five feet. They were to be armed with six 24-pound carronades, and three of Paixhan's new guns, carrying a hollow twelve-inch shell shot. The French had nine armed steamships afloat in 1830, and nine under construction. A writer in the *United Service Journal* in 1831 says, "It is really surprising—melancholy—to find there is not one steam man-of-war on our (the Royal) Navy list,"—"the construction of engines has not even commenced in our dock-yards."

1830.—FIRST STEAMER ON THE DANUBE.—The first attempts to navigate the Danube by steam were made by French and German engineers, who were so confident of success that they did not even try the vessel, but before trial, invited the Emperor Francis I. to honor them with his presence on their first trip to Pesth. His Majesty embarked, and a favorable passage was made *down* the stream. On arriving at Pesth with the emperor on board the vessel created no little sensation; salutes were fired from the batteries, the curiosity was intense, and to celebrate the great event public balls and other festivities were given. At the end of these joyous proceedings His Majesty intimated his intention of returning to Vienna. But when orders were given to "go on with all speed" it was found the engines had insufficient power, and that the stream was carrying the boat *down* the river. All attempts to propel the boat against the current proving inefficient, His Imperial Majesty was obliged to land and proceed to Vienna through a country where the roads were so bad that his carriage frequently stuck fast in the mud.

In 1830, Mr. J. Pritchard, an Englishman, succeeded in conquering the Danube, and passing the rapids of Floresdorf in his steamer, returned to Vienna, where his vessel was visited by the imperial family and permission given to name her the "Francis the First." A concession was granted to Mr. Pritchard by the Austrian government for the exclusive right of carrying on steam navigation on the Danube for fifteen years.

1830.—FIRST ENGLISH MAIL STEAMER.—The first English steamship to carry foreign mails was the "Meteor." The *United Service Journal* for 1830 says, "It has long been contemplated for the conveyance of the foreign mails. H. M. steam-vessel 'Meteor,' Lieutenant William H. Symons, is to proceed to the Mediterranean on this service. The first adoption of steam in the conveyance of the foreign post-office mail has taken place. H. M. steam-vessel 'Meteor,' Lieutenant William H. Symons, left Falmouth February 5, for the Mediterranean. We look on this as an era in steam navigation which bids fair to introduce its more general adoption for the purposes of government."

1830.—FIRST STEAMER ON THE RED SEA.—The Hon. East India Company's armed steamer "Hugh Lindsay," Captain Wilson, of four hundred and eleven tons burden, and two engines of eighty horse-power each, arrived at Suez, April 20, 1830, from Bombay. She was the first steam-vessel that ever navigated the Red Sea. It had been for some time a favorite object of Sir John Malcolm, the governor of Bombay, to establish a steam conveyance for dispatches between that place and England, and the "Hugh Lindsay" was built for the purpose at a cost of forty thousand pounds; yet the blunder was committed of her having only the capacity to carry six days' coal. In consequence the "Hugh Lindsay" was thirty-three days in reaching Suez from Bombay, having lost twelve days in the ports of Aden, Mocha, Jiddah, and Cosseir, coaling.

The letters sent by her reached England in less time than any ever received before from India. Colonel Campbell was the only passenger by her, from want of room, as the cabin and every other available place was occupied by coal. She was so deep in the water on leaving Bombay that she was à fleur d'eau, and her wheels could hardly revolve. The distances between the several places on her route are: From Bombay to Aden, 1710 miles; from Aden to Mocha, 146 miles; from Mocha to Jiddah, 556 miles; from Jiddah to Cosseir, 430 miles; from Cosseir to Suez, 261 miles, which at twenty days' navigation is 155 miles a day, or six miles and a fraction per hour. She was the first vessel that made so long a voyage entirely by steam.

A letter from the captain of the "Hugh Lindsay" details this the first attempt to establish a steam conveyance upon the Red Sea, where the Lord opened a path for the Israelites of old, and where Pharaoh and his host so miserably perished:

"HON. COMPANY'S ARMED STEAMER 'HUGH LINDSAY,'
"SUEZ, April 22, 1830.

"SIR,—I have much pleasure in acquainting you with the arrival of the 'Hugh Lindsay' at Suez this day from Bombay, which place she left 20th of March. The passage has occupied more time than was expected, owing to the delay occasioned by receiving coal at Aden and Jiddah. At the former place we were detained *six* days, and at Jiddah five. We also touched at Mocha, which detained us a day. The present trip being an experiment, I was instructed, if time permitted, to visit you at Alexandria, for the purpose of communicating with you on the subject of steam navigation in the Red Sea; but the season being now so far advanced, it is necessary we should use the utmost dispatch to insure our return to Bombay previous to the setting in of the southwest monsoon, for which reason we shall leave Suez as soon as we have received what coal there is. We touched at Cosseir to take what fuel was there also, and we are apprehensive we shall find scarcely enough on the Red Sea to take us to Bombay.

"The 'Hugh Lindsay' is four hundred and eleven tons burden, and has two eighty horse-power engines. By the builder's plan, she appears to have been intended to carry about six days' coal; but in order to make the passage from Bombay to Aden she was laden as deep as could be, and left with her transom in the water. Notwithstanding, on our arrival at Aden after a passage of eleven days, we had only about six hours' coal remaining, which circumstance alone shows her unfit for the performance of the passage. Her being so deep, too, materially affected her speed. I met with greater detention in getting off coal at Aden and Jiddah than I had anticipated. Arrangements might be made to expedite the shipment of coal at those places, but I am now of opinion the fewer depots the better, and that if steamers were built of a class that would be propelled by engines whose consumption of coal would not exceed nine tons in the twenty-four hours, and which should carry conveniently fifteen days' coal at that rate of consumption, then the navigation of the Red Sea would be best carried on in two stages, one from Bombay to Aden, and from thence to Cosseir or Suez direct. I think, too, there is no necessity for proceeding up as far as Suez, as every object might be equally well attained by going to Cosseir only. As far as the passengers are concerned, the majority, I should suppose, would prefer being landed at that place, for the purpose of viewing the antiquities on the route from thence to Alexandria, and the arrival of dispatches would be very little delayed when we take into account the time occupied by a steamer on going from the parallel of Cosseir to Suez, which, when northwest winds prevail, could not be done in less than two days and a half.

"I inclose a copy of the log of the 'Hugh Lindsay' from Bombay to Suez, conceiving it might possess some interest as the journal of the first steam-vessel which has ever navigated the Red Sea.

"I am, sir, etc."

1831.—April 23, 1831, Giraud patented in the United States "a screw or spiral lever for propelling."

1831.—THE FIRST STEAMER TO CHICAGO.—The first steamer arrived at Chicago, Illinois, in 1831. Nothing could exceed the surprise of the sons of the forest on seeing this steamer move against wind and current without sails or oars. They lined the shores and expressed their astonishment by repeated shouts of "*Taiyoh nichee!*" an expression of surprise. A report had been circulated among them that a "big canoe" would soon come from the noisy waters, which by order of the Great Father of the "Chemo Komods" (*Yankees*), would be drawn through the lakes and rivers by a sturgeon, and this served to verify the report.

1832.—IRON STEAMBOATS.—March, 1832, Bennett Woodcroft patented a screw formed by a circular line coiled round a cylinder, increasing the pitch throughout the length and producing greater speed with fewer revolutions, to be fixed forward of the middle post by cutting away part of the dead wood. Sauvage also experimented this year.

The introduction of wrought-iron hulls for steam-vessels produced great improvements. It enabled builders to combine a strength and lightness of draught peculiarly advantageous in some branches of trade and in certain localities. The "Alburkha," of fifty-five tons, built as a companion to the "Quorra" for the Niger expedition in 1832, gave great satisfaction. Messrs. Laird, of Liverpool, their builders, immediately commenced the "Garryowen," to run between Limerick and Kilrush. The "Garryowen" was one hundred and twenty-five feet on deck, twenty-one feet six inches beam, with engines of fifty horse-power each. The "Garryowen" was driven on shore in the great hurricane which happened soon after, but escaped uninjured. This evidence of the power of iron vessels to withstand the casualties of the sea so raised their estimation that they were rapidly increased in number and their size greatly extended. The "Garryowen" was the first steamer built that had a *regular arrangement of water-tight bulk-heads.*

1820.—THE "AARON MANBY."—The first steam-vessel ever constructed of iron was the "Aaron Manby,"[1] launched in 1820, and named for her builder. She was constructed at the Horsely Iron-Works in sections, and was sent to London and put together in dock. September, 1821, Captain—afterwards Rear-Admiral—Sir Charles Napier, a partner in the speculation, took charge of her and navigated her from London to Havre, and thence to Paris, without unloading any of her cargo. She was the first, and for *thirty years afterwards* the only, vessel that sailed direct from London to Paris. In 1843 she was in good condition, and to that time had required no repairs on her hull. She was broken up in 1855, after thirty-five years' service.

1832.—The third steamer to cross the Atlantic was the "Royal William," built at Quebec in 1831 by Mr. George Black for the Quebec and Halifax Steam Navigation Company. She is described as $360\frac{44}{94}$ tons burden, one deck, three masts, one hundred and sixty feet long; breadth above the main wales, forty-four feet; between paddle-boxes, twenty-eight feet; schooner-rigged, carvel built. She was towed to Montreal, where she was fitted with marine engines with side levers by Messrs. Bennett and Henderson. The ship created a profound sensation, and especially upon the officers of one of his Majesty's frigates, who fired at her as she was steaming through the Gulf, and she was compelled to lay to until convinced that there was nothing diabolical in her construction. The only cargo she carried on her trip across the Atlantic was coal, which was nearly all used on the voyage. The good people of Cockaigne thronged to see the strange craft in the Thames, and were heard to remark that the "Indians" were not unlike themselves, the hallucination being strengthened by the fact that the ancient mariners were talking French. While in the Thames the "Royal William," according to our informant, was sold to the Spanish government, and became the "Isabella the Second," and the first war-vessel of the Dons.

Mr. Joseph George Dauten, who was the second engineer of the "Royal William" on this Atlantic trip, was in Montreal in 1880.

Her Majesty's ship "Rhodamanthus" arrived at Barbadoes May 17, 1832, from Plymouth. She was the first vessel of the Royal Navy to make the voyage to the West Indies, and the Portsmouth *Herald*, in announcing her intended departure, says, "we are anxious to learn what may be the effect of the climate on the engines, fittings, etc."

1832.—THE FIRST IRONCLAD BATTERY.—Robert L. Stevens

---

[1] Previously noted.

conceived the Stevens battery in 1832. It was to be an iron-armored ship, two hundred and fifty feet long, and twenty-eight feet beam. His brothers, J. C. and E. A. Stevens, assisted in the experiments, and the keel of the battery was laid in 1843. In 1854, the improvement in projectiles having got ahead of the growth of the battery, the old designs were abandoned and the keel of the Stevens battery, as it was called, was laid. It was designed to be forty feet over all, and forty-five feet beam, with a draught of twenty-two feet, and six thousand tons displacement. Powerful engines devised by Mr. Stevens were to give the battery a speed of fifteen and three-quarter knots. Mr. E. A. Stevens at his death left one million dollars to complete the vessel, directing that it should be given when completed to the State of New Jersey. This million, together with nearly as much expended before, was used up. The heirs claimed the battery and began a suit to have it declared theirs. The New Jersey courts held that the title was in the State, and the heirs appealed to the United States courts for the reversal of the decision. Meanwhile, the battery stood on property belonging to the Stevens' estate valued, it is claimed, at one hundred and fifty thousand dollars. The heirs desired to make the property remunerative, and in order to get the battery away asked the chancellor to have the battery sold.

In 1880, in pursuance to a decree of the Court of Chancery of New Jersey, the whole of the still unfinished Stevens battery, together with three steam-engines used in the workshops and in the construction of the hull, an immense quantity of iron, bolts, and screws, and a lot of tools, wrenches, punching- and bolting-machines, were sold at auction, at the yard in Hoboken, to William E. Laimbeer, of New York, for sixty-two thousand seven hundred and ninety dollars. It had cost nearly two million dollars.

The battery and material were divided into eight lots. The first lot, comprising the hull of the vessel so far as it was completed, with the engines and boilers on board, a locomotive boiler and Worthington pump, and a quantity of rope and trestle-work and shed beneath which the battery is housed, was offered for sale as soon as the master in chancery had read the decree and stated the conditions of sale, as follows: On each of the seven small lots ten per cent. of the purchase-money to accompany the purchase, and the remainder on October 20. On lot one, the vessel, ten per cent. of the purchase-money down, sixteen per cent. on October 20, and the rest, if the vessel, etc., should be removed in one lot or remain on the ground for completion, before the 1st day of January, 1881; or if removed piece-meal, in installments as the material is removed, at the rate of twenty dollars per ton. The bidding opened at twenty-five thousand dollars, and rose quickly by one thousand-dollar bids to thirty-two thousand dollars, then by five hundred dollars a bid to forty-seven thousand dollars, after which it dragged at two hundred and fifty dollars a bid to fifty-five thousand dollars, at which figure it was knocked down to Mr. William E. Laimbeer, of No. 51 East Thirty-first Street, New York. The only bidders besides the purchaser after thirty-five thousand dollars had been offered were Mr. Purves, of Purves & Son, Philadelphia, and Mr. Clancy, of Boston.

In 1832 the "General Jackson" was the only steamer running in the Sound between New York and Norwich. She was thought in her time a splendid craft, and no one ever imagined that any improvements could be made in regard to her beauty, speed, or comfort. But time works wonders. "She had no state-rooms, her passengers being compelled to sleep in berths below the water-line. These were roomy enough, but at times they were not numerous enough to accommodate the throngs that took passage. On these occasions Captain Havens used to resort to a lottery. Whenever he saw that all could not get berths he'd send a boy on deck with a big bell, which he'd ring and tell the passengers to step into the cabin for berths. When all had assembled he would place slices of paper with numbers corresponding to the berths, and as many blanks, and shake 'em up. Then each man or woman would step up, draw a slip, and if there was a number on it, that berth was placed at the disposal of the lucky one. If not, it was a matter of solicitude to find a soft place on the cabin floor. It was a rare thing, however, for a lady to be compelled to rest that way, as the more fortunate males gallantly surrendered their privileges and slept where they could find a place."

1833.—THE FIRST MAIL CONTRACT.—The first contract for carrying the mails in steamers was made by the British postmaster-general in 1833, with the "Mona Isle Steam Company," to run semi-weekly between Liverpool and the Isle of Man at eight hundred and fifty pounds per annum. After this a contract was made in 1834 with the "General Steam Navigation Company," for the weekly conveyance of the mails between London and Rotterdam and London and Hamburg at seventeen thousand pounds per year. Both these contracts continued in force twenty years or more.

1833.—EARLY STEAMBOATS ON THE LAKES.—Mr. Randall, of Philadelphia, in 1833, built the "Wisconsin," two hundred and eighteen feet long by thirty-eight feet wide, at Detroit, and ran her through three of the lakes on round trips of two thousand miles. In 1845 he designed and navigated the "Empire," two hundred and fifty-one feet long, thirty-eight feet beam, sixteen statute miles per hour. Soon after the "City of Buffalo" and the "Western Metropolis" were sent afloat. They were sister boats three hundred and forty feet long, forty-two feet beam, and only nine and one-half feet draught of water, light laden. By a report in the Cleveland *Herald* the trip between Buffalo and Cleveland at that early date was made at an average speed of twenty-one miles an hour by the "Metropolis," the "City of Buffalo" making even greater speed.[1]

1833.—H. M. steam-packet "Firebrand" traversed, in sixty-six days, eleven thousand five hundred miles in two voyages from Falmouth to Corfu, and one from the same port to Lisbon. In the same year the "Royal William," of one thousand tons burden and one hundred and eighty horse-power engine, built on Three Rivers, in Lower Canada, made the voyage from Pictou, Nova Scotia, to Cowes, in the Isle of Wight, being the *third* transatlantic voyage[2] of a steamer. She was employed for three or four years between England and Ireland. She afterwards made several voyages across the Atlantic. The people of the provinces claimed for her the credit of the first ocean transit by steam. The Historical Society of Chicago has the original working plans of this vessel, presented by James Gouchie, a Scotch ship-builder, who, in 1880, was a resident of that city. She was launched at Quebec in 1831, and made the trip from Pictou to London in twenty-five days. In 1837 "The City of Dublin Steam Packet Company" purchased the "Royal William," and she made her first voyage from Dublin to Liverpool, October 9, 1837, in nine hours and forty-eight minutes. Soon after she was sold to the Spanish government for ten thousand pounds, and converted into a man-of-war. She sailed from Pictou to cross the Atlantic April 1, 1833.

1834.—Up to the year 1834 steamboats in the United States had burnt wood only. The "Novelty" burnt forty cords each trip from New York to Albany. In 1836 experiments were made with anthracite coal for fuel on board the ferry-boats in New York with success, but wood was principally used for American coast-steamers for several years after.

The advent of ocean steam navigation soon led to the almost uni-

---

[1] In 1860, Mr. Randall designed and modeled a vessel for an ocean steamship line to be called the "Philadelphia and Crescent Steam Navigation Company," organized for constructing vessels for trading between Great Britain and Philadelphia, which obtained an act of incorporation from the State Legislature of Pennsylvania. This vessel was to be five hundred feet long, fifty-eight feet moulded beam, and to measure eight thousand tons. Her motive-power was to consist of two sets of wheels. She was to have ample accommodations for three thousand passengers and three thousand tons of cargo, and to be a regular "twenty-mile ship." She was to have ample fuel room sufficient to run eight thousand miles without stopping for coal; a main saloon of three hundred and fifty feet of uninterrupted length and one hundred and seventy-five family state-rooms, with double beds in each of extra size, etc. A dining-room and drawing-room, each one hundred and fifty feet long, a social hall, reading-room, smoking-room, and library, etc.—*Lindsay's Merchant Shipping*, vol. iv., pp. 157, 158.

Unfortunately, this magnificent design of Mr. Randall was never put to a practical test at that time, but he only anticipated the large ocean steamships of to-day.

[2] The "Savannah," 1819, from Liverpool, was the first; the "Curaçoa," from Antwerp to Curaçoa, the second.

versal use of coal,—bituminous and anthracite,—even the steamboats on the Mississippi having adopted the former.

1834.—The first steamer on the Merrimac River, Massachusetts, was called the "Herald." She was built above Pawtucket Falls, launched in 1834, and made regular trips between Lowell and Nashua when Lowell had but fourteen thousand inhabitants and Nashua a few hundred. In 1888 she was lengthened, and could carry five hundred passengers. In 1840 she was floated over the falls to Newburyport, and taken to New York, and run as a ferry-boat between New York city and Brooklyn.[1]

1835.—John F. Smith, of Charlestown, Massachusetts, September 18, 1835, patented a screw revolving in a cavity made by giving the hull the form of a double vessel from amidships to the stern, the forepart being in the ordinary shape.

Edward P. Fitzpatrick, of Mount Morris, New York, November 23, 1835, patented a spiral screw, the shaft swelling in the middle like a double cone, surrounded by a spiral thread, also wider in the middle than at the ends.

1836.—FRENCH STEAMBOATS.—The whole number of French steamboats in 1836 was eighty-two; the majority were of small size and only suited to the navigation of the French rivers. Forty-four were passenger-boats, seventeen freight-boats, and twenty-one employed in towing ships. The aggregate horse-power of these eighty-two steamboats was two thousand eight hundred and sixty-three, an average of thirty-five horse-power to each boat. The average tonnage was estimated at one hundred and eighty tons, or fifteen thousand in all.

Twenty-seven steam-vessels were also in the French Royal Navy, eighteen afloat, six on the stocks, and three employed as *tugs*. Of the eighteen afloat, eleven had one hundred and sixty horse-power each, and seven one hundred and fifty horse-power and under, and were armed with six guns each, two being Paixhan or *steel* guns. Fifty-four steam-vessels were also preparing for the service of the Post-Office Department in the Mediterranean.

THE ORIGIN OF OCEAN STEAM NAVIGATION, 1832.

No thought was entertained of the application of steam to ocean navigation until 1832, when the subject was first brought before the public by an American citizen, a graduate of Yale College of the class of 1802, Junius Smith, LL.D., who had resided in London over forty years, engaged in active business pursuits with this country. In 1832 he crossed the Atlantic on the British ship "St. Leonard," arriving in New York in October, after a passage of fifty-four days. He returned to London in the packet-ship "Westminster," sailing from New York in December, making the passage to Plymouth, England, in thirty-two

[1] Newburyport *Herald.*

days. These two passages forced upon his mind the idea of transatlantic steam navigation, and writing to his correspondents in New York, under date "London, June 28, 1833," he says,—

"Thirty-two days from New York to Plymouth is no trifle; *any ordinary sea-going steamer would have run it with the weather we had in fifteen days with ease.* I shall not relinquish the project unless I find it absolutely impracticable."

After giving the subject thoughtful examination, his mind became thoroughly imbued with the project, and he entered upon it with enthusiasm, first introducing the scheme to leading business-men and bankers of London, and to shipping merchants engaged in the American trade. The novel project was received with indifference and scouted as visionary, and presenting insurmountable obstacles. These objections he regarded as the offspring of ignorant prejudice, which it was his province to overthrow. He issued a prospectus embodying facts and figures to disprove such objections, which he distributed personally. He failed to meet with the slightest encouragement, but, on the contrary, with unqualified ridicule, as a visionary, and an outspoken opposition from all the sailing-packet interest, whose craft would be endangered if the enterprise should prove successful. Nothing daunted by these difficulties, which served only to furnish him new arguments favorable to his project and to enlarge his ideas, he issued a second and then a third prospectus, giving a wider scope to his idea on a more extended basis. Thus, his first prospectus contemplated a company with one hundred thousand pounds sterling capital to build steamers of one thousand tons, while his third prospectus proposed forming a company with one million pounds sterling capital to build steamers of eighteen hundred to two thousand tons. These prospectuses presented calculations based upon facts connected with the commerce and shipping interests of the two countries which could not be controverted, the only remaining point was to satisfy the public of the practicability of the scheme.

Here was a direct issue, for which no precedent was furnished, and it seemed for a time a formidable objection. Although the fact that a vessel might be safely and expeditiously navigated by steam-power from port to port in the coasting trade was fully demonstrated, it was universally thought impracticable to cross the Atlantic by the same means. It was an Herculean task to turn such currents of thought, but to this great change his efforts were directed. In accomplishing this he set about organizing a company under the title of "The British and American Steam Navigation Company," by securing a board of directors upon the basis of his third prospectus, as stated, with a capital of one million pounds sterling. To further this he waited upon leading merchants and bankers, soliciting the use of their names, borrowing them as a man would borrow money, with the promise to return it as soon as he could do without. After great labor he succeeded in securing a list of directors. With these he came before the public, opening books of subscription to the stock. Here it may be proper to remark that a more difficult task can scarcely be conceived than the introduction to the British public of a new project embracing such physical objections as Atlantic Ocean steam navigation for a consecutive number of days, for the reason that they are a conservative and peculiarly cautious people, slow to move, while ready with their vast wealth for great enterprises. The books of subscription were opened in July, 1836, shares were liberally subscribed, sufficient being allotted to warrant contracting for their first steamship, which was made with Messrs. Curling & Young, ship-builders at Blackwall, London. Relative to this Dr. Smith wrote his New York correspondents,—

"I have the pleasure to inform you that the directors of the 'British and American Steam Navigation Company' have contracted for the building of the largest and intended to be the most splendid steamship ever built, expressly for the New York and London trade. She will measure one thousand seven hundred tons, two hundred feet keel, forty feet beam, three decks, and everything in proportion. She will carry two engines of two hundred and twenty-five horse-power each, seventy-six-inch cylinder, and nine feet stroke. The expense of this steam-frigate is estimated at sixty thousand pounds. These large undertakings require time to mature, but I think the business will at last be done effectually."

The contract for the engines was made with Messrs. Claude, Girdwood & Co., of Glasgow, which firm, after completing about two-thirds of the work, was obliged to suspend and went into bankruptcy, which proved a serious disappointment, involving a year's delay. A new contract was then made with Mr. Robert Napier, of Glasgow, and as the building of the ship progressed the views of the directors enlarged, resulting in the completion of the "British Queen," of *two thousand four hundred tons*. The delay consequent upon the failure of the first contractors for the engines, coupled with the importance of practical demonstration of the feasibility of crossing the Atlantic Ocean by steam, determined the company to charter the steamer "Sirius," of about seven hundred tons, for a voyage from London to New York and return. She was dispatched from London April 1, 1838, and arrived at New York on the 17th, making the passage in sixteen days' consecutive steaming, encountering very tempestuous weather, completely demonstrating the feasibility of crossing the Atlantic by steam. She was soon succeeded by the "British Queen," which left London in July, 1839, and arrived in New York after a passage of fourteen and a half days. It is certainly of value as a matter of record to give the prospectus under which the enterprise was originated. The following is a verbatim copy of the original:

"BRITISH AND AMERICAN STEAM NAVIGATION COMPANY.

"CAPITAL, £1,000,000, IN 10,000 SHARES OF £100 EACH.

"DIRECTORS:

"Henry Bainbridge, Esq., Chairman,
"Chas. Enderby, Esq., Col. Aspinwall, U. States Consul,
"Capt. Thomas Larkins, Junius Smith, Esq.,
"Capt. Robt. Locke, Jos. Robinson Pim, Esq.,
"Capt. Robt. Isaacke, Liverpool,
"Paul Twigg, Esq., Dublin, Jas. Beale, Esq., Cork.

"Bankers—Messrs. Puget, Bainbridge & Co., 12 St. Paul's Churchyard.

"Secretary—Macgregor Laird, Esq.

"The object of this company is to establish a regular and certain communication by steamships between Great Britain and the United States. The vessels are intended to depart alternately from London and Liverpool to New York; their average passage will not exceed fifteen days. The company's first vessel, the 'British Queen,' has capacity for five hundred passengers, twenty-five days' fuel, and eighty tons measurement goods, exclusive of provisions, stores, etc.

"The successful voyages of 'Sirius' and 'Great Western' steamships having placed the success of the undertaking beyond a doubt, the Directors are now preparing contracts for other vessels of similar description to the 'British Queen,' and will be able in 1839 to dispatch their vessels for New York on the 1st and 16th of each month from London and Liverpool alternately.

"Applications for shares may be made to Macgregor Laird, Esq., at the Company's offices, 78 Cornhill; to Buxendale, Tathem, Upton & Johnston, 7 Great Manchester Street, London; to Isaac Miller, Esq., Liverpool, and to Boyle, Low, Pain & Co., Duane Street, Dublin."

Such was the modest prospectus under which a system of ocean steam navigation, now extending throughout the entire globe, was inaugurated.

The Duke of Wellington, in answer to a letter addressed to him by Dr. Junius Smith, replied "he would give no countenance to any scheme which had for its object a change in the established system of the country."[1]

1830.—THE FIRST STEAMERS IN CHINA.—In the "Life of E.

---

[1] These facts were furnished to the New York *Evening Post* by Henry Smith, of the firm of Wadsworth & Smith, New York, who is in possession of all the correspondence from the first inception of the enterprise.

C. Bridgeman, the Pioneer of American Missions in China," the arrival of the first steamer at Macao is thus mentioned in his diary:

"*May* 1, 1830.—Arrived at Macao on the 19th (April) in the steamer 'Forbes,' the first ship of the kind that has ever visited these shores. She's a wonder to the Chinese; they call her *Fo Shune*,—The Fire-Ship."

In 1832 a Canton paper contained an advertisement of the steamer "King-fa." It said, "She carries a cow, a surgeon, a band of music, and has rooms elegantly fitted up for cards and opium-smoking."

In 1835 an attempt was made by the foreign residents to place a small steamboat called the "Jardine" upon the Canton River, to run between Lintin, Macao, and Whampoa. In consequence of the opposition of the Chinese authorities, as shown in the following correspondence, the undertaking was temporarily abandoned. The editor of the Canton *Register* remarks, "We understand that the project of running the steamer in the way set forth in the letter is not abandoned, notwithstanding the deputy-governor's refusal to accede to the proposition of the whole of the foreign community of Canton. Perhaps the arrival of the new governor will be a favorable opportunity to reurge this reasonable and judicious plan of communication with the shipping at Lintin and with Macao. A united and determined perseverance on the part of the foreigners is all that is wanted to carry this or any other reasonable project into effect.

"We notice with unfeigned pleasure the unanimous feeling of the foreign community on this subject. The name of every foreign merchant in Canton was signed to the letter to Howqua, including the three East India Company's agents, whose names head the list. *O si sic omnia!*"[1]

"To Howqua, Senior Hong Merchant —— Canton:

"Sir,—We, the undersigned, merchants of all nations residing at Canton, having for years past experienced much inconvenience from the tardiness and uncertainty of our communication with Macao, where our wives and children reside, as well as from the difficulties attending the conveyance of letters to and from vessels arriving and departing, have lately procured from Europe, at considerable expense, a traveling boat of a modern construction propelled by steam and capable of moving against wind and tide.

"The said boat having arrived at Lintin, we intend to order her up without delay; and, as the officers stationed at the different forts, never having seen a traveling boat of this description, may entertain erroneous ideas regarding her, and may attempt to impede her passage up the river, which might terminate in disaster, the motive of our now addressing you is to request the favor of your forwarding a true state-

[1] Canton *Register*, December 29, 1835.

ment to the government officers, in order to preclude the possibility of misunderstanding or trouble.

"Being all personally known to you, it is superfluous to assure you of our peaceable dispositions and the rectitude of our intentions.

"Our boat is purely a passage-boat, and no cargo can ever be admitted. Neither is she provided with a defensive weapon of any description, such is our unbounded confidence in the protection of the Imperial government. Any officer doubting our statement can satisfy himself by personal inspection.

"The regularity of communication thus established will leave no inducement to resort any longer to Chinese fast-boats for the conveyance of letters or passengers, which has so frequently led to petitioning at the city gate, removing at once one of the chief sources of trouble to the Hong merchants as well as to ourselves.

"The boat is expected at Canton in seven days, when we shall be happy to see you, sir, or any gentleman of your honorable country, on board.

"With compliments we affix our names.

"We herein state her length 85 feet, beam 17 feet, draught of water, 6 feet. Reduced to Chinese feet in the Chinese letter, being 70 feet length, 14 beam, 5 draught of water."

To this letter the Hong merchants replied:

"We respectfully inform you, benevolent elder brethren, that yesterday we received your letter, the contents of which we immediately submitted to *Tuhheĕn*. Now, we have received the *Tuhheĕn's* reply, which we have faithfully transcribed, and we present it praying that you, benevolent elder brethren, will all inform yourselves thereof. You, gentlemen, and the established authorities of your honorable country, should obey the orders that the said steamship is not permitted to enter the port. When there are letters, ships' boats, as heretofore, should be ordered to make a clear report and bring them up for delivery. We earnestly request your particular attention to this matter. Directed to Mr. Jardine and the constituted gentlemen for their information.

"Signed by *Wootaeyung*, and ten others.

"11th moon, 6th day,—25th December, 1835."

The acting-governor also wrote to Hong merchants in reply to the petition of the foreign merchants:

"*Ke*, Guardian of the Prince, Acting Governor-general of the two *Kwang*, *Seunfoo* of Kwantung, proclaims to the Hong merchants, who have presented the petition of the English foreign merchant *Tanele* (Daniel) and the others, in reply,—

"I have examined, and find that each ship of every nation arriving in the Chinese waters (of Canton province) have hitherto been cargo-ships, and, consequently, they have been permitted to come up to Whampoa; with these exceptions, ships are not allowed to enter the port. As the ships that remain at anchor in the offing have letters for delivery and such-like business, heretofore it has been the custom to order ships' boats to make a clear report at the custom-houses, and then allow them to enter the port; these are the reported and fixed regulations. Now, as the English have brought hither a steamship, it is proper to manage the affair agreeably to the regulations. The said Hong merchants must immediately transmit the orders to the foreigner of the said steamship, that if he has letters he should order ships' boats to make a clear report, and then enter the port and deliver the letters, he must not hastily bring in the steamship; if he presumes obstinately to disobey, I, the acting-governor, have already issued orders to all the forts that when the steamship arrives they are to open a thundering fire and attack her. On the whole, since he has arrived within the boundaries of the Celestial Dynasty, it is right that we should obey the laws of the Celestial Dynasty. I order the said foreigner to ponder this well and act in trembling obedience thereto.

"TAOUKWANG, 15th year, 11th moon, 6th day,—25th December, 1835."

Hoppo followed this letter with this edict three days later:

"*Pang by Imperial appointment Controller-General of the Customs at Canton, etc.:*

"I have examined and find that the reported and fixed regulations are that the foreign ships of every nation, when they arrive in the waters of Canton, should, as the law directs, make a clear report and receive a pilot to bring them up to Whampoa. In the transmission of letters hitherto open boats have been used to enter and leave the port, which waited to be examined; this has been the custom for very many years, and there has neither been delay nor impediment; and most assuredly these regulations are unchangeable. It is now authenticated that the English have petitioned respecting a newly-built steamship. This is scarcely a credible affair. She is not permitted to enter the port. I order the head Hong merchants and all the others immediately to direct their most assiduous attention to the explanation of the orders to the said foreigners, that they should be obedient to the fixed regulations as established by the Emperor, and that they should use ships' small open boats for the conveyance of letters in going and returning, and reverently obey the laws of the Celestial Dynasty; they are not allowed presumptuously to make changes and oppose the prohibitory laws. Forthwith obey my former orders on this business, and await the reply of the acting-governor.

"TAOUKWANG, 15th year, 11th moon, 9th day,—December 28, 1835."

The doubt expressed by *Pang* as to the credibility of the "affair" of the steamer is pointed at the manner in which he supposes she may be employed; he does not believe that she is merely intended as a passage-boat and packet, and seems afraid there is some ulterior design on the part of the foreigners.[1]

In Williams's "Middle Kingdom" (vol. i. pp. 573, 574, edition 1876) there is a description of a steamer which " was attached to drawings made by the Chinese when the English attacked Canton in 1841 :"

> "She's more than three hundred cubits long,
> And thirty-odd in height and breadth;
> Iron is used to bend her stiff and stout,
> And she's painted black all round about;
> Like a weaver's shuttle is her shape;
> On both sides carriage-wheels are fixed,
> And, using fossil coal to make a fire,
> They whirl around as the race-horse flies.
> Of white cloth all the sails are made,
> In winds both fair and foul she goes.
> On her bow is the god of the waves,
> At stem and stern is a revolving gun;
> Her form is truly terrific to men.
> The god of the North displaying his sanctity,
> The sunken rocks there shoaled the steamer;
> All who saw it witnessed to the justice of heaven.
> None of the plans of the foreigners took effect,
> Which greatly delighted the hearts of men."

In this connection, referring to the American steamers trading in Canton waters, Mr. Gideon Nye wrote,—

"Premising that several steamers under the British flag preceded the coming of any but a very small one under our own, I merely recall that this one was the 'Firefly,' sent out in pieces by R. B. Forbes, Esq., of Boston, to run between Canton and Whampoa; that he sent next the 'Spark' (that is still running to Macao, after having been lengthened about sixteen feet), also in pieces, chiefly for account of the late Mr. J. B. Endicott; and another called the 'Midas,' that went hence to Brazil. These all came out during my absence from Canton,—that is, after 1845 and before 1850."

---

[1] "The steamer 'Jardine' was sailed out as a schooner from Aberdeen (Scotland), and arrived in September, 1835, at Lintin, where her machinery was put in working order; and she made several trips to the Bogue (Bocca Tigris) in November, being intended as a passenger and mail conveyance between Macao, Lintin, and Canton. But, although every foreign merchant residing at Canton signed a letter to Howqua for submission to the governor, stating the purpose of her employment and engaging that she should be restricted to it, the chief authorities refused consent to her entering the river; and this was peremptory, notwithstanding the admiral's disposition to admit her, having visited her and allowed her to take his own junk in tow up and down Anson's Bay, after which he freely acknowledged that there could be no harm in her running."—GIDEON NYE, in *China Review*, Hong-Kong, 1875.

HISTORY OF STEAM NAVIGATION.   147

"During the same period three British steamers were running between Canton and Hong-Kong,—the 'Corsair,' the 'Canton,' and the 'Hong-Kong.' In 1854 the late Mr. Robert Sturgis, Mr. J. B. Endicott, and myself sent to New York for a larger class steamer for this river trade, and in her (under command of Captain Sampson) came the late Captain George U. Sands as chief engineer; she being called, I think, the 'Fung Shung' when she left New York, but the new name of 'River Bird,' suggested by my partner, Mr. Tuckerman (late United States Minister in Greece), was given her here. In 1854 the steamer 'Carolina' was bought for me in California, and brought over by Captain Sampson in 1855; but I sent her to Calcutta, where also the 'River Bird' was sent by Mr. Sturgis after the war of 1856 stopped the river traffic. Hostilities here continued until 1860, though after the treaty of Tientsin, in 1858, there was a partial resumption of business. Meantime, Captain Sampson had returned to California and brought over the 'Williamette.' Soon after the 'White Cloud' came out from New York, chiefly for Mr. Sturgis's and Captain Sands's account, and next the 'Hankow,' both under steam, followed later by the 'Kiushau' in pieces, to be set up at Whampoa. The 'Fire-Dart' was sent down from Shanghai, followed thence, later, by the 'Po-yang' and 'Kiu-Kiang.' The 'Hankow' was destroyed by fire here, and the 'Po-yang' was lost in a typhoon near Macao."[1]

1836.—PROPOSED INVULNERABLE STEAM BATTERY AND TORPEDO-BOAT.—The New York *Times*, in 1836, says, "Clinton Roosevelt, of New York, has invented an invulnerable steam battery. It is rendered invulnerable by making the bow and stern of the vessel alike sharp and plating them with polished iron armor, with high bulwarks, and a sharp roof plated in like manner, with the design of glancing the balls. The means of offense are a torpedo made to lower on nearing an enemy, and driven by a mortar into the enemy's side under water, where, by a fusee, it will explode. There is also a large cannon at each end of the battery, and mortars to throw combustibles upon the sails and decks of opponents. There are means to prevent balls reaching any part of the machinery, and the design is always to fight the vessel end-on."

This device seems not to have been put to practical experiment, but most of the ideas have been adopted or incorporated in vessels of a later date.

1836.—COMMODORE BARRON'S PROW-SHIP.—A model of Commodore James Barron's prow-ship was exhibited in the rotunda of the Capitol at Washington in 1836, and is now preserved in the Seamanship building at the Naval Academy, Annapolis, Maryland. Its in-

---

[1] Gideon Nye, author of "History of American Commerce with China," to Thomas Gibbons.

ventor thus described this, the first steam ram ever proposed, under date February 11, 1836:

"I would propose that a vessel be constructed of solid logs of light timber, the gravity of which would not exceed four-tenths that of water, and be of such bulk that the upper part of the solid log-work of the centre vessel would float six or eight feet above its surface.

"Let this vessel, or combination of vessels, be of large dimensions, say from one hundred and fifty to two hundred or two hundred and thirty feet long, and seventy or eighty feet wide, and resembling in their form a steamboat of the treble construction. The prow should be very strong, and for a few feet aft a little sharp; but not so much so as to impair its strength. The point of it should not be reduced to a less thickness than three or four feet, and not exceeding in its whole length beyond the bow of the centre vessel fifteen or twenty feet, and that prominence covered with iron plates from three to four inches thick, eight or ten inches wide, and six or eight feet long on each arm, formed into an acute angle to fit the shape of the prow, and enlarged at their junction on the point of the prow to about eight or ten inches in thickness, and rounding outwards in sharp-pointed knobs, cut in large diamond form. These plates should be placed four or five inches apart from each other, and let half their thickness into the wood, which will produce a saw-shaped space upon the prow, and prevent the glancing of the vessel from her object, either up or down, or sideways.

"The logs that form the prow should be at least two feet square, thirty or forty feet long, and of the hardest and toughest wood, such as oak or elm, and occupy a space of ten or twelve feet up and down, and be supported on each side by the same kind of timber. The iron plates should be securely bolted through the whole mass, but particularly so through these logs of hard timber. To protect the crew and machinery from shot, let the guard-vessels without the centre vessel be built twelve or fifteen feet wide, and of solid white pine timber, and projected a sufficient distance from the sides of the centre vessel to embrace the paddle-wheels. These barricade vessels should be of sufficient elevation to cover the upper part of the paddle-wheels. Each of the lower parts must form a bottom similar to the centre one, and be secured to it forward and aft by the cross logs of which the centre vessel is constructed, projecting from her sides to such a distance as to allow spaces for the paddle-wheels on each side, and from as many points above the water between the paddle-wheels as might be required for strength.

"The water is admitted to these paddle-wheels between the bows of these vessels through a channel formed by a long inverted arch, the lowest point of which must descend below the level of the lower part of the wheels. The solid log-work, forward and aft of the centre vessel, should form a mass of at least twelve or fifteen feet in thickness, or as the side vessels.

"Over the top of these vessels lay a tier of logs about two feet square, which will serve as a protection to the crew and machinery from any assaults by boarding, etc. The middle vessel may be hollowed out, at a proper distance from her extremes, if more buoyancy is required than the timber itself gives, except amidships, and there the log-work should be continuous from the prow all the way aft.

"The object of this vessel is to destroy men-of-war by running into them with such impetuosity as to break down their sides sufficiently to admit water in such quantities as would defy all possible efforts to prevent immediate sinking.

"Only about ten or twelve feet of the prow of this vessel ought to be allowed to strike the ship that is assailed; the other parts, above and below, should recede or incline aft, and this ten or twelve feet space should be so situated as to come in contact with the side of the enemy five or six feet above the water and five or six feet below its surface. The resistance to the stroke would be less impeded than it would be were it given by a prow of greater extent, and of course it would be more certain to pierce or break down that part of the side of the enemy's ship which it might come in contact with. Three steam-engines, of one hundred and twenty horse-power each, would propel such a vessel at the rate of eight or ten miles, or more, per hour, and should be preferred to larger ones, as they would be less liable to damage from the shock to which they might be exposed when the vessel should come at her full speed in contact with the enemy.

"Let those who are curious or doubtful of the efficiency of this plan calculate the effect which would be produced on a stationary body by a concussion so violent as would be occasioned by a stroke of the prow of this massive vessel. To make it apparent that the strongest ships in the world are entirely inadequate to resist such force, it need only be observed that they seldom come in contact with each other with any violence without sinking or sustaining a most destructive degree of damage.

"Ancient as well as modern history furnishes us with many proofs of the decided effects of this mode of attack. The Romans and Carthaginians were in the practice of running into each other's vessels at their greatest speed, impelled by their oars; and it is recorded of them that when they found their enemies entangled with their friends, so as to render them stationary for the moment of their assault, that it seldom failed to produce that description of destruction contemplated by the adoption of this invention; but the power of steam and the solid construction of this vessel would give this mode of attack a decided advantage over all other attempts of a similar nature ever heretofore resorted to, and beyond a doubt insure success.

"The proof of the effects of an attack made by a whale on the ship 'Essex' of New Bedford, in the year 1819, is conclusive that no construction of a ship now known could resist the shock of such a vessel as the one I have described. A circumstance not very dissimilar occurred to Captain Jones, in the United States ship 'Peacock,' in the Pacific Ocean.

"The instances of destruction occasioned to vessels by one running into another are too numerous to admit of a doubt that if the plan recommended above should be adopted on a proper scale, it could never fail of effecting its object.

"The rudder is attached to the centre vessel, and must be moved by a wheel, which may be placed on the upper surface of the centre vessel, under the roof or main covering, either forward or aft; but I should prefer its being aft, and it should be considerably forward and lower down than in ordinary cases. A breast-work should be raised aft, for the protection of officers and others; also for the chimneys and steam-pipes, in their proper places, which should be circular.

"The timber alluded to in the above description is the white pine,—'*Pinus strobus*,'—poplar,—'*Liriodendron tulipifera*,'—and some species of the gum, none of which exceed four-tenths of the gravity of water.

"The prow mentioned in the first part of this description is not of such a form as I would either use myself or recommend to those whom I would allow to use my invention: that form might become fixed in the body assailed, but the form represented by the drawing will surely clear itself.

"In speaking of the different presentations of the prow and its momentum, it is to be considered as in contact with a solid body.

"Dimensions, etc., of the steam prow-ship:

	Length. Feet.	Width. Feet.	Depth. Feet.	Number of Cubic Feet.
"Middle vessel	150	20	30	90,000
Side vessels	each 125	12	30	both 90,000

Number of cubic feet in the three vessels, 180,000.
Weight of each cubic foot of white pine in the three vessels, 24 pounds.
Specific gravity of the three vessels, 4,320,000 pounds, or 1963 tons.
Specific gravity of the three vessels multiplied by their velocity gives, as the whole momentum of the three vessels, 43,200,000 pounds.
Momentum on each foot of the prow, 900,000 pounds."

1836.—STEAM TOW-BOATS ON THE DELAWARE.—Steam towboats were introduced upon the Delaware in 1836, as appears from the following advertisement which appeared in the first number of the Philadelphia *Ledger*, March 25, 1836:

"PHILADELPHIA STEAM TOW-BOAT CO.

"A meeting of the stockholders will be held on Saturday evening next, at the room of the Board of Trade, in the Exchange, at 7 o'clock.

"Merchants generally, who take an interest in facilitating the navigation of the Delaware by means of steam tow-boats, are respectfully invited to attend.

"By order of the Board of Directors,
"D. B. STACEY, *Secretary*."

1836.—REGISTERED STEAM-VESSELS OF GREAT BRITAIN.—The number of registered steam-vessels in Great Britain in 1836 was three hundred and ninety-seven. One hundred and fifty-three were under fifty tons, and one hundred and eighteen more under one hundred tons. The number above one hundred tons was one hundred and twenty-six. The largest, the "Monarch," of London, measured only five hundred and eighty-seven, and no other exceeded four hundred tons. The newspapers of this year speak of "an *immense* steam-frigate, to be called the 'Gorgon,' to be built in London. She is to be eleven hundred tons, and will carry twelve guns, and is larger than the old seventy-fours."

In 1837 the number and tonnage of steam-vessels belonging to the British empire, distinguishing British possessions in Europe from the British plantations, was—

	Vessels.	Tonnage.
England	482	37,240
Scotland	109	13,368
Ireland	87	18,437
Total for United Kingdom	628	69,045
Isles of Guernsey, Jersey, and Man	6	832
British Plantations	44	8,411
Total for all	678	78,288

THE FIRST PRACTICAL SCREW-STEAMERS.

1836.—Captain John Ericsson,[1] a native of Sweden, who had for some time previous to the date of his patent for propelling vessels been a resident in England, and was well known as a mechanician of originality and skill, obtained a patent in England, July 13, 1836, for a spiral propeller consisting of two broad thin hoops with eight fans, each fixed on a shaft, the outer hoop revolving in a contrary direction and at a greater velocity to the inner one. This propeller was to be entirely submerged *abaft the rudder*, the shaft passing through the stern-post; the rudder was divided into two parts, connected by a strong iron stay on each side, having a wide bend to allow the rudder to traverse clear of the shaft. Before the construction of his first vessel, Captain Ericsson experimented in a circular bath in London with a model boat, which was propelled by a screw. This model boat was fitted with a small engine supplied with steam by a pipe leading from a steam-boiler

---

[1] Eric is in Scandinavian countries the same as Enrico in Italian, Enrique in Spanish, Heinrich in German, Henri in French, and Henry in English. So that Mr. Ericsson may be called Mr. Henryson.

over the centre of the bath and descending to within a foot of the water-line, where it was branched off by a swivel-joint and connected with the engine in the boat. Steam being admitted in this pipe, the engine in the boat was put in action, and motion was thus communicated to the propeller. This model, though less than three feet long, performed its voyage about the basin at the rate of upward of three miles an hour.

His next step in the invention was the construction of a wooden boat forty-five feet long, eight feet beam, three feet draught of water, with *two propellers*, each five feet two inches in diameter. So successful was this experiment that when steam was turned on for the first time the boat moved at once upward of ten miles an hour without any alteration in her machinery. This vessel was named by the inventor the "Francis B. Ogden," in compliment to the United States consul at Liverpool, who was the first to appreciate and encourage his efforts. The vessel was built at Wapping, by Mr. Gulliver, boat-builder, and was constructed solely for the purpose of testing Ericsson's propeller.

The following description of her motive-power was published in the London *Mechanics' Magazine* for June, 1837:

"The propelling apparatus is placed at the stern, and works entirely under the water. It consists of a peculiar application of the old and well-known principle of the water-screw, by which a great propelling power is concentrated in a small space. Of the degree of power concentrated no better proof can be adduced than the fact that the speed of four and a half knots, against wind and tide, was produced by an apparatus measuring only five feet two inches in diameter, of two feet two inches wide, weighing only six hundred and fifteen pounds, and worked by a high-pressure engine having two cylinders of fourteen-inches stroke and twelve inches diameter, and which, during the experiment, made only sixty strokes per minute, and showed a pressure of not more than fifty pounds to the square inch. The new propelling apparatus consists of two short cylinders of thin wrought iron supported by arms of a peculiar form, which are placed entirely under the water at the stern and made to revolve in contrary directions round a common centre. To the outer periphery of each cylinder is attached a series of spiral planes or plates, which may be placed at any angle, according to the effect sought to be obtained, whether it be great speed or great propelling power.

"The apparatus may be made to ship and unship at pleasure, the engine that works it may also be loco-movable, so as to be worked upon deck and any part of the deck, and in these two peculiarities we are inclined to think the chief advantage of this new step in steam-navigation will be found to consist. Sailing-vessels may by this means command all the aid that steam can give them without divest-

HISTORY OF STEAM NAVIGATION. 153

ing themselves of any peculiar fitness for long sea voyages or undergo any change in their original construction."[1]

As noticed, the "Ogden" when first tried, April, 1837, upon the Thames, attained a speed of *ten miles an hour*. She subsequently towed schooners of one hundred and forty tons seven miles an hour, and the American packet-ship "Toronto," of six hundred and fifty tons register, at the rate of more than five English miles an hour, according to the following certificate:

"PACKET-SHIP 'TORONTO,'
"IN THE THAMES, 28th May, 1837.

"We feel pleasure in certifying that your experimental steamboat, the 'Francis B. Ogden,' has this morning towed our ship at the rate of four and a half knots through the water, and *against* tide.

"E. NASHLY, *Pilot*,
"H. R. HOOEY, *Mate*.
"To CAPTAIN ERICSSON."

The London engineers looked upon the experiment with silent neglect, and when the subject was laid before the British Admiralty it failed to attract its favorable notice. Accounts of the experiments, with favorable mention, appeared in the *Times*, and other public journals; also in the *Civil Engineer's and Architect's Journal*, the London *Journal of Arts and Sciences*, the London *Mechanics' Magazine*, and similar publications.

Perceiving its peculiar and admirable fitness for ships of war, Ericsson was confident that the Lords of the Admiralty would at once order the construction of a war-steamer on the new principle. He therefore invited them to an excursion in tow of his experimental boat. Accordingly the Admiralty barge was ordered to Somerset House, and Ericsson's little steamer was lashed alongside of it.

A lecture before the Boston Lyceum in December, 1843, by John O. Sargent, supplies the following graphic description of the trip:

"The barge contained Sir Charles Adam, senior Lord of the Admiralty; Sir William Symonds, surveyor of the British navy; Sir Edward Parry, the commander of the second British North Pole Expedition; Captain Beaufort, the hydrographer of the royal navy, and other scientific and naval officers.

"In anticipation of a severe scrutiny from so distinguished a personage as the chief constructor of the British navy, the inventor had carefully prepared plans of his mode of propulsion, which were spread on the damask cloth of the magnificent barge. To his utter astonishment, as we may well imagine, this scientific gentleman[2] did not appear to take the slightest interest in his explanations. On the con-

[1] Vol. xxvii. p. 130.   [2] Sir William Symonds.

trary, with those expressive shrugs of the shoulder and shakes of the head which convey so much without absolutely committing the actor,—with an occasional sly, mysterious undertone remark to his colleagues,—he indicated plainly that though his humanity would not permit him to give a worthy man cause for unhappiness, yet 'he could an' if he would' demonstrate by a single word the utter futility of the invention.

"Meanwhile, the little steamer proceeded at a steady progress of ten miles an hour through the arches of the Southwark and London bridges towards Limehouse and the steam-engine manufactory of the Messrs. Seward. Their lordships having landed and inspected the huge piles of the marine-engines intended for his Majesty's steamers, with a look at their favorite propelling apparatus, the 'Morgan paddle-wheel,' re-embarked, and were safely returned to Somerset House by the noiseless and unseen propeller of the new steamer.

"On parting, Sir Charles Adam, with a sympathizing air, shook Ericsson cordially by the hand, and thanked him for the trouble he had been at in showing him and his friends this interesting experiment, adding that he feared he had put himself to too great an expense and trouble. Notwithstanding this ominous ending of the day's excursion, Ericsson felt confident that their lordships would not fail to perceive the importance of the invention. To his surprise, however, a few days afterwards a letter written by Captain Beaufort, at the suggestion, probably, of the Lords of the Admiralty, was put into his hands, in which that gentleman, who had witnessed the experiment, expressed his regret that their lordships had been very much disappointed at its results. The reason was altogether inexplicable to the inventor; for the speed attained at the trial far exceeded anything that had been accomplished by any paddle-wheel steamer on so small a scale.

"An accident soon relieved his astonishment. The subject having been started at a dinner-table where a friend of Ericsson was present, Sir William Symonds ingeniously remarked that 'even if the propeller had the power of propelling a vessel, it would be found altogether useless in practice, because the power being applied in the stern, it would be absolutely impossible to make the vessel steer.' It may not be obvious to every one how this naval philosopher derived his conclusion; but his hearers doubtless acquiesced in his oracular proposition, and were amused at the idea of 'undertaking to steer a vessel when the power was applied in her stern.'

"But we may well excuse the British Admiralty for exhibiting no interest in the invention when the engineering corps of the empire arrayed itself in opposition to it, alleging that it was constructed upon erroneous principles and was full of practical defects; regarding its failure as too certain to authorize any speculation of its success. The plan of screw propulsion was specially submitted to many distinguished engineers, and publicly discussed in the scientific journals; and there was scarcely any one but the inventor who refused to acquiesce in the numerous demonstrations proving the vast loss of mechanical power which must attend the substitute for the old-fashioned paddle-wheel."

In August, 1837, a lithograph of the apparatus of the "F. B. Ogden" was published in London. The machinery was subsequently removed and applied to other purposes.

THE "NOVELTY."—In the winter of 1837 the "Novelty," a canal-boat, was fitted with Ericsson's propeller, and sent to ply on the canal between Manchester and London, England. The propellers were but two feet six inches in diameter, and were driven by an engine of ten horse-power; nevertheless, the boat realized a speed of eight or nine miles an hour. This is the first screw-boat ever employed for commercial purposes, but in a short time she was laid up, owing to the failure of her owners.

Although Ericsson's invention was treated with indifference by the highest naval scientific authority of England, Mr. Ogden did not lose his interest or belief in it. He was distinguished for his attainments in mechanical science, and is entitled to the honor of having first applied the principle of the expansive power of steam, and of having originated the idea of right-angular cranks for marine engines. His practical experience and long study of the subject—for he was the first to stem the waters of the Ohio and Mississippi, and first to navigate the ocean by steam alone—enabled him at once to perceive the truth of the inventor's demonstrations.

Other circumstances consoled Ericsson for the rejection of his propeller by the Admiralty. The subject was brought to the notice of Captain Robert F. Stockton, United States navy, then in London, who was induced to accompany the inventor on one of his experimental trips on the Thames. Captain Stockton must be credited with being the first naval officer who dared to act upon the suggestions of Ericsson as to the application of his propeller to ships of war. He saw the importance of the invention, and his acute judgment enabled him to predict it was destined to work a revolution in naval architecture. After making a trip in the "Ogden," from London Bridge to Greenwich, he ordered Mr. Ericsson to build for him forthwith two *iron* boats, for the United States, with steam machinery and propeller on the plan rejected by the British Admiralty. "I do not want," said Captain Stockton, "the opinions of scientific men: what I have seen this day satisfies me." At a dinner at Greenwich, Captain Stockton made several predictions respecting the new invention, all of which have been realized. To the inventor he said, in words of no unmeaning compliment, "We will make your name ring on the Delaware as soon as we get the propeller there."

Captain Stockton not only ordered, on his own account, two *iron* boats, but at once brought the subject before the government of the United States, and had numerous plans and models made at his own expense, explaining the peculiar fitness of the new invention for ships of war. So completely was he persuaded of its importance, and so determined his views should be carried out, that he assured the inventor the government of the United States would test the propeller on a large scale; Ericsson was so confident that the perseverance and energy of Captain Stockton would accomplish all he promised that he abandoned his professional engagements in England and set out for the United States at once.

The "Enterprise."—Before leaving England, however, he built for Mr. John Thomas Woodhouse an iron screw-propeller, which was named the "Enterprise," to run as a passenger-boat on the Ashby-de-la-Zouch Canal. Her length was about seventy feet; beam, seven feet; and her engine about fourteen horse-power; her speed, from nine to ten miles an hour. She commenced running on the canal in August, 1839, and having run the season through without profit was afterwards used as a steam-tug on the Trent and Mersey.

The *Naval Magazine* for November, 1837, published at New York under the auspices of the United States Naval Lyceum, and which contains a description and drawing of Ericsson's propeller for steamboats, says, "We do it from a conviction that this ingenious engineer has discovered a most valuable improvement in the mode of propelling vessels by steam," and adds, "If it succeeds on a large scale as well as it has on the trials already, *it must create an entire revolution in the mode of propelling by steam.*"

1838.—The "Robert F. Stockton."—The iron vessel built for Captain Stockton was launched from the yard of Messrs. Laird & Co., of Birkenhead, the 7th of July, 1838, and named the "Robert F. Stockton." A drawing of this vessel as rigged for her voyage across the Atlantic illustrates Woodcroft's "History of Steam Navigation."

On a trial below Blackwall the 12th of January, 1839, in the presence of thirty gentleman, a distance of nine miles (over the land) was passed with the tide in thirty-five minutes, proving her speed in the water to be between eleven and twelve miles an hour. The "Stockton" was seventy feet long, had ten feet beam, and drew six feet nine inches of water. The diameter of her propeller was six feet four inches.

To test the power of her propeller, she was made to tow four coal-barges with upright sides and square ends, each of fifteen feet beam and drawing four and three-quarters feet of water, from Southwark to Waterloo Bridge. Steam being set on, full speed was attained in one minute, and the distance between the bridges, which is precisely one mile, was performed in eleven minutes.

Considering the square form of the barges, and that they presented together fifty-eight feet one inch beam, with an average draught of four feet four inches, besides the sectional area of the steamer, which was fifty-three square feet, and that the propeller, only six feet four inches in diameter, occupied less than two feet six inches in length behind the stern of the boat, the result was considered very satisfactory.

The "Robert F. Stockton" left England for the United States early in April, 1839, under the command of Captain Crane. Her crew comprised four men and a boy. She was forty days making the passage under sail, and for his daring in crossing the Atlantic in this small vessel Captain Crane was presented with the freedom of the city of New York. Her machinery was arranged so that either one or two propellers could be used. In her experiment on the Thames she was worked with a single propeller.

THE "NEW JERSEY."—In 1840 Captain Stockton sold the "R. F. Stockton" to the Delaware and Raritan Canal Company, permission having been obtained, by a special act of Congress, to run her in American waters, her name at the same time being changed to that of "New Jersey." From that date she was in constant employment as a steam-tug on the Delaware and Schuylkill, both winter and summer, as she was the only vessel capable of towing through the drift ice, paddle-wheel steamers being of little use for that purpose. The "New Jersey" was the first screw-propeller vessel practically used in America, although numerous unsuccessful experiments with the screw had been previously made.

In the autumn of 1839, Ericsson came to the United States, and still lives (1883) in a green old age to plan new and to perfect his old inventions on steam navigation. Before he had been long in America he had an opportunity of introducing his propeller into the United States navy.

THE "PRINCETON."—The "Princeton" war-steamer was built and fitted with Ericsson's screw; the engines also designed by him were so constructed as to lie beneath the water-line, and therefore more out of reach of shot. These were the first engines made upon this principle, and we believe her engines, though compact and eminently successful, have never been duplicated in any other vessel in the United States.[1]

THE "POMONE."—When Ericsson left England he consigned his interests to the guardianship of Count Adolph E. de Rosen, and in 1843, Count Rosen received an order from the French government to fit a 44-gun frigate, the "Pomone," with a propeller on Ericsson's plan, with engines of two hundred and twenty horse-power, which were to be kept below the water-line. In 1844 the English government had the "Amphion" frigate fitted on the same plan, with engines of three hundred horse-power. These were the first engines in Europe which were kept below the water-line. They were also the first direct-acting

[1] A full description of the "Princeton" will be found in the next chapter.

horizontal engines employed to give motion to the screw. Both vessels were completely successful.

1836.—SMITH'S ARCHIMEDEAN SCREW.—In 1835, Francis P. Smith, a farmer at Hendon, first directed his attention to screw propulsion. In the spring of 1836 he obtained the co-operation of Mr. Wright, a banker, and his first patent was granted the 31st of May, 1836. A model boat, constructed under his supervision and fitted with a wooden screw, was then exhibited in operation upon a pond on his farm at Hendon and at the Adelaide Gallery in London. At the Adelaide Gallery it was inspected by Sir John Barrow, the secretary of the Admiralty, and Messrs. Harris & Bell, of Alexandria, offered to purchase the invention for the Pasha of Egypt; but their offer was declined.

The results with the model boat were so satisfactory that in the autumn of 1836, Mr. Smith and his friends constructed a boat of six tons burden, and about six horse-power, to further demonstrate the advantages of the invention. This boat was fitted with a wooden screw of two turns. On the 1st of November, 1836, she was exhibited to the public in operation on the Paddington Canal, and continued to ply there and on the Thames until the month of September, 1837. During one of her trips on the Paddington Canal, in February, 1837, an accident occurred which first pointed out the advantage of diminishing the length of the screw. The propeller having come in contact with some object in the water, about one-half of its length was broken away, and no sooner had this been done than the boat quickened her speed and was found to realize a better performance than before. In consequence of this discovery, a new screw was fitted, of a single turn, and with the vessel thus improved, very satisfactory results were obtained.

Although these experiments established the eligibility of the screw as a propeller for canal and river vessels, nothing had yet been done that was known or remembered to show that it was applicable to vessels navigating the sea. To this point, therefore, Mr. Smith directed his attention, and he determined to carry his small vessel to sea with the view of ascertaining if she would there exhibit the same efficiency displayed in canal and river navigation. Accordingly, on a Saturday evening, September, 1837, he proceeded in his miniature vessel from Blackwall to Gravesend, and having at three in the morning taken in a pilot, went on to Ramsgate, and reached that place during divine service. From Ramsgate he proceeded to Dover, where a trial of the vessel's performance was made in the presence of Mr. John Wright and Mr. Peak, civil engineer. From Dover he went on to Folkestone, and thence to Hythe, returning again to Folkestone. The distance between Hythe and Folkestone, about five miles, was accomplished in three-quarters of an hour. On the 25th of September he returned to London, in weather so stormy and boisterous that it was accounted dangerous for any vessel of so small a size to put to sea. The courage of the undertaking, and the unexpected efficiency of the propeller, rendered the little vessel during this voyage an object of great interest; and her progress was watched with solicitude from the cliffs by nautical and naval men, who were loud in their praises. These favorable impressions reached the Admiralty, and produced a visible effect there.

In March, 1838, the Lords of the Admiralty requested Mr. Smith to have the vessel tried under their inspection.[1] Two trials were accordingly made which were considered satisfactory, and thenceforth the adoption of the propeller for the naval service was deemed not improbable.

Before finally deciding, however, upon the adoption of the propeller, the Lords of the Admiralty considered it desirable that an experiment should be made with a vessel of at least two hundred tons, and Mr. Smith and the gentlemen associated with him in the enterprise accordingly resolved to construct the "Archimedes."

1839.—THE "ARCHIMEDES."—This vessel, of two hundred and thirty-seven tons burden, was designed by Mr. Pascoe, laid down in the spring of 1838, and launched on the 18th of October following, and made her first trip in 1839. She was fitted up with a screw of one convolution, which was set in the dead-wood, and was propelled by two engines of the collective power of ninety horses. Her cost was ten thousand five hundred pounds. She was built under the persuasion that her performance would be considered satisfactory if a speed was attained of four or five knots an hour, and that in such an event the invention would be immediately adopted for the service of the navy. Nearly twice that speed was actually obtained.

After various trials on the Thames and at Sheerness, the "Archimedes," on the 15th of May, 1839, proceeded to sea. She made the trip from Gravesend to Portsmouth, under adverse circumstances of wind and water, in twenty hours. At Portsmouth she was tried against the "Vulcan," one of the swiftest steam-vessels in her Majesty's service. The trial took place before Admiral Fleming, Captain Crispin, and other competent authorities, who acquired from the result a high opinion of the efficiency of the screw as a propeller, which they expressed in writing to Mr. Smith.

The following description of the "Archimedes" is from a newspaper of the time:[2]

"The 'Archimedes' is rigged as a three-masted schooner, with her masts raking. Her length is one hundred and twenty-five feet; average draught of water, ten feet; capacity, two hundred and forty tons; power of engines, eighty horses.

"The mode of propulsion may be said to be by a portion only of

---

[1] This was a year or more after their trip in Ericsson's "F. B. Ogden."
[2] The Inverness *Courier*.

the Archimedean screw. When the vessel was first tried, a full turn of that species of screw was employed. The inventor afterwards, for the sake of compactness, introduced the double-threaded screw, with half a turn of each thread, as more applicable to this vessel, although he prefers the other. This is of iron, and is fixed in an opening on the run of the vessel, above the keel, and about ten feet forward from the rudder. The screw works transversely with the keel, radiating the water all round as it turns with a backward movement. Its diameter is five feet nine inches, and the length fore and aft about five feet. It almost appears incredible that so small a portion of machinery could propel a vessel of such length, but the hold it takes of the water, and the velocity with which it turns, are the elements of its power. It is quite under the surface, and is therefore invisible to spectators, either on board or on shore. It is worked by a spindle forming its axle, which runs fore and aft and is connected with the steam-engine, the velocity being acquired by a combination of spur-wheels and pinions. Each revolution of the larger wheel turned by the cranks of the engines gives, by the multiplied power, five and one-third revolutions of the screw, which consequently revolves at the rate of from one hundred and thirty to one hundred and fifty turns in a minute, according to the speed of the engine. In consequence of the powerful stream thus propelled against the rudder, the ship is actually found to obey the helm much more readily and to be therefore more under command in steering than either a common steam- or sailing-vessel, so that she can easily turn round in one and a quarter or one and a half of her own length, while it is well known that an ordinary steamer cannot do so with the paddles in less than six times her length.[1] The shafts of the steam-engine work fore and aft, the cranks turning transversely, so as to communicate the power directly, by cog-wheels, to the screw; and there is one considerable advantage arising from this arrangement of the machinery,—namely, that the cylinders, and in fact the whole weight of the engine, rests immediately over the keel, where the vessel is the least liable to straining or twisting from the effects of undue pressure. The larger wheel is toothed or cogged with hornbeam (timber).

"The action of the screw is different from the operation of 'sculling,' in the particular that in sculling there are but two motions, the chief force being derived from the lateral; whereas the screw exerts an equal degree of power for every part of its surface towards the periphery in the direction of the radii. The successive columns of water, as fast as presented, are forced away by the act of rotation, pretty much as the earth is turned away from the mold-board of a plow. The action of the screw may be said to bear the same relation to 'scull-

---

[1] This was a confounding answer to Sir William Symond's opinion of Ericsson's boat,—"It would be absolutely impossible to make the vessel steer."

ing' which the use of paddle-wheels does to the ordinary mode of propulsion by oars.

"The 'Archimedes' has made several trips and works well. Her speed is not quite so great as that of a first-rate steamboat in calm weather, but this is believed to result from the fact that her engines are on a new principle, and made by an inexperienced engineer. The full power of the boat is eighty horse-power, but in reality they do not work up to more than sixty.

"One of the greatest advantages of this invention, as applicable to all descriptions of shipping, is the circumstance that the screw may be thrown out of gear in two minutes and the vessel be put under sail alone. The screw is then turned by the motion of the vessel, but the drag is not more than half a mile in ten. Even the drag itself admits of being removed, as provision is made for totally unshipping the screw and bringing it upon deck.

"The advantages of the screw over the paddle-wheels in ocean-steamers, it will be readily seen, must be very great. The leaning over of the ship often throws one of the paddle-wheels out of water and immerses the other too deeply. The screw is always in the water. The saving of fuel will be considerable, as the fires may be extinguished on board a ship propelled by the screw and the vessel used as a sailing-ship when the wind is full and fair. As a vessel of war the advantages would be palpable. This opinion has been expressed by officers of the royal navy who have witnessed the performance of the 'Archimedes.' When it is recollected that this invention is yet in its infancy, and that the 'Archimedes' is the first vessel on a large scale that has been constructed on the new principle, we may readily infer that the introduction of the screw in the construction of steamers is destined to work an important change in one of the most essential features of naval architecture."

Soon after this the "Archimedes" had to return to London, an accident having occurred to her boilers, and new boilers were fitted, which occupied five months. She was then sent to the Texel, by request of the Dutch government, whose interest her performances had excited; but on the way she broke the crank-shaft of one of her engines. She was consequently put into the hands of Messrs. Miller, Ravenhill & Co. for a complete repair, and at the same time the form of her screw was altered by dividing the one whole turn into two half-turns, which, being placed on the opposite sides of the axis, gave to the propeller the character of a double-threaded screw of half a turn. In April, 1840, the Admiralty dispatched Captain Chappell, of the royal navy, and Mr. Lloyd, chief engineer of the Woolwich Dock-Yard, to conduct a series of experiments upon the vessel at Dover. These experiments were carried on during April and May, and the speed of the "Archimedes" was tested relatively with that of the mail-packets on the

Dover station. The result was a highly favorable report to the Admiralty, stating that the success of this new method of propulsion had been completely proved. Immediately after these experiments the vessel was placed at the disposal of Captain Chappell, who, accompanied by Mr. Smith, performed in her the circumnavigation of Great Britain, visiting every seaport of importance. Everywhere the vessel became an object of wonder and admiration. Heretofore engineers had been almost unanimous in opinion that a screw would occasion a loss of power from the obliquity of its action, and the consequent dispersion of the water, and concluded, therefore, that it would be ineligible as a propeller. But it was impossible for them to resist facts such as the performance of the "Archimedes" afforded.

The London *Nautical Magazine* at this time took decided ground against the screw as a means of propulsion in the following article:

"PADDLE–WHEEL *versus* SCREW. *Trial of Strength.*—A few days ago the following experiment was made in the river to test the power of the Archimedean screw, as compared with the common paddle-wheel, in presence of Mr. Fawcet, the eminent steam-engine builder of Liverpool, Mr. Barnes, and other gentlemen. The 'Archimedes,' with Mr. Smith's screw-propeller, and the 'William Gunston' tug-boat, with common paddles, were lashed together, stern to stern, with an interval between them of from twenty to thirty feet. The former vessel has two engines of twenty-five horse-power each; the latter, two of twenty.

"The 'Archimedes' was employed to tow the 'William Gunston' with her engines and paddle-wheels in a state of rest, and this she did with ease, the object of this preliminary trial being to ascertain that the working efficiency of the screw was not impaired by the relative position of the two vessels. The steam was then let on to the engines of the 'William Gunston,' and a fair trial of strength commenced between them. In a little while the 'Archimedes' was seen to have lost all power over her rival; a minute or two more and the 'William Gunston' was tugging the 'Archimedes' after her in spite of the superior engine-power employed on the opposite direction, and in spite also of her much-lauded screw-propeller,—at first slowly, and as it were intermittingly, but at a constantly increased rate of speed, till at last it reached the usual tug-boat speed of from eight to nine knots per hour.

"So complete and convincing an experiment, as recorded in the above extract from the *Mechanic's Magazine*,[1] must indeed have been a most interesting sight, the result of which has fully confirmed our opinion of Mr. Smith's invention, as being one of those that are *theoretically most ingenious, but in practice deficient.* In the midst of the laudatory accounts of the doings of the 'Archimedes,' which fol-

[1] Vol. xxxii. p. 149, No. 885, for July.

lowed her all round the coast, we briefly recorded our opinion among our 'Shakings,' and that too in spite of her beating an old government steamer at Liverpool. 'We ask then, 'Where is the power of the "Archimedes" to contend with the ocean waves?' And 'echo answers, Where?' Let her keep to still water, and Mr. Smith's propeller will prove as good in practice as it has in theory. We understand it is being adopted on canals."[1]

After the "Archimedes" had accomplished the circumnavigation of Great Britain, she made a voyage to Oporto. This voyage was performed in sixty-eight and a half hours, and was at the time held to be the quickest on record. She also visited Antwerp and Amsterdam, passed through the North Holland Canal, and made a great number of trips to other places, leaving everywhere the impression that she had succeeded in demonstrating the practicability of propelling vessels by a screw in an efficient manner. She was next loaned to Mr. Brunel, who fitted her with screws of several different forms, and performed various experiments with her at Bristol. The result of his experiments was so satisfactory that the "Great Britain," orginally intended to be propelled by paddles, was altered and adapted for the reception of a screw.

Meanwhile, the Admiralty determined upon adopting the screw for the navy, and in the merchant service an opinion had arisen equally favorable to its eligibility.

In 1840 and 1841 the "Princess Royal" was built at New Castle, the "Margaret" and "Senator" were built at Hull, and the "Great Northern," a vessel of fifteen hundred tons burden, was laid down at Londonderry, in Ireland.[2] These were merchant screw-vessels. In 1841 the "Rattler," the first screw-vessel built for the British navy, was laid down at Sheerness as a paddle-wheel steamer, but while on the stocks was changed to a screw-steamer. This vessel, of eight hundred and eighty-eight tons burden, was launched in the spring of 1 843 The "Rattler" was fitted with a screw in every respect the counterpart of the screw of the "Archimedes,"—viz., a double-threaded screw of half a convolution. The length of the screw was subsequently reduced, and it was found that best results were obtained with a length of screw answering to one-sixth of a convolution. In the years 1843, 1844, and 1845 an extensive series of experiments were made on the "Rattler" upon screws of various forms, and under varying circumstances of wind and water. The performance of the vessel was so satisfactory that the Lords of the Admiralty ordered twenty vessels to be fitted with the screw, under Mr. Smith's superintendence. The screws introduced into these vessels in every case were double-threaded screws, set in the

---

[1] London *Nautical Magazine*, September, 1840.
[2] A description of these vessels will be found in the next chapter.

deadwood, after the fashion adopted in the "Archimedes" and the "Rattler."

Such are the respective merits of Smith and Ericsson in connection with the practical introduction of the screw-propeller. Ericsson had the advantage in mechanical capacity, and Smith in persistency of character. Ericsson, previous to his connection with the screw, was an accomplished engineer. Smith was only an amateur, with everything except the leading idea to learn. Ericsson's mechanical resources gave him means of overcoming difficulties which Smith did not possess; and Smith had to accept expedients then usual among engineers as his starting-point, while Ericsson could reject those expedients in favor of others which his own ingenuity suggested. In bringing up the speed of his screw, Smith had to use gearing, as that was the expedient which was approved by orthodox engineers; but Ericsson, throwing the dogmas of the engineers to the winds, coupled the engine immediately to the propeller. This comparative destitution of mechanical resources must have added to the difficulties of Smith. Smith's patent was taken out on May 31, 1836; Ericsson's patent was taken out on the 13th of July, 1836. The first trial of Smith's experimental boat was the 31st of May, 1836, and the first trial of Ericsson's experimental boat was on the 30th of April, 1837. In the summer of 1837, Ericsson exhibited his vessel to the Lords of the Admiralty, but without result, owing, as is alleged, to the anticipated difficulty of steering. In September, 1837, Smith carried his vessel to sea, and showed, by repeated experiments, that the objection entertained to Ericsson's plan did not exist in his. Ericsson's vessel appears to have been more efficient than Smith's. Its engine-power was greater, and the mechanical details of its construction more perfect. But Smith's vessel was also completely successful. She towed the "British Queen" steamer in the river, and also the "Lord William Bentinck," a heavily-laden ship, at a speed of two and a half miles an hour, although there was an opposing breeze. Both vessels were therefore successful.

1837.—STEAMERS ON THE DANUBE.—On the 18th of February, 1837, six steamers launched by the Austrian government commenced running between Pesth and the ports of Lower Hungary. This step was hailed in Germany as an important inception of the entire navigation of the Danube by the Austrian government.

Of the steam-packets which were to run between Marseilles and Constantinople, and between Marseilles and Alexandria, seven vessels were this year assembled at Toulon. The "Scamandre" was the first vessel to start for Constantinople. She left during the month of April. A Russian steamer left Constantinople for Odessa on the 20th of each month; fare, twenty-two dollars. An English steamer was running from Constantinople to Trebizond at the beginning and middle of each month, the distance being five hundred and thirty miles. An Austrian steamer, however, placed on that station in May, 1837, made the passage once a week.

The steamer "Maria Dorothea" left Constantinople for Smyrna every Monday, and made the voyage in thirty-six hours. An English steamer, the "Crescent," made the same passage in thirty hours. The Levant steamer, which had hitherto run between Smyrna and Athens twice a week, made the voyage in about forty-eight hours. The Ionian steamers left Corfu for Zante twice a month, the voyage being made in about fourteen hours. The English steamer left Corfu the 29th of each month, touched at Patras to take the mail, and thence proceeded to Malta, touching at Zante, and on to Falmouth, making the voyage of nineteen hundred miles in about twenty days.

Upper cabins in steamers on the great American lakes were first introduced in 1837, on board the steamer "Great Western," by Captain Augustus Walker, who died at Buffalo, New York, 1865, aged sixty-five years.

1837.—ATLANTIC STEAM NAVIGATION.—The *Edinburgh Review*, in 1837, in a long article on steam navigation across the Atlantic, which was attributed to Dr. Lardner, maintained that until further improvements should be made in the construction and management of steam-vessels, or the economy of fuel, it would be impossible, as an ordinary thing, to make a continuous voyage from New York to Liverpool, and especially from Liverpool to New York. The New York *Journal of Commerce*, in June, 1837, referring to this article, approved of its conclusions, and supported them in a long article, concluding, "Whatever difference of opinion may exist as to the practicability of an Atlantic steam voyage, it must be admitted upon all hands that its extent, for an uninterrupted run, comes to the extreme verge of the possible powers of steam navigation." "To be successful, the nearest points of approach to the Eastern and Western continents should be chosen as the points of arrival and departure, to increase the probabilities of success." [1]

The London *Nautical Magazine* for March, 1837,[2] says, "The time is fast approaching when the famous prophecy of the Rev. Dr. Dionysius Lardner, delivered in Dublin and redelivered in Bristol, 'that it is as easy to go to the moon as to go direct from a port in England to New York,' will be tested. There are two vessels at present building to run direct from Bristol and London to New York. The Great Western Steamship Company is building a vessel at Bristol, which will probably make her first trip next August. She is intended to carry twenty-five days' coal. The British and American Steam Navi-

[1] See *Army and Navy Chronicle*, June 29, 1837, for the *Journal of Commerce* articles and several others.
[2] See also *Army and Navy Chronicle* for April 13, 1837.

gation Company, of London, have contracted for a vessel of seventeen hundred and ninety-five tons. This, the largest steam-vessel ever yet propelled, will have a capacity for twenty-five days' fuel, eight hundred tons measurement goods, and five hundred passengers. We sincerely wish both the Bristol vessel and the London one all manner of success; and when we reflect that sixty thousand people have landed at New York from January 1 to September 1, and twenty-seven thousand in Quebec last year, the increase that will naturally take place when the passage is shortened to *fifteen* days instead of *thirty-seven*, the present outward average of the New York packet-ships, we do not think that any of the numerous plans before the public hold out stronger inducements to the capitalists.

"It is difficult to calculate the natural benefits that will accrue to both countries by the establishment of steam communication between them. This much we may affirm, it will greatly improve both countries and render perpetual the peace that now happily exists between them."

1837.—THE FIRST STEAM-WHISTLE.—The first steam-whistle used upon a steamboat was on Narragansett Bay, Rhode Island, upon the "King Philip," Captain Thomas Borden, running between Fall River and Providence, in 1837, by Stephen D. Collins. He is still (1882) engineer of the "Canonicus," of the same line, having been in service forty-five years. Having seen a whistle on a locomotive, Mr. Collins ordered one to be made for the "King Philip." It was not liked at first, but its usefulness as a signal led to its rapid adoption.

1838.—STEAMBOATS IN UNITED STATES WATERS.—A letter prepared by the Secretary of the Treasury of the United States, in answer to a resolution of inquiry of the House of Representatives, 20th of June, 1838, communicated many interesting particulars concerning the employment of steam-vessels in the United States, and the accidents that had happened to them.

"The number of accidents resulting in loss of life or much injury to property from the use of marine steam-engines of every kind in the United States is computed to have been about 260. Of these, 253 are ascertained, and the rest are estimated. Accidents, by explosions and other disasters to steamboats, appear to have constituted a great portion of the whole, and are estimated to have equalled 230, two hundred and fifteen of which are ascertained. The first of these is believed to have occurred in the 'Washington,' on the Ohio River, in 1816.

"Since the employment of steamboats in the United States it is computed that 1300 have been built here. About 260 of these have been lost by accident, as many as 240 worn out, and the rest are running.

"The largest boat in the United States is the 'Natchez,' of 860 tons, and about 300 horse-power, designed to run between New York

HISTORY OF STEAM NAVIGATION. 167

and the Mississippi. The 'Illinois' and the 'Mattison,' on Lake Erie, are next in size, the first being 755 and the last 700 tons. The 'Massachusetts,' on Long Island Sound, is the next, being 626 tons, and the 'Buffalo,' on Lake Erie,' next largest, being 613 tons.

"The largest boats passing Louisville in 1837 were the 'Uncle Sam,' of 490 tons, and the 'Mogul,' of 414 tons; below Louisville the 'Mediterranean,' of 490 tons, and 'North America,' of 445 tons, on the Ohio, and the 'St. Louis,' of 550 tons, on the Mississippi, were running.

"The whole number of steamboats ascertained and estimated to be in this country (1838) is 800. In England, in 1836, the whole number of steamboats in that country was computed to have been 600. On the Western and Southwestern waters near 400 were supposed to be running in 1838, where none were used till 1811, and where, in 1834, the number was computed to be but 234. On the Ohio River, in 1837, 413 steamboats are reported to have passed through the Louisville and Portland Canal, not including many below and above, which never passed through. It is deserving of notice that of the 413 near 60 went out of use by accidents, decay, etc., within the year; and 104 of the others were new, and many of them were probably destined to run on other rivers. As an illustration of the rapid increase of steamboat business on the Ohio, the steamboat passages through the Louisville Canal increased from 406, in 1831, to 1501, in 1837, or about fourfold in six years. Seventy boats were running in 1870 on the Northwestern lakes, where a few years since the number was very small, having been as late as 1835 only 25. Of the 800 steamboats now in the United States the greatest number ascertained to be in any State is 140, in the State of New York.

"The tonnage of all the steamboats in the United States is computed to exceed 155,473. Of this, 137,473 is in boats reported. By the official returns, the whole tonnage now would probably equal near 160,000 tons, having been in 1837 153,660. Many boats included in those returns have since been lost or worn out, and several new ones have been built.

"The tonnage of each boat averages about 200, and the estimates, where the returns have been defective, were on that basis. In England the tonnage is estimated to have been 67,969 in 1836.

"The greatest loss of life on any one occasion in a steamboat was by a collision, and the consequent sinking of the 'Monmouth,' in 1837, on the Mississippi, when 300 lives were lost. The next greatest were by the explosions of the 'Oronoka,' in 1838, on the Mississippi, by which 130 (or more) lives were lost; and of the 'Moselle,' at Cincinnati, Ohio, by which between 100 and 120 persons were destroyed. The greatest injury to life by accidents to boats from snags and sawyers appears to have been 13 lost, in 1834, on the 'St. Louis,' on the

Mississippi River. The greatest by shipwreck was in the 'Home,' in 1837, on the coast of North Carolina, when 100 persons perished. The greatest by fire happened in the 'Ben Sherrod,' on the Mississippi River, in 1837, when near 130 perished. The number of steamboats built in the United States in 1834 was 88; in 1837 it was 184, having increased over 200 per cent in three years. The greatest number of steamboats and other steam-machines appear to have been constructed at Pittsburg, Cincinnati, and Louisville, on the Western waters, and New York, Philadelphia, and Baltimore, on the Atlantic. At Louisville alone, from 1819 to 1838, there were built 244 steam-engines, 62 of which were for boats. The fuel originally used in steamboats in the United States was wood; of late years bituminous coal has been substituted in many instances, also anthracite coal. The latter, from the small space it occupies, seems to possess a decided advantage for sea-going vessels, as well as locomotives.

"Some steamboats made of iron are believed to be in use in Georgia, if not in other parts of this country, though none of that material have been manufactured here; it is computed that their cost is less than those of wood, and as they draw less water with the same freight, they are most useful on shallow streams.

"The number of steamboats built in the United States during the years ending on the 30th of September, 1838 and 1839, were 90 and 125 respectively."[1]

1837.—WHAT DR. LARDNER SAID ABOUT TRANSATLANTIC NAVIGATION.—It has been frequently said, and it is generally believed, that Dr. Dionysius Lardner publicly asserted before the voyages of the "Great Western" and "Sirius" were accomplished facts, that a steam voyage across the Atlantic was a *physical impossibility*. What he did say was, however, quite different,—viz., that such vessels could not be made a paying investment for such a voyage without government assistance or a subsidy, in the then state of steam navigation.

He says,[2] "It cannot be seriously imagined that any one who had been conversant with the past history of steam navigation could entertain the least doubt of the abstract practicability of a steam-vessel making the voyage between Bristol and New York.

"A vessel having as a cargo a couple of hundred tons of coals would, *cæteris paribus*, be as capable of crossing the Atlantic as a vessel transporting the same weight of any other cargo. A steamer of the usual form and construction would, it is true, labor under comparative disadvantages, owing to obstructions presented by her paddle-wheels and paddle-boxes; but still it would have been preposterous to suppose that these improvements could have rendered her passage to New York

---

[1] Extract from the Report of the Secretary of the Treasury to Congress, June 30, 1830.

[2] Museum of Science and Arts, vol. x., 1856.

HISTORY OF STEAM NAVIGATION. 169

impracticable. But, independently of these considerations, it was a well-known fact that long antecedent to the epoch adverted to, the Atlantic had actually been crossed by the steamers 'Savannah' and 'Curaçoa.' . . . Projects had been started, in 1836, by two different and opposing interests, one advocating the establishment of a line of steamers to ply between the west coast of Ireland and Boston, touching at Halifax, and the other a direct line making an uninterrupted trip between Bristol and New York. In the year 1836, in Dublin, I advocated the former of these projects, and in 1837, at Bristol, at the next meeting of the British Association, I again urged its advantages, and by comparison discouraged the project of a direct line between Bristol and New York. When I say that I advocated one of these projects, it is needless to add that the popular rumor that I had pronounced the Atlantic voyage by steam impracticable is utterly destitute of foundation."

The meeting took place August 25, 1837, and the report of the *Times'* special reporter which appeared in that paper on the 27th says, "Dr. Lardner said he would beg any one, and more especially of those who had a direct interest in the inquiry, to dismiss from their minds all previously-formed judgments about it, *and more especially upon this question* to be *guarded against the conclusions of mere theory;* for if ever there was one point in practice of a commercial nature which more than another required to be founded on experience, it was this one of extending steam navigation to voyages of extraordinary length. He was aware that, since the question had arisen, it had been stated that his own opinion was averse to it. *This statement was totally wrong;* but he did feel that great caution should be used in the means of carrying the project into effect. Almost all depended on the first attempt, for a failure would *much retard the ultimate consummation of the project.*

"Mr. Scott Russell said that he had listened with great delight to the lucid and logical observations they had just heard. He would add one word. Let them try this experiment with a view only to the enterprise itself, but on no account try any new boiler or other experiment, but have a combination of the most approved plans that had yet been adopted.

"After some observations from Messrs. Brunel and Field, Dr. Lardner, in reply, said *that he considered the voyage practicable,* but he wished to point out that which would *remove the possibility of a doubt,* because if the first attempt failed it would cast a damp upon the enterprise and prevent a repetition of the attempt."[1]

"What I did affirm in 1836–37," continues Dr. Lardner, "was that the long sea-voyages by steam which were contemplated could not at that time be maintained with that regularity and certainty which are indispensable to commercial success by any revenue which could

[1] London *Times*, August 27, 1837.

be expected from the traffic alone, and that without a government subsidy of a considerable amount such lines of steamers, although they might be started, could not be permanently maintained.".

He then proceeds to show, up to 1851, the commercially non-success of transatlantic steamers that were not subsidized, and adds,—

"Thus it appears, in fine, that after a lapse of nearly fourteen years, notwithstanding the great improvements in steam navigation, the project advanced at Bristol, and there pronounced by me to be commercially impracticable, signally failed."[1]

It is a pity that he could not have looked a little farther into the future and seen the commercial success of later steamships, consequent upon their increase of size and the economical improvements adopted, as also from the demand for the agricultural products of the United States furnishing return cargoes.

1839.—SIR JOHN ROSS'S IDEAS ABOUT STEAM WAR-VESSELS.— Sir John Ross, royal navy, the distinguished Arctic voyager, in his "Treatise on Navigation by Steam,"[2] says, "The ships and vessels proper in steam navigation will admit of a still greater variety than sailing-vessels; and although none have as yet been constructed of a greater tonnage than one thousand tons, there is no good reason why they may not be twice as large, or of as much tonnage as the largest ship in the navy; for although there may be a limit to the size of the boiler, shafts, and other parts of the machinery, there can be no objection to two sets, if the ship is too large for one." He then proceeds to say, "There can be no doubt that in a future war a fleet of men-of-war, and indeed a small squadron, will scarcely be effective without a considerable, if not an equal number of steam-vessels to act under various circumstances; and, among other things, their province will be to tow or increase the velocity of the ships in calms or light winds, and particularly in action." Such vessels, he adds, should have the parts containing the machinery fortified against shot at distances where it would take effect upon her consort; and he also proposes a class of steam gunboats for coast defense, having their guns and paddles covered by a *semicircular shield-deck of iron;* he gives sectional illustrations of this proposed defense.

He says also in the same volume, "It is believed by those who have not devoted much time and attention to the subject of steam navigation that *it cannot be extended to perform foreign voyages,* and it must be confessed that the experiments which have been made seem rather to confirm than to alter that opinion; but it will be shown here that the trials which have hitherto been made have not been of such a

---

[1] Museum of Science and Arts, vol. x., 1856.

[2] Treatise on Navigation by Steam, etc., and an Essay towards a System of the Naval Tactics peculiar to Steam Navigation, as applicable both to Commerce and Maritime Warfare. By Sir John Ross, C. B. Second edition. 1 vol., quarto. London: John Weale, 1837.

nature as to justify a decided opinion." He also gives in the volume, illustrated by diagrams, a system of naval tactics, in which the steam-vessels are represented either as towing ships of the line on the off-side, or as whippers-in of a convoy in time of war.

In 1837, Mr. Samuel Hall, of Basford, the inventor of the tubular condenser, patented a wheel having its floats placed obliquely, but so arranged that every three of them were set in an opposite direction; and about the middle of 1838 a patent for another oblique paddle-wheel was taken out by Lieutenant W. S. Hall, of the Eighteenth Regiment. These and other inventions for the improvement of the paddle-wheel preceded the invention of the Archimedean propeller, improperly called the Archimedean screw, being only a small segment of a screw, and resembling more a short fan than a screw. The system was taken from a kind of small windmills called "water-snakes" employed in low countries like Holland to draw water off the plains.

1837.—THE GERM OF THE UNITED STATES STEAM NAVY.

After the destruction of the steam-battery "Demologos," or "Fulton 1st," the steam galliot "Sea-Gull," a purchased vessel of one hundred tons, was employed in Porter's mosquito fleet for the suppression of piracy in the West Indies in 1822–25. She was employed as a receiving-vessel at Philadelphia for many years, and finally sold out of the service in 1840. But "Fulton 2d," launched in 1837, from the New York Navy-Yard, was the pioneer steam war-vessel of our present naval organization, and the second war-vessel built by the United States.

She was designed and intended for a floating battery for the defense of New York harbor, as a substitute for the "Demologos." With machinery of great power, she attained for that time a high rate of speed, but was virtually inadequate for an ocean steamer, although she did make one trip to the West Indies and back.

Her hull was built solid of the best live-oak. Strength rather than speed was consulted in its lines, her midship cross-sections being the same for one-third of her length, with a bluff bow, partially relieved by a hollow line and finer lines aft. Heavy bulwarks were built up from her decks for the protection of her crew and battery, beveled in all directions to glance off an enemy's shot. She had three masts and was rigged as a topsail schooner. Her principal dimensions were: Length between the perpendiculars, one hundred and eighty feet; extreme beam on deck, thirty-four feet eight inches; depth of hold, thirteen feet four inches; estimated tonnage, nine hundred and seventy-three tons. At thirteen feet draught she displaced fourteen hundred and thirty-three tons of sea water. She had two horizontal condensing engines on the spar-deck, supported by wooden frames. The boilers were of copper, set in flues wagon-shaped and four in number, each with its separate smokestack. The paddle-wheels were twenty-two feet ten inches in diameter; the buckets eleven feet six inches wide and three feet broad. Her armament consisted of eight long 42-pounders and one 24-pounder. Her total cost, hull and equipments, engines, wheels, and boilers, was two hundred and ninety-nine thousand, six hundred and fifty dollars.

There are no logs extant of the performances of this vessel, but in a letter to Captain Matt. C. Perry, dated February 18, 1838, from Chas. H. Haswell, the chief engineer, the speed in smooth water in New York Bay is given at fifteen statute miles per hour with a boiler-pressure of thirty pounds per square inch, cutting off at three eighty the stroke with the old-fashioned canboid cut-off, the engines making twenty-six double strokes of piston per minute. The average draught of water was ten feet six inches. The coal-lockers contained coal for two days' consumption.

"Fulton 2d" remained for several years a useless hulk at the New York Navy-Yard, until 1853, when she was hauled upon ways, lengthened and repaired, and fitted with new machinery, and became known as "Fulton 3d."[1]

The "Fulton 2d" lay at the New York Navy-Yard for many years a useless hulk, until 1852, when the old engine was condemned and she was fitted with new engines of different arrangement, two iron boilers being substituted for the copper. The new engine was a single, inclined, condensing one, with circular, double-drop return flue boilers.

The hulk was hauled upon the ways and thoroughly repaired. The upper deck and heavy bulwarks removed and a complete change made in her internal arrangements, but none in her lines. She was rigged as a two-masted fore-topsail schooner. Her armament consisted of one pivot 8-inch Paixhan gun forward, and four medium 32's in broadside.

The hull of this "Fulton 2d" was launched August 30, 1851, and on the 1st of January, 1852, a trial trip was made in the harbor of New York, embracing a run of seventy-one miles, under steam; average miles per hour 13.34; consumption of coal per hour, 2280 pounds; average revolutions per minute, 21; horse-power developed, 899; draught, 10 feet. After cruising in New York harbor for the relief of distressed vessels, she sailed on the 25th of February to join the Home Squadron in the Gulf of Mexico. On the 31st of March she steamed from Havana to Pensacola, five hundred and fifty miles, on an air-line in fifty-five hours, said to be at that time the quickest trip ever made between those two ports. Going down the bay from Pensa-

---

[1] For full particulars of "Fulton 1st," 2d, and 3d, see the Naval and Mail Steamers of the United States, by Engineer-in-Chief Chas. B. Stuart, U.S.N., 1853.

cola to the navy-yard, she ran the six miles in twenty-two minutes, accurate time, a rate equivalent to 17.73 miles per hour.[1]

"Fulton 3d" was in ordinary at the Pensacola Navy-Yard when it was taken possession of by the rebels in 1862, and was then destroyed.

October 31, 1837.—The Secretary of the Navy authorized Captain M. C. Perry "to appoint two first-class and two second-class assistant engineers; the appointments to be confirmed by the commandant of the station." "The engineers must receive from you," he adds, "a letter of appointment revocable at any time by the commanding officer of the station, upon complaint of intemperance, incapacity, insubordination, negligence, or other misconduct, preferred by the commander of the steamer, if proved to the satisfaction of the commanding officer of the station. The commander of the steamer, of course, to have the power of suspending them from duty if necessary. The engineers must be required to sign some proper instrument of writing which will legally make them liable to this law for the government of the navy, but to be exempt from corporal punishment, which instrument is to be transmitted to the Secretary of the Navy, with their letters accepting their appointments."

November 7, 1837.—The Secretary wrote Captain Perry that the "Fulton," as recommended by the Commissioners of the Navy and approved by the Navy Department, was allowed,—two first-class engineers, at eight hundred dollars per annum each; two second-class engineers, at five hundred dollars per annum each; four coal-heavers, at fifteen dollars per month; and eight firemen, at twenty-five dollars to thirty dollars per month.

Both the firemen and coal-heavers were to sign the ship's articles, and were to be removable "at the pleasure of the commander of the vessel," as authorized for the reduction of petty officers and seamen. "If additional coal-heavers should be found necessary, some of the seamen or ordinary seamen of the vessel might be designated by the commander to perform that duty." He next wrote,—

"NAVY DEPARTMENT, November 21, 1837.

"CAPT. M. C. PERRY, Com'dg Str. 'Fulton,' New York:

"SIR,—Your letter of the 16th instant, relative to the engineers of the 'Fulton' and their uniforms, has been received.

"*The adoption of a uniform such as you may approve, if agreeable to those at whose expense it is to be provided,* meets with the sanction of the Department, and it is also desirable, as mentioned in your letter, that none be appointed engineers but those of the very best standing.

"I am, respectfully, &c.,

"M. DICKENSON,

"*Secretary of the Navy.*"

[1] Stuart's Naval and Mail Steamers of the United States.

A letter dated December 19, 1837, authorized Captain Perry to employ, agreeably to his request, four additional firemen.

December 21, 1837, the Secretary wrote him, "Your communication of the 17th instant has been received, with its several inclosures, and the appointments of assistant engineers which you have made, as well as the measures you have taken in regard to the engagements, etc., of the engineers, firemen, and others, of the steamer 'Fulton,' are approved by the Department."

February 13, 1838, the Secretary wrote Captain Perry that he approved of his suggestion, and says, "I have directed Commodore Ridgely to place on board the 'Fulton' five *apprentices* to the navy, who are to be under the particular charge of the engineers (one to each) and exclusively attached to the engineers, and to be shipped and paid as other apprentices."

February 21, 1839, the Secretary authorized the pay of the second assistant engineers on the "Fulton" to be increased from five hundred to six hundred dollars from the 1st of March.

March 1, 1839, he authorized "the salary of such engineers as now receive eight hundred dollars to be increased to nine hundred."

In this connection it is interesting to note the rapid rise in importance of our steam navy in the past forty-one or forty-two years. Its *personnel* in 1882 consists of

Ten chief engineers on the active list ranking relatively with captains in the navy, one of whom, as chief engineer of the bureau of steam engineering, has the relative rank of commodore; 15 chief engineers with the relative rank of commander; 45 chief engineers with the relative rank of lieutenant-commander; 81 passed assistant engineers with the relative rank of lieutenant; 17 passed assistant engineers with the relative rank of master; 11 assistant engineers ranking as masters; 51 assistant engineers with the relative rank of ensign; 62 cadet engineers, graduates; 74 cadet engineers at the Naval Academy,—viz., 25 first-class; 25 second-class; 24 third-class.

One chief engineer on the retired list, with the relative rank of captain; 1 chief engineer with the relative rank of commander; 6 chief engineers with the relative rank of lieutenant-commander; 18 passed assistant engineers with the relative rank of lieutenant; 25 assistant engineers with the relative rank of master.

While the rank of engineer officers has been increased the pay has similarly advanced. The engineer-in-chief now receives $5000; chief engineers, from $4000 to $2800, on duty; passed assistant engineers, from $2200 to $2000, on duty; assistant engineers, from $1900 to $1700, on duty; cadet engineers, from $1000 to $500, on duty; and their right to leave pay has been recognized. When retired they receive three-fourths of their highest pay on the active list.

CHAPTER IV.—1838–1858.

The Inauguration of Regular Transatlantic Steam Navigation.—Arrival of the City of Kingston at New York from Cork, April 2, 1838.—Arrival of the Sirius from Cork and the Great Western from Bristol at New York, April 28, 1888.—The President, 1839.—The British Queen, 1839.—Dimensions of the Earliest and Largest Transatlantic Steamships, 1840.—Miscellaneous Notes.— The Cyclops, Steam Frigate, 1840.—The Nemesis, 1840.—The Screw Steamer Archimedes, 1840.—The Argyle, Chili, and Peru, 1839.—The Cunard Line Inaugurated, 1840.—The Bangor, 1842.—The French Steam Navy, 1840.— Screw Steamers in Great Britain, 1842.—Steam Navigation on the Indus, Established 1842.—The Driver, the First Steamship to Circumnavigate the Globe, 1842.—United States Steamship Princeton, the First Screw Steam War-Vessel, 1843.—H. M. Ship Rattler, the Second Screw Steam War-Vessel, 1843.—The Great Britain, 1843.—First English Steam Collier, 1844.—The Midias and Edith, the First Steam Screw Vessels to China, 1844–45.—The Witch, 1845.—American Mail Steamships to Havre and Bremen, 1845–50.— The Propeller Massachusetts, 1845.—Thames Steamboats, 1845.—The North River Steamer Oregon, 1846.—The First French Atlantic Steamer, 1847.— First American Steamer to the Pacific, 1848.—The Gemini Iron Twin Steamer, 1850.—Screw Steamship Himalaya, 1851.—The Francis Skiddy, 1852.—The Australian, 1852.—The Argo, the Second Steamship and First Screw to Circumnavigate the Globe, 1854.—The Golden Age, 1854.—The Cunard Steamer Persia, 1855.—Steam Vessels of the Royal Navy, 1856.

1838.—Daniel Webster, in a lecture at Boston, said, in allusion to steam-power, " In comparison with the past, what centuries of improvement has this single agent comprised in the short space of fifty years! . . . What further improvements may still be made in the use of this astonishing power, it is impossible to know, and it were vain to conjecture. What we do know is, that it has most essentially altered the face of affairs, and that no visible limit yet appears beyond which its progress is seen to be impossible." When Webster spoke thus, the grand problem of ocean steam navigation had not been solved; in fact, the possibility of a steamship crossing any ocean was generally denied both by practical and scientific men.

At a meeting of the directors of the Great Western Railway, October, 1835, one of the party spoke of the enormous length, as it then appeared, of the proposed railway from London to Bristol. Mr. Brunel exclaimed, " Why not make it longer, and have a steamboat to go from Bristol to New York, and call it the Great Western?" The suggestion, treated at first as a joke, soon engaged the serious attention of three of the leading members of the board. A tour of the great ship-building ports of the kingdom was made in order to collect information. In the report of the result of the inquiry Mr. Brunel inserted a paragraph which laid down the principles on which the success of oceanic steam navigation wholly depended. It was this, that the resistance to the passage of vessels through the water increases at a lower rate of progression than their tonnage. At equal speeds a vessel twice the size of another will encounter four times the resistance. But its capacity, or tonnage, will be eightfold that of the smaller vessel. By a well-proportioned increase of size, therefore, it is possible to employ far more powerful engines, to carry enough coal for the consumption of a long voyage, and at the same time to have ample accommodation for passengers and goods. So true is this, that it is now admitted that the economical limit to the size of vessels is imposed rather by the dimensions of ports and harbors than by the exigencies of the shipwright. Speed, also, can be considerably increased by the employment of more powerful engines; the limit to ocean speed being imposed by another physical law, that the resistance increases as the cube of the velocity.

The keel of the "Great Western" was laid, and assurance given that she would be followed by a splendid line of vessels, which would consign the packet-ships to the care of the historian as "things that were."

The project was simultaneously started by two opposing interests, one advocating a line of steamers to ply between the west coast of Ireland and Boston, touching at Halifax, the other a direct line between Bristol and New York. The former, the "British and American Steam Navigation Company," resolving not to be left astern by the company in Bristol, which was getting the "Great Western" ready for sea, chartered the "Sirius," a steamer which had been built to run between London and Cork, to run against the "Great Western," and she made two voyages in their employ.

1838.—April 2, 1838, the British steamer "City of Kingston" arrived at New York from Cork, Ireland, being the second British steamship that crossed the Atlantic. Subsequently she went to the West Indies and returned to Norfolk and Baltimore.

1838.—THE "SIRIUS."—The "Sirius" arrived at New York on St. George's day, the 23d of April, also the anniversary of the birth and death of Shakespeare. The New York papers of that date say, "Myriads of persons crowded the Battery to have a glimpse of the first steam-vessel which had crossed the Atlantic from the British Isles and arrived safely in port." The "Sirius," of seven hundred tons' register and engines of three hundred and twenty horse-power, sailed from Cork at 10 A.M. Wednesday, April 4, 1838, and was followed by the "Great Western," which sailed from Bristol (the port which sent out the Cabots), April 8, both vessels arriving at New York April 23, 1838, the "Sirius" a few hours in advance of the "Great Western."

The "Sirius" was advertised to return May 1, and the Chevalier Wickoff was one of seven passengers who met on the tug-boat which was to convey them on board. He says in his reminiscences, "We moved off amid the hurrahs of excited people who came on every kind of craft to wish us God speed." Among the passengers was James Gordon Bennett, the remarkable founder of the New York *Herald.* He says, "Perceiving a tall, slim man near me, I entered into conversation. His physiognomy was striking: lofty forehead, prominent nose, firm mouth, and the general expression, though somewhat stern, not forbidding. After chatting for some time I remarked,—

"'I hear the famous Bennett is on board.'

"'Yes, I believe he is,' said the tall man, with a smile.

"'Do you feel at all nervous about it?'

"'Not in the least,' was the reply.

"'Well, for my part,' I continued, 'I am not altogether comfortable on the point.'

"'Why?' asked my companion.

"'Because he is so given to saying sarcastic things of people.'

"'That depends a good deal,' he answered, 'whether they are worth it.'

"'Do you know him by sight?' I inquired.

"'Very well.'

"'Then do point him out if you see him on deck.'

"'He is standing before you. My name is Bennett.'

"'What!' I exclaimed, on recovering my breath; 'are you the man so fiercely assailed, and whose humorous sallies I have read with such delight these six months past?'

"'*Ecce homo!*' he retorted.

"All went merrily the first week. Then stormy weather set in, and our little steamer was put to a tougher test than I had expected. She was dreadfully knocked about, but was stanch and steadfast in the worst gales.

"When only a couple of days from the English coast, the coal was nearly exhausted, and they economized by going at half-speed, but towards the last we were forced to burn up whatever could be spared. On entering the English Channel the vessel became enveloped in a dense fog. Suddenly the mist cleared off and it was found we were heading on to one of the Sicily Islands, and in half an hour would have been a wreck. On the seventeenth day we put into Falmouth for coal and provisions, and thence started for London."

The "Sirius" ran afterwards on the line of steam-packets between Dublin and Cork, and ran on the rocks of Bally Cotton Bay January 16, 1847, and was wrecked, when twenty lives were lost.

The "Great Western" made her return trip to Bristol in less than twelve days. Steam traveling across the Atlantic was thus inaugurated.

The following account of these pioneer steamships, and of their first voyage across the Atlantic, is from the New York *Express* of April 24, 1838.[1]

[1] The New York *Courier and Enquirer*, of April 23, 1838, has this notice of the arrival of the "Sirius:"

"ARRIVAL OF A STEAMER FROM EUROPE.

"*Seven days later from London. Six days later from Liverpool.*

"Last night our news schooner 'Eclipse' boarded the steamer 'Sirius,' Lieutenant Richard Roberts, R. N., commander, from Cork, whence she sailed on the 4th inst. She has performed the voyage without accident, save a slight one which befell her on coming in the Hook, where she grounded. Since her departure she has used only fresh water in her boilers, having on board Mr. Hall's condensing apparatus."

Under the head of marine news is reported: "Steam-packet 'Sirius,' Roberts, from Cork, sailed April 4, with forty-six passengers, etc., to Wadsworth & Smith. The 'Sirius' went ashore on the point of the Hook last evening about ten o'clock. She did not sustain any damage, and will be got off on the rising tide."

The same paper contains the following advertisement:

"BRITISH STEAM-PACKET SHIP FOR LONDON, TO SAIL FROM NEW YORK, MAY 1, 1838.

"The new and powerful Steamship

"'SIRIUS,'

"700 tons burthen and 320 Horse-power,

"LIEUTENANT R. ROBERTS, *Commander*,

is intended to sail from London, March 28th, touching at Cork, and thence, on the 2d of April, for this port, returning from New York to London on the 1st of May.

"This vessel has superior accommodation, and is fitted with separate cabins, for the accommodation of families, to whom every possible attention will be given.

"Cabin, $140, including provisions, wines, etc.

"Second cabin, $80, including provisions.

"This superior steamship has been chartered by the directors of the British and American Steam Navigation Company of London, to meet the pressing demands of the public, in anticipation of the steamship 'British Queen,' now building; is a new vessel, about six months old, and has proved herself superior to any steam-vessel in British waters in speed and seaworthy qualities.

"Further information afforded on application; and for freight and passage apply to

"WADSWORTH & SMITH,

"4 Jones Lane (rear 103 Front Street),

"*Agent of the American and British Steam Navigation Company.*"

The following is the first advertisement of the "Great Western" in the New York *Courier and Enquirer*, April 24, 1838:

"BRITISH STEAM-PACKET SHIP

"'GREAT WESTERN,'

"JAMES HOSKINS, R. N., Commander,

"Having arrived yesterday from Bristol, which place she left on the 8th inst., at noon, will sail from New York for Bristol on Monday, 7th May, at 2 o'clock P.M.

"She takes no steerage passengers. Rates in the Cabin, including Wines and

"STEAMSHIPS 'SIRIUS' AND 'GREAT WESTERN.'—SPLENDID SIGHT FROM THE BATTERY.

"Yesterday was a day of unusual excitement in this city, it being universally considered the beginning of a new era in the history of Atlantic navigation. The steamship 'Sirius' having arrived Sunday night, thousands assembled to see her, as the news spread about the city. She anchored a short distance from the castle, and crowds upon the Battery had a view of her from that promenade. The sun shone clear, and the weather was as fine as could be wished.

"The 'Sirius' sailed from Cork on the evening of the 4th instant, and made the Highlands of New York at six o'clock P.M. on the 22d, making the passage in eighteen days, and having on board forty-seven passengers. During the day she was thronged by small boats filled with passengers to view her. About one o'clock it was announced by telegraph that the steamer 'Great Western' was off the Hook, when thousands poured down Broadway; and the Battery at two P.M. presented a brilliant appearance. The crowd reminded one of the landing of the 'Nation's guest,' Lafayette. The smoke of the 'Great Western' was seen in the horizon ascending in black volumes long before her hull was visible. The ship, as she came in sight and passed Bedloe's Island, received a salute from the fort of twenty-six guns. She approached the Battery through a fleet of row-boats and small craft, cheered by every one. She soon ranged alongside the Castle, sailed around the 'Sirius,' which saluted her, and the crowd from the wharves, Castle, boats, etc., gave three hearty cheers, returned by those on board. She then went up the East River, and anchored near Pike Street. This successful experiment of steam-packets between New York and England gave life and joy to all.

"The 'Great Western' left Kingroad, Bristol, at two o'clock, April 7th, and she was, at two o'clock, April 23d, only sixteen days, in New York, thus bringing England nearer to us than many parts of our own country. This has been done in a season of the year, not of summer sunshine, but of gales, storms, sleet, and hail,—and *steam*

Provisions of every kind, 30 guineas; a whole state-room for one person, 50 guineas. Stewart's fee for each passenger, £1.10s. sterling. Children under 13 years of age half price. No charge for letters or papers. The captain and owners will not be liable for any package unless a bill of lading has been given for it. One to two hundred tons can be taken at the lowest current rates.

"Passage or freight may be engaged, a plan of the cabin may be seen, and further particulars learned, by applying to

"RICHARD IRVING, 98 Front Street."

The "Great Western" continued to sail from the Severn, and subsequently from the Mersey, and made seventy-four transatlantic passages before passing into the hands of the West India Company. On her second trip from New York she reached Bristol in twelve and a half days.

navigation across the Atlantic is no longer an experiment, but a plain matter of fact. The thing has been done triumphantly.

"The 'Great Western' was built at Bristol, by the Great Western Steamship Company, and intended to commence a regular line between Bristol and New York. She was launched on the 19th of July, 1837. Her length between the perpendiculars, from the forepart of the stem to the afterpart of the stern at the keel, 212 feet; length of keel on the blocks, 205 feet; length of cabin-deck (saloon), 75 feet; length over all (from figure-head to taffrail), 235 feet; breadth between paddle-wheels, 34 feet 4 inches; depth under deck to top of floors, 23 feet 3 inches; scantling floors on the side of keel, 15 inches, sided; ditto, 16 inches, moulded; length of floors, 24 feet; thickness of bends, 7 inches; bottom plank, 5 inches; top sides, 4 inches; sheer streaks, 5 inches; upper-deck clamps, 8 inches; diagonal riders, 5 inches, 3 feet apart; iron diagonals, 4 inches by ¾; bilge planks, 6 inches; keelson, 20 by 21 inches.

"Tonnage, 1320 tons; best berths, 150; berths for crew, 26; berths for engineers, firemen, and officers, 40; two engines, by Maudsley & Field, 400 horse-power, 200 each; diameter of cylinder, 73½ inches; length of stroke, 7 feet; coal stowage, 600 tons, or enough for thirty tons per diem for twenty days.

"Her whole cost amounted to about £50,000, £21,373 15s. 10d. of which has been expended for ship-building, £18,500 for the engines, about £1000 for the fitting up, furniture, and painting of the grand saloon, and the remainder for rigging, equipment, stores, and coals.

"The 'Sirius' is a beautiful model, seven hundred tons, three hundred and twenty horse-power, schooner-rigged. Notwithstanding rough weather, she came over with perfect safety. Passengers were delighted with her performance. Her boilers were supplied with fresh water by a distilling apparatus which converted the salt into fresh water. The distilling worms (small copper tubes) measured, as reported, near *four miles!*

"The following is the journal of her voyage:

"4th April.—Started; light breezes from N.E. Draft of water, 15 feet 2 inches.

"5th.—Heavy at N.E. to N.N.E., windy; fresh gale, much head-sea, slight rain. Exchanged numbers with the bark 'Dale,' of Liverpool. Weighted one ton of coal, which lasted 1 h. 30 m.; pressure on the boilers, 53.4 pounds.

"6th.—Stormy, W.N.W. breezes, with squalls and heavy head-sea. Passed two brigs, one standing east and the other north.

"7th.—Same, strong gales and squally, with rain,—vessel laboring heavy. Passed two large ships standing to the eastward, under double-reefed topsails. Very squally. Passed a barque. Heavy sea, with long swell; took in water on deck.

"8th.—Same, with hazy weather. Stopped engine, owing to one of the braces working loose—started the engine in an hour after—heavy rains.

"9th.—Wind still W.N.W., and a heavy head-sea—clear. Passed a brig standing east. Set a single-reefed foresail and double-reefed mainsail.

"10th.—Spoke ship 'Star,' of New York, longitude 24 W.—fresh gales and squally—shipped a great deal of water.

"11th.—Winds E.N.E.—passed a ship standing to the south—light breezes.

"12th.—Light winds, easterly—stopped engine to pack the stuffing-boxes—light winds and fair.

"13th.—S.E., light breezes. Spoke the 'Roger Sherman,' of Bath, 36 days from New Orleans, bound to Havre—hoisted colors to a Falmouth packet—three sails in sight—reduced the weight to 33.4 lbs. on boilers.

"14th.—S.W. light breezes—passed a ship standing to the westward—observed a change in the color of the water.

"15th.—Heavy W.N.W. gale; dark and foggy.

"16th—N.W. to W. gales; heavy head-sea and snow—vessel laboring—stopped engine three-quarters of an hour to fasten screws.

"17th.—N.W. by W. winds; squally, with hail and snow.

"18th.—S.W. winds and squalls.

"19th.—Same.

"20th.—W. by N., heavy sea and hard rain—stopped engine, and was boarded by Her Majesty's ship "Coromandel," from Bermuda, bound to Halifax, with Eleventh Regiment.

"21st.—Ditto—exchanged signals with an Austrian brig.

"22d.—Made light for the pilot off the Highlands. Not getting a pilot, the 'Sirius' ran in, and then touched off the Hook—receiving, however, no damage."

Her Majesty's consul historically records the event of her arrival in the following letter addressed to the commander of the "Sirius:"

"HER MAJESTY'S CONSULATE,
"NEW YORK, April 23, 1838.

"SIR,—I have the honor and happiness to congratulate you on the arrival of your steamship across the Atlantic, at a season when strong gales so generally prevail, thereby having proved that British skill has accomplished a most important enterprise, which will produce a revolution in commercial and social intercourse, of which we are incapable of forming any just conceptions. Permit me, sir, to add that I have, in common with my fellow-subjects of Her Majesty in this city, a further cause of rejoicing, that the honor of accomplishing the enterprise has been achieved by a son of the British navy, and that it was completed on St. George's day.

"I have the honor to be, sir,
"Your humble servant,
"JAMES BUCHANAN."
"RICHARD ROBERTS, Esq., R. N.,
"Commander of the Steamship 'Sirius.'"

"LOG OF THE 'GREAT WESTERN.'—We published yesterday an abstract from the log-book of the 'Sirius,' showing her daily progress, and the sort of weather she had to encounter, and we now give an extract from the log-book of the 'Great Western':

Dates.	Course.	Distance.	Latitude.		Longitude.		Wind.	Remarks on Weather.
			Acct.	Obs.	Acct.	Chron.		
April 8...	10 P.M.		Sandy I.				N.W. N.N.W	Strong gale.
" 9...	West.	240		50.27		07.82	N.N.W. and S.W.	Moderate.
" 10...	78-80 W.	213	49.55	00.00	12.50	12.16.45	W. by N. and S. W.	Moderate.
" 11...	W. by S.	206	49.04	48.11	17.25	17.10	S.W. and E. by S.	Moderate and hazy, rough at night.
" 12...	W. 1-2 S.	231	47.47	47.17	22.48	22.05.10	E. by S.E. to S.E.	Moderate and cloudy.
" 13...	W. 1-4 S.	218	46.56	46.56	28.09	28.27	E.S.E.	Light winds.
" 14...	W. 3-4 S.	215	46.26	46.28	33.40	34.09	S.W. and S.S.W.	At 10 P.M. squally, with small rain.
" 15...	W. by S.	241	45.24	45.19	39.43	39.38.30	S.E. to S.W. by S.	Strong and squally, vessel lurched deeply but easy.
" 16...	W. 3-4 S.	243	44.46	44.84	45.19	45.31	Variable.	Squally.
" 17...	W. 3-4 S.	185	44.07	44.10	49.46	49.21	S.W. to W.N.W.	Strong gales and heavy sea.
" 18...	W.S.W.	169	42.02	42.58	52.55	52.30	W.N.W. to W. by N.	Moderate.
" 19...	W. 1-4 S.	206	42.02	42.02	56.50	56.49.45	S.W.	Strong winds and heavy sea.
" 20...	W. 3-4 S.	183	41.36	No ob	60.54	No ob	S.W. W.N.W.	Strong winds and heavy sea, ship very easy.
" 21...	W. 3-4 S.	192	41.05	40.30	65.05	64.24.13	N.N.W.	Light winds and cloudy.
" 22...	S. 83 W.	198	39.48	39.41	68.38	69.03.30	N.N.W. to W.N.W.	Strong winds and frosty.
" 23...	S. 79 W.	230					N.N.W. and N.	Fine weather; at 10 received a pilot.

To harbor, 50; 3223 miles steaming.

A passenger on the "Great Western," on this her first transatlantic voyage, in a communication to Chambers's *Edinburgh Journal*, says,—

"A number of daring passengers—for daring they were thought in that day—took berths for the voyage in the 'Great Western;' and on 8th April, 1838, at noon, the gallant ship steamed away from her anchorage at the mouth of the river Avon, and majestically descended the Severn, bound for New York. One of her passengers says, when they were fairly under way, 'Whatever misgivings might previously have assailed us in the contemplation of our voyage, I believe that at this moment there was not a faltering heart among us. Such stability, such power, such provision against every probable or barely possible contingency, and such order presented itself everywhere on board, as was sufficient to allay all fear.'

"Suffice it that the 'Great Western' entered the harbor of New York at full speed on the afternoon of 23d April, having performed the passage in the then unprecedentedly short period of fifteen days, in which only four hundred and fifty-two tons of the six hundred tons of coal on board had been consumed. The fort on Bedloe's Island saluted the steamer with twenty-six guns, answering to the number of States of the Union at that time.

"'It had been agreed among us,' says one passenger, 'some days previously, that before we left the ship one of the tables should be christened Victoria, the other the President. Wine and fruit had been set upon them for this purpose: we were standing round the former of them; the health of Britain's Queen had been proposed; the toast was drunk; and amidst the cheers that followed, the arm was just raised to consummate the naming, when the fort opened its fire. The fire was electric. Our colors were lowered in acknowledgment of the compliment, and the burst which accompanied it from our decks— drinking the President and the country, and breaking wine again— was more loud and joyous than if at that moment we had unitedly overcome a common enemy. Proceeding still, the city became more distinct,—trees, streets, the people,—the announcement of the arrival of the ship by telegraph had brought thousands to every point of view upon the water-side; boats, too, in shoals, were out to welcome her, and every object seemed a superadded impulse to our feelings. The first to which our attention was now given was the "Sirius," lying at anchor in the North River, gay with flowing streamers, and literally crammed with spectators,—her decks, her paddle-boxes, her rigging, mast-head high! We passed round her, receiving and giving three hearty cheers, then turned towards the Battery. Here myriads seemed collected,—boats had gathered around us in countless confusion, flags flying, guns were firing, and cheering again,—the shore, the boats, on all hands around, loudly and gloriously, seemed as though they would never have done. It was an exciting moment,—a moment which, in the tame events of life, finds few parallels: it seemed the out-pouring congratulations of a whole people, when swelling hearts were open to receive and to return them. It was a moment of achievement! We had been sharers in the chances of a noble effort, and each one of us felt the pride of participation in the success of it, and this was the crowning instant. Experiment then ceased; certainty was attained; our voyage was accomplished.' In explanation of the allusion in the above to the 'Sirius' we may here state that this steamship, which had sailed from Cork before the 'Great Western' left Bristol, had arrived a day or two before the latter vessel; but the 'Sirius' only partially used her engines, not having stowage for sufficient fuel to keep them constantly plying."

1839.—The Charleston (S. C.) *Mercury* says, August, 1839, "Major

John Lind, of Charleston, S. C., an officer of the United States Engineers, is justly entitled to the credit of the application of the *screw* in the place of the paddle-wheel to the steamboats. More than five years since[1] he explained the principle, and experimented successfully with a small model boat on the canal near Washington City."

1839.—The New Jersey *Journal*, August, 1839, says, "Mr. Samuel Dow, of Elizabethtown, upward of *twenty years since*, made two small boats from twenty to twenty-five inches in length, one with a screw, and the other with paddle-wheels, in order to test the superiority of the screw. Each had a mast and cord, the standing part of the latter fast to and wound around the shaft or axle, and over a sheave in the mast-head, with equal weight attached. At the going off the wheel would go ahead; but before the race the screw would over-haul and shoot ahead.

"Mr. Dow built a boat twenty-five feet in length, with a screw on each side, to ship and unship as might be advantageous. It was worked by four men with a crank and cog-wheels."

1839.—SAIL VESSELS TO BE PROPELLED BY STEAM.—The Norfolk *Herald*, October 7, 1839, says Mr. Benjamin Harris, of that borough, had conceived a plan by which sail-vessels of every description might be propelled with the aid of steam, by paddles operating vertically in the bottom of the vessel above the keel, connected with the machinery above by a perpendicular shaft working in a metal cylinder, constructed to exclude the water. In the larger class of ships, the boilers, engines, and all the machinery could be stowed away *below the water-line.*

Mr. Harris tested his idea on a skiff fourteen feet long and three wide, which, propelled by the hand, by a crank turning a paddle-wheel two and a half feet in diameter, made the rate of five miles an hour.

Many ingenious plans were proposed up to 1839, when the utility of the screw-propeller was fully demonstrated, and a number of screw boats were placed on the lines of inland navigation connecting Lake Ontario with the St. Lawrence.

THE "LONDONDERRY" OR "GREAT NORTHERN" SCREWS, 1842.—There is a good representation of the "Great Northern," which was launched the latter part of 1842, with sections of the stern showing the screw, in the London *Illustrated News*, for January 24, 1843. The vessel is represented as ship-rigged, with the smokestack aloft the mainmast and having a line of painted ports along her side. The paper states, "Her great length, breadth, and depth exceeds, we believe, the dimensions of any steam vessel ever in existence. She was built at Londonderry by Captain Wm. Coppin[2] (an experienced ship-builder

---

[1] The screw as a method of propulsion was devised nearly half a century earlier.
[2] Captain Coppin has obtained in England and in this country (March 28, 1882) a patent for a compound ship constructed of three hulls of narrow beam, the two

and inventor), and is a remarkable monument of marine architecture. She is propelled by the Archimedean screw, which works on each side of the rudder: the engine is of three hundred and sixty horse-power. No paddles are required, and but for the funnel which is seen amidships, she might pass for a square-rigged ship of the larger class. She has three masts with lower and upper yards, and is rigged in every respect like a frigate or sloop-of-war. We were favored by one of her officers with the following dimensions: Length from taffrail to stern, two hundred and seventy-four feet; beam, thirty-seven feet; depth, fifty feet. On her passage from Londonderry she ran upon an average thirteen and a half knots without her engine, which can be spared or used as circumstances may require. When it was necessary to put on the engine she ran nine knots head to wind. The space for storage is most capacious. Standing aft and looking forward on the orlop deck the distance seems immense, exceeding indeed the largest first-rate in the navy. With all this room there is at present a want of arrangement for cabins, but we understand she will be fitted up in the best style. With respect to her external appearance the vessel seems a huge monster steamer, but pleasing in her mould and trim. (This the cut shows.) A beautiful female figure is placed over the cut-water and her stern is richly decorated with carving, gold and color. In consequence of the heavy mast, yards, and rigging, she will require an immense quantity of ballast. At present it is not decided whether she is to run to and from Ireland or be employed in other service. During her stay many persons entered the dockyard to gaze upon this truly wonderful object."

Extracts from her log from Cowes to London, beginning December 25, 1843, and ending December 29, when she steamed into the East India port docks, which are given, show that her sailing qualities were not impeded by the screw propeller.

1842.—In March, 1842, Lieutenant W. W. Hunter, United States navy, took out a patent for a submerged *horizontal* wheel, for the propelling of steamers. The first essay was made in the canal at Washington, D. C., on a small boat called the " Germ." The result obtained was represented as so favorable it was determined by the United States government to build a wooden vessel of 1000 tons to test this method of propulsion. This vessel, named " The Union," was built at the Norfolk (Virginia) Navy-Yard, and was of the following dimensions: Length on deck, 184 feet 6 inches; beam on deck, 33 feet 6 inches; beam at wheels, 26 ; depth of hold, 16¾ feet; deep drop, 13 feet; displacement at 11 feet draft, 900 tons. *Engines*,—Two iron condensing

outer hulls being longer than the central hull, and the whole decked over and combined as one vessel. The centre vessel is entirely devoted to machinery and has a screw at both ends. The design bears promise of great speed and carrying capacity and great stability, but has not yet been put to a practical trial.

horizontal disconnected engines, built at the Washington Navy-Yard. Diameter of cylinders, 24 feet; strokes of piston, 4 feet.

The Hunter wheel consisted of a plain drum revolving in a horizontal plane beneath the water upon the sides or periphery of this drum; the paddles placed vertically and radically from the centre. In the Hunter wheel the paddles acted in the same manner as the Orsman paddle-wheel, excepting that they revolved horizontally instead of vertically.

"The Union" was rigged as a three-masted schooner, was never off the United States coast, and did but very little steering, and never after several alterations attained a speed of over six knots. Her total cost with alterations was $172,475. Her armament was four 65-pounders mounted in the centre of the vessel on swivels. After various trials she was put in orders and sent to the Philadelphia Navy-Yard, where her machinery and boilers were taken out and sold, and the hull turned into a receiving ship, and finally sold and broken up.

Two other vessels were built for the United States Navy with Hunter's submerged horizontal wheels,—viz., the "Hunter," a small vessel, lost at Sacrificio on her first voyage, in 1841, and the "Allegheny," an iron vessel of large tonnage, but which was only partially a success.

1843.—THE "GREAT BRITAIN."—The keel of the "Great Britain," built at Bristol from designs and on calculations made by Mr. Brunel, was laid down in July, 1839, and launched on the 19th of July, 1843, His Royal Highness Prince Albert, the Prince Consort, honoring the event with his presence. The "Great Britain" was originally intended for a paddle-steamer, but the company having been unable to induce any forge-master to undertake the forgings required for the paddle-shafts, necessity compelled the adoption of the screw-propeller. After her launch she was imprisoned several months in Cumberland dock, Bristol, owing to the locks being narrower than the ship, which necessitated their being widened. She was released from her long and ludicrous durance December 12, 1844, and early in 1845 steamed round to London. Her propeller was fifteen and a half feet in diameter. She was of large dimensions for the time, having an extreme total length of 322 feet, 51 feet width of beam, 32 feet 6 inches depth of hold, and 3448 tons burden by the old measurement. The "Great Britain" was among the first ocean-going steamships built of iron, and also among the first of that now numerous class navigated by a screw propeller. Originally she had six masts, which were afterwards reduced to three. The screw was worked by engines of 1000 horse-power, but were changed to engines of 500 horse-power nominal. She was intended to be employed between Bristol and New York as the companion ship of the "Great Western." Besides being very strongly framed, she was divided into *six water-tight* compartments, which proved their utility when on her voyage from Liverpool to New York, with one hundred

HISTORY OF STEAM NAVIGATION.   187

and eighty-five passengers on board, she was stranded on the 22d of September, 1846, in Dundrum Bay, on the Irish coast, where she lay till the 25th of August, 1847, exposed to all the storms which swept that rugged and tempestuous coast. When floated off she was found to have sustained little or no damage. During the Crimean war she was employed by the British government as a transport, and afterwards run to Australia as a passenger-ship, with machinery and equipments modified to suit the service. She was still on that route in 1876.[1]

The " Great Western" ran regularly between Bristol and New York till the end of 1846. In 1847 she was sold to the West India Royal Mail Steam Packet Company, and was considered one of their best vessels. She was broken up in 1857, at Vauxhall, being unable longer to compete profitably with the new class of steamers.

1838.—THE "LIVERPOOL."—The "Liverpool" was built in the city for which she was named, and was dispatched to New York, October 20, 1838, by Sir John Tobin, a well-known merchant, and put back to Cork, October 26. She again proceeded on her voyage on the 6th of November, and made the passage in sixteen and a half days, arriving at New York November 23. She was at first of 1150 tons, but her tonnage was subsequently increased to 1543, and she obtained the name of the "Great Liverpool." She made in all six voyages to and from New York, when she was transferred to the Peninsula and Oriental Company, and in 1846 was totally wrecked off Cape Finisterre.

1839.—THE "PRESIDENT."—The "President" was launched December 7, 1839, with great *éclat*, and sailed on her first trip to New York August 1, 1840; but her career was very brief, and may be summed up in a few words. When due from New York in April,

---

[1] This vessel, which has a history of more than ordinary interest, was yesterday offered for sale by Mr. C. W. Kellock (Messrs. Kellock & Co.) at their salesroom, Walmer Buildings, Water Street, and the event attracted a very large attendance of gentlemen who are closely identified with the shipping interests of the port. The "Great Britain," lying in the West Float, Birkenhead, was described in the "bill of particulars" as of 3270 gross tonnage, and 1795 tons net register. It is further stated that "she was for many years in the Australian trade, and well-known by her rapid passages as a most successful ship. Her construction is of great strength, and the iron used was Low Moor of the finest quality. For the cattle trade across the Atlantic she is admirably adapted, her high 'tween decks and side ports affording grand ventilation; she can carry live stock on three decks. For a sailing ship her beautiful lines peculiarly adapt her, and with the machinery taken out she is calculated to carry 4000 tons dead weight. Her engines are by J. Penn & Sons, of Greenwich, and are in good condition; her boilers by Fawcett, Preston & Co., of Liverpool; and though this steamer has been built many years, her iron was so good, and strength of construction so great, with a certain outlay she could be made a most desirable merchant ship. Dimensions,—Length over all 325 feet, breadth 50·6 feet, depth 31·5 feet." The bidding began at £2,000, then went to £5,000, and before long £6,500 was offered. There being no advance on this price, Mr. Kellock announced that the vessel was withdrawn.—*Liverpool Mercury*, July 29, 1881.

1841, she failed to make her appearance: tremendous weather having been experienced in the Atlantic, with unusual quantities of ice in very low latitudes, and the greatest anxiety was felt for her safety. She was never again heard of, nor was any trace of her wreck ever discovered. Her figure-head was a bust of Washington after Canova.[1]

1839.—THE "BRITISH QUEEN."—The "British Queen" sailed from Portsmouth, England, on her first trip, July 13, 1839, with a full complement of passengers, a crew of one hundred men, eight hundred tons of goods, and six hundred tons of coal. She cost three hundred thousand dollars, and when leaving the harbor was said to have afloat in her property to the value of seven and a half millions of dollars. She was sold to the Belgian government in 1841.

The "Columbia," of the Cunard Line from Liverpool to New York, was wrecked on the rocks off Seal Island July 2, 1843. No lives lost.

In 1840 Lieutenant Wall, royal navy, communicated interesting papers to the *United Service Journal* "On the Construction, Proportions, and Power best adapted to Sea-going Steam Vessels," in which he presented arguments in favor of building and supplying large steamers with three instead of two engines, and set forth the advantages which would counterbalance the increased expense, weight, and friction of a third cylinder.

The same year M. Scott Russell arrived at this "very remarkable result:" "That in a voyage by a steam-vessel in the open sea, exposed of course to adverse winds, there is a certain high velocity and high portion of power which may be accomplished with less expenditure of fuel and of room than at a lower speed with less power."

The Secretary of the United States navy, in 1840, in his official report, stated that England, in 1836, had six hundred steamers at home and abroad, and in 1840 the number of steamers in the United States was eight hundred, of which six hundred belonged to the Western waters, where in 1834 there were about two hundred and fifty-four. About one hundred and forty belonged to the State of New York. In tonnage, in 1840, the United States had one hundred and fifty-five thousand tons of steam-shipping, and Great Britain sixty-eight thousand.

The Society of Arts awarded Mr. Jennings a silver medal in 1840, for his invention of night signals for steamers. A small iron steamer

---

[1] On the 23d of April, 1841, in lat. 41, long. 70, a Portuguese brig saw a large steamship under sail going about four miles an hour. No smoke issued from the funnels (the "President" had two), and the paddle-wheels were not in motion. The captain of the brig saw the steamer on the following day, and even approached within three or four miles of her while pursuing his homeward route. She did not hail the brig, nor did she appear to be at all in a disabled state. A British man-of-war and two Portuguese vessels were sent to cruise in search of the "President," but without success.

was built in England, appropriately named "The Anthracite," especially adapted to burning that kind of coal.[1]

July 10, 1840, the "Cyclops" steam frigate, "the largest and most powerful steam man-of-war in the world," was launched at the Pembroke Dock-Yard. Her dimensions were: length, 225 feet; beam between paddles, 38 feet; depth of hold, 38 feet; tonnage, 1300. She was two hundred tons larger than the "Gorgon," launched from the same slip two years before. She had a complete gun-deck, as well as an upper or quarter-deck, and on her main deck mounted eighteen long 36-pounders, on the upper deck four 48-pounders and two 96-pounders, "tremendous guns on swivel carriages, carrying a ball ten inches in diameter, and sweeping around the horizon two hundred and forty degrees."

She was commanded by a post-captain, the "Gorgon" being the only steamer in the royal navy at that date taking post rank. Her crew consisted of two hundred and ten men, twenty engineers and stokers, and a lieutenant's party of marines, *who had charge of the guns.* All the guns were mounted upon sliding fixed pivot carriages. She was schooner-rigged, and with six months' stores and twenty days' fuel, drew only fifteen feet of water. Her orlop-deck could store eight hundred troops and their officers with comfort. She was built in six months, on plans of Sir William Symonds, and had engines of three hundred and twenty horse-power.

The steamer "Nicholai," of eight hundred tons, was built at Deptford in 1839, to run between Lubeck and St. Petersburg, and the Messrs. Laid & Woodside, of Liverpool, shipped in sections the hulls of three iron steamboats to be set up in Montevideo.

1838.—THE "COLUMBUS."—The "Columbus," of Liverpool, built in 1838 for transatlantic voyages, was fitted with Howard's *vapor* engine, and hence obtained the name of the "*quicksilver*" steamer. She was brig-rigged, had two very low funnels, and burned *anthracite* coal, so that "no smoke was emitted." She was a vessel of 330 tons, builder's measurement, had 21¼ feet beam, was 145 feet long on her keel, and her depth of hold was 13½ feet; horse-power, 110. She had two 55 feet engines (her cylinder being 40¼ inches in diameter), her piston had 3¼ feet stroke, and her paddle-wheels were 17½ feet in diameter. Her speed was ten and a half statute miles per hour. Her furnace was not applied immediately to the water, but to a pan of quicksilver, which it was proposed to maintain at its boiling-point, but very much above the boiling-point of water. On this surface of hot quicksilver water was injected, which instantly converted into steam containing more heat than was sufficient to maintain it in vaporing form. This superheated steam worked the piston, and being subsequently condensed by a jet of fresh water, the mixture of warm water produced

[1] *Mechanics' Magazine.*

by the steam and the water injected was conducted through the cooling pipes, and subsequently used to supply the water evaporation, thus not only dispensing with the boiler, but also with sea water, the same distilled water constantly circulating through the cylinder and condenser. The experimental results were satisfactory, and a small boat fitted with Howard's engine was plying between London and Richmond during the summer of 1838. The result of the trial of the "Columbus" I have not ascertained, but it was probably unsuccessful, as this is the only notice of "Howard's quicksilver engine" I have been able to find.

1838.—THE "RAINBOW," built by John Laird, of Liverpool, for the General Steam Navigation Company in 1838, was an *iron* steamer of 580 tons, 190 feet between perpendiculars, 25 feet beam between the paddle-boxes, and 12¾ feet depth of hold. Her engines were of 180 horse-power. On one occasion she made the trip between London and Antwerp, a distance of one hundred and ninety nautical miles, in fourteen hours,—the quickest that had been made. On this vessel Professor Airy experimented on the effect of iron on the compass.[1]

1839.—THE "NORTH AMERICA," the first vessel with which it was attempted to open a steam communication between Halifax and Boston, performed the voyage in the autumn of 1839 from one place to the other in thirty-six hours, and on a second trip in twenty-nine hours, with very heavy weather.

1839.—STEAMERS TO INDIA.—The "Queen of the East," an iron steamship, the first of a line of steamers to ply between England and Calcutta, launched in 1839, was an iron ship of 2618 tons and 600 horse-power. Her extreme length was 312 feet, and between the perpendiculars 270 feet; beam, 45 feet; depth of hold, 30 feet; cylinder, 84 inches diameter; 9 feet stroke.

The "India," the first vessel of the India Steam Navigation Company *via* the Cape of Good Hope, was one thousand two hundred tons, and had accommodation for eighty passengers. Her extreme length was two hundred feet; beam forty; depth forty. Her cargo capacity was four hundred tons. She had two plate iron bulkheads across the engine to confine accidental fire and prevent a leak spreading from one division to another. Three additional steamers were on the stocks for this company, and others to be immediately commenced.

1840.—THE "PROSERPINE" war-steamer of four hundred and seventy tons, built in England, 1840, had four sliding keels, nine water-tight bulkheads, two of which were longitudinal, running the entire length of the engine-room, and was armed with four long guns on non-recoil carriages. Her draught was four feet; her two engines were of forty-five horse-power each, and her paddle-wheels could be disconnected.

1840.—THE "PROPELLER," a small steamer with engine of

[1] *Nautical Magazine*, 1829.

twenty-four horse-power, built in England in 1840, had propellers of single blades of iron on each side, broad and large, which dipped into the water perpendicularly. The appearance of the propellers was like that of the legs of grasshoppers, and when in motion their action resembled the legs of that insect in its work.[1]

1841.—THE "CAIRO," built for the navigation of the Nile in 1841, was flat-bottomed to adapt her for the shallow waters of the Nile, having a draught of only two feet. She had two oscillating engines of sixteen horse-power each. She was an iron vessel and divided by water-tight bulkheads, with five compartments, and could accommodate one hundred persons in her cabins. Her average speed was guaranteed by her builders to be fifteen miles an hour.

1841.—THE "FIRE-FLY," of about two horse-power, fitted with a locomotive boiler, vibrating engines, and Ericsson screw propeller, attained a speed of nine miles an hour on the Thames at Oxford.

1839.—SCREW STEAMER "R. F. STOCKTON."—January 29, 1839, the "R. F. Stockton" (screw) towed the American packet-ship "Toronto," six hundred and fifty tons, and drawing sixteen and three-quarters feet of water, from Blackwall to the lower points of Woolwich, three and a quarter miles, in forty minutes, against a flood-tide running two to two and a half miles an hour.

"The fact of this ship having been moved at the rate of upward of six miles an hour, by a propeller measuring only six feet four inches in diameter, and occupying less than three feet in length, is one which, scientifically considered, as well as in a practical and commercial point of view, is of immense importance."[2]

1840.—THE "NEMESIS."—Captain W. H. Hall sailed from Portsmouth in the "Nemesis," March 28, 1840. She was the first iron steamer that ever rounded the Cape of Good Hope. She arrived at Table Bay July 1, left on the 11th, but meeting with severe gales, put into English River, Delagoa Bay, to refit, which occupied three weeks, when she resumed her voyage up the Mozambique Channel to India and China, where she performed gallant service. She was one hundred and sixty-eight feet long, twenty-nine feet beam, and six hundred and fifty tons burthen. She was fitted with five water-tight compartments.

The "Archimedes," an iron screw steamer, in 1840 made an experimental trip around the island of Great Britain, or seventeen hundred and twenty-two miles in two hundred and ten hours, being on an average about eight and a half miles an hour.

The "Archimedes" was built by F. P. Smith's Archimedean Screw Propeller Company. After the experimental trials were over the engines were taken out and she was sold for a sailing-vessel.[3]

---

[1] *London Times*, Oct. 10, 1840.
[2] Timbs, in the Year-Book of Facts for 1840.
[3] See *ante*, Chapter III.

The first application of Hall's reefing paddle-wheels was to the iron steamer "Lee," in 1840.

COMPOUND ENGINES, 1829–1839.—A comparatively little known work, by C. A. Tremtsuk, published at Bordeaux in 1842, contains some interesting particulars of the steamers plying at that time on the Gironde and the Garonne. One of these vessels, the "Union," launched in June, 1829, had a compound-engine constructed by Hallette, of Arras. This engine had two inclined cylinders, the connecting-rods taking hold of the same crank-pin. The cylinders had diameters of 15 and 15.8 inches respectively, and the stroke in each instance was 26 inches. The engine was run at thirty revolutions a minute under a pressure of sixty-six pounds of steam. Another example of an early compound engine was in use in 1842 on board the steamer "Le Corsaire Noir." It was built in 1837 by Fol, Sr., of Bordeaux, and had three oscillating cylinders, two of them being each 10.78 inches in diameter, with 39.4 inches stroke, and the third having a diameter of 21.27 inches, with a stroke of 32 inches. The three cylinders acted on three different cranks. The two smaller cylinders received the steam from the boiler at a pressure of seventy-four pounds, and discharged it into an intermediate receiver, from which it passed to the large cylinder and then to the condenser.[1]

1839.—The steamer "Argyle" sailed from Liverpool April 6, 1839, for New Orleans *via* Cadiz and Madeira; and the "Chili" sailed from Falmouth, and the "Peru" from London, July 2, 1839, for Valparaiso and Callao *via* Rio Janeiro.

1839.—THE FIRST TRIAL OF STEAMERS IN BATTLE.—The attack upon St. Jean d'Acre, November 3, 1839, by the allied squadrons of England, Austria, and Turkey, under the command of Commodore Sir Charles Napier, was the first occasion on which the advantages of steam was tried in battle. Four English paddle-wheel steamers—viz., the "Phœnix," "Gorgon," "Stromboli," and "Vesuvius"—were engaged in the action, and the shells thrown from them did prodigious execution; they were enabled with rapidity to take up the most advantageous positions and rendered great assistance during the bombardment.

1840.—A VESSEL PROPELLED BY PRESSURE-PUMPS.—The Edinburgh *Observer* of 1840 says, "An ingenious mechanic residing at Grahamstown has been for a long period engaged in constructing a small vessel to be propelled by pressure-pumps. The boat was launched into the Forth and Clyde Canal at Bainsford Bridge, and proceeded along the reach at a rate of not less than fifteen miles per hour, con-

---

[1] Benjamin, in his paper on "Ocean Steamships," in the *Century*, September, 1882, says, "The compound engine was invented by Hornblower in 1781." Also "that Allaire made such an engine for Eckford in 1825."

Hornblower's engine is not mentioned in the Abridgment of Patents for Marine Propulsion, published by the British Patent Office.

ducted by the inventor alone, who worked the pumps. He had no doubt that his invention would entirely supersede the use of paddle-wheels."

The London *Morning Chronicle* for 1840 says, "Experiments were tried with a model of an entirely new form of steam-vessel, and with every prospect of a successful result. In this remarkable invention there are no paddle-wheels nor external work of any kind. The whole machinery is in the hold of the vessel, where a horizontal wheel is moved by the power of steam, and, acting upon a current of water admitted by the bows and thrown off at the stern, propels the vessel at a rapid rate. By a very simple contrivance of stop-cocks, etc., on the apparatus, the steamer can be turned, retarded, stopped, or have her motion reversed."

An officer of the United States navy obtained a patent in 1840 for a similar improvement; his model was examined by scientific gentlemen in Washington, who highly approved of it. The whole machinery was situated below the water-line, out of reach of shot.

1840.—THE CUNARD LINE ESTABLISHED.—Samuel Cunard, of Halifax, in 1840, started the line of ocean steamers known by his name. It was the first permanently successful line of transatlantic steamers. The "Britannia," the first regular steamer of the line, left Liverpool, July 4, 1840, and arrived at Boston, July 18, 1840, fourteen days and eight hours from Liverpool.

Cunard had for years conducted a line of packet-brigs between Halifax and England,—tub-like vessels widely known as coffins, several having foundered under the wintry waves of the Atlantic. Mr. Cunard accepted a subsidy and laid the keels of four steamers of eight hundred tons to run from Halifax to Boston. On his return by the "Great Western" he was encountered at Bristol by news from America. Resolutions favoring the enterprise had been presented at a large meeting in Boston and adopted by acclamation. With these in hand, Cunard waited on the Admiralty. "See," he says, "my predictions are verified. I told you the boats were too small; the Bostonians say they must come through to Boston, and that they will settle the question of the Northeast boundary. Give me ten thousand pounds more and I will enlarge the steamers and extend my route to Boston." They gave him the additional sum; he went back to Glasgow, broke up the keels already laid, and built the "Britannia," "Acadia," "Caledonia," and "Columbia," the pioneers of his line to America. The "Unicorn," a chartered vessel, was the first vessel of the Cunard line to cross the Atlantic, but the "Britannia" was the first regular vessel to arrive at Boston.

1842.—The paddle-wheel steamer "Bangor," from Boston, *via* Halifax and Pictou, arrived at Fayal on the 19th September, 1842, in ten days from the latter port, and left on the 21st for Constantinople, touching at Gibraltar and Malta. She was at one time the steam-yacht of the Sultan, and later employed in conveying Mohammedan pilgrims towards Mecca. She was a side-wheel steamer, built in New York to ply between Boston, Portland, and Bangor, Maine, and was some time on that route. On her voyage to Gibraltar her lower cabins were converted into coal-bunkers and her upper cabins removed.

1840.—THE FRENCH STEAM NAVY.—The French steam navy in 1840 consisted of the following paddle-wheel steamers,—viz., the "Lavoisier," 220 horse-power; "Véloce," 220; "Caméléon," 220; "Gassendi," 220; "Majeur," 160; "Sphinx," 160; "Ardent," 160; "Crocodile," 160; "Fulton," 160; "Chimère," 160; "Styx," 160; "Météore," 160; "Vulture," 160; "Phare," 160; "Achéron," 160; "Papin," 160; "Cerberus," 160; "Tartar," 160; "Etna," 160; "Brandon," 160; "Cocytes," 160; "Phaéton," 160; "Tonnerre," 160; "Euphrates," 160; "Grégeois," 160; "Grondeur," 160; "Ramier," 150; "Castor," 150; "Brasier," 100; "Coureur," 80; "Flambeau," 80; "Corsair," 60; "Erebus," 60; "African," 40; and seven other boats on the stocks,—viz., the "Asmodeus," "Pluto," "Infernal," "Gomore," "Tonare," "Cuvier," and "Chaptal," which gave France an effective force of forty-one steamboats, whilst the English had nearly twice as many. The "Gomore," of four hundred and fifty horse-power, was to carry thirty-four guns under a covered battery, and the "Infernal" was of three hundred and twenty horse-power.

On the other hand, the English had the "Cyclops," which could mount sixteen long thirty-twos, four pieces of forty-eight on its quarter-deck, and two of ninety-six,—twenty-two guns in all. She could carry coal for twenty-five days' steaming, and take one thousand soldiers on her deck, four hundred troops across the Atlantic, or three hundred to India. Her usual rate of sailing was eleven knots an hour. She beat in sailing, and without using the engine, the "Pantaloon," the fastest sailing brig in the royal navy, in a passage of three hundred miles. Her crew comprised two hundred and twenty seamen in time of war, and one hundred and seventy-three during peace. Independent of her war steamboats, Great Britain had immense resources in her commercial steam navy, which consisted of eight hundred and ninety-nine steamboats, aggregating a force of sixty-eight thousand one hundred and forty-five horse-power. Among these were thirty-three steamboats, of from four hundred and fifty to seven hundred horse-power, which traded to the United States, South America, and India.

1842.—EARLY SCREW STEAMERS IN GREAT BRITAIN.—The London *Nautical Magazine* for 1842 notes the following vessels with *screw propellers* as having been built or then being built in Great Britain,—viz.:

HISTORY OF STEAM NAVIGATION.

ALREADY BUILT.

"Archimedes," 237 tons, 70 horse-power, belonging to London.
"Princess Royal," 101   "   45   "   "   Brighton.
"Bee,"   80   "   10   "   "   Portsmouth.
"Beddington," 270   "   60   "   "   South Shields.
"Novelty," 300   "   25   "   "   London.

BUILDING.

"Great Britain," 3600 tons, 1000 horse-power, belonging to Bristol.
"Rattler,"   800   "   200   "   "   "
Two for the French government of 230 horse-power.
One   "   "   "   " 350   "

Propellers had been fitted to other vessels with various success. The old river steamer "Swiftsure" was fitted with one, and an increased speed attained by it. The "Great Britain" is described as the "largest vessel in the world;" but the most notable feature about her is her newly-improved screw-propeller, patented by Mr. Smith, of London, and applied by him with complete success to the "Archimedes."

Henry Winhault, who launched the "Novelty" on the Thames, in 1843, claims she was the first screw propeller ever used to carry freight.

The "Napoleon," of one hundred and thirty horse-power, built in Havre in 1842, was the first French steamer propelled by the screw.

In 1842 steam navigation was established on the Indus. The iron steamers "Planet" and "Satellite," originally intended for the Rhine, were purchased by the East India Company, sent out in sections, and put together in the dock-yards in Bombay. In 1844–45 the "Napier," "Conqueror," and "Menace" were added to the line; all these had engines of sixty horse-power.

In 1842 her Britannic Majesty's steamship "Driver" circumnavigated the globe, the first steamship to perform this feat.

1841.—THE FIRST STEAM LAUNCH.—The "Jane," a steamer twenty-six feet long, with five feet beam, and of less than three tons tonnage and one horse-power, attained in smooth water a speed of seven miles an hour. She was built by Mr. Blaxand, of Greenwich, and her propelling power was two screw paddles at the stern. The machinery was worked by straps and friction-pulleys, so arranged as to avoid the wear and tear of gears.

1842.—Captain Carpenter, of her Majesty's steamship "Geyser," in 1842 had her pinnace fitted with his patent propeller and a small engine of five to six horse-power. The pinnace was thirty feet in length, nine feet wide, and capable of carrying three tons. Her "disk" engine weighed six hundredweight, and measured three feet by one and a half. The engine and boiler were so fitted to the pinnace that they could be taken out or replaced in five minutes.

1841.—An Ice-Cutting Steamboat was invented by M. C. Hiorth, a Dane, in 1841, which could cut its way through the thickest ice with a speed nearly equal to that of an unimpeded navigation.

1843.—The "Princeton."—Screw propulsion was introduced into the United States navy, and, it may be said, into the United States, in 1843 by the construction of the "Princeton," a steamship classed as a second-rate sloop-of-war.

This vessel was designed by and constructed under the superintendence of Captain John Ericsson, a Swede by birth, but a resident of New York. *She was the first screw steam war-vessel ever built.*[1]

Her dimensions were:

Length on deck	164 feet.	
Length between perpendiculars	156 "	
Extreme beam on deck	30 "	6 inches.
Depth of hold to berth-deck	14 "	
Depth from berth to spar-deck	7 "	"
Total depth of vessel	21 "	"
Measurement burden	673 tons.	
Launching weight of hull	418 "	
Displacement at 16¼ feet draught	954 "	
" " 18 " "	1046 "	"
Immersed midship section at 16¼ feet draught	846 square feet.	
" " " " 18 " "	390 "	"
Draught of water at deepest load, with 200 tons of coal on board	19 feet 4 inches.	
Draught of water, with 100 tons of coal in, after bunkers and provisions and water for the crew half out	forward 14¾ feet. aft 18¼ "	
Mean draught of water with half coal out and all other weights full	17 feet.	

The peculiarity of her model consisted in a very flat floor amidships, with great sharpness forward and excessive leanness aft, the run being remarkably fine, with a great extent of dead-wood terminating in a stern-post of the unusual thickness of twenty-six inches at the centre of the propeller-shaft, but tapering above and below. This deadwood and stern-post was pierced by a hole thirteen inches in diameter.

Other of her peculiarities were that for the *first time in a vessel of war all of her machinery was placed entirely below the water-line, out of reach of shot.* She was also the first war-steamer to burn anthracite coal, thus avoiding the dense volumes of black smoke which revealed all foreign war-steamers. She was also the first steamer provided with telescopic funnels, to be lowered out of the way of the sails, and the first to use blowers. She was provided with direct-acting engines. Ericsson, who devised her, was the first also to couple the screw directly to the engine.

An eye-witness has described a remarkable race between the "Princeton" and the "Great Western," the fastest ocean paddle-wheel steamer of the day. The "Great Western" was aware that the new

---

[1] Her Majesty's ship "Rattler," the second screw war-vessel, was launched after the "Princeton."

HISTORY OF STEAM NAVIGATION. 197

United States war-vessel propelled by an unseen instrument intended to run with her a sufficient distance for a fair trial of the relative speed of the two vessels, and was therefore fully prepared.

On the day in question, shortly after the "Great Western" had passed the Battery in the New York harbor, with volumes of dense smoke pouring from her pipe, her paddle-wheels leaving a snow-white wake behind them, the "Princeton" came down the Hudson at great speed. She looked like a fine model of a sailing-ship, with yards squared and not a stitch of canvas spread; no smoke-pipe visible, it being lowered level with the rail; no smoke to be seen, anthracite being the fuel supplied, but propelled by a noiseless and unseen agency. She soon reached and passed the "Great Western" and steamed around her, and passed her a second time before the two reached their points of final separation.

Captain Stockton, who may be said to have been her originator, superintended her construction and was her first captain. In a letter to the Secretary of the Navy, he thus describes the "Princeton."

UNITED STATES SHIP "PRINCETON,"
PHILADELPHIA, February 5, 1844.

SIR,—The United States ship "Princeton" having received her armament on board, and, being nearly ready for sea, I have the honor to transmit to you the following account of her equipment, etc.:

The "Princeton" is a full-rigged ship of great speed and power, able to perform any service that can be expected from a ship of war. Constructed upon the most approved principles of naval architecture, she is believed to be at least equal to any ship of her class with her sail, and she has an auxiliary power of steam, and can make greater speed than any sea-going steamer or other vessel heretofore built. Her engines lie snug in the bottom of the vessel, out of reach of an enemy's shot, and do not at all interfere with the use of the sails, but can at any time be made auxiliary thereto. She shows no chimney and makes no smoke, and there is nothing in her external appearance to indicate that she is propelled by steam.

The advantages of the "Princeton" over both sailing-ships and steamers propelled in the usual way are great and obvious. She can go in and out of port at pleasure, without regard to the force or direction of the wind or tide or the thickness of the ice. She can ride safely with her anchors in the most open roadstead, and may lie to in the severest gale of wind with safety. She cannot only save herself, but will be able to tow a squadron from the dangers of a lee shore. Using ordinarily the power of the wind and reserving her fuel for emergencies, she can remain at sea the same length of time as other sailing-ships. Making no noise, smoke, or agitation of the water (and, if she chooses, showing no sail) she can surprise an enemy. She can take her own position and her own distance from an enemy. Her engines and water-wheel being below the surface of the water, safe from an enemy's shot, she is in no danger of being disabled, even if her masts should be destroyed. She will not be at daily expense for fuel as other steam-ships are. The engines, being seldom used, will probably outlast two such ships. These advantages make the "Princeton," in my opinion, the cheapest, fastest, and most certain ship-of-war in the world.

The equipments of this ship are of the plainest and most substantial kind, the furniture of the cabins being made of white pine boards, painted white, with mahogany chairs, table, and side-board, and an American manufactured oil-cloth on the floor.

To economize room, and that the ship may be better ventilated, curtains of American manufactured linen are substituted for the usual and more customary and expensive wooden bulkheads, by which arrangement the apartments of the men and officers may in an instant be thrown into one, and a degree of spaciousness and comfort is attained unusual in a vessel of her class.

The "Princeton" is armed with two long 225-pounder wrought-iron guns and twelve 42-pounder carronades, all of which may be used at once on either side of the ship. She can consequently throw a greater weight of metal at one broadside than most frigates. The big guns of the "Princeton" can be fired with an effect terrific and almost incredible, and with a certainty heretofore unknown. The extraordinary effects of the shot were proved by firing at a target, which was made to represent a section of the two sides and deck of a 74-gun ship, and timbered, kneed, planked, and bolted in the same manner. This target was five hundred and sixty yards from the gun. With the smaller charges of powder the shot passed through these immense masses of timber (being fifty-seven inches thick), tearing it away and splintering it for several feet on each side and covering the whole surface of the ground for a hundred yards square with fragments of wood and iron. The accuracy with which these guns throw their immense shot (which are *three feet* in circumference) may be judged by this: the six shots fired in succession at the same elevation struck the same horizontal plank more than half a mile distant. By the application of the various arts to the purposes of war on board the "Princeton," it is believed that the art of gunnery for sea service has for the first time been reduced to something like mathematical certainty. The distances to which these guns can throw their shot at every necessary angle of elevation has been ascertained by a series of careful experiments. The distance from the ship to any object is readily ascertained with an instrument on board, contrived for that purpose by an observation which it requires but an instant to make, and by inspection without calculation. By self-acting locks the guns can be fired accurately at the necessary elevation, no matter what the motion of the ship may be. It is confidently believed that this small ship will be able to battle with any vessel, however large, if she is not invincible against any foe. The improvements in the art of war adopted on board the "Princeton" may be productive of more important results than anything that has occurred since the invention of gunpowder. The numerical force of other navies, so long boasted, may be set at naught. The ocean may again become neutral ground, and the rights of the smallest as well as the greatest nations may once more be respected. All of which, for the honor and defense of every inch of our territory, is most respectfully submitted to the honorable Secretary of the Navy, for the information of the President and Congress of the United States.

By your obedient and faithful servant,

R. F. STOCKTON,
Captain U. S. Navy.

To Hon. DAVID HENSHAW,
Secretary of the Navy.

The "Arrogant," the first war-propeller vessel planned as such by the English,[1] four or five years after the date of the United States steamer "Princeton," had cylinders of nearly the same capacity as her American prototype, yet her engines occupied two thousand eight hundred and twelve cubic feet, while those of the "Princeton" occupied but seventeen hundred and thirty-eight feet. The "Princeton's" en-

---

[1] The "Rattler" was originally laid down for a paddle-wheel steamer, and her plans changed on the stocks to a screw.

HISTORY OF STEAM NAVIGATION. 199

gines weighed eighty-five tons; the "Arrogant's," built by the eminent engineer, Penn, were much heavier.

The hull of the "Princeton," having been built of white oak, was found to be too rotten for repair in 1849 and was broken up. Her performance was not excelled by any screw steamer of her time, relatively with the fuel she consumed. At sea she worked and steered admirably, either under sail alone or with sail and steam. She was a very dry vessel, but, owing to the sharpness of her hull fore and aft the midship section, she pitched in a rough sea with great violence. With a fair amount of canvas and a moderate wind she would careen to an extent unusual in a vessel of her class, but, though she thus easily went down to her bearings, it took additionally a very large quantity of canvas and a strong wind to depress her sensibly further. In a heavy gale clawing off a lee shore she carried sail to a greater extent than was considered prudent by other sailing sloops of war in her company; all of them, and some frigates, she beat out to windward, dragging her propeller.

After the hull was broken up the machinery of the vessel remained in store at the Boston Navy-Yard until the summer of 1851, when the department ordered a new clipper hull to be built at that yard, of increased dimensions, to receive the Ericsson semicylinder engines, to have new boilers, and a propeller of suitable proportions for this enlarged "Princeton." The new vessel, built of live oak and copper fastened, was beautiful to look at, but her performance did not equal expectation. It was a case of putting old wine into new bottles. She performed very little service at sea, was used as a receiving vessel at Philadelphia, and was sold in that city in 1867. Her armament was four 8-inch guns of 58 hundredweight and six 30-pounder guns of 82 hundredweight. Her dimensions were: Mean length at loadline, 177.5 feet; extreme beam, 32.66 feet; depth, 25.75 feet; displacement at mean load-line, 1370 gross tons. She was ship-rigged.

1840.—The Royal Steam Navy in 1840 consisted of between thirty-eight and fifty paddle-wheel steam-vessels of all classes. During the next three years—1842-44—eight screw vessels were *ordered* to be built, but the "Rattler" was the first that was launched. This number was augmented by twenty-six in 1845. In 1848 there were forty-five screw steamers in the Royal Navy.

In 1845 the Queen reviewed the channel fleet, the *steam* branch being on that occasion represented by one solitary ship, the "*Rattler*," the first screw steamship added to the Royal Navy. In 1853, when the Queen again reviewed the fleet at Spithead, the steam branch had increased in the intervening eight years to twenty-seven paddle-wheels and thirteen screws, while there were only three sailing-ships present.

An official report of the result of various trials of the performance of screw steamers, dated May, 1850, states it "as highly probable that fine sailing-vessels, fitted with auxiliary screw-power, would be able, if not to rival, at least to approach full-powered and expansively-acting steamships in respect of their capability of making a long voyage with certainty and in a reasonably short time." "Another application of the screw, although inferior in general importance to its application as a propeller to ordinary ships," says the same report, "is as a manœuvrer to those large ships in which engines of considerable power cannot be placed, or in which it is considered unadvisable to place them. No doubt can be entertained of the efficiency of such an instrument worked by an engine of even fifty horse-power. The full extent of its utility, however, cannot perhaps be thoroughly appreciated until it shall have been extensively used in Her Majesty's navy."

1843.—The H. M. S. "RATTLER," the first screw vessel of war of the Royal Navy, was ordered to be altered when on the stocks to test the method of screw propulsion. She seems to have been built to see if a propeller would really propel a vessel. Her engines were a set of ordinary paddle-wheel engines attached to the screw by means of gearing, and of course projecting above the water-line. That the experiment might be conclusive, so far as a trial could be made between two vessels, she was constructed on the same lines as the "Alecto" (her afterpart being lengthened for the insertion of the screw), and she was fitted with engines of the same power, and on a plan which had previously been tried with paddle-wheel vessels. So doubtful were the Lords of the Admiralty of her success that the space on her broadside where paddle-wheels were usually inserted was kept clear of gun-ports that wheelhouses might be appended in case of the non-success of her screw; and this was the state of her broadside when she was in China, in 1853-54.[1]

The "Rattler" was launched from Sheerness Dock-Yard in April, 1843. She was considered a remarkably fine model, and of very unusual length in proportion to her beam, her dimensions being one hundred and ninety-five feet extreme length, thirty-three feet extreme breadth, and eighteen and one-half feet mean depth of hold. Her burden was eight hundred and eighty-eight tons. The river trials of the "Rattler" lasted from October, 1843, to the beginning of 1845, and showed that the screw-shaft might be advantageously reduced in diameter, and the blades reduced by one-third of their length; an alteration which greatly reduced the weight of the screw, and facilitated the shipping and unshipping of it, and also rendered unnecessary the wounding or weakening to so great an extent the after part of the vessel. The result of the experiments with the "Rattler" was that the aperture in future vessels might be of very moderate dimensions without lessening the propelling power of the screw, and that in smooth water the screw was not inferior to the paddle-wheel. Early in 1845

---

[1] My informant of this fact was Captain Abel Fellowes, R. N., who commanded her at that time.

the "Rattler" proceeded, in company with the "Victoria and Albert" and the "Black Eagle," from Portsmouth to Pembroke. When rounding Land's End, both these vessels steaming against a strong headwind, their paddles being constructed on the feathering principle, proved superior to the "Rattler," which left an unfavorable impression as to the efficiency of the screw against wind and sea in heavy weather, and this impression continued for several years, although when next tried, in a run from the Thames to Leith, in speed she was decidedly superior to paddle-wheel steamers of greater tonnage. Before joining the squadron of Rear-Admiral Hyde Parker, in July, 1845, the "Rattler" was employed to tow the "Erebus" and "Terror" to the Orkney Islands on their fatal expeditions to the North Pole.

In 1843 Count Adolph E. de Rosen, the agent of Ericsson, received an order from the French government to fit a forty-four gun frigate, the "Pomone," with an Ericsson propeller with engines of two hundred and twenty horse-power, which were to be located beneath the water-line, as in the case of the "Princeton." The next year the English government gave Count Rosen instructions to fit the frigate "Amphion" with a propeller and with engines of three hundred horse-power, which were to be fixed below the water-line like those of the French "Pomone." The engines of these vessels were the first engines in Europe which were kept below the water-line. They were also the first *direct acting* horizontal engines employed to give motion to the screw. Both vessels were completely successful.[1][2]

When the screw propeller was first tried in the British navy it was not supposed by anybody that the small section at present used would be enough; it might for anything that was then decided be a screw of one complete turn upon its axis. Upon that supposition the "Rattler" was lengthened by the stern sufficiently for a long aperture; in consequence the run at the fore part of the aperture was constructed of such a degree of fineness as to be most favorable to the efficacy of the screw. The correctness of form in this case was purely accidental.

1844.—THE FIRST STEAM WHISTLE ON THE MISSOURI.—The use of the steam-whistle on the Missouri River dates back to 1844. At that time the settlers on the Missouri River were in the habit of making yearly visits to St. Louis to do their trading for themselves and friends. They were not provided with daily intercourse with the outside world, and many who lived back from the river seldom if ever saw a steamboat more than once a year. During the fall of the year 1844 the new steamboat "Lexington" started up the Missouri River loaded down to the guards with freight. Among the passengers were Judge Joseph C. Ransom, Theodore Warner, of Lexington, and Ben Holliday, afterwards the famous overland stage proprietor; Colonel

---

[1] Bourne on the screw propeller.   [2] See page 157.

Pomeroy, of Lexington, and a planter of Platte County, named George Yocum.

The steamer "Lexington" was provided with a steam-whistle,—the first used on the Missouri,—and no one knew about it except Warner, who was a wag and a lover of a joke. The night after leaving St. Louis the passengers were collected together playing cards in the cabin, when the talk turned upon steamboat explosions, then very common. "I feel perfectly safe on this boat," said Warner, as he dealt the cards.

"Why?" inquired Yocum, the planter.

"Why?" echoed the rest of the company.

"I will tell you why," said the wag, carefully studying his cards; "this boat is provided with a new patent safety-valve, which notifies the passengers on board when it is about to blow up. It is a concern which makes a most unearthly noise, and when you hear it, it is time to get back aft or jump overboard."

Notwithstanding that Warner told his story with the most solemn and earnest countenance, some were skeptical. Not so, however, the planter. Next morning, when the "Lexington" was steaming up the straight stretch of river below Washington, Missouri, the passengers were at breakfast, and busily engaged in doing justice to the meal. Suddenly the whistle commenced to blow for the first time on the trip. The passengers looked at each other a moment, and horror and dismay spread itself over their faces. The first man to realize the situation was Yocum, the planter, who, with hair erect and blanched face, jumped up, crying,—

"Run, run for your lives; the derned thing's going to bust. Follow me, and let's save ourselves."

Of course, there was a stampede for the rear of the boat, and it was only by the exertions of some of the crew that the more excited were restrained from jumping into the river.

1844.—THE FIRST ENGLISH STEAM COLLIER was built in 1844. She was bark-rigged. The "King Coal," as she is appropriately called, one of the latest, was contracted for in 1870, and cost complete for sea fifteen thousand pounds. She carries nine hundred tons coal cargo, with burden space for one hundred tons more, and has extra water-ballast when she has no cargo on board; against strong winds her speed is eight and a half knots an hour loaded, and from nine and a half to ten knots in fine weather when light; her power, ninety horse-power, nominal. She has a saloon-cabin on deck for the captain, with four berths aft, and accommodation for chief mate and steward forward. Her crew, all told, is seventeen. Her voyages from New Castle to London and back usually occupy six to eight days. Hoisting sails, lifting the anchor, and other heavy work are done by steam winches. The crew have a roomy and well-ventilated forecastle level with the main-deck; the seamen occupy one side, the stokers the other, with a bulkhead between. The engineers have cabins on deck in the bridge-house. The wheel-house is amidship and the helmsman is protected from the weather.

The ordinary sailing collier delivered in the course of the year under the most favorable circumstances three thousand five hundred tons of coal. The screw collier, with a complement, all told, of seventeen men, conveys annually, on the same round, fifty thousand tons. Steam colliers have been generally adopted in the United States, and the Reading Company has quite a fleet of them.

1844.—Steam propellers, carrying principally freight, but some passengers, commenced navigating Long Island Sound in 1844. The first was called the "Quinebaug."

1844.—THE "MIDAS."—The propeller schooner "Midas," Captain William Poor, owned by R. B. Forbes, of Boston, left New York for China, November 18, 1844. She was the first American steam vessel that passed beyond the Cape of Good Hope, and was the first American screw steamer to ply in the waters of China. She was disabled by neglect to her boilers, and came home *via* Rio Janeiro under sail, and ran for a long time after between Savannah and Rio Janeiro as a sailing-vessel.

1845.—THE "EDITH."—The propeller bark "Edith," Captain George W. Lewis, owned by R. B. Forbes, left New York for Bombay and China January 18, 1845. She proceeded from Bombay to China in twenty-one and one-half days, beating all competitors. She was the first American steamer that visited British India, and the first square-rigged propeller that went to China under the American flag. She was purchased by the United States government during the war with Mexico, and after running in the Gulf of Mexico for a year went around Cape Horn, and was lost near St. Barbara, on the coast of California.

THE "IRON WITCH."—In April, 1845, R. B. Forbes contracted with Ericsson to build an iron paddle-wheel steamer of great speed, called the "Iron Witch." She was about three hundred feet long, and was the first *iron* passenger steamer that plied on the North River. She had side propellers in place of paddles, but was not fast enough to compete with the Albany boats. Her engines were, therefore, taken out and put into a wooden vessel called the "Falcon," which was bought by George Law, and was the first steamer under the American flag that plied to Chagres, in connection with the California route.[1]

1845.—AUXILIARY STEAMSHIPS FOR THE ROYAL NAVY ORDERED.—The commissioners appointed to inquire into the state of the national defenses of Great Britain recommended that several ships of the line should be fitted with steam machinery and screw propellers, and the Board of Admiralty in 1845 issued an order to prepare the

[1] See account of George Law's line in succeeding pages.

"Blenheim," "Ajax," "Edinburgh," and "Hague," 72-gun ships, for adaptation to screw steamers. Four 42-gun frigates were ordered to be similarly prepared. The "Blenheim" was lengthened and altered at an outlay of above forty-three thousand pounds on her hull, and twenty-five thousand pounds for machinery before she was completed as a guard ship. The expense of altering and adapting the other vessels was much less.

The term "auxiliary," which has been found a most convenient application when a steam vessel does not come up to the anticipated speed, came from England, and in the British navy was never designed for new vessels, but only for those sailing vessels already built which could not be driven beyond a moderate speed. The screw was added to save condemnation.

1845.—THE "EREBUS" AND "TERROR."—The two vessels of Captain Franklin's ill-fated expedition in search of the Northwest passage, which sailed from England on the Queen's birthday, May 24, 1845, were provided with a small steam-engine and screw, intended for use in calms.

1845.—Early in 1841, Thomas Butler King, of Georgia, for many years chairman of the committee of the United States House of Representatives on naval affairs, introduced a resolution directing the Secretary of the Navy to advertise for proposals for mail steamships to European ports, and for a coastwise line between the North and South. Persevering in his efforts from session to session, he succeeded in having a bill passed in 1845 placing the arrangement for the transportation of the mails to foreign countries under the direction of the Postmaster-General, and authorizing him to solicit proposals for several routes. This led to the formation of the Ocean Steam Navigation Company of New York, which in 1847 built and placed the "Washington" and the "Hermann" on the route to Southampton and Bremen. They were the first American ocean steamships after the "Savannah," and at the time of their construction the best specimens of sea steamers our constructors and engineers had produced. Their average passages from Cowes to New York were thirteen days, fourteen hours, and fifty-three minutes; from New York to Cowes, fourteen days, seven hours, and seventeen minutes. The contract between this "Ocean Steam Navigation Company" and the United States was for them to carry the United States mails between New York and Bremen twice a month, touching at Cowes, the compensation to be two hundred thousand dollars per annum. The two steamships were two hundred and twenty-four feet long, thirty-nine feet broad, and twenty-nine feet deep, and measured seventeen hundred tons. At the expiration of the contract the line was discontinued, the steamers were sold, and transferred to the Pacific, where in 1863 the "Hermann" was broken up, and a few years later the "Washington" was wrecked.

HISTORY OF STEAM NAVIGATION. 205

1845.—THE UNITED STATES STEAMER "WATER WITCH."—The first iron steamer built for the United States navy was the "Water Witch." She was intended as a water-tank to supply the vessels of the Portsmouth (Va.) Navy-York with water, and was originally fitted with Hunter's horizontal submerged wheels. She proved too large for the purpose intended, and was then fitted for a harbor vessel and tug. Her performance not being satisfactory, she was taken to Philadelphia, cut in two, and lengthened thirty feet at the centre, the width being also increased six inches. The whole machinery was taken out and she was fitted with a Losser propeller. In 1849 she was again fitted with entirely new machinery, without alteration of hull, and fitted with ordinary paddle-wheels at the sides. In 1852 the iron hull, as originally constructed, proving too narrow for an efficient and safe war steamer, it was used as a target for experiment gun-practice at Washington, and a new one of wood of enlarged proportions and greater strength was ordered by the Department. Thus, like the boy's jack-knife that by repairs was changed, both blades and handle, until it was questionable whether he could call it the old knife or a new one, the iron submerged wheel, water-tank, propeller, and paddle-wheel steamer "Water Witch" became at last a wooden paddle-wheel boat of increased dimensions, having both a new hull and new engines. She was finally surprised and captured by the rebels during our Civil War and destroyed by them.

1845.—THE "MASSACHUSETTS."—Captain R. B. Forbes says, "In 1845 I built the auxiliary steam propeller 'Massachusetts' for myself and others, and sailed in her on the 15th of September, or thereabouts, from New York for Liverpool, and arrived on the 2d of October, having used steam nearly eleven days out of seventeen and a half. This was the first packet-ship under steam that started and performed more than one complete voyage between the United States and England under the American flag, and was the first propeller that was put into the trade." The propeller "Marmora" went to England before the "Massachusetts," on her way to the Mediterranean, and the steamer "Bangor" (paddle), which had been a packet between Boston and Portland, Maine, went to Gibraltar; but the "Massachusetts" was the first regular steam packet-ship between the United States and England under our flag.

The propeller of the "Massachusetts"[1] was of composition metal, nine feet in diameter. She had two cylinders of 17,640 cubic inches each, set at right angles. The propeller was contrived to take out of the water at pleasure, and when out of water the ship was a perfect sailing-ship of about seven hundred tons. She made two voyages from New York to Liverpool and back, and was then chartered, and after-

[1] Portraits of the "Massachusetts" and "Edith" are preserved in the Naval Library and Institute at the Boston Navy-Yard.

wards sold to the War Department. General Scott had his flag on board the "Massachusetts" at the taking of Vera Cruz. She was transferred to the Navy Department and went through the Straits of Magellan to California.

During the Civil War her engines, which were designed by Ericsson, were taken out and she was refitted as a storeship and renamed the "Farralones." After the war she was sold in San Francisco and renamed the "Alaska," and was engaged in carrying wheat from that port to Liverpool, and, for aught I know, "still lives."

1846.—STEAMBOATS ON THE THAMES.—In 1846 there were eleven steamboats running between London and Westminster Bridges on the Thames at *one penny* the trip, making thirty-two trips in the hour, or three hundred and twenty trips per diem. Assuming forty as the average number of passengers for each trip, the daily total would be fifteen thousand, and the return trip being the same, one hundred and twenty-five pounds was about the daily receipts of these boats. The time of each trip varied from one-quarter to one-half hour.

1846.—THE "OREGON."—The Hudson River steamer "Oregon," the most magnificent steamer afloat in 1846, it is said maintained a speed against a west-northwest gale and head sea of twenty miles per hour. In calm weather she made an average speed of twenty-five miles per hour. Her length was three hundred and thirty feet, by thirty-five feet width of beam, and her measurement one thousand tons, with berth accommodations for six hundred passengers. Her engine was of eleven hundred horse-power, and had a seventy-two-inch cylinder with eleven feet stroke. On the main deck, the inclosed space from the ladies' cabin forward formed a promenade two hundred feet long. The massive engine in the centre, and four or five side parlors, fitted up with ten or twelve berths each, opened out over the guards, as also a smoking-room, denominated the "Exchange," and the wash-room and barber's-shop,—the latter fitted up with marble slab, Croton water, wash-bowls, etc. In the main cabin a continuous line of berths extended over three hundred feet from end to end of the boat, numbering some two hundred. This included the after-cabin, which was connected by an ample passage-way with the forward one. Five hundred yards of carpeting covered the floors in these cabins. Each berth was fitted with Mackinaw blankets and Marseilles quilts, having the name of the steamer worked in them. A thirty-pound mattress, and also bolsters and pillows, with linen of the finest quality, completed the equipment of the berths. The curtains were of satin de laine of rich tints, with embroidered inner curtains.

"A portion of the after-cabin was set aside for ladies, and distinguished by extra trimmings, blue and gold curtains, etc. The dining-saloon accommodated two hundred and fifty persons. The table service was of the richest French china, every article marked with the name of the steamer; the glassware was heavy star-cut. The silver-plated ware was of Prince Albert pattern, very heavy and costly. But the transition from this show-room to the ladies' upper cabin was as great as from that of a common ferry-boat cabin. There the magnificent fittings dazzled the eye. Nothing was wanting which could add richness, splendor, or luxury. There were seven tiers of berths and three state-rooms upon each side, the cabin being seventy feet long. At the extreme stern was the wash-room, fitted with even more comfort than that for gentlemen. Each side of the entrance were full-length mirrors that at first glance were often mistaken for doors opening into another cabin. The state-room doors were of enameled white, richly gilt, and their interior embellishments, like the cabin, splendid and beautiful. The front of the ladies' cabin from the main-deck was splendid. The architecture was plain, with an enameled white ground profusely gilt, with raised flowers upon the gilt pillars. A time-piece was placed over the door and stained glass around it."

The "state-room hall" on the upper deck was two hundred and twenty feet long by sixteen wide, except the space occupied by the engine in the centre. Out of it opened sixty state-rooms, furnished in sumptuous style; three were double ones, and a fourth was fitted up as a "bridal-room" with good taste, and with a wide French bedstead, etc.

Forward of this hall was a lounge, from which there was an unobstructed view ahead of the progress of the boat and passing objects. Astern was a promenade-deck. State-room hall and main cabin were adorned with superb mirrors set in rich frames. The cost of the furniture and fittings was thirty thousand dollars, and of the boat itself one hundred and thirty thousand dollars. She was built under the superintendence of her commander, Captain St. John, and her symmetry, the beauty of her model, and the arrangement of her engines, which gave her unrivaled speed, were the result of his long and practical experience.

1846.—FIRST AMERICAN MAIL STEAMSHIPS.—The first regular American ocean mail steamship was the "Southerner." She was built in 1846 and put on the route between New York and Charleston, South Carolina. She was followed by the "Falcon" and others in the trade to Southern ports.

1847.—The first French Atlantic steamer arrived at New York from Cherbourg on the 8th of July, 1847.

1847.—THE "UNITED STATES."—W. H. Webb in 1847 built for Messrs. C. H. Marshall & Co., the owners of the celebrated Black Ball line of packet-ships, for the New York and Liverpool trade, the steamer "United States," of two thousand tons burden, which in April, 1848, sailed on her first voyage to Liverpool. She was the first American steamer built for the Atlantic Ocean freight and passenger trade, made several voyages, did not pay, was withdrawn and sold to parties in Bremen, and was added to the navy of the new German Confederation. She had a flat bottom with a concave floor. In several respects she differed from any vessel previously constructed. She was also the first commercial steamship constructed to be of use to the government naval service. She could be armed with two tiers of guns, had plenty of room in which to work them, and could carry coal enough for a voyage to Europe. Her first trip to Liverpool occupied thirteen days and consumed forty tons of coal daily,—five hundred and twenty tons. She was two hundred and fifty-six feet long, fifty feet broad, and thirty and a half feet deep.

1849.—THE LAW LINE.—This at one time highly successful line of mail steamers was established by Law, Roberts & Co., under a government contract with A. G. Sloo, made in conformity with the law of Congress of March 2, 1847, for carrying the United States mails between New York and California and Oregon. The line owed its origin to the enterprise, intelligent policy, and business capacity of George Law, of New York, who at an early day in the history of California did much to hasten the introduction of civilization and comfort upon the shores of the Pacific, and to convey the countless thousands of immigrants to their new homes and bring back intelligence of their arrival.

The "OHIO" was the first vessel built for this line under the law of Congress in 1849. Her hull was strongly built and had a diagonal bracing of three-inch *round* iron extending the whole length of the vessel between the keelson and main-deck beams. The "Georgia," a sister vessel, was framed in the same manner, but was of different model. She exhibited in her model the first signal departure from the sail-packets that had been so celebrated. The general dimensions of these two steamers were,—

	"Ohio."	"Georgia."
Length on deck	248 feet.	255 feet.
Breadth of beam	45½ "	49 "
Depth of hold	24½ "	25½ "
Tonnage	2397 tons.	2695 tons.
Average draught	15½ feet.	17 feet.
Diameter of paddle-wheels	36 "	36 "

Their engines were of the side-lever variety and had double-balanced valves, the steam-valve being worked by one eccentric so adjusted as to cut off the steam at any part of the stroke, while the exhaust-valve, being worked by a separate eccentric, could be set to give any desired lead. Each steamer had two engines. Diameter of the cylinders, 90 inches; stroke of piston, 3 feet. There were four iron boilers in each,—two forward and two abaft the engines. Each boiler was 21½ feet long, 15 feet wide, and 14 feet high, with five rows of flues and four furnaces with grates 8 feet in length. The arrange-

HISTORY OF STEAM NAVIGATION.   209

ment of the flues was different from any previously built. The average speed of these vessels in good weather was 12 knots.

The "ILLINOIS," the next vessel built for the line, was constructed under the immediate direction of George Law. Her length on deck was 267 feet 9 inches; length of keel, 255 feet; breadth of beam, 40 feet 8 inches; depth of hold to spar deck, 31 feet. She was fitted with two oscillating engines. The diameter of the cylinder was 85 inches; stroke of piston, 9 feet; diameter of paddle-wheels, 33 feet 6 inches; breadth of paddle-wheels, 10 feet 6 inches. She had four return tubular iron boilers, with two smoke-pipes, and was barquentine rigged. Her maximum speed was 13½ miles per hour. On one occasion she ran from Chagres to New York, one thousand nine hundred and eighty miles, in six days and sixteen hours, being an average or nearly twelve and a half miles per hour the whole voyage.

Besides these vessels the company chartered the "Falcon,"[1] which was chiefly employed in carrying the mail between Havana and New Orleans. Her length on deck was 206 feet; beam, 30½ feet; depth of hold, 21 feet; average draught, 12 feet; tonnage, 875 tons; average speed, 9 knots.

These steamers were all running on the line between Chagres and New York in 1853.

1847.—THE BREMEN LINE.—The first *American* transatlantic steamers after the "Savannah" (1818) were the "Washington" and the "Hermann," constructed in 1847 to form a monthly communication between New York and Bremen. The hulls of these sister ships were built by Westervelt & Mackay and the machinery by Stillman, Allen & Co., of New York. The following were their general dimensions:

	"Washington."	"Hermann."
Length on main-deck	230 feet.	235 feet.
Length on spar-deck	236 "	241 "
Breadth of beam	39 "	40 "
Depth of hold	31 "	31 "
Average draught	19½ "	19½ "
Tonnage C. H. measurements	1700 tons.	1800 tons.
Kind of engines	two side lever.	two side lever.
Diameter of cylinders	6 feet.	6 feet.
Length of stroke	10 "	10 "
Diameter of paddle-wheels	34¾ "	36 "
Average speed per hour	11 knots.	. . .

Several alterations were made in the boilers and paddle-wheels after their first construction.

1850.—THE HAVRE LINE.—The "Franklin," constructed in 1848, and the "Humboldt" in 1850, built to be added to the Bremen Line, were built and equipped by the same firms as those of the Bremen

---

[1] The "Falcon," it will be recollected, received the engines of the "Iron Witch," the first iron Hudson River boat.

Line, but were placed by Messrs. Fox & Livingston to run between New York and Havre. Their average passages from New York to Cowes, from January 1 to December 1, 1852, were 12 days, 17 hours, 9 minutes, and from Cowes to New York 12 days, 22 hours each.

The general dimensions of these two steamships were,—

	"Franklin."	"Humboldt."
Length on deck	263 feet.	292 feet.
Breadth of beam	41¼ "	40 "
Depth of hold	26 "	27 "
Average draught	18 "	19½ "
Breadth across the paddles	32 "	72 "
Diameter of paddle-wheels	32½ "	35 "
Engines	two side lever.	two side lever.
Diameter of cylinders	7¼ feet.	95 inches.
Length of stroke	8 "	9 feet.
Tonnage	2400 tons.	2850 tons.

Each had four iron flue boilers, placed back to back.

The New York and Havre Steam Navigation Company, to which these steamships belonged, was established in 1848, to ply between Havre and New York, stopping at Southampton both going and returning, and obtained a contract for carrying the United States mails, for which they were to receive one hundred and fifty thousand dollars per annum for a fortnightly service. The "Franklin" was launched in 1848, and made her first voyage in 1850. In July, 1854, she was wrecked and totally lost on Long Island. The "Humboldt" made her first voyage in 1851, and was wrecked entering Halifax, Nova Scotia, in October, 1853.

To preserve the mail contract, the service was supplied by chartering unsuitable steamers at heavy cost until 1855–56, when the "Arago" and the "Fulton" were built and placed on the line. On the breaking out of the Rebellion, in 1861, the line was withdrawn. The "Arago" was sold to the Peruvian government, and the hull of the "Fulton" was broken up, dry rot rendering her useless as a sailing-ship. Her engines were utilized elsewhere.

The "Fulton" (1856) was built by Smith & Denison under the superintendence of Captain Wm. Skiddy; the engines by the Morgan Iron Works. Her dimensions were: Length on deck, 290 feet; breadth of beam, 42 feet 4 inches; breadth over all, 65 feet 6 inches; depth of hold, 31 feet 6 inches; tonnage, custom house, 2300 tons; tonnage, cargo, and measurement, 3000 tons; diameter of cylinder, 65 inches; length of stroke, 10 feet; diameter of paddle-wheels, 31 feet; length of paddles, 9 feet; number of paddles on each wheel, 28 feet; width of paddles, 18 inches; and shafts of wrought iron. She had two iron Martin boilers with vertical seamless brass tubes, 12 feet long, 30 feet wide, drawn from ingots by the American Tube Company, Boston, and a fire and heating surface of 9100 square feet. The

"Fulton" had three decks. On the berth-deck she had accommodation for 150 first- and second-class passengers, and could accommodate 300; and she could carry 800 tons of coal and 700 tons of freight. Her draught of water was seventeen and a half feet. She was furnished with two inclined oscillating engines.

Mr. Rainey, in his work on "Ocean Steam Navigation," says, "When one of our first American mail steamers sailed for Europe, no practical marine engineers could be found to work her engines. She took a first-class engineer and corps of assistants from one of the North River packets; but as soon as the ship got to sea and heavy breakers came on, all the engineers and firemen were taken deadly seasick, and for three days it was constantly expected the ship would be lost."

1848.—THE "CALIFORNIA."—The steamer "California," which left New York on the 6th of October, 1848, was the first steamer to bear the American flag to the Pacific Ocean, and the first to salute with a new life the solitudes of that rich and untrodden territory. She was soon followed by the "Panama" and the "Oregon," and in due time by the "Tennessee," the "Golden Gate," the "Columbia," the "John L. Stevens," the "Sonora," the "Republic," the "Northerner," the "Fremont," the "Tobago," the "St. Louis," and the "Golden Age." These steamers found nothing ready to receive them in the Pacific. The company was compelled to construct large workshops and foundries for their repair, and had also to build their own dry-dock, that of the government at Mare Island not being ready until 1854. For a large portion of the early time the company had to pay thirty dollars per ton for coal, and once as high as fifty dollars per ton.[1]

1848.—THE USE OF IRON FOR STEAMERS DISTRUSTED.—In the report of a Parliamentary committee on the state of the British navy in 1848, it was said, "Contradictory evidence was given the committee as to the applicability of iron to the construction of war steamers, and the committee therefore offer no opinion on the matter. The present Board of Admiralty distrust the use of iron in the construction of war steamers; and the committee consider that while so important a question is in abeyance, the expenditure of a large sum for constructing such vessels must be regarded as an inconsiderate outlay of the public money."

DUBLIN AND HOLYHEAD PACKETS.—In 1848 the "Banshee" and the "Llewellyn" commenced to run between Dublin and Holyhead as mail packets, and on their trial trips attained a speed of upward of eighteen statute miles per hour.

The public soon required faster and more commodious steamers, and in 1860 the "Connaught," "Ulster," "Munster," and "Leinster," iron steamboats, were built, of the following dimensions: Length between the perpendiculars, 334 feet; beam, 35 feet; depth, 21 feet.

[1] See account of this company under head of Ocean Steamship Company.

They had a central keel-plate 3 feet deep, ⅜-inch thick, with two bars 9 inches deep. They had nine iron water-tight bulkheads. The "Leinster," on her trial, made twenty and a half statute miles. The "Connaught," twenty and three-quarter statute miles. Each of these vessels cost near £80,000 when complete in all respects for sea.

1849.—THE "MINT."—R. B. Forbes, of Boston, Massachusetts, in 1849, sent to California, on the deck of the ship "Samoset," an iron steamer called the "Mint," about seventy-five feet long by fifteen beam. She was stowed on the starboard side of the ship, the deck-house being removed over to the port side to balance her, *and was launched under steam.* She was the first American steamer to ply on the Sacramento. In 1850 he sent an iron paddle-wheel steamer in two parts to China on the deck of the brig "Rolling Wave," on account of Captain J. B. Endicot.

1849.—The "Sansom," the first screw steam tug in the United States, was built by Messrs. Cramp & Sons in 1849.

1850.—FIRST STEAMER ON LAKE TITICACA, PERU.—A small iron *steamboat* was built by Mr. George Birbeck, Jr., of New York, intended to ply on Lake Titicaca, Peru. She was 55 feet keel, 12 feet beam, and 5 feet hold, and was propelled by two high-pressure engines of 10 horse-power each, connected at right angles. Her wheels were of wrought iron 10 feet in diameter. The boat was put together in New York, and each piece marked. She was then taken apart to be shipped. No piece was to exceed 350 pounds, as on its arrival at Lima it was to be transported on mule-back to Lake Titicaca, which is 140 miles long.

1850.—THE TWIN STEAMER "GEMINI."—In the autumn of 1850 Mr. Peter Borrie launched what he called a "safety iron twin steamer," which he appropriately named the "Gemini," adapted for carrying goods, passengers, cattle, and all sorts of vehicles, and for either ocean or river navigation.

This vessel was chiefly constructed of iron, having two separate hulls placed side by side (with a space between them in which the paddle-wheel worked) strongly connected together at the deck (which passed over all), and also by a plate-iron arch and stays between the hulls. The hulls thus joined afforded a great extent of deck-room with a very small amount of tonnage, or of resistance from the area passing through the fluid; and, as both ends were exactly similar, it was expected the vessel would steam with equal facility either way without turning. The keels and stems were not placed in the centre of the hulls, but towards the inside of them, thus making the water-lines very fine on the inside, to diminish the tendency of the water to gorge up between the hulls, found to take place in twin steamers as usually constructed; which gorging tends to separate the two hulls and increases their resistance in passing through the water. The inner bilges of the two hulls were fuller than the outer ones, to afford a greater degree of buoyancy on the inside, necessary to support the weight of the deck, etc., between the hulls. The vessel was adapted for river navigation, at a high degree of velocity; but a vessel for sea purposes would require to be made broader in proportion to her length, according to the trade in which she was to be placed.

The "Gemini" was one hundred and fifty-seven and a half feet long and twenty-six and a half feet broad on deck, each hull being eight and a half feet broad, with a space of nine and a half feet between them. Her frames were of angle-iron and spaced, the outside plating being securely riveted to them. The keels were formed by curving the plates downward so as to form channels for the bilge-water inside of the hulls; but in sea-going and other vessels, where the draught of water would be greater, Mr. Borrie proposed keels of iron bars, and to rivet the garboard strakes upon them in the usual way. The plating was not carried to the top of the frames on the inside of the hulls, except at the space in the middle for the paddle-wheel, but was carried up to the deck, so as to form an arch between the two hulls, which were also bound together with iron stays at the springing of the arch. The deck-beams were of T-shaped iron, securely fastened at the ends to the frames, and at the middle to the top of the arch. The deck-planks were fixed to the beams by screws passing through the flanges of the beams, and calked and made water-tight in the usual way. Each of the hulls was divided into compartments by water-tight bulkheads. There were also fenders of angle-iron, one at each end, to prevent boats, etc., from getting into the canal or space between the hulls. The deck was bounded by bulwarks, which had two large gangways on each side, hinged at the lower side to the decks, and lifted up or lowered by winches attached to the bulwarks. On each end of the paddle-box were a number of deck-houses,—a cook-house, with apparatus in it for cooking by steam, a state-room, a dining-room, engineer's room, etc. On the top of the deck-houses and paddle-box was a platform, or hurricane-deck, upon which the steering-wheels were placed; and, being properly railed in, could be used as a promenade for passengers.

The vessel, having to steam with equal facility either way without turning, was fitted with a rudder at each end. The rudder was in the middle of the canal between the hulls, and was formed of an iron plate upon a shaft or spindle coming up to the deck, which shaft was not in the centre of the plate but about one-third of its length from the one side, so that the pressure of the water against the rudder acted partly on both sides of its centre of motion; but when the rudder was left free it always accommodated itself to the direction of the vessel's motion, one end being longer than the other from the centre of motion.

The steering-wheels were on the top of the paddle-box in the middle of the vessel; thus the man at the wheel, from his elevated position, had a clear view. The clear area on deck for passengers, including the hurricane-deck above the accommodations at each end of the paddle-box, was two thousand six hundred square feet, and the area of the cabin floors was six hundred square feet, so that there was ample accommodation to carry from eight hundred to one thousand passengers with ease and safety.

1851-52.—AVERAGE PASSAGES OF THE CUNARD AND COLLINS STEAMERS.—There was great rivalry in 1851-52 between the Cunard and Collins lines of steamships between England and the United States, which resulted as follows:

In 1851 the Collins Line in fourteen trips from Liverpool to New York, averaged 11 days, 8 hours. The quickest trip was made by the "Baltic," in 9 days, 13 hours. The longest by the "Atlantic," in 13 days, 17 hours, and 30 minutes. In fourteen trips from New York to Liverpool the average time per trip was 10 days, 23 hours. Quickest trip by the "Baltic," 10 days, 4 hours, 45 minutes. Longest by the "Baltic," 12 days, 9 hours.

In 1851 the Cunard Line, in fourteen trips from Liverpool to New York, averaged 11 days, 23 hours, 30 minutes. Quickest trip by the "Africa," 10 days, 16 hours, 50 minutes. Longest by the "Europa," 17 days, 2 hours, 50 minutes. In fourteen trips from New York to Liverpool the average time was 10 days, 13 hours. Quickest trip by the "Africa," 10 days, 5 hours, 35 minutes. Longest by the "Europa," 14 days, 3 hours.

In 1852 the Collins Line averaged, in thirteen trips from Liverpool to New York, per trip, 11 days, 22 hours. Quickest trip by the "Atlantic," 10 days, 3 hours. Longest by the "Pacific," 15 days, 4 hours, 30 minutes. In thirteen trips, the same year, from New York to Liverpool, the average was 11 days, 1 hour. Quickest trip by the "Arctic," 9 days, 13 hours, 30 minutes. Longest by the "Baltic," 12 days, 21 hours.

In 1852 the average of thirteen trips of the Cunard Line from Liverpool to New York per trip was 13 days, 3 hours, 3 minutes. Quickest trip by the "Asia," 10 days, 19 hours. Longest by the "Niagara," 20 days, 19 hours. In thirteen trips from New York to Liverpool the average was 11 days, 5 hours. Quickest trip by the "Asia," 10 days, 5 hours, 10 minutes. Longest by the "Asia," 12 days, 21 hours, 30 minutes.

In 1860 the Collins steamer "Baltic" made the trip from New York to Liverpool in 9 days, 13 hours, 30 minutes.

1851.—THE "HIMALAYA."—The screw steamship "Himalaya" was launched on the anniversary of the Queen's birthday, May 24, 1851. The launch was witnessed by the directors of the Peninsular and Oriental Company, for which the vessel was built, and a noble and fashionable assembly. The naming was by Lady Matheson, wife of Sir James Matheson, chairman of the company. On a given signal, shortly before high tide, the vessel glided gently into the water amid the cheers of the spectators.

The "Himalaya," designed and built under the inspection of F. Wattman, Jr., at Blackwall, was commenced in November, 1850; her length between perpendiculars was three hundred and forty feet; breadth, forty-six feet two inches; depth of hold, thirty-four feet nine inches; and she was three thousand five hundred and fifty tons burden, and had engines of seven hundred horse-power. She was intended to have paddle-wheels, with engines of twelve hundred horse-power, but before she was too far advanced it was decided she should be fitted with a screw propeller and engines of seven hundred horse-power on the most approved principle. She carried twelve hundred tons of fuel, with accommodation for four hundred cabin passengers, five hundred tons measurement goods, and had ample space for mail-rooms, etc. In strength of build and form for speed the "Himalaya" was at that day unrivaled, having six water-tight bulkheads, and she was fitted with every appliance for safety. She was provided with "Trotman's improved Porter's" anchors, the bower-anchors weighing respectively forty-eight and fifty hundredweight, in lieu of ordinary anchors of five tons each. The cabin arrangements with regard to ventilation were excellent, and combined elegance with simplicity.

1852.—THE "FRANCIS SKIDDY."—The magnificent side-wheel steamer "Francis Skiddy," which plied between New York and Albany in 1852, was built by George Colyer. She was three hundred and twenty-five feet in length, thirty-eight and a half feet beam, eleven and a half feet depth of hold. Her engine was of one beam, seventy-inch cylinder, and fourteen-feet stroke. Her water-wheel was forty feet in diameter, twelve feet face, thirty-three-inch bucket. She had four low-pressure boilers, twenty-four feet long, nine feet face, capable of seventy pounds of steam, with a blowing-engine attached to each of twelve-inch cylinder and twelve-inch stroke. Her consumption of fuel was two thousand pounds per hour. Her draught of water, five and a half feet. As a provision against danger she had three fire-pumps,—two to work by hand and one by steam, with six hundred and fifty feet of hose attached, together with fire-buckets, a life-preserver for every passenger, and a supply of Francis's metallic life-boats, etc. Her appointments were magnificent. The main cabin, three hundred feet in length, was capable of seating five hundred people, and was arranged in the most commodious manner. There was also an immense saloon, opening upon sixty state-rooms. This was surmounted with a dome or arch, decorated with stained glass, which cost ten thousand dollars.

1852.—THE "AUSTRALIAN," THE FIRST MAIL STEAMER TO AUSTRALIA.—The "Australian" was the first to make the mail steam voyage from England to Australia. She was built at Dumbarton, for

Messrs. Cunard & Co., for the Canadian trade. She steamed from Plymouth, England, on her first voyage to Australia June 5, 1852, and reached King George's Sound, West Australia, August 20; Adelaide, August 29; Melbourne, September 2; and returned January 11, 1853, having completed the voyage in two hundred and twenty-one days, one hundred and sixty-five of which were under steam and sails, and fifty-six in port, taking in mails, coal, and lading. The following account of her voyage *out* is extracted from *Chambers's Journal* for 1854:

"The public mind was excited to a pitch of feverish anxiety concerning the gold discoveries in Australia, and, in order to provide for the delivery of mails to and from the colony with greater speed and regularity, a company was formed, pledged to effect this by a line of great steamships. Even then people who ought to have known better confidently predicted that direct steam communication with Australia was impracticable. As in the case of crossing the Atlantic, nothing would convince them or settle the question but actual performance. Now, as the distance to be run is little short of sixteen thousand miles, it is obvious that no ship, unless of enormous size, could carry sufficient fuel to perform the entire voyage under steam without stopping to take in coal at stations on the way; and this has caused hitherto considerable delay and great additional expense. The pioneer was the 'Australia,' a large new Clyde-built iron steamship that first started from London, and, after some accidents and delays, finally left Plymouth with the mails on the 5th of June, 1852, under command of Captain Hoseason. She anchored at St. Vincent on the 16th to take in coal, which had previously been sent to the depot there from England. This occupied three days. The ship then proceeded on her vayage, and, after coaling at St. Helena, reached the Cape of Good Hope on the 19th of July, where she again coaled, sailing from Table Bay on the 22d, and anchored in King George's Sound, West Australia, on the 20th of August. There she received coal from a ship sent out with a cargo from England expressly for her, and a few days afterwards proceeded to Adelaide, which she reached on the 29th, and Melbourne on the 2d of September. This was the first voyage performed by a steamer from England to the antipodes. In some respects it was a badly-managed voyage, much unpleasantness occurring among both passengers and crew, repeated accidents happening to the machinery, and the coal running short between the stations, so that at times the engines stopped, and the vessel had to lie to or proceed under canvas. Nevertheless, it effectually demonstrated the practicability of the enterprise. She was followed by the 'Great Britain,' and steamships now perform with punctuality and dispatch the voyage to and from Australia, calling at the Cape both on the outward and homeward passage to land and receive mails and passengers, equal to that which distinguishes the Atlantic and Mediterranean steamers. Taking into consideration the prodigious expanse of ocean to be traversed, this is a triumphant realization of the most sanguine hopes of those who have watched the progress of steam navigation."

1852.—FASTEST STEAMERS IN THE ROYAL NAVY.—The second edition of Murray's "Marine Engine," published in 1852, states that the "Terrible," the "Sidon," and the "Odin" are "probably the *fastest* war steamers properly so called in the Royal Navy. Of these, the 'Terrible,' with 226 feet length, 42 feet beam, 28 feet hold, and 17½ feet load draught, attained a speed of ten knots per hour on trial with sea stores and guns on board. The 'Sidon' (Sir Charles Napier's ship) with 210¾ feet length, 36¼ feet beam, and 27 feet hold, and with two engines of 6½ feet stroke, and 86¼ inches diameter, has a speed on trial of ten knots; while the speed of the 'Odin' is superior to either, being eleven and one-quarter knots, also on trial; the average sea speed of the three being not to exceed nine knots. The few steamers then in the navy of the United States equaled in speed these at that time exceptionally fast steamers of the Royal Navy."

1852.—Commodore M. O. Perry, in a letter to the Secretary of the Navy, February 8, 1852, wrote, "An ocean steamer of 3000 tons is of the maximum dimensions for safety and efficiency, whether for *war* or commercial purposes." He did not foresee the immense ironclads and passenger steamers that a quarter of a century would develop.

1852.—THE PENINSULA AND ORIENTAL COMPANY was the first to adopt screw steamers for its regular service. In 1852 the "Chusan," of seven hundred and sixty-five tons, and the "Formosa," of six hundred and seventy-five tons, were placed upon the route between Hong-Kong and Shanghai. These were succeeded by the "Bengal," of two thousand one hundred and eighty-five tons, and the "Candia," of nineteen hundred and eighty-two tons, between Suez and Calcutta.

In 1852 the iron steamer "Thistle," while proceeding along the coast, struck a rock on the north of Ireland, and steamed thence without assistance to Greenock, seventy nautical miles across the north channel, with the fore-deck under water, the fore and after compartments filled with water, and only the centre or engine compartment free. She returned to Greenock by the power of her own engines without assistance. The fact of a vessel of only six hundred and seventy tons steaming across the Irish Channel safely, with her holds and cabins full of water, the mid-compartment only free, affords a strong testimony of the efficiency of water-tight bulkheads.

1853.—THE ASPINWALL LINE, originally established by Messrs. Howland and Aspinwall of New York, by an arrangement with the Law Line, performed mail service exclusively between Panama (on the Pacific coast), California, and Oregon, under government contract.

The steamers of this line in the mail service in 1853 were the

"Golden Gate," the "Tennessee," the "Columbia," the "Panama," the "California," the "Oregon," and the "John L. Stevens." The "Golden Gate" was completed in 1851, and made a trial trip to Annapolis, where she was visited by the President of the United States, members of his Cabinet, and other distinguished persons.

The following were the principal dimensions of these steamships:

Dimensions.	Columbia.	Tennessee.	Panama.	California.	Oregon.	Golden Gate.	J. L. Stevens.
Length on deck	220 feet	212 feet	200 feet	200 feet	200 feet	285 feet	200 feet
" keel	219 "						270 "
Breadth of beam	29 "	35 feet	32 feet	33 feet	34 feet	40 feet	40 "
Depth of hold	13 "	22 "	21 "	20 "	20 "	22 "	26 "
Tonnage			1087 tons	1050 tons	1100 tons	2030 tons	2450 tons
Engines	side lever	side lever	side lever	side lever	side lever	oscillating	oscillating
Diameter of cylinders	57 inches	75 inches	70 inches	70 inches	70 inches	85 inches	85 inches
Stroke of piston	5 feet	8 feet	8 feet	8 feet	8 feet	9 feet	9 feet
Diameter of paddle-wheels	22 "	32 "	26 "	26 "	26 "	31 "	32 "

1853.—The "Forforo," a small iron screw steamer of forty-three tons and forty horse-power, rigged as a three-masted schooner, sailed July 17, 1853, from Liverpool for the West coast of South America, and arrived at Valparaiso November 15. The passage occupied one hundred and twenty-one days,—forty-six under steam and sail, and twenty-eight under sail alone. She used in all one hundred and sixty tons of coal, and averaged six knots all the way. She was the smallest steamer that ever performed so long a voyage.

1854.—The First Steamer to Circumnavigate the Globe.—In 1854 the English screw steamship "Argo," eighteen hundred and fifty tons register, returned to England from Australia *via* Cape Horn, and was the first steamer that had circumnavigated the globe. She made the passage out to Australia *via* Cape of Good Hope in sixty-four days, and returned *via* Cape Horn in the same time. Since the ancient days of Jason and his "Golden Fleece" several celebrated ships have borne the renowned name of "Argo," and certainly we consider the present steamer not the least worthy of the number to be chronicled in history. She has proved herself one of the most notable pioneer ships of the nineteenth century.

1853-54.—The "Golden Age."—The American paddle-wheel steamer "Golden Age" arrived at Liverpool in 1853, where she attracted much notice. She was of great size and power, built with all the latest transatlantic fashions and improvements, one of which was she had no bowsprit!—something our English brothers then thought—though they have learned to know better—as indispensable as the nose on a man's face. Her owners resolved to send her to Australia, and she made the quickest passage out on record up to that time. But her subsequent voyage was far more memorable and important. On the

HISTORY OF STEAM NAVIGATION. 219

11th of May, 1854, she left Sydney, and in thirteen days reached Tahiti, where she took in the enormous weight of twelve hundred tons of coal. This occupied her six days; and on the 31st she sailed direct for the Isthmus of Panama, which she reached on the 19th of June, the passage from Sydney, including the long stoppage mentioned, thus being performed in about thirty-nine days! This wonderful feat was rendered more remarkable from strong head-winds during the first part of the voyage and an estimated current against her course equal to an extra seven hundred and sixty-eight miles. From Tahiti, however, the sea was so smooth and the passage so mild that a canoe might have come the whole distance in safety. She arrived at Panama just in time to transfer two hundred passengers, her mails, and a million sterling in gold to the West Indian steamer "Magdalena," at Chagres, and consequently letters from Sydney to the 11th, and from Melbourne to the 5th of May—only sixty-seven days from Sydney!—were received in London on the 18th of July, 1854.

"Thus to American skill and enterprise," says the *Edinburgh Journal*, "credit is due for first opening direct steam communication across the vast Pacific, in that manner connecting Australia and Europe by the medium of Panama. We cannot read without regret that the spirited proprietors of the 'Golden Age' have incurred a dead loss of several thousand pounds by the experiment, solely owing to the cost of coal at Tahiti. But they have shown what can be done, and nothing can be more certain than that ere long arrangements will be made sufficiently economical to enable a regular line of noble steamships to traverse this novel route, and so bring us within two months' distance of Australia. To quote a newspaper paragraph, 'Ever since Columbus set out across the Atlantic in search of India it has been the dream of commerce to reach the East by the West, and from the time that Balboa caught a glimpse of the great trans-American ocean from the heights of Darien, the world has looked forward to the junction of the two oceans at one point or another as the commencement of a new era in the history of commerce. Nevertheless, the Pacific has hitherto been a field of adventure rather than of regular commerce. Till recently it has been cut off from all direct communication with the trade and civilization of Europe and America. No maritime nations of importance have occupied any part of the extensive line of coast by which it is circumscribed, and within which it has lain in silent repose rather like a secluded lake than a mighty ocean. But a new destiny is beginning to dawn upon it. The 'Golden Age' breaks in upon its isolation, and arouses it from its slumbers. She inaugurates an era in which its commerce will probably as far transcend that of the Atlantic as the latter eclipsed that of the Mediterranean.'"

1854-56.—SIDE-PROPELLERS ON THE LAKES.—Side-screw propellers were advocated in 1856 as a substitute for the paddle-wheel.

In 1854 the lake steamer "Baltic" was thus altered at Buffalo. Her high-pressure paddle-wheel engines were taken out and replaced with side-propeller engines. She carried double the weight and run with half the fuel at a higher rate of speed after the change, notwithstanding her new engines rated sixty per cent. less power than her old ones. The "Baltic" was the first vessel to which this mode of propulsion was applied.[1]

In 1848 Gardner Stow patented a screw propeller on each side of the vessel, so that the inclined vanes of sheet iron or wood should dip into the water.

1855.—The steam frigate "Mississippi" (paddle), flag-ship of Commodore M. O. Perry on the Japan expedition, sailed from Norfolk, Virginia, November 24, 1852, arrived at the navy-yard, Brooklyn, New York, April 23, 1855, and was the first war steamship of the United States navy to circumnavigate the globe. She went to Japan *via* the Cape of Good Hope and returned *via* Cape Horn, or rather through the Straits of Magellan, having been absent two years and five months.

The "Mississippi" run aground in the attack upon Port Hudson in 1863, and was set fire to and abandoned to avoid her surrender.

April, 1856.—The steamer "Baltic" (Collins's Line) had bulkheads put into her hold in New York after making her last trip from Liverpool. These bulkheads should have been of iron instead of wood, which was cheaper. Why is it that water-tanks for vessels are made of iron, and the *fire-tanks*, or the encasement for boilers and engines, are made of wood, neither fire-proof nor water-proof? Iron bulkheads are lighter, less bulky, and cheaper, if the safety of life is taken into account.

1856.—STEAM VESSELS OF THE ROYAL NAVY.—On the 1st of April, 1856, the steam-vessels belonging to the Royal Navy were,—[2]

	Guns.	Horse-Power.
48 line of battle-ships	3797	22,940
24 frigates and mortar-vessels	889	10,560
90 paddle-wheel vessels	500	24,640
76 corvettes and sloops	761	16,202
47 troop-ships	37	7,300
155 gunboats	580	8,240
435	6564	89,882

In 1857 the American steamship "Vanderbilt" made the run from New York to "the Needles," the western extremity of the Isle of Wight, in nine days and eight hours, and on her return trip in nine days, nine hours, twenty-four minutes.

---

[1] The Hudson River steamer "Iron Witch" had *side*-propellers in 1845. See *ante*, page 203.

[2] Lardner's "Museum of Science."

CHAPTER V.—1858–1882.

THE GREAT EASTERN, 1858; Description of the Vessel, etc.; Her First Voyage to New York and Arrival described.—The Emperor, a Steam Yacht, presented to the Japanese, 1859.—The Scotland and England purchased by the Prince of Satsuma, 1861.—The MONITOR, First Turreted Steam War-Vessel, 1861.—The Faid Rabani Yacht of the Khedive, 1863.—Number of British Inventions patented in the Ten Years preceding 1866.—Steamers on Lake Memphremagog, 1867.—The Kate Corser, the First Steamer on the Great Salt Lake, 1869.—An Extraordinary Inland Voyage, 1869.—Coal-Saving Discovery, 1872.—The Cable Steamer Faraday, 1873.—A Chinese Steamboat Enterprise, 1874.—The Bessemer Anti-Sea-Sick Steamboat, 1875.—The Double-Hulled Castalia, 1875.—The Iona, 1876.—Steamboats in Corea, 1878.—The Solano, 1879.—The Remarkable Voyage of a Wrecked Steamer, 1880.—The Comet on Lake Bigler, 1880.—A Mountain Steamer on Twin Lakes, 1880.—The Three Brothers transferred to the British Flag, 1880.—A Canal-Boat propelled by Air, 1880.—The Hochung, the First Chinese Steamer to cross the Pacific, 1880.—The Chinese Steamer Meefoo arrives at London with a Cargo of Tea, 1881.—Taggart's Screws, 1880.—The Anthracite, the Smallest Steamer that has crossed the Atlantic, 1880.—The Harriet Lane, 1881.—The Dessoug, 1881.—A Hydraulic Ship, 1881.—A Novel Steam Yacht, 1881.—The Kittatinny, 1881.—Steamboat Disaster, 1881.—The Fall River Line, 1882.—A West India Steamship Enterprise, 1882.—The Colossus, 1882.—RECENT NOVEL INVENTIONS AND EXPERIMENTS.—Morse's Unsinkable Ship.—Lundborg's Twin-Screws.—Root's Side-Screw Steamship.—Coppin's Triple Steamship.—Fryer's Buoyant Propeller.—Rosse's Catamaran Steam Tugs.

1858.—THE "GREAT EASTERN."—Experience had shown that a sea steamer of eighteen hundred tons, making the quickest passages to and from England and Australia, with a full cargo and complement of passengers, lost by the voyage from one thousand to ten thousand pounds. A great portion of the expense was from the necessity of supplying coal depots at different points where the steamer could touch during her voyage. These deviations from the shortest route also protracted the passage so that clipper-ships made as quick passages as steamers, at less expense, so that they superseded steamers. The problem then to be solved was: Supposing a steamer could be built to move eighteen miles an hour, what must be the size of a steamer to carry out and back fuel for a voyage from England to Australia,—twenty-five thousand miles? To work a steamer profitably, it was found that the tonnage must be nearly a ton to a mile. Mr. Brunel, therefore, conceived the idea of constructing a steamer of from twenty to twenty-five thousand tons burden, capable of carrying coal for full steaming on the longest voyage, to be built on the tubular plan, with both the screw and the paddle, and fitted also with sail for propelling power.

The Eastern Steam Navigation Company was formed to carry out his idea, with a capital of one million two hundred thousand pounds, in shares of twenty pounds each, with power to increase the capital to two million pounds. The place where the great ship was to be built, on the bank of the Thames at Millwall, consisting of a layer of mud thirty feet thick on a bed of gravel, was prepared by driving over fourteen hundred piles in lines parallel to the river, as the vessel was to be launched *sideways*. The first plate of the vessel was laid May 1, 1854.

The ship was built with an inner and an outer skin,—two feet ten inches apart, with longitudinal webs at intervals of six feet running the whole length of the vessel; and these were subdivided by transverse plates into water-tight spaces of about six feet square, so that should the outer skin be damaged the water could only get in between the webs and inner skin. The ship is divided by transverse bulkheads into twelve water-tight compartments below the lower deck, and nine above the lower deck, so that should both the outer and inner skin be fractured the water could only enter one of these compartments,—two of which could be filled without danger to the safety of the vessel. Besides these transverse bulkheads, there are two which extend from the bottom of the ship to the upper deck, and run longitudinally for a length of three hundred and fifty feet. There are also two tubular iron platforms extending from the gunwale to the longitudinal bulkheads, running fore and aft, thirty-six feet apart, and connected together about every sixty feet by iron platforms seven feet wide. The greatest care was taken to make the bow strong enough to withstand any impediment, and to enable the vessel to resist the constant vibration of the screw.

The vessel has no keel, the bottom being flat. A keel-plate was first laid along a level platform prepared for it about five feet from the ground; then the centre-web, which somewhat resembles the keel of an ordinary ship.

The iron plates of which the skins of the vessel are composed are three-quarters of an inch thick, except the keel-plate, which is one inch thick. Their average size is about ten feet by two feet nine inches, and their weight eight hundred and twenty-five pounds. For the stern-post and keel some enormous plates were required. Two were twenty-seven feet long, three feet three inches wide, one and one-quarter inches thick, and weighed two tons each; others were twenty-five feet long, four feet wide, and one and one-quarter inches thick, and weighed two and one-quarter tons each. About thirty thousand plates, of an average weight of six hundred pounds each, were used in the construction of the hull. Each plate, before being placed in its proper position, was a separate study to the engineer. For each a model in wood was made, and by steam-shears the plates were cut according to the pattern; the proper curve was given to it, and the holes for the rivets were punched by machinery. They were riveted together by rivets, fastened at a white heat, some seven-eighths of an inch and some three-quarters of an inch in diameter, about two and a half inches apart where the plates were to be made water-tight, and from four to six inches apart in other places. The total number of rivets were not far from two million. About eight thousand tons of iron were used in her hull. The estimated weight of the whole vessel when voyaging with every article and person on board was twenty-five thousand tons.

For the purpose of launching the vessel two ways were constructed, with pile foundations, one at the fore part of the vessel and one at the after part, each three hundred feet long and one hundred and twenty feet wide, with about one hundred and twenty feet of space between them. The cradles, two in number, were of the same width as the ways. Their bottom was composed of iron plates seven inches wide and one inch thick, placed at intervals of one foot apart, with their edges carefully rounded off so as to offer the least resistance to the railway metals of the ways down which they would pass.

The first attempt to launch the vessel was made November 3, 1857, and the vessel was moved six feet down in her ways. Several unsuccessful attempts were made on different days, until January 31, 1858, when she was afloat. The cost of building and launching the vessel in round numbers was seven hundred and thirty thousand pounds, exceeding the original estimate by two hundred and thirty thousand pounds. In November, 1858, the Eastern Steam Navigation Company, finding it impossible to go on, was dissolved, and a new corporation, called "The Great Ship Company," was formed, with a capital of three hundred and thirty thousand pounds. Of this capital one hundred and sixty thousand pounds was to be paid to share-holders of the former corporation; the fitting and finishing would cost about one hundred and twenty thousand pounds, so that it was estimated fifty thousand pounds would be left for working expenses.

The "Great Eastern" was christened by Miss Hope, now Duchess of Newcastle, daughter of the chairman of the Great Eastern Steam Navigation Company.[1]

[1] W. S. Lindsay, in his "History of Merchant Shipping," says, in the summer of 1857, accompanied by Robert Stephenson and Brunel he visited the "Great Eastern." Preparations for her launching had commenced. After his inspecting the vessel, Brunel asked him what he thought of her. He replied, she was the strongest and best built ship he had ever seen and a marvelous piece of mechanism. "Oh," he said, rather testily and abruptly, "I did not want your opinion about her build. I should think I know rather more how an iron ship should be built than you do. *How will she pay?*"

SUMMARY OF STATISTICS OF THE "GREAT EASTERN."

Length of upper deck	692 feet.	*Paddle-Engines.*	
Length between perpendiculars	680 "	Nominal horse-power	1000
Breadth across paddle-boxes	118 "	Number of cylinders	4
		Diameter of "	6 ft. 2 in.
Breadth of hull	83 "	Weight of cylinders, including piston and rod	38 tons.
Depth from deck to keel	58 "		
Number of decks	4	Length of stroke	14 feet.
Number of masts	6	Strokes per minute	14
Diameter of masts	2 ft. 9 in. to 3 " 6 "		
Quantity of canvas under full sail	6500 sq. yards.	*Paddle-Engine Boilers.*	
Number of anchors	10	Number of boilers	4
Number of boats	20	Furnaces to each	10
Tonnage (old measurement)	22,500 tons.	Length of boilers	17 ft. 6 in.
		Width of "	17 " 9 "
Storage for cargo	6000 "	Height of "	13 " 9 "
Capacity of coal-bunkers	12,000 "	Weight of each	50 tons.
		Weight of water	40 "
Draught of water, unladen	15 ft. 6 in.	Area of heating surface	4800 sq. feet.
		Number of tubes	400
Draught of water, laden	30 feet.	Thickness of plates	⅜ and ₁/₁₆ in.
Number of water-tight compartments	12		
		Screw Propeller.	
		Diameter of screw	24 feet.
Paddle-Wheels.		Pitch of screw	37 "
Diameter of paddle-wheels	56 feet.	Number of fans	4
		Weight of screw	36 tons.
Weight of paddle-wheels	185 tons.	Length of propeller-shaft	160 feet.
Length of floats	13 feet.		
Width of "	3 "	*Screw Engines.*	
Number of floats to each wheel	30	Nominal horse-power	1600
Length of paddle-shafts	38 feet.	Number of cylinders	4
Weight of "	80 tons.	Diameter of each cylinder	84 inches.
Length of intermediate cranked shaft	21½ feet.	Length of stroke	4 feet.
Weight of intermediate cranked shaft	31 tons.	Number of revolutions per minute	50

"Ah," replied Mr. L., "that's quite a different matter."

Seeing Mr. L. did not care to answer his question, he repeated it, adding, "If she belonged to you, in what trade would you place her?"

"Turn her into a show," said Mr. L., with a laugh, "something attractive to the masses. She will never pay as a ship. Send her to Brighton, dig a hole in the beach, and bed her stern in it, and if well set she will make a substantial *pier*, and her decks a splendid promenade. Her hold would make magnificent salt-water baths, and her 'tween decks a grand hotel, with restaurant, smoking and dancing saloons, etc. She would be a marvelous attraction for the cockneys, who would flock to her by thousands. Candidly, this is my opinion, for I really don't know of any other trade at present in which she will be likely to pay so well."

Stephenson laughed, but Brunel was offended.

HISTORY OF STEAM NAVIGATION.

Screw Boilers.		Passenger Accommodation.	
Number of boilers	6	Number of passengers (first-class)	800
Funnels to each boiler	12	Number of passengers (second-class)	2000
Length of boiler	18 ft. 6 in.	Number of passengers (third-class)	1200
Width of "	17 " 6 in.	Aggregate length of saloons and berths	350 feet.
Height of "	14 feet.	Number of saloons	10
Weight of "	57 tons.	Length of principal saloon	100 feet.
Weight of water	45 "	Width	36 "
Area of heating surface	5000 sq. feet.	Height	13 "
Number of tubes	420	Length of berths	14 "
Thickness of plates	$\frac{7}{16}$ and $\frac{1}{2}$ in.	Width of "	7 to 8 ft.
Number of auxiliary engines	4	Height of "	7 ft. 4 in.
Number of donkey-engines	10		
Total horse-power, about	12,000		

Nothing can stand comparison with this great steamship except Noah's ark, and even Noah's ark could not match it. The length of the ark was three hundred cubits, its breadth fifty cubits, and its height thirty cubits. The Scripture "cubit," as stated by Sir Isaac Newton, is twenty inches and about sixty-two hundredths. Bishop Wilkins makes it somewhat more,—namely, twenty-one inches and about sixty-eight hundredths. Reducing these to English feet, and calculating the tonnage after the old law, we have approximately the following table:

	Noah's Ark according to Sir Isaac Newton.	Noah's Ark according to Bishop Wilkins.	Great Eastern.
Length between perpendiculars	515.62	547.00	680.00
Breadth	85.94	91.16	83.00
Depth	51.56	54.70	58.00
Keel or length for tonnage	464.08	492.31	630.02
Tonnage according to old law	18,232	21,762	28,093

So Noah's ark is quite overshadowed. Magnitude is not, however, the only peculiarity which the "Great Eastern" possesses. No other vessel afloat has two sets of engines and two propellers, nor was the cellular construction to be found elsewhere in marine architecture.

To comprehend the immense size of the ship one must go on the main deck. From that stand-point every foot of the deck is seen except the very shadow of the masts and chimneys. The wave of the hand can be seen by the steersman or any officer on watch on any part of the deck. Go on to the bridge between the paddle-boxes and look towards the bow, and you see a space in extent equal to the entire length of a very large steamer,—near two hundred and fifty feet,—and then turn your eye towards the stern and you have double the distance in that direction, the entire length of the deck being a little short of seven hundred feet and the width eighty-four feet. This expanse of deck covers about an acre of surface, or one hundred and sixty square rods, stretched out into a long oval one-eighth of a mile, or forty rods, in length. The deck of the ship is double, or cellular, after the plan of the Britannia tubular bridge, and is formed of two half-inch plates at the bottom and two half-inch plates at the top, between which are webs which run the whole length of the ship.

This deck is planned to be of such strength that were it taken up by its two extremities and the entire weight the vessel is to carry were hung upon its middle, it would sustain the whole unaided.

The deck is six hundred and ninety-two feet in length, or more than as long again as that of the steamship "Great Britain." It is nearly three times as long as that of the British line-of-battle ship the "Duke of Wellington"; eighty-eight feet more would make it as long again as the "Persia," the longest vessel, previous to the launch of the "Great Eastern," afloat upon the ocean.

"This ship," says a writer just after the launch, "is one of the wonders of this fast age, but whether, like some of the monstrosities of past ages, she is to be a mere curiosity and a monument of the folly of her builders, or whether she is to introduce a new age of progress in steam navigation yet remains to be demonstrated. The first step in the solution of the problem is her safe and rapid passage from England to America."

"Granting, then," said the Liverpool *Albion,* just previous to her launch, "that the mammoth ship is merely an extended copy of all other iron steamers built on the wave-line principle, let us see what are the 'one or two exceptions,' so modestly alluded to by Mr. Russell last week before the British Association of Dublin. The most prominent in reality, though the feature which escapes unprofessional visitors, is the cellular construction of the upper deck and the lower part of the hull, up to the water-line, or about thirty feet from the bottom, which is as flat as the floor of the room. This system, while it gives greater buoyancy to the hull, increases her strength enormously, and thus enables her to resist almost any outward pressure. Two walls of iron, about sixty feet high, divide her longitudinally into three parts, —the inner containing the boilers, the engine-rooms, and the saloons, rising one above the other, and the lateral divisions the coal-bunkers; and above them the side-cabins and berths. The saloons are nearly sixty feet in length, the principal one nearly half the width of the vessel, and lighted by skylights from the upper deck. On either side are the cabins and berths, those of the first-class being commodious rooms large enough to contain every requirement of the most fastidious landsmen. The thickness of the lower deck will prevent any sound from the engine-rooms reaching the passengers, and the vibrations from being at all felt by them. Each side of the engine-rooms there is a tunnel through which the steam and water-pipes are carried, and also rails for economizing labor in conveyance of coal. The berths of the crew are forward, below the forecastle, which it is intended to appropriate to the officers.

"Below the berths of the seamen are two enormous cavities for cargo, of which five thousand tons can be carried, besides coal enough for the voyage to Australia, making about as many tons more.

"The weight of this huge ship being twelve thousand tons, and coal and cargo about eighteen thousand tons more, the motive-power to propel her twenty miles an hour must be proportionate. If the visitor walks aft and looks down a deep chasm near the stern, he will perceive an enormous metal shaft one hundred and sixty feet in length and weighing sixty tons; this extends from the engine-room nearest the stern to the extremity of the ship, and is destined to move the screw, the four fans of which are of proportionate weight and dimensions. If next he walks forward and looks over the side, he will see a paddle-wheel considerably larger than the circle at Astley's; and when he learns that this wheel and its fellow will be driven by four engines having a nominal power of one thousand horses, and the screw by a nominal power of sixteen hundred horses, he will have no difficulty in conceiving a voyage to America in seven, and Australia in thirty-five, days.

"The screw-engines, designed and manufactured by Messrs. J. Watt & Co., are the largest ever constructed, and when making fifty revolutions per minute will exert an effective force of not less than eight thousand horses. It is difficult to realize the work which this gigantic force would perform if applied to the ordinary operations of commerce: it would raise one hundred and thirty-two thousand gallons of water to the top of the London Monument in one minute, or drive the machinery of forty of the largest cotton-mills in Manchester, giving employment to from thirty to forty thousand operatives.

"There are four cylinders, each of about twenty-five tons, and eighty-four inches in diameter. The crank-shaft, to which the connecting-rods are applied, weighs about thirty tons. The boilers are six in number, having seventy-two furnaces, and an absorbent heating surface nearly equal in extent to an acre of ground. The total weight of the engines exceeds twelve hundred tons, yet they are so contrived that they can be set in motion or stopped by a single hand.

"Sails will not be much needed, for in careering over the Atlantic at twenty miles per hour, with a moderate wind, they would rather impede than aid; but in the event of a strong wind arising, going twenty-five miles per hour in the course of the vessel, sails may be used with advantage. The 'Great Eastern' is provided, accordingly, with seven masts, two square-rigged, the others carrying fore and aft sails only. The larger masts are iron tubes, the smaller of wood. The funnels, of which there will be five alternating with the masts, are constructed with double castings, and the space between the outer and inner casting will be filled with water, which will answer the double purpose of preventing the radiation of heat to the decks and economizing coal by causing the water to enter the boiler in a warm state. Her rigging will probably cause most disturbance of ideas to nautical observers, for, besides the unusual number of masts, she will want two most striking features of all other vessels,—namely, bowsprit and figure-head. Another peculiarity is the absence of a poop. The captain's apartment is placed amidships, immediately below the bridge, whence the electric telegraph will flash the commander's orders to the engineer below, helmsman at the wheel, and lookout man at the bows. In iron vessels, great precaution being necessary to prevent the compass being influenced by the mass of metal in such attractive proximity, various experiments have been made with the view of discovering the best mode of overcoming this. It was originally intended to locate the compass upon a stage forty feet high, but this plan has been abandoned, and a standard compass will be affixed to the mizzenmast at an elevation beyond the magnetic influence of the ship.

"Whatever misgivings there may be as to the length and the weight she will carry amidships will be set at rest before she touches the water by the mode of her launching, as great a novelty as the ship herself. Hitherto the plan has been to build the vessel on an inclined plane at right angles with the water; but in the 'Great Eastern' this was impossible, on account of her great length, to say nothing of the expense of building a vessel of her dimensions in a position which would elevate her forecastle nearly a hundred feet above the ground. These considerations led Mr. Brunel to launch her *sideways*, with which view she has been built parallel with the river. In constructing the foundation of the floor upon which it stands provision has been made at two points to insure sufficient strength to bear the whole weight when completed. On these two points she will rest when ready, and thus her strength will be tested in the severest and therefore most satisfactory manner. Two cradles will be introduced at these points, and she will then be moved by two hydraulic engines. Timber ways are laid down to low-water mark, with an incline of one foot in twelve, and iron rails of peculiar construction are to be laid upon these transversely. A tell-tale will indicate the rate at which the two ends are descending, and any difference that may occur will be immediately rectified by strong check-tackles. It is calculated that she will advance twelve feet per minute, at which speed her submersion will be effected in twenty minutes. The cradles will then be drawn from under her, and she will be towed over to the opposite side of the river, where she will lie until ready for sea."

The London *Times*, after describing the ship, thus discourses,—

"With these principal figures gone through, let us imagine the 'Great Eastern' afloat and on her voyage to Bombay or Melbourne, with her ordinary complement of passengers on board. The first idea that strikes us is the multitude on board. It will, in fact, be a town afloat, and more than a town of four thousand population, because it will be a floating town of four thousand grown-up persons, with comparatively few exceptions, each of them being an 'individual,'—by which we mean a human being of size to command notice, and having, to appearance, a mind and will of his own, with a formed air, tone, and manner peculiar to himself. In this sense even young ladies are individuals. All this crowd of individuals will be collected within the dimensions of seven hundred feet by sixty. What a new shape of human society! Take the eight hundred first-class passengers by themselves, and what room does even this number afford for the formation of all kinds of different circles and sets, which will know nothing of each other, one man only knowing another by sight, and hardly that! How many immeasurable social charms will be collected within a few hundred feet! How many Mr. Smiths will there be who will not speak to Mr. Jones during the whole voyage because he is not in the same set! How many Mr. Joneses will pay back Mr. Smith in the same coin! Between how many 'nice' young ladies and 'proper' young gentlemen will there not be a great gulf fixed, because in the eyes of anxious mothers the said young gentlemen are not desirable persons, but mere penniless bipeds! What flirtations will there not be behind boats, what rivalries, and, if many Americans voyage by the 'Great Eastern,' what duelings may we not expect on that ample deck! In short, what an epitome or camera obscura of the world will the 'Great Eastern' present! It will be worth any aspiring novelist's while to take his berth to Australia or India and back again simply for the great convenience of having so much human nature brought before him within so small a compass. It will be the mountain brought to Mahomet, the world condensing itself before his eyes for the sake of being observed and examined; the rapid succession of faces will bewilder him at first, but individuality will come out in time, though he must be sharp about his work, otherwise the 'Great Eastern' will have stopped her screw and paddles before he has got any results. If his material is enlarged his time is much curtailed on the new system. Farewell to long voyages with their appropriate quarrels and matches, their love-makings, reconciliations, and irrevocable unions; voyage-life has entered on another phase. For what is a month? It is gone before we begin to think about its going. How will the old voyagers look back to the romantic days when a roomful of persons were their own company for four months, gradually forming enemies or friendships, when attachments rose up among 'young people' unconsciously, and by the mere passive influence of the scene! We are growing a busier nation every year, and cannot afford time for more than one chapter of this sea romance."

After hopes deferred, and delays almost innumerable, the mammoth steamship "Great Eastern" made a highly successful trip across the Atlantic, and moored at the dock prepared for her in New York.

The event marks an era in the history of steam navigation. That a vessel so monstrous in its proportions—by the side of which the first steamer of Fulton would be but a cock-boat—should have been propelled across the ocean by the power of steam alone shows what strides have been made since 1818, when the "Savannah" first ventured to cross the Atlantic, steaming when the wind was not fair, and sailing with favoring gales.

The "Great Eastern" differs from all ships which have been built before it in three respects, the chief of which is her excessive magnitude. Nothing like it ever before floated. We have given the figures of her huge dimensions, but these naked numerals convey only a vague idea.

The steamships in the English and American navies hardly equal half her length or breadth, and yet the "Himalaya" the "Persia," the "Adriatic," and the "Niagara" were previously regarded as absolute prodigies in marine architecture.

The "Great Eastern" had thirty-eight passengers and eight guests on her first voyage to the United States. There names were: Miss Herburt, Mr. and Mrs. Gooch, Mr. and Mrs. Stainthorp, General Watkins, Lieutenant-Colonel Harrison, Captain Morris, R.N., Captain McKennan, R.N., Major Balfour, Captain Drummond, Captain Carnagee,[1] R.N., Rev. Mr. Southey, Mr. A. Woods, correspondent London *Times*; Mr. J. S. Oakford, London agent Vanderbilt Line; Mr. Murphy, New York pilot; Mr. Russell, Zerah Colburn, Mr. Holly, correspondent New York *Times*; H. M. Wells, Mr. McKenzie, G. S. Roebuck, Mr. Skinner, D. Kinnedy, G. E. M. Taylor, G. D. Brooks, Mr. Taylor, T. Harnley, H. Marin, Mr. Cave, A. Zuravelloff, Mr. Merrifield, Mr. Field, Mr. Barber, R. Marson, G. Hawkins, H. Cangtan, W. T. Stimpson, Mr. Beresford, Mr. Hubbard, George Wilkes.

The following is the official report of the run of the "Great Eastern," on her first voyage to New York:

June 18, latitude 49° 27′, longitude 8° 45′; run since yesterday, 285 miles.
" 19, " 48° 41′, " 16° 12′; " " 296 "
" 20, " 47° 40′, " 27° 54′; " " 276 "
" 21, " 46° 16′, " 30° 08′; " " 304 "
" 22, " 44° 50′, " 56° 22′; " " 280 "
" 23, " 42° 50′, " 42° 40′; " " 302 "
" 24, " 41° 01′, " 48° 52′; " " 299 "
" 25, " 40° 58′, " 56° 10′; " " 325 "
" 26, " 40° 58′, " 63° 41′; " " 333 "
" 27, " 40° 13′, " 68° 56′; " " 254 "
" 28, " 40° 28′, " 74° 00′; " " 284 "

Total . . . . 8188 "

[1] Captain Carnagee and Mr. Gooch were directors in the Great Ship Company, and Mr. Russell was a son of J. Scott Russell, architect of the ship.

HISTORY OF STEAM NAVIGATION. 231

The greatest speed attained during the passage was 14¼ knots an hour, and she consumed 2877 tons of coal.

The New York *Herald* gave an account of the trip, from which we extract a few passages:

"THE START.—The 'Great Eastern' was advertised to sail on Saturday, the 16th of June. Workmen were engaged on her up to five o'clock in the afternoon of that day, and before they could be disembarked the weather, which had been stormy since noon, became thick and hazy, so that it was felt by the pilot it would be dangerous to take so large a vessel through the intricate channel of the Solent in the uncertain light of the evening. She lay, therefore, in Southampton water till Sunday morning, when about 7 A.M. orders were given to unshackle the mooring-chains. The ponderous character of these cables is such that it was forty-five minutes before this could be effected.

"The morning was raw and gusty, with the wind blowing down the water. The tide had canted the vessel athwart the channel, which she appeared to half block up, but on hoisting the fore-staysail she slowly paid off and got her head pointed in the direction she was to go. Steam was admitted into the cylinders of the paddle-engines about ten minutes past eight, and shortly after the order was given, 'Easy ahead with the screw,' and the 'Great Eastern' steamed slowly out on her first voyage to sea. It has been a remark in all trials, that no motion is felt when this ship is under way. It was not until objects on shore began to recede that one could realize the fact of this huge ship being fairly on her journey. A few minutes steaming brought us abreast of Calshot Castle, where the colors were dipped in acknowledgment of a similar courtesy from the fort. With this exception our departure was ungreeted. The men on board the few vessels we saw had seen so much of the big ship that she excited no emotion in their minds, and we passed without a single cheer. The ship rounded the bell-buoy and ran into the Solent with the handiness of a yacht. As we passed Yarmouth our presence was acknowledged by the lowering of the ensign of the Yacht Club-House, a civility returned by the ship. In two hours we were abreast of the Needles. At twenty minutes past ten o'clock we discharged our Southampton pilot. In a few minutes we were again under way, with the screw making twenty-seven and the paddles seven and a half revolutions per minute, and ran down channel. The ship on starting drew twenty-two feet of water forward and twenty-six aft. Her right trim is on an even keel, so that her condition was unfavorable to her best performance. She had five thousand five hundred tons of coal in the bunkers. Being stored principally aft, this had something to do with her being down by the stern. The object of the trip was not to get any great amount of speed out of the ship, but to get the machinery and men in working order.

"The 'Great Eastern' so outrages all received notions of ship and of sea-life, that when strolling about one of her spacious unoccupied lower decks a party of English and American gentlemen are discovered in an odd corner engaged in a great international skittle-match, one accepts it as a matter of course, and is fully prepared to find a billiard-table in full blast in some other unexplored compartment of the vessel. It is certainly the first time skittles were played in crossing the Atlantic; but the idea is a good one, as enabling those fond of athletic sports to divert the tedium of a sea-passage by first-rate physical exercise. Several exciting foot-races have come off round our ample deck, and the distance to be run in making the complete circuit has been found quite sufficient to give the competitors a very decided 'breathing.'

"For those whose tastes do not lie in the direction of gymnastics there is a well-selected library of the English classics, which the accommodations of the saloons enable one to enjoy most luxuriously. Quite an interesting feature in our trip has been evening concerts in the ladies' saloons. Mr. Macfarlane, the conductor of the ship's band, and an able pianist, has added much to the general enjoyment by the excellent manner in which the band has rendered a selection of musical duets for the piano-forte and the cornet-à-piston. Vocal amateurs among the officers and passengers have varied the performance, and Captain Hall has shown that to his other accomplishments must be added that of his being an excellent musician; his proficiency on the flute being very seldom equaled by amateurs.

"Thursday, June 28.—Ran under easy steam all night, and at twenty-five minutes past seven o'clock (ship's time) this morning reached the light-ship at Sandy-Hook, thus making the run, in spite of the long route taken, the loss of time by encountering the Gulf Stream, and the delay from fogs, in eleven days two hours, including the difference of time. The distance run by the ship was three thousand two hundred and forty-two miles; deducting the loss of time by the fog, this gives a speed of about thirteen knots, proving that with a clear bottom and full pressure of steam she would overrun Brunel's estimate of fourteen and a half knots an hour for a long run.

"The passage being, all things considered, decidedly fine, it was still sufficiently checkered to settle the important point of the 'Great Eastern' being the most comfortable passenger-ship in the world, her movements in a sea-way being so long, slight, and easy that no inconvenience is produced. Sea-sickness may be considered as annihilated and the attendant discomfort of a sea-passage reduced to a minimum."

Mr. George Wilkes, editor of *Wilkes' Spirit of the Times*, a passenger on the "Great Eastern," has furnished a graphic account of his trip. The getting on board and the first day of the voyage he makes of but little account, but after a night on board he writes as follows:

"Monday, June 18.—I was awoke this morning by the sun shining brightly through my port-hole (I should rather use the plural, for my sumptuous apartment was lit by two), and I rose to enjoy the luxury of dressing in a carpeted space as large almost as a room in the St. Nicholas. Before I got up, however, I lay for a few minutes to observe the silence and quiet of the vessel. In fact, there seemed to be no motion to her at all, and had it not been for the barely perceptible buzz of her bow—to which I was very near—as it split the water and passed it humming along the vessel's beautiful wave-line, I should not have been able to decide with certainty whether she was going on or standing still. Vibration there was none, and as for the usual clatter of machinery, which is the distinguishing feature of a steamship, it could not be heard at all. Moreover, there was not any of the squeaking and squealing of timbers and tortured wood-work, which makes up a hideous serenade on all other vessels, for our party-walls, our state-room floors and ceilings, are of iron, and so ribbed and morticed, and joined stiffly with the hull, that the ship, while passing through still water, seems to be one solid tube or beam. Indeed, I could not make it certain to my senses that she had not stopped, until, looking out of my port-hole, I saw the ocean passing by, and our vast mass moving gradually through it like a floating castle. When I went on deck I found the air cool and bracing, but all there was of wind was caused by our own motion. At eight o'clock her paddle-engines gave ten revolutions, and those for the propeller twenty-nine, while the log, which was heaved a few minutes afterwards, credited her with a rate of ten knots. After timing the stroke of the engines I took a look at the rapidly-revolving paddles, and found that their original diameter of fifty six feet, which had proved to be too large, had been reduced to fifty feet by reefing or drawing in the floats, or paddles, three feet on each arm. A large projection of useless iron consequently extends beyond the actual wheels to make an unnecessary resistance to the water, and I am told that the wheel would do better still if the floats were reefed in yet farther.

"I now took my first promenade around the deck, and though well instructed in its vast proportions, I could not help wondering, as I went on, to see the space unroll before me as it did. Standing at the stern and looking forward, the vessel seems almost to terminate amidships, but when you reach that point there appears to open up another ship before you. This allusion proceeds from the fact that two large life-boats, which had hung outside towards the bow, had been brought in at the request of the Board of Trade, and set on blocks in the centre of the ship to divide the view. These, however, will be removed as soon as the vessel gets into port, and then there will be restored a clean, unobstructed double avenue, through which our friend Hiram Woodruff might drive a double team, and go only four times round to make a mile. The deck is flush from stem to stern, and its only obstructions are the six masts, the five smoke-funnels in between, the raised skylights for cabin ventilation, and seven low structures, all of which run in a line with the masts and smoke-stacks. The two outermost of these—stem and stern—are sheds for the donkey or auxiliary engines; two are erections for the main cabin entrances; one spacious one in the centre of the quarter-deck is allotted to the captain; another of like character is the double residence of the first and second officers, and another still, of tolerable size, is given to the passengers as a smoking-room. These are the only obstructions which are found on deck, while around them runs a clean twelve-foot promenade, one side of which has been named Broadway and the other Fifth Avenue. The floor of the deck, like the hull of the ship, is of iron, and built like the sides, on the tubular principle, with twenty-one inches of space between its walls, and interlaced and strapped, crossed and recrossed, with welded bars, so as to give it not only the buoyancy of a life-preserver, but almost incalculable strength. The facing of this floor is pine. Two men are usually placed at each of the wheels, so that eight are enabled to steer her; and four auxiliary wheels can be added, by which a force of thirty-two men can be brought to bear. Only four, however, are now guiding her through the calm, mild weather of the morning. The course is given by the first officer, the man next the compass guides the motions of the rest; and if the direction of the ship requires a sudden change, an auxiliary compass, or indicator, which receives its impulse from the central bridge, directs them immediately what to do. But for this device it would be difficult to guide the ship without great loss of time; but now orders are communicated from end to end with the speed of light, and the leviathan answers to her rudder and points its nose as readily as if drawn with a hook, or 'led' by its tongue with a cord.

"At noon, as the bugle summoned us to lunch, I timed the paddle-piston at ten revolutions and the propellor at thirty and a half, and the log at the same time reported twelve and a half knots. The run of the ship for the last twenty-six hours was reported as three hundred miles. Latitude 49° 27', longitude 8° 45'. When we came up from lunch we found that a light breeze had set in upon our larboard quarter, and our jib and forward trysails were spread to take advantage of it. The wind freshened as the afternoon grew on, and at three o'clock the billows began to crispen at their tops and indicate a rising sea. At four o'clock a drizzling rain set in, and the still strengthening wind gave promise of a stormy night. Some of us had been apprehensive, from the mild manner in which we had set out, that the voyage might run through the entire length of its term in the same dull way, and thus, while it deprived us of the least possibility of becoming heroes, land us at New York without any further knowledge of the ship and her sea-going qualities than we could have learned by studying her while anchored in the Thames. The fear of such disappointment, however, was dispelled by the time we wiped our beards from dinner, for on ascending to the deck at six o'clock and taking our position on the elevated grating in her bow, we saw the leviathan, before so dead, so apparently inert, and which had been passing through the waters like some spectral island, quicken with life and bend with a slow grandeur to the motion of the sea. 'Thank God, she rolls!' exclaimed an experienced officer on her first trial trip, when she was caught in a series of heavy billows off Portland Race, and it was with something like the same ebullition of delight that we saw the mighty ship cast her silent disposition off and make her obeisance to the still mightier deep. Her motion was a gentle and majestic swing from side to side, the extent of three or four degrees, and now and then when a billow fell away from her bow and a swell at the same time would roll underneath her stern she would mildly yield her head,—not short and sudden, with a plebeian start, but with a monarch's measured grace, as if she felt herself to be the master, and only yielding to the courteous laws of life. It was a great treat to see her thus leaning her way from side to side through the parting waters, while good-sized ships, which were then in sight, were rolling uneasily or pitching from stem to stern. It was like some accomplished swimmer, who sweeps forward gracefully hand over hand, compared to a clumsy novice who barely manages to keep himself afloat through the rapidity of a short digging motion. The 'Great Eastern' was alive; but mighty as she was, still she was amenable to that vast throb and pulsation of the sea which is mightier than the mightiest. Nevertheless she proved, by the comparison before us, her superiority to all ordinary ships, as well as to any disturbing motion. In fact, her soft undulations gave actual relief and pleasure to every one who stood upon her deck. And all the while this motion was upon her the skittles were played at one of the afterholds. Nevertheless, let it be noted here that the theory that ships above a certain size will march through the wave superior to the perturbation of the sea is ended by our experiment forever. No ship can be made large enough to entirely ignore the gigantic pulsation of the ocean. The foresail and fore-topsail were drawing well at dark, and the wind, which now struck us almost astern, was whistling through our cordage with great noise.

"A GALE.—Tuesday, January 19, I was awakened a little after midnight by the howling of the wind, the shouts of the men taking in sail, and a great tramping overhead. The vessel was rolling more than she had at any time before,—say about eight or nine degrees,—and I could now feel a little vibration of her bow, imparted by the screw as it smote and scudded into the water whenever the motion of the vessel lifted its blades above the surface. I went to my window, but the night was too thick for anything but darkness to be seen, and all I could distinctly hear was the measured wail of one hundred and twenty men (for both watches had been called up) in chorus, to 'haul the bowline, haul,' while engaged in trying to take in the mainsail and main-topsail. The wind seemed to soften a little at two o'clock, but perhaps that was the notion of my drowsiness, for I fell asleep at that hour, while the men were still as busily engaged at the mainsail as ever. I afterwards learned that it had employed them five hours to furl it in the furious tempest that prevailed. The cause of this difficulty was partly owing to the violence of the gale acting upon the immense area of the sail, and partly to the unhandy size of the tackle by which it must necessarily be worked. Everything is exaggerated in the way of size on board the 'Great Eastern,' and to be handled aloft as other ships she requires an extra breed of men. The gale subsided a little in its fury at four o'clock, but when I arose, at seven, I still found it blowing very hard, and the sea covered with a thread-like foam, which filled the hollows as well as whitened on the billow tops. Still the ship rolled only eight degrees, and her stately nod did not disturb a plate upon the table. The storm-rack was laid at breakfast to protect the dishes, but it was not needed, for my full tea-cup sat outside of it without being in the slightest peril of a slip. Nevertheless, a three-thousand-ton vessel would have been pitching sadly. The motion did not succeed in making a single person sea-sick, though there were among her passengers several who had never been to sea before.

"The wind moderated still more during the afternoon, and we set all our topsails, but the ship kept up her motion, and went frolicking along her path as full of life as a clipper-brig or a pilot-boat. Nothing could be more beautiful than to stand upon an elevated grating in her bow and see her stern lift itself majestically against the sky as we dropped into some yielding wave before us, or to behold her rising sideways to her equilibrium, like some frolicking beauty lifting her shoulder in her downy bed. I could hardly realize, as I viewed her buoyant step upon the deep, that ten thousand plates of iron, representing twelve thousand tons of inert metal, clamped by three million rivets, and bearing within, besides her ponderous engines, six thousand tons of coal, could career thus, cork-like, upon the bosom of the thin and shifting element below. Yet there she rode, ship-like and sweet, 'a thing of beauty and a joy forever.' The most striking idea of her size, however, and the greatest demand upon your wonder that she swims so lightly, is obtained by going down by her sponsons, outside and aft the paddle-boxes, which enables you to see her entire towering section abaft the wheel. From that point you face up and down her massive sides and see the black warehouse, for it looks not like a ship, grandly rise and fall in the hissing and downy foam which the wheels send flying by her run. This flying foam unites beneath her stern, and is there strewn into lace-work by the propeller, and goes seething on its broad path for miles. I think the scene from this lower platform of the gangway gives the finest idea, while in motion, of the vast power and grandeur of the ship. The deck and rigging, on the other hand, being seen altogether, lose in a little while their command upon the wonder, for their great symmetry so wins upon the eye that they mingle together in apparently usual degrees. It is only when in comparison with some other object that the 'Great Eastern' sensibly exhibits her huge proportions to an accustomed eye, and then everything else is dwarfed by her neighborhood.

"Wednesday, June 27.—Fine weather, with a breeze which kept four of our trysails set, continued during the afternoon, but at six o'clock a very heavy fog set in, which condensed itself upon the rigging in huge drops that fell upon the deck like rain. So dense did this all-pervading mist become that the lookouts could scarcely see ten feet from the ship, and our lights could not have been distinguished at the distance of a hundred yards ahead; so out of mercy to the unwary who might possibly be in our path, at near reach to shore, we slackened our speed down from fifteen to seven and a half knots, and ran at this rate, with frequent warnings from our whistle, all night. Under this state of affairs it was thought prudent, moreover, that we should make soundings to ascertain with certainty exactly where we were, but the effort failed at every attempt, in consequence of the great height we were above the water, requiring more line than we could pay out while the vessel was in motion. We slowed her down to six knots, then to four, and then to two, but still it would not answer, and the order went from the captain that the ship must be absolutely stopped.

"It had been the particular pride of Mr. McLenan, the chief engineer, who is a perfect enthusiast in his duty, that the ship's engines, which had been so much abused and misrepresented for the last year, should perform what scarcely, if ever, had been done before, and that was to make a first Atlantic voyage without a single moment's pause from port to port. When, therefore, he heard the order to stop the ship, he received it like a man who was smitten with a sentence, and asked with the greatest earnestness if we could not get along without. The answer was against him, and the lungs of the monster were folded from their respirations, and after ten minute's run with silent wheels and blades, and final reversal of her wheels, she sat still upon the waters. This event took place at 11.40, but a cast of one hundred and fifteen fathoms of line gave us no bottom, and we went on again, at twelve o'clock, still, however, continuing only at half speed. At ten minutes to five this morning we made another pause to heave the lead again, and this time with a cast of sixty-five fathoms we found bottom on George's Bank, and at ten minutes past five went on again. The fog having lifted, we now resumed our speed and proceeded at our usual rate of thirteen and fourteen knots. During these two pauses the engineer rapidly examined such of the screws and nuts as were not accessible during the action of the engines, but did not discover one that was out of place or that required tightening,—a great proof of the excellence and condition of her machinery.

"Thus ended the first transatlantic voyage of the 'Great Eastern,' and though it may be regarded as a failure in the way of speed, it will be perceived there were interests at stake which transcended that consideration, and which doubtless justified the commander in the unusual care he took to keep the great ship safe.

"Captain Vine Hall is one of the most experienced navigators of the English East India trade, but in addition to the caution which he naturally felt incumbent on him from the fact that he had never crossed the Atlantic before, he was doubtless deeply impressed with the paramount importance, not only to his employers and the cause of science, but to England and the whole world, of giving a substantial proof that ships of the size of the 'Great Eastern' could safely cross the deep. It was therefore properly a matter of secondary consequence to him whether the enthusiasm of his passengers or the ardor of his engineers or officers should chafe at his divergences or extra care; he accomplished the great point that was required, and we who left England with him but ten days before are here to approve his action. When he returns to England in September he will give the leviathan its head, and she will then prove for herself that speed is one of her attributes as well as safety. In fact, she has proved it already by the manner in which she has accomplished this voyage, and there is not a passenger who crossed in her but views her as beyond all comparison the most superior passenger-ship that ever floated. The extra distance which she ran on this trip is certainly equal to more than a day's travel, and when we add to this that twenty-four hour's margin is always allowed to a new ship's first voyage, and take into consideration also that not an officer on board ever made a voyage in her, that the men were all raw recruits, fresh levied within three days of starting, and that even the stokers did not know how to spread coal to advantage on the fires, we cannot help regarding even the *time* she made as a great triumph. As to her comfort and convenience as a passenger-ship, it is hardly possible to say too much in praise of her. She meets all the requirements of the most luxurious hotel, and when the weather drives her inhabitants below they can promenade through her cabins upon long walks, or lounge about upon superb divans, listening to music that would not discredit the most pretentious concert. By her continued steadiness sea-sickness is entirely ignored, and in the way of strength no iron structure that ever has been made can at all compare with her.

"This was impressed upon us by every sway of the sea, and the idea which she continually enforces on the mind, above all others, is her absolute safety from all ordinary dangers of the ocean. Against the risks resulting from contact with a solid body she is beyond all calculation stronger than anything which has been seen afloat. The manner in which her vast weight stood poised upon two single rests in the builder's yard for weeks before her launch, and the thundering against her sides of the huge battering-rams that smote her inch by inch towards the water, give evidence of what she can endure. No shoal or beach could break her before all her passengers could escape, for 'her scales are her pride, shut up together as with a close seal. They are joined one to another, they stick together that they cannot be sundered.'

"Above all other ships she should be chosen by the timid, and it really is a puzzle to me how so many intelligent men who had read the history of her construction, and who were about crossing to New York at the date of her departure, could be induced to choose any other vessel. She is certainly exempt from all the ordinary dangers of the sea, and any one who will go into her bow and look at the fourteen feet of matted iron in that welded beak will credit her with sufficient power and impulse to split and push aside any ordinary iceberg."

ARRIVAL AT NEW YORK.—The "Great Eastern" arrived at the bar at about seven o'clock on Thursday morning, and as it was known she would be detained until high water (two o'clock), ample time was afforded to everybody who wished to go down the bay to meet her, or to witness her approach to the city. Messrs. Grinnell, Minturn & Co., consignees of the ship, with their friends and the press, went down in a steamer and came up on board the "Great Eastern." The New York *Times* gives the following sketch of the passage of the bar and the trip up the bay:

"About two o'clock the order was given to cast off the steamer's tugs, which lay like two long-boats under her quarters, and Mr. Murphy, the pilot, with Captain Hall, mounted the starboard wheel-house, and the word was passed, 'Head slow with the paddles.' In another moment the enormous wheels were in motion, and the ship began to move. Slowly her great prow was turned off shore and headed towards the light-ship, for the purpose of getting a good entrance to the ship-channel. At 2.30 P.M. both the paddles and screw were in rapid motion, the ship heading towards Sandy Hook. The speed of the ship was now increased, so that the half-dozen steamboats which followed in her wake could with difficulty keep up with her. At three o'clock the ship was on the bar, when the paddles were slowed, as is the custom in passing that point with all vessels of heavy draught. She went over, however, without any difficulty, and the long-dreaded bar was safely passed. Full steam was now given to both the screw- and paddle-engines, and she made excellent time in coming up with and passing the Hook. Here the telegraph station was decked out with a profusion of flags, and as 'they had no guns to fire,' the fog-bell was vigorously tolled, a greeting to the passing steamer. This was replied to by cheers from the passengers gathered on the port side, in which Captain Hall joined; the ensign was also dipped. Meantime, an *extempore* lunch was prepared below for the newly-arrived guests, whom Captain Carnagee welcomed to the ship in a few words, to which Mr. Grinnell responded, giving as a sentiment the Press of New York, which was acknowleged briefly by Mr. Raymond and Mr. Erastus Brooks.

"Steering well to the southward to give ample room in which to turn the only remaining point of difficulty,—the Southwest Spit,—the order was given to slow the paddles to half speed; the helm was put hard a-port, and in less time than it takes to describe the operation she made the circuit of the spit with all the ease of a pilot-boat. No description could do justice to the scene of animation and enthusiasm which now surrounded the steamer as she approached the Narrows. Steamers of all sizes and descriptions swarmed about her, crowded with ladies and gentlemen cheering and waving their salutations.

"At a few minutes after 3 P.M. the 'Great Eastern' was dimly discerned in the foggy distance of the lower bay. Then she disappeared behind the bluff, and an hour passed before, over the walls of the new fort, at the distance of four miles, the tall masts of the great ship were seen rapidly passing. With an uncontrollable impulse a shout arose from the vast crowd on the old quarantine grounds and from Burr's Gardens. Opposite Fort Hamilton she stopped, and the fort gave her a rousing salute of cannon. When she resumed her 'onward march, her triumph o'er the deep,'—which at this point meant the bay of New York, that it was said she never could enter,—she in due courtesy replied in cannon. As she passed the various landings on the islands she was also greeted with gunpowder, and her health and the good wishes of the spectators were drunk, not in as much lager beer as would float her, but certainly in a great quantity of lager beer. As she passed the shore of the island she was admirable in her appearance. Though at a distance of more than a mile and a half, with the smoke of her cannon mantling about her and partially obscuring her magnificent proportions, she announced herself as the leviathan of the bay. By the rule of parallax, her size was indeed enormous, for she seemed to shut from observation miles of Long Island Heights over and below Greenwood and Gowanus. Her appearance as she passed up the bay took everybody by surprise. Not only was no voice of detraction heard, but all spectators were almost madly enthusiastic in her praise.

"The effort to round her to at the foot of Hammond Street was unsuccessful, it being necessary to moderate her speed so much that steerage-way was lost as soon as the engines were stopped. She accordingly swung with her head up-stream, and the efforts of two tugs, with hawsers at her bow, could not wind her. After drifting with the flood-tide, backing and going ahead for a long time, she was turned round, and at about eight o'clock P.M. was snugly got into her berth and made fast.

"There was no lack of admiration for the vast proportions, the graceful lines, and the internal arrangements and ornamentation of the ship. There was much surprise expressed at the neglected condition of the decks, which appeared as if they had neither been cleaned, scraped, holystoned, or varnished since she was launched. The planks in many places appeared badly shrunken, and suffering for want of wetting down. The same was observed of the platforms on both sides of the paddle-boxes, and other portions of wood-work of the ship. The smoke-pipes look as if they had encountered the storms of a voyage from India instead of England, and there is a general dirty appearance of the whole outside portion of the ship. It is understood that it will take several days to put her in condition to receive the visits of the public."[1]

1858.—On the Emperor of Russia's birthday, September 21, 1857, the stern-post of the "General Admiral" was laid in Wm. H. Webb's ship-yard, New York, in the presence of the Russian Minister and

---

[1] The Hon. John McLeod Murphy, once an officer of the United States navy, in a lecture on "American Ships and Ship-Builders," delivered at Clinton Hall, New York, December 29, 1859, took occasion to say,—

"I am not a prophet, nor the son of a prophet, but I hazard little in expressing the conviction that a monster ship, far exceeding the 'Great Eastern' in model and build, *will yet be launched in this country;* but her keel will not be laid until it is clearly demonstrated that she can be *made to pay*. Perhaps in the calm waters of the Pacific, when our trade shall have been fairly opened with Japan, the vessel that shall bring her enchanting fabrics and people will outstrip in magnitude and strength and speed the gigantic form of that which was conceived in the feverish brain of Brunel."

When they examined the hull of the "Great Eastern," in 1875, they found 52,000 square feet of iron plate incrusted with mussels, in some places to the thickness of six inches. The total weight of these incumbrances was estimated at 800 tons, enough to load two brigs or thirty freight cars.

The Manchester (England) *Examiner* reported in 1880 that the "Great Eastern" would be sold by auction soon, unless previously disposed of by private treaty. The step proposed was foreshadowed in the last report of the directors of the company, as will be gathered from the following paragraph : " During the past year several proposals for the employment of the ship have been made, but have fallen through from some cause or other; the directors are, however, using their best exertions to attain that object, which now becomes imperative, as the funds available for the maintenance of the ship are approaching exhaustion, and under these circumstances the directors feel it desirable to take powers from the shareholders to dispose of the ship in case no favorable proposal for chartering her should be received." The balance to the debt of profit and loss account at the close of the last year was eight thousand four hundred and thirty-one pounds. Considerable expenditure was made on the vessel last year, when she had new upper decks and part new masts. It may be stated that the capital of the company is one hundred thousand pounds, and that she stood in the books at the close of 1880 at eighty-six thousand seven hundred and fifteen pounds. She has been employed in various ways, but perhaps in none more successfully than the laying of the Atlantic cable. She is stated now to be in excellent condition.

many invited guests, the event being further celebrated by a prayer in the Russian language and a banquet at the Clarendon Hotel. A silver plate was placed in a mortice in the keel inscribed in Russian, "*The 70-gun ship "General Admiral" was begun in the presence of the Baron de Stoeckel, Russian Minister at Washington, September 21, 1857, at New York, after the plans of Wm. H. Webb, American ship-builder.*" The mortice was then closed, and the first copper bolt driven into the ship, every guest present giving a blow.

Precisely one year afterwards, on the birthday of the Grand Duke Constantine, after whom she was named, the "General Admiral" was launched with great *éclat*. Her cost was about $1,125,000. On her trip to Europe she made the voyage to Cherbourg in eleven days and ten hours, part of the time under canvas alone, with her propeller lifted clear of the water, her average speed being twelve knots an hour. In acknowledgment of her success the Emperor of Russia presented Mr. Webb with a gold snuff-box enriched with diamonds, and the British government immediately built two vessels after the same general design and model, which, however, never equaled her in speed.

She was 325 feet long, 55 feet wide, and 34 feet deep, and had two horizontal engines of 800 horse-power. A board of United States navy officers, consisting of Commodore (afterwards Rear-Admiral) A. H. Foote, Chief-Engineer W. E. Everett, and Naval Constructors S. M. Pook and B. F. Delano, reported to the Secretary of the Navy "that the workmanship and disposition of materials was excellent, and fully equal those of any vessel constructed by our government, and in regard to location of beams relatively to the parts she is superior, from the fact of the armament having been determined before building the vessel."

1858.—Thomas Rainey in his book entitled "Ocean Steam Navigation of the Ocean *Post*," says, "In offering to the government and public his volume he is conscious of his inability to present any new views, but there is no work in any country which treats of marine steam navigation in its commercial, political, economical, social, and diplomatic bearings, or discusses the theory and practice of navigation so as to develop the costs and difficulties attending high speed on the ocean or of the large expenses incurred in making regular and reliable statements."

1859.—STEAMING ON THE AMOOR.—Steam navigation was introduced upon the Amoor River, China, in 1859, by private means. The first steam vessel, called the "Admiral Kozawitch," was launched upon the waters of that river in the summer of that year. She was built in the United States, brought over in pieces, and put together at Nicolajefsk. She was constructed of timber, and had one paddle-wheel, and that astern. On her first trip she went up the river to the confluence of the Shika, and returned to Nicolajefsk. She then went up the river as far as the thriving town of Michael Semenofsky, at the mouth of the Soongari, and finally to Nianchoorsky, near Algoon, where she remained for the winter.

1858.—STEAMERS ON THE YANG-TSE-KIANG.—In 1858, it being questioned how far the Yang-tse-Kiang was navigable, a British squadron, composed of the "Retribution," Captain Barker, senior officer commanding; the "Furious," Captain Sherard Osborn (on board of which were Lord Elgin and staff); the "Cruiser," Commander Bythesea; the "Dove," gunboat, Commander Ward; and "Lee," gunboat, Lieutenant Jones, steamed up the river towards Hankow. The "Retribution" grounded and did not reach that port, but all the others did, and were the first foreign vessels to penetrate so far into the interior of China, a service which Lord Elgin availed himself of to insist that Hankow should be opened to foreign commerce. The expedition left Shanghai November 9, 1858, and returned January 1, 1859.

1860.—In February, 1860, the Yang-tse was for the first time opened by treaty to the ships of other nations, and the "Scotland," commanded by Captain A. D. Dundas, R.N., and belonging to W. S. Lindsay,[1] an auxiliary screw steamship of eleven hundred tons gross register, was the first foreign merchant vessel which loaded a cargo from Shanghai to Hankow, bringing back teas for transshipment to Europe and America; but it was not until 1863 that any English vessel loaded a cargo direct from Hankow for Great Britain. The "Scotland" sailed from Shanghai with a full cargo for Hankow in June, 1860. She drew seventeen feet of water. Two light-draught trading steamers preceded her; one an American boat, and the other a Russian vessel from the Amoor. On the 8th of May, 1860, the auxiliary steamship "Robert Lowe," of twelve hundred and fifty tons, left Shanghai for Hankow for the purpose of loading a cargo of teas *direct* for London. Two other vessels, however, had preceded her. The engines of the "Robert Lowe" were only eighty nominal horse-power, and her passage between Shanghai and Hankow, a distance of six hundred and eight miles, occupied ten days. One day was lost in changing her propeller, which she had to anchor every night. The current averaged three knots, and at times was fully five knots an hour against her. The cargo of the "Robert Lowe," for Hankow and London, consisted of nine thousand five hundred and sixty-eight chests, two hundred and thirty-four half-chests, and two thousand and fifty-four boxes of black teas; five hundred and thirty-five bales of cotton and sundries; and her freights amounted to ten thousand three hundred and fifteen pounds, and four hundred and eighty pounds passage money.

Owing to the repudiation by the Chinese of the treaty of Tientsin, the defeat of the British forces at the Peiho and the subsequent war

[1] Author of "Merchant Shipping." See p. 467.

measures which resulted in a new treaty, the formal opening of the Chinese ports was deferred until the spring of 1861.

The first merchant steamer that anchored at Hankow after Lord Elgin's treaty was the "St. Theodosius," under a German flag; the second, the "Fire-Dart," an American side-wheel steamer belonging to Heard & Co.; the third was the British steamer "Governor-General," all within a few days of each other.

The "Fire-Dart's" imagined they were the first until they found the Germans had stolen a march upon them. Her trip was a most interesting one and had some of the excitement of an exploring expedition. They had no charts except some tracings obtained by Mr. John Heard from one of the officers of Lord Elgin's expedition. They touched at a great many places, and were absent from Shanghai from April 16 to May 14, 1861. The rebel forces occupied some two hundred and fifty miles of the river, and the "Fire-Dart" had several adventures with them.

1863-64.—There were nine steamers loading between Hankow and Shanghai,—five British and four American,—some having a capacity for two thousand tons of tea, and all vessels of great speed, making the passage to Hankow in four days, and returning under favorable circumstances in less than half that time.

1873.—The "Hankow," and three other paddle-wheel steamers of a similar class, were built at Glasgow expressly for the navigation of the Yang-tse. The "Pekin," "Shanghai," and "Ichang" were finished in 1873, and the "Hankow" in April, 1874. Their dimensions were as follows:

Dimensions.	Pekin and Shanghai.	Ichang.	Hankow.
Gross tonnage	3076	1681	3168
Length on load water-line	292 feet	242 feet	306 feet
Breadth moulded	42 "	36 "	42 "
Depth	15 "	12½ "	16 "
Load Draught	10 "	9 "	11 "
Dead weight capacity	664 tons	460 tons	840 tons
Measurement capacity in tons of 40 feet	3668 "	1972 "	3800 "
Passenger accommodations, European	14 "	10 "	14 "
" " Chinese, 1st class	16 "	6 "	18 "
" " 2d class	164 "	166 "	170 "
Speed on trial	13 knots	12 knots	12⅞ knots
Diameter of cylinder	68 inches	62 inches	72 inches
Stroke	12 feet	10 feet	14 feet
Indicated horse-power	1450	1200	1840
Pressure of steam	27 lbs.	33 lbs.	35 lbs.
Consumption of fuel at full power per hour	27 cwt.	27 cwt.	40 cwt.

Steamers of the above type in 1876 left Hankow and Shanghai daily, one dispatched by Russell & Co., an American company, the other by Butterfield & Swine, an English firm.

1877.—On the 15th of March, 1877, the United States steamer "Monocacy," Commander Joseph P. Fyffe, steamed from Hankow to Ichang, three hundred and fifty miles above Hankow and one thousand miles from the sea. April 5 the formal opening of Ichang took place, and the American flag was hoisted over the newly-established consulate, being the first foreign ensign raised thus far in the interior of China, and the "Monocacy" the first foreign vessel to reach Ichang.

1861.—STEAMERS IN JAPAN.—In 1861 the Prince of Satsuma purchased the "England" and the "Scotland," two British screw steamships of eleven hundred tons gross register, being the first foreign vessels purchased by the Japanese, except by the government. As evidence of the skill and ingenuity of the Japanese, they made boilers of copper for the "England" within twelve months of the time when she came into their possession. The "England" was seized and scuttled in August, 1863, by the English at the bombardment of Kagosima, and sunk in deep water. The "Scotland" was still in the service of the Japanese in 1870.

The first steamer owned by the Japanese was the "Emperor," a yacht presented them by Lord Elgin on making his commercial treaty in 1858–59. Since then the Japanese have become owners of steamers with astonishing rapidity.

1861.—THE "MONITOR."—A resolution of the United States Senate, July 24, 1868, requested the Secretary of the Navy to communicate to that body the facts concerning the construction of the ironclad "Monitor." In answer, Secretary Welles made an elaborate report[1] detailing the history of her construction, together with that of two other ironclads,—the "New Ironsides" and the "Galena," constructed differently, as recommended by a board of navy officers September 16, 1861, composed of Commodores Joseph Smith and Hiram Paulding and Commander Charles Henry Davis.

The Secretary visited Connecticut in September, and while at Hartford, C. S. Bushnell, Esq., brought him the plan of the original "Monitor," invented by Captain John Ericsson, of New York. It received the instant approval of the Secretary, who requested Mr. Bushnell to proceed to Washington without delay and submit it to the board. He was assured that in case of unavoidable delay beyond the time limited for receiving proposals, an exception should be made in favor of this novel invention of a submerged vessel with a revolving turret, and that it should be embraced among the plans on which the opinion of the board would be required.

The board of officers in their report say, with regard to Mr. Ericsson's proposition,—

"This plan of a floating battery is novel, but seems based on a plan which will render the battery shot- and shell-proof. We are apprehensive that her properties for sea are not such as a sea-going vessel should possess. But she may be moved from one place to an-

---

[1] Executive Document, No. 86, Fortieth Congress, second session.

other on the coast in smooth water. We recommend an experiment be made with one battery of this description on the terms proposed, with a guarantee and forfeiture in case of failure in any of the properties and points of the vessel as proposed. Price, $275,000; length of vessel, 172 feet; breadth of beam, 41 feet; depth of hold, 11½ feet; time, 100 days; draught of water, 10 feet; displacement, 1255 tons; speed per hour, 9 statute miles."

In accord with this recommendation, on the 4th of October, 1861, John Ericsson, John F. Winslow, John A. Griswold, and C. S. Bushnell contracted with Gideon Welles, the Secretary of the Navy, on behalf of the United States, to build the original "Monitor," as she was later named by her inventor, and to have her and her equipments in all respects ready for sea in one hundred days after the date of the contract. The agreement was "to construct an ironclad, shot-proof steam battery of iron and wood combined on Ericsson's plan; the lower vessel to be wholly of iron, and the upper vessel of wood; the length, one hundred and seventy-nine feet; breadth, forty-one feet; depth, five feet, or larger if the contractors thought it requisite to carry the armament and stores required." Masts, spars, sails, and rigging were to be furnished sufficient to drive the vessel six knots an hour with fair breeze of wind; steam-power was to be supplied to give her a speed of eight knots, and she was to carry provisions, water, and stores of all kinds for one hundred persons for ninety days, and fuel for her engines for eight days; the deck, when loaded, was to be eighteen inches above the load-line amidships. It was also expressly stipulated that no member of Congress or officer of the navy, or any person holding office under government, should share in the contract or in any benefits arising from it,—a wise provision.

The payments made to the contractors, as per agreement, the last being only five days before the "Monitor" sailed from New York, were as follows:

1861, November 15, first payment, $50,000, less 25 per cent.	$37,500
" December 3, second payment, $50,000, less 25 per cent.	37,500
" December 17, third payment, $50,000, less 25 per cent.	37,500
1862, January 3, fourth payment, $50,000, less 25 per cent.	37,500
" February 6, fifth payment, $50,000, less 25 per cent.	37,500
" March 3, sixth payment, $25,000, less 25 per cent.	18,750
" March 14, last payment, reservations	68,750
Total	$275,000

By the terms of the contract the reservations were to be retained until the points and properties of the vessel were fully tested, not exceeding ninety days. Her performance from New York to Hampton Roads and her encounter with the "Merrimac" were deemed satisfactory tests, and the payment of the reservations was made within one

HISTORY OF STEAM NAVIGATION. 245

week after that action, as will be seen by the date of the last payment. Erroneous newspaper statements were made that the "Monitor" "was built by the contractors at their own risk, and that the government was not to be called upon for remuneration until the vessel had been tested in action. Strong in faith, receiving but a negative support from the Navy Department, the contractors completed the 'Monitor' at their own cost." It was also stated that a member of the House of Representatives from New York "advanced the money and paid the expense of getting the 'Monitor,' which met the 'Merrimac' at Hampton Roads, built." The truth is the money applied to build the "Monitor" was appropriated by Congress in August, and the money promptly handed over to the contractors, agreeably to their contract, as the work progressed. While building, the novel experiment received ridicule and abuse, but after her wonderful achievement in Hampton Roads the tone was changed, and persistent efforts were made to deny the Navy Department any credit for her adoption and construction.

The "Monitor" left New York March 6, 1862, under command of Lieutenant John L. Worden, and on the 8th reached Hampton Roads, and the next day her memorable encounter with the "Merrimac" took place.

The hull of the "Monitor" was built by Mr. T. F. Rowland, at Greenpoint, from Captain Ericsson's drawings,[1] and under his personal supervision, the material being furnished by his associates, Messrs. Griswold, Winslow, and Bushnell. The turret was built at the Novelty Iron Works, agreeably to his plans and under his supervision, with plates, rivets, etc., furnished by his associates. Being too heavy for transportation, it was taken down and placed in sections on the deck of the vessel. The port-stoppers, of heavy hammered wrought iron, were made at the steam-forge of Mr. C. D. DeLancey, in Buffalo. After the guns were discharged and run back into the turret, the stoppers were swung over the port-holes, to prevent any shot from entering the ports. The closing, being regulated by machinery, was instantaneous, and that side of the turret swung away from the enemy, the guns loaded and swung back again, and guns discharged. Thus the ports were constantly protected, either by the guns obstructing or by the ports being closed by the stoppers.

The entire internal mechanism of the turret was built to Captain Ericsson's working plans at the Delamater Iron Works. The hull and side armor was put up by Mr. Rowland. The mode of launching was planned by him. To prevent the vessel, when fully equipped with machinery, turret, and armor, from plunging under water, Mr. Rowland constructed large wooden tanks, securing them under the stern. The result of these joint efforts was that within one hundred

---

[1] "A Brief Sketch of the First 'Monitor' and its Inventor," a paper read before the Buffalo Historical Society, January 8, 1874, by Eben P. Dorr. 8vo. Pp. 49.

days from laying the keel-plates of the hull the whole work was completed and the engines of the vessel put in motion under steam.

The "Monitor" was launched on the 30th day of January, 1862, and her first trial trip and delivery to the navy-yard was February 19, 1862. She had two trial trips afterwards. On her second trial she could not be steered, and went no farther than the foot of Wall Street, New York. On the third trial trip, about March 4, she went down to Sandy Hook and tried her guns, having on board a board of officers consisting of Commodore Gregory, Chief-Engineer Garvin, and Constructor Hart, who reported favorably of her performance.[1]

How the name "Monitor" was given to this first turreted ironclad—a name that has since become generic for all this class of vessels—is told in the following letter from its inventor ten days before her launch:

"NEW YORK, January 20, 1862.

"SIR,—In accordance with your request I now submit for your approbation a name for the floating battery at Greenpoint.

"The impregnable and aggressive character of this structure will admonish the leaders of the Southern Rebellion that the batteries on the banks of their rivers will no longer present barriers to the entrance of the Union forces.

"The ironclad intruder will thus prove a severe monitor to those leaders. But there are other leaders who will be startled and admonished by the booming of the guns from the impregnable iron turret. 'Downing Street' will hardly view with indifference this last 'Yankee notion,' this monitor. To the Lords of the Admiralty the new craft will be a *monitor*, suggesting doubts as to the propriety of completing those four steel-clad ships at three and a half millions apiece.

"On these and many similar grounds I propose to name the new battery 'MONITOR.'

"Your obedient servant,
"J. ERICSSON.

"To GUSTAVUS V. FOX,
"Assistant Secretary of the Navy."

When the "Monitor" was nearly ready for commission, Lieutenant Worden was authorized to select a crew for her from the receiving-ship "North Carolina," or any other vessel of war in New York harbor.

---

[1] Previous to 1854, Ericsson's mind had dwelt upon the idea of planning and constructing an iron-plated shot-proof ship of war, and on the 26th of September, 1854, he forwarded from New York to Napoleon III. a plan of such a ship, with a synopsis of his plans, which shows beyond all cavil that America is the birthplace of the "Monitor," and that John Ericsson, the Swede, is its sole inventor. Ericsson's letter was promptly acknowledged by the Emperor, but he did not embrace the opportunity offered, and the first monitor was built for the United States in the early period of its civil troubles.

HISTORY OF STEAM NAVIGATION.

Under that authority he asked for volunteers from the "North Carolina" and the frigate "Sabine," and after fully stating to the crews of those vessels the probable dangers of the passage to Hampton Roads, and the certainty of important services to be performed there, he had many more volunteers than was required. It is unnecessary, and would be out of place here, to detail the fight in Hampton Roads,— the first naval duel between ironclads; that belongs more properly to the naval history of the period. Suffice it to say, the little turreted vessel, mounting but two guns, stood up successfully to the defense of twenty-one ships of war, mounting two hundred and ninety-six guns, all alike defenseless against the attack of the ironclad "Merrimac." She was a modern David, taking the forefront of the battle against a modern giant Goliath, while the hosts stood by anxious spectators of the conflict.

From the 10th of March until the destruction of the "Merrimac," on the 11th of May, the "Monitor" remained at Hampton Roads, guarding the Elizabeth and James Rivers, always ready for the "Merrimac." During this time her pilot-house was strengthened by heavy pieces of oak and three one-inch layers of iron plates. May 8 she engaged the battery on Sewell's Point in company with the fleet. May 12 she led the vessels that went to Norfolk when that city was evacuated by the rebels. On the 15th she participated in the engagements of Fort Darling, seven miles below Richmond. From that time until the retreat of the army from the Peninsula she was employed patrolling the James River, and arrived at Newport News August 31, being the last vessel that came down the James River. In September the "Monitor" proceeded to the Washington Navy-Yard for repairs, and sailed again for Hampton Roads in November.

On the 29th of December, 1862, under the command of Commander John P. Bankhead, she sailed for Beaufort, North Carolina, in company with the United States steamer "Rhode Island," her convoy, and on the night of the 30th she foundered near Cape Hatteras. About half of her officers and crew were carried down with her, the others escaped to the "Rhode Island." The cause of her foundering is not known. "It may, perhaps," says Mr. Dorr, "be assigned to the fact that she had lain all summer in the hot sun of the James River. The oak timber which had been fitted to the top edge of the iron hull had shrunk so that when in the heavy sea there was two or three feet of water over it most of the time on the weather side, and the water found its way through this space and flowed in great volume into the ship with fatal effect." There can be, I think, no doubt that the battering the great overhang of her deck received from the heavy seas caused it to separate from the hull to which it was fastened, and allowed the water to flow in which sunk her. The report of the board of officers who recommended her construction says they were "somewhat apprehensive that her properties for sea are not such as a sea-going vessel should possess," and this opinion was fully borne out by this result.

1863.—THE "FAID RABANI."—A beautiful steamer, the "Faid Rabani," or "Divine Favor," was built as a river pleasure yacht for the Pacha of Egypt by an English firm in 1863. She was an exquisitely-modeled vessel of the following dimensions,—viz., keel and forerake, one hundred and eighty feet; breadth of beam, twenty feet; depth of hold, nine feet; draught of water, three feet; power of engines, one hundred and fifty horses. The yacht was furnished with oscillating engines, had feathering paddles, and performed thirteen knots an hour without the slightest perceptible vibration. Her engines were bright with brass and steelwork, and finished with the same taste and care used in turning out a gold watch. Although the vessel had an ordinary escape-pipe, it was not used, for the steam was blown into the water from the sides of the yacht. She had three safety-valves and a beautiful small brass donkey-engine, independent of the others, for supplying the boilers with water when the large engines were still. The principal features of the "Faid Rabani," however were her splendid interior furnishings and decorations, including no less than four hundred and fifty pictures of separate subjects, set in frames. His Highness's reception-room, which was in the poop, was an apartment of unrivaled beauty, fitted up with the richest rosewood bulkheads, door, etc., the panels of which were filled with beautiful pictorial designs on *papier-mâché*. The divans extending round the saloon were covered with costly cloth of gold, from the front of which was suspended gold-embroidered needle-work and massive gold-bullion fringe. Between the windows were pictures of fruit and flowers, birds, etc., and vases enriched by precious stones, executed by a new patent gem-enameling process. The ceiling between the beams— which were of mahogany, French polished—was filled with designs of fruit and flowers on *papier-mâché* panels, enriched with gold-border mouldings. His Highness's bedroom was fitted up in a corresponding style of elegance. The cabins were decked out in a style of great costliness and magnificence; the fore-cabin contained twelve apartments for the pacha's officers and suite. A beautiful awning covered the main deck and poop. In point of decoration the outside of the yacht was worthy of the interior. Round all the windows, from stem to stern, were carved and gilt architraves, and the bulwarks were ornamented with carved fretwork, relieved with gold. The paddle-boxes were also highly ornamented, and on a shield in the centre was the vessel's name in Arabic. The figure-head was composed of his Highness's crest, supported by two lions richly gilded. The hull was painted a very rich green color, and was literally one blaze of gold from stem to stern.

1864.—Winan's Cigar-Shaped Steamship.—In 1858, Messrs. Winans, of Baltimore (see *Harper's Weekly*, October 28, 1858, where drawings were given), built a cigar-shaped steamer which was expected to revolutionize transatlantic steam navigation. In 1864 they built at Millwall, London, a somewhat similar vessel. She was a great iron tube, tapering away to a point at each end, and presenting the strangest possible form for a ship, her deck being merely the arc of a circle, on which were riveted stanchions for rails, and between these a raised platform with seats on each side. She had neither keel nor cut-water, and, in the language of her inventor, there was "no blunt bow standing up above the water line to receive blows from heavy seas, no flat deck to hold, or close bulwark to retain, the water that a rough sea may cast upon the vessel, neither masts, spars, nor rigging."[1] The length of the vessel was one hundred and eighty feet, or sixteen times its breadth of beam, the whole length being made available to secure water-lines favorable to fast speed. She was fitted with high-pressure engines, and her boilers were on the principle of those used on railway locomotives. The propelling power was a novel application of the screw. She appears to have failed for want of sufficient stability.

Messrs. Perkins & Sons, of London, subsequently patented a similar design, and proposed to construct and run an experimental fast express steamer from England to New York. It was proposed that she should be *eight hundred* feet in length, with forty feet beam, and have a flat bottom. She was not to draw more than eleven feet of water with her cargo, passengers, and five hundred tons of coal on board.[2]

1865.—The "Dunderberg" or "Rochambeau."—The steam ram "Dunderberg" was launched from the yard of W. H. Webb, New York, July 22, 1865. Her length was 378 feet, breadth 73 feet, depth of hold 23 feet, tonnage, 7060 tons. Her sides, five feet thick, were covered with a five-inch plating of iron. Her guns threw shells of 500 pounds, and she was driven fifteen nautical miles by an entirely concealed force of 1200 horse-power. After offering her to the United States government, which had about wound up its expensive civil war when she was launched, Mr. Webb sold her to the French government, who renamed her the "Rochambeau," but in their hands she did not prove a success. Having been built of unseasoned white oak, she soon required extensive repairs, and was finally broken up without having performed any war service.

The "Dunderberg" was built under the general superintendence of Rear-Admiral F. H. Gregory, U.S.N. The following description

---

[1] We see here a rude type of the domed steamships of 1882, expected to make great speed in crossing the Atlantic.

[2] See W. S. Lindsay's "Merchant Shipping," vol. iv., pp. 568–573.

of this novel vessel and her launch is derived from the New York *Sun:*

"At three minutes past nine o'clock on Saturday morning, at Webb's yard, New York, was launched the great naval curiosity of the age, the monster iron ram 'Dunderberg,' the mightiest vessel in the world. Admiral Francis H. Gregory, with Commander Ringgold, and other members of his staff, occupied a stand decorated with bunting, on shore and near the bow of the vessel. A large number of other distinguished personages were present.

"The 'Dunderberg,' on reaching the dock, was found to be drawing only fifteen feet aft, thirteen feet amidships, and nine feet six inches forward. The lightness of this draught is truly wonderful, and it is far less than many people supposed it would be. The ship, dressed off in flags and streamers, and her decks covered with ladies and gentlemen, made a splendid appearance in the water.

"Early in the beginning of the late Civil War, the builder of the 'Dunderberg,' Mr. W. H. Webb, prepared the general plan for the construction of a vessel to combine the requirements of the most powerful war-vessel afloat, before the monitors began to dot our coast line. The demand for vessels for blockading and swift cruising monopolized the attention of those who had the subject in charge. At last the order was given and the keel of the 'Dunderberg' was laid.

"Due care has been taken to render the 'Dunderberg' safe in a heavy seaway, being intended for a sea-going vessel. The prime necessity of offering the utmost resistance to the missiles of an enemy, was by no means lost sight of, and the advantages of an angular surface to receive the enemy's fire has been combined with a great mass of timber and the protective powers of four and a half inches of solid armor plating. In general appearance she will resemble, when afloat, a huge fort embrasured for a score of the heaviest ordnance yet placed upon the deck of any vessel. Her magnitude and novel design will be rendered pleasing to the eye by her spars and outward fittings; but the lack of the common symmetry displayed in marine architecture will lose its quaintness and be changed into a feeling of admiration of her grandeur and power.

"The whole object in the construction of this noble vessel has been to make the most terrible war-vessel in existence; one that could protect our large harbors, but, if required, launch out in mid-ocean to meet the enemy, or cross over and place under contribution any of the ports of Europe, or crush out any naval force that attempted to impede her progress.

"The hull of the 'Dunderberg' is built of several thousand feet of solid timber of the finest quality and choicest selection. The bottom is flat, the sides angular and sharp, surmounted by a casemate of sixteen guns, although pierced for twenty-one. The hull is built of square logs, bolted together, leaving no openings, and caulked inside as well as outside. This massive structure is strongly trussed with diagonal braces of iron fastened inside of the solid frame, in such a manner it seems impossible she could be damaged by any ordinary disaster. The hull is three hundred and eighty feet four inches in extreme length, and seventy-two feet ten inches extreme beam. The main hold is twenty-two feet seven and a half inches in depth. Her tonnage is set down by the naval authorities in the register as five thousand and ninety tons.

"The 'Dunderberg's' bulkheads are such she may properly be described as a double vessel, one being built inside the other. The outer vessel destroyed or seriously injured, the inner one would be able to buoy up the mass. The bulkheads run longitudinally as well as transversely, inclosing the engines, and furnishing ample space for the coal-bunkers, which, when filled with coal, give security to the engines and boilers against shot or a ram driven by the enemy.

"The *ram* is *the* feature of the 'Dunderberg,' and will attract observation and comment. It is a portion of the ship itself. It is the bow of the vessel fashioned into a huge beak, and is a solid mass of timber extending back fifty feet, arranged with a wrought-iron front-piece to protect it from shot and abrasion in contact.

"The planking of the outer hull is five inches in thickness. Outside the outer planking is the covering of logs. This commences at nothing and widens out at the top to seven feet, so that at the bilge it is three feet, and at the water-line six feet in thickness. On the cushion, which is filled in solid, is placed the armor.

"The captain's cabin is on the main deck and in the casemate aft. The ward-room is on the berth-deck aft, and forward of it will be the steerage, for the junior engineers, midshipmen, and mates.

"She will be provided with four heavy anchors, two 'bowers' and two sheet anchors, with several hundred fathoms of chain of the finest quality of iron. She will have a number of stream anchors and kedges. Two capstans will be placed on deck, one forward and one aft, while forward is a windlass of great power.

"Very large and improved magazines and shell-rooms are placed, one forward and the other aft.

"The engine department is provided with several large and powerful pumps, for clearing the ship of water in event of a leak, as well as protection against fire. In addition are two sets of hand-pumps, which can be used for like purposes, and besides are two eight-inch steam-pumps which are worked independent of the engine. The vessel is supplied with one of Normandy's fresh-water condensers capable of providing two thousand gallons of drinking-water per day.

"*The Armor.*—The armor required for the 'Dunderberg' will be about one thousand tons. The side-armor, of the best hammered iron, is manufactured into slabs, from twelve to fifteen feet in length, by three feet in width. These plates are three and a half inches, and are screw-bolted to the armor cushion by one-and-a-half-inch bolts. The plates are placed vertically, and not horizontally, as in the case with the iron-clad vessels of Europe. The armor of the casemate is four and a half inches thick, placed vertically on the sloping sides, and screw-bolted with one-and-a-half-inch bolts, which enter the woodwork to the depth of eighteen inches, none of the fastenings passing through the sides; so there will be no nuts or bolts flying about the deck in action. These slabs are twenty-eight inches in width, and are eight feet in height. The top of the casemate will have a light bomb-proof armor. The main deck outside of the casemate will be covered with thick armor, and will be secured to the deck by three-quarter-inch iron bolts with counter-sunk heads. The armor will extend out over the shelf which serves as a protection to the screw and the two rudders.

"The pilot-house is six feet in diameter, seven feet in height, and ten inches in thickness, and is on the forward upper deck of the casemate.

"In guarding against the assault of the enemy in the rear, Mr. Webb has arranged the stern with a view to obtain the greatest strength and protection, combined with lightness of construction, to avoid the drag of the water as well as the jar in a seaway, this necessary projection pounding upon the waves. This marvel of strength, with its braces and supports, is generally conceded deserving of the highest praise as a piece of skill and ingenuity.

"Beneath this shelf is the enormous propeller, weighing 32,000 pounds, the largest ever cast of composition. The screw shaft has no out-board bearing, but works upon a massive metal stern bearing, lined with strips of *lignum vitæ*. The screw is twenty-one feet in diameter, four feet in diameter at the hub, and tapering down to three-quarters of an inch at the edge of the four blades, and has a pitch of from twenty-seven to thirty-feet.

"The main rudder is abaft the propeller, and is a massive wooden structure. Forward of the screw, and over the propeller shaft, is a spare rudder, which can be put in service should any accident occur to the main rudder.

"The casemate of the 'Dunderberg' surmounts her hull, and is a tower of strength. It is constructed of square logs, each one foot in thickness, and is built to the height of seven feet in the clear, and covered over with a bomb-proof deck, on which it was intended to place two turrets, similar to those in use on board of the monitors. The casemate will contain twelve to fourteen 11-inch Dahlgren, and four 15-inch Rodman smooth-bore guns, making it the heaviest armament of its number ever placed on the deck of any vessel. The

'Dunderberg' contract price was one million four hundred thousand dollars.

"The hull of the vessel from below the water-line rises to the gunwale at an angle of about thirty-five degrees, when it joins the casemate, which inclines inward at an angle of about fifty-five degrees. This, it is expected, will 'shed' shot with perfect ease and certainty.

"To support the immense weight, and give strength to the bottom of the fabric, the vessel has an enormous keel and four keelsons, on which rest the bed-plates of the engines, and furnish the foundation for the upright stanchions or supports which aid in holding up the weight of the casemate and its contents.

"The 'Dunderberg' will be rigged as an hermaphrodite brig,—*i.e.*, having yards upon her foremast and fore-and-aft sails upon her mainmast. She will spread several thousand yards of canvas, which will steady her in a seaway and aid her in making a passage across the ocean or cruising at sea or along our shores. She will be provided with boats to accommodate six hundred souls.

"GENERAL DIMENSIONS OF THE SHIP.

Extreme length	380 feet 4 inches.
Extreme beam	72 " 10 "
Depth of main hold	22 " 7 "
Height of casemate	7 " 9 "
Length of ram	50 "
Draught when ready for sea	21 "
Displacement	7000 tons.
Tonnage	5090 "
Weight of iron armor	1000 "

"DIMENSIONS OF ENGINES, BOILERS, ETC.

Cylinders (two) each	100 inches.
Stroke of pistons	45 "
Boilers—six main and two donkey.	
Depth of boilers	18 feet.
Height of boilers	17 " 6 inches.
Front of boilers	21 " 6 "
Weight of boilers	450 tons.
Boiler surface	30,000 feet.
Grate surface	1,200 "
Condenser surface	12,000 square feet.
Diameter of propeller	21 feet.
Pitch of propeller	27 to 30 feet.
Weight of propeller	34,580 pounds.
Capacity of coal-bunkers	1,000 tons.
Actual horse-power	5,000 horse.
Nominal horse-power	1,500 "

"*The Engines.*—The 'Dunderberg' will be propelled by two horizontal back-acting condensing engines of five thousand actual horsepower, subjected to the most critical inspection at the instance of the

Navy Department, and pronounced without fault or blemish in any respect. They are massive, beautiful, and powerful, and reflect credit upon their builders. The cylinders are two in number, and each one hundred inches in internal diameter, with forty-five inches stroke of piston. These enormous cylinders were bored out horizontally to prevent springing. The engines have one of Allen's patent surface condensers, of the tubular pattern, ten feet in width, twenty-six feet long, and five feet deep. The air-circulating and condensing pumps are worked independently. The air-pump has two steam cylinders, 36 x 36 inches, working the pump, which is also 36 x 36 inches. The circulating pumps, two in number, and the condenser pumps, 33 x 36 inches, with 36-inch cylinders and 45-inch stroke. There is one bilge-pump for each engine, and two donkey-pumps with 9-inch cylinders and 12-inch stroke. There are four blowers for ventilation, driven by independent engines.

"The main engines are reversed by two small engines which can be controlled by a small boy. The engines will make sixty revolutions per minute, ordinary speed, on a pressure of twenty-five pounds of steam. The pumping, air-condensing, and circulating engines will run at forty-five revolutions per minute. A prominent feature of the engine department of the 'Dunderberg' is the mechanical skill displayed in the placing of the line-shafting and bearing of the propeller-shaft. The main bearings are forty inches in length, and are provided with hollow brasses for water circulation. The thrust-bearing has thirteen thrust-collars on the shaft, and in addition a ball-thrust is attached. Steam is furnished to the engines by six horizontal tubular boilers, each thirteen feet in depth, seventeen feet six inches in height, and twenty-one feet five inches front. The furnaces are situated in two tiers, with ten furnaces to each boiler, making a total of sixty furnaces in the main boilers. There are two donkey-boilers, each with four furnaces. The smoke-pipe is thirteen feet in diameter, and where it passes through the gun-room it is shot-proof. It contains a grating to prevent anything being thrown down to damage the boilers. Some idea can be formed of the size of the smoke-stack when we state that it is sufficiently commodious, standing upright, to accommodate twenty persons seated around a table placed inside. Bulkheads of iron are placed transversely at each end of the space occupied by the boilers and machinery; these extend from the floors up to the spar-deck, and form water-tight compartments of sufficient capacity to float the ship in case of an emergency. The coal-bunkers have a capacity of one thousand tons. The propeller shaft is in four sections, and is one hundred and eighteen feet in length; it is eighteen inches in diameter, and is supported by four main journals. The stern bearing is of brass and extends outside of the vessel two feet. The engines are expected to give the screw sixty revolutions per minute, working at an ordinary and regular rate of speed, although it is believed in case of need they can be worked up as high as seventy-five or eighty turns. The former rate can be attained with twenty-five pounds pressure of steam, but by the addition of the donkey-boilers and full firing, steam can be raised to forty pounds. The contract calls for a speed of fifteen knots per hour. The 'Dunderberg' will carry from ten to fifteen days' coal. The cost of the engines and boilers will be over half a million of dollars."

1866.—THE DOUBLE-TURRETED MONITORS "MONADNOCK" AND "MIANTONOMOH."—This class of vessels was never designed for cruising purposes, but for harbor defense and operations upon the coast of the United States, and, owing to the foundering of the original "Monitor" off Cape Hatteras, and another of these vessels in the blockade off Charleston, an impression prevailed that they could not be sent with safety outside the harbors in which they were constructed. To dispel this false impression the Secretary of the Navy decided to send the "Miantonomoh" across the Atlantic to Europe and return, and the "Monadnock" *via* the Straits of Magellan to California, but not without accompanying vessels to tow them if needed, and to insure the safety of their crews in case of disaster or shipwreck. The "Monadnock," after navigating the Atlantic and Pacific, reached San Francisco in safety and was placed in ordinary at Mare Island Navy-Yard, where an iron vessel of the same name and similar dimensions has since been built, to receive her engines and machinery, the old wooden hull having become decayed. The "Miantonomoh," a vessel of the same size and type, crossed the Atlantic, passed up the Baltic to Cronstadt, visited many of the principal ports of Europe, and returned in safety to the United States. Like her sister vessel, her wooden hull, having become decayed, has been replaced by an iron one, and her iron plating has been exchanged for one of compound steel.

The "Monadnock," under command of Lieutenant-Commander Francis M. Bunce, sailed from Hampton Roads, Virginia, November 2, 1865, in company with the "Vanderbilt" and the "Powhatan," paddle-wheel steamers, and the "Tuscarora," a screw ship, and arrived at St. Thomas, West Indies, November 11, after a somewhat stormy passage of nine days. "The 'Monadnock' behaved so well at sea," says Commodore John Rodgers in his official report, "as to inspire her officers not only with confidence, but with enthusiasm at her performance as a sea-boat. They do not doubt her ability to go anywhere." At St. Thomas she was visited by Santa Anna, ex-president of Mexico. Captain Bunce, in his report from there, says, "The engines have not stopped except in obedience to the bell. She has made an average speed of 5.85 knots per hour, the greatest distance run in any one day being 162; the least, 79.5. In scudding she behaves well, her propeller guarding the rudder against heavy shocks. A head sea has but little effect on her. Her motion is greatest with the sea abaft the beam; but her roll, though quick and short, is easy." On her voyage to St. Thomas she consumed 213 tons of coal, or an average of 23 tons 8 cwt. daily. On the 26th of November she arrived at Salute Island, French Guiana, having made an average speed of 6.01 knots per hour on an average daily expenditure of 25 tons, 19 cwt. of coal. On the 10th of December she was at Ciara, Brazil, after a passage from Salute Island of nine days, five hours, having made an average speed of 5.34 knots per hour on a daily expenditure of 27¼ tons of coal. On the 26th of December she arrived at Bahia in company with the attending squadron, having stopped at Pernambuco; her steaming performance continued equally, and she aided her engines with extemporized sails, which added from a knot to a knot and a half to her speed. On the 3d of January the squadron arrived at Rio Janeiro, and on the passage from Bahia to Rio her average speed was seven knots on a daily expenditure of 26½ tons of coal. At Rio the emperor of the Brazils, Dom Pedro II., visited the "Monadnock." From Rio to Montevideo she averaged a speed of 7.37 knots. From Montevideo to Valparaiso her average speed was 7.1 knots. Commodore Rodgers, in his report from Valparaiso, March 2, 1866, says,—

"Any difficulties in the voyage to San Francisco which may have been anticipated are believed to end here. It would be something unusual were we to encounter any weather which an ordinary steamboat could not resist. The powers of the monitor have been much more than equal to the difficulties that we have thus far met, and the result amply vindicates the judgment of the department in directing a voyage which was generally thought perilous, but of the success of which I had no doubt. In the long seas of the Pacific to the southward of this I observed that the 'Monadnock' took very little water upon her decks, rising over the waves easily and buoyantly." Her commander, the same, reports, "The machinery has worked admirably. The passage through the Straits of Magellan and Sarmiento Channel to the Gulf of Penar presented no difficulties which were not easily overcome. I feared, in passing through the narrow places and abrupt turnings, the length of the ship would give trouble, but in practice found none whatever."

On the 25th of April the "Monadnock" arrived at Callao, Peru, and on May 13 at Panama, having stopped at Payta, with her usual average of speed and expenditure of coal. Her next stopping-place was Acapolio, in Mexico, May 29, and on the 22d of June she arrived at San Francisco. On the 28th of June, Commodore Rodgers reports, "I have the honor to announce the safe arrival of the 'Vanderbilt' and the 'Monadnock' at the navy-yard, Mare Island. The 'Monadnock' found no weather on her voyage from Philadelphia to this place which seemed to touch the limit of her sea-going qualities.

The engines have performed as satisfactory as the hull, and have arrived in complete order. The success of the voyage amply vindicates the judgment of the department in undertaking it, and the hopes of the most sanguine of 'Monitor' people are fulfilled in this crucial experiment."

Lieutenant-Commander Bunce, in his report, says, "During the recent passage of this ship from Philadelphia to this port (San Francisco) the 'Monadnock' has run by log 15,385 knots. Her average speed has been 6.32 knots. The engines have been run about sixty revolutions per minute, that being the point judged to be most economical in fuel and in wear and tear of machinery. Not a single piece of the spare machinery has been used, and the engines are all now in good working order; they have been able to perform all work demanded of them. The vessel is an excellent sea-boat, and has received no damage from any weather we have encountered.

" In her present condition she is as perfectly safe and trustworthy a vessel for cruising in any part of the world as a vessel can be relying on steam alone for its motive-power, and twice as safe as most steamers, for she has two independent pairs of steam-engines, either of which are sufficient to keep the ship under control in any weather, and to propel her in ordinary conditions of wind and sea five knots per hour. At sea she has never needed or received assistance of any kind whatever from other vessels, and therefore I regard her, or any vessel of her class, as a thoroughly competent, independent cruiser."

Such was the successful voyage of the first turreted vessel from the Atlantic to the Pacific. It was followed soon after by the safe voyages of two single-turreted monitors to Callao, which had been sold to the agents of the Peruvian government by the government of the United States.[1]

THE "MIANTONOMOH" AND HER VOYAGE.—We now turn to the voyage of the sister ship, and her crossing and recrossing the Atlantic. The "Miantonomoh" left New York under the command of Commander J. C. Beaumont, and under the escort of the paddle-wheel steamship "Augusta" and the double-ender "Ashuelot," May 6, and arrived at Halifax on the 10th; left Halifax on the 18th, and arrived at St. John's, Newfoundland, on the 23d, and at Queenstown,

---

[1] The two monitors, "Catawba" and "Oneota," of 1054 tons, fitted with Ericsson's patent trunk engines, were purchased from the United States government by the agents of the Peruvian government, and added to the navy of the republic under the names of " Manco Capac" and " Atahuallpa." They arrived at Callao in May, 1870, after a prolonged voyage of eighteen months, having steamed 12,000 miles, the engines having made 4,500,000 revolutions. In latitude 44° 50′ S. in the Pacific they encountered a very heavy gale, which not only tried the strength of the ship, but its sea-going qualities. The monitors proved splendid sea-boats, their heaviest rolling being but seven degrees, while their convoy was rolling twenty-eight degrees.

Ireland, June 16, at 4 P.M., after a pleasant passage across the Atlantic of ten days, and having been in tow of the "Augusta," "as a matter of convenience or precaution" more than necessity, a great portion of the way, the "Miantonomoh" consuming a fair proportion of coal. Captain Murray, in his report, says, "I think she could have crossed over alone. Heavy weather does not appear to materially affect the speed or rolling of the monitor, for while the other vessels were lurching about, their progress being checked by heavy seas, she went along comparatively undisturbed or unchecked." On the 23d of June the "Miantonomoh" arrived at Portsmouth, England. Mr. Fox, Assistant Secretary of the United States Navy, joined her at Halifax and took passage in her to Queenstown, where he left her, being a special messenger to the emperor of Russia, bearing the congratulations of the people of the United States on his escape from assassination. He rejoined her, however, at Cherbourg, France, but left her again at Kiel. The "Miantonomoh" afterwards made an extended cruise in the Mediterranean, visiting most of the principal naval ports, and returned to the United States *via* the West Indies, arriving at Philadelphia in July, 1867, after having steamed 17,767 miles. Her performance was in every respect as satisfactory as was that of the "Monadnock." Everywhere she was an object of interest and attention. In England she was visited by the lords of the Admiralty, the Prince of Wales, the Dukes of Edinburgh, Argyle, and Sutherland, and other high dignitaries; in Copenhagen, by the king of Denmark and the royal family; and her arrival at Cronstadt with the "Augusta" was the occasion of a great naval fête. Indeed, her whole cruise in Northern Europe proved one continued ovation. At Hamburg, Rear-Admiral Popoff, the distinguished naval constructor of the Russian navy, came on board, and with his staff took passage in her to Cronstadt, and was delighted with his trip and the performance of the monitor.

The recrossing the Atlantic was accomplished under the most favorable circumstances as regards weather, but the monitor, in consequence of a foul bottom, did not behave as well, her average speed being but six and a half knots instead of seven, which was the average made during the run from St. John's to Queenstown. On both passages she was aided a greater part of the time by the tow-line of the "Augusta." From Naples to Philadelphia, a distance of 7500 miles, head winds were encountered in only two instances,—viz., on the second day out from Naples, and the day before she arrived in the Delaware.

After these two voyages no doubt remained that the larger class of monitors were seaworthy vessels, capable of crossing the Atlantic or visiting the most distant seas, when necessity required them to, though their particular province is the defense of our coasts and harbors.

The tonnage of the "Monadnock" and the "Miantonomoh," then building, is stated in the United States *Navy Register* for 1864, by the old measurement, to be 1564 tons each. In 1866, by the new measurement, the "Miantonomoh" was 1225 tons; the "Monadnock" 1091, which infers a difference of model. They continued to be so reported until the register of 1881, where both are stated to have a tonnage of 1226 tons, and a displacement of 3815 tons.

It seems more than probable that the seaworthiness of these vessels suggested the idea of the domed and mastless steamship "Meteor," now (1882) building, which is to make a rapid transit of the Atlantic, if the expectation of her constructor and owners is fulfilled.

1866.—BRITISH STEAM INVENTION FOR TEN YEARS PRECEDING.—The British Patent-Office has published a series of classified abridgments of specifications of patents in fifty-five handy volumes, which contain all the patents of the particular subjects treated in each volume that have been reported from the establishment of the patent-office up to a late date. No such index of American invention has been issued by the United States Patent-Office, and the inquirer has to search through the records of one hundred years to select what he particularly wants.

Thus the two 12mo volumes, of 333 and 340 pages respectively, "on marine propulsion, exclusive of sails," contain abridgments of every patent on that subject issued from the British Patent-Office from 1618 to 1866.

The second volume shows that during the ten years comprised between January, 1857, and December, 1866, 17 patents were taken out for air expelled to propel a vessel, 26 for air-pump to steam-engine, 26 for fire-bars to steam-engine, 163 concerning boilers, 8 for canal navigation, 5 for cranks, 119 for cylinders, 74 for condensers, 6 for vessels supported on drums, 212 for steam-engines, 75 for feathering paddles, 100 concerning furnaces, 35 for governors, 7 for gauges, 69 for hydro-propulsion, 11 for preventing the incrustation of boilers, 10 for life-boats, etc., 8 for atmospheric-engines, 4 for gas-engines, 5 for heated air, 32 for paddle-floats, 98 for paddle-wheels, 10 for submerged wheels, 340 for screw propellers, devices of various kinds, etc., 15 for refrigerators for engines, 70 concerning shafts for paddle-wheels or propellers, 3 for starting-gear, 4 for stopping vessels, 52 for steering, 4 for submarine vessels, 29 for superheating steam, 11 for towing, 27 for turbines, 71 for valve and valve gear, 3 for revolving vessels, 2 for vessel separate for engine, and many other minor inventions; and the first volume (1618–1857) contains thirty pages of index, showing quite as many more.

1867.—STEAMERS ON LAKE MEMPHREMAGOG, NEW HAMPSHIRE.—The Memphremagog Steam Navigation Company had three steamers in 1867 plying upon that lake in New Hampshire, and two more upon the stocks. A traveler describes a trip in one of these boats to inspect another upon the stocks that year.

"Friday last," he says, "I took a trip upon the 'Mountain Maid' to Magog to inspect the new boat. She exceeds the best of the Winnipiseogee boats in her construction, in speed, and in her appointments, and will equal the largest of them in size. She is not an American boat, although American capital has been liberally invested in her. She will fly the flag of the new Dominion of Canada (supposing that to be different from the British bunting).

"The name of the steamer is taken from Mount Oxford, the highest mountain in Canada, which stands a sentinel at the outlet of the lake, rearing its pyramid almost five thousand feet from its waters. The hull is iron, the plates having been made and fitted upon the Clyde. Her length is one hundred and seventy feet; her low pressure engine has a thirty-six-inch cylinder and ten feet stroke, and is of superior finish.

"The company has purchased the 'Mountain Maid' and rebuilt her. The 'Oxford' is to make two trips a day through the lake. The 'Maid' will run as an auxiliary freight- and tow-boat."

The "Mountain Maid" being insufficient to meet the wants of pleasure-seekers, an iron steamer was built and placed on the lake. The hull was built on the Clyde. It was brought over, and the steamer completed at Magog. It is one hundred and seventy feet long, and is divided into four water-tight compartments, and is conveniently fitted up with dining-saloon and ladies' cabin. It was christened the "Lady of the Lake." It runs seventeen miles an hour, makes two daily trips between Newport and Magog, and takes three hours to make the run from one end of the lake to the other, including stops.

In addition to the "Lady of the Lake," there are a number of smaller steamers at Newport.

1869.—STEAMER ON THE GREAT SALT LAKE.—The "Kate Corser," the first steamer to cross the American "Dead Sea,"—the Great Salt Lake,—and employed for some time in transporting ties to the Union Pacific Railroad, in 1869 made a successful trip up Bear River to Corinne. The local newspaper says, "On nearing the city the circus band-wagon containing the band, with several other carriages, started to meet her. About one mile below she steamed to shore and took them aboard. She stemmed the current admirably, and bore up to the city like a swan, amid the sound of swelling music, the deafening boom of anvils, and the cheers of the throng upon the river's bank." Bear River was found to be perfectly free from falls or rapids; the current, however, was very strong.

EXTRAORDINARY INLAND VOYAGE.—On the 5th day of August, 1869, the steamer "Helen Brooks" left Baltimore, Maryland, for Bayou Teche, Louisiana. She left Baltimore by way of the Chesapeake Bay, and passed through the State of Delaware by canal; up the Delaware River to Trenton, New Jersey; through the State of

HISTORY OF STEAM NAVIGATION.

New Jersey by canal; down the Raritan River to New York City; up the Hudson River to Troy; through the State of New York by the Erie Canal to Buffalo; thence by way of Lake Erie to Chicago; down through the Illinois Canal to the Illinois River; and thence down the Mississippi River, arriving at Napoleon October 14, 1869, after a circuitous journey of over three thousand miles.

THE MERCANTILE STEAMERS OF THE WORLD, 1870–74.

NATIONALITY.	Number.			Average Size in Tons.			Tonnage.		
	1870.	1873.	1874.	1870.	1873.	1874.	1870.	1873.	1874.
American	597	408	613	861	1199	1254	513,792	483,040	768,724
Asiatic	..	..	6	..	..	576	..	..	3,459
Austrian	74	91	81	599	925	1025	44,312	84,155	83,039
Belgian	14	42	39	746	725	1039	10,462	30,444	40,536
British	2426	3061	3002	681	857	1005	1,651,767	2,624,481	3,015,778
Central American	..	..	9	..	..	592	..	..	5,332
Danish	44	71	67	275	486	582	12,085	34,498	38,976
Dutch	82	95	107	481	766	876	39,406	72,753	93,723
French	288	392	315	739	808	1012	212,976	316,765	318,757
German	127	200	220	827	1024	1222	105,131	204,894	268,828
Greek	8	8	9	408	424	592	3,267	3,390	5,329
Italian	86	103	110	423	826	827	36,358	85,045	91,011
Norwegian	26	88	112	282	478	453	7,321	41,602	51,108
Portuguese	18	17	23	729	855	802	13,126	14,586	18,452
Russian	62	114	144	458	592	771	28,422	67,522	111,072
South American	..	..	72	..	..	728	..	..	52,387
Spanish	148	202	212	492	686	733	72,845	138,675	155,417
Swedish	83	148	195	224	373	397	18,633	53,327	77,440
Turkish and Egyptian	..	9	29	..	339	949	..	3,049	27,580
Various	49	109	..	481	643	..	23,550	70,067	....
Totals	4132	5148	5365	676	841	974	2,793,452	4,328,193	5,226,868

1872.—From 1841 to 1872 forty-four steamships, employed on voyages between the United States, England, and the Continent, were lost. Four of these were wooden paddle-wheel steamers, the remainder were iron vessels.

The "President," "City of Glasgow," "City of Boston," "Pacific," "Tempest," "United Kingdom," and "Mina Thomas" foundered at sea, and were never heard from. Between 1857 and 1864 nine iron steamers, running from the mouth of the St. Lawrence to Portland, Maine, were lost.

1867.—PETROLEUM AS FUEL ON BOARD STEAMERS.—Under authority of an act approved April 27, 1866, appropriating five thousand dollars for testing the use of petroleum as a fuel under marine boilers, an elaborate series of experiments was made at the Boston Navy-Yard on board the United States steamer "Palos," a first-class screw tugboat of 350 tons, to ascertain the value of crude petroleum as a fuel for generating steam in marine boilers, the burning apparatus being the invention of Mr. Henry R. Foote. The steamer made a successful excursion down the harbor and back, and the experiments were continued at the wharf for several months, but the general result was not considered satisfactory. About the same time other experiments were made at the Brooklyn Navy-Yard with the same fuel and the boilers and apparatus invented by Clark Fisher, an engineer of the United States navy. Also, among other systems of burning petroleum under the same boilers, was tried that of Mr. Simon Stevens.[1]

The conclusion arrived at was that convenience, health, comfort, and safety were against the use of petroleum in steam-vessels, and that the only advantage shown was a not very important reduction in the bulk and weight of fuel carried.

1867.—Up to 1867 the largest and fastest merchant ocean steamer built on the American continent was the "Adriatic," of the Collins Line. The hull was 343$\frac{1}{12}$ feet long on the load-line, and her extreme breadth 343$\frac{1}{12}$ feet. Her displacement was 5233 tons.

1870.—The "Palos."—The first United States steamer to pass through the Suez Canal was the "Palos," fourth-rate, Commander L. A. Beardslee, which entered the canal at Port Said on the morning of August 9, 1870. Leaving it on the 11th at 7 A.M., the steamer arrived at Ismailia at 3 P.M., having been detained three hours in the "gares" waiting for steamers coming from the southwest to pass, and after several other detentions at "gares" arrived at Suez at 1.30 P.M., August 13, 1870, having been *under way* in the canal seventeen hours.

Commander Beardslee reported that the canal for its entire length at that date had a nearly level floor, with from 24 to 28 feet of water, 72 feet wide, and that a vessel drawing 16 feet had a channel 116 feet in width.

1870.—The "Hotspur," the first ironclad, constructed chiefly as a ram for the royal navy, was launched in 1870.

1870.—Compound Engines in the Royal Navy.—The wooden screw corvette "Briton" was taken out of Sheerness harbor on the 10th of June, 1870, for a final trial of her engines and the *newly invented* plan of reheating the steam on its passage from a small to a large cylinder. The London *Times* said, "The value of the invention was amply proved; the trial having finally disposed of the long-vexed question as to the best means of economizing fuel in steamships." The "Briton" was kept in full speed for four consecutive hours, the engines making seventy-seven revolutions, the speed being over twelve knots, and the consumption of coal only 1.3 pounds per horse-power per hour, the average consumption of coal on her Majesty's steamers having before ranged from 3 to 4 pounds per horse-power per hour. A previous trial of the "Briton" had not been so successful.

1871.—Compound Engines in the United States Navy.—This year Chief-Engineer J. W. King, U.S.N., made a strong report in favor of compound engines, in which he stated that the Fairfield Works on the Clyde had completed one hundred and thirty *pairs* of

---

[1] See Report of Secretary of the Navy, December 2, 1867. Report of the Chief of the Bureau of Steam Engineering.

compound engines, and had then, at the time of his visit, twenty-two pairs under construction, all for ocean steamers. That firm or company was then regarded as the pioneer of the compound system, and its productions were accepted as the best types.[1]

In consequence of this favorable report, the Honorable Secretary of the United States Navy ordered all new vessels and those requiring new engines to be fitted with those of the compound type.[2] In December, 1872, Chief-Engineers Charles H. Loring and Charles H. Baker made a very strong report to the Secretary of the Navy in favor of compound engines.

1872.—FUEL-SAVINGS EXPERIMENT.—In 1872 a discovery was made by which the cost of steam-power, it was claimed, was reduced sixty per cent. It was put into practical operation at the Atlantic Works in Boston. By a novel process the great amount of heat that escapes into the air in the waste or exhaust steam from engines is utilized by conducting it through the tubes of a boiler filled with the bisulphide of carbon, "a fluid which boils at 110° F., and at the temperature of exhaust steam gives a pressure of sixty-five pounds to the inch in the boiler;" the vapor formed in this boiler is used to drive an engine, instead of steam, and after being used, is condensed by cooling, pumped into the boiler again, and used continuously without loss.

Careful experiments proved that the fuel required to produce one hundred horse-power with the best engines then in use would by this process produce two hundred and fifty horse-power, a gain of one hundred and fifty per cent. in the power obtained by the same consumption of fuel.

For making a careful test of this process, two new engines of the same size and construction were put up at the Atlantic Works. One was run by steam in the usual manner, while the heat that escaped in the exhaust from this engine was used to heat a boiler and drive the second engine. A careful measurement of the power produced by each of the engines showed that while the first engine, worked by steam in the usual way, produced 6.23 horse-power, the second engine, worked entirely by the waste heat escaping in the exhaust from the first, produced 9.12 horse-power, the two together producing 15.35 horse-power with the fuel required to drive the steam-engine alone.

The coal required to run a steam-engine of one hundred horse-power, of the best class in use, is about four thousand pounds per day, or six hundred tons a year. It was claimed by this discovery that the same engine could be run with sixteen hundred pounds of coal per day, or two hundred and forty tons per year, saving three hundred and sixty tons of coal a year for each hundred horse-power produced.

[1] Report of J. W. King, U.S.N., Chief of Bureau of Steam Engineering, to the Secretary of the Navy, October 30, 1871.

[2] See Secretary of Navy Report, 1872.

For steam-vessels the advantages of this process would be greater than for stationary engines, as a large amount of room occupied by coal would be saved, and could be used for freight. The vessel could also carry fuel to last through a much longer voyage, enabling steam- to compete with sailing-vessels on long voyages advantageously.

1873.—THE CABLE STEAMER "FARADAY."—This vessel was built in 1873 for laying Atlantic cables. She is 366 feet in length, has 52 feet beam, is 36 feet in depth, and measures 5000 tons gross, but can carry 6000 tons dead weight. Her iron hull, in addition to the requirements of "Lloyds," was enormously strengthened to fit her for the service for which she was built. She is fitted with three cable tanks constructed of plate-iron, which form a series of double arches supporting the sides of the vessel. These tanks are united together and to the general fabric of the hull by five iron decks. The vessel is doubled-bottomed, the space between the two bottoms being a net-work of iron girders for carrying the cable tanks, and at the same time giving longitudinal strength to that portion of the hull. The space is further utilized for carrying water ballast, to trim the vessel as the cable is run out, and to enable her to make a voyage across the Atlantic without cargo or other weight beyond fuel. In outward appearance the "Faraday" is unlike other ocean steamers, her bow and stern being of the same form, and she is fitted with a rudder at each end. She has two surface condensing engines, each working a separate screw. The object of this arrangement is to obtain increased steering or manœuvring power, which is a very important condition in cable laying.

1875.—THE DOUBLE-HULL "CASTALIA."—To provide ample accommodations for all classes of passengers under shelter as well as on deck, to reduce the motion of rolling and pitching to a minimum, and to keep the draught to six feet, so that the steamer could enter the channel ports on both sides at every state of tide, the "Castalia" was built at the Thames Iron Works. She may be roughly described as the two halves of a longitudinally divided hull, 290 feet long, placed 26 feet apart, and strongly bound together. Under this deck worked a pair of paddle-wheels, *side by side*, on two separate shafts, so that each wheel could be worked independently by two pairs of engines, one pair on each half of the vessel. The division of the hull provided a deck *sixty feet* wide. Before and behind the engine were state-saloons enclosed by the hurricane deck running the whole width of the vessel. There were also decks below running fore and aft to within a few feet of the double bow in the separate hulls. The "Castalia" had accommodation for one thousand passengers.

A correspondent of the London *Times* says of this steamer,—

"Returning from our autumnal tour, we determined to give the 'Castalia' a trial. The weather was unusually boisterous; at Calais it was difficult to stand against the gust of wind which swept across the pier. Outside, the sea ran high, and the usual discomforts of the passage presented themselves to us. The 'Castalia,' when she left the pier, seemed to glide to the turbulent waters outside. For a moment it puzzled one to find the deck as firm and level as a dinner-table, and yet waves breaking all around. We performed the passage to Dover in about two hours and a quarter; the motion was very slight indeed, about as much as in the ordinary steamers after they get within the harbor of Dover or Calais,—every few minutes there was one single roll of about three degrees. There was no tremulous motion from the paddles. I explored the saloons for indications of straining, but found none; the surface of the paint was without a shadow of a crack, and throughout the passage there was no creaking noise. When we arrived in Dover the decks before and aft of the funnels were as dry as when we left Calais. The sea was enough to try the regular steamers, but on board the 'Castalia' children were playing about, every one was perfectly comfortable, and I can safely state that it is the first time I ever crossed the Channel without seeing a sign of sickness."

1875.—THE "BESSEMER."—This vessel was constructed for the Channel service to combine great speed, a light draught, and the least possible rolling and pitching motions, and to afford passengers crossing the Channel the quickest transit with the greatest amount of ease, at an immersion so small that the vessel could enter the existing English and French harbors at all times of the tide. The "Bessemer" was designed by E. J. Reed, ex-constructor to the royal navy, with the exception of her anti-seasick swinging saloon, which was the invention of Mr. Bessemer. The vessel was so novel in her construction as to be an object of great interest. She was three hundred and fifty feet long at the water-line, and forty-eight feet at each end; the deck was only four feet above the line of flotation, so that in rough weather the sea would wash over these low ends. The decks on this portion of the vessel had a considerable curve, and the sides of the ship were rounded off so that the water might escape. This form of end was selected to obviate any tendency to pitching. Above these low decks was a breastwork eight feet high, two hundred and fifty-four feet long, and all the width of the vessel. The whole of this breastwork deck was for the use of the passengers, and portions fore and aft of the paddle-boxes were protected with stanchions. The vessels were propelled by *four* paddle-wheels, and ninety feet of space between the paddles was occupied by the swinging saloon. Beyond this and at each end the space nearest the saloon was occupied by the engines and the boilers. At one end of the breastwork there was accommodation for the crew, and beneath their quarters stowage-room for passengers' luggage, etc. At the opposite end of the breastwork the space was fitted with cabins for the ladies, and below these cabins was a saloon fifty-two feet long, fitted with sofa seats all around. Along the sides of the breastwork deck, between the paddle-boxes, were other cabins, smoking- and refreshment-rooms. The "Bessemer" swinging saloon was about seventy feet long, thirty-five feet wide, and twenty feet high. The weight of the saloon was borne by four large bearings, one at each end and two near the centre. The end bearings were fixed on iron transverse bulkheads, which were well-stiffened by fore-and-aft ways to prevent their buckling. The saloon was a superbly-fitted apartment. The top of it formed a promenade-deck, and was fitted all around with seats. The saloon was entirely under the control of machinery invented by Mr. Bessemer, and it was expected that the passengers would not feel any more unpleasant sensation than they would in going up or down the Thames.

The swinging saloon was in the centre of the vessel, and was entered by two broad staircases leading to a landing connected with the saloon by a flexible flooring. The aftermost of the two central supports was hollow, and served as a part of the hydraulic machinery for regulating the motion of the saloon.

The nominal horse-power of the engines of the "Bessemer" was 750, but they could be worked up to an indicated power of 4600, and were calculated to drive the vessel at a speed of from eighteen to twenty statute miles an hour. The paddle-wheels, one hundred and six feet apart and twenty-seven feet ten inches in diameter, were fitted with twelve feathering floats.

May 8, 1875.—The "Bessemer" crossed from Dover to Calais and back again, when her speed was about the same as the ordinary boats.

THE "CALAIS-DOUVRE."—Another twin boat for crossing the Channel between England and France, called the "Calais-Douvre," in some respects an improvement on the "Bessemer," has been built and is in successful service. Her length is three hundred and two feet; breadth over all sixty-one feet; depth, thirteen feet nine inches; water-space between the hulls, twenty-four and a half feet; draught, seven feet; speed, fourteen and a half to fifteen knots. The diameter of her cylinders is sixty-three inches; stroke of piston, six feet; cut-off, three-tenths of stroke; revolutions of her paddle-wheel, thirty-five per minute; steam pressure, thirty pounds; diameter of wheel, twenty-four feet; beam of each hull, eighteen feet three inches; horse-power, 3600. She was built at Newcastle-upon-Tyne.

1875.—HIGH-SPEED BOATS IN RUSSIA.—In 1875 a high-speed boat was built at St. Petersburg on an improved plan, whose outer hull was made entirely of Muntz metal, it being cheaper than copper as a sheathing for wooden vessels. In a trial with one of the fastest boats she was victorious, and accomplished nineteen miles per hour, the engines making an average of nearly six hundred revolutions per minute, working with steam at one hundred pounds per square inch. This vessel is described as forty-eight feet long at the load-line, having six and one-half feet beam, and three and one-half feet depth of hold, while her mean draught was one foot nine inches. She had compound engines of superior workmanship in every respect, which drove a screw two feet nine inches in diameter, having three feet four inches in pitch.

1876.—THE "IONA."—The "Iona," a paddle-wheel steamer employed in the passenger traffic between Glasgow and the Western Highlands, had cabin accommodations for twelve hundred passengers, and her long range of saloon-houses, with plate-glass windows fore and aft, gave her a graceful appearance. Her dimensions were: Length, 250 feet; beam, 25 feet. She was propelled by a pair of oscillating engines with a continued nominal power of 180 horses. Her draught, when fully laden, did not exceed six feet, and her speed under favorable circumstances was from twenty to twenty-one miles per hour. She was the fastest steam-vessel in Great Britain, and, one or two steamers of the United States excepted, in the world.

1878.—THE "IRIS."—There was in the British navy in 1878 a man-of-war capable of steaming twenty-one miles an hour. She was a vessel named the "Iris," of nearly four thousand tons measurement, having a nominal speed of seven thousand horse-power. When fully equipped and armed she may not have been so fleet, but the surprising speed realized at Portsmouth was not considered the maximum that the "Iris" was capable of making. A previous trial of the ship's engines had not been so satisfactory. At that time a huge, four-bladed screw was fitted, and the improvement in the fleetness of the vessel was due to reducing the surface of the screw, and employing two blades instead of four. The engines, powerful as they were, had been overweighted by the screw.

The "Iris" was the forerunner of a steel flotilla of six corvettes and two dispatch-boats of a similar character.

By employing steel in lieu of iron, it has been possible to construct much lighter craft, with finer lines to the vessels, without sacrificing their strength and solidity. The steel corvettes are to be fleet boats, but have the high speed of the "Iris" or the "Mercury." They are intended for swift cruisers, and, though comparatively lightly armed, each of them have a pair of 7-inch or armor-piercing guns. They are named, respectively, "Carysfort," "Champion," "Cleopatra," "Comus," "Conquest," and "Curaçoa." The "Iris" and the "Mercury" armaments consist of sixty-four pounders; but their speed is such that they will always have the option of fighting or running away.

1878.—STEAMBOATS IN COREA.—A steamboat built by the Coreans is thus referred to in the *North China Daily News* of March 28, 1878:

"Everything European, just because it is so, is despised, but the

Coreans try hard to originate wonderful undertakings. For about eight months they have been working at a steamboat, and some ten thousand *taels* have been used up. There is the shell with three keels, which makes the thing rather flat. The bow is sharp, and there are port-holes for cannon; a smoke-stack, which has been observed at work, but the wheels are wanting. Meanwhile, for fear the Japanese might benefit by the sight, this masterpiece was covered in with a wooden frame. Ten years ago they made an iron vessel, but it unfortunately sunk when launched."

1879.—THE "DURBIN."—The fastest long-distance voyage on record was made by the steamer "Durbin," with telegrams from Zululand to England, in 1879. She left Table Bay a little before 8 P.M., and averaged 298 miles a day to Madeira, where she stopped April 14 for four and a half hours. She made Plymouth at 6 P.M. on April 20. The entire distance, about 6000 miles, was run at an *average of* 13.1 *knots.* Faster speed has been made across the Atlantic, but this is the best for so long a distance.

1879.—STEAM *vs.* SAILS.—At the end of the year 1879 there were registered as belonging to the United Kingdom, including the Channel Islands, 20,538 sailing-vessels, of 4,068,742 tons, and 5027 steam-vessels, of 2,511,733 tons, making in the whole 25,565 vessels, of 6,579,795 tons, being 24,811 tons more than at the end of the year 1878.

The numbers for 1879 compared with those of 1866 show in the fourteen years a decline of 5602 in the number of sailing-vessels, and of 834,910 tons in the tonnage; and in steam-vessels an *increase* of 2196 in the number, and of 1,635,548 tons in the tonnage.

The shipping belonging to the United States on the 30th of June, 1879, was classified as follows: 17,042 sailing-vessels, of 2,422,813 tons; 4569 steam-vessels, of 1,176,172 tons; 2394 barges, of 466,878 tons; and 1206 canal-boats, etc., of 103,721 tons; total, 25,211 vessels of all kinds, and tonnage, 4,169,584 tons.

How rapidly steam has superseded wind as the motive-power of ships on the Atlantic is shown in the statement of exports of grain in bushels from New York, from January 1 to October 31, for five years, —viz.:

Year.	Steam.	Sail.
1878	28,151,191	47,493,409
1879	33,847,952	52,046,708
1880	43,955,065	57,203 079
1881	46,212,288	17,788,421
1882	34,500,000	5,200,000

1879.—THE "SOLANO."—The largest ferry-boat in the world was given a trial December 1, 1879, at San Francisco, and behaved satisfactorily in every respect. The "Solano" was built for the transportation of passenger- and freight-cars across the Straits of Carquinez from Port Costa to Benicia. Her dimensions are: Length over all, 424 feet; length on bottom (she has no keel), 406 feet; height of sides in centre, 18 feet 5 inches; height of sides on each end, from bottom of boat, 15 feet 10 inches; molded beam, 64 feet; extreme width over guards, 116 feet; width of guards at centre of boat, 25 feet 6 inches; reverse, sheer of deck, 2½ feet. She has two vertical-beam engines of 60-inch bore and 11-inch stroke, built at Wilmington, Delaware. The engines have a nominal power of 1500 horses each, but are capable of being worked up to 2000 horse-power each. Upon the deck of the "Solano" are *four railroad tracks* extending her entire length, with a capacity of carrying forty-eight loaded freight-cars, or twenty-four passenger-coaches of the largest class. Her four rudders are worked by an hydraulic steering-gear, operated by an independent steam-pump. They are also connected with the ordinary steering-gear, so that, in case of any disarrangement of the hydraulic apparatus, the vessel may be guided by it. The advantage is that this immense craft can be handled by one man, whereas, if the ordinary wheel and system of steering were used, six men would be required at the wheel.

1880.—CHINESE ENTERPRISE.—In 1874 fifty British steamers were profitably engaged in the local trades in Chinese waters. That year the natives organized the China Merchants' Steam Navigation Company, with the imperial consent and support. The first year the company had six steamers in operation. The next year four were added, and in 1877 the company's fleet numbered sixteen vessels. A fierce competition was waged with foreign companies, during which rates were cut from fifty to seventy per cent. of the former amounts. The result was that the foreign "Shanghai Steam Navigation Company" was killed, and its twenty-six vessels and wharf property were bought by the native company. The aggressive policy thus begun has been continued, until now the Chinese look to a general navigation of the high seas, and in August, 1880, the "Hongchong," one of the original six vessels of the China Merchants' Company, entered the harbor of San Francisco. China enjoys the cheapest labor on the planet; has enormous coal-fields and large iron deposits; and a firm of British builders have decided to transfer their capital to China, with a view to beginning the work of ship-building, for which so abundant materials and advantageous conditions for labor exist. Japan is acting with like vigor, and has already several steam lines in operation.

1880.—A REMARKABLE VOYAGE OF A WRECKED STEAMER.— On July 14, 1880, the Chilian transport "Rimac," an iron screw-steamer of twelve hundred and twenty-seven tons, carrying a regiment of cavalry and a valuable cargo, was captured by the Peruvian corvette "Union" and taken to Callao. After the Peruvian defeat at Chorillos and Miraflores the "Rimac" was burned and sunk. The hulk was raised by the Chilians, and, although severely damaged, it was found that it could be rendered serviceable, and that the machinery was only slightly injured. Every particle of wood-work was burned out of her, and she presented more the appearance of an empty fire-worn stove than of a vessel with which the sea could be navigated. The deck-beams were cracked and twisted as if they had been thin iron wires; some stanchions still stood upright, but more had assumed shapes which would have astonished any ship-builder, and the bulwarks were bulged in and out, and shriveled as if they had been run through some powerful crimping-machine. Damaged as she was, it was the desire of the Chilian government, whose prize she had become, and of the South American Company, who had become her purchasers, that she should be taken back to Chili, and Captain James Hart was called upon for an opinion as to the possibility of taking her to Chili. He reported favorably, although declaring there was much risk, and the voyage was agreed upon. Only the most absolute and trivial repairs were effected, and, after the sides had been boarded up to prevent her filling, this damaged iron tank—for it could scarcely be called a vessel—took its departure from Callao. The machinery worked well. But as the engines were intended to drive a heavy vessel, and they were now employed in propelling a light and unladen hull, they were too powerful for their work. They drove it along at a good speed, it is true, but the vibration caused thereby was severe in the extreme. Very heavy weather was encountered, and, as the vessel would dip into the sea so it would strike her abeam, the water would rush into the hold, threatening to swamp her, and keeping the pumps constantly at work. All hands were wet through the entire trip, no cabins having been put up. Several of the damaged deck-beams broke, through the severe straining of the sides, and one day the remains of the bridge tumbled into the hold, carrying with it the binnacle and the wheel, which had been temporarily fixed up. The compass was useless, it being impossible to place reliance in it owing to the vibration causing the needle to revolve the whole time. Steering was done by guesswork, the direction of the sea, which runs from the southward, and the heavens serving as a substitute. The voyage fortunately was performed in safety, and the wreck was finally moored to Valparaiso. The distance from Callao to Valparaiso is fifteen hundred and fifty-eight miles, head to wind all the time. The "Rimac" is now being repaired, and within a few months she will be again ready for sea.

1880.—THE "COMET" ON LAKE BIGLER.—A new pleasure-steamer, called the "Comet," was built for Lake Bigler in 1880. It was exclusively for the use of passengers and pleasure-parties, and made the trip around the lake in a day. It was fitted up in splendid style.

1880.—THE "THREE BROTHERS."—In 1880 the well-known

American ship "Three Brothers," formerly the steamship "Vanderbilt," and the largest sailing merchant-vessel afloat, was sold to merchants in Liverpool for eight thousand pounds, and she will hereafter sail under the British flag.

1880.—A MOUNTAIN STEAMER.—Steam navigation among the mountain ranges of Colorado is one of the peculiarities of that wonderful region. A Denver paper says, "A sail over the placid and translucent waters of Twin Lakes will convince the traveler that Colorado affords some of the most beautiful aquatic scenery in nature. Twin Lakes are located three miles from Twin Lake Station, Denver and South Park Division, Union Pacific Railway, or one hundred and fifty-seven miles southwest of Denver, at the eastern base of the Sawache Range, at an elevation of nine thousand three hundred and thirty-three feet above the level of the sea. The lower lake covers fifteen hundred and twenty-five, and the upper four hundred and seventy-five acres, and they are united by a small, swift, clear stream, about half a mile in length, which winds through grassy meadows studded with scattering shade-trees, affording delightful picnic- or camp-grounds. On the north stands Mount Elbert, fourteen thousand three hundred and sixty feet above the sea, or five thousand and twenty-seven feet above the lakes. Directly opposite (at the south side of the lakes) are the Twin Peaks, also giants of the Rocky chain. The sheets are, therefore, thoroughly mountain-locked." The paper above quoted says the little steamer plying on Twin Lakes "has the distinguished honor of being nearer to heaven than any other craft in the wide, wide world."

SHIPS THAT WERE NEVER HEARD FROM.—The following European steamers have never been heard from after leaving port: The "President," sailed from New York, March 11, 1841; had among her passengers Tyrone Power, the famous Irish comedian, and a son of the Duke of Richmond. The "City of Glasgow," never heard from after leaving Glasgow in the spring of 1854; four hundred and eighty lives lost. The " Pacific," never heard from after January 23, 1856, when she left Liverpool; two hundred lives lost. The "Tempest," never heard from after she left New York, Feburary 26, 1857. The "City of Boston," left New York January 25, 1860; about one hundred and sixty lives lost. The "Ismailia" left New York, September 26, 1878, and was never heard from.

1880.—A CANAL-BOAT PROPELLED BY AIR.—A novelty in canal-boats in Charles River, Massachusetts, attracted considerable attention in 1880. It was called a "pneumatic canal-boat, and was built at Wiscasset, Maine, as devised by the owner, R. H. Tucker, of Boston, who held patents for its design in England and the United States. The boat shown on Charles River, designed to be used on canals without injuring the banks, was a simple structure, sixty-two feet long, twenty feet wide, three feet in depth, and drew seventeen inches of water. It was driven entirely by air, Root's blower No. 4 being used, and was operated by an eight horse-power engine. The air was forced down a central shaft to the bottom, where it was deflected, and, being confined between the keels, passed backward and upward, escaping at the stern through an orifice nineteen feet wide, so as to form an air wedge between the boat and the surface of the water. The force with which the air struck the water propelled the boat at a speed of four miles an hour, but required a thirty-five horse-power engine to develop its full capabilities. The patentee claimed a great advantage in dispensing with the heavy machinery of screws and side-wheels, and believed that his contrivance gave full results in proportion to the power employed. It was also contrived for backing and steering by air propulsion. Owing to the slight disturbance it caused to the water, it was thought very well adapted for work on canals.

1880.—THE FIRST CHINESE STEAMER TO CROSS THE PACIFIC. —On the 31st of August, 1880, the Chinese steamer "Hochung" entered the custom-house of San Francisco, California, paying the regular tonnage dues of thirty cents per ton, and one dollar per ton extra dues on alien ships, the latter under protest. Extra duties of 10 per cent. on the cargo were also paid under protest, and the whole matter was referred to the decision of the Secretary of the Treasury. She was also the first Chinese steamer that ever visited the Hawaiian Islands in November, 1879, and carried to Honolulu 431 Chinese immigrants.

A San Francisco paper said of this arrival, under the heading, "China's Début upon the Sea,"—

"The arrival at San Francisco on the 30th of August of the first Chinese steamer that has ever crossed the Pacific deserves commemoration. This steamer, the 'Hochung,' appeared at the Golden Gate, seeking admission to a foreign port, nearly forty years after the isolation in which for ages China was encased was broken and five of her ports were opened to the commerce of the civilized world. The treaty of 1842, by which this concession was secured to foreign trade, has borne fruit slowly; but the tardiness of the Chinese to undertake maritime enterprises is due not so much to their love of seclusion as to the difficulty of acquiring the art of navigation. This art is, and ever has been, one of the later acquisitions of nations. . . . It is no wonder, therefore, that the Chinese have taken forty years to master the nautical skill requisite for the accomplishment of this feat. But the beginning of ocean traffic is now made; and this field of commercial competition once fairly broken, there is reason to hope the Orientals will find it profitable. . . . In this maritime enterprise they are favored by the immense coal-supply of the Middle Kingdom. Baron Richthofen, who carefully examined the coal-fields of China, says it is 'among the most favored countries of the world as regards the distribution of mineral fuel.' This able geographer computes from his own inspection that the 'quantity of very superior coal available for cheap extraction is so large that, at the present rate of consumption, the world could be supplied from Shansi alone for several thousand years.' This vast coal-bed is reached by the Yang-tse-Kiang (river), China's great commercial highway, navigable for large vessels twelve hundred miles from its mouth, and easily ascended by ocean steamers as far as Hankow, seven hundred miles from the sea. With such magnificent deposits of mineral fuel suited for use on steam-vessels, the day is not distant when the Chinese, renowned for ages as dexterous mechanics, will be able with a little nautical training to carve out a bright maritime future for their nation."

A telegraphic dispatch, dated London, December 7, 1881, announced that "the 'Meefoo,' the first of a regular line of steamers under the Chinese flag, arrived in the Thames with three thousand tons of tea." [1]

1880.—TWIN GAIN SCREWS.—Mr. John Taggart, of Boston, in 1880, invented a method of propelling steamers by two screws, differing in almost every particular from the ordinary propeller. These screws are described as long, hollow, iron cylinders, with what are called "gain" screws with two threads. The threads are near together at the bow, and gradually diverge towards the stern, thus giving them the name of *gain* screw. It is claimed a great power is gained by this means at once at the bow, and the gradually-increasing width between the threads diminishes to a great extent the friction and dead weight of the water. The cylinders, being hollow, are very buoyant. The journals of these cylinders run in strong yokes projecting from the iron heel at the bow and stern. These cylinders are run by an endless chain. The threads are large, and answer to the blades of a propeller, but, having a greater surface, give an increased power. It is claimed that with these screws a river-boat could be run at the rate of *thirty-seven miles an hour;* that a tug thus equipped could, with engines of the same power, pull ordinary tugs backward, and that an ocean steamer could cross the Atlantic in four and a half days. A practical test of the invention is proposed by building a tug on this new plan.

1880.—The tonnage and value of the steamers of the mercantile navy of Great Britain in 1880 was,—

	Tons.		Value.
Under 500 tons	339,505	£12	£4,074,060
From 500 to 2000	1,913,445	20	38,268,900
From 2000 upward	341,184	25	8,529,600
Total	2,594,134		£50,872,560

[1] Are not the Chinese now in advance, considering that we, who claim to hold the most advanced opinions of the age, exclude their emigrants under the recent shameful act of Congress?

This was the value of the vessels completely fitted and provisioned for sea, with allowance for the average of the various ages in the different classes.

1880.—THE "ANTHRACITE," the smallest steamer that ever crossed the Atlantic, arrived at New York in August, 1880, and went thence to Philadelphia. She sailed from the latter port on the 23d of August, and arrived at Falmouth, England, September 14, after a voyage of twenty-two days and fourteen hours. She steamed three thousand three hundred and sixteen miles, doing the entire distance with the consumption of less than *twenty-five tons of coal*, steaming thirteen hundred and fifty-three miles with only nine tons. The "Anthracite" had a new system of boilers, which, her inventor claimed, would revolutionize the utilization of steam for propelling vessels.

The "Anthracite" was built expressly for this Atlantic voyage, to show that the difficulty previously encountered in vessels with high-pressure engines of retaining steam could be overcome by substituting for ordinary piston-packing a metal peculiar to the Perkins system. Economy in expenditure of heat and water was also claimed.

Of the "Anthracite's" eighty-four feet of length, her engines, furnaces, and boilers take up a space of twenty-two feet six inches, leaving a hatchway, kitchen, and forecastle-cabin in the forepart of the boat, and a water-tight bulkhead. Abaft the engines are three cabins, with sleeping-bunks, with a water-tight bulkhead in the stern. The screw is of the ordinary fish-tail pattern, with two blades. Her gross tonnage is 70.26 tons, and her registered tonnage is 27.91 tons. Her average consumption of coal on the voyage from England to Newfoundland and thence to New York was one ton of Welsh bituminous coal a day. The weather was very rough, consequently the sails could be little used. The counter registering the revolutions of her screw was set at 0 before she left England, and on arrival at New York marked three million nine hundred and eighty thousand. In the voyage over the natural draught of the furnace only was used, but she has a fan-blower, which can be brought into use if increased consumption of fuel and a high pressure of steam are desired.

The peculiarity of the machinery which effects the economy of fuel lies in the means employed for using steam at very high pressure safely, and without undue wear and strain. The average boiler pressure on the voyage over was from *three hundred and fifty to four hundred pounds to the square inch, but the boilers had been tested up to two thousand five hundred pounds per square inch* by hydraulic pressure. The body of the boiler consists of a series of horizontal tubes, welded up at each end, and connected together by a vertical tube, and the several sections are connected by a verticle tube to the top ring of the fire-box, and by another to the steam-collecting tube. The fire-box is formed of tubes bent into a rectangular shape. The boiler is surrounded by a double casing of thin sheet-iron, filled between with non-conducting material to prevent loss of heat. The cylinders and valve-boxes are steam-jacketed, and further protected by jackets of non-conducting material, so that, although all the parts are kept at a high temperature, the heat given out in the engine and fire-room is much less than is usual in ordinary marine engines.

The difficulty from friction and imperfect joints in practically working machinery at high pressures was one of the serious obstacles encountered in developing this system. After a series of experiments, the inventor adopted an antifriction alloy, of which the packing-rings and internal rubbing surfaces are made. No lubrication is required beyond that furnished by the steam. He states that cylinders fitted with piston-rings made of this metal have been several years at work, showing no signs of wear, the only wear occurring on the rings, which can be easily and cheaply replaced. Not only is the cost of oil and grease saved, but the destructive action on the machinery and boiler of the acids generated from lubricants is avoided.

For the use of steam at these high pressures three different-sized cylinders are employed, all jacketed with spiral tubes cast in the metal, which are supplied with steam direct from the boilers, and keep up the temperature of the cylinders. The cylinders are arranged one above the other, and their pistons are connected to a common piston-rod. The operation is thus described by Mr. Loftus Perkins, the inventor, in a paper read before the Institution of Mechanical Engineers, London:

"The high-pressure steam is introduced into the upper end of the first cylinder, where there is no gland, and where the piston is formed so as to require no lubricating material. The steam is cut off at half-stroke in this cylinder, and when admitted for the return-stroke into the bottom of the second cylinder, of four times the area, the temperature is so much reduced as to cause no difficulty when brought into contact with the piston-rod gland. From the bottom of the second cylinder the steam expands into the top of the same cylinder, which is of larger capacity than the bottom, and serves as a chamber, and is in direct communication with the valve-box of the third cylinder. This last is double-acting, and is arranged to cut off at about a quarter-stroke, and at the termination of the stroke exhausts into the condenser, with an expansion of about thirty-two times."

It is some years since Mr. Perkins began to advocate the merits of this system, and he has taken out many patents connected therewith, but the difficulties attending its practical working, and the disposition to oppose it by those who had large sums invested in old style machinery, have, it is asserted, prevented its general adoption, although in several cases in England it has been successfully introduced. The boilers and engines of the "Anthracite" contain all the latest improvements of the inventor, and are thought to afford a practical demonstration of the entire success of the Perkins system, and show how all stationary and marine engines can be run at an expense of less than one-half the present cost for fuel.

Two and a half pounds of coal per horse-power per hour is considered very economical running, and some of our best-managed ocean steamers use one hundred tons of coal a day in their voyage. To demonstrate the practicability of reducing this more than one-half, thereby not only saving the cost of fuel, but giving more space for freight, was the purpose of the visit of the "Anthracite" to American waters.

1880.—FIRST STEAMBOAT ON THE UPPER DELAWARE.—The steamboat "Kittatinny," the first that ever reached Port Jervis, New York, arrived at Delaware Water Gap April 28, 1880, without accident, having run the fifty miles in less than five hours. This steamboat was sixty feet long, fourteen feet wide, and carried seventy persons, the navigation of the Upper Delaware being thus proved feasible by steam. Great excitement prevailed throughout the region traversed, and hundreds of persons flocked to see the boat.

1881.—THE "HARRIET LANE."—The United States revenue steam-cutter "Harriet Lane," built in 1859 for that service, was placed at the disposal of the Prince of Wales during his visit to this country, and at the outbreak of the Rebellion was turned over to the Navy Department. On New Year's night, 1863, her decks were the scene of one of the most desperate hand-to-hand encounters of the war, when her captain and first lieutenant were killed. Transformed into a sailing bark, and named the "Elliott Ritchie," this famous craft was peacefully lying at Philadelphia awaiting a cargo, December 10, 1881.

1881.—THE "DESSOUG."—The steamer "Dessoug," which conveyed Cleopatra's Needle from Egypt to New York, was built in England, and was for years used as a trader until the Khedive of Egypt bought and converted her into a yacht. Purchased for the purpose of bringing the obelisk to America, she was sold and altered and rebuilt as a freight steamer for the New York and Savannah cotton trade.

1881.—AN HYDRAULIC SHIP, built in Germany in 1881, on her trial accomplished nine knots an hour. Two hundred years before that the experiment was made of propelling vessels by expelling water from the stern, and failed, as sufficient speed was not attained. This new method is based on the assumption that the propelling force depends on the contact of surfaces, and not on the sectional area of the flowing mass, so a number of tubes with narrow outlets are used instead of one large tube.

1881.—A NOVEL PROPELLING POWER.—A steam-yacht with a

novel propelling power was built in 1881. Instead of a screw, as in ordinary propellers, there is a flat blade of iron under the rudder at right angles to the keel. This blade was hinged in the centre. The blade worked backward and forward on a hollow shaft, with a stroke of three feet forward and aft. As the blade moves forward under the overhang of the vessel, by means of an inside shaft, it shuts up, and makes no resistance to the water. When it goes back again it opens, and virtually pushes the water astern. As the engine can work the blade with a stroke of one hundred and twenty to the minute, it is calculated that extraordinary speed will be attained. The yacht is about thirty feet long over all, and is provided with a patent engine resembling a pump-engine, with a pump-cylinder. The propelling-blade or pusher is three feet in length and fifteen inches wide.

1881.—THE " MONARCH."—The first freight steamer to engage in the interoceanic trade arrived at San Francisco in 1881. She left Barrow, England, on the 31st of August, 1881, and stopping to coal at the Cape Verde Islands, and at Coronel, on the West Coast of South America, arrived at San Francisco on the 8th of September, having been sixty-nine days on the passage. She had as freight on her voyage 2000 tons of steel rails, and it was the result of the desire of railroad builders on the Pacific slope to get the equipments needed as speedily as possible. The shipment might have been made by a sailing vessel at not over $5 per ton, but in this case it is understood $16.75 were paid, making the shipment cost, when landed, over $20,000 more than would have been the case under ordinary conditions. The "Monarch" was chartered before her arrival in San Francisco to carry a load of grain to Liverpool, at £3 17s. 6d. per ton, a trifle over that paid to sailing vessels when the contract was made. Premising that the steamer carries the same weight of grain she has of rails, her gross freight money would amount to about $72,000 for the round voyage. Out of this, deducting the money paid for coal, and assuming that she consumed twenty-five tons of fuel each day, which would cost, when on board, not less, on an average, than $10 per ton,—not a high valuation, considering that the coal was taken in large part at outlying stations,—and that she steamed on the round voyage one hundred and twenty-eight days, this would amount to $32,000, leaving $40,000 for ordinary running expenses and profits. A sailing vessel, which carried an equal amount of cargo would, with freight-rates as they have been, obtain for making the same round trip $22 per ton, which would give a gross freight of $44,000, or ten per cent. more than the sum made by the steamer after deducting coal charges. The saving to the steamer would be that she could make five round voyages while a sailing vessel was making three. But it must be remembered that steamers are not likely to have the same favorable outward freight offered to them. If they can only command 2s. 6d. more per ton than sailing vessels in carrying a perishable article like grain from San Francisco, it is safe to assume, that as a rule, they will not get more than the slower craft for carrying steel rails or other outward cargo. The conclusion to be drawn is that for the present steamers cannot profitably compete with sailing vessels on such a long route as that between California and Europe.

1881.—COST OF OCEAN STEAMSHIPS IN ENGLAND.—The following were the prices per ton paid for screw steamers built, equipped, and ready for sea in 1881 by builders on the Mersey, Clyde, and east coast of England, suited to the trade indicated; and the enormous losses by wreck and foundering have resulted in a sober second thought; and the lead-pencil type model, long and narrow, says an English paper, is giving place to more beam. The length and contracted breadth, with a profusion of water ballast, is compelled to give place to more beam and greater stability:

Trade.	Class.	Net Tonnage.	Knots per hour.	Consumption of coal, 24 hours. Tons.	Price, U. S. Gold.
CARGO STEAMERS:					
Adapted for general Atlantic trade	100 A 1	1484	10.5	28	$167,894
Especially fitted for cattle	100 A 1	2000	10¼	36	214,126
Especially fitted for cattle	100 A 1	. .	11	24	228,859
For general and cattle trade	20 years L	2000	10¼	25	243,325
Three-decked rule	100 A 1	1500	10	27	170,327
Spar deck	20 years L	1370	10	16	175,194
And passengers if required	100 A 1	1849	9¼	20	160,594
Also suitable for cattle	100 A 1	1180	9¼	17	128,962
" "	100 A 1	1090	9	12	131,395
" "	100 A 1	910	9	10	107,063
But easily arranged for passengers	100 A 1	916	9½	12	105,608
Awning deck especially built for cotton	100 A 1	1270	9¾	18	145,995
Awning deck especially built for cotton	100 A 1	2060	13	35	291,990
Spar deck for Atlantic trade	100 A 1 & 20 years L.	1747	11	28	184,927

1881.—THE LARGEST TORPEDO-BOAT afloat in 1881 was built in England for the Danish government by Messrs. Thornycroft & Co. Her displacement was fifty-five tons, or forty per cent. more than that of the largest torpedo-boats in the British service; but her dimensions were still within the limit which would permit her to be conveyed by rail from one part of the coast to another. Her armament consisted of four of the largest Whitehead torpedoes, each of which carried a charge of eighty pounds of gun-cotton, and, in addition, she mounted a Hotchkiss revolving gun. She had a coal capacity of ten tons, estimated as equivalent to 1200 miles, at a speed of eleven knots, and her full speed, as shown at the trial, as well as during a run of three

HISTORY OF STEAM NAVIGATION. 279

hours at the measured miles, was twenty knots, which was two knots in excess of the stipulation.

1881.—The " DESTROYER."—The first public exhibition of Captain Ericsson's torpedo-boat, "Destroyer," was made at Hoboken, November 14, 1881. Several prominent officers of the army and navy were present. The chief object of the exhibition was to demonstrate the practical working of the submerged gun, by which the torpedo missile is sent upon its deadly errand ; also to show the ability of the torpedo to penetrate protective net-work around a fleet or a single ironclad.

A dummy projectile of wood was used without a torpedo charge. In the test the dummy was discharged from the cannon by the use of twelve pounds of giant powder at a target net of Manilla rope and wooden slats three hundred feet distant. The muzzle was six feet and six inches below the surface, and the projectile passed through the target five feet under water, appeared on the surface one hundred feet further in shore, and rode on the water at a considerable speed for two hundred feet more, making a distance of six hundred feet traveled in all. The *projectile*, which was *twenty-five inches in length*, traveled through the water to the point of appearance on the surface, four hundred feet, in three seconds, and this with a charge of but twelve pounds of powder. The gun is fired by electricity by the wheelsman, who, through his lookout, must aim and discharge the gun in accordance with his best judgment as to effectiveness. The experiment was under the direction of V. F. Lassoe. It was the fifty-second time the gun had fired the projectile, and at no trial since the boat has been put in working order has it failed with the same charge to throw the dummy torpedo three hundred feet in three seconds or less. The French officers were especially interested in the experiment, and though they at first pronounced it an impossibility to operate a gun constructed on such principles, and with submerged muzzle, successfully, they were obliged to acknowledge that the theory had proved correct. Astonishment was depicted in every line of their countenances when they saw the projectile rise to the surface beyond the target, after having traversed the distance from the muzzle of the gun and through the netting without making even the faintest ripple on the surface.

In actual service the torpedo projectile is to carry three hundred and forty pounds of dynamite,—enough to destroy the largest ironclad. The gun will be discharged with a force sufficient to carry the projectile from three hundred to seven hundred feet through the water.

1881.—THE FALL RIVER LINE.—The "Bristol" and "Providence," of the Fall River Line of Sound steamers between Boston and New York, for size, proportions, and general magnificence of appointments have attracted the attention and admiration of travelers from every portion of the world. They are 373 feet long, 83 feet beam, 3000 tons register, and cost $1,250,000 each. During the Centennial season, 1876, the passengers carried in safety and comfort by these mammoth steamships were numbered by hundreds of thousands. Over one thousand persons frequently made the trip in one of these steamers without discomfort or crowding. The fresco-work and gilding of the interior is elegant and elaborate, the shading and coloring having a most harmonious and beautiful effect. The main saloons, galleries, and cabins are carpeted richly and tastefully, and the furniture elegantly upholstered. All the state-rooms are connected with the main office by electric bells. Some idea of the size of their engines may be formed when it is stated that the Corliss engine, which attracted so much attention at the Centennial, was not one-half the size nor had one-half the capacity of the engines on either the "Bristol" or "Providence." In provisions for safety the arrangements are perfect. Every portion of the boats where fire is used is absolutely fire-proof, and each steamer is provided with all the improved life-saving appliances.

The "Pilgrim," the new steamer launched August, 1882, from Roach's yard for this line has 300 state-rooms and accommodations for 1000 passengers, and is 15 feet longer and 4 feet wider than the "Bristol." She is 384 feet long over all; 370 feet long at water-line; 87 feet wide over guards, and 17 feet 6 inches deep at sides. Her double hulls are divided into 96 water-tight compartments, bearing a pressure of 5 pounds per square inch. Steam is supplied from four Redfield boilers, and there is one immense beam-engine, having a cylinder 110 inches in diameter, with 14 feet stroke. This cylinder was cast at Mr. Roach's Morgan Iron Works, in New York, and is said to be the largest cylinder ever cast in this country. It required 45 tons of gun-metal, which it took three hours and ten minutes to melt. The 90,000 pounds were then transferred by the labor of 100 men to two huge tank-ladles, each with a capacity of about 14 tons, and having two large crane-handles. The tanks were connected with the mould by pipes, and the crane-handles were attached to huge cranes. The mould was filled, under Mr. Roach's personal supervision, in two and a half minutes, the molten metal roaring like a wild beast, and emitting showers of twenty colors. It required about ten days for the metal to thoroughly cool, and for several days it remained red-hot. When perfectly solidified the upper part of the mould was demolished, and the cylinder dug from its resting-place in the ground. The two main shafts for this engine are 40 feet long and 27 inches in diameter, forged from wrought iron, and each weighing 85,000 pounds.

1881.—STEAMSHIP DISASTERS.—As the tonnage of the merchant steam marine increases, so do disasters of steam-vessels grow. The records of 1881 show the disasters to steam-vessels for the year to

HISTORY OF STEAM NAVIGATION.

have been 198. A dozen of these were repaired and put into service, but nearly all were total wrecks. A few were also sunk at their piers through carelessness while loading or discharging cargoes, as in the case of the "Braunschweig," loading coal in the harbor at Bremen. Others were stranded and floated off without receiving damage. Included in the record for 1881 is the loss of the Polar expedition steamer "Jeannette," in the Arctic Ocean.

The record for 1881 shows 141 of the disasters were to British steamships; 15 were American; 6 French; 6 Danish; 5 German; 3 Dutch; 4 Swedish; 1 Brazilian; 3 Belgian; 4 Spanish; 2 Chilian; Mexican, Chinese, Austrian, Japanese, and Norwegian, 1 each; of 3 the nationality could not be learned. Of these, 4 were of steel, 5 of wood, and the remainder iron vessels. The total tonnage lost in 1881 was 200,000 tons, 151,041 tons of which were British; 11,568 American; 4390 Dutch; 2488 Swedish; 1000 Brazilian; 6486 French; 4643 Belgian; 3274 Danish; 4562 German; 4177 Spanish; 680 Mexican; 1233 Chinese; 808 Austrian; 947 Japanese; 697 Norwegian, and 1750 Chilian. Of the disasters, 99 vessels were stranded; 30 sunk by collision; 40 foundered; 7 burned; 11 are missing; 6 were abandoned at sea; 2 were sunk by ice; 1 broken in two, and 1 was destroyed by explosion. Eleven of the vessels were laden with grain; 23 with coal; 11 with iron; 2 with cotton, and 1 each with copper ore, petroleum, provisions, wool, and sugar.

The greatest number of disasters were in October; the records for that month are unprecedented, the total number lost being 32, of which 18 were British; France, Germany, and Norway lost 2 each; Austria, Belgium, Brazil, Chili, Holland, Russia, Spain, and Sweden, 1 each. It is estimated that no less than 43,033 tons of produce were lost in the October gales.

The steamship "Bath City" foundered off Newfoundland, December 3, 1881, and the sufferings of the crew were terrible. Sighted on November 30, two hundred and fifty miles from the port of St. John's, Newfoundland, by a steamship which could have assisted her into port, she was left mastless, rudderless, and leaking, to her fate, which came three days afterwards. The vessel went to the bottom, and the crew were launched on the stormy ocean in their life-boats. Four were drowned by the capsizing of one of the boats, and six, including the captain, perished from cold and exposure. The other castaways, having suffered three days and nights in these open boats, were rescued.

1881.—BRITISH STEAMSHIP SUBSIDIES.—The report of the British post-office for the year ended March 31, 1881, states the sums paid to various steamship companies for the conveyance of the ocean mails, together with the receipts from ocean postages and the net payments under the several contracts during that year, was as follows:

Countries.	Contract Compensation.	Receipts from Postages.	Net Payment by the Government.
East Indies, China, and Japan	£356,900 [1]	£60,000	£208,000
East Coast of Africa	30,000	500	29,500
United States	65,811	38,000	27,000
Halifax, Bermuda, and St. Thomas	17,500	1,000	16,500
West Indies	84,782	35,000	50,000
West Coast of Africa	7,969	6,000	1,900
	£562,462 Estimated	£140,500	£332,900

For the service in the English Channel, between Dover and Calais, the sum of £11,274 were paid for the same year; and for the service in the Irish Channel, between Holyhead and Kingstown, £85,000 were expended, a sum equal to more than one-quarter of the total net payment by the government for its ocean postal service.

The service to Brazil coast the government nothing, the postage earned having been sufficient for the compensation asked for. Nearly the whole of the expenditure specified was made for the maintenance of postal communication within the limits of the British empire. Besides which several of the colonial governments are under contract with steamship companies for their own immediate ocean mail service.

AUSTRIAN STEAMERS.—The first Austrian Lloyd steamer for New York sailed from Trieste, January 25, 1881. She was to touch at Messina, Palermo, Barcelona, Malaga, Cadiz, and Lisbon, and had on board a full cargo, 600 tons of it being for New York.

1882.—"THE PEACE."—A missionary steamer, whose hull and machinery weighed only six tons, was recently moored in the Thames, near London. The vessel was named "Peace," and was built for the Baptist Missionary Society, who destined it for the service of the mission in the upper reaches of the Congo River. The boat could be taken to pieces rapidly for transport purposes, and the total number of pieces, none of which were too heavy for a man to carry, were eight hundred. The greatest possible use was made of all available space, and the two cabins were admirably fitted. A kitchen adapted for a stove and other cooking appliances formed part of the equipment. A substantial awning covered the deck, and between this and the sides of the vessel a wire awning was fitted to stop arrows and other missiles. It was intended to take the steamer to pieces and pack the sections in boxes, which would be sent to the mouth of the Congo. From thence they were to be borne by eight hundred men three hundred miles up to Stanley Pool, where the steamer would be reconstructed by the missionaries.

1882.—THE "COLOSSUS."—The latest addition to the British

---

[1] Of this amount, £88,000 were contributed by the government of British India.

HISTORY OF STEAM NAVIGATION. 283

royal navy is the double-screw steel armor-plate turret-ship "Colossus," launched at Portsmouth, March 21, 1882. She is of 9146 tons burden, and her engines are of 6000 horse-power,—a striking advance upon Fulton's "Clermont," the wonder of three-quarters of a century ago.

The "Colossus" has been in process of construction for some eight years past, but the work on her has been seriously pressed only since 1879. She is a twin-screw turret-ship, with a central armored citadel, her principal dimensions being: total length between the perpendiculars, 325 feet; extreme breadth, 68 feet; with a displacement of 9146 tons. Considerable delay has been experienced with respect to the turrets, which cannot be proceeded with until the nature of their armament is determined. It is probable that each turret will be armed with two of the new 46-ton breech-loading rifle-guns. A novel feature in the armament of the ship will be the mounting of four 6-inch guns on the top of the after superstructure, and a couple of guns on the forward superstructure, with rifle-proof covering-boards for the protection of the gunners.

The vessel is to be fitted with a manganese bronze propeller, in place of the one of gun-metal originally ordered. This decision was arrived at after a series of comparative experiments made with the two metals. Bars of both metals, one inch square, were placed on supports twelve inches apart, and first subjected to a steady pressure applied in the middle of the bars, and afterwards to impact, by a weight of fifty pounds falling from a height of five feet. With a steady pressure the gun-metal bars slipped between the supports or broke with a strain of twenty-eight hundred-weight, while the manganese bronze bars required fifty-four hundred-weight to break them. Tested by impact, the gun-metal bars broke with from seven to eight blows, when it took from thirteen to seventeen blows to break the manganese bronze bars. The ultimate bend of the latter was also in both cases more than that of the gun-metal, thus showing fully double the strength, with superior toughness. The advantages claimed for the manganese bronze over gun-metal are, first, a considerable saving of actual weight of machinery; and, secondly, that it enables a thinner and consequently a better blade to be made, offering less resistance to the water, and equaling in strength the gun-metal blade of greater dimensions.

Since the launch of the "Colossus" another ironclad, to be called the "Rodney," has been laid down and commenced at the Chatham Dock-Yard. She is to be a barbette ship, and will carry ten heavy guns. Her length between the perpendiculars is 325 feet; extreme breadth, 68 feet; depth of hold, 28 feet $2\frac{1}{2}$ inches. She is to have engines of 7000 horse-power, and will have a gross tonnage of 9158 tons.

1882.—THE "DUNCAN" AND THE "CAMPERDOWN."—The English government, having determined to build two ironclads which will match the Italian ironclad "Duilio," on the 26th of September, 1882, the Admiralty ordered the construction of two ships, to be named "Duncan" and "Camperdown," of the following dimensions: Length, 330 feet; extreme breadth, 63 feet 6 inches; displacement, 10,000 tons on a mean draught of water of 26 feet 9 inches. These new ships are to have twin screws, with engines of 9800 horse-power, estimated to give a speed of 16 knots an hour, being an excess of two knots over the Italian turret ship. The "Duilio" is 341 feet long. Her extreme beam, 64 feet 9 inches, and displacement, 10,434; her engines being of 7500 indicated horse-power. The armor of the English ships will be carried to a depth of 5 feet below the water-line, with a protecting belt rising 2 feet 6 inches above the water-line, the armor comprising compound plates of the following thickness: side, 18 inches; bulkhead, 16 inches; barbette towers, 14 and 12 inches. They will have vertical ventilation by tubes from the flying to the lower decks. As at present determined upon, their armaments will each consist of four 63-ton breech-loading rifle guns, and six 6-inch breech-loading guns, with a number of Nordenfelts and Gatlings, and Whitehead torpedoes. They are to carry 900 tons of coal, and their complements will consist of 450 officers and men. Their cost is estimated to be not less than £1,000,000 sterling each, or two-thirds of the amount which is appropriated for the annual expenditure for the whole navy of the United States.

1882.—NEW FRENCH IRONCLADS.—As a result of a number of experiments lately carried out in France with armor plates of a variety of patterns, and obtained from various sources, both French and foreign, a contract has been concluded between the Minister of Marine and the managers of the Creusot Works for the supply by the latter of the armor for the "Formidable" and the "Capitaine Baudin," two new ironclads of 11,441 tons each, or of almost exactly the same size as the English "Inflexible;" the displacement of the latter being 11,406 tons. The plates are to be 22 inches thick at the strongest, and 14 inches thick at the weakest part of the armor; and consequently the new French vessels will be defensively stronger than any English ironclad at present either afloat or being built. The Creusot firm is also at the present time supplying the armor plates for the "Terrible," a vessel of 7184 tons, and for the "Furieux," a ship of 5695 tons; the plates for both the vessels being nearly 20 inches thick.

1882.—Among the costly steamers built at Pittsburg, Pa., in 1882, none possess more points of interest than the "Chattahoochee." Her hull is the first constructed *entirely* of steel in this country. Steel hulls have been built in Pittsburg, but in these the braces, angles, etc., were of iron. In the "Chattahoochee" steel is solely used. The steel plates used vary from a "light" three-sixteenth inch in thickness up to one-fourth inch, according to their locality in the hull. The contract for the boat was let to the Duquesne Engine Works, by the People's Line, of Columbus, Ga., for $47,000. The trade calls for a boat of light draught, strength, and speed, and these seem all embodied in the "Chattahoochee." Her hull is 158 feet long, 31½ wide, and 4½ deep. She is a stern-wheeler, with engines of 15-inch cylinder and 5-foot stroke, fitted with the Rees "cut-off" and other modern improvements. Her wheel is eighteen by twenty-four feet, with a steel shaft. There is more steel about the "Chattahoochee" than any other boat of her size afloat. Five electric lights make the "Chattahoochee" a thing of beauty by night. Her draught is only twenty-two inches.[1]

At the steam-yacht race at Nice, France, on the 16th of March, 1882, nine yachts competed for the *Prix de Monte Carlo*, or $1000 and a gold medal. Eight were English, and the smallest, the "Le Few-Follet," of French nationality. The course was fifty miles long, and done in three hours, fifty-six minutes, and ten seconds,—a speed about thirteen and seven-tenths knots per hour. The "Condace," built in Leith and engined in Glasgow, Scotland, won the first prize; the "Black Swan," engined by the same firm, took the second; the "Le Few-Follet," the third. Only two yachts contested in 1881, and the increase in 1882 indicates the future of steam-yacht racing.

In 1882 the little steam-tug "Game Cock," a craft only seventy-five feet long, — feet wide, and drawing eleven feet of water, steamed from London to Panama in thirty-one days. She indexes in a marked manner the wonderful improvements made lately in the efficiency of steam craft. The recent introduction of steel as a building-material in the construction of these "lightning" steam craft—torpedo-boats, launches, etc.—has made. results probable that a short time ago were thought impossible.

1882.—CHAIN-STEAMERS.—The Leipsic *Gartenlaube*, June, 1882, contains an interesting article on chains used in the navigation on the Elbe River. The following are the main points of the article:

On the waves of the Elbe, impatiently floating towards Hamburg, a steamer goes up the stream, pulling along a long row of heavily-laden boats. But it is not only the force of steam that conquers the stream. Below, on the bottom of the river, a heavy iron chain is resting, that gives the steamer a hold, and enables her to overcome the force of the water. From this chain such vessels are called chain-steamers, and the whole navigation going on in such a way is called chain navigation.

In the middle of the channel, along the whole length of the navi-

---

[1] This steamer should not be confounded with one of the same name launched in 1882, by John Roach, at Chester, for the Ocean Steamship Company of Savannah.

gable part of the river, a chain has been sunk, firmly anchored at its two ends. This chain, lifted out of the water, is received by an arm at the bow of the vessel, and thence by conducting rollers moved to two steel drums in the middle of the deck. Around these drums, provided with grooves, the chain winds three times in such a manner that it goes from the first groove of the first drum to the first groove of the second drum, thence to the second groove of the first drum, and then to the second groove of the second drum, etc. Finally the chain, in a conducting groove obliquely descending, is taken to the stern of the ship, where it goes down into the water again. The engine sets the two drums in motion, and all the parts of the drums encircled by the chain receive and dismiss an equal portion of it, moving the vessel forward a corresponding distance.

The chain on the bottom of the river to which the steamer is attached by the two drums, so that she can go only forward or backward, is, according to the pulling force of the ship and the depth of the water, lifted a certain length in front of the vessel. The point where it remains unlifted is, as it were, the anchoring point of the vessel, the weight and friction of the chain supplying the anchor. The chain-steamer, with the whole load of vessels attached to and towed by her, is thus, as it were, constantly at anchor on going up the stream, and she cannot, even by the most rapid current, be forced back one inch of the way made. Because the vessel by the chain firmly resists the water, the power of the engine can be used to its fullest extent.

The chain, of course, does not rest tightly in the river bed. The raised portion of it permits the vessel, by means of the rudders, to go sufficiently far to the right or left, out of the way of other vessels. This is of particular importance at the bends of the river.

On account of the burden caused by the lifting of the chain, the depth of the water must not exceed a certain limit. In a river from thirty to fifty feet deep chain navigation would not be profitable, because the chain would become too heavy. As to the use of chain vessels, a depth of eight metres has proved a practical limit of the depth of the water. The essential advantage of chain navigation consists in the fact that it permits vessels to go up a stream with a very rapid current, where other tow-boats cannot go along any farther with the barges attached to them.

It is self-evident that the strength of the chain must correspond to the depth and rapidity of the river. The links of the chain placed in the Elbe have the size of the palm of a hand, and are of two and one-half centimetres thick, each link weighing a little over one kilogramme. The weight of the chain placed in the Elbe River exceeds ten million kilogrammes.

The chain-steamers have the same shape at both ends, and are provided with two rudders, one at the bow and one at the stern. The engine usually has a strength of from one hundred to one hundred and fifty horse-power. To a chain-steamer in the Elbe usually from ten to twelve freight vessels are attached, connected by ropes. She takes the train of boats up the river, until another chain-steamer meets her and relieves her of her load. Such a place is made a station, and may be any point of the chain. The relieved motor returns until it meets another train of vessels coming up, which it receives in turn in the mode described, towing it up the stream. In order to move independently of the chain, the majority of the steamers are provided with propellers. For detaching a steamer from the chain simply one of the locks of the chain is opened, with which it is regularly provided in intervals of half a kilometre. Or, if necessary, a link of the chain is broken by a chisel, and after the chain has been taken off from the drums, its two parts are united again by a lock.

The first chain-steamers were successfully used in France in 1830. E. Bellingrath, of Dresden, inventor of the hydrostatic truck, is the chief of the chain navigation in the Elbe River, Germany. The Elbe River rises in Austria (Bohemia) and flows through the central part of Germany into the North Sea. In the latter country six hundred and thirty kilometres and in the former about forty kilometres of chain have been placed in the river, while the number of chain-steamers is about thirty.

The chain does not always occupy the same place in the river, but its position is constantly changed by the steamers. For this reason only one can be used in the river. Two or more chains or ropes made of metal wires would become entangled.[1]

1882.—THE HOPPER STEAM DREDGER.—This new dredger, built at Renfrew for the Harbor Commissioners of Otago, New Zealand, was recently tried on the banks of the Clyde,[2] "and dredged at the rate of

---

[1] Experiments have been recently made on the canal from Antwerp to Liége with a system of mechanical traction of boats by means of a moving cable (the invention of M. Rigoni). An endless cable made of Bessemer steel is set in continuous motion by fixed engines on the banks of the canal. It is supported along the bank by special pulleys, and directed by return pulleys of large diameter lodged in chambers of masonry under the level of the tow-path. The length of the cable is eight kilometres, or five miles. Thus a canal is divided into as many sections, each worked by fixed engine, as this length of five miles is contained in it. The steam-engine acts on the cable through a pinching-pulley, similar to the Fowler pulley. The attachment of the boats to the cable is by means of checkered nippers embracing the cable. On coming to a supporting pulley, or a pulley at a curve, the nippers pass without releasing the cable. The principal advantages of the system are, first, a considerable increase of speed. At present the daily stretch covered in hauling with horses is about seventeen kilometres, and with men only about twelve kilometres. By the new method it is easy to make five kilometres an hour. Further, there is considerable economy both in the capital required at first and in the cost of working over other systems.—*Boston Transcript*, November 1, 1881.

[2] *London Engineering*, October, 1882.

400 tons per hour, which was plunged into its own hold, or hopper cavity, capable of containing 1300 tons of soil; at the same time it loaded the new government steamer "Perseverance," which came alongside. Afterwards, by steam appliances, its bucket-girder was elevated, the moorings let go, its twin screws put in motion, and the vessel steamed away down the Clyde to the measured mile, where the loaded speed was tested at $7\frac{1}{4}$ knots per hour; it then steamed down the Firth of Clyde, where its large cargo was instantly deposited, through its bottom, in sixty fathoms water. The trial of dredging, steering, speed, manœuvering, and depositing was considered very satisfactory by the respecting gentlemen on board. This vessel dredges from 5 feet to 35 feet depth, has twin screws, and is propelled and worked by two independent sets of compound engines, of 700 horsepower, and, besides loading its own cargo, it can, if required, fill a fleet of barges on the old system. It will steam out to New Zealand, and is the tenth and largest Hopper dredger constructed by Messrs. Simons & Co., who are the inventors and originators of the system. It is also worthy of note that, owing to the enterprise of the above small colony, they have now a dredger the equal of which is neither in Europe nor America."

1882.—THE RAILROAD IRON FERRY-BOAT "NEWBURGH," built for the West Shore Railroad Company, was launched in October, 1882, at Newburgh, the christening being by Miss Carrie Fry, daughter of the superintendent of steam motive power of the railroad. The dimensions are: Length over all, 205 feet; breadth of beam, 36 feet; over the guards, 65 feet; depth, $14\frac{1}{2}$ feet. Her hull is of the best quality of iron, and of great strength, as she will have to contend with heavy ice in the winter. The keel-plate is $\frac{3}{4}$ inch thick, the bottom and bilge-plates $\frac{1}{2}$ inch, the water-line strake $\frac{3}{4}$ inch, shear strake $\frac{7}{16}$, and the gunwale-plate $\frac{1}{2}$ inch by 24 inches wide. The frames are 3 x 4, spaced 21 inches apart, and the reverse iron is 3 x 3. There is a 10-inch belt frame on every eighth frame, and the floors are 16 inches deep. The stem-posts are of the best hammered iron, 8 x 4 inches. Each end of the hull is fitted with a water-tight, wrought-iron bulkhead, extending for about 30 feet from the stem; there are 4 keelsons, running from bulkhead to bulkhead, and the bottom of the hull inside is cemented with the best Portland cement.

The motive power of the vessel is a vertical beam engine, of 50 inches bore by 10 feet stroke, fitted with Hayward's patent cut-off. The gallows frame of the engine is of iron and of great strength. The water-wheels are wholly of iron, 21 feet in diameter and of $8\frac{1}{2}$ feet face. The shafts are 15 inches in diameter, each one, with its wheel, weighing, complete, about 26 tons. The boiler is of steel, $10\frac{1}{2}$ feet in diameter, and 33 feet long, with two furnaces, and weighs about 30 tons. Everything about the engine and boiler departments is of the

HISTORY OF STEAM NAVIGATION. 289

newest and best description. In short, the boat is all that experience and skill can make her, for safety, utility, and comfort.

The cabins on two sides of the boat are made very inviting. They have tile floors; the wood-work is in the Queen Anne style, of California red-wood, cherry, and mahogany, finished in oil and touched with gold. The seats are of perforated veneering, with "Austrian bentwood arms." The windows in the sides of the cabins are each one single light of plate glass, 6 feet high and 3 wide, with a transom of stained glass above. The doors to the cabins are of mahogany, with stained glass transoms overhead; the wheel bulkheads are each provided with two large bevel-edged mirrors. She was to be completed about the 15th of December.

RECENT NOVEL INVENTIONS AND EXPERIMENTS.

1882.—MORSE'S UNSINKABLE STEAMSHIP.—Mr. Joseph W. Morse, a veteran artist and engraver of Brooklyn, New York, has invented a safety ocean steamship, which he claims is unsinkable. He says he conceived the invention twenty-five years ago, and built a model of it nine years ago, which he kept in his office in Franklin Avenue, where many persons saw it. He thinks that Lorrillard and others who are building the "Meteor" are infringing upon his invention, and that it probably suggested the idea of the dome steamer. Last July, describing his vessel to a visitor, he said, "One advantage I have over the proposed new line is that my vessel *cannot be sunk.* No matter how heavy a storm may be, she will ride it safely. If she should run into an iceberg, or collide with another vessel, it would be impossible to sink her.

"Her safety will not consist in numerous air-tight compartments, but why it will be impossible to sink her is my secret. You can look at the model," he added, pointing to it standing on a table in the corner of the office.

The model boat is that of a low, rakish-looking vessel. The principal feature is that she has no deck, being rounded on top after the manner of the lower part of the hull. The bow tapers gradually from the centre, after the fashion of a steam-yacht. There is also a gradual tapering from the centre to the stern, which overhangs the rudder to some extent, but the stern is as sharp as the bow. The vessel is a long, narrow cylinder, sharpened at both ends, the lines being neatly and artistically drawn. She has two tall smoke-stacks, leaning fore and aft.

"You see," continued the inventor, "she is built for speed as well as for safety. Having no rigging, and with her shape, she will meet with little resistance of either wind or water. She is modeled so that she will glide through the water with scarcely a ripple. The water will run along her bottom with as much ease as though running down hill. Her upper part is built on the same principle, so that the speed will not be impeded by the wind. There will be no projections from the upper part, save the pilot-house and smoke-stack. They will be built of iron and strongly braced, and modeled in the same manner as the vessel. You will notice that I have studied the wind as well as the water, and speed as well as safety. A steamship built after my model will make a voyage to Europe in one-quarter less time than the fastest steamship afloat at the present day.

"That apparent forward smoke-stack is the pilot-house. The vessel has but one smoke-stack. The pilot-house being on a level with the smoke-stack, the pilot will have a longer range of vision, and be beyond the reach of the sea in case of storm. The pilot-house and smoke-stack will be forty feet above the surface of the water, about the usual height of a look-out on a vessel. Below the pilot-house there will be an opening for the purpose of pumping air into the ship. This pure air will be continually passing through the ship, and out again through the smoke-stack. Aft of the pilot-room, in the stack, will be an elevator for the transportation of the men up and down."

The pilot-house and smoke-stack are not circular tube-shaped, but are flattened on the sides, and sharp fore and aft, on the same principle as the bow and stern of the ship.

"People may object to being sealed up in your cylinder-shaped vessel during an entire voyage to Europe," the visitor remarked. "In case of an accident there would be no opportunity to escape."

"A great many people object to going to Europe on account of the danger they are exposed to on board the present vessels," said the inventor. "Could they be convinced that there was no danger in making a voyage to Europe, there would be many more who would make the trip. On my vessel there would be no danger whatever; as I said, it is impossible to sink her. The only accident that could happen would be a break-down in the machinery. But each ship would carry duplicate machinery, so that an accident could be repaired immediately. Then, my ship would be fitted up as comfortably as a hotel. There will be heavy plate-glass windows running along the sides of the ship, and the ventilation will be perfect. I intend having a railing along the upper part of the vessel, so that in pleasant weather the passengers may take a promenade, if they wish. In bad weather they don't want to be outside. In a heavy storm, when the sea is pitching over a vessel, —seas that would wrench and disable an ordinary ship,—my boat will ride it as safely as though she was steaming up the East River. The passengers will feel as safe as though they were sitting in their own parlors. The water, when rushing over the deck of an ordinary ship, carrying away the bulwarks and rigging, will run off my vessel like the water off a whale's back. The boat is so modeled that if she should turn over,—which will be impossible, as the centre of gravity will be below the water-line,—but if she should turn over, she would float as well one way as the other. All that the passengers would have to do would be to stand on their heads. To be sure, that might inconvenience them some, but then there is no danger. There is a picture that will illustrate how she will weather a storm," and the inventor, artist, and engraver pointed to a picture hanging on the wall.

The painting is of his patent safety steamship in a terrible storm, executed by the inventor himself. The hurricane is blowing due east, and heavy black clouds hover about in close proximity to the smokestack. The sea is running "mountain high" and breaking over the ship from a represented height of forty feet. Part of the ship is obscured, from her being submerged amidships. The bow is about plunging into a great sea, while the stern projects from another. Away up in the pilot-house the captain is seen with his face glued to the glass, his hands firmly grasping the wheel, the sea breaking about him in a white, foamy mass. In through the plate-glass windows the passengers are forming a set for a quadrille, as unconcerned as though they were sailing up the Hudson on an excursion barge.

"Here is another," said the inventor, shortly afterwards, pointing to a picture on the other wall, "which presents the ship in another light."

The painting represented the ship in smoother water, under sunshine, evidently steaming along at a rapid pace. A little astern is a sea-gull. The reporter interpreted it as a race between the patent safety steamship and the gull, in which the bird is beaten.

"What will be the dimensions of your ship?" the reporter inquired.

"My figures," replied the inventor, "are 360 feet in length, 25 feet beam, and 35 feet deep. She can be built larger, if necessary.[1]

1882.—CAPTAIN LUNDBORG'S TWIN-SCREW STEAMSHIP.—His design, which he has patented in the United States and Europe, is based on a novel form of vessel, which renders high speed possible, while adding greatly to the carrying capacity and stability of the vessel.

The design, while affording ample space for passengers and valuable cargo, has the primary object of attaining a velocity of twenty to twenty-one knots an hour, with a comparatively moderate expenditure of power. The prominent idea is that of making the main body of the ship divide the water horizontally instead of vertically. By adopting this system of construction he says it becomes possible to build a ship of the greatest capacity for a given draught,—an advantage which speaks for itself. But, besides this, it is stated that this ship of shallow draught and great capacity can have admirable lines, and her resistance may be reduced to a minimum. The principle, he claims, admits of the naval architect imparting to his ship a splendid clean run aft, and the screws can be carried far astern and yet be well supported. The advantages to be derived from thus placing the screws far astern have

[1] *Brooklyn Eagle*, July 17, 1882.

been insisted on by the late Mr. Froude. No scheme has been put forward which is so perfectly adapted to the use of twin-screws. If desired, the stern of the ship can be carried farther aft, to protect the screws. There is ample room provided for engine-power, notwithstanding the fine run of the hull aft. The principal dimensions, etc., of Captain Lundborg's proposed ship are:

Length of hull below water on the plane of greatest beam	450 feet.
Greatest breadth	66 "
Length on load water-line	444 "
Breadth on load water-line	58 "
Draught of water on load water-line	23 "
Length over all on upper deck	475 "
Breadth on upper deck at greatest transverse section (outside of frames)	62 "
Depth from top of upper deck beams to bottom plating	41 "
Height between the upper and second decks	9 "
Height between second and third decks	9 "
Height between third and orlop decks	8 "
Area of greatest immersed transverse section	1,412 square "
Coefficient of greatest immersed transverse section	0.09808
Area of load water-plane	15,255 square feet.
Displacement to load water-line	380,836 cubic "
Displacement	10,881 tons.
Horizontal distance of centre of buoyancy from the submerged stern	225 feet.
Vertical distance of centre of buoyancy below load water-line	11,456 "
Height of metacentre above centre of buoyancy	7,469 "
Height of metacentre above centre of gravity of the ship when fully equipped and loaded	8,458 "
Height of metacentre above centre of gravity of the ship at 14 feet draught of water, with no cargo, coal, stores, water, or ballast, and no water in boilers, but otherwise completely fitted and fully rigged	5,060 "
Height of metacentre above centre of gravity of the ship at 9.6 feet draught of water, the hull being complete, with masts in and rigged, but empty, without engines or boilers	11,389 "
Wet surface when immersed to load water-line	38,040 "
Angle of obliquity of load water-line at the bow	5° 50′
Angle of obliquity at the stern	6° 30′
Mean angle of obliquity at entrance	7°

The ship is to have two propellers of 16 feet diameter and 28 feet pitch; the propelling power to consist of *four* compound engines, two on each propeller shaft, developing each, when making 90 revolutions per minute, 4500 indicated horse-power, or for all four engines together, 18,000 indicated horse-power. With this power the speed, according to Professor Rankine's formula, would be 20.7 knots per hour; but that speed would in all probability be exceeded, as little power will be lost by wave-making, the water having a clean run astern, being divided horizontally by the lower part of the hull.

The ship would have room to accommodate about 600 first-class and

HISTORY OF STEAM NAVIGATION. 293

1000 second- and third-class passengers, and carry 3000 tons of cargo, 23 feet draught of water, besides 2700 tons of coal.

The ship is designed to be built of iron or steel, with a double bottom, and with a great number of water-tight compartments, transverse and longitudinal.

The peculiar form of the hull makes it possible to unite great carrying capacity with the finest lines for high speeds. The submerged stern, which divides the water horizontally, admits of the finest possible run aft, and affords a perfect support and protection to the propeller shafts. With this construction the propellers act constantly in solid water, unaffected by stern-post, rudder, and the overhanging part of the stern, as in ships of the usual form. This feature secures an economy of power, or, what is the same thing, an increase of speed.

A vessel of this form will not roll and pitch as much as other vessels, as the body of water above the projecting part of the hull offers considerable resistance to such motions.

The rudders may be nearly balanced, and will require but little power to work them, and, on account of the peculiar form of the stern, the rudders may have considerably less area than those of the common model, as it requires less power to move the stern laterally.

The form of the hull, while permitting very sharp entrance and run, affords ample room for the application of the greatest engine-power compatible with carrying capacity.[1]

1882.—ROOT'S SIDE-SCREW STEAMSHIP.—A vessel of this kind is being built at Greenpoint, Long Island, by Samuel Pine, for Señor Diaz, for lighterage service in Cuba. This vessel embodies in the arrangement of her propelling wheels the ideas set forth by Mr. Root before the American Society of Mechanical Engineers. The hull is one hundred feet long, thirty-two wide, and with one hundred tons of cargo draws only three feet of water. She is decked over and has a flat bottom, with vertical sides, longitudinal strength being obtained by three fore and aft bulkheads, and she is the first example of what is thought by experts will be a revolution in the science of screw propulsion.

A high rate of speed is not expected, but her performance will exemplify the economy which Mr. Root claims for his novel application of screw-propelling wheels. These wheels are set on the ends of an athwartship shaft, the plane of their faces being fore and aft, and not as the common type of screw propeller is, at right angles to the line of motion of the vessel. They are driven by a vertical direct-acting engine. The boiler is a vertical tubular, which will drive the wheels from one hundred and fifty to two hundred revolutions per minute. The "true-screw" type of wheel is used, six feet in diameter.

---

[1] The *Scientific American*, October 21, 1882, has a view of the ship complete, and also of her stern. She is represented as having three funnels and four masts, three of which are square rigged.

In his experimental workshop Mr. Root has a trough of water, in which he exhibits the speed of different models moved by clock-spring machinery, turning various types of propelling wheels. It is interesting and instructive to see one model in particular spinning down the trough, propelled by a screw-wheel revolving horizontally under the bottom, the propelling force being generated by a current of water sucked in by the revolutions of the screw, between it and the incline of the bottom of the boat. There seems no limit to the power that could be exerted by this oblique-acting current, excepting in the size and speed of the screw-wheel, and the illustration of Mr. Root's theory by the action of this model is conclusive as to its theoretical correctness. It presented an amusing and instructive paradox in the propelling effect produced by a vertical screw-shaft, its thrust being at right angles to the line of motion,—the propeller blades working horizontally and parallel with the keel instead of at right angles to it, as all propellers do that are now used. "In the present method of applying the screw-propeller wheel," says Mr. Root, "the maximum propelling effect has without doubt been obtained, for it is well known that an increase of engine-power gives nothing like a proportionate effect in speed. Sixty per cent. of all the power is wasted somewhere, Mr. Froude calculates, and accounts for this great loss of power in the present method of stern screw-wheel propulsion in the fact that a screw-wheel at the stern of a vessel draws the water away from the after body, creates a suction, as it were, and, of course, increases thereby the head resistance, such increase varying with the size of the column of water acted upon by the wheel.

"It is a fact in practice that all craft propelled by a stern screw-wheel, when they reach a certain velocity, settle down by the stern; and, pile on the power as you may, beyond that point no more speed can be obtained. They can and do settle, however, which fact shows clearly that a vacuum is formed when a high rate of speed is obtained, and that the screw-wheel, operating in the vacuum, becomes, more or less, a retarding instead of a propelling force, as such 'minus-pressure' adds directly to the head resistance. It has lately been found in England that at high speeds the power does not follow the speed produced in a uniform ratio, as in some speeds it may vary as the cube; beyond them it drops down as low as the square of the velocity. Fluid action around a vessel is something of an enigma, and the columns of water acted upon by a screw-wheel at the stern, in its reactionary thrust, is more so. The fact of the enormous waste of power in the best examples of steam screw-wheel propulsion is incontrovertible."

Mr. Root proposes to change the position of the wheel, and make the currents generated by their revolutions force the vessel through the water by their oblique action on the sides of the after-body or "run" of the vessel. His system has been patented in the United States and abroad, and is analogous in its application to the action of fishes when swimming, the power being applied laterally. At a point in the "run" of his craft where the water begins to close in laterally he places his wheels. The shaft is at right angles to the keel, and the wheels some sixteen feet apart. The proper pitch, etc., of these wheels has to be determined by experiment, but they will drive a current inboard along the sides of the run (which will be made concave, vertically) that, in its impinging force upon the converging sides of the hull, will propel it forward. It is like the snapping of a bean between your fingers, and the larger the wheels and the greater their velocity the more power they will exert, as they work always in solid water.

1882.—COPPIN'S TRIPLE STEAMSHIP.—Captain William Coppin is an old and well-known constructor and inventor. As early as 1842 he built the "Londonderry," a screw steamship of 1500 tons, the largest screw steamer that had up to that time been built.[1] She was sometimes called the "Great Northern," and antedated the "Great Britain," which was laid down as a paddle-wheel, but before launching altered to a screw. Captain Coppin's United States patent is dated March 28, 1882, and his idea, which has yet to be put to a practical test, has been approved and indorsed by several distinguished officers, both line and staff, of the United States navy, and William Pearce, of the well-known firm of William Elder & Co., who, under date of September 11, 1880, says, "I am satisfied that twenty knots an hour will be very readily attained with this (your) form of vessel, and of the power, displacement, and dimensions contained in your estimates."

The invention consists of a compound ship, consisting of three ship hulls united as one vessel, the two outer hulls being of equal length and longer than the central hull, and the whole being decked over. The three hulls are rigidly connected by iron or steel bulkheads, box-girders, and iron or steel decks, or frames, so as to form complete platforms or decks, and leave considerable extra space between the ships. The centre ship is to carry the engines, and is provided with a propeller at each end. This arrangement brings the screws well towards the centre of the outside hulls and prevents a possibility of the pitching motion lifting the propeller out of the water. The three hulls are tapered from the centre, both longitudinally and vertically, and come to a rounded point at both ends, so as to enter the wave and reduce the pitching motion to a minimum, the rolling being done away with by the extent of the water-space between the ships. The decks extend in the centre three-fifths (more or less) of the length of the outside ship. The remaining portion of the ends are covered over for passing through the waves. For smooth-water ferry-boats and the like, the decks are proposed to be the entire length of the outside hulls.

Captain Coppin claims that his improvements are "specially ap-

[1] See page 184.

plicable to war-ships, and enable a large amount of armor-plating to be carried, and give an extended battery platform to carry guns of the largest calibre, and that turrets of increased thickness of armor-plate can be employed with safety. Complete protection is also given to the engines, screw-propellers, and steering apparatus, increased accommodation for a large number of troops and horses, with a speed at least one-third faster than the present class of transports; and the construction is such that one of the three ships might be completely riddled with shot or damaged by a ram, and yet be supported by the other two." There can be no question that a vessel of this description will have great stability, and can be armor-clad, and that the outer hulls will have to be penetrated before the central hull, containing the engine, can be reached, and that the broad platform of her deck would be admirably adapted for carrying guns of heavy calibre. As a ferry-boat she seems also to unite many advantages, and her broad decks and stability seem to adapt her particularly for a railroad ferry barge. Her ability to turn rapidly in a seaway and to withstand Atlantic gales, and also the speed she might attain, has yet to be put to a practical test.

1882.—THE FRYER BUOYANT PROPELLER "ALICE"—A VELOCIPEDE OR LOCOMOTIVE.—A working model of this queer craft stands in a brick-yard at Hastings-on-the-Hudson, where it is an object of great curiosity. The model consists of a triangular frame-work resting on three wheels, which are in the same relation to each other as the wheels of a tricycle. These wheels are spheroidal in shape, about six feet in diameter, and are housed above with dome-shaped covers. Each sphere is a propeller, having flanges or buckets at the sides at right angles to the vertical diameter, and acting upon the water like a paddle-wheel. These spheroids are driven by steam. At the same time they serve as floats, and are submerged about one-sixth of their capacity. Another feature of the propellers is that they have an iron tire or keel, by means of which they may be made to serve as wheels, and carry the vessel along a track on dry land. An engine rests on the frame-work between the two propellers that are opposite each other. The frame-work forming the deck is supported on the axes of the wheels, so that it is several feet above the surface of the water.

Robert Fryer, the inventor, conceived the idea of his water-car about twelve years ago, and has been engaged in making experiments ever since. His first model was made on a small scale. It consisted of three hollow copper globes connected by axles to a frame superstructure, and of the same form as the larger model. The spheres were twelve inches in diameter, made to revolve by springs placed inside and wound up by keys. After repeated experiments in a tank, it was rigged with a small sail and launched on the Harlem River, with good results. Daily experiments were subsequently made with the steam model on the Harlem, much to the astonishment of those who saw it. It was found that it could be turned in its own length; that there was no appreciable slipping, and that it was little affected by the action of the wind or tide. When the "Alice" was taken to Hastings it made part of the distance on dry land, steaming along the road like a great lumbering wagon.

The plan proposes a huge hollow semi-cylinder for the superstructure, containing saloons and state-rooms, with masts and rigging above for carrying sails. One claim made for the buoyant propeller is that it cannot be overturned in the roughest sea, on account of its triangular shape, and that its oscillation in a violent sea will be less than that of an ordinary vessel on comparatively smooth water. The advantage from this is that passengers would have no fear of sea-sickness. The inventor believes that his ship will excel the steam-vessels now in use in point of convenience and comfort, and be a safer means of transit, as the ship proper would stand thirty feet above the water, and out of reach of the waves even in a stormy sea. He also designs to apply the same principle to the construction of dispatch- and life-boats. If this water-car comes up to the expectations of its inventor, it will make the passage of the Atlantic between Sundays.[1]

1882.—ROSSE'S CATAMARAN STEAM-TUG.—This novel steam-vessel, which was built at Brown's ship-yard, in Tarrytown, is now in the harbor of New York, waiting trial. Its inventor, Captain J. Rosse, will claim the reward offered by the government for a steamboat that can run in canals without washing or otherwise injuring the banks. The practical utility of the craft has not yet been proved, but it is believed that it will prove very powerful in towing canal-boats

---

[1] Two correspondents of the Manchester *Times*, in October, 1882, referring to Fryer's Marine Velocipede, say,—

"In June, 1866, a patent was granted in America to A. Blomquist and C. Cooke (patent No. 56,851) for a 'marine car' on three spheres, with paddles attached, on the same principle as that described by your correspondent 'Mechanic.' What made me notice his account is the fact that about five years ago I made a model of the vessel for Mr. Blomquist, of Brooklyn, New York, one of the original patentees.
"ANOTHER MECHANIC,
"Late of Brooklyn, New York."

"'Mechanic,' Carlisle, describing the vessel invented by Robert Fryer, of New York, would almost make us believe there *is* something new under the sun. But though the remarkable vessel may be new, the idea is not. I once inquired of the editor respecting a machine on which a man walked on the river Tyne, and was told that my question was not sufficiently explicit. The machine described by 'Mechanic' corresponds exactly with the invention to which my question referred. If I recollect rightly, the machine I saw was a marine velocipede, on three long, spider-like legs, stretching from what formed a seat for the rider. These legs were fixed in hollow tin spheres, sufficiently large to bear his weight, and wide enough apart to enable him to maintain his balance. The rider had flanges or flappers fitted on his feet, and was thus enabled to propel himself. Although the speed was not very great, it was sufficient to enable him to keep pace with the boats around him,— namely, the procession of barges on the day when George IV. was crowned.
"DRIFFIELD, South Shields."

without making a destructive washing against the bank. The boat is built of two very narrow hulls, fifty-three feet in length, with the machinery and weight thoroughly balanced on them. She lies low, so as to pass under the canal bridges. A huge belt, which runs fore and aft over two drums at right angles with and between the two hulls, has buckets or paddles fixed across its outer surface. The power is applied to the drums, and the belt is moved around from forward to aft, taking the water easily, and leaving it without making a commotion. The novelty has so far made satisfactory speed.[1]

1882.—A Boat Propelled by Electricity.—The *Scientific American* for November 11, 1882, has a description and an engraving of a small boat propelled by electricity, lately tried on the Thames River near London. It also gives transverse and longitudinal sections and a deck-plan of the boat. The hull is of iron, 25 feet long, 5 feet beam, drawing 21 inches of water forward and 30 inches aft. She is a screw boat, the propeller being of the Collis-Browne type, 20 inches in diameter, and with a 3-foot pitch. The screw is calculated to make 350 revolutions per minute. Twelve persons can be accommodated on board, though only four were actually carried on the trial trip. The electric engines are nothing else than a pair of Siemens's dynamos, of the size known as D3, and their motive power is furnished by Sellon-Volckmar accumulators. These accumulators are a modification of those of Plante and of Faure, but are made of specially compact design for the purpose of electric navigation. The cells each contain forty prepared plates, and weigh about forty pounds. They are about ten inches square and eight inches high, and are charged, while the boat is lying at anchor, by wires which come across the wharf from the factory, bringing currents generated by dynamos fixed in the works. There is room for a battery of fifty-four such cells to be stowed away, as will be seen upon the drawings, where the battery cells are marked B B. Only forty-five cells were used at the trial trip. They had a total electromotive force of ninety-six volts, and were capable of furnishing continuously for nine hours a current exceeding thirty ampères.

When in action the counter-electromotive force of the motors reduces the apparent strength of the current according to Jacobi's well-known theory of electro-magnetic engines. The accumulators have a total weight of somewhat less than a ton. The motors of electric engines are arranged so that either or both of them may be furnished with the current, there being a switch to each lead. There is also a commutator to switch into circuit any number of cells from forty upward. One of the motors can be thrown in or out of gear by means of an Addyman's friction clutch, which permits the pulley to be started and stopped with great facility without shocks. A reversing gear for the two motors is

---

[1] Engravings of this catamaran, the Fryer propeller, and the domed steamship "Meteor" can be found in *Harper's Weekly*, October 7, 1882.

contrived by the very simple device of arranging two pairs of brushes for each collector or commutator, one pair having an angular lead forward, the other a lead backward. By a simple lever arrangement either pair of brushes can be pressed at will against the segments of the commutator. In practice this arrangement works well, the boat being very readily stopped by reversing the engines in this fashion. As will be seen from the drawings, the motors are connected by belts to pulleys on a countershaft, from which a belt passes down to a pulley on the propeller axis, whose speed is thus reduced in the proportion of 950 to 350 revolutions per minute. The steering is managed by the same person who operates the switches, seated in the central cabin. A whistle being impossible in the absence of steam, this necessary feature is replaced by a large electric bell, also worked by the accumulators. The calculated average speed is nine miles per hour. This speed, says *Engineering*, was actually attained on the trial trip from Milwall to London Bridge and back.

1882.—A STEAMSHIP BRAKE.—The stopping of steamers suddenly, when under way, has long been a problem unsolved. But a near approach to an effective "brake," as it is called, is in operation on one of the small craft plying between City Point and Long Island, in Boston harbor. A trial of the device, invented by Mr. John McAdams, on the steamer "City Point," was made in the harbor in November. The arrangement is simple, and is seen at once from a glance at the working model. The essential parts are two large metal fins on the after part of the hull, one on either side, which can by a simple movement be thrown at right angles to the body of the boat, presenting a broad surface to the water and effectually checking the boat's headway. The fins can be made of any size, those of the "City Point" being five feet by four. The fins are hinged securely on the stern post, and are sustained when open by three strong telescope braces and a chain, the last-named also serving to close the apparatus. When closed the appearance is of two closed port-holes. The material is steel. A strong spring opens the fins, just starting them a few inches, and the force of the water throws them open to the full extent. There are two levers for working the apparatus, one in the pilot-house and one on the forward deck. An additional and automatic arrangement has also been invented, consisting of a long lever to hang from the end of the bowsprit of large vessels, and serving to work the apparatus automatically in case of sudden collision. In case of necessity one fin can be worked alone, not only checking the speed, but also turning sharply aside. The "City Point" got under way, and, while at full speed, the signal was given and the fins thrown back. The motion of the boat was checked with a sharp shock, and before ten feet of space were covered she lay perfectly still. The effect of forty square feet of steel braced suddenly at right angles to the vessel may be imagined. Several trials were made, both with steam on and with steam shut off at the moment the fins were opened, and in both cases the motion was quickly stopped. The patent has only been issued a few weeks, and nothing has been done looking to the general introduction of the brake, but its success on trial certainly shows that steps have been taken in the right direction towards preventing the numerous collisions of steamers and the consequent loss of life and property.

OCEAN MERCANTILE STEAMERS.—The net tonnage of the maritime nations of the world, according to the French Bureau Reports in 1882, was,—

Countries.	Net tonnage.
Great Britain	8,133,458
United States	408,496
Norway	53,340
Germany	234,680
Italy	75,646
France	302,432
Russia	87,997
Sweden	66,204
Spain	144,691
Holland	81,048
Greece	11,019
Austria	66,852

1882.—There are sixty-five steamers in the British merchant marine of considerable coal-bearing power that possess an ocean speed of upward of thirteen knots, and the P. & O. Line possess forty-eight steamers with a speed of over twelve knots.

1882.—THE LIMIT OF STEAM PRESSURE.—In the time of Watt the ordinary limit was seven pounds. Ten times this pressure is usual now, while ninety pounds is not uncommon. The rise within the past ten years has been twenty-five pounds, and with the constant study of boiler structure and boiler capacity for work and strain, we may expect to see at least an equal rise during the coming ten years. Pressures of one hundred pounds and over are occasional now, but are yet far from being the rule. The increasing use of steel in boiler construction must lead to developments that will help the solvement of the problem.

1882.—A NOVEL APPLICATION OF THE SCREW.—The screw propeller at the stern has maintained its position unchanged, though often varied in its form and in the pitch, or number of its blades, since it was first brought into general use. It has been tried at the bow, where it worked well enough, until it proved troublesome when brought in contact with drift-wood. It has been placed at the sides, where it operated only as an imperfect paddle-wheel. Recently it has been tried in an entirely new position. The vessel to which this new method of placing the screw has been applied is a lighter, designed for carrying heavy freight upon a crooked and shallow river. Her wood hull is about ninety feet long and thirty-two feet wide, and draws about thirty-nine inches when loaded with one hundred tons of freight. In general appearance the boat does not differ from the ordinary steam-lighters used in American waters. Her hull is of the usual shape, except at the stern; there the after-body turns abruptly inward at the water-line, making a double curve towards the stern-post. Below the water-line the hull carries a lip or projection that follows the ordinary lines of a ship's stern. In the concave recess on *each side of the stern* is placed a single screw, facing outward,—that is, the shaft carrying a screw at each end extends directly *across the hull.* This shaft is just at the water-line, and carries each screw half-submerged. The deck above each screw overhangs the hull, as in American river-boats. The engine is placed between the two screws and directly connected with the shaft. On turning the two screws placed in this position, it would appear that they would act as paddle-wheels. They do so, but the amount of work performed in moving the boat is thought to be very small. Experiments seem to prove that the movement of the boat is caused by the streams of water turned by the screws against the wedge-shaped hull. The water thrown into the concave part of the stern cannot easily escape, and the result is the hull is thrust forward by the action of the water against it. The actual trials of the boat show that she can be moved with a full load, in rather rough water, at a speed of from *four to five knots* an hour. This is considered good speed for such a boat, with her small engine-power. On the second trial trip careful measurements were made of the power utilized by the screws. The boat was towed at her usual speed, and the amount of strain on the tow-line found by the aid of a dynamometer. The power needed to move the boat, compared with the actual working power of the engine, was found to be over fifty per cent. In other words, one-half the actual power of the engine seems to be realized in moving the boat. This is considered a favorable showing for the position of the screws. The trial trips of the new boat are regarded as interesting contributions to the question of screw propulsion. The positions of the screws give a good economy for the power employed, and in new and faster boats, that are to be built upon the same pattern, more interesting results may be expected.[1]

1882.—THE DOME STEAM-YACHT "METEOR."—There is now building at Nyack-on-the-Hudson a steamboat of naval construction which is rapidly approaching completion. This craft is the design, model, and invention, both in hull and machinery, of Captain A. Perry Bliven. She will be launched on the 1st of August. Her dimensions are: Length over all, 153 feet; water-line, 136 feet; on keel, 128 feet; extreme beam, 21 feet 6 inches; beam at water-line,

[1] *The Century* for November, 1882.

17 feet; extreme depth of hold, 17 feet; draught forward, 6 feet; draught aft, 11 feet; tonnage, old measurement, 512$\frac{80}{100}$. This vessel is an entirely new departure from the principles and designs of the steamers now afloat, and is the pioneer vessel of the American Quick Transit Company of Boston. The "Meteor" will be followed by large steel steamers of the same model, and with the most powerful machinery ever yet placed in ocean steamships. The "Herald," to be built in Boston, on the "Meteor's" model, will be of the following dimensions: 425 feet long; 56 feet beam; 48 feet hold; draught forward, 17 feet; draught aft, 26 feet; capacity, 7500 tons, old measurement. She will have four steel boilers, new pattern; three double compounded steel engines, twelve cylinders; actual horse-power, 18,000; capable of making a speed of 28 to 30 miles per hour.

It appears that the inventor's aim is to make a self-righting boat by carrying the sides over the deck in the form of a dome. The side frames are made continuous, and meet over the centre of the hull, or, in other words, the frames begin at one side of the keel, rise directly at an angle of about forty-five degrees to the water-line, and then curve inward over the deck and back on the same lines to the keel. A section of the hull taken in the centre is thus of a wedge shape, with a sharp edge below and rounded top above. This wedge-form is preserved through the entire length of the hull. There are no hollow lines in the boat, and the sharp, overhanging bow is intended to part the water near the surface, and to form a long, tapering wedge. The widest part of the hull is exactly at the middle, both ends being precisely alike. This is quite different from the flat bottom and straight sides, with comparatively bluff or rounded bows, of the ordinary ocean steamship.

The boat is intended to be much deeper aft than forward, and the deck will be much higher above water at the bows than at the stern. There will be no houses or raised constructions of any kind on deck, except the dome-shaped pilot-house, the ventilators, and the smoke-stacks. There will be an open railing around the centre of the deck, so that it can be used as a promenade in pleasant weather, or whenever the seas do not break over the boat. The object of this unbroken dome-shaped deck is to enable the boat to throw off all waves that break over the bows or sides in rough weather. It is thought that, instead of shipping tons of water and retaining it on deck till it can be drained off, the boat will shed or throw off the water from the long, sharp bows and open deck, and will at once relieve herself of the weight of the water. Waves striking the rounded deck will have no hold on the boat, and their force will thus be spent harmlessly. The sharp wedge-shape and rounded top of the hull, and the fact that even when fully loaded the centre of gravity will be below the water-line, makes the model self-righting.

From experiments with a small model, this claim of the inventor seems to be clearly proved. In laying out the boat only the spar-deck will be used for passengers, the main-deck and all below being intended for cargo, coal, and engines. The state-rooms will be arranged along the outside, each room having a port in the side of the boat, while the ceiling will be formed of the curved deck above. The saloons will be the whole width of the ship, and on the spar-deck. For lighting the saloons there will be skylights in the centre, and as these in rough weather may be covered by the seas that sweep over the deck, they will be very strong, and will be air-tight. To secure ventilation there will be steam-fans, kept in motion at all times, and maintaining a good circulation of air through every part of the boat. For this purpose the fresh air will be taken through wind-sails on the deck, and the exhaust air from the rooms will be turned into the blast used in forcing the boiler fires. No boats are to be carried on deck; the life-rafts and boats will be kept in an apartment under the domed deck at the stern, and when they are to be launched doors will be opened in the deck, and the boats launched in the usual way from davits through these doors. The pilot-house will be at the bows, and will be entirely inclosed. It will not rise much above the deck, and will be entered from below.

There will be no masts or sails, as it is intended to depend wholly on the engines for propulsion. In constructing the hull, to secure great strength, three heavy trusses, or "hog frames," are to be placed on the keel, each one rising to the spar-deck, and securely fastened to the side frames of the boat. The ceiling will be double, and placed diagonally on the frames. In the larger steamships the absence of sailing power will be compensated for by two extra engines and two supplementary screws, that can be employed in case the larger screw is lost, or the main engines break down.

1882.—HERR BECK'S GUNPOWDER ENGINE.—A patent has been taken out in Germany for a gunpowder engine. Years ago, before Savery and Newcomen introduced their rude attempts at steam-engines, Huyghens and others, notably Papin, endeavored to utilize the force of exploding gunpowder as a means of obtaining motive-power, and engines were constructed which demonstrated at least the *possibility* of the idea. A tall cylinder, having a touch-hole at the bottom, was fitted with a heavy piston, to which ropes were attached passing over pulleys. A sufficient quantity of gunpowder was placed inside the cylinder to drive the piston nearly to the top when the powder was fired, and then the gases escaping through the touch-hole, and being also condensed, the atmospheric pressure forced the piston down, and men who were holding on to the ropes were hauled up. Of late the idea has been utilized in the construction of a pile-driver, the "monkey" being driven down by the force of exploding gunpowder. Herr Beck has recently devised an engine the piston of which is driven backward and forward by small charges of gunpowder supplied at each end by an automatic arrangement. The ignition is effected by the motion of the piston, which draws in a flame of gas or spirit, the access being regulated by slide valves, which also opens outlets for the escape of the gases of combustion.

1882.—A NEW MOTOR.—A new motor has been discovered, which, it is claimed, will supersede steam. The material from which the energy is generated is bisulphide of carbon, which is utilized as a motor agent in the form of vapor, and the advantage claimed for it over steam is that, while water expands in the ratio of 1 cubic inch to 1700, bisulphide of carbon has an expansive property of 1 to 8000. When the vapor is generated it passes into the steam-chest of the engine and moves the piston-rods. A pipe attached to the engine conveys the exhaust vapor directly through a condenser back to the tank in its original liquefied form, to be regenerated. The system of generation and condensation is similar to the heart-action; and with machinery perfectly constructed it is claimed that a single supply of the bisulphide of carbon can be used with reinforcement for an indefinite period. The cost of fuel is trifling, it being claimed that from the peculiar properties of the bisulphide an ordinary house fire can develop a power sufficient to run an ocean steamer. Water boils at 212°, and it takes 320° of heat to make steam available, while the new agent takes the form of vapor at 180°. The invention is owned by J. R. Blumenburg, a German, who has been exhibiting it to Philadelphia capitalists with such success that they are likely to try it on a large scale.

CHAPTER VI.

THE GREAT OCEAN STEAMSHIP COMPANIES.—GENERAL REMARKS, OCEAN TRAMPS, ETC.—The Cunard, 1840.—The Peninsular and Oriental, 1840.—Pacific Steam Navigation, 1840.—Royal West India Mail, 1841.—Collins Line, 1847.—Pacific Mail Steamship Company, 1848.—Warren Line, 1850.—Inman Line, 1850.—The Messageries Maritimes, 1851.—Allan Line, 1854.—Hamburg American Packet Company, 1855.—Anchor Line, 1856.—North German Lloyds, 1857.—Leyland Line, 1860.—Compagnie Générale Transatlantique, 1862.—National Steamship Company, 1863.—Williams & Guion Line, 1866.— Old Dominion Line, 1867.—White Star Line, 1870.—American or Keystone Line, 1871.—City Line.—State Line, 1872.—Red Star Line, 1873.—The Monarch Line, 1874.—Harrison Line.—Ocean Steamship Company of Savannah.— The Mitsu-Bishi Steam Navigation Company, 1875.—The Atlas Steamship Company.—Roach's United States and Brazil Steamship Line, 1875.—The Mallory Line.—The Red "D" Line, 1879.—New York, Havana, and Mexican Mail Line.—Boston and Savannah Steamship Company, 1882.—Thingvalla Line, 1882.—West India Steamship Enterprise.

I AM indebted to the courtesy of the managers, agents, and owners of the several ocean steamship lines for the major part of the information contained in this chapter, but I have also drawn from printed histories and circulars and communications which I have found in magazines and newspapers since these sketches of ocean steamship lines were written, and in part printed in the UNITED SERVICE.

The *Century*, in its September number, has published an interesting article on ocean steamships, by S. W. G. Benjamin, which has been supplemented by an anonymous communication entitled " More about Ocean Steamships," published in the Boston *Transcript*. The writer seemed to be well posted up in his subject, better even than Mr. Benjamin, and as his communication contains some interesting facts which I have not given, I take the liberty to quote from him a few paragraphs to supply the deficiency.

"The steamships of the world," he says, "may be roughly divided into three classes. These are, first, those belonging to mail lines, carrying passengers and mails, and leaving and arriving at certain ports at an advertised time, and with the greatest regularity possible under the circumstances. The second class consists of steamers not carrying the mails, and sometimes but a few passengers, chiefly devoted to the carrying trade,—cattle, grain, miscellaneous cargoes of ore and general products,—but plying with a certain regularity between stated ports. The third class comprises all steamers which, having no fixed route, go to any port which offers the best terms for freight, wandering around the globe, and hardly touching at the same place twice. These latter are the 'ocean tramp' class of steamships, on which in many cases opprobrium has been unjustly heaped."

Of the first class of steamers, the two largest lines in the world are the British India Steam Navigation Company and the Austro-Hungarian Lloyds. It is hard to say exactly which is the larger, but at present the steamers owned by each number about seventy-seven and seventy-nine respectively. The British India Company does its chief business, as its name indicates, with India and its dependencies, and the map which represents its different routes is a net-work of bewildering lines. Every port in India is in communication with Calcutta, Bombay, and Madras by this company's steamships, and communication with London is kept up by fortnightly steamers. This company runs steamers every fortnight also from London to the Persian Gulf and Bagdad, calling at Algiers; and it has lately started a line to Brisbane in Queensland *via* Batavia. Its steamers have until lately been of medium size, but it is now building larger ships. Its vessels are named after Indian towns, etc., and the names are mostly very pretty, as " Merkara," " Dorunda," " Ellora," and others.

"The chief lines from London to the Cape direct are the Union Steamship Company (thirteen steamers), and Donald Currie & Co.'s Castle line (twenty steamers), mostly large and fine ships, while the trading stations on the West Coast of Africa are supplied by the African Steamship Company, and the British and African Steam Navigation Company, with smaller steamers, more or less devoted to freight, although carrying the mails.

"Lamport & Holt also run a line from London to Brazil and the river Platte, some of the steamers returning to Liverpool *via* New York. This line has some thirty steamers of moderate size, named after scientific men, painters, and poets.

"The City Line (City of London, of Venice, of Khios, etc.) is owned by George Smith & Sons, of Glasgow, who also own a large fleet of sailing ships. There are ten steamers in this line, all fine ships of 3000 tons. The Hall Line (Werneth Hall [4100], Breton Hall, etc.), owned by the Sun Shipping Company, and the Star Line ("Vega," "Orion," etc.) are favorite lines for India, as is also the Ducal Line (Duke of Lancaster, etc.), which has some very fine ships, seven in all. These last-named lines all come more or less under the second heading of combined passenger and freight steamers.

"Hamburg sends out lines to Panama (Hamburg-American Steamship Company), to Brazil (Hamburg-South American Steamship Company), to Valparaiso (Kosmos Steamship Company). It is not generally known, however, that the French Transatlantic Company by no means confines its operations in America to its New York business, but has some fine steamers running to Aspinwall, Vera Cruz, and the West Indies.

"Turning to the Pacific Ocean, we find only one English line connecting America with Asia,—the Oriental and Occidental Steamship Company, which is really a part of the White Star Line. The fine steamers "Arabic" and "Coptic," of 4300 tons each, which were built last year, and ran a short time on the Atlantic, have now their place in the O. and O. Company's fleet.

"Turning, then, to the second class of steamers, the organized lines of 'freighters,' we find in this category many lines of fine ships, so many, in fact, it will be impossible to mention more than a few. At the head of this class stands the firm of Thomas Wilson, Sons & Co., of Hull. They own fifty ships, averaging fully one thousand five hundred tons each, their names all ending in 'o.' Besides the lines of steamers running from Hull to Boston and New York,—only a tithe of their immense business,—Wilson & Co. dispatch ships to all ports of the Baltic, to Germany, Holland, and France, and even to Constantinople. Their business is rapidly increasing, and they have built within a few years a number of large ships, chiefly for their Atlantic trade.

"McGregor, Gow & Co., of Glasgow, own the Glen Line of steamers (not to be confounded with another line of Glen steamers owned by Lindsay, Gracie & Co., of Leith), fifteen in all, employed in the China and Japan trade, noted as tea-ships. They are of moderate size, and of a good model. The 'Stirling Castle,' of 4423 tons, which has earned the name of being the fastest steamer in the world, belongs to another 'tea' line of nine steamers, owned by Thomas Skinner, of Glasgow, named after Scottish castles. Another China line is the Ocean Steamship Company, owned by Alfred Holt, Liverpool, twenty-four steamers of about 2000 tons, named from Homeric characters. Warren & Co., of Liverpool, although they own only three steamers (the ships not named after States being, according to the registers, chartered), have in those three, the 'Missouri' (5146), the 'Kansas' (5276), and the 'Iowa' (4329), the largest freighters on one line in the world. The 'Hooper' (4935) has been taken off the Boston Line for some time, and now, with her name changed to the 'Silvertown,' is running in her old capacity of a telegraph ship. Another line of 'freighters' of large tonnage is that owned by Nott & Hill, of London,—the 'Notting Hill,' the 'Tower Hill,' and the 'Ludgate Hill,'—all over 4000 tons. In fact, large freight steamers are fast becoming common, and lines which have hitherto built ships of 2000 tons are now building vessels of 4000 tons and over. A line of steamers which has recently sprung into prominence, and which illustrates the rapidity with which steamers are built nowadays, is the 'Clan Line,' owned by Messrs. Cayzer, Irvine & Co., of Liverpool. In 1878 this company had about five steamers, but such has been the wonderful growth of the line that at present there are twenty-one steamers, either now running or in course of construction; most of them 2200 tons. They are all named after Scottish clans, as the 'Clan Cameron,' etc. They run from Liverpool to Calcutta, the Cape, and Mauritius."

"The Marquis de Campo, of Cadiz, has lately become prominent as a ship owner, employing steamers in the Manila and the Havana and the Mexican trade. Nearly all his ships have been bought of other lines, and we may discover among them some old friends. Every one who has crossed the Atlantic in the famous old 'China' will be glad to know of her present situation. She is now the 'Magellanes' of De Campo's Line, while the 'Siberia' figures as the 'Manila,' and the Warren steamer 'Minnesota' assumes her place as the 'Cristobal Colon.'

"Passing over many important regular freight lines, we come to the third class, the general freighter, the vagabond class of steamer, the 'ocean tramp,' which may be in Boston one month, Odessa the next, and Archangel the third. This is a much-abused class. Popular opinion is decidely against them. They are all supposed to be worthless, rotten, poorly manned, and liable to founder in any sea heavier than that of a mill pond. That there are a great many to which this description will apply is too true. They founder, like the 'Escambia,' almost within the harbor, or more frequently are simply reported 'missing.' These unfortunate vessels mostly belong to individual owners or small lines. But there are large fleets of newly-built, stanch steamers employed in this useful trade, and at the head of the list stand Messrs. Watts, Ward & Milburn, of London, with about forty steamers, most of them comparatively new. Their steamers are found everywhere. Messrs. Appleby, Ropner & Co., London, is another large firm. The number of new companies started within the last few years for this business is surprising. At present they usually number some half a dozen vessels each, generally named as a distinct system. To enumerate them would be tedious; but we may single out Messrs. Rankin, Gilmour & Co., for their splendid steamer 'St. Rouans,' of 4484 tons, a magnificent vessel, equal in every way in appearance to a transatlantic passenger steamer.

"The few persons who pursue the shipping news have undoubtedly noticed the numbers of freighters arriving at Philadelphia and Baltimore from Benisaf and Rio Marina. These two places, which maps completely ignore, are situated in Algeria, near Bona, and in the island of Elba respectively. The freighters go there for ballast of iron ore, which they take to our Southern ports, receiving a full cargo for Europe in the place of the ore.

"Of all these thousands of steamers so few are totally lost every year that when we think of the powers of Nature and the carelessness of man in sending unseaworthy ships to sea, we cannot help being surprised at the smallness of the number of casualities."

1840.—THE CUNARD LINE.—Mr. Samuel Cunard was one of the first to foresee the great results that might be achieved by the establishment of steamer communication between the United States and England, and as far back as the year 1830, in his quiet home in Nova Scotia, was thinking over the best means of carrying out this project. In 1838, Mr. Cunard went to England, bent upon putting his idea into operation, and, introduced by Sir James Melville, of the India House, he presented himself to Robert Napier, the eminent marine engineer, and the result of their deliberations was that Mr. Cunard gave Mr. Napier an order to build four steamships for the Atlantic service. The four vessels were to be of 900 tons each, and 300 horse-power. Mr. Napier advised the building of larger vessels, and ultimately it was arranged that the four vessels should each be of 1200 tons burden and 440 horse-power.

The project now assumed a proportion beyond the resurces of a private individual, and Messrs. Cunard and Napier, taking counsel together, hit upon the idea of forming a company. Messrs. Burns, of Glasgow, and Messrs. MacIver, of Liverpool, after having run coasting steamers in keen rivalry for several years, in 1830 amalgamated their undertakings, and this firm of Burns & MacIver was at the time that Mr. Cunard came to England one of the most prosperous shipping companies in Great Britain. The proposal to form an Atlantic steamship company was mooted to Messrs. Burns & MacIver by Mr. Napier, and the outcome was the establishment, in 1839, of the "British and North American Royal Mail Steam-Packet Company." This official title being rather lengthy for hurried utterance, a convenient substitute was found in the simple phrase, "*Cunard Line.*" This phrase has now become familiar as a nautical term from Sandy Hook to the Suez Canal, and from Scotland to the West Indies. Samuel Cunard may be justly regarded as the father of the line, and his enterprising partners, the MacIvers and Burnses, have shown themselves to be quite adequate to the grave responsibilities which they then assumed. About this time the government decided, on grounds of public convenience, as well as with the view of promoting the extension of steam navigation, to abandon the curious old brigs which had been used for so many years for the conveyance of the mails across the Atlantic and to substitute steam mail-boats. The Admiralty accordingly advertised for tenders for this service, and the Great Western Steam Shipping Company and the newly-formed company of Messrs. Cunard, Burns & MacIver were the only competitors. The tender of the latter firm was accepted, and a seven years' contract was entered into between the Lords of the Admiralty on the one part, and Samuel Cunard, George Burns, and David MacIver on the other part, for the conveyance of mails fortnightly between Liverpool and Halifax, Boston, and Quebec, in consideration of the annual sum of £60,000. One of the conditions of the bargain was that the ships engaged in this service should be of sufficient strength and capacity to be used as troop-ships in case of necessity. The first four ships built under Mr. Napier's direction for the Cunard Company were the "Britannia," the "Acadia," the "Caledonia," and the "Columbia." The "Unicorn" was dispatched from Liverpool on the 16th of May, 1840, to be placed on the branch route to Newfoundland, and made the passage to Boston in nineteen days.

There was considerable excitement in Boston on the afternoon of Tuesday, June 2, 1840, when it was announced that Mr. Cunard's steamship "Unicorn," Captain Douglas, was entering the harbor. The arrival of the first regular steam-packet from Europe had been looked forward to with interest, as marking a most important epoch in the commercial relations of the New World and the Old. The people, young and old, men, women, and children, assembled as the "Unicorn" approached Long Wharf, and the scene on water and land was inspiring and enthusiastic. Cheers rent the air, handkerchiefs and hats were waved, as the "Unicorn" approached. The United States ship-of-the-line "Columbus," moored in the channel, hoisted the English ensign at the fore, and her band played the national tunes of England and the United States, and the revenue cutter "Hamilton," which made a gallant appearance dressed in flags and bunting, fired a salute. For a short time the "Unicorn" "lay to" off the wharf, and as Captain Sturgis, commanding the "Hamilton," stepped on board and tendered a welcome to Captain Douglas, a round of cheers went up from the crowd. Then the "Unicorn" steamed along the water-front and wharves to the vicinity of the navy-yard, and proceeded to the Cunard wharf at East Boston, which had been recently built, and at that time was considered elegant and spacious in every respect. As she passed the revenue cutter she was again saluted, and returned the salute. Salutes were also fired from the wharf. On two lofty flag-staffs erected on the extremity of the wharf British and American ensigns were hoisted. When moored at the wharf many people hastened on board to exchange congratulations with the captain, officers, and passengers.

The "Unicorn" encountered a good deal of rough weather on her voyage, but proved a good and stanch boat. Her machinery worked well, and the passengers were well pleased with their accommodations. She brought out twenty-seven cabin passengers to Halifax, and twenty-four to Boston, and files of London papers to the 15th of May, of Liverpool papers to the 16th, and of Paris papers to the 13th.

The day following her arrival the Boston newspapers were full of copious extracts from the foreign papers which the "Unicorn" brought, and which were appended to the short notice of the important event. Regret was expressed that the political and commercial intelligence by the arrival was not more important, but the heading, "SIXTEEN DAYS LATER FROM EUROPE!" clearly indicated that one of the most important advantages that was anticipated by the opening of steamship communication between Boston and Liverpool was the quicker exchange of news with the Old World.

The arrival of the "Unicorn" was the talk of the city, and the city felt called upon to take proper recognition of so significant an occurrence, and three days later, on Friday, June 5, the city authorities extended a welcome to Samuel Cunard, Jr., a son of Samuel Cunard, and Captain Douglas, commander of the "Unicorn," at Faneuil Hall. The cradle of liberty was beautifully festooned with the flags of the United States and Great Britain, and was otherwise decorated in a very tasteful manner. The city officials and invited guests marched in procession to the hall from the old City Hall, where a banquet had been prepared for about four hundred and fifty persons. Hon. Jonathan Chapman, the Mayor of Boston, acted as the presiding officer and master of ceremonies. In his address of welcome he enlarged upon the vast importance to Boston of steam navigation with Europe in connection with the western railroad. The sentiment which he offered in conclusion was: " Commercial enterprise—it waked up the dark ages; it launched mankind upon the sea of improvement; it guided the bark and spread the sail until a sail is no longer needed to join the two continents together." Mr. Cunard, Jr., was then called up, and made a pleasant response, and the band played " God Save the Queen." Commander Douglas gave a brief account of the voyage, and said the steamers that were being built for the line were to be much larger, and he had reason to believe that the passage would be made in fifteen days. To a toast in honor of England and America, Hon. Mr. Grattan, her Britannic Majesty's consul, responded, and then, the Mayor calling for volunteer toasts, there followed the most sparkling wit and sentiment. Hon. Robert C. Winthrop, then Speaker of the House, made an eloquent speech, and, referring to the dictum of Dr. Dionysius Lardner, that steam navigation across the ocean was physically impossible, said that, to all appearances, it was quite as improbable as the scientific doctor's late elopement to France with Mrs. Heaviside. The poet Longfellow offered this beautiful sentiment: "Steamships,—the pillar of fire by night and the cloud by day, which guide the wanderer over the sea." The Chevalier de Friederichsthal, attached to the Austrian embassy at Washington, M. Gourand, from Paris, and other distinguished foreigners, John P. Bigelow, John C. Park, Hon. George S. Hillard, Nathaniel Greene, then postmaster of Boston, and others, offered appropriate sentiments, and Governor Everett, who was not present, sent a letter.

The celebration was creditable to the city and the event it commemorated, but nevertheless evoked the criticism of censorious individuals, who evidently did not understand or agree with the old proverb, that the way to a people's heart is through their stomach. In comparison with steamships which now enter Boston and New York, the "Unicorn" was small and insignificant, and yet the arrival of no craft was ever looked forward to with greater anticipation or more genuine pleasure.

With the arrival of the "Unicorn" began the steam traffic between Boston and London and Liverpool, which has since assumed such large proportions. Its coming marked a new era in civilization, and was the harbinger of an immense commercial traffic, and a wonderful rapidity of communication between the New World and the Old. Over forty years have elapsed, and ocean steamers daily arrive, but they excite little interest now.

The "Unicorn" was followed by a coincidence which was entirely unintentional by the departure on the 4th of July from Liverpool of the "Britannia," under command of Lieutenant Woodruff, R.N., for Halifax and Boston, the first regular vessel of the Cunard Line. Liverpool was in a condition of great excitement on the day of the vessel's departure; thousands of people crowded the quays to watch her out, and it was felt that a new era of oceanic intercourse had been begun by this memorable event.

The "Britannia" entered Boston harbor after a run of fourteen days and eight hours. The ship came to her moorings on a Saturday evening, but the inhabitants of Boston thronged the wharves to welcome her, and salvos of artillery were fired in honor of the occasion. Mr. Cunard, Sr., accompanied the vessel, and so great was the enthusiasm created by his enterprise that he received eighteen hundred invitations to dinner within twenty-four hours after his arrival. On the 17th of August the "Acadia" arrived at Boston, after a passage of twelve days and eighteen hours; the shortest passage between the two continents which had been made. Three days later a public banquet was given in honor of the event, at which Hon. Josiah Quincy presided. For seven years these four steamers, re-enforced by two others, carried out the contract with the government. At the end of that time the British government called upon the company to double the number of its sailings, and every new steamer was, in some respects, an improvement upon its predecessors.

Charles Dickens crossed in the "Britannia," and one of the most amusing chapters of his "American Notes" is devoted to the voyage.

Some readers may recall how comically he contrasts his actual experiences with his anticipations of what the ship would be like, his imagination having been fed previous to his going on board by the lithographic pictures of the line,—what "an utterly impracticable, thoroughly hopeless, and profoundly preposterous box" he found his state-room to be; and how he describes the saloon as "a long, narrow apartment, not unlike a gigantic hearse with windows in the sides; having at the upper end a melancholy stone, while on either side, extending down its whole dreary length, was a long, long table, over each of which a rack, fixed to the low roof and stuck full of drinking-glasses and cruet-stands, hinted dismally at rolling seas and heavy weather."

A notable event in the history of the "Britannia," the pioneer ship of the Cunard Line, which became a great favorite in Boston, was the cutting a channel for ten miles in length, in Boston harbor, in 1844, through the ice, in order that she might sail at the appointed time. "Those who remember the month of February, 1844, will recall one of the most astonishingly cold periods of the last fifty years. The first of the month was agreeable enough for winter, but three or four days of intense cold came upon us about the middle of it. Ice rapidly formed in the harbor, and soon the whole distance from the wharves to Fort Warren was frozen over. Men, women, and children enjoyed the novel experience of walking all over the harbor. Skaters went to the outermost edge of the ice. Horses and sleighs entered on the ice-field from South Boston. Booths were established for the supply of creature comforts, bonfires lighted to warm the hands and feet of pedestrians, the earliest ice-craft with extended sail was seen skimming over the smooth surface, and the days and nights in the harbor partook of a carnival. But it was a serious matter to the agent of the Cunard Line, who had the steamer 'Britannia' in port, and she was under contract to carry the mails, and must somehow get out to sea. Bostonians had some interest in the matter, too, for the line had but recently been established, and here was a fulfillment of the prophecy of the jealous New Yorkers, who had said it was an ice-locked harbor in winter. With characteristic energy and public spirit the merchants met at the Exchange one day, as the time for the sailing of the steamer neared, and no south wind had come to loosen the frost's hold on the waters, and resolved upon the undertaking of cutting a channel for the steamer from her dock to the open bay,—a pathway of over ten miles. Mr. John Hill, with some experience in ice-cutting, was selected for the job, but it proved too much for him. At this juncture Mr. Jacob Hittinger, of Gage, Hittinger & Co., large ice-cutters upon Spy Pond, in West Cambridge, contracted with the merchants to liberate the steamer. The task was accomplished, and the 'Britannia,' on her appointed sailing day, moved majestically through the canal, a hundred feet wide, to the open ocean, amid firing of cannon and the cheering of thousands, the multitudes not only lining all the wharves, but flocking upon the solid ice in countless numbers. Probably never again will we witness the spectacle of an ocean steamer moving down the harbor accompanied by thousands of people running or skating by her side. The tug-boats which have come into service by scores have rendered the freezing of the harbor practically impossible, as on the slightest indication of ice they are abroad to break it up. Gage, Hittinger & Co. received ten thousand dollars for this immense job, which actually cost them twenty thousand dollars, but they enjoyed the satisfaction of being recognized as enterprising and successful men in the venture." [1]

The Cunard steamers in the transatlantic trade, 1850, were:

	Tons	H. P.		Tons	H. P.
Caledonia	1250	500	Niagara	1800	700
Hibernia	1400	550	Europa	1800	700
Cambria	1400	550	Asia	2250	800
America	1800	700	Africa	2250	800
Canada	1800	700			

All these were paddle-wheel steamships, and the general length of the six largest was 275 to 300 feet, and beam from 40 to 42 feet. Their cylinders were 90 inches in diameter, and the length of stroke of the piston of the 700 horse-power engines was 8 feet, and of the 800 horse-power engines 9 feet. The diameter of the paddle-wheels was 32 and 36 feet.

In 1852 the Cunard Company established steam communication between Liverpool and the Mediterranean ports. Their steamers have also performed the mail service between Glasgow, Greenock, and Belfast. They have had lines of steamers plying between Liverpool and Glasgow and Glasgow and Londonderry, and they likewise have had steamers carrying the mails between Halifax, Bermuda, and St. Thomas.

Prior to 1852 the fleet of the Cunard Company consisted entirely of paddle-wheel wooden steamships. In that year the "Andes" and "Alps," both iron vessels *with screws*, were added to the long "catalogue of the ships." These were afterwards taken by the British government for transport service in the Crimea, and were followed in 1854 and 1855 by the "Jura" and "Ætna," iron screws, and both for the Atlantic trade. In 1855, with the "Persia," the experiment was tried of building an *iron* paddle steamer.

1855.—On the 3d of March the steamship "Persia," the first *iron* paddle-wheel ship built for the Cunard Company, was launched from the building-yard of Messrs. Robert Napier & Sons, at Govan. She was the largest steamship then afloat in the world, exceeding in length, strength, tonnage, and steam-power the "Great Britain" or the "Himalaya," and by twelve hundred tons the internal capacity of the largest of the Cunard liners of that time. Her chief proportions were as follows:

Length from figure-head to taffrail	390 feet.
Length in the water	360 "
Breadth of the hull	45 "
Breadth all over	71 "
Depth	32 "

[1] *Commonwealth* newspaper.

The lines of beauty had been so well worked out in the "Persia" that her appearance was singularly graceful and light. Yet the mighty fabric, so beautiful as a whole, was made up of innumerable pieces of metal, welded, jointed, and riveted into each other with exceeding deftness. The keel consisted of several bars of iron about thirty-five feet in length, each joined by long scarfs, and as a whole thirteen inches deep by four and a half inches thick. The framing was constructed in a peculiar manner to secure the greatest amount of strength. The iron stern-post was thirteen inches in breadth by five inches in thickness, carrying the rudder, the stack of which was eight inches in diameter. The framing of the ship was very heavy. The space between each frame was only ten inches, and the powerful frames or ribs were themselves ten inches deep, with double angle-irons at the outer and inner edges.

The plates, or outer planking of the ship, were laid alternately, so that one added strength to the other, forming a whole of wonderful compactness and solidity. The keel-plates were eleven-sixteenths of an inch in thickness; at the bottom of the ship the plates were fifteen-sixteenths of an inch in thickness; from that section to the load waterline they were three-fourths of an inch; and above that they were eleven-sixteenths of an inch in thickness. The plates round the gunwales were seven-eighths of an inch in thickness.

She had seven water-tight compartments. The goods were to be stowed in two of the divisions. The goods store-rooms or tanks were placed in the centre line of the ship, with the coal-bunkers on each side of them. The vessel was constructed with a double bottom under the goods-chambers, so that if the outer were beat in, the inner would protect the cargo dry and intact. The chambers were water-tight, and in the event of accident to the hull the tanks would of themselves float the ship.

She was followed in 1862 by the "Scotia," also built of iron, and of still larger dimensions.[1] It soon became apparent that iron was the

---

[1] In the summer of 1879 the "Scotia" was bought by the British Telegraph Construction and Maintenance Company. Her paddles were removed and new engines and twin screws placed in her, and she sailed from the Mersey for Singapore. The "Scotia" was the last and grandest of the paddle-wheel vessels added to the Cunard fleet: a strong ship, of great engine power, and in her day the most magnificent vessel engaged in the transatlantic trade between Liverpool and New York. But times changed with the "Scotia," as they do with all other things mundane. Her engines, though still of unrivaled power, consumed an enormous amount of coal, and coal was not only costly, but its storage filled an undue proportion of the available space. Science had introduced a new order of things in marine engines. The cumbrous paddles were superseded by the more compact screw, and the compound system of engines allowed of an equal power being realized at a far less expenditure of fuel. These improvements decided the fate of the "Scotia." We may well suppose that it was not without a severe qualm that the Cunard Company came to the resolution that their splendid "Scotia," while almost a new ship, must

best material for ocean steamers, and that the screw furnished the best means of propelling them, and in all subsequent additions to the fleet these truths have been recognized and acted upon.

Between 1840 (when the Cunard Company, strictly so-called, came into existence) and 1876 it had built one hundred and twenty-two steamers, and owned in that year a navy of forty-nine vessels,—viz., twenty-four in the Atlantic mail service, twelve in the Mediterranean and Havre line, five plying between Glasgow and Belfast, three between Liverpool and Glasgow, three between Halifax and Bermuda, and two between Glasgow and Derry. The money value of the Atlantic mail boats alone was estimated at between fifteen million and twenty million dollars, and it would not be an exaggeration to state that the value of the entire fleet was double the amount. According to an official statement, made by the company about this time, a Cunard transatlantic steamer had sailed at first once a week, subsequently twice a week, and latterly three times a week from Liverpool, and another from New York or Boston, making over four thousand voyages across the Atlantic, an aggregate distance of over twelve million miles, carrying more than two million passengers without the loss of a life or even of a single letter.

Few people suspect that at least three of the old favorites are still running from New York to Europe; for how could they recognize the "Russia," enlarged to nearly twice her former size in the "Waesland," the "Java," in the "Zealand," or the "Algeria," which disappeared so quietly as hardly to be missed in the "Pennland?"

It was said that the steamship "Russia," the last vessel built by the Cunard Company under a subsidy contract, cost more by £30,000 than she would have cost if built for an independent service.

For ten years in the early history of the Cunard Company each vessel carried a naval officer as a representative of the Admiralty (in those days the mail contracts were made by the Lords of the Admiralty instead of by the postmaster-general, as now), who was clothed with power to act in certain emergencies, and who had control of the royal mails. The company, after a time, paid a round sum to be relieved of the presence of these officials. At a later period, representatives of the post-office were placed on board, who sorted and made up the mails on the voyage.

give way to the new order of things. Screw steamers like the "Russia" and the "Scythia" were doing as good work under more favorable conditions, and the "Scotia" was withdrawn from the service. She was sold, and for a long time lay at Birkenhead, superannuated and almost neglected. And it should be borne in mind by those who criticise the deterioration of our navy that the "Scotia" was built after the commencement of our Civil War as a specimen of the finest steamship afloat, and that three years ago, only seventeen years after her construction, she was sold, having been for some time superannuated.

THE FLEET OF THE CUNARD LINE, 1882.

Name.	Built.	Tonnage. Gross.	Tonnage. Net.	Name.	Built.	Tonnage. Gross.	Tonnage. Net.	Name.	Built.	Tonnage. Gross.	Tonnage. Net.
Aleppo	1865	2050	1398	Malta†	1865	1132	1149	Scythia*	1874	4557	2928
Atlas†	1860	2398	1552	Marathon†	1860	2408	1552	Servia*	1881	8500	6500
Batavia	1870	2553	1627	Morocco	1861	1855	1193	Sidon†	1861	1858	1198
Bothnia*	1870	4586	2928	Olympus	1860	2415	1585	Tarifa†	1865	2058	1399
Catalonia*				Palmyra	1866	2043	1382	Trinidad	1872	1899	1228
Demerara‡	1872	1904	1231	Parthia*	1870	3166	2088	Aurania	bldg		
Gallia*				Samaria†	1870	2605	1694	Cephalonia‡	1882	5600	4350
Kedar‡	1860	1875	1215	Saragossa	1874	2262	1429	Pavonia†	1882		

* Between New York and Liverpool.   † Between Boston and Liverpool.
‡ Mediterranean service.   ₰ Arrived at Boston on first trip, September 4, 1882.

The transatlantic steamers of this line sail every Wednesday and Saturday from New York and from Boston for Liverpool, and as often from Liverpool for each of those ports.

The report of the directors of the lately-formed Cunard Stock Company shows the net profits of the year 1880 amounted to one hundred and ninety-three thousand eight hundred and eleven pounds.

The three steamers recently built are of steel. The "Aurania" is of seven thousand tons, and has engines of eight thousand five hundred horse-power; and the "Pavonia," and her sister ship, the "Cephalonia," are of five thousand six hundred tons. The "Servia," one of the latest additions to the Cunard Line, arrived at New York at 11 A.M., December 8, 1881. She left Queenstown at 10 A.M., November 28, and, taking into consideration the boisterous weather she encountered, the passage was a remarkably quick one. Her purser, Mr. William Field, said that he never experienced such a rough time, though he has held his present position for twenty-five years, having served in every ship on the line, and made over four hundred passages. No damage whatever occurred to the big craft.

The "Servia" brought one hundred and seventy-one cabin passengers and one hundred and fifty-five in the steerage. In point of size the "Servia" is only exceeded by the "Great Eastern," while, as regards engine-power, it is claimed that she surpasses anything afloat.

Mr. John Burns, of the Cunard Company, in a communication to the London *Times* when the "Servia" was on the stocks, said, concerning her,—

"This vessel has been designed, after lengthened consideration, to meet the requirements of our traditional service, and we have adopted in every detail of the ship and engines the most advanced scientific improvements compatible with the safe working of so great a vessel. Among the important matters into which we have crucially inquired has been that of the employment of steel instead of iron, and after a practical and thorough examination into the merits of both materials we have adopted steel for the hull and boilers, but under a provision so stringent that every plate, before acceptance, will undergo a severe and rigid test by a qualified surveyor appointed and stationed at the steel manufactory for that special purpose, and that the manipulation of the steel by the builders shall be subject to an equally careful supervision by qualified engineers of our own appointment. The steel is to be made on the Siemens-Martin process, and all rivets as well as plates throughout the ship are to be of steel."

The substitution of steel for iron has not only improved the steamship, steel being more ductile and stronger than iron, but it has a great advantage economically. The "Servia" weighs six hundred and twenty tons less than she would have done if she had been built equally strong with iron; and of course she has so much greater carrying capacity.

The "Servia's" dimensions are: Length, 533 feet; breadth, 52 feet; depth, 44 feet 9 inches; gross tonnage, 8500 tons. A better idea, perhaps, of the vast size of the vessel may be gathered from the following facts: Her cargo capacity is 6500 tons, with 1800 tons of coal and 1000 tons of water ballast, the vessel having a double bottom, on the longitudinal bracket system. The anchor davits are 8 inches and the chain-cable pipe 22 inches in diameter. The propeller-shaft weighs $26\frac{1}{2}$ tons, and the propeller, boss, and blades are 38 tons in weight. The machinery consists of three cylinder compound surface condensing engines, one cylinder being 72 inches and two 100 inches in diameter, with a stroke of piston of 6 feet 6 inches. It is anticipated that the indicated horse-power will amount to 10,500. There are in all seven boilers, six of which are double- and one single-ended, and all are made of steel, with corrugated furnaces, the total number of furnaces being 39.

Practically, the "Servia" is a five-decker, as she is built with four decks and a promenade. The promenade, which is reserved for the passengers, is very large and spacious. On the fore part of it are the steam steering-gear and house, the captain's room, and flying bridge. On the upper deck forward is the forecastle, with accommodations for the crew, and lavatories and bath-rooms for steerage passengers, while aft are the light-towers for signaling the admiralty lights, with the lookout bridge on the top. Near the midship-house are the captain's and officers' sleeping-cabins. Next to the engine sky-light is the smoking-room, which can be entered from the deck or from the cabins below. It is unusually large for a smoking-room, being 30 feet long by 22 feet wide. Near the after-deck house is the ladies' drawing-room, to which access can be obtained either from the music-room or from the deck. Abaft of this, and in the upper end of the upper deck, is the music-room, which is 50 feet by 22 feet in dimensions, and which is fitted up in a handsome manner, with polished wood panelings. Immediately abaft of the music-room is the grand staircase leading to the main saloon and the cabins below on the main and lower decks. At the foot of the stair leading to the saloon, and also in the cabins, the panelings are of Hungarian ash and maple wood. The saloon is very large, being 74 feet long by 49 feet wide, with sitting accommodation for 350 persons, while the clear height under the beams is 8 feet 6 inches. The sides are all in fancy wood, with beautifully polished inlaid panels. All the upholstery of the saloon is of morocco leather. Right forward of the after-deck are the baths, lavatories, and state-rooms. The total number of state-rooms is 168, and the vessel has accommodation for 450 first-class and 600 steerage passengers, besides a crew of 200 officers and men. For two-thirds of its entire length the lower deck is fitted up with first-class state-rooms. The ship is divided into nine water-tight bulkheads. There are in all twelve boats equipped as life-boats.

The arrangement of the water-tight doors in the engine- and boiler-spaces is admirable, as in case of accident they can be shut from the upper deck in two seconds or so. The keel is built in five layers, having a total thickness of six and three-quarter inches. The upper deck, which is of steel, has a covering of yellow pine; the main deck, which is also of steel, is covered with teak, and the lower deck, again of steel, is shielded with teak above the engine- and boiler-spaces. The deck-houses and deck-fittings, which in unusually heavy weather might otherwise be liable to be carried away, are made of iron and steel, and are riveted to the decks underneath. The "Servia" is built with a double bottom, so that in the event of her running on the rocks and having a hole knocked in her hull, she would still be perfectly safe as long as the inner skin remained intact. She has three masts of the special Cunard rig, and they carry a good spread of canvas to assist in propelling her. She is fitted with steam stearing-gear, steam winches, and a second steering-gear, independent of the steam apparatus. The latest scientific improvements have been adopted in all parts of the vessel; steam is used for warming the cabins and saloons, and every passage has its own seriers of ventilators.

On her trial trip she repeatedly attained a speed of $20\frac{1}{2}$ miles an hour. This is equivalent to about 18 knots. During the trial she carried 2500 tons of dead weight aboard.

In former days it was held that the ratio of indicated horse-power in the engines to the tons burden of the vessel should be as one to four. In the "Great Eastern," with her propeller and paddle-wheels the ratio was as one to fourteen. But in the "Servia" and other new boats the number of indicated horse-power is greater than the number of tons burden. The engines are exceedingly powerful, even when the size of the vessel is considered; and hence the frame-work of the hull has to be made with great rigidity and with the utmost care. The increase in speed attained by these changes can only be demonstrated by experience; but it seems to be the opinion of many nautical men that, with such heavy engines, the jar given to hull will make the "Servia" and vessels of her class less comfortable as passenger crafts than some of the older and smaller transatlantic steamers.

In 1859 in recognition of the great service he had rendered to the United Kingdom, the queen, upon the recommendation of Lord Palmerston, conferred a baronetcy upon Mr. Samuel Cunard. He was succeeded, on his death, both in his business and his title, by his son Edward, who continued his connection with the company up to the time of his decease, in 1869, when the title devolved upon the present baronet, Sir Bache Edward Cunard. Sir Bache, who is a great polo player and intimate of the Prince of Wales, was born in 1851, and has not been connected with the undertaking originated by his distinguished grandfather. The only member of the Cunard family now associated with the Cunard steamship enterprise is Mr. William Cunard, the second son of Sir Samuel, and uncle of the present baronet.

Mr. David MacIver died a few years after the formation of the line. Sir Samuel and his son, Sir Edward, died later. George and James Burns retired from business in favor of two sons of the former, John and James Cleland.

Until the year 1868 the management of the Cunard Company was carried on, as it were, in three divisions. There were the Messrs. MacIver, at Liverpool, the Messrs. Burns, at Glasgow, and the Messrs. Cunard, in America. Together they constituted the Cunard Company, but they conducted the business as three distinct undertakings. In 1863 a fresh deed of partnership was executed, by which Messrs. Cunard, Burns, and MacIver became the sole partners, as well as joint managers. This arrangement continued in force until May, 1878, when the concern was merged into a limited liability company, with a capital of $2,000,000. Of this, $1,200,000 was taken by Messrs. Cunard, Burns, and MacIver as part payment for the property and business which they transferred to the new company. No shares were offered to the public. By a rule of the London Stock Exchange, however, two-thirds of the capital of any undertaking quoted in their official list must be allotted to the public. To meet this requirement, Messrs. Cunard, Burns, and MacIver consented to relinquish £533,340 of their capital for the benefit of the public. This was done in March, 1880, and the demand for shares thrown open was enormously in excess of what was available.

Mr. William Cunard, one of the managing directors of the company in 1881, is the second son of Sir Samuel, who founded the company, and was created a baronet by the queen for his enterprise in transatlantic steam navigation. For many years the Cunard Company received a subsidy of £176,340 per annum under its mail contracts, but for some years past the only compensation the line has received for carrying the mails has been one-third of the actual postage paid. The

HISTORY OF STEAM NAVIGATION.   321

steamships of the company are, however, as formerly, inspected on the day before sailing from England by officers of the Board of Trade. When first established they carried an officer of the Royal Navy as mail agent; but that practice has been discontinued.

It is remarkable to note the extraordinary progress achieved since the "Britannia" made her first voyage in 1840. Measuring 1139 tons, she had capacity for but 225 tons of cargo, whereas the "Bothnia," of 4335 tons, built in 1874, takes 3000 tons of cargo, or nearly fourteen times as much, though only four times larger. The "Britannia" carried ninety passengers, whereas the "Bothnia" can carry three hundred and forty-nine, or close upon four times as many. The former steamed eight and a half knots, the latter steams thirteen knots an hour, or more than half as quick again, with less than half the coal per indicated horse-power per hour, and at about the same quantity of fuel for the actual number of miles run. The "Persia," the finest vessel afloat in her day, took six tons of coal to carry a ton of freight across the Atlantic. The "Arizona," double the size of the "Persia," takes only a fifth of a ton.

The "Cephalonia" was launched in the Mersey May, 1882, and is the largest steamer ever built on that river. Her dimensions are as follows: Length on upper deck, 440 feet; length between perpendiculars, 430 feet; beam, 46 feet; depth in hold, 34 feet 6 inches; tonnage, B. M., 4350 tons; gross register, about 5600 tons. The "Cephalonia" is constructed of iron, and is fitted to carry upward of one hundred first-class passengers, and one thousand, five hundred steerage. She has four decks, three of which are of iron, covered with wood-planking. Her rig is that of a barque. The masts are of steel,.the fore and main being in one piece up to the top-mast head, and mizzen in one piece its whole length. The engines are two thousand five hundred horse-power, and have two cylinders, the high pressure one being fifty-two inches diameter, and the low pressure ninety-three inches diameter, with a stroke piston of five feet six inches. The propeller is four-flanged, and of the best steel. The boilers are six in number. The appliances for discharging cargo include five very powerful steam winches. The capstans and the steering apparatus are also worked by steam.

The "Cephalonia" has several unique features, distinguishing her from other large ocean steamers. One is that of Sir George Thompson's sounding machinery, by which soundings can be made to a depth of sixty fathoms while the vessel is going at the rate of fifteen miles an hour. She has also appliances for steering, both by steam and by hand, there being two for the former and three for the latter. She carries six officers, eight engineers, and two electricians. The "Cephalonia" excels in the completeness of the electric light system, which, in some respects, is in advance of anything yet used on the Atlantic.

There are three hundred and forty of the Swan incandescent lamps on board, ready for use in the day as well as night. They are so contrived that the light falls within the chimney of a regular oil-lamp, which can be used in case of accident to the former. A pair of powerful engines and one of Dr. Siemens's electric machines are steadily employed under the management of an electrician for the production of the light.

She left Liverpool on her first trip August 24, 1882, at 3 P.M., and arrived at Boston, September 4, bringing 141 cabin and 406 steerage passengers. No fair wind was had during the whole trip, and in consequence the "Cephalonia" was not able to utilize her square sails, but with the exception of one or two stoppages to attend to the requirements of the machinery, no delay was encountered. The speed attained during the trip was fourteen knots.

The new Cunard steamship "Pavonia," Captain McKay, arrived at Boston, October 30, 1882, from Liverpool. The "Pavonia" is a sister ship to the "Cephalonia." Her length is 430 feet, breadth 46 feet, and depth 47 feet. There are accommodations for over 200 cabin and 1000 steerage passengers. The saloon extends across the vessel, and the smoking-room is situated on the promenade deck. The ladies' cabin, which is a marvel of beauty, is situated on the main deck. The vessel has eleven water-tight compartments, with three solid iron decks. A special feature in the construction of this steamer is the strength and number of her transverse water-tight bulkheads, the eleven compartments being divided into smaller ones. Besides the steam stearing-gear, which is located aft, but is worked from the bridge, there is a powerful screw-gear and an arrangement for working the vessel with ropes in the event of any accident. The forecastle, which is 92 feet long, contains storage-room for the passengers and accommodation for the seamen. Back of the forecastle, in the after deck, there is a pleasant promenade to the turtle back, the deck being clear on both sides. The first-class state-rooms are on the main deck, and their average size is about 11 x 6 feet. Each state-room is provided with an electric light which can be regulated by the occupant. The engines are of the two-cylinder, inverted, vertical type, being 53 and 92 inches in diameter, and having 5 feet 6 inches stroke. The "Pavonia" was built by Messrs. J. & G. Thomson, of Glasgow, and is intended to go at the rate of fourteen knots per hour at sea.

The "Gallia's" model received a first-prize gold medal at the Paris Exhibition. She was barque-rigged, and built after the general design of the "Scythia" and "Bothnia," but she is longer and wider than either. Her length is 450 feet over all, her molded width 44 feet, and her depth of hold 36 feet, with a measurement capacity of 4809 tons. Her machinery includes the latest improvements. She has three compound direct-acting cylinder engines, two of them being 84 inches in diameter, and the third 61 inches; the piston-stroke being 60 inches,

HISTORY OF STEAM NAVIGATION. 323

affording a nominal force of 700 horse-power, which, however, can be increased, should necessity demand, to over 3000 horse-power. She has state-room accommodations for 480 first-class passengers, and has equally large accommodation for steerage passengers. The cabin fittings and arrangements, and the state-rooms, are unusually fine. The principal dining-saloon is on the spar deck, and is lighted by a series of top and side lights. It is floored with oak parquetry of Belgian manufacture, and the walls are inlaid with Japenese paneling upon a ground of red jasper, with gold tracery. There are sideboards and mirrors, a piano, and a large library. The second dining-saloon (on the main deck) is furnished with taste, and both have revolving sofa chairs at the tables. On the upper deck there is a " Ladies' boudoir," and a " Ladies' cabin" on the spar deck, the latter being paneled with Brazilian onyx, and richly upholstered in blue. A commodious and beautifully fitted smoking-room for gentlemen is on the main deck. The state-rooms and berths are large, well ventilated, and fitted with many improvements, including stationary wash-basins and steam-heaters of a new pattern. They all communicate by means of pneumatic bells in the steward's department. The vessel carries a crew of one hundred and thirty men.

With a history extending over forty busy years, with a fleet that has comprised from the beginning one hundred and twenty-six large steamers, with a constant floating population of many thousands to protect, and with all the dangers of wind and wave to battle against, it might naturally be supposed that the Cunard Company would have a long list of disastrous accidents, shipwrecks, and losses to recount; but it is the boast of the proprietors of the Cunard Line that from 1840 down to the present time not one of their passengers has lost his life by accident in any of the thousands of voyages that have been made across the Atlantic in their ships, and the few accidents which have happened to the machinery or otherwise have only resulted in temporary delays, without endangering the safety of the passengers. Many things have combined to secure to the Cunard ships this astonishing immunity from disaster. In the first place, the company have always insisted on having their vessels built of the best possible materials; they have enjoined the most thorough workmanship; they have kept their vessels under such careful supervision as to insure the discovery of the slightest defect in strength or seaworthiness, and they have never allowed a steamer to start on a voyage unless they have been satisfied of its being complete, perfect, and efficient. In the next place, they have chalked out separate routes for outward bound and homeward bound steamers, somewhat apart from the direct course; and although by adopting this plan they may have lengthened their voyages by a few hours, this has been more than atoned for by the increased sense of security which has been induced. The care and skill exercised by the navigation of the Cunard Line of steamers have been amply rewarded by the prosperity and success which have attended them.

From the year 1840 down to the present time (November, 1882) the company have built 126 steamers, and their entire fleet now comprises 31 steamships, having an aggregate tonnage of 87,604 tons and 55,445 effective horse-power. The company employ, one way and another, from 10,000 to 12,000 men. Upward of 1500 are constantly engaged in the work of loading and unloading, and nearly that number in fitting and repairing vessels. They have always from 7000 to 8000 sailors employed, and these men may be regarded as among the finest men to be found in the whole merchant service.

1840.—THE PENINSULAR AND ORIENTAL STEAM NAVIGATION COMPANY.—The career of this company, the first to undertake to convey the mails overland to the East, is interesting. During the earlier part of its career, by agreeing to carry the Peninsular mails for a sum considerably less than the Admiralty packets, with a speed and regularity hitherto unknown, it conferred an undoubted boon upon the public.

In 1815 Mr. Brodie McGhee Wilcox, a young man without influence and but limited pecuniary means, commenced business in London as a ship broker and commission merchant. He soon after engaged a youth from the Orkney Islands, Arthur Anderson, as his clerk, who became his partner in 1825, under the title of Wilcox & Anderson. In 1834 the Dublin and London Steam-Packet Company chartered the steamer "Royal Tar" to Dom Pedro through the agency of the firm. Soon afterwards the Spanish minister in London induced Messrs. Bourne, of Dublin, to put on a line of steamers between London and the Peninsula, for which Wilcox & Anderson were appointed agents. A small company was formed to carry out this undertaking. Previously to September, 1837, the Peninsular mails were conveyed by sailing-packets, which left Falmouth, England, for Lisbon every week, "wind and weather permitting." The Peninsular Company of Steam-Packets, some little time established, on the 29th of August, 1837, contracted to convey the Peninsular mails for £29,600 per annum, subsequently reduced to £20,500 per annum. This service may be considered the nucleus of the great company which now conveys the mails to all parts of the Eastern world. The "Iberia," the first steamer dispatched with the Peninsular mails, sailed in September, 1837.

The mails were conveyed to and from India up to September, 1840, by steamers plying monthly between Bombay and Suez, and thence by British government steamers from Alexandria to Gibraltar, where they received the mails brought out by the Peninsular Company from England. In 1839 the British government entered into a convention with the French government for sending letters to and from

India through France by way of Marseilles. The irregularities that ensued caused the British government to apply to the managers of the Peninsular Company to run a line of superior steamers direct from England to Alexandria, and *vice versa*, touching only at Gibraltar and Malta. The vessels approved by the Admiralty were the "Oriental," of 1600 tons and 450 horse-power, and the "Great Liverpool," of 1540 tons and 464 horse-power, which was originally intended for the transatlantic service. These were now dispatched with the mails from England to Alexandria, Egypt, thus combining the two mail services and constituting the Peninsular and *Oriental* Steam Navigation Company. In 1842 the East India Company contracted with the Peninsular Company to establish a line of steamers between Calcutta and Suez, and September 24, 1842, its new ship, "Hindostan," of 1800 tons and 520 horse-power, was sent from Southampton to open a line between Calcutta, Madras, Ceylon, and Suez. The government went into another contract with the company for a monthly service from Ceylon to Penang, Singapore, and Hong-Kong, and in 1854 the company undertook another line between Bombay and Suez. They next extended a line between India and the Australian colonies. All these lines were heavily subsidized. The urgent requirements of government for conveying troops to the Black Sea and the Baltic on the outbreak of the Crimean war obliged the company, towards the close of 1854, to discontinue the line to Australia and to reduce the Bombay and China service from a fortnightly to a monthly line. During the Crimean war this company had eleven of their steamers, measuring 18,000 tons, in the transport service, which conveyed during the continuance of hostilities 1800 officers, 60,000 men, and 15,000 horses. The "Himalaya," the largest vessel of the line at this time, was 340 feet in length, 44½ feet width of beam, and her engines were 2050 indicated horse-power. She was 3540 tons, old measurement, and cost £132,000 when complete for sea.

Thus, step by step, the company advanced, until we learn from its annual report ending September 30, 1874, its paid-up capital at that time amounted to £2,700,000 and £800,000 debenture stock, and that it was the intention during the year to increase it up to £4,300,000, of which £600,000 would remain unpaid. Of this capital, £3,757,000 consisted of stock in ships; £221,000 of freehold and leasehold property and docks and premises in England, Calcutta, Bombay, Singapore, Hong-Kong, and other stations; and £413,000 in coal and naval victualing stores. Its fleet at the same time consisted of 50 sea-going steamers, measuring 122,000 tons, and of 22,000 horse-power,—thirty-four being employed in the Mediterranean, Adriatic, India, and China services; four in the Australian service between Ceylon, Melbourne, and Sydney; five in the China and Japan local services; two used as cargo vessels; five undergoing repairs and in reserve. The company also possessed twelve steam-tugs and three cargo- and coal-hulks, and gave permanent employment to 12,600 persons, exclusive of coal laborers and coolies on shore; about 90,000 tons of coal were usually kept constantly in stock at its coaling-stations. This was a navy which many governments might be proud to own.

The iron screw steamship "Khedive," of this line, built in 1873, is of the following dimensions: Length, 380 feet; breadth, 42 feet; depth, 36 feet. Her builders' measurement is 3329 tons; her gross register, 3742 tons; and her net register, 2092 tons. She is fitted to accommodate with the space and style now required for Eastern travel 164 first-class and 53 second-class passengers. She has store-rooms to hold 380 tons; rooms for mails and baggage to contain 142 tons; bunkers to hold 846 tons of coal; and holds which can receive 2003 tons of cargo, of 50 feet to the ton. The contract price for the ship fitted complete for sea was £110,000. Her engines are compound, vertical, direct-acting, of 600 nominal horse-power, with 4 feet 6 inches length of stroke. The diameter of her cylinders, 69 and 96 inches respectively; and of her four-bladed screw, 17 feet 6 inches; its pitch being 22 feet 6 inches and 24 feet. She has 4 boilers and 16 furnaces. The five-bar surface is 320 square feet, and the heating and condensing surface 11,720 and 6059 square feet respectively. The loaded pressure is 55 pounds on her boilers.

We have nothing in ancient times to compare with this model modern steamship, with her long, low hull, unless it be the rowing-galley, and to propel a vessel of the size and weight of the "Khedive" at the rate of four miles an hour through the smoothest water would require at least two thousand rowers, while the average speed of the "Khedive" on a voyage from Alexandria to Southampton, a distance of 2982 miles, was ten knots, and on the return voyage eleven knots or nautical miles per hour.

A new contract has been made with the Peninsular and Oriental Steam Navigation Company for the conveyance of the mails to India and China, for a period of eight years from the 1st of February, 1880, at the reduced subsidy of £370,000, being £60,000 per annum less than the sum paid under the then expiring contract. This payment may be further reduced at the option of the post-office authorities by £10,000 per annum, in consideration of the penalties not being made absolute. In this case, also, simultaneously with a reduction of cost, an increase of speed has been secured. The company is liable to a penalty of £100 for every twelve hours in excess of the contract time between Brindisi and Bombay on its outward voyages, and of £200 for every twelve hours in such excess on its homeward voyages.

In the service to and from the Cape of Good Hope, the two contracting companies, when their voyages go beyond three days in excess of the time allowed by their contracts (heavy penalties being incurred for one or more of these three days), are liable to a penalty of £6 5s. an hour for each complete hour in addition consumed on the voyage out or home.

1840.—THE PACIFIC STEAM NAVIGATION COMPANY.—The Pacific Steam Navigation Company sends out its ships from London eastward to Melbourne, westward to Valparaiso, and does a large coasting business on the west coast of South America. Its ships run to Australia under the name of the Orient Line, and are splendid specimens of steamers. To this line belong the "Orient," 5386 tons, and the lately-finished steamer "Austral,"[1] whose tonnage is 5588 tons gross. The Orient steamers go to Australia both *via* the Cape of Good Hope and *via* the canal.

The first steamer on the Pacific coast was a small craft named the "Telica," commanded and owned by a Spaniard named Mitrovitch, but his career, as well as that of his vessel, was a short and melancholy one. In a fit of despair at his want of success he fired his pistol into a barrel of gunpowder, blowing up his vessel in the harbor of Guayaquil, and destroying himself and all on board except one man. This lamentable occurrence retarded the introduction of steam on the Pacific coast. But Mr. William Wheelwright, a native of Newburyport, Massachusetts, then United States consul at Guayaquil, saw the great advantages of steam communication along the coast and between the several South American republics, and spent six of the best years of his life in arranging for such communication. Failing to obtain the needed aid and encouragement for his plans in the United States, he proceeded to England, and on the 17th of February, 1840, just about the time that transatlantic steam navigation was an assured success, he obtained, "under letters patent," a charter for the establishment of the Pacific Steam Navigation Company, with a small subsidy for the conveyance of the British mails.

The capital of the company was at first limited to two hundred and fifty thousand pounds, in five thousand shares of fifty pounds each. The whole capital was subscribed for, but only an amount was called up sufficient at the time to enable the directors to provide two boats,— the "Chili" and "Peru,"—which were dispatched to commence operations towards the close of 1840. These vessels were wooden paddle-wheel steamers, sister ships of about seven hundred tons gross register, though with a capacity of not half that tonnage, with engines of about one hundred and fifty horse-power, their extreme length being one

[1] A telegram from Sydney states that the belief which was first entertained that the foundering of the Orient steamer "Austral," November, 1882, entailed no loss of life proves to have been mistaken. The purser and four of the crew were drowned. Further telegrams received at Lloyd's state that the "Austral," while coaling, keeled over and sank at her moorings. She had 1500 tons of coal on board and a cargo of only 200 tons of iron.—*The Penny Illustrated Paper*, November 18, 1882.

hundred and ninety-eight feet and extreme breadth fifty feet.[1] They were at that time considered fine vessels, and on their arrival at Valparaiso they were received with great rejoicings and with salvos of artillery, everybody wishing to visit them, "the President of the Republic, accompanied by his ministers, being among the first to welcome the steamships to the shores of the Pacific."

The company in its early days had many difficulties to overcome, the scarcity of fuel being one of the greatest, and during the first five years sustained a loss of no less than seventy-two thousand pounds upon a paid-up capital of ninety-four thousand pounds. In face of this heavy loss the share-holders resolved to persevere, and in December, 1847, the directors were enabled to give to the share-holders for the first time a dividend, though only two and one-half per cent., on their paid-up capital.

In 1850 four new steamers, viz., the "Lima," "Santiago," "Quito," and "Bogota," of one thousand tons and two hundred horse-power each, in pursuance with a contract with the Admiralty, and costing one hundred and forty thousand pounds, were added to the line, to be employed in a bimonthly service between Valparaiso and Panama.

From 1860 the trade of the Pacific rapidly developed. Steam here, as elsewhere, opened up new and hitherto unthought-of branches of commerce, and from that date the progress of the company has been of unexampled success.

In 1865 the chartered powers of the company were extended to the establishment of lines "between the west coast of South America and the river Plata, including the Falkland Islands and such other ports or places in North and South America and other foreign ports as the said company shall deem expedient."

The directors by degrees applied the compound engine after 1856 to all their steamships, and it is worthy of record that they were not only among the first, if not the first, to adopt the compound engine for ocean-going steamers, but were almost singular in this respect for upward of fourteen years.

During these years the profits of the undertaking had been steadily increasing, and at a special meeting of the share-holders, held December, 1867, it was determined to add to the operations of the company a monthly line from Liverpool to the west coast of South America *via* the Straits of Magellan.

This entirely new and important though hazardous branch of the service necessitated an increase of the capital of the company to two million pounds. In furtherance of their views the "Pacific," of two thousand tons register and four hundred and fifty horse-power, was

---

[1] Lindsay's "Merchant Shipping," vol. iv., has an illustration of the pioneer steamer "Peru."

sent from Valparaiso in May, 1868, as the pioneer of the new mail line.

The project was successful, and in 1869 the profits of the four new steamers, which had made nine voyages from Liverpool to Valparaiso, were so satisfactory that in 1870 it was determined to extend the voyage from Valparaiso to Callao. Seventeen voyages made in the course of that year with still greater success induced the directors to recommend that the departures thenceforward should be three a month; and in December, 1871, the capital was authorized to be increased to three million pounds, so that the company might be enabled to dispatch every week one of their steamers on this distant voyage.

In July, 1872, the capital was increased to four million pounds.

In 1877, when in command of the United States squadron in the South Pacific, I wrote a letter to the Navy Department, in which I gave the following information in regard to the then condition of this line:

"I forward herewith an advertisement exhibiting the names and tonnage of the *forty-eight* vessels[1] which now compose the steam fleet of the English 'Pacific Steam Navigation Company' on this coast. A few of these vessels have paddle-wheels, but nearly all are iron screw-steamers of power, speed, and good model. Relieved of their light passenger decks and armed, they would in the event of war prove an efficient and formidable auxiliary to the British naval force in these seas as cruisers and 'commerce destroyers.' The schedule and average speed of the coasting steamers of this company, ten knots, is considered their *economical* rate of steaming.

"The *eighteen* steamers of the 'Straits' Line are barque-rigged, have an average tonnage greater than the five 'first-rates' of our navy, are superior to them in speed, are capable of being as heavily armed. In addition to a profitable freight, they carry coal for *forty* days, steaming at the rate of eleven knots per hour under all conditions of wind and weather, the latter a good desideratum for a country like the United States, having no colonies, and its ships dependent upon home ports for a supply of coal, which are now classed as 'contraband of war.'

"The following memorandum of the performance of the 'Aconcagua,' one of the steamships of the Straits Line, I took from her abstract log by permission of her commander:

"'The Pacific Steam Navigation Company's steamship "Aconcagua," 4106 tons, left Liverpool June 13, 1877, at 8 P.M., and arrived at Callao, Peru, August 9, 1877, at 7 A.M., stopping in the voyage at Pauillac, Lisbon, St. Vincent, Rio Janeiro, Montevideo, Sandy Point, Valparaiso, Arica, and Mollendo, the time occupied on the voyage being 56 days, 5 hours, 50 minutes; the actual *steaming* time, 40 days,

---

[1] Mr. Lindsay, in his "Merchant Shipping," says the company owned in 1876 four steamships, aggregating 119,870 tons and 20,895 horse-power.

11 hours, 35 minutes. The distance run was 11,033 nautical miles. Coal consumed, 1900 tons. She also expended 656 gallons of oil, 132 pounds of tallow, and 74 pounds of waste. She received on board at Liverpool 1746 tons of coal, and at St. Vincent, 760 tons.'

"The following was her expenditure of coal between the several ports stopped at:

	Tons.		Tons.
Liverpool to Pauillac	189	Sandy Point to Valparaiso	295
Pauillac to Lisbon	148	Valparaiso to Arica	147
Lisbon to St. Vincent	256	Arica to Mollendo	22
St. Vincent to Rio Janeiro	461	Mollendo to Callao	66
Rio Janeiro to Montevideo	155		
Montevideo to Sandy Point	211	Total	1900

"The average of her voyage,—speed, 11.36 knots; revolutions, 50.75 per minute; pressure, 63; coal, 46.91 tons per day. The least average speed made in any twenty-four hours during the voyage was 9.6 knots.

"On her previous voyage the 'Aconcagua' touched at one less port, ran 11,003 nautical miles, and consumed 1776 tons of coal. The 'Aconcagua' has but one smoke-stack, others of the line have two. The Straits steamers have steam-cutters, and all the ships of the company are furnished with steam-capstans."

Two of the ships of this company, viz., the "Iberia" and "Liguria," built in 1873, are each 4671 tons gross register, with a capacity of 4000 tons of cargo, space for 916 tons of coal additional, and accommodation for 800 third-class passengers. On their trial trips these steamers attained a speed of 15 knots per hour. Their length is 425 feet between perpendiculars, and 449 feet over all. Their breadth is 44½ feet; depth of hold, 35¼ feet. The engines, which are compound, have each three cylinders, one of 4 feet 8 inches diameter, and two of 6 feet 6 inches diameter, with 5 feet length of stroke.

When we consider that the tonnage of the navy of the United States in 1881, distributed in 22 sailing-vessels, 83 screw-steamers, 26 iron-clads, and 7 side-wheel steamers, in all 138 vessels of every class and type, amounts to only 143,338, tons, it may be profitable to compare it with the 120,000 tons of this private company, invested in steam-vessels combining the latest improvements in machinery for economy and speed.

The services of the steamers of this company on the west coast of South America have of late been subjected to the depressing influences of the war between Chili and Peru, but the steam trade of the Pacific has steadily and marvelously increased since first opened out by the energy of our countryman, Wheelwright. The people of Chili, sensible of their indebtedness, have erected a bronze statue to his honor in one of the principal plazas of Valparaiso.

The commanders, officers, and engineers of this company are all

Britons. The company owns an island in the Bay of Panama, where they have a *gridiron* for hauling up their vessels for cleaning or repair. They have also erected shops at Callao, Peru, fitted with the requisite apparatus, implements, and tools, and maintain there a staff of well-trained workmen. Connected with the establishments at Callao, Panama, and Valparaiso, the company contributes liberally to the support of schools, and for the maintenance of clergymen of the Established Church; and it is also interested in the iron floating-docks at Valparaiso and Callao.

The splendid, we may say, stupendous results of this company are the outgrowth of the project of William Wheelwright, a native of Newburyport, Mass., who, after presenting his plans to the capitalists of New York, and their being rejected by them, presented them in Liverpool, where they met with better success. Thus through the far-seeing of our English brethren the sceptre of the commerce of the Pacific has passed into their hands, and it will require on our part, notwithstanding the predilection our South American cousins have for us, a long pull, a strong pull, and a pull all together before we can regain it or any portion of it.

The "Austral," built on the Clyde by Elder & Co., is 474 feet long over all, has a breadth of beam of 48 feet 3 inches, and her molded depth is 37 feet. Her displacement on the load-line is about 9500 tons. She is ten feet longer, two feet broader, and two inches deeper than the "Orient," but as her lines are finer, her tonnage will not much exceed that of the "Orient." She is built throughout of mild steel, and has 3 steel decks. Between the inner skin and the double bottom she is divided into 19 water-tight compartments. The hull proper is divided by 13 water-tight bulkheads, 10 of which are carried up to the main deck. Above the main deck the ship is divided into 7 fire-proof compartments, and there are ample arrangements for flooding any of the compartments or for extracting water from them, the pumps having a capacity for throwing 2928 tons of water per hour. She has four masts, two of which are square rigged. The cabins are all placed within the area of the ship, with a gangway four feet wide, running along the vessel *outside* the state-rooms and at frequent intervals across the ship. This permits each state-room to have *windows* instead of air-ports, and the air-port in the side of the ship may be kept open even in rough weather without any fear of the water entering the cabin. This arrangement of the cabins and state-rooms coincides exactly with one proposed by R. B. Forbes, Esq., of Boston, in a pamphlet published by him in 1866. It seems an arrangement that must be universally adopted, as it not only allows the passenger to obtain an abundant supply of fresh air, but prevents his inhaling the foul air which comes up from the hold through the skin of the ship into his state-room when the state-room is built against the sides.

The "Austral" belongs to what is known as the Orient Line of this company, and, as well as the "Orient," is specially designed for the importation of frozen meats from Australia. She is fitted with refrigerating machinery of the capacity of about seven hundred tons, the largest refrigerator room fitted on any ship. At the trials at sea of the machinery it produced a continuous stream of cold, dry air for the meat-chamber, the temperature of the air flowing from the machine being 85° Fahrenheit below zero, and the large chamber kept steadily at zero, or 32° below the freezing point. As the weight of an Australian sheep is about eighty pounds, this enormous freezing machine will keep *twenty thousand sheep* frozen in a perfectly fresh state for any length of time necessary before shipment. The public rooms, engine-room, pantries, and passageways are lighted by the electric light fitted up by Messrs. Siemens with nine arc lamps and one hundred and seventy Swan lamps.

1841.—THE ROYAL WEST INDIA MAIL STEAM-PACKET COMPANY.—Soon after the Atlantic Ocean began to be regularly navigated by steam-vessels, the importance of a rapid and more frequent means of intercommunication with the West Indies led to the formation of this company, which contracted with the Board of Admiralty in March, 1841, for the conveyance of the mails between England, the West Indies, and the Gulf of Mexico. It commenced operations on a much more comprehensive and grander scale than either the Cunard Company or Peninsular and Oriental. Fourteen large steamships were at once ordered to be built for the service; they were to be of such strength as would enable them to carry guns of the largest calibre then in use on board Her Majesty's war-steamers, with engines of not less than four hundred cohesive horse-power. The contract required one of these vessels to be ready to take the mails on board twice in each calendar month, and to proceed *via* Corunna and Madeira to the island of Barbadoes, and after staying not more than six hours, thence *via* St. Vincent to the island of Grenada, where the stoppage was limited to twelve hours; thence in succession to Santa Cruz and St. Thomas, Tricola Mole, in Hayti, Santiago de Cuba, and Port Royal, in Jamaica. After a stay of not exceeding twenty-four hours at Port Royal, the steamer was to proceed to Savana la Mar, and thence to Havana; returning, she was to call at Savana la Mar, Port Royal, Santiago de Cuba, Tricola Mole, and Samana, in Hayti, delivering mails at each place, "care being taken that the said steam-vessel shall always arrive at Samana aforesaid (after performing the said voyage from Barbadoes under ordinary circumstances of wind and weather) on the twenty-second day after the arrival from England of the mails at Barbadoes;" and after delivering and receiving the mails at Samana, "the steam-vessel shall make the best of her way back from Samana to such port in the British Channel as the said Commissioners of the Admiralty shall from time to time direct.". In consideration of this service the company was to receive at the rate of two hundred and forty thousand pounds per annum in quarterly payments. Notwithstanding this large subsidy, the close of the first year's operations showed a loss of seventy-nine thousand seven hundred and ninety pounds, sixteen shillings, eight pence to the company.

By the original arrangements the annual mileage traversed would have been six hundred and eighty-four thousand eight hundred and sixteen miles. Government, however, in answer to the company's appeal, reduced the distance to be performed to three hundred and ninety-two thousand nine hundred and seventy-six miles, without reducing the subsidy. Though these liberal concessions had been made, they were more than counterbalanced by the loss of two valuable ships during the second year. Yet the trade increased so rapidly as to leave in 1848 a surplus of receipts over expenditures of ninety-four thousand two hundred and ten pounds, and in 1844 of one hundred and forty-seven thousand seven hundred and forty-nine pounds. From this time the prospects of the company have steadily improved. In 1850 the mail contract was renewed for ten years from 1st January, 1852, the annual subsidy being increased to two hundred and seventy thousand pounds, the company agreeing to a monthly service to Brazil, and an increase of the mileage to five hundred and forty-seven thousand two hundred and ninety-six miles. The company was also required to increase the speed of the West Indian line from eight knots to ten knots per hour, and to add to their fleet five new steamers of two thousand two hundred and fifty tons and eight hundred horse-power each. In 1864 a third contract was entered into whereby the annual subsidy was reduced to one hundred and seventy-two thousand nine hundred and fourteen pounds, and the speed increased to ten and a half knots per hour in the West India transatlantic service. In 1866 it was agreed each alternate fortnightly packet should proceed from St. Thomas direct to Colon (Aspinwall), instead of first touching at Jamaica, thus shortening the route between England and Panama.

In 1874 the annual subsidy for the conveyance of the West India mails was reduced to eighty-four thousand seven hundred and fifty pounds, not much more than one-third of what the company originally received.

In 1875 a contract was entered into with Her Majesty's government to carry on the Brazilian and River Plata mail service for a payment according to the weight of letters, etc., conveyed.

The early ships of this line were the finest class of paddle-wheel steamers built of wood then afloat, or that had been sent to sea either for naval or mercantile purposes. Thus, the "Forth," one of the original fleet, was somewhere about nineteen hundred tons gross or builder's measurement, eleven hundred and forty-seven tons register, and four hundred and fifty nominal horse-power. She was built at Leith in 1841. As government reserved the right of purchasing any of these ships at valuation, she was, like the others, constructed in accordance with a specification from the Admiralty, under the survey and immediate control of officers appointed for the purpose. Ill luck, however, attended the early days of the company, for though the course of the vessels was a comparatively safe one, they lost six of their ships in the first eight years. The "Isis" sunk off Bermuda, October 8, 1842, having previously struck on a reef. The "Galway" was lost April 15, 1843, twenty miles west of Corunna, when her captain, surgeon, various passengers, and a portion of her crew, consisting in all of sixty persons, perished. The "Medina" was wrecked on a coral reef near Turk's Island, May 12, 1844. The "Tweed," of 1800 tons and 450 horse-power, was lost February 12, 1847, on the Alicranes, a reef off the coast of Yucatan, by which accident seventy-two of the one hundred and fifty-one persons which composed her crew and passengers were drowned. February 1, 1849, the "Forth" was lost on the same rocks which had caused the destruction of the "Tweed," while the following year the "Actæon" was wrecked while rounding the point near Carthagena. Some of these disasters no doubt arose from the intricate character of the navigation among the West India Islands, and others, as it was alleged, "by those sudden changes of weather—hurricanes, squalls, 'northers,' etc.—with which the West India Islands, Spanish Main, and Gulf of Mexico are so frequently visited." But as the company has met with much fewer disasters of late years, incompetency probably had something to do with these almost periodical losses. In November, 1852, the "Demerara," which had been launched the preceding September from the banks of the Severn, was stranded across the river, and so injured that she had to be broken up, and her engines utilized on the "Atrato," an iron paddle-wheel steamer. The "Demerara" was, at the time of her launch,[1] the largest steamship save

[1] The launch of the "Demerara" took place at Bristol. The morning being a fine one, large numbers of persons assembled to witness the floating out; and the vessels in the floating harbor were dressed gayly. Owing, however, to delays, and the water having fallen some eighteen inches or two feet, the spectators were doomed to disappointment, as she could not be got out until the evening's tide, when she floated gracefully upon the water, having been christened by the wife of Lieutenant Hast, R.N., Commodore of the West India Squadron, and future commander of the "Demerara." With the exception of the "Great Britain," the "Demerara" was the largest steamship afloat. Her length of keel was 276 feet; length between the perpendiculars, 282 feet; length over all, 816 feet; or 6 feet shorter than the "Great Britain." Her breadth of beam was 41 feet, and the extreme width, from the outside of the paddle-boxes, 75½ feet; depth to the main-deck, 26 feet 8 inches; depth of spar-deck, 7 feet. Tonnage—by old measurement, 2318 tons; by new measurement, upward of 3000 tons. She was built of sound British oak, teak, and pine, was diagonally trussed with iron, had copper fastenings throughout to the 21 feet mark, and iron fastenings above that. She was propelled by two engines made by Messrs. Caird & Co., of Greenock, which were constructed on the side-lever prin-

the "Great Britain" afloat. She was 316 feet long over all, 282 feet between the perpendiculars, and 276 feet keel, and was 2318 tons by the old, and upward of 3000 tons by the new, measurement.

The "Atrato" was launched by Messrs Caird & Co., from their yard at Cartsdyke, in May, 1853. Early in 1852 the "Demerara," built on the Severn, was stranded across the river soon after her launch, as stated above, and so much injured that she had to be broken up. For this ship Messrs. Caird & Co. had the engines ready, and the directors immediately gave orders to construct an iron vessel to be fitted with them. That ship was the "Atrato." To suit the machinery it was requisite to maintain the same width as the "Demerara" had been, but the length was considerably increased. The "Great Britain" was of about thirty tons greater capacity, but the "Atrato" was longer by forty feet. Her dimensions were:

	Feet.
Length over all	350
Length of keel and forerake	315
Extreme breadth, including wings	72
Breadth of beam	42
Depth of hold	34

The dimensions of the great war-steamer "Duke of Wellington," three-decker, the largest ship then belonging to the Royal Navy, may be stated by way of comparison:

	Feet.
Extreme length	278
Length of keel and forerake	240
Breadth	59
Depth	24½

The "Duke" was thus less than the "Atrato" by about seventy feet in length and ten feet in depth; the width of the latter being, from the cause we have mentioned, less by seventeen feet. The height of the "Atrato" from the keel to top of bulwark-rail was forty-three feet. Her bow was surmounted by a spirited representation of an Indian deity, the work of Mr. Peter Christie, of Greenock.

The "Atrato" had four decks, seven and eight feet respectively in height. The spar-deck was flush from stem to stern, affording a promenade the length and breadth of a good street,—three hundred and thirty feet by thirty-eight. She had two funnels and three masts. The standing rigging was light and graceful, being formed of galvanized iron. The masts were fitted with Sir Snow Harris's lightning conductors. The main- and foremasts were "great sticks" of Quebec pine, the former measuring ninety feet long by seven in circumference.

ciple, of the combined power of 750 horses, or 24,500,000 pounds, 96-inch cylinders, and 9 feet stroke, and they were attached to a pair of Morgan's patent feathering float-paddles.

An elegant *déjeûner* was afterwards given at the White Lion Hotel, at which between forty and fifty gentlemen sat down.

The keel of the ship was formed of nine enormous pieces of iron, and the stem- and stern-posts were each one piece, and both carried besides some distance along horizontally. In the framing and fitting of the paddle-boxes, the beams and stringers, all of patent iron, presented an extraordinary contrast to the great logs used for the purpose in the other ships. The paddle-spaces were forty feet by twelve and a half wide, the wheels of thirty-seven feet diameter, patent feathering principle. The ship was divided into seven water-tight compartments by iron bulkeads. Thirteen hundred tons of iron were used in the construction of the hull. She was propelled by two beam-engines of the collective power of eight hundred horses, and she had accommodations for two hundred and twenty-four first-class passengers.

But by far the greatest disaster which befell any of this company's ships was the destruction of the "Amazon" by fire; nothing could be more terrible than the loss of this ship and the sufferings of those who perished with her. The "Amazon" was launched at Blackwell on the 28th of June, 1851. She was the largest wooden merchant steamship which up to that time had been constructed. She was 310 feet in length, 42 feet in width, 72 feet over the paddle-boxes, and 32 feet in depth; she was about 3000 tons burden, or 2256 tons register, and was fitted with engines of 800 horse-power, the diameter of the cylinders being 96 inches each, and the stroke 9 feet. The engines made 14 revolutions of her wheels, which were 41 feet in diameter, per minute, giving her a speed by log of 11 knots. Her cost was upward of £80,000, and when ready for sea somewhat over £100,000. When surveyed by the Admiralty before her departure from Southampton she was reported capable of carrying fourteen 32-pounders and two 10-inch pivot guns of eighty-five hundred-weight each, and her coal-bunkers were constructed to carry 1000 tons of coal, sufficient for sixteen and one-half days' full steaming. On the 2d of January, 1852, the "Amazon" sailed from Southampton on her first outward voyage. On the 4th of January, when about 110 miles W.S.W. of the Scilly Islands, the watch on deck discovered that a fire had broken out suddenly on the starboard side forward, between the steam-chest and the galley, the flames at once rushing up the gangway in front of the foremost funnel. All efforts to check the progress of the fire proved futile, and the most terrible consternation and confusion prevailed, the gale which howled overhead and around them increasing the terror of the awful calamity. The boats were burnt where stowed or swamped when lowered, save two of the life-boats and a small dingy, in which sixty-five of the one hundred and sixty-one souls on board managed to escape from the burning wreck; ninety-six, including the captain, perished in the ship.

These losses left the company only the "Orinoco," "Magdalene," and "Paraua" for the direct service between Southampton and Colon;

but, stimulated rather than depressed by misfortune, they chartered other vessels, and entered into the construction of steamers of a still finer description. When the government relieved them from the condition of building wooden vessels adapted for purposes of war, and the directors discovered that iron was preferable to wood, and the screw a better mode of propulsion than the paddle, they produced vessels equal to most of those engaged in transatlantic navigation.

There are not now many finer vessels afloat than the "Tagus" and "Moselle," launched in 1871, and the later ships of this line. The "Moselle," of about 3200 tons gross register, and engines of 600 horse-power, made 14.929 knots per hour as the average per four runs over the measured mile; and the "Tasmanian," an iron screw-vessel, also fitted in 1871 with compound engines, accomplished her first voyage to St. Thomas in fourteen days and two hours, on a consumption of only 466 tons of coal, though before the alteration in her engines she had consumed 1088 tons in making the same voyage.

The fleet is now a fine one, consisting of twenty-four steamships of from 3472 tons registered tonnage down to 1000, and nearly all iron screw-vessels.

1847.—THE COLLINS LINE.—In 1847 Mr. Edward K. Collins, with others, emulous of the success which had attended the Cunard Line, contracted with the government of the United States to convey the United States mails between New York and Liverpool, agreeing to make twenty voyages in each year, and to employ five first-class vessels in doing so. For the fulfillment of this agreement the Collins Company was to receive $19,250 per voyage. The company was unable to get the vessels ready within the stipulated time, and the time for their completion was extended. It was also favored with an advance of $25,000 a month on each vessel from the date of its launch

[1] Edward K. Collins, founder of the first American line of steamships between New York and Liverpool, was buried June 26, 1878, from his former residence, at Madison Avenue. The remains were taken to Woodlawn Cemetery. Representatives from all the large steamship lines in the vicinity attended. He was born at Truro, Massachusetts, in 1802. He entered upon mercantile pursuits in early life, and on settling in New York City soon acquired a reputation for great activity and enterprise in commercial affairs. He organized a line of sailing-packets between that city and New Orleans, and Vera Cruz, Mexico, which were so successful as to induce him to turn his attention to the passenger traffic between New York and Liverpool. He accordingly established the Dramatic Line of sailing-packets, comprising the fine ships "Shakespeare," "Garrick," "Siddons," and "Roscius." He had them constructed with full poops, with a view of affording increased accommodations for cabin passengers, which was considered quite an improvement over the "old liners" then in use, and as a consequence he soon distanced his competitors in gaining the patronage and favor of the public. The Dramatic Line became famous and was a successful pecuniary enterprise. The great success attending his efforts in this direction finally led him to entertain the idea of establishing a steam line of packets. In nautical circles the project at once excited considerable interest, and also secured the sympathies of the people. A subsidy from Congress was granted for carrying the mails.

until the sum should amount to $385,000. It was also agreed on the part of the government that the company should not be compelled to complete its fifth vessel. Then, in consideration of the company's making twenty-six instead of twenty annual voyages, the subsidy was increased from $19,250 to $33,000 per voyage, or to $878,000 yearly. For these pecuniary considerations the company was urged by the United States government, and endeavored, as well as agreed, to make the fastest passages between England and America. This endeavor was made with great spirit, and statements submitted to Congress show that it cost nearly half a million of dollars annually to effect the saving of a single day or a day and a half on the passage to Liverpool. Notwithstanding its large subsidy, the Collins enterprise, after sustaining the loss of two out of four of the company's ships, completely failed.

The history of the Collins fleet, the ships of which were in their day the finest afloat, both as to accommodations and speed, is soon told. The "Arctic" was run into by the French steamship "Vesta" in mid-ocean, September 27, 1854, and sunk; the "Pacific," with 240 souls on board, including the wife of Mr. Collins, was never heard from after sailing from Liverpool. The "Atlantic" was the pioneer steamship of the line. She sailed from New York April 27, 1849, and arrived in the Mersey May 10, thus making the passage in about thirteen days, two of which were lost in repairing the machinery; the speed was reduced in order to prevent the floats from being torn from the paddle-wheels. The average time of the forty-two westward trips in the early days of the line was 11 days, 10 hours, and 26 minutes, against the average of the then so-called fastest line of steamers, 12 days, 19 hours, and 26 minutes. The "Atlantic" was broken up in New York in 1879. On her arrival at Liverpool, in 1850, she was found to be too large for any of the docks, so of necessity lay out in the river.

The "Adriatic," the queen of the fleet, the only screw-ship of the line, was purchased by an English company, and is now used as a coal-hulk. To such base uses do we come at last.

This leaves only the "Baltic," a vessel which cost $700,000, to be accounted for. It is claimed that she made the quickest trip under steam alone that had ever been made in crossing the Atlantic. The White Star steamships, which later have made such rapid passages, spread nearly an acre of canvas, while the "Baltic" had comparatively no canvas.

After the failure of the Collins Line, the "Baltic" was in government service during the Civil War, and afterwards, altered into a sailing-ship, made several trips from San Francisco to Europe with wheat, her freight sometimes amounting to more than $70,000. She was sold to a German company, who hoped to sell her to Russia during the Turkish war, but the war ceasing, she was sold to private owners, and on her passage from Bremen to Boston met with a terrific gale, which strained her so badly that it was determined to break her up for the material in her. Soon, said a Boston paper of October, 1880, all that will be left of the "Baltic" will be a collection of old junk and a smoking hulk at Apple Island, the graveyard of many a fine vessel. So ended the last of the Collins Line, all of which were paddle-wheel steamships, excepting the "Adriatic," which never made a trip on the line.

The "Adriatic" was launched April 8, 1856. Her length was 345 feet; beam, 50 feet; depth of hold, 33½ feet; registered tonnage, 4144.75. The "Adriatic" was purchased by the Galway Company in 1861. The transfer of this ship to the English flag does not seem to have reduced her speed or detracted from her sea-going qualities, for she made the run from Galway to St. Johns in six days, the specified time, and having completed this passage to New York in one day fifteen hours, and three-quarters less than the contract time, returned from St. Johns to Galway in *five days, nineteen* hours and three-quarters, perhaps the quickest passage on record from port to port across the Atlantic.[1]

The principal dimensions of the "Atlantic" and of the "Pacific," a sister vessel, were: Length between the perpendiculars, 276 feet; beam, 45 feet; across the paddles, 75 feet; depth of hold, 31 feet 7 inches; diameter of wheel, 36 feet; tons burden, 2860, and she was said to be the largest steamship that had been built.

The "Arctic," the fastest steamer of the line, was modeled by George Steers, who designed the yacht "America;" her tonnage was 2856 tons; length of deck, 282 feet; breadth, 45 feet; and depth below main deck, 24 feet. Her cylinders were 95 inches diameter, stroke 10 feet. On her eighth passage from New York to Liverpool she made the then extraordinary time of 9 days, 17 hours, and 12 minutes. Her paddle-wheels were 35 feet 6 inches diameter, and contained each thirty-six floats. She burned about 87 tons of coal a day.[2]

---

[1] Appendix No. 6 to the Report of the Committee of the House of Commons. For a history of the Galway Line, which was unsuccessful, see Lindsay's "Merchant Shipping," vol. iii.

[2] Sir Edmund Cunard testified, in 1860, that the Collins Line got at first for twenty-four voyages $401,040 from the United States government, and that afterwards it received $893,750 for twenty-six voyages, or double his own subsidy, considering that he made two voyages to one. The capital of the Collins Line, $8,500,000, he said, would have been entirely sunk but for the loss of two ships, by which they got $1,250,000 from the English underwriters.

He said if his contract was withdrawn he had better sink his ships than try to keep them, for they were not adapted for mercantile uses. The "Scotia" cost him $900,000. Cunard's original subsidy, for twenty-four voyages a year, was $300,000 per annum for seven years. In 1852 he agreed to make a weekly service for $865,000 a year, to last ten years; five years afterwards he demanded a larger extension

From the start the Collins Company suffered from want of capital. Although the four vessels of this company cost $2,944,142 its paid-in capital only amounted to $1,200,000. It began, therefore, with a debt of $1,744,122, which was a continual drain for interest and commissions. With careful management this difficulty might have been overcome, for its receipts from the government for the transportation of mails during the first five years amounted to more than the cost of the vessels. Its receipts from other sources were large, and when the "Arctic" and "Pacific" were lost they were insured for their value at the time. Mr. Collins submitted to Congress the following statement, dated February 17, 1855:

Total receipts for passengers and freight	$4,460,867
" " mail service	3,413,966
	$7,874,833
Total disbursement	7,207,291
Leaving a nominal surplus of	$667,542

which was more than disposed of, as follows:

Loss of the Arctic	$255,000
Depreciation of investment	258,000
7 per cent. interest on capital	408,000
	$921,000

The all-controlling desire which seemed to outweigh every consideration of prudence was principally in relation to speed. Mr. Olds, of Ohio, in the United States House of Representatives, expressed the feeling of multitudes in the country when he said, "We have the fastest horses, the prettiest women, and the best shooting-guns in the world, and we must also have the fastest steamers. The Collins Line must beat the British steamers. Our people expected this of Mr. Collins, and he has not disappointed them."

The Collins Line were as substantially and economically built vessels as any of their time. After running six years their cost for repairs was more than the previous cost of the ships, or eighteen per cent. per annum.[1]

of the contract, so he could borrow money to build faster steamers than Collins. Collins's original four steamers cost $2,994,000, and his last experiment, the "Adriatic," ruined him. The average cost of each of his early voyages was $65,215, and the corresponding receipts $48,287, yet he carried more passengers from the beginning to the end than the Cunarders.

Mr. Collins's first proposition to the government of the United States was in 1845, but no contract was concluded with him until 1847. The "Adriatic" was the first to take her departure for Europe, in April, 1850, the "Pacific" followed in a few weeks, then the "Adriatic," and the "Baltic" soon after. These vessels were alike in model and in dimensions.

[1] Raney's *Ocean Post.*

1848.—PACIFIC MAIL STEAMSHIP COMPANY.—This company was compelled at the outset to form an establishment of the most effective character four or five thousand miles away from home, and it was at that time thirteen thousand miles distant. The country was wholly new, so much so that it was, in most parts of the field which it had to occupy, extremely difficult to procure ordinary food for their operations. Their ships had to make a voyage more than half of that around the world before they arrived at their points of service, and they found themselves without a home when there. The steamer "California," 1086 tons, which left New York on the 6th of October, 1848, was the first of the line to bear the American flag to the Pacific Ocean, and the first to salute with a new life the solitudes of that rich and untrodden territory. She was soon followed by the "Panama," 1088 tons, and the "Oregon," 1099 tons, and in due course by the "Tennessee," the "Golden Gate," 2068 tons, the "Columbia," 778 tons, the "John L. Stephens," 2189 tons, the "Sonora," 1614 tons, the "Republic," 850 tons, the "Northerner," 1010 tons, the "Fremont," 576 tons, the "Tobago," 189 tons, the "St. Louis," 1621 tons, and the "Golden Age," 2280 tons.

These steamers found nothing ready to receive them in the Pacific. The company was compelled to construct large workshops and foundries for their repair, and now have at Benicia a large and excellent establishment, where they can easily construct a marine engine. They had also to build their own dry-dock. They had also to make shore establishments at Panama, San Francisco, and Astoria, which, with coal depots, etc., were extremely costly, owing to materials having to be transported so far and labor at the time being so high owing to the rush to the gold-diggings. For a portion of the time the company had to pay thirty dollars a ton for coal, and in one instance fifty dollars. The success of building up this large establishment in the Pacific was simply an accident, and that accident the discovery of gold.

It is impossible in these notes to give even a brief sketch of all the fortunes and misfortunes of this great steamship company, but it is sufficient to say it still lives. All the early steamers were wooden paddle-wheelers, but, as in the case of all the ocean steamship companies, the fleet is now composed of iron screw ships. In 1876 it had a fleet of thirty-three steamers of an aggregate capacity of 74,000 tons of cargo, exclusive of the large space assigned to passengers; but that fleet has since been very much reduced. It had then thirty-five chief agencies, and its steamers called at forty-seven ports in the Pacific and those in the Atlantic.

The China and Japan Line was not started until the 1st of January, 1867, when the first of its fleet passed out of the Golden Gate of California bound across the Pacific to those ancient nations. The "Great

Republic," "China," "Japan," and "America," all of them wooden vessels with paddle-wheels and walking-beam engines, soon followed. These vessels, of about 4000 tons each, made the voyage from San Francisco to Yokohama in twenty-two days, thence to Hong-Kong in seven days, the whole distance, including the stoppage at Yokohama, occupying thirty days.

In 1874 the company added to the line the "City of Tokio" and the "City of Peking," two magnificent iron screw steamships of 5560 tons burden, 423 feet in length, 48 feet wide, and 38 feet deep, being the largest steamships that had ever carried the American flag. They have since started a line of steamers to Australia and the Hawaiian Islands.

The voyage of the Pacific Mail Steamship Company's steamer "City of New York," from New York to San Francisco in 1876, was remarkable. The total distance, 13,552 miles, was performed in 59 days, the actual steaming time being 54 days, 14 hours. The entire passage was made on the coal shipped at New York, none having been taken on board *en route*. The runs were as follows:

New York to Cape Virgin, west entrance of the Strait of Magellan	7074 miles.
Through the strait	840 "
Cape Pillar, east entrance of Strait of Magellan, to San Francisco	6138 "
Total revolutions of the engines during the voyage	3,888,105
" distance, by observation run	13,552 miles.
" " by screw	14,235 "
" amount of coal consumed (dock to dock)	1485 tons.
" " " " at anchor (port consumption)	45 "
" " " " for steaming	1440 "
Average consumption of coal per day	26.4 "
" " " mile	239 lbs.
" revolutions per day, running time	61,250
" " minute	42.53
" speed per day, running time	248¼ miles.

The following are the dimensions of the "City of New York": Length, 353 feet; beam, 40½ feet; tonnage, 3019. Engines, 1000 horse-power.

The following table gives the name, class, tonnage, and passenger capacity of the present fleet of the company, but does not give the foreign connecting lines in the Atlantic and South Pacific.

These vessels are *all* iron screw steamships.

The "City of Para" and the "City of Rio de Janeiro," formerly of the Brazilian Line, now belonging to the Pacific Mail Steamship Company, are sister ships. Each measures 368 feet 6 inches over all; beam, 38 feet 8 inches; hold, 28 feet 7 inches, with compound engines 42½ and 74½ inches in diameter; stroke, 5 feet. Each ship has six boilers, 10 feet 6 inches long and 13 feet in diameter. The register is 2548 tons; gross tonnage, 3500.

FLEET OF THE PACIFIC MAIL STEAMSHIP COMPANY, OCTOBER, 1882.

Vessels.	Tonnage.	Length.	Beam.	Passengers.	
				Cabin.	Steerage.
Atlantic Line.					
Acapulco	2572	300	43	190	800
City of Para	3532	345	38.6	..	..
Colon	2686	280	40	190	300
San Blas	2075	300	36	..	..
Panama and San Francisco Through Line.					
Colima	2906	312	40	190	800
Granada	2572	280	40	190	800
San José	2081	300	36	..	..
San Juan	2076	300	36	..	..
Central America and Mexican Line.					
City of Panama	1490	248	36.1	55	150
Clyde	2017	263	37	100	200
Costa Rica	1457	227	35	120	600
Honduras	1816	261.4	38.8	60	250
South Carolina	2099	257.1	35	80	200
China Line.					
City of Peking	5080	423	48	150	1500
City of Tokio	5080	425	48	150	1500
City of Rio de Janeiro	3548	344	38	..	..
Australian Line.					
City of New York	3019	339	40.2	150	600
City of Sydney	3017	358	40	150	500
Australia (*chartered*)	2737	376.9	37.4	..	..
Calandia (*chartered*)	2730	377	37.1	..	..

Steamships of the line sail from New York on the 10th, 20th, and 30th of each month, and from San Francisco on the 4th and 19th of each month *via* the Isthmus of Panama.

The voyage between New York and San Francisco occupies twenty-five days: nine days between New York and Aspinwall; one day in crossing the Isthmus, including the transfer by steam-tug to or from steamers in the Bay of Panama; and fifteen days on the Pacific Ocean. Steamers call at no California port except San Francisco, and at no port between New York and Aspinwall. Connections are made at Aspinwall with Royal Mail, West India and Pacific, Transatlantique, and Hamburg-American steamers for ports on the Atlantic coast of Central, South, and North America, and the West India Islands.

At Panama, with Pacific Steam Navigation Company, for all Pacific ports of South America and Australia.

At Yokohama, with Mitsu-Bishi Mail Line, for Japanese ports and Shanghai.

At Hong-Kong, with Peninsular and Oriental, Messageries Maritimes, Jardine, Matheson & Co., and Douglas, Lapraik & Co.'s steamship lines for all China, India, and Eastern ports, and *via* Suez Canal for all European ports. Also with steamers for Manilla and Batavia.

At Auckland, with Union Steamship Company, for all New Zealand ports.

At Sydney, with Australian Steam Navigation Company, for Australian ports; with Union Steamship Company, for all New Zealand ports; with Eastern and Australian Steamship Company, for Keppel Bay, Bowen, Townsville, Somerset, and *via* Torres Straits for Batavia, Singapore, and Calcutta; with Peninsular and Oriental steamers, for Melbourne, Adelaide, King George's Sound, Ceylon, etc., also with steamers for New Caledonia and Hobart Town; with Tasmanian Steam Navigation Company, for Hobart Town and Launceton.

1850.—THE WARREN LINE OF STEAMSHIPS, BOSTON AND LIVERPOOL.—The nucleus of this line was the once celebrated sailing-packets of Enoch Train & Co.,—viz., the "Plymouth Rock," "Washington Irving," "Daniel Webster," "Anglo-American," "Anglo-Saxon," etc., ships of from one thousand to fifteen hundred tons; supplemented as the requirements of speed were called for by the clippers "Star of Empire," "Chatsworth," "Staffordshire," "Cathedral," and "Chariot of Fame," of from fifteen hundred to two thousand tons.

This line is a Boston enterprise for carrying freight and passengers between Boston and Liverpool. At times each ship has brought from four hundred to eight hundred emigrant passengers, and the pressure has been so great that other ships have been chartered.

Between 1850 and 1860 steam worked its way into the Atlantic carrying trade, and the Warren Company was among the first to substitute steam- for sailing-ships. Its first vessels were the "Propontis," "Bosphorus," "Delaware," "Meletia," "Peruvian," etc., bringing large cargoes, and an average of seven hundred emigrant passengers. Return cargoes were sought for in other ports.

In 1872 the trade had increased enough to warrant the placing of such large steamships on the line as the "Minnesota," "Victoria," and "Palestine," carrying from 2200 to 2800 tons of merchandise. The "Iowa" has the capacity of carrying 3300 tons of merchandise, exclusive of coal, and makes an average passage of ten and one-half days between Boston and Liverpool. Other ships of this line are the "Canopus," "Milanese," "Pharos," "Glamorgan," and "Pembroke," to which have been recently added the "Missouri," of 4300 tons, and the "Kansas," of 4500 tons dead-weight capacity.

In 1880 this line dispatched from Boston in eighty-four steamers 20,031 tons of merchandise, 28,176 oxen, 11,323 swine, and 18,053 sheep.

The "Missouri," Captain A. H. Burwell, arrived at Boston Friday, June 10, 1880, having sailed from Liverpool on the 29th of May, making her first ocean voyage in about twelve days.[1] She was built on the Clyde, and is pronounced one of the finest of the Atlantic steamers. Her dimensions are: Length, 425 feet; breadth, 43 feet 6 inches; depth, 35 feet 6 inches, and the tonnage under deck 5000. Her engines are 300 horse-power, constructed on the compound principle, which are supplied with steam from four steel boilers at a working pressure of eighty pounds to the square inch. The steamer is fitted with four decks; three are iron, throughout the entire length, and sheathed with wood planking. She is divided into eight water-tight compartments, and has water-ballast capacity to the extent of 700 tons, and her dead-weight cargo and coal capacity will be 5000 tons. The steam stearing-gear can be worked from aft, or in the pilot-house or on the bridge amidships.

1850.—THE INMAN LINE.—The history of the Inman Line owes its inception to William Inman (who died in 1881) and his copartners, is the history of all the great institutions in England,—a good basis, sure foundations, and the gradual growth of a legitimate plan. It was the first regular line of steamers across the Atlantic, consisting entirely of iron ships, propelled by the screw. December 10, 1850, the "City of Glasgow," of 1600 tons and 350 horse-power, the first steamship of what was then called the Liverpool, New York, and Philadelphia Steamship Company, sailed from Liverpool for Philadelphia, having previously made several successive and successful voyages to New York,[2] under other owners. In June, 1851, the "City of Manchester" was added to the line. It was not until February, 1875, that the line was converted, in honor of its founder, into the "Inman Steamship Company," limited.

New York having just become the port of the Cunard fleet, the new line did not wish to enter into direct competition with the older

[1] Captain Burwell died on his passage to Boston in command of one of the company's steamers, September, 1882.

[2] The "City of Glasgow" left Liverpool last for Philadelphia, March 1, 1854, and is supposed to have foundered at sea, as she was never heard from. The vessel and cargo were valued at $850,000.

Mr. Inman, having watched the performances of the "City of Glasgow" on her first trip to America, was convinced of the advantages she possessed over not merely sailing-ships, but over paddle-steamers, and therefore recommended her purchase to his partners. Acting on his advice, they bought and dispatched her with four hundred steerage passengers in the winter of 1850 across the Atlantic, and thus inaugurated what is now known as the "Inman Line." The "City of Glasgow" did her work well, and falsified the prophecies of disaster. The "City of Manchester" left a profit of forty per cent. the first year of her movement.

company, but in 1857 the "Inman" went also to New York, and having decided to name their ships for the leading cities of the world, had already added to its line the "City of Philadelphia,"[1] "City of Baltimore," "City of Washington," and "Kangaroo," and in 1860 they added the "City of New York," when the company's service became a weekly one.

In 1863 the "City of London," "City of Cork," "City of Limerick," and "City of Dublin" were added to the line, and the number of the trips increased to three times a fortnight, and afterwards to twice a week. The fleet in 1880 consisted of eleven vessels, varying in gross tonnage from 2536 to 5490 tons, and in nominal horse-power from 350 to 1000. Five ships have been built within the last seven years, four being among the largest and finest merchant steamships afloat,—viz., the "City of Chester," "City of Richmond," "City of Berlin," and "City of Rome."

The "City of Berlin" was launched October 27, 1874. She has a gross tonnage of 5491, is 4634 tons, builder's measurement, and has a net register tonnage of 3139 tons. Her engines are 1000 nominal horse-power, but capable of being worked up to five times that amount of power. She is 513 feet in length over all, has four decks, and a molded width of 45 feet. These dimensions give her accommodations for 200 saloon, or first-class, and 1500 intermediate, or steerage, passengers, and a crew of 150 men. The contract with her builders was that she should indicate 5000 horse-power and steam about 16 knots. On her trial trip, at the measured mile, her engines indicated 5200 horse-power. She is propelled by a pair of inverted, direct-acting, compound high- and low-pressure engines. The low-pressure cylinder of these engines is 120 inches, and the high-pressure cylinder 72 inches in diameter, with a piston-stroke of 5 feet 6 inches. She has 12 boilers, heated by 36 furnaces, and they are so arranged that any number of them can be cut off. Her saloon is amidships, and is 44 feet in length by 43 in width, longitudinally divided by two rows of walnut columns surmounted by gilded Corinthian capitals. It is lighted in the day time by an elegant cupola skylight.

The following description of this vessel by a passenger may well be compared with that of the "Thalmamegus," described by Athenæus, and built by Philopater, king of Egypt, which was 420 feet long, 57 feet broad, and 72 feet high from the keel. The element of steam was of course wanting.

"There is certainly no finer steamer afloat, none more comfortable. Seated at dinner in her saloon, lounging in her smoking-room, or chat-

---

[1] The "City of Philadelphia," on her passage from Liverpool to Philadelphia, struck on Cape Race, September 17, 1854, and was lost; the vessel and cargo being valued at $600,000,—passengers and crew saved. In 1870 the "City of Boston" sailed for Europe and has never since been heard of.

ting with the ladies in their divan, you may easily forget you are at sea. The 'City of Berlin' has two decks, both of them superior to anything I have ever seen. You can have a promenade of nearly five hundred feet straight ahead, and the clean sweep of the lower deck from one end to the other is something superb. The lower deck looks like a little town, and it is a great deal pleasanter than most little towns. There is a row of handsome-looking houses, with a street open to the sea on either side. These houses, bright and neat, with their descriptions engraved on each in English, French, and German, are the officers' rooms, ladies' room, smoking-room, etc., all opening upon the deck on both sides, so that their ventilation and comfort are perfect. The smoking-room has electric bells and other conveniences. The ladies' public room is spacious, and filled with sofas and seats, so that the occupants can sit and chat with their male friends outside, or draw a curtain and shut themselves from all observation, or retire to a private room below (which opens upon lavatories and bath-rooms), and is one of the snuggest apartments in the ship, furnished in excellent taste, and provided with luxuries and comforts undreamed of in private houses. In the companion-way hangs a list of the crew, and the boats to which they belong. The call is made every day; each man has his number, and in case of danger he knows exactly what to do. . . . The staterooms are lighted from the deck by protected windows. In the best rooms, in addition to the usual berths, is a sofa made so that it can be converted into a berth large enough for two. The washing conveniences are such that you turn the taps in your state-room to wash with more confidence than if you had a London reservoir to draw from, there being between three and four miles of lead piping in the ship. The bath-tubs are all of white marble. You arrange the business of getting a bath with the steward. At the entrance of each bath is a slate, on which is inscribed the passenger's name and the time at which the bath is devoted to him. Should he fail to appear, the others go on in rotation.

"The saloon is furnished in Spanish mahogany and purple velvet. There are four rows of tables, and the menu and wine-card is something to be remembered. The captain presides at one, the purser at another, the surgeon at a third, and some favored passenger at the fourth. The ship comprises within its vast domain a barber-shop, a butcher-shop, vegetable-store, kitchen, with lifts and shoots for the convenience of cooks and waiters, a bakery, a laundry, a surgery, hospital and infirmaries, and ice-houses. Indeed, nothing is wanting: even a light-house is provided. The sleeping accommodations are so arranged that by writing early, families or parties of eight, sixteen, and twenty-four can be berthed in private rooms."

The "City of Paris" in 1869 conveyed his Royal Highness Prince Arthur (now Duke of Connaught) to America in *six days, twenty-*

one hours, the quickest passage ever made to any part of the New World from Cork. The prince attended divine service at Queenstown on Sunday, embarked at 4 P.M. that day, and was landed at Halifax, Nova Scotia, at half-past 10 A.M. on the following Sunday in time for morning service at that place, which, to his credit, he also attended.

In 1874 the average time made by the fifty-one sailings of the Inman steamers between Queenstown and Sandy Hook, New York, 2775 miles, was 10 days, 22 hours, 1 minute. The same year the "City of Chester" and the "City of Richmond," the newest and swiftest of the line, made seven passages each, none of which exceeded 9 days, the longest being the "Richmond's," in 8 days, 21 hours, 41 minutes, and the shortest the "Chester's," in 8 days, 1 hour, 38 minutes. The passages covered the whole of 1874, the vessels being subject to all the phases of the variable Atlantic. In December, 1875, the "City of Brussels" made the passage from New York to Queenstown in 7 days, 20 hours, 33 minutes, the "City of Richmond" in 7 days, 18 hours, 50 minutes, and in September and October the "City of Berlin" made passages *both ways* in 7 days, 18 hours, 2 minutes, 7 days, 15 hours, 48 minutes, and 7 days, 14 hours, 12 minutes.

The Inman was the first line to make special provisions for emigrant passengers, and during the ten years ending in 1863 had carried a yearly average of 30,000 passengers, or 300,000. The next ten years exhibited even better results, the number of passengers carried exceeding 787,000, or an annual average of 78,700.

From 1850 to 1860 no mails were carried, Mr. Inman holding that "ocean postage" was the proper way of paying for mail services rather than by monopolies and subsidies. When the Collins Line of American steamers was withdrawn the Inman came into the gap and carried the American mails, receiving for the service eight pence per half-ounce for letters, the postage being one shilling per half-ounce. The *Inman Company has never had a subsidy*, and has never been paid but for work done. When they came to agreement in 1867 with the Cunard Company to run a tri-weekly service to New York, they were paid £35,000 per annum for one sailing a week, which was less than one-half the remuneration they would have been paid under the ocean postage system. Thus the company carried the royal mail from 1868 until December, 1876, in conjunction with the Cunard. In 1877 the British government entered into arrangements with the Inman, Cunard, and White Star Lines (exclusively) to run the mails tri-weekly—viz., Tuesday, Thursday, and Saturday—to New York.

On the 30th of December, 1881, the "City of Brussels" took from Liverpool to New York seven hundred and sixty sacks of mail matter, the largest shipment of that kind ever sent to New York.

The "City of Rome," launched on the 14th of June, 1881, at Bar-

HISTORY OF STEAM NAVIGATION. 349

row-in-Furness, by the Barrow Ship-Building Company, was regarded as the most appropriate name which could be given to the latest addition to the Inman fleet. Not many years ago Barrow was a handful of houses; it is now a town with thousands of inhabitants, whose prosperity depends upon the enterprise and ability which have led to the construction of the "City of Rome." The builders and owners of the vessel united to make the occasion memorable. A conspicuous proof of the friendly rivalry between the transatlantic companies was shown by the presence at the launch of representatives of the Cunard, White Star, National, and Allan Lines. The launch was successfully accomplished; the ceremony of christening being performed by Lady Constance Stanley. The vessel arrived in the Mersey from her trial trip on the 14th of September following.[1]

The decoration of ocean steamers is generally of a hybrid sort, and not always in the best of taste. In the "City of Rome" a consistent design has been harmoniously executed, and finds expression in richness of material rather than emphasis of color. An inspection of her saloons and cabins carries away a recollection of noiseless carpets, neutral hues, the flashings of beveled mirrors, gold and ebony panelings, embroidered curtains, silver lamps, stained glass, yielding cushions of green velvet, and faint designs of tapestries. The decorations belong to the modern æsthetic, and have been chosen for their utility, appropriateness, and beauty. The figure-head, about three times life-size, represents a Roman emperor, Hadrian, modeled from the statue in the British Museum in strict conformity with its model. The stern is enriched by festoons on either side, the centre being marked by a carving of the arms and crest of the city of Rome. As a compliment, the municipality of the ancient metropolis sent a copy on vellum of the arms and crest of the city, which are hung up in one of the principal apartments of the vessel.

The dimensions of the "City of Rome" are: Length, 586 feet; extreme breadth, 52 feet 3 inches; depth of hold, 37 feet; tonnage, 8826 tons; horse-power indicated, 10,000. The weight of this great steamer is 8000 tons, and her displacement, at 26 feet mean draught, is 13,500 tons; so that she has a dead-weight carrying power of 5500 tons. The cubical contents of her hold give her a measurement capacity of 7720 tons, at 50 cubic feet to the ton. She has 4 masts, 3 funnels,

[1] The "City of Rome" sailed from Liverpool for New York April 6, 1882, on her first trip. She made her last trip as one of the Inman Line to New York in September. She has since been transferred to the Anchor Line, and is advertised by that line to sail from New York in October. She was returned to her builders by the Inman Company, because she failed to come up to the contract in many important respects, notably in speed, carrying capacity, and draught of water. The Barrow Ship-Building Company agreed to take her back and pay every expense the Inman Company had gone to with her rather than stand a suit for £125,000 sterling damages which the Inman Company had commenced.

and has 11 compartments formed by water-tight bulkheads, each extending to the main-deck. The largest of these compartments is 60 feet long; and supposing one filled with water, the trim of the vessel would not be materially affected. The stern frame is the largest forging ever made for such a purpose, the finished weight being 33 tons. The framing of the vessel is of the ordinary type: the floors are 34 inches deep at the centre line. The frames are in one length from centre line to gunwale, and are of angle-iron 7 inches by 4 inches, and 60 feet in length. The reverse frames are in one length of 4 inches by 4 inches angle-iron. The beams are of the Butterley bulb sections, each rolled in one length. The vessel has two complete iron decks above, while the lower deck is complete for half the length, and has wide plating on each side of the remainder. The "City of Rome" has nine keelsons. The five central ones are of uniform height, and are carried unbroken through the engine- and boiler-seatings. The shell plating is on the principle that has been applied to all the large transatlantic steamers built in Barrow. The inside plates form a complete skin, fitted edge to edge and butt to butt, with covering plates half the width of the inside strakes fitted outside. The hold stanchions are arranged in two tiers, one on each side, the better to support and strengthen the long beams. The question of propelling the ship at so high a speed as 18 knots per hour demanded careful consideration, and it was ultimately decided that it would be best to adhere to the single-screw arrangement, and adopt a propeller 24 feet in diameter, driven by three sets of inverted "tandem" engines, working on three cranks disposed at an angle of 120 degrees with one another. The "tandem" engine has the high-pressure cylinder placed in a line behind or above the low-pressure cylinder. The crank-shaft is a built shaft, and, with the screw shafting, was made by Sir Joseph Whitworth & Co. of their fluid compressed steel. The leading particulars of the engines are: there are three high-pressure cylinders 43 inches diameter, and three low-pressure cylinders 86 inches diameter, and 6-feet stroke. The diameter of the crank-shaft is 25 inches, and of the crank-pins 26 inches. The length of the main bearings is $33\frac{1}{2}$ inches, and of the crank-pins 28 inches. The crank-shaft weighs 64 tons; had it been made of iron, and solid, the weight would have been 73 tons. The propeller shafting is 24 inches diameter, and the hole through it 14 inches diameter. The thrust-shaft has thirteen collars $39\frac{1}{2}$ inches diameter, giving a surface of 6000 square inches. This piece of shafting weighs 17 tons. The propeller-shaft is 25 inches diameter and $30\frac{1}{2}$ feet long, and weighs 18 tons. The bed-plate weighs 100 tons. The cooling surface of the condensers is 17,000 square feet, equal to nearly 17 miles 360 yards of tubing. There are two air-pumps, 39 inches diameter, and 3 feet stroke, worked by levers attached to the aft and forward engines. There is a pumping-engine, which can be used for pumping heavy leaks, or can also discharge through the condenser. There are also three auxiliary pumping-engines, for feeding the boilers, for bilge-pumping, and for deck purposes. Steam is supplied by eight cylindrical tubular boilers, fired from both ends. Each boiler is 14 feet mean diameter, and 19 feet long, with a steam-receiver 13 feet long and 4 feet diameter; and has 6 furnaces 3 feet 9 inches diameter, 3 at each end : 48 furnaces in all. The fire-bars are 6 feet long, giving a grate surface of 1080 square feet. The shell plates of the boilers are 24 feet 8 inches long, 4 feet $4\frac{1}{2}$ inches wide, and $1\frac{1}{4}$ inches thick, and weigh nearly $2\frac{1}{2}$ tons each; all the holes are drilled. Each furnace has its separate combustion-chamber. These boilers are constructed for a working pressure of 90 pounds per square inch. The engines are intended to work constantly at 8000 indicated horse-power, but are capable of developing 10,000 horse-power, indicated.

It is difficult to convey in words an adequate idea of the engine-room. Four Serrin lamps render it as bright as day. These lamps have no glass shades, and give no trouble. It may help a little to realize what her engines are when we state the engine-room is 50 feet wide and of the same length. The engines are 47 feet 8 inches high from the bottom of the frames to the tops of the high-pressure cylinders; that is to say, as high as an ordinary four-story house. Access to the engine-room platforms is by iron staircases, which will take three persons abreast. Entering from the upper deck, nothing is to be seen but the three high-pressure cylinders and the lids of the low-pressure cylinders, a close grating concealing all the rest of the machinery below. Descending the first flight of stairs, which runs fore and aft, we are on the second platform surrounding the low-pressure cylinders, which is the only hot place in the engine-room. Passing between the cylinders and the steps we have descended, we come to a second flight, aft of the engines, and running athwartships, and descend to the third platform, from which access is got to the two stuffing-boxes in the lower lid of each low-pressure cylinder. Standing here, and looking forward between the frames, we have a sight unique. We see the three mighty cross-heads, with their guides, and the jaws of the great connecting-rods moving up and down in rhythmical sequence in the vivid glare of the electric lamps, which cast strong shadows on the white bulkheads. Passing to the lower floor again, we have before us the like of which can nowhere else be seen. Here is ample room to walk about; there is no steam to indicate the presence of an engine, for the cylinders are high over our heads. We look up and see the black covers looming far above; straight before us is the crank-shaft. As we look at it we realize that it is the largest crank-shaft in the world; it weighs 66 tons. Each of three cranks, with its shafting, occupies a length of 14 feet, and weighs 22 tons. A tall man, standing beside one of the cranks, is dwarfed. Each crank-pit is a chasm.

The rush of water from the pipes over the bearings is caught, and the crank, which has given so much trouble, scatters a light spray, the drops gleaming like jewels in the electric light. The noise is monotonous, but not wearisome. The great connecting-rod brasses are just a little slack, and the want of lead in the slides makes the pistons slow in getting away from the cylinder-covers; and we have, as the cranks revolve, not a blow or a knock, but a soft, all-pervading thud, as each centre is turned. Away aft runs the main screw-shaft, 24 inches in diameter. The thrust-shaft has 12 collars 4 feet in diameter, and weighs 17 tons. Following it down the long tunnel we lose by degrees all the sights and sounds of the ship. Then a noise, as of a village waterwheel, a pattering and murmuring of water, reaches us. Standing on an angle-iron brace, we look through a hole in the last bulkhead in the ship, and see by the light of an engine-room lamp a small pool of water under the end of the stern-tube, and in this pool dips the last coupling, 4 feet in diameter, like its fellows; and the nuts and the heads of the bolts of the coupling patter in the water, and make the sounds which have different associations. It may be well to explain, with reference to the engines, that the bald figures of horse-power do not express the true significance of the progress which has been made in that department of naval science. The engines now in use are not only infinitely more powerful, but they are relatively more economical. The engines, with which earlier vessels were equipped, have been superseded by compound condensing-engines, which accumulate force and utilize the steam more fully, so that with a reduced consumption of fuel there is an increased power of propulsion. Without this progress in engineering skill the development of steam navigation would have been impossible. Either the vessels could not have carried a sufficiency of fuel, or the storage of it would have engrossed so large a proportion of the cargo space that they could not have been worked profitably.[1]

An example of the revolution in the engine-room may be cited from one of the Inman steamers. The "City of Brussels" was placed on the line in 1869, when she was regarded as a model of nautical excellence,—the "crack" ship of her day. But within seven years of her launch, while her hull and sailing appointments were in undiminished efficiency, her machinery had become antiquated, and she was furnished with entirely new engines. This costly renovation was made with the result that by the new compound engines equal power was attained on a much smaller consumption of coal. It is needless to explain that to save 40 to 50 tons of coal per day was a direct economy of fuel, and a gain of space for the stowage of freight-earning cargo. In fact, by the change of engines the consumption of fuel was reduced from about 110 tons per day to less than 65 tons, and the cargo space

---

[1] This fulfills Dr. Lardner's famous opinion or prediction.

augmented by about 800 tons, with an increase of propelling power. Compound engines have introduced a revolution almost as complete as did first the paddle-wheels and next the screw, and are now universal in ocean-going steamers, one of the largest sets ever constructed being fitted on board the "City of Rome."

On the trial trip of the "City of Rome," working at three-quarters speed, with 45 revolutions per minute, the measured mile was performed at the rate of $15\frac{3}{4}$ knots per hour; but as the engines at full speed make 58 or 60 revolutions per minute, the ship will, it is expected, in practice attain a speed of 17 or 18 knots per hour. In the series of tests the engines worked with great smoothness, and it was demonstrated that they could be brought to a dead stop in two seconds by the turning of a single lever, and that from going full speed ahead they could be reversed to full speed astern in the space of five seconds.

The internal arrangements of the "City of Rome" are of the most complete nature. The promenade-deck carries at the fore end the saloon skylight. In the hurricane deck-house the captain's and chief officer's cabins are placed close to the steering-house and lookout bridge, so that they are always near in case of necessity. Abaft this is the upper saloon, and abaft this the upper smoking-rooms is a novel feature, it being thought advisable, in view of the large number of passengers, to fit two smoking-rooms, with separate stairs to the cabin-deck. In the after deck-house is a saloon or lounge for ladies, fitted up in the most elegant manner, to prevent the going below in showery weather. Abaft is a companion leading to the sleeping-cabins. At the sides of the hurricane-deck are twelve life-boats, one fitted up as a steam-launch. On this deck are placed capstans, and at each of the cargo hatchways steam-winches for working the cargo. On the upper deck is the drawing-room, one hundred feet long, for the use of passengers. This apartment, which is fitted very handsomely with lounges, is in the form of a wide gallery, with a rectangular opening into the dining-saloon below, thus giving height and light to the latter apartment. Above is a large skylight, richly ornamented; at the fore end is a grand piano, and at the after end the grand staircase to the dining-room below. Here, also, is the lower smoking-room, which is fitted similarly to the upper; the paneling of these rooms is in wainscot oak, the floor is laid in mosaic pavement, and the upholstery in morocco leather. Abaft this are the rooms for the officers and engineers. The height in the 'tween decks is 9 feet. The grand dining-saloon is 72 feet long, 52 feet wide, and 9 feet high, or 17 feet in the opening to the drawing-room above. This opening, surmounted by the skylight, forms an effective and elegant relief to the flat and heavy ceiling. The paneling and decorations are artistic and unique. The apartment accommodates two hundred and fifty first-class passengers. The chairs are of polished teak-wood, neatly fluted, with the Inman monogram carved in open work. They revolve on pivots, and are numbered to correspond with the state-rooms. At night the saloon is lit by thirty-two Swan incandescent electric lamps, pendent from the ceiling, giving the whole a brilliant appearance. A paneled dado, of quaint design, three feet high, is carried entirely round the saloon, and from the dado cornice to the line of the ceiling the wall is treated with rich panels of figured mahogany, bordered with a margin of satin-wood, alternating with the side-light casings. These side-lights are more architectural than is usually found on board steamships. An architrave is carried in a square form round the side-lights, inclosing a secondary sill, and runs down to the top of the dado. From the centres of each of the intermediate panels the corbels (elaborate pieces of molded and carved oak) spring, making the lines of the ceiling construction, and carrying them down on the walls. At the level of the corbel capitals the ceiling rises upon elliptic arches between the beams, suggesting the fan vaunting, which is so beautiful in Gothic architecture. The music-room is immediately above the saloon, and is rather more severe in its style, being finished in black and gold. The room is surmounted by a handsome circular skylight, twenty feet long by ten feet wide, which throws down a flood of light to the dining- and music-rooms. A special feature in this skylight is the introduction of oval lights, enlarged to double the area where they pass into the ceiling of the dining-saloon. An organ is in the dining-saloon, and a grand piano in the music-room. The ladies' boudoir, on the main-deck, is fitted in a very handsome manner, the walls being paneled in figured brocaded silk, and the ceiling in Japanese leather paper. The couch is upholstered in blue velvet, with tapestry curtains. Alongside are baths, etc., for the lady passengers. On the hurricane-deck is another boudoir, treated in a contrast, with black and gold. The furniture and upholstery of this boudoir is of amber-colored plush velvet, and the window-hangings and door portière are of Roman cloth of the same tone, banded with stripes of plush. The smoking-rooms are beautifully fitted, that on the saloon-deck having a novel treatment of wall paneling of original Japanese water-color sketches of birds and flowers. The seats are covered with pig-skin leather. The woodwork of the walls, etc., in the upper smoking-room is of pencil cedar-wood; in the lower of mahogany, oak, and walnut. The floors of those apartments are laid with parquetry. Abaft the music-saloon are the repositories for the plate and dishes for the service of the table, and abaft of these the cook's and steward's portion of the ship. The breadth and general style of the kitchen may surprise many, but when the number of passengers is taken into account wonder at the gigantic proportions for feeding them will cease. Four hundred cabin passengers and 1800 steerage, with about 240 of a crew, may have to be provided for on a voyage, and in that aspect the rooms for cooks and stewards are none too many. Going aft beyond the regions where the cook presides, we come on the engine-room. Nearer the stern we come to the quarters of the steerage passengers, and these, though of course not rich like the cabin, are roomy and clean to a degree that would surprise old Atlantic stagers. Still aft there is an engine for the service of the electric light, with which the whole ship is to be fitted. An ominous notice warns all who come near that instantaneous death may result from the incautious handling of the wires. At the stern there is a ponderous steering apparatus, although the place from which the steering is to be done is far off on the captain's bridge, where there is the now familiar little wheel which is used in steering by steam.

The crew numbers, when the full complement is aboard, 240. There are berths for 54 firemen and 50 seamen, while over 100 are in the cook and steward's department, and 12 directly connected with the engine-room.

Opening through double spring-doors at the foot of the grand staircase, and under, is an American luncheon-bar, with the usual fittings. On each side, from the saloon to the after end of the engine-room, are state-rooms, providing for 300 passengers. Amidships are retiring-rooms, baths, and lavatories, barber's shop, etc. Accommodation is provided on the main-deck for 500 emigrants, and on the lower deck for 1000 more, making a grand total of 1500. The berths are arranged in single tiers or half-rooms, each separated by a passage, and having a large side-light, adding greatly to the light, ventilation, and comfort of the passengers, besides the advantage of a lesser number of persons in each room. Comfortable and properly equipped wash-rooms are provided for both sexes.

In proportions and design the "City of Rome" presents a remarkable contrast to the "Great Eastern," to which she stands next in magnitude in the mercantile marine. Brunel's vessel suggests a stately ark, with towering walls and ponderous hull, massive, stupendous, rather than elegant. The conditions are reversed in this vessel. The "City of Rome" is of great length, tapering form, symmetrical lines, and graceful mold, so that the inexperienced observer is unable to realize her enormous dimensions. The difference of proportions between the two vessels shows how scientific theory is modified by practical experiment. In designing the "Great Eastern," Brunel had no other guide than his scientific knowledge; there were no gradations between the puny vessels of five-and-twenty years ago and the leviathan he constructed; and he reckoned the length, beam, and depth on bases which the practice of later ship-building has not confirmed. The tendency of naval construction in the merchant navy is to lengthen the hulls, without, in any appreciable degree, increasing the beam or depth of the hold. This is apparent by comparing the dimensions of these typical vessels, the "Great Eastern" and the "City of Rome."

The length of the former is 680 feet; her breadth of beam, 83 feet; depth, 60 feet. The measurements of the "City of Rome" are: Length, 586 feet; breadth of beam, 52 feet 3 inches; and depth of hold, 37 feet; while in length she closely approximates to her rival, in breadth and depth she is little more than half the magnitude. It is in these differences of proportion that the disparity of tonnage is to be found. The "Great Eastern" is of enormously greater cubical capacity from her breadth and depth; though less tall and bulky of hull, the "City of Rome" is of great cargo capacity. Her length and beautiful lines suggest an impression of buoyant grace rather than of vast magnitude; yet her carrying power, notwithstanding her clipper bow and rounded stern, is greater than any other vessel afloat, except the "Great Eastern."

The fleet of the Inman Line is now (1882) composed of the following steamships: "City of Berlin," 5491 tons; "City of Richmond," 4607 tons; "City of Chester," 4566 tons; "City of Paris," 3500 tons; "City of Montreal," 4490 tons; "City of Brussels," 3775 tons; "City of New York," 3500 tons, which leave New York for Liverpool Thursdays or Saturdays, and Liverpool for New York Tuesdays or Thursdays.

With the latest vessels added to the fleets of the Cunard, the Inman, the Guion, and the Anchor Companies, it is possible to gain an idea of the ocean ships of the future. So far as size, speed, and comfort are concerned, these are as much in advance of the Atlantic liners of which we were so proud a quarter of a century ago as those were improvements on the earliest specimens of river passenger steamers. A great point was thought to be reached when the Cunard Company built the "Scotia" and the "Persia," or when the Inman Company became possessed of the "City of Glasgow;" but the finest of these steamers was not much above half the size of the "Servia" or the "City of Rome," whilst its engine-power was comparatively infinitesimal. No better illustration of the changes that have taken place in our ocean fleet could be given than a reference to the statistics bearing on the size of some of the early and some of the latest Atlantic liners. The Cunarder "Scotia," which was launched on the Clyde in 1862, and was then considered the best specimen of her type, measured 379 feet in length, and had a breadth of 47 feet 8 inches, and a depth of 30 feet 5 inches. Her tonnage was 3871, and she was fitted with side-lever engines indicating 1000 horse-power. The "City of Glasgow," belonging to the Inman Company some years earlier, measured 277 feet long by 32 feet 7 inches broad, and 24 feet 7 inches deep. She was 1600 tons burden, and her engines were 380 horse-power. According to popular theory, the limits of practicable ship-building were reached when the "City of Berlin," five years ago, was introduced into the Inman fleet, she being then the largest vessel afloat (excepting the "Great Eastern"), and it being assumed finality had been reached in the magnitude of ocean-going steamers. Her measurements, in contrast with the pioneer of the service, testify to the progress which twenty-five years have witnessed in the development of steam navigation. Her length is 520 feet; breadth, 44 feet; depth to spar-deck, 37 feet; and her gross measurement 5481 tons. Her engine-power being 900 horse-power nominal, but capable of working up to 4800 horse-power indicated. Compare these figures with the dimensions of the "Servia" or the "City of Rome." The "Servia" has a length of 530 feet, a beam of 52 feet, a depth of 41 feet, a carrying capacity of at least 8500 tons, and is fitted with engines calculated to develop an indicated horse-power of 10,500 tons. The "City of Rome" is: Length, 586 feet; breadth, 52 feet 3 inches; depth, 37 feet; tonnage upward of 8000; and engine-power, 10,000. These facts are striking, but they fail to exhaust the comparisons which might be drawn between the vessels formerly engaged in the ocean traffic and the ships which are taking their place. Those who inspect the "Servia" or the "City of Rome" will become aware of an untold number of ingenious contrivances by which the comfort and safety of the passengers are now assured. The vessel of the future is not only a model of speed and of large cargo capacity, it also is a model of luxury.

Where, it may be asked, is this peaceful rivalry in the production of big ships to stop? Are ship-builders and ship-owners to go on increasing the size of the ocean-liners until they rival the "Great Eastern"? It is impossible to place any limit on such an enterprise; but it may safely be taken for granted that if ships of the dimensions of the "Great Eastern" become necessary, the errors which have made her failure conspicuous will be avoided. It is evident if Mr. Brunel, in building that vessel, could have adopted the principle of the compound engine, her fate might have been different. Instead of being under the necessity of putting the great ship up to auction after a by no means brilliant career, the share-holders might be enjoying the profits which are to be reaped in ocean transport. The danger is that in the race for the possession of huge floating palaces the steamship companies may outrun the wants of travelers. If the ocean fleets of the future are to be composed of such vessels, an enormous increase of the traveling public will be essential to the continued prosperity of the industry. Any improvement in the facilities with which a transatlantic voyage can be made is sure to bring its own reward. The time when ocean travel was attended with misgivings, or was a luxury reserved for men of wealth and leisure, has passed. With the appearance of ships that will traverse the Atlantic in less than a week, a holiday trip to Europe may be as cheap as restorative. The president of the Scotch Engineers' and Ship-builders' Society recently declared that in a few years "we shall have steamships starting from each side of the Atlantic every morning, noon, and night, and arriving on the opposite shores with as much regularity as our present express railway trains arrive at the termination of a journey of four or five hundred miles."

In passenger accommodations the ships of the Inman Line are superior to most Clyde-built ships, and their design shows an inclination to break from the restrictive and uninventive habit which is said to hamper the British ship-builder. "Give an English carpenter a certain space in an unfinished ship, and tell him to fit it up as, for instance, a chart-room," a gentleman connected with one of the lines recently said, "and he will repeat exactly what he did in fitting up the previous ships, without stopping a moment to consider if some change is not desirable and possible. An American carpenter, on the contrary," this critic, who was an Englishman, continued, "will rack his brains for improvements, and the ship he fits up to-day is sure to be more comfortable than the one he fitted up yesterday."

The following vessels have been bought and built or have passed through the Inman Company's hands since its establishment in 1850:

NAME.	Built.	Length.	Breadth.	Depth.	TONNAGE. Gross.	TONNAGE. Net.	NAME.	Built.	Length.	Breadth.	Depth.	TONNAGE. Gross.	TONNAGE. Net.
City of Rome*	1881	586	52	37	8415	...	City of Boston	1864	313	39	26	2213	1649
City of Berlin	1874	489	45	36	5491	2957	Ætna‡	...	309	37	27	2190	1564
City of Richmond	1873	450	44	35	4607	2824	City of Dublin§	...	318	36	26	1999	1548
City of Chester	1873	444	44	35	4566	2713	Edinburgh‖	...	300	40	25	2197	1494
City of Montreal	1872	419	44	34	4489	2939	City of Philadelphia¶	1854	294	39	26	2168	1648
City of Brussels	1869	390	41	35	3775	2434	Glasgow	...	262	36	25	1962	1152
City of New York (enlarged)	...	...	...	...	...	...	Vigo**	...	270	35	25	1953	1250
City of Paris	1865	375	40	33	3499	2380	City of Manchester††	1851	262	36	25	1906	1296
City of London	1866	398	41	26	3081	1975	Kangaroo‖	...	257	36	27	1719	1169
City of Brooklyn	1863	374	41	26	2765	1880	City of Glasgow¶	1850	227	33	25	1609	1087
City of Washington	1869	354	43	27	2911	1980	Nemesis	...	353	42	28	2717	1587
City of Bristol	1853	358	40	26	2870	1951	City of Cork††	...	265	33	26	1547	1082
City of Antwerp	1860	349	38	27	2655	1805	City of Halifax§	...	204	30	18	770	523
City of Limerick	1867	332	39	26	2991	1626	City of Durham§	1865	201	29	17	697	588
City of New York	1863	331	34	30	2536	1724	Bosphorus	1856	174	24	15	448	383
City of Baltimore†	1865	326	40	28	2360	1679	Hercules	1856	122	23	10	211	174
	1854	326	39	26	2472	1774	Ajax	1856	108	23	9	163	138

* Returned to the builders as not fulfilling the contract, and since transferred to the Anchor Line, October, 1882.
† Sold March, 1874, and now running between Liverpool and Bombay.
‡ Purchased from Cunard Company.   § Sold 1872.   ‖ Sold 1869.
¶ Lost 1854.   ** Sold 1861.   †† Sold 1871.

The present fleet of the transatlantic steamers of the Inman Line are:

NAME.	Built.	Gross Tons.	NAME.	Built.	Gross Tons.
City of Berlin	1874	5491	City of Montreal	1872	4490
City of Richmond	1873	4607	City of Brussels	1869	3775
City of Chester	1873	4566	City of New York	1865	3500
City of Paris	1865	3091	City of Rome	1881	8415

1851.—THE MESSAGERIES MARITIMES.—Much the largest maritime undertaking engaged in the trade of the Mediterranean and elsewhere is that of the Messageries Maritimes, formerly the Messageries Imperiales, monopolizing, as it does, nearly the whole of the steam tonnage of France. Indeed, apart from the vessels owned by this company, and one or two highly subsidized, the French may be said to have no steamers. In 1873 the whole steam tonnage of France amounted to one hundred and eighty-five thousand one hundred and sixty-five tons net register, and in 1875 the gross tonnage of the fleet of Messageries Maritimes was one hundred and twenty-four thousand nine hundred and seventy-six tons. The Messageries Maritimes is a pure creation of the government, raised with the greatest care from its infancy, and maintained by large grants from the public purse. Previously to 1851 the company had been chiefly engaged as carriers by land, and was under contract for the conveyance of the mails throughout a considerable portion of France. In July, 1851, the company entered upon its first over-sea contract for the conveyance of the French mails to Italy, the Levant, Greece, Egypt, and Syria, and in 1852 added to their service the principal ports of Greece and Salonica.

In 1854 the managers contracted for the transport of all troops and military stores between France and Algeria, besides the conveyance of the mails, and having increased their fleet to meet the requirements of the Crimean campaign, were in 1855 enabled to open between Marseilles, Civita Vecchia, and Naples a direct weekly line of steamers, independently of the postal service. After the close of the Crimean war, in 1856, the directors employed their disposable vessels in increasing the frequency of services to Algeria, and in establishing a postal service between Marseilles and the ports of the Danube and along the east coast of the Black Sea. In 1857 they entered into arrangements for the conveyance of the French mails between Bordeaux, the Brazils, and the La Plata. At that time the fleet of the company had reached fifty-four ships of eighty thousand eight hundred and seventy-five tons and fifteen thousand two hundred and forty horse-power, and they obtained from their government in 1861 a contract for the conveyance of the French mails to India and China. In 1871 their fleet, measuring one hundred and thirty-seven thousand three hundred and thirty-four tons, of twenty thousand eight hundred and eighty-five horse-power, performed service on the India and China routes of two hundred and thirty thousand one hundred and thirty-five French leagues; on the Mediterranean and Black Seas, one hundred and fifty-three thousand four hundred and seventy-eight; and on the Brazilian, fifty thousand and four. In all, four hundred and twenty-three thousand six hundred and seven leagues annually, independently of various extra services. Since then their Brazilian and La Plata lines have been doubled. At the first their vessels were built in England, but the company now possesses large establishments of its own, where they construct screw steamers of iron of the largest size. The ships of the Messageries Maritimes, like those of their great competitors for the trade of the East, the Peninsular and Oriental Company, now pass through the Suez Canal.[1]

*1855.—*THE HAMBURG-AMERICAN PACKET COMPANY.—The Hamburg-American Packet Company, which has now a weekly service between New York and Hamburg, touching at Havre on the western trips and at Plymouth and Cherbourg on the eastern, was established in 1847 at Hamburg, its first vessels being first-class sailing-ships. Mr. Adolf Godeffroy, of Hamburg, elected president of the company at its formation, still retains that responsible position. Its ships, which were built expressly for its service, had excellent cabin accommodations, and quarters in the steerage for emigrants even superior to anything that had previously been offered to that class, and the new line met a want that had for some time existed, supplying direct and first-class accommodation for travelers between Germany and the United States. The first two vessels were the "Deutschland" and the "Nordamerica," which came to New York first in 1848, and were followed in succession by the "Elbe," "Rhein," "Oder," "Donau," "Alair," "Weser," and "Neckar;" and while sailing-ships were the best means of transport between the two countries, the vessels of this line were not surpassed by any others until by the famous American lines of sailing-ships between New York and Liverpool.

The introduction of lines of screw steamers, however, between Liverpool and New York, and their keen competition for the German and French emigrants, convinced the directors that if this line desired to retain its supremacy it must avail itself of the most approved method of transport, and, foreseeing that steam must inevitably supersede canvas as a method of propulsion for sea-going vessels, measures were taken to increase the capital of the company, and Caird & Co., of Greenock, Scotland, were ordered to build two screw steamships. The result of this order was the launching in 1855 of the "Hammonia" and the "Borussia." Just then, however, there was an active demand for transports sailing under a neutral flag, and the company chartered its two new steamers to the allied French and English governments, and they were sent to the Crimea. Their charters expired in the spring of 1856, and on the 1st of June in that year the "Borussia" left Hamburg for New York, arriving here on the 16th of June, she being really the pioneer of the present line, for the old sailing-packets were soon all replaced by steamers. The "Hammonia" left Hamburg on the 1st of July, and from that time a monthly steam service was maintained. The new ships were fine vessels, ably com-

---

[1] The English Peninsular and Oriental Company, in 1875, for a service of 1,171,092 miles, received £430,000, while the Messageries Maritimes, for a service of 631,514 miles, or little more than half as much, received £399,838. It will be perceived that both were pretty heavily subsidized.

manded and officered. Close attention was given by the company's agents on either side of the water to the proper working of the steward's department, and the line became a favorite from the start. The management of the company was already popular in connection with the sailing-vessels, and their adoption of a steam line in its stead was the cause of much gratification to those who had friends in Germany desiring to come to this country.

The Hamburg Company met with sufficient encouragement to induce them to double their steamers and increase the service from a monthly to a semi-monthly one, and in 1856 the "Bavaria" and the "Teutonia" were added to the fleet. They were built at Greenock, and were 2273 and 2034 tons measurement respectively. Next year was a year of panic and great commercial depression, and the new enterprise of the Hamburg Company had to bear its share of the general disaster; nevertheless, in this year another new steamer was added, the "Saxonia," of 2404 tons. All the old sailing-ships were now sold off as fast as practicable, and the line became a steam line solely.

Although their steamers were as fast as any afloat and were noted for their excellence as sea-boats, the aim of the management was to secure regularity of passage and perfect safety rather than great speed. No racing passages were, therefore, ever allowed.

In 1861 the service was again increased, a steamer being dispatched from New York every Saturday. This change had been contemplated for some time, but was hastened by the charter of the Vanderbilt steamers to the United States government, and the United States mails were given to the Hamburg Company in addition to the direct German mail, which it had carried from the first. This extra service necessitated the addition of more steamers, and in 1863 the "Germania" was built by the Messrs. Caird & Co., at Greenock, followed the next year by the "Allemannia," built by Messrs. Day & Co. at Southampton.

In 1867 the first steamer "Hammonia" was sold, and her name changed to the "Belgian," and the Hamburg Company built a new steamer "Hammonia" at Greenock. This steamer was 300 feet long, 40 feet beam, and 33 feet deep, and registered 2967 tons. The "Cimbria," of about the same size, was also built in 1867. Next year the "Holsatia" and "Westphalia" were built, being larger vessels than either of the previous steamers, the "Holsatia" being 3134 and the "Westphalia" 3500 tons. In 1869 the "Silesia," of 3156 tons, was added, and in 1870 the "Thuringia" was launched at Greenock.

The older steamers were now withdrawn from the New York Line, and a new line was established by this company between Hamburg and New Orleans, and an attempt made to maintain a service from Hamburg to the West Indies and Aspinwall. Here it came into keen competition with the North German Lloyd, and as there was not sufficient business for both, the two companies finally agreed that the North

German Lloyd should have the New Orleans Line; and the Hamburg Line kept the West India service, with Aspinwall as the final port of destination.

The Franco-German War, in 1870, caused an interruption of the Hamburg Company's service for three months, after which the weekly service to New York was resumed. In 1872 the "Frisia" was built at Greenock. In 1873 the "Pomerania" was added from the same builders, and in 1874 the "Suevia." This, the last steamer built by the Hamburg Line, is the largest. She is 360 feet long, 41 feet beam, and 26 feet deep, and registers 3624 tons. Like all the other boats, she is brig-rigged and is propelled by two compound inverted direct-acting engines fitted with surface condensers. Her cylinders are 48 and 80 inches respectively in diameter, with 5 feet stroke of piston. She is divided into compartments by seven water-tight bulkheads, and is a first-class vessel, having no superior in the ocean service. Below, her arrangements for passengers are on the most liberal scale, her rooms for cabin passengers being of extra size and well ventilated, while the quarters for steerage passengers are convenient and commodious. Her great power and fine model insured a regularity and rapidity of passage which has never been interrupted.

The years which immediately followed the building of this steamer were years of reverse to the Hamburg Company. The panic of 1873 in this country had checked emigration, and in addition to this the establishment of the Eagle Line between New York and Hamburg caused a competition which was ruinous. With the decrease in the number of passengers came, of course, a surplus of freight-room, and freights from all European ports fell greatly in consequence. All these causes were felt so severely by the Hamburg-American Packet Company that in 1875, for its own salvation, it was obliged to buy up the floating property of the Eagle Line, which forthwith went into liquidation. By this operation the steamers "Herder," "Lessing," "Gellert," and "Wieland" were added to the New York Line. These were all very fine steamers, built at Glasgow expressly for the Eagle Line, and would have been a great acquisition to the Hamburg Line if they had not been too much in the nature of too much of a good thing. They were about 3500 tons each; the "Herder" was built in 1873; the "Lessing" and "Wieland" in 1874; and the "Gellert" in 1875. Still, although the company was saddled with a surplus of steamers, the vexatious opposition was removed, and the New York service again became profitable. The threatened war between Russia and England in 1878 enabled the Hamburg Company to dispose of some of its surplus steamers, and the "Holsatia," "Hammonia," and "Thuringia" were sold to the Russian government.

The fleet of the Hamburg-American Packet Company in 1882 consists of twenty-four ocean steamships,—viz., "Albingia," "Allemannia," "Bavaria," "Bohemia," "Borussia," "Cimbria," "Cyclop," "Frisia," "Gellert," "Hammonia," "Herder," "Holsatia," "Lessing," "Lotharingia," "Rhenania," "Rugia," "Saxonia," "Silesia," "Suevia," "Teutonia," "Thuringia," "Vandalia," "Westphalia," "Wieland,"—besides a number of smaller steamers employed as feeders for the West India Line and elsewhere, and a large number of river passenger steamers, tugboats, lighters, floating steam-winches, steam-sloops, etc., which are necessary accessories to so large a service.

1856.—THE ANCHOR LINE.—Some fifty years ago four small Scotch boys started from the Clyde in little smacks, then served consecutively in schooners, brigs, barks, ships, and steamers, until conversant with every detail connected with all these types of vessels; with knowledge acquired and sterling integrity, and practicing economy, they grew up to manhood, and saw attempts made to establish steam traffic between Glasgow and the Western Continent, and as often saw them fail. In due time they banded together, and these little Scotch boys became the well-known firm of "Handyside & Henderson," of Glasgow, the originators of the "Anchor Line." Their first efforts were in small sailing-vessels in the Mediterranean fruit trade, and they finally purchased the steamer "Inez de Castro" and another small craft. They then altered the ship "John Bell" into an auxiliary steamer, and another sailing-ship, the "Tempest," in the same manner, and with these two vessels inaugurated the *Anchor Line.* The story of the "Tempest," the pioneer of this line, is soon told: "*The good die young.*" She was lost on her second return trip.

The Anchor Line came into existence, with these two converted vessels, in 1856, and as early as 1872 seventeen steamships had been constructed for its service between New York and Glasgow, besides thirty steamships for its service in the Mediterranean. At the present time (1882) steamships of the line, carrying the United States mail, sail from New York every Saturday, calling at Londonderry on the voyage to Glasgow, and from Glasgow every Thursday, also from London every Saturday, sailing the same day of the week from New York for London. There is also a branch of this line sailing between Barrow-in-Furness (touching at Dublin) and New York about once a fortnight. For several years the company applied its energies in developing the Peninsular and Mediterranean branch of their service. Steamships of this line sail from Glasgow every fourteen days for Lisbon, Gibraltar, Genoa, Leghorn, Naples, Messina, and Palermo. In 1863 they determined to vigorously prosecute the Glasgow and New York trade, and built the "Caledonia" and the "Britannia." In 1868–70 serious disasters befell the company, and in a few months they chronicled the losses of the "Hibernia," "United Kingdom," and "Cambria."

On the arrival of the "Iowa" at New York, June 29, 1867, the dwarfs, Tom Thumb and wife and Commodore Nutt and wife, who were passengers, united in a letter of thanks for the care and attention they had received.

The company flag which gives name to the line is a white burgee, on which is borne a red anchor horizontally.

On the 14th of August, 1872, the owners and agents of the Anchor Line signalized the advent of their latest and at that time best steamer, the "California," an iron screw steamship of 3208 gross tons, 361.5 feet length, 40.5 feet beam, and a working horse-power of 1047, by an excursion to Long Branch. The company numbered four hundred, and after an absence of eight hours returned to New York City. The band of the Seventh Regiment and two bagpipers in Highland costume entertained the company, and the whole four hundred guests were at *one time* seated at tables spread between decks, provided with every delicacy that the markets of the Old and the New World afforded.

A passenger describing the "California" says, "The grand saloon, forty-five feet long by forty wide, is finished in a scale of magnificence which is carried out in every part of the floating palace. The paneling is of polished oak, interlaid with rich dog- and white-wood, adorned with rich carving and gold. The smoking-saloon is luxuriously fitted, and painted in a tint of sea-green, and silver-plated chandeliers drop from the ceiling. Each state-room has its electric bell. Two large bath-rooms are on each side of the vessel. The ladies' boudoir is decorated in sea-green tints, dotted and striped in gold, with delicate birds perched in the centre of each broad panel. She has accommodations for one hundred and fifty first-class and nine hundred steerage passengers."

The present fleet of the Anchor Line is as follows; the names of the vessels, with few exceptions, end in "*ia*":

TRANSATLANTIC, PENINSULAR, MEDITERRANEAN, AND ORIENTAL STEAMSHIPS OF THE ANCHOR LINE IN 1882.[1]

Name.	Service.	Built.	Registered Tonnage.	Name.	Service.	Built.	Registered Tonnage.
Acadia	Med. and Or.	1866	1081	Ethiopia	Transatlantic	1873	4004
Alexandria	"	1870	1629	Furnessia	"	1881	5496
Alsatia	"	1876	3000	Galatia	Med. and Or.	..	3125
Anchoria	Transatlantic	1875	4176	Hesperia	"	..	3125
Armenia	Med. and Or.	..	3380	Hispania	"	..	3380
Assyria	"	1871	1623	India	"	1869	2299
Australia	"	1870	2243	Ischia	"	..	3125
Belgravia	"	..	5000	Italia	"	1872	2245
Britannia	"	1863	2200	Justitia	"	..	3125
Bolivia	Transatlantic	1873	4050	Macedonia	"	..	2272
Caledonia	Med. and Or.	1872	2125	Olympia	"	1872	2060
California	"	1872	3287	Roumania	"	..	3500
Castalia	"	1873	2200	Scandinavia	"	1865	1135
Circassia	Transatlantic	..	4200	Scotia	"	1866	1108
City of Rome	"	..	..	Sidonian	"	1870	1285
Columbia	Med. and Or.	1867	2000	Trinacria	"	1871	2107
Devonia	Transatlantic	..	4200	Tyrian	"	1869	1088
Dorion	Med. and Or.	1868	1038	Utopia	"	1873	2731
Elysia	"	1873	2733	Victoria	"	1872	3242

[1] The date of building is given when known. Those whose date of building is not given have been built since 1873.

To obviate the risk of collision, lessen the dangers of navigation, and insure fine weather, the owners of the Anchor Line have adopted Maury's system of separate steam lane routes for their Atlantic steamships, whereby the most southerly route practicable is regularly maintained throughout all seasons of the year.

The "Furnessia," the latest addition to the fleet, the "City of Rome" excepted, was built at Barrow-in-Furness, Lancashire, England, and was, when launched, the largest vessel ever built in England save the "Great Eastern." She has since been surpassed by the "City of Rome," "Servia," etc. Her dimensions are: Length, 445 feet; beam, 44 feet 6 inches; depth of hold, 34 feet 6 inches; her registered tonnage is 5496; gross tonnage, 6500 tons; and her displacement when drawing twenty-six feet of water, 9900 tons. She is brig-rigged, and has two funnels. Her engines are 3500 horse-power. The diameter of the propeller is 20 feet 6 inches. The engines, fitted with Rogers's patent exhauster, have special fire-engines and emergency pumps for pumping in case of collision or accident. She has steam steering-gear, winches, cranes, etc., and her hull is divided into nine water-tight compartments.

The promenade-deck, which stretches from nearly amidships to the stern of the steamer, is surmounted by a deck-house, of which one-half is utilized as a comfortable smoking-room. Opposite the entrance to the smoking-room is a staircase which descends to the music- or drawing-room on the spar-deck. The walls of this music-room are lined with panels of walnut and satin-wood. The seats around the apartment are upholstered in brown morocco, and around the staircase leading to the main-deck are ornamental boxes filled with exotic plants. It is also furnished with a Broadwood piano, a Mason & Hamlin organ, and a well-stocked library. A broad, airy corridor, lighted and ventilated by skylights at frequent intervals, leads from the music-room aft, on either side of which are state-rooms elegantly and comfortably fitted up, having two berths and a sofa in each. Descending from the music-room by a broad staircase, the dining-saloon is reached. The port-holes of this saloon are hid by window-frames with stained glass, and the carpets, curtains, and other accessories display the taste and elegance which are everywhere evinced.

The dining-saloon is heated by steam, furnished from two Baltimore heaters fitted into white marble mantels. A corridor, similar to that on the spar-deck, stretches from the main saloon aft, giving access on both sides to state-rooms, which are each fitted for the accommodation of four persons. There are two state-cabins furnished with special magnificence, which, in place of the ordinary berths elsewhere provided, are supplied with Parisian electro-plated bedsteads.

1857.—THE NORTH GERMAN LLOYD STEAMSHIP COMPANY was founded by a number of enterprising business men of the ancient and wealthy city of Bremen, a city belonging to the so-called Hansa-Bund, or commercial confederation of German free cities, whose merchants in the thirteenth century sent their ships out over the German Ocean and up the Baltic, and gave the first incentive to the trade of northern Europe, which they controlled for centuries. True to the traditions of their forefathers, the inaugurators of this new line of communication with the Western Hemisphere determined to offer to the public in place of the slow and uncertain sailing-vessels, by which all living and dead freight had been forwarded from the port of Bremen, a quick, safe, and commodious fleet of steamers.

The founders of the line were sensible that, in order to succeed in the new undertaking, it would be necessary to conduct the management with a jealous regard for the comfort, safety, and well-being of the passengers. They had to contend with the prejudice of many who were unable to comprehend the grand revolution in ocean transportation taking place, and who would not intrust their lives or goods on these new-fangled arrangements driven by steam and moved by complicated machinery, liable, as they believed, to continual derangement. Founded on the maxim that that company serves its own interest best that serves the public best, the line, in spite of the opposition of early years and the eager competition of later days, grew and prospered. Up to December, 1878, the steamers of this company had made two thousand five hundred and fourteen voyages across the Atlantic, and carried more than six hundred and eighty thousand persons over the ocean. Of this number more than one hundred and eight thousand were cabin passengers, all of whom were conducted safely and well over its stormy sea. This is a record few steamship lines can equal, and that hardly any can excel.

The transatlantic steamers of this line, thirty in number, except four built on the Humber, were all built on the Clyde. They are iron screw steamers with flush decks, built according to the English Lloyd rule. Their length on an average is 360 feet; breadth of beam, 40 feet; and depth, 32 feet, the length being about nine times the breadth. Tonnage, about 3500 tons. They are provided with iron decks, and seven water-tight compartments. Their draught without cargo is 17 feet, and with cargo 21 feet. They are brig-rigged, spreading 14,000 square feet of sail, carry ten iron life-boats, 28 feet long, and the other usual appliances for saving life. The engines of nearly all of these ships are of the compound type. The screws are of iron, with four blades about 15 feet in diameter, and with a pitch of about 24 feet. The large steamers have twelve main boilers, with two furnaces and one auxiliary, and the average speed of the mail steamers,—viz., "Neckar," "Oder," "Mosel," "Rhein," "Main," "Donau," "Weser," and "America,"—plying between Bremen and New York, is stated as fourteen and one-half knots per hour.

A new steamer, called the "Elbe," has been built on the Clyde and placed on the line between Bremen, Southampton, and New York.

The "Elbe" is of 5000 tons measurement, and her dimensions are 420 feet in length by 45 feet breadth of beam, and 40 feet depth of hold. She is provided with seven water-tight compartments, and fitted with four masts, the fore- and mainmasts square-rigged, and the two mizzen-masts schooner-rigged. The upper-deck fore and aft is covered over. She has a hurricane-deck amidships 180 feet long, as a promenade-deck for first-cabin passengers, on which the ladies' cabin is placed near the mainmast.

The "Elbe" has the most approved steam steering-gear, operated from the wheel-house, which is placed under the bridge and at the forward end of the hurricane-deck.

Her engines are of 6000 horse-power, indicated, and consist of three cylinders, the high-pressure of 60 inches diameter, and the two low-pressure of 85 inches diameter each, and guaranteed to obtain a speed of sixteen knots an hour. The crew is 160 all told.

The "Mosel," from Southampton for New York, went on shore near the Lizard in a thick fog and calm, August 9, 1882, and became a total loss, breaking up about September 4. Her six or seven hundred passengers and the mails were landed by the steamer "Rosetta," of Falmouth. Her dimensions were: Length, 365 feet; beam, 40 feet; depth of hold, 35 feet. Her gross tonnage was 3500, and her bunkers carried 1000 tons of coal. She was full brig-rigged, had eight metallic life-boats and two gigs, and her decks were of East India teak. Her original machinery was powerful and fine, consisting of inverted direct-acting engines of 800 horse-power, nominal, with the capacity of working up to 2500. She had two cylinders, 72 inches in diameter, with 5 feet stroke. The boilers were six in number, with four furnaces to each. The "Mosel" was finely furnished throughout, and could accommodate 90 first-class, 126 second-class, and 680 steerage passengers, and she cost a little over $500,000. She was valued at $425,000. In September, 1881, she was repaired and refitted at an expense of $125,000. Her hurricane-decks and turtle-backs were renewed, and the second cabin was removed to the main-deck forward. New engines were placed in her, greatly exceeding in power her old ones. In 1875 a memorable crime was committed by a passenger on the "Mosel" while she was lying in Bremerhaven. A case of dynamite was exploded on the wharf, sixty-eight persons being killed and thirty-three severely wounded. The vessel was but little injured. The author of the catastrophe, W. H. Thomassen, who had been a blockade-runner during the American rebellion, but had latterly lived in Germany, was tried and legally put to death.

THE LEYLAND LINE.—This line has a large fleet, all of which, except the Boston steamships, run to Mediterranean ports, for which there are four departures a week. The steamers of this line bear names ending with the letter "n," and have the further peculiarity of being ranged in classes according to the letters with which their names begin, the names of sister ships always beginning with the same letter. Thus, the steamers of the Boston service are always spoken of as the "B's" and the "I's,"—the "Bavarian," the "Batavian," and the "Bohemian," and the "Istrien," the "Illyrien," and the "Iberien."

The "Flavian," repaired in Boston, replaced the "Bohemian," lost, in the Boston service of the company. The disaster which overtook her obliged the giving up temporarily of a projected line to Baltimore. She is different from the regular boats of the line running to Boston, being smaller and shorter than the large four-masters, of lighter draught, and of greater beam in proportion to her length, which is 335 feet. She has only two masts. Her tonnage is about 1400 by measurement. She is finely fitted, and has comfortable quarters for officers and crew. She was built at Jarrow-on-Tyne, a name hardly known this side of the Atlantic, but which has the greatest iron ship-building yard in the world. It employs seven thousand men, and everything is done on the premises. The iron is taken from the company's mines three miles up the river, enters the yard as crude ore, and leaves it a complete steamship. The *coal is mined in the yard*. At Jarrow there are three monster steamers building specially for the Boston service of the Leyland Line, and they will probably begin running in the autumn of 1882. Two are called the "Virginian" and the "Valencian;" the third will have a name beginning with V. The three "V's" will be steamers of 5000 tons and about 500 feet long, much larger than any of the present boats, but resembling them in build.

The steamer "Bohemian" was wrecked in Dunlough Bay, February 6, 1881. She sailed from Boston on January 27, 1881, for Liverpool, and went ashore on the Irish coast during a dreadful storm. Thirty-two of those on board were drowned, and twenty-one of the crew, including the second officer, were saved. Another survivor was seen on a rock, separated from the mainland, but all efforts to rescue him failed. Two life-boats were capsized in the attempt.

The "Bohemian" was fifteen years old, and had been on the Leyland Line five years.

1862.—THE COMPAGNIE GÉNÉRALE TRANSATLANTIQUE.—This company, established in 1862, maintains a regular line between Havre and New York. It receives a subsidy from the French government for its West India and New York and Havre lines; other independent services are not subsidized. In 1880 a contract was entered into between the company and the French government for its line between Marseilles, Algerian, and Tunisian ports, and a small subsidy granted.

The company has lately added to its lines a new weekly line from Marseilles to Genoa, Leghorn, Naples, Messina, Syracuse, Malta, etc.

HISTORY OF STEAM NAVIGATION. 369

The following table shows the *fleet* of the company, 1881:

FOR THE ATLANTIC.

	Tonnage.	Horse-power.		Tonnage.	Horse-power.
Amérique	4500	900	Salvador	900	250
France	4500	900	Saint-Domingue	800	250
Labrador	4500	900	Venezuela	800	250
Canada	4500	900	Alice	800	100
Saint-Germain	3650	850	Caravelle	700	250
Péreire	3300	900	Colomba	600	200
Saint-Laurent	3400	900	Caraïbe	600	125
Ville de Paris	3300	900			
Lafayette	3400	800	TUG.		
Washington	3400	800	Belle Isle	150	100
Olinde-Rodrigues	3000	660			
Saint-Simon	3000	660	TRANSPORT STEAMERS.		
Ferdinand de Lesseps	3000	660	Bixio	2280	250
Ville de Marseille	3000	660	Flachat	2280	250
Ville de Bordeaux	2600	660	Le Chatelier	2227	250
Ville de Brest	2600	660	Fournel	2000	250
Ville de Saint-Nazaire	2600	660	Clapeyron	1760	180
			Provincia	1700	180
Colombie	2800	660	Martinique	1600	200
Caldera	2800	660	Picardie	1500	200

FOR THE MEDITERRANEAN.

	Tonnage.	Horse-power.		Tonnage.	Horse-power.
Moïse	1800	450	Mohammed-el-Sadeck	800	250
Saint-Augustin	1800	450	Malvina	800	250
Isaac Péreire	1800	450	Manoubia	600	200
Abd-el-Kader	1800	450	Ville de Tanger	600	200
Charles-Quint	1800	450	Dragut	500	150
Ville de Madrid	1800	450	Mustapha-ben-Ismail	500	150
Ville de Barcelone	1800	450	La Valette	500	150
Kléber	1800	450	Insulaire	400	150
Ville d'Oran	1800	450			
Ville de Bone	1800	450	RESERVES.		
Afrique	800	250	Guadeloupe	1600	400
Ajaccio	800	250	Désirade	1400	400
Bastia	800	250			
Corse	800	250	SHIPS BUILDING.		
Immaculée-Conception	800	250	Ville de Rome	1800	450
Lou-Cettori	800	250	Ville de Naples	1800	450
Maréchal Canrobert	800	250	Ville de New York	..	..

The "Ville de New York," now building at Barrow-in-Furness for the company, is to be the largest steamship that has entered the port of Havre. According to the plans, her length between perpendiculars will be 460 feet; depth of hold, from bottom of keel to spardeck, 37 feet 6 inches. Her beam is to be proportioned with her draught, which cannot exceed 23 feet in depth on account of the bar or entrance on the river Seine, and its breadth is to be fifty feet. In her length she is to be divided into ten water-tight compartments, two of which will be occupied by the boilers, which can be separated in case of emergency. One-half of the boiler-power can be used without stopping the vessel, and will give a speed of almost eleven knots. A water-tight bottom, which is to extend her whole length, can also be used for ballasting the vessel and giving her uniform draught, and a system of pumps worked by steam will insure her speedy and adequate drainage. The "Ville de New York" will have four masts and two smoke-stacks. She will have all the latest improvements and most recently devised accommodations.

There are to be four decks and a promenade-deck extending alongside on top of the main-deck, and supported forward by stanchions. This one will be entirely reserved for the first- and second-class passengers. No sailors will be permitted on it, as all their work will be done on the deck below, which is also to be used by the third-class passengers. Forward and aft on the promenade-deck there are to be two turrets, which will contain the signal-fire and the double foot-bridge for the officers on watch. The pilot-house, which is to be fitted with steam stearing-gear, and the captain's house will be located here too. The arrangements for the crew will be such that every department will do its work without interfering with the passengers. The officers' rooms will be situated forward under cover, so as to be convenient to the bridge, where they have to be on watch, and the engineers' berths are to be arranged around the engine-room, so that they may not be obliged to go on deck.

The first-class passengers' saloon and cabins will be in the centre of the vessel, forward of the machinery, where the pitching is felt least. Twenty-four of the cabins will contain single berths, and have skylights for admitting air in all weathers. All will be lighted by means of electricity. The second-class passengers are to be located aft of the machinery, and third-class at the end of the first-class cabins, between decks. Splendidly furnished dining-rooms, saloons, and reading-rooms will form one of the vessel's attractions, and there will be a system of baths and all arrangements likely to contribute to comfort.

The machinery will be compound, with cylinders set one above the other. Each of the three compound engines will have its own crankshaft and condenser. The air and circulating pumps will be independent. The six cylinders will have a stroke of 5 feet 7 inches. The diameter of high-pressure cylinders will be $35\frac{1}{4}$ inches, and that of the low-pressure cylinders 75 inches. The whole condensing surface will be 10,300 feet, and every one of the circulating pumps will be able to supply at full speed 250 gallons of water per second.

The boilers supplying the steam to the main engine will have in all 36 furnaces, with a fire surface of 21,600 square feet; besides, there will be a large donkey boiler, with two furnaces having 550 square feet of fire surface, for supplying steam to the hoisting engines, donkey-pumps, and other steam apparatus. The main boilers will carry a steam-pressure of 90 pounds per square inch, and the power of the engines, it is claimed, can be estimated at 7000 horse-power on trial, giving a speed of 16½ knots.

1863.—THE NATIONAL STEAMSHIP COMPANY.—The year in which this line, between Boston, New York, and Liverpool, was started was a most unpromising one for the inauguration of such a commercial enterprise, as it was the year in which commercial men in the Northern States were distracted with apprehensions for the future of the Union, and when trade, except in war material, was practically at a stand-still. Such was the period, however, chosen by a little knot of far-seeing commercial men in Liverpool for commencing the operations of the National Steamship Company. They have been more than justified by the result, and their success is at once a testimony to their pluck and commercial foresight.

The National Steamship Company was the first and for some years the only steamship company trading across the Atlantic between Liverpool and the United States established upon the principle of a limited activity, that is, to maintain the reputation of its steamers for safety and such expedition on the voyage as is consistent with safe navigation. And as an additional guarantee for safety, the company takes upon itself the entire insurance of each of its steamers, and a considerable sum per annum is distributed between the captain and officers of each steamer, as a bonus, provided that their vessel is navigated free of accident. The efficacy of these regulations is proved by the fact that, although the National Line has carried nearly 650,000 passengers, not a single passenger has been lost from accident of the seas, and though it was started with a capital of £700,000, in one of its recent years its gross earnings exceeded that amount, and it has not only paid good dividends during the years of its existence, but has accumulated an insurance fund of over £200,000, while its property in 1877 was valued at £1,200,000, and must now have increased to more than double the original capital. From the start the directors had to face the fact that it could expect no assistance from mail subsidies, and that it had to compete with formidable rivals. It was necessary, therefore, that it should strike out a line for itself, and it was decided that the line should consist of ships not built for great speed, but capable of carrying large cargoes without interfering with comfortable arrangements for passengers. This was the model adopted, and experience has shown that the policy of the company was a wise one. The result is that to-day the vessels of the National Company are among the largest engaged in the transatlantic traffic.

The company commenced its operations in 1863 with three of the largest vessels then afloat, viz., the iron screw steamships " Louisiana,"

"Virginia," and "Pennsylvania" respectively, of a gross tonnage, one of 3000 and two of 3500 tons each. The following year the fleet was increased to six vessels by the addition of the "Erin" the "Queen," and the "Helvetia," each of a larger tonnage than the pioneer vessels, with which number a weekly service was commenced. After two years' trading this fleet proved insufficient, and two other vessels—the "England," of 4900 tons and 600 horse-power, and the "Denmark," of 3724 tons and 350 horse-power—was added to the line in 1865. In 1868 the "Italy," of 4169 tons and 500 horse-power, built and engined by Messrs. John Elder, of Glasgow, became one of the National liners. It should be mentioned that the "Italy" *was the first Atlantic steamship in which engines upon the compound principle were used.* In 1869 the "Holland," of 3847 tons and 350 horse-power, was added to the line. The company signalized its increasing prosperity in the year 1871 by adding to the line two of the largest steamships then afloat (the "Great Eastern" excepted) in the "Egypt," of 4670 tons, and the "Spain," of 4512 tons. The "Egypt" is 455 feet long and 44 feet beam, and the "Spain" 440 feet long and 43 feet beam. Each of these vessels has frequently made the passage from Queenstown to Sandy Hook in nine days. In 1872 the "Canada," of 4276 tons, and the "Greece," of 4310 tons, were added to the line. At the present time (1882) its fleet consists of the following vessels:

Name.	Built.	H. P.	Tons.	Name.	Built.	H. P.	Tons.
Spain	1871	600	4871	Canada	1872	450	4276
Egypt	1871	600	5089	Greece	1872	450	4310
England	1865	600	4900	France	1866	450	4281
The Queen	1864	450	4471	Holland	1869	350	3847
Helvetia	1864	500	4588	Denmark	1865	350	3724
Erin	1864	500	4577	Italy	1868	500	4341

Comprising twelve of the largest steamers (belonging to one company) in the Atlantic passenger service, capable of accommodating 1200 cabin and 15,000 steerage passengers. With this fleet a weekly service is maintained, one vessel starting from Liverpool every Wednesday and another for New York every Saturday. In addition there is a special weekly service maintained between London and New York, in which six vessels of the company are engaged.

At the outbreak of the Abyssinian campaign the "England" and the "Queen" were chartered by the government as transports, and continued in service until the close of the campaign. They made the shortest run of any of the transports between Liverpool and Bombay, and the "Queen" steamed home from Bombay to Liverpool, by way of the Cape of Good Hope, in forty-nine days, which was claimed as the shortest time ever made by that route.

Four of the company's steamships—the "Egypt," the "Spain," the "England," and the "France"—were engaged in the year 1879 to convey troops to South Africa, and the present year the "Holland," the "France," the "Italy," and the "Greece" were employed to take troops to Egypt. The "Holland" sailed from London on the 1st of August with a portion of the Household cavalry, and by special request of Her Majesty passed inside the Isle of Wight, and she was visited by the Prince and Princess of Wales and their daughters, who boarded her from the Royal yacht "Osborne."

On the 9th the "Greece," commanded by Captain W. Pearce, sailed from Southampton, having had the honor of receiving four royal visits during the day. She had on board 246 horses and about 300 officers and men of the Fifth Dragoon Guards, under the command of Lieutenant-Colonel Pope. The first distinguished visitor to arrive on board the steamer was Prince Edward of Saxe-Weimar, who, with his suite, made a careful inspection of the vessel and the arrangements for the accommodation of the troops, and expressed themselves highly satisfied. Shortly afterwards his Royal Highness the Duke of Cambridge and suite paid a visit to the "Greece," and after a thoroughly official examination of the provision made for the officers, men, and horses, expressed the greatest satisfaction. About three o'clock in the afternoon the Prince and Princess of Wales, accompanied by the three princesses, Louise, Victoria, and Maud, and the two royal middies, Prince Albert Victor and Prince George of Wales (just returned from their two years' cruise round the world), and Miss Knollys, went on board the "Greece," inspecting with much interest every portion of the fine vessel, their examination even extending to the lower decks of the vessel, where the horses are carried. The Princess of Wales was most particular in examining minutely all the fitting and accommodation for the men and horses, and was especially enthusiastic in her commendation of the arrangements of the vessel. Immediately after their departure the royal yacht "Alberta" was sighted, and Her Majesty the queen, arriving from Osborne House, accompanied by the Princess Beatrice, the Duchess of Connaught, and attended by several ladies, was received on board the "Greece" by Admiral Ryder and Captain Brookes. The queen, who evinced the liveliest interest in the fitting out of the transport, was much pleased with her visit, and before Her Majesty left the steamer, several officers who were going on active service in the East were presented to her in the saloon.

The steamships of this line have been constructed by the most celebrated builders in Great Britain, and are of great strength and power and of beautiful model, enabling them to make regular passages in all kinds of weather. They are built entirely of iron and steel (except the merely decorative parts), and divided into water-tight and fire-proof compartments, with steam pumping, hoisting, and steering-gear, and provided with fire-extinguishers, improved sounding apparatus, and generally found throughout in everything calculated to add to their safety, and to the comfort and convenience of passengers, heretofore unattained at sea.

The saloons are some of them one hundred and fifty feet in length, and are particularly well lighted and ventilated. The state-rooms, all on the main-deck, are exceptionally large, light, and airy, and are furnished throughout with every requisite to make the ocean passage a comfortable and easy one. Pianos, ladies' saloons, both on deck and below, gentlemen's smoking-room, and ladies' and gentlemen's bathrooms, are provided. The *cuisine* is of the very highest order.

Special attention has been given in the construction of the steamers to provide for the comfort of steerage passengers, the accommodation being unsurpassed for airiness and room, light, good ventilation, and general arrangements.

The steamers have covered-in decks over their whole length, allowing passengers in good weather an unobstructed length of promenade, and affording in bad weather a complete protection from wet and exposure, while allowing spacious room for exercise. The deck space is over four hundred feet in length, and from forty-two to forty-five feet wide.

The sleeping apartments are well lighted, warmed, and comfortable, the height between decks being greater than in most steamers. Married couples, with their young children, are berthed by themselves; single men and women in separate rooms, apart from each other. During the day all can associate together and mess at the same table. Stewardesses are in attendance on women and children. Medicine and medical attendance free to every passenger.

From the beginning of its operations it has been the settled practice of the company to make the safety of the passengers its first consideration, and the speed of the passage the second. It is the uniform practice of the managers to require from each captain a sailing chart, showing his course out and home, the instructions being that he is never to go higher than a certain line of latitude with the idea of getting a shorter sailing line. These charts are regularly examined and filed. The articles in the Company's Book of Instructions on these matters are as follows: "During the ice months, that is to say, from the 1st of February until the 31st of August, inclusive, the commanders will shape their courses so far south as will in their judgments avoid danger from field icebergs. Between the above dates they are not to cross the region of the banks higher than 43° north latitude on the outward passages (easterly), and not higher than 42° north latitude on the homeward (westerly) passages. From the 1st of September until the 31st of January, inclusive, the banks are to be crossed at a safe distance south of the Virgin Rocks.

HISTORY OF STEAM NAVIGATION. 375

"The commanders, while using every diligence to secure a speedy voyage, are prohibited from running any risk whatever that might result in accident to their ships. They must ever bear in mind that the safety of the ships and the lives and property on board is to be the ruling principle that shall govern them in the navigation of their ships, and no supposed gain in expedition or saving of time on the voyage is to be purchased at the risk of accidents. The company desires to establish and maintain the reputation of the steamers for safety, and expect such expedition on their voyage as is consistent with safe navigation."

From the soundness of the positions it has taken and the policy it has pursued, it is not too much to prophesy from its past an equally prosperous future.

1866.—THE WILLIAMS & GUION LINE.—This line was established in August, 1866. It was originally the Black Star Line of packet-ships, which were run from Liverpool to New York for twenty-four years, carrying some sixty thousand passengers yearly, and never losing a ship or a life by accident. From 1866, when the steamship line was established, to 1873 the line run six steamers, each making eight round trips per year, carrying, on an average, six hundred passengers to New York and one hundred from New York each trip, making seven hundred passengers per round trip, or a total per year of thirty-three thousand six hundred, and a grand total of passengers, between 1866 and 1873, of fully two hundred and fifty thousand. In January, 1868, the "Chicago," of this line, ran ashore near Queenstown and became a total wreck, all hands being saved. Since then the "Colorado" was run into in the Mersey, and six passengers jumped overboard and were drowned. All the others were saved.

In August, 1866, the iron screw steamer "Manhattan" sailed from Liverpool for New York, being the pioneer of the company's new fleet. The "Minnesota," "Nebraska," "Colorado," "Idaho," "Nevada," "Wisconsin," and "Wyoming," named for the States and Territories of the Union, each of about three thousand tons, and built of iron specially for the line, followed in rapid succession. In 1873 the "Montana," of three thousand five hundred tons, was added, and in 1874 the "Dakota," a sister ship. The incorporate name of the company is the "Liverpool and Great Western Steamship Company," but it is best known as the "Guion Line."

The "Alaska," the latest addition to the Guion Line, arrived in New York on her first trip after a prolonged and stormy passage, having left Queenstown Tuesday, November 1, during a severe storm, which during the night turned into a complete hurricane. The steam steering-gear gave way, as also did the hand-gear, which compelled a stop for ten hours to repair the damage. The next day a small steam-pipe broke, which filled the engine-room with steam and obliged the engineers to leave their posts and put out the fires. It was only a water-pipe used to lessen the noise of escaping steam, but it caused great inconvenience and obliged them to work up to sixty-five pounds of steam only, when the vessel is capable of working under one hundred. An average of sixteen knots an hour was made, but it is expected the "Alaska" will make regularly eighteen and one-half knots an hour and record four hundred and forty miles a day. She made four hundred and two miles one day with only sixty-five pounds of steam.

Mr. Guion, accompanied by a number of personal friends and members of the press, went down the bay in a special tender to meet the steamship. When the tender was off Staten Island the huge ship was sighted steaming through the Narrows decked gayly with flags, floating the national ensign at the fore and the flag of the royal naval reserve at the stern. When off quarantine the "Alaska" dropped her anchor, and the health-officer, with those who had gone down to inspect her, went on board.

As the vessel lay at anchor in the stream she presented a fine appearance, but only when on board of her could one get an idea of her size. The principal dimensions of the "Alaska" are: Length, 526 feet; breadth, 50 feet 6 inches; depth, 40 feet 7 inches to upper-deck, or 48 feet 7 inches to promenade-deck. Her gross tonnage is 8000 tons. The engines are of the compound inverted, direct-acting, three-cylinder type, the high-pressure cylinder 68-inch diameter, and the two-ton pressure cylinders 100 inches diameter each, with a stroke of 6 feet. Steam is supplied by boilers of the usual cylindrical form at a pressure of 100 pounds. The indicated horse-power is about 1000.

The "Alaska" has two smoke-stacks and four masts, bark-rigged. There are altogether seven decks. The first, or promenade-deck, extends the whole length and breadth of the vessel, excepting the parts in the bow and stern forming the "turtle." The second deck is an open one. Along the sides of the vessel and along the middle are the quarters for the officers and engineers, and a number of state-rooms for intermediate passengers. In the third, or main-deck, accommodations are provided for three hundred and forty first-class, sixty second-class, and one hundred and eighteen steerage passengers. This deck, amidships, is taken up entirely by the state-rooms and dining-saloons for first-class passengers. The entrance to the main saloon is by a spacious stairway from the second deck, and is handsomely arranged. The main saloon is 50 feet wide and 64 feet long, and has a seating capacity for 280 people. The ceiling is 9 feet high, but a cupola of stained glass, 23 feet long and 15 feet wide, makes the centre of the main saloon 20 feet high. The sides of the saloon are finished in hard woods, with panels of maple, teak, satin, and oak inlaid. The upholstery is in blue Utrecht velvet. Near the saloon is the ladies' cabin, upholstered with rich brocaded tapestry, with sofas well arranged for comfort and ease. Communicating with this room are the ladies' bath-rooms, which are complete in every particular. The smoking-room is 28 feet wide and 24 feet long. It is floored in parquetry. There are four bath-rooms on the main-deck, as well as lavatories at convenient places. The fourth deck is devoted to steerage passengers, and will accommodate one thousand persons. The fifth deck is used entirely for cargo. The "Alaska" is fitted with steam-windlass, steam steering-gear, steam-winches, and all the most improved appliances for navigation and for promoting the comfort of the passengers. There are electric bells communicating with the chief steward's office throughout the ship, and she is fitted with Swan's electric lights.

1867.—THE OLD DOMINION STEAMSHIP COMPANY succeeded the New York and Virginia Steamship Company, which ran the route previous to the Civil War.

The service of the Old Dominion Steamship Company now embraces the following lines of passenger travel: Main Line—New York to Norfolk, Portsmouth, Newport News, Petersburg, and Richmond, Virginia. Norfolk Division—Norfolk to Old Point Comfort (Fortress Monroe), Hampton, Newport News, Smithfield, Yorktown, Matthews, Gloucester, and Cherrystone, Virginia. North Carolina Division—Elizabeth City to Washington, South Creek, Makeley's, Newberne, and Riverdale, North Carolina; Washington, North Carolina, to Greenville and Tarboro, North Carolina, etc. Delaware Division—New York to Lewes, Delaware; Franklin City, Virginia, to Chincoteague, Virginia, etc. West Point Division—New York to West Point, Virginia; freight only.

The line commenced with three steamers of less than 3000 tons burden combined. The following named are its present fleet:

The "Roanoke," iron propeller, freight and passengers, 2354 tons, New York.

The "Guyandotte," iron propeller, of the same class and build as the "Roanoke."

The "Old Dominion," iron side-wheel steamship, freight and passengers, 2222 tons.

The "Wyanoke," iron side-wheel steamship, freight and passengers, 2068 tons.

The "Richmond," iron propeller, freight and passengers, 1436 tons.

The "Manhattan," iron propeller, freight and passengers, 1400 tons.

The "Breakwater," iron propeller, freight and passengers, 1110 tons.

The "Rapidan," wooden side-wheel, freight, 868 tons.

Steamer "Widgeon," Swift, master.

Steamer " Transfer."

The " Northampton," wooden side-wheel, freight and passengers, 600 tons.

The " Accomack," wooden side-wheel, freight and passengers, 434 tons.

The " Shenandoah," wooden side-wheel.

The " Luray," wooden side-wheel.

The " Newberne," iron propeller, freight and passengers, 400 tons.

The " Pamlico," wooden propeller, 252 tons.

And about 2000 tons in barges, propellers, lighters, etc., or about 20,000 tons in all.

The passenger accommodations of the Old Dominion steamships are of the most comfortable and superb character; the saloons are substantially and elegantly furnished, the tables well supplied, and in fact they are wanting in nothing calculated to make a trip upon them desirable and pleasant. During the company's career of fifteen years *not a single life intrusted to its care has been lost*. Through the worst storms and series of marine disasters these steamships have always passed in perfect safety.

The movement of freights northward by this line consists of the products of mine, field, and forest,—ores, marble, granite, logs, lumber, and their products, cotton, tobacco, rice, peanuts, and every variety of produce, fish, oysters, etc.

South-bound, all kinds of merchandise.

Besides points immediately reached by steamers, intimate rail connections exist with all parts of the South, Southwest, and West, and freights and passengers transferred to and from the same.

An almost daily line is maintained. During August, 1882, forty-five arrivals of this company's boats were entered in New York. They probably handle, agents of the company say, as great a volume of business in tons as any other company, either foreign or domestic, in this country.

The " Roanoke," and the " Guyandotte," of 1355 tons each, built at Roach's ship-yard, Chester, Pennsylvania, are two iron screw steamships of a very superior character. The dimensions are: Length, 270 feet; breadth of beam, 41 feet; depth of hold from base line, 26 feet, 9 inches. The steamers were built under the special inspection and in accordance with the rule of the American Shipmasters' Association, and are classed for twenty years in the " Record of American Shipping." They are supplied with water-tight bulkheads, and have every appliance for the safety and comfort of passengers. There are three decks and a hurricane-deck. Excellent accommodations are supplied for 100 cabin passengers, state-rooms for which are of large size and elegantly upholstered and appointed, having all modern conveniences. The saloons are finished in a choice variety of hard woods, and handsomely upholstered and furnished. Thorough ventilation is supplied, and everything done which experience can suggest to make these steamships among the best in the coasting trade. They have compound engines, the high-pressure cylinders being 38 inches in diameter, and the low-pressure 74 inches. The length of stroke of the piston is 4½ feet. Four steel boilers, 13 feet in diameter, 12 feet long, and tested to carry 90 pounds of steam, insure a good rate of speed.

1870.—THE WHITE STAR LINE.—The White Star Line was originally composed of a fleet of fast-sailing American clipper-ships, by the "Champion of the Seas," "Blue Jacket," "White Star," "Shalimar," etc., sailing to Australia. To this line Messrs. Imray & Co. succeeded, and still carry it on with fast vessels, built of iron.

In 1870 the establishment of the line of steamships taking this name was claimed as a new departure in ocean steamship management. The ships of the line differed in model, internal arrangements, and equipment from all their predecessors. They were designed to combine the highest speed with unprecedented comfort and convenience for passengers.

Nautical critics are conservative, and look with great distrust upon marked innovations in naval construction, and these vessels were the subject of unfavorable comments. They might do for summer passages, but doubts were expressed whether they would endure the test of a North Atlantic winter. It was an innovation that the vessels of the line should be built at Belfast instead of upon the Clyde, the stipulation being that the ships were to be constructed of strength, size, and power to equal, if not surpass, anything upon the Mersey. The builders were not limited by contract, but left to fulfill the general instructions given. When the first vessels of the line were brought to Liverpool from Belfast they created a "sensation," and became the subject of comment and observation. Events have proved that the builders reached a high degree of speed and safety, and that no steamships have been better able to cope with the winter storms of the Atlantic. For ten years, in winter as in summer, the steamships of the White Star Line have lived down adverse criticism. The best evidence of the value of the improvements introduced by the White Star Company is that they have been adopted by rival lines. The White Star steamers range from 3700 to 5000 tons, and are among the largest in the world. They are built with regard to strength no less than speed, and constructed on the floating-tube principle, with seven water-tight and fire-proof iron bulkheads. They are steered by steam, and have the principal saloon and state-rooms amidships. A complete inspection by the commanding officer is made before every voyage, when the men are put through a boat-service drill and a drill in defense of fire, which is repeated once or twice at sea on each voyage. The discipline is as pronounced as on board ships of the royal navy. From

February to July, when the ice is drifting with the Gulf Stream, the White Star vessels are navigated by a southerly track, and *vice versa* from August to January. When the ice has drifted, and the northern parallels are clear of ice and fog, the boats take the northern track.

The average passages of the steamships of the White Star Line, both ways between Queenstown and New York, have been under nine days, and many passages have been under eight days. In July, 1875, the " Germania" made the passage from Queenstown to New York in 7 days, 23 hours, 7 minutes, and the return passage in August in 7 days, 22 hours, 8 minutes. The " Adriatic" and the " Baltic" have made passages under eight days, and in February, 1876, the "Germania" eclipsed herself and all other vessels of the line by steaming from Sandy Hook to Queenstown in 7 days, 15 hours, 17 minutes, having traversed 2894 knots, equal to 15.8 knots per hour for the entire passage. In 1877 the " Germania" made the passage in 7 days, 11 hours, 27 minutes. The " Britannia" made the passage in 7 days, 10 hours, 53 minutes.

A passenger describing these vessels says of them:

"In their internal arrangements the White Star ships are even more strikingly a ' new departure' in steamship architecture than in their model. The main saloon, instead of being at the stern, and hemmed in by state-rooms, making a long, narrow, badly-lighted apartment, is placed in the very middle of the vessel, and extends from side to side, forming a grand hall 75 feet long and 45 feet wide, lighted not only by the ample skylights but by large windows at the sides. A broad staircase, well lighted by night and day, leads to the saloon, where there is ample room for dining two hundred persons, giving to each diner his or her own seat, not of undefined capacity on a settee, but a chair with revolving seat, which is kept at every meal for the passenger to whom it is allotted at the commencement of the voyage, and can be approached at any time during the progress of the meals without disturbing the others. There is nothing to indicate that you are on shipboard; indeed, there is every appearance of hotel life of the most elegant and comfortable style, including even an open marble fireplace, which substitutes the customary stove and gives an additional air of homeliness to the scene.

" The state-rooms are also arranged amidships, at either end of the saloon, and are large, well-lighted, and furnished with every convenience, including electric bells. Bath-rooms are within easy reach, and nothing that can promote the comfort of the passenger is omitted. The smoking-room is not, as too often, a close little den, but a large and handsome apartment; and the ladies' saloon is on a more liberal scale than usual, and far more attractive in its appointments. From their situation and the great length of the ships, the main saloon, the state-rooms, and all the rooms for the general use of the passengers, are almost entirely free from motion, except in the worst of weather, thus reducing the risk of sea-sickness to a minimum.

"Five water-tight bulkheads run from the top to the bottom of the ship. These are supplemented by self-closing doors, and other appliances designed to confine a leak or the effect of an accident to that part of the vessel to which the mishap may have occurred. These doors are perfectly self-acting and almost independent of human agency. In one compartment, containing the after-set of boilers, the door which leads to the next compartment is arranged for prompt water-tight closing. Should the water find its way into the neighboring compartment, the engineer in charge has only to turn a lever and the ponderous door falls into its place, regulated in its descent by an air cylinder, which checks the door and causes it to fall in jerks. In another compartment you find that the iron way, upon which you walk, is automatic. Should the sea find its way beneath, the door (for the flooring upon which you have passed is, after all, only a kind of iron bridge) rises by the action of the water, and confines the water to a section of the vessel. There is nothing more remarkable in the fittings of these steamers than these self-acting doors, which are always kept in perfect order, working with a simplicity only equaled by the importance of the work they can accomplish."

The managers of the line have adopted "ic" as a termination for the names of their vessels, as " Adriatic," " Celtic," " Baltic," " Britannic," " Germanic," " Republic," etc.

At a meeting of the passengers assembled in the saloon of the steamer "Britannic," off Sandy Hook, on the evening of August 17, 1877, on the completion of the voyage from Queenstown in the unprecedented time of 7 days, 10 hours, and 53 minutes, it was " *Resolved*, To ask Captain Thompson to accept a souvenir, suitably inscribed, to commemorate this achievement." Thirty passengers and a number of invited guests were present. The souvenir consisted of a silver pitcher, with this inscription: " Presented to Captain Wm. H. Thompson, of S. S. 'Britannic,' by the passengers, to commemorate the voyage from Queenstown to New York, August 10 to August 17, 1877." The presentation speech by D. W. James humorously contrasted the discomforts of ocean travel twenty years ago with the speed and conveniences which modern vessels afford.

A silver cup, appropriately inscribed, was also presented to the chief engineer of the "Britannic," Thomas Sewell, as a mark of the passengers' appreciation of his skill and care during the voyage, September 29, 1877.

The " Coptic," the latest addition to the White Star Line, arrived at New York December 3, 1881, after an exceedingly rough passage of sixteen days. The " Coptic" is a sister ship to the " Arabic," of the same line, and was built at Belfast, Ireland. The material used in her construction is milled steel, which was chosen on account of its strength and toughness. Her dimensions are: Length, 430 feet; breadth, 42 feet; and depth of hold, 34 feet. Her registered tonnage is 4368 tons, but she will carry about 6000. She is propelled by two double-cylindered compound engines of 450 horse-power at 90 pounds pressure of steam. These were built by the Victoria Engine-Works, Liverpool. The main shaft is a built one. In the engine-room are the very large pumps. In the next room are two dynamos, which furnish electricity for the Swan electric lights used throughout the ship. There are three double elliptical boilers, which require twelve fires to heat them, and have been tested to 180 pounds. While the "Coptic" is intended to be used more for carrying freight than passengers, the accommodations for passengers are very good. The staterooms are large and supplied with all the conveniences known to modern ship-builders. The main saloon is handsomely upholstered in dark olive velvet, and is approached through an entrance hall from the main staircase. The saloon is paneled in wood made to simulate embossed leather. The chairs are cane-seated and revolving. The light all through the ship is furnished by the Swan electric lamps, which consist of carbonized threads inclosed in hermetically sealed glass bulbs. The hull of the "Coptic" is divided into eight compartments, either one of which might be stove in without endangering the vessel. The principle upon which the doors of these compartments are worked is comparatively new, and has been so highly approved by the English Admiralty Board that the government has adopted it in building vessels for the navy. The "Coptic" has four masts, three being square-rigged, and the fourth being fore- and aft-rigged. There are three decks, braced in every direction, and turtle-backs fore and aft.

The "Coptic" left Queenstown, on her first trip, on the 17th of November, 1881. Her captain said of her, "She behaved very well. We had about as heavy weather as I have seen, and nothing could be more satisfactory than the 'Coptic.' When we were in about forty degrees west we were struck by a hurricane. On the 28th she was struck aft by a sea which stove in the after turtle-back over the rudder, swept everything loose away, stove in two boats, and carried two sailors overboard. We could do nothing to save them, because no boat could live in such a sea. The iron plates over the wheel were broken in. The stout iron rods were bent and twisted by the water as though they had been light wires in the hands of a strong man."

The chief engineer said of the engines, "They work beautifully. One man can, by moving six little levers, work the whole engine with one-half the effort ordinarily required to manage a small stationary engine. It works rapidly too. On this side is the signal-plate which connects with the bridge. The engineer can in less than a minute after receiving the order to stop, go ahead at full or half speed, or back. They are as easily managed as any engines I have ever seen. The new lights make the engine-room as light as day."

The "Coptic" and her sister ship, the "Arabic," are intended for the carrying of freight and emigrants. The "Coptic" will probably be sent to the Pacific in two or three years, to run between San Francisco and Hong-Kong. She will carry more freight, run faster on a given amount of coal, said her captain, than any vessel now running between New York and England. The "Coptic," on her first trip, brought a few saloon passengers, three hundred emigrants, and a full cargo of freight.

NAVIGAZIONE GENERALE ITALIANA.—This great steamship company, whose head-quarters are in Rome, with departments at Genoa and Palermo, is a union of Florios and Rubattinos companies, and have service extending all over the Mediterranean, and up the Adriatic and Black Sea, and to India, also to New York. The I. & V. Florio Company, of Palermo, began operations about twenty-five or thirty years ago, and five years ago absorbed the Trinacria Company, of Palermo, making their fleet about forty-five steamers of various sizes. Later, they consolidated with the Rubattino Company, of Geneva, whose business was, in a great part, to the East, through the Suez Canal, the combined fleet consisting now of ninety-two steam vessels, exclusive of several very large ones which are being constructed. In the New York trade they now have employed three steamers regularly of large tonnage,—viz., the "Archemede," 4500 tons; the "Washington," 4000 tons; and the "Vincenzo Florio," 4000 tons; besides three other steamers of somewhat smaller tonnage, employed as trade requires. Three other steamers are being built for the New York Line, and it is anticipated six steamships will be running regularly on that line in the course of a year. A recent newspaper says, speaking of this company,—

"The Italian government is rendering essential aid to the efforts of its citizens to extend the commerce of the country. Under the promise of large bounties from the government, two great shipping firms at Genoa have united and have given orders to English builders for *twenty steamers, all of them ranging between* 4000 *and* 5000 *tons register*. For many years the traffic of the great Italian port has been stationary, Marseilles having outrun it under the changed conditions of modern commerce. An effort is now to be made to restore the prosperity of former days, and immense new docks have been constructed. The new steamers will not be confined to the Mediterranean trade, but lines will be established to both coasts of the American continent."

The company's steam fleet consists of the following-named steamships,—viz:

BELONGING TO THE GENOA BRANCH.

Name.	Tons.	Name.	Tons.
Abissinia	3600	Italia	600
Adriatico	1200	Liguria	550
Africa	1200	Lombardia	500
Alessandro Volta	600	Malabar	1900
Arabia	1400	Malta	1000
Asia	1300	Manilla	4800
Assiria	1600	Messina	1200
Bengala	1600	Montcalieri	600
Birmania	3200	Palestine	900
Calabria	1400	Palmaria	1000
Candia	1000	Persia	1400
Caprera	600	Pertusola	800
China	5000	Pianosa	100
Cipro	1100	Piemonte	400
Christoforo Colombo	500	Roma	2200
Conte Menabrea	200	Sardegna	400
Corsica	200	Sicilia	800
Egitto	1800	Singapore	4500
Elba	200	Sumatra	2200
Giava	3600	Tortola	150
Gorgona	200	Torcana	400
India	1400	Umbria	300

Raffaele Rubattino, 5000 tons (building).

BELONGING TO THE PALERMO BRANCH.

Name.	Tons.	Name.	Tons.
Alfredo Cappellini	150	Marsala	2300
Amerigo Vespucci	400	Mediterraneo	1800
Ancona	700	Milano	400
Archemede	4500	Moretto	100
Bagnaria	1200	Napoli	450
Barone Ricasoli	200	Oreto	700
Campidoglio	500	Orlegia	2200
Cariddi	1200	Pachino	1200
Dripane	2000	Palermo	480
Egadi	2600	Peloro	2500
Egida	100	Principe Amedeo	1200
Elettrico	450	Principe Oddone	1200
Enna	2000	Scilla	1200
Etna	500	Sagesta	2500
Faro	1500	Selinunte	1800
Firenze	450	Simeto	2300
Flavis Gioja	400	Solunto	2500
Galileo Galilei	400	Taormina	1800
Imera	1800	Tigre	400
Jonio	1500	Tirreno	800
Leone	550	Venezia	900
Liliteo	1200	Vincenzio Florio	4000
Marco Polo	400	Washington	4000

1871.—THE AMERICAN STEAMSHIP COMPANY OF PHILADELPHIA was organized in 1871 with a capital of $2,500,000, and a contract was given to Messrs. Cramp & Sons, of Philadelphia, for the construction of four first-class iron steamships of 3000 tons burden, and to have an average speed of thirteen knots an hour. The steamers were intended to carry the mails and conduct a general freight and passenger business between Philadelphia and Liverpool, calling at Queenstown. The "Pennsylvania," the pioneer steamship of the line, was launched in August, 1872, and made her first voyage in May, 1873. The "Ohio," "Indiana," and "Illinois" followed at regular intervals. They are 360 feet long, 42 feet beam, and 33 feet depth of hold. Their engines are nominally 500 horse-power, and capable of being worked up to 3000. Their great breadth of beam, in proportion to their length, tends to increase their steadiness at sea. This line is now the only transatlantic line sailing under the American flag, and the fleet in 1881 embraced the following nine first-class steamships:

	Tons.		Tons.
Pennsylvania	3104	Lord Gough	3655
Ohio	3104	British Crown	3487
Indiana	3104	British Queen	3558
Illinois	3104	British King	3558
Lord Clive	3386	British Prince	3858

A steamer of the fleet sails every Wednesday and Saturday between Liverpool and Philadelphia from each port, calling at Queenstown. They are capable of carrying 100 first-class, 75 intermediate, and 800 steerage passengers, with from 3500 to 4500 tons of freight. A portion of the main-deck is set apart for the special accommodation of "intermediate" passengers. Families can secure separate rooms, and have their meals served apart from the other passengers, at about half the price paid by the holders of first-class tickets, and the bill of fare is ample and varied. The accommodations for steerage passengers are excellent, and great pains is taken to secure comfort and to provide wholesome and unstinted food for this class of voyagers.

The largest vessel of the line, the "British Prince," is 419 feet long, has 42 feet beam and 28 feet depth of hold, and is 3858 tons register.

The shortest passage of any steamship of the line was made by the "Illinois," October, 1880, from Queenstown to Cape Henlopen, in eight days, ten hours, and thirty-four minutes, beating the "Pennsylvania's" shortest time of eight days, nineteen hours, and twelve minutes. The average passage is about ten days. The "Illinois," in her 59 round voyages, or 118 passages, has had six years, ten months, and thirteen days *sea service*. In 59 passages out to Queenstown she traveled 173,000 miles, and in 59 home to Henlopen, 171,092 miles, a distance of 344,092 miles, to which must be added 10,620 miles up and down the Delaware, and 27,966 miles from Queenstown to Liverpool, making the total nautical miles 382,678, equal to 441,093 statute miles.

Safeguards against loss of life at sea are a feature in the equipments of these steamers. In addition to the usual complement of life-boats of the ordinary construction, each carries a number of life-rafts, provided with bread- and water-tanks, always kept supplied. These rafts can be thrown into the water with scarcely a moment's delay; and have appliances for the accommodation of passengers on both top and bottom, and are always right side up. They are more available in a storm than ordinary life-boats, which have to be lowered with caution, and are frequently stove against the side of the ship and rendered useless.

General Grant, on starting upon his trip around the world, on the 17th of May, 1877, took his departure from Philadelphia in one of these steamers, the "Indiana."

The five latest additions to the line were built in Great Britain, two being constructed by Harland & Wolff, of Belfast, and three by the Lairds, of Liverpool. Although of greater tonnage, they are not fitted to carry as many *first-class* passengers as the American-built ships.

CITY LINE OF OCEAN STEAMSHIPS.—The steamships of this line sailing fortnightly *via* the Suez Canal from Glasgow and Liverpool to Calcutta direct and back to London, are so called because they are named for the principal cities of the world. They are owned by Messrs. George Smith & Sons, of Glasgow, and comprise twelve steamships, varying in tonnage from 3750 to 2328 tons,—viz.:

	Tons.		Tons.
City of Damascus	3,750	City of Edinburgh	3,212
City of Agra	3,412	City of Canterbury	3,212
City of London	3,212	City of Carthage	2,650
City of Khios	3,246	City of Mecca	2,290
City of Venice	3,206	City of Oxford	2,328
City of Manchester	3,125		
City of Cambridge	2,829	Total tonnage of the fleet	35,972

THE STATE STEAMSHIP LINE was established in 1872 by a British company, in Glasgow. The steamers comprising the fleet have all been built on the Clyde, by the Glasgow Engineering and Ship-Building Company, especially for the North Atlantic passenger traffic. Each steamer is constructed with an especial view to safety, which is invariably the first consideration in all deliberations regarding the operations of the company. It is due to the care and vigilance of the company's officers that the line has been so fortunate in escaping accidents.

The officers of this company are supplied with, and instructed to use carefully and often in case of fogs, and on all occasions of uncertainty, the log, patent log, head-line, and Sir William Thomson's sounding-machine. Officers are also instructed as to the necessary precautions in the avoidance of danger from collision with fishermen off the Banks, and from icebergs. Intemperance is uncompromisingly dealt with, and no officer employed or retained who is addicted to the excessive use of spirituous liquors.

The cabins are situated on the main-deck, in the portion of the steamer where the least motion is felt, and consequently the less liability to sea-sickness. The state-rooms are arranged with two berths and a sofa; are large, light, and well ventilated. For the convenience of ladies, there are private baths and dressing-rooms in the main saloon, and reception-rooms on deck. There are also provided for gentlemen, baths, smoking- and reading-rooms, and everything necessary for their comfort and enjoyment during the voyage. For the general use of passengers there are comprehensive libraries of selected books, pianos, and other musical instruments, and most tastefully arranged concert-halls. The main dining-saloons, which are luxuriously furnished, extend entirely across the steamers, and are provided with revolving chairs, and other improvements for convenience and comfort.

The tables are always supplied with all seasonable delicacies, and an abundance of the best quality of the more substantial and necessary eatables, *à la carte*. Attentive stewards are at the disposal of passengers.

Experienced surgeons also accompany each steamer.

The second cabins of this line are in the centre portion of the steamers on main-deck. The berths are similar to those in the first cabin, with plenty of clean linen, and the floors are carpeted, the only difference being that there are four in a room, and occasionally more. Second-cabin passengers are not permitted in the saloon or smoking-rooms. There are separate dining-tables, and well-prepared meals are served three times daily. During the busy season the sexes are separated; but whenever it is practicable to book families together it is invariably done.

Steerage passengers receive special attention by the State Line Company, and this company has made special arrangements for the convenience of families, who are allotted to special rooms wherever practicable. The proper separation of the sexes and the provision for the privacy of single women has also been looked after in the State Line steamers. Good provision is made for ventilation and other necessary comfort. There is always a liberal supply of well-cooked food on hand, which is served out unsparingly. The surgeon visits the steerage apartments three times regularly every day, and oftener when necessary. Special hospitals are also arranged on deck for the isolation of patients when necessary.

During the year 1881 the company added to their fleet two new and large steamers,—the "State of Nebraska" and the "State of Florida." Both of these are specimens of marine architecture of which the company may well be proud. They are about 400 feet long, 42 feet wide, and have a tonnage measurement of between 4000 and 5000. There are accommodations for about 100 first-class saloon, 80 second-cabin, and several hundred steerage passengers.

The saloons, which are on the main-deck, extend entirely across the steamer, are provided with six long dining-tables with revolving chairs of the most approved pattern, securely fixed so as to afford the greatest ease for passengers while enjoying their meals. The saloons are lighted by skylights from above, and the usual side port-holes. In the upper portion of the saloon is a circular balcony or gallery, at one end of which is a piano and at the other a pipe-organ, and around the sides are elegantly upholstered seats. This room is called the concert-hall.

The state-rooms are both forward and aft of the saloons, and they are unusually large, well lighted and ventilated. They are fitted with two berths each, and a sofa berth, which may be utilized by children or members of the same family, if they so desire.

From the ladies' saloon a wide companion-way leads up to the hurricane-decks, which extend the entire breadth of the vessels, and are 125 feet in length, affording a splendid promenade.

The ladies' private dressing-rooms, gentlemen's smoking-rooms, libraries, bath-rooms, etc., are all well arranged and provided with all necessary appointments for convenience and luxury.

The second cabins are situated forward of the saloons, and are provided with a comfortable saloon and separate tables. The state-rooms are about the same as those in the saloon,—the floors carpeted, and plenty of bedding provided,—so that while the passengers by this class are not allowed the extra privileges of the saloon passengers, yet they certainly have here most comfortable quarters.

The steerage berths are also situated on the main-deck, and are unusually convenient and comfortable. The berths are arranged and classified so as to afford more retirement and privacy to single women, and large rooms for families where they may remain intact. There are also provisions for good ventilation and cleanliness, and also hospitals for the sick in case such are required.

ROUTE, LENGTH OF TRIP, ETC.—The route of the State Line steamers is from New York, every Thursday, to Glasgow direct. From Glasgow steamers sail every Friday, calling at Belfast, from which port a steamer sails every Saturday. The average length of voyage is nine to ten days between New York and Glasgow, and *vice versa*. The steamers of this line take the direct course across the Atlantic, passing the north coast of Ireland, thus avoiding the unpleasant experience of a trip through St. George's Channel.

The company's fleet is composed of the "State of Nebraska," about 4500 tons; "State of Florida," about 4000 tons; "State of Indiana," about 3000 tons; "State of Nevada," about 3000 tons; "State of Pennsylvania," about 3000 tons; "State of Georgia," about 3000 tons; "State of Alabama," about 3000 tons; "State of ———," building.

1873.—THE RED STAR LINE.—The Red Star Line, of Belgian Royal Mail Steamers, between Antwerp and New York and Philadelphia, was inaugurated in 1873, under the auspices of the King of the Belgians, and now comprises seven large, full-powered steamers, forming a weekly line, sailing from Europe and America every Saturday. The latest additions to the fleet, the "Belgenland," the "Rhynland," and the "Waesland," are built with all the modern appliances for comfort and safety, and are among the largest and fastest steamships in the Atlantic trade.

The fleet comprises the following first-class steamers:

STEAMERS.	Built.	Tons.	Beam.	Length.
Waesland	1880	5000	43 feet.	445 feet.
Rhynland	1879	4000	40 "	418 "
Belgenland	1879	4000	40 "	418 "
Switzerland	1874	3000	39 "	345 "
Nederland	1873	3000	39 "	345 "
Vaderland	1872	3000	39 "	330 "
Zeeland	1878	8500	43 "	370 "
New Steamer (building)	...	5000	43 "	445 "

The "Belgenland" and the "Rhynland" were added to the fleet in 1879, and were built by the celebrated Barrow Ship-Building Company, of Barrow, England. Their engines are compounded, of about 2200 indicated horse-power, and consume from forty-five to fifty tons of coal per day, producing an average speed of fourteen knots per hour. They have accommodations for 150 cabin and 1000 steerage passengers.

The "Waesland," added in 1880, is from the ship-yards of Harland & Wolff, of Belfast. She is of 5000 tons burden, 445 feet long, 43 feet beam, and 34 feet 8 inches depth of hold. She has four decks, three of them of iron, and four iron masts, two of which are square-rigged. She can accommodate 150 cabin and 1500 steerage passengers. These vessels are of the highest class in every respect, having been built under the special survey of the Inspectors of British Lloyds and Bureau Veritas, the leading authorities on the classification of ships. The state-rooms and saloons are in the centre of the ship, where the least motion is felt, and are supplied with the latest improvements in ventilating apparatus, electric bells, commodious bath- and smoking-rooms, etc.

The second cabins and state-rooms are situated above the main-deck (the same deck as the first cabin), in the after part of the ship. They have the same perfect ventilation as the first cabins, and are unsurpassed in cleanliness and convenience, being admirably adapted for families and passengers generally who may wish to exercise a moderate amount of economy in their voyage to and from Europe.

The American Line (running between Philadelphia and Liverpool) and the Red Star Line (running between New York and Antwerp) are under one management, and first-class round-trip tickets issued for one line are good to return on the other. Holders of first-cabin excursion tickets by the Red Star Line who may be in England, and not caring to recross the English Channel, can therefore return by the American Line direct from Liverpool to Philadelphia, by applying to the agents of the American Line at Liverpool.

To those who wish to go direct to the Continent, the Red Star Line offers unusual inducements. The voyages to Antwerp are direct and uninterrupted, and on landing at that port the passenger finds himself but a short distance from Paris, and within easy travel of the leading continental cities.

1874.—THE MONARCH LINE.—The legal and corporate name of this company is "The Royal Exchange Shipping Company" (limited), but it is better known as the Monarch Line, from the nomenclature adopted by the company for the ships of its fleet. The ships are all well built of iron and steel, with a double hull and six water-tight compartments, the bulkheads running from the keelson to the upper-deck. They are 400 feet in length, 45 feet beam, 33 feet depth of hold, and are of a gross tonnage of 4500 tons, with engines of 2500 horse-power. They are built under the British Admiralty Survey, to comply with their stringent rules for government transport service. Their accommodations are similar and equal to those of the steamers of other transatlantic lines. Several of the ships of this line have been taken up as transports by the English government in the several wars it has been engaged in since 1874.

The "Grecian Monarch," the latest addition to the line, and which arrived from London at New York, September, 1882, on her first trip, is thus described in the *Daily Graphic* of the 16th:

"Lying at her dock next the Pavonia Ferry in Jersey City, her huge sides exposed to view, and her masts, which are of iron, glistening in the sunlight, the steamer looked a craft of rare beauty. She is not large as compared with some of the modern monsters in the shape of vessels that now cross the sea, but she is symmetrical and strongly built, the main purpose of her construction being evidently safety rather than a high rate of speed. Over all she is 400 feet long, while her breadth of beam is 43 feet and her hold 33 feet. She is 4364 tons burden, and above the spar-deck has a hurricane-deck 166 feet long and 30 feet wide. She has accommodations in the steerage for 1000 passengers, and in the cabins for 112. The ship is divided into water-tight compartments, and, besides a handsome dining-saloon, smoking-room, and ladies' cabin, has three hospitals,—two located near the steerage and one on deck. Of the first two, one is set apart for men, while the other is appropriated to the use of women. The third is for patients who may chance to fall ill of an infectious disease. It is completely isolated, and forms an improvement worthy of special note. Like her sister vessels, the "Grecian Monarch" is peculiarly fitted for troop service, and is on the English Admiralty list for that purpose. The steerage is more commodious, however, than on the other ships, and the ventilation afforded better than on most ships that come into this port. The state-rooms are of average size, but beautifully and comfortably furnished. The berths are tempting retreats. The saloon, which is almost amidships, is as elegant as that of any first-class hotel. An upright piano of rich ebony is one of its attractions. The apartment is finished in carved oak and maple, and has white ceilings decorated with gold stars. The upholstering is of blue morocco leather and velvet. The captain, officers, and crew, numbering one hundred men, were selected with care. The captain is Mr. R. J. W. Bristow, a gentleman of long experience at sea. He was the late commander of the "Egyptian Monarch," and formerly in the service of the Cunard and White Star Lines. The vessel ran at the rate of fourteen knots per hour in coming from London, but as usual during a first trip there were little hinderances to speed, which will be done away with when the machinery works more smoothly."

The "Assyrian Monarch," in 1882, was honored by having as a passenger from England the celebrated elephant Jumbo. He received royal honors *en route*, the boy crews of the training-ships manning yards as he went by. Lady Burdett-Coutts and party traveled from London to bid the great brute farewell. The Baroness on reaching the "Monarch" went to the forward part of the ship, between decks, to visit the elephant, and gave him a last bun and bid him good-by. The Baroness left a sum of money to purchase sweets, etc., for the "Monarch's" passage. So much interest in England was manifested for Jumbo that the "Monarch" took out elastic bags to be dropped into the sea at intervals in regard to his health, etc., a skillful means of advertising the enormous beast. As she left the Millwall docks she was gayly dressed with flags.

The Monarch Line forms a direct communication between London and New York, and has connections with Havre, Paris, Hamburg, Bremen, Antwerp, Gothenburg, and Copenhagen.

The present fleet consists of the following-named steamships:

Name.	Built.	Registered Tonnage.	Name.	Built.	Registered Tonnage.
Norman Monarch	1875	1482	Persian Monarch	1880	3908
Danish Monarch	1878	1338	Egyptian Monarch	1881	3916
Celtic Monarch	1879	2014	Lydian Monarch	1881	3916
Assyrian Monarch	1880	3917	Grecian Monarch	1882	4364
Roman Monarch	building	4400			

THE HARRISON LINE.—This line of steamships, running between New Orleans and Liverpool, has started up since the Civil War, and is the outgrowth of a line of sailing ships which were running as early as 1850. The owners of this line are Thomas and James Harrison, of Liverpool. The following is a list of their steamers in 1882:

NAME.	Tons Reg.	NAME.	Tons Reg.
Alice	1182	Governor	2650
Architect	1934	Historian	1830
Author	1393	Inventor	2291
Chancellor	2052	Legislator	2126
Chrysolite	702	Mariner	1443
Cogniac	702	Mediator	2011
Commander	1550	Merchant	1443
Counsellor	2251	Orator	1842
Discoverer	2251	Professor	2630
Editor	1393	Statesman	1851
Engineer	2750	Warrior	1231
Explorer	2010		

THE OCEAN STEAMSHIP COMPANY OF SAVANNAH.—This company runs a line of ocean steamships between New York and Savannah and Philadelphia and Savannah, and owns at present a fleet of nine vessels,—viz., the "City of Augusta," "City of Macon," "City of Savannah," "Juniata," "Dessoug," "Tallahassee," "Chattahoochie," and "Wacoochie." The three last have been recently launched from Roach's yard at Chester. The "City of Columbus" and the "Gate City," formerly of this company, were sold in September, 1882, to a Boston company, which will run them as a connecting line with the Ocean Steamship Company, using the docks of the latter company at Savannah. The "Dessoug," used as a freight boat, is noted for having brought to New York the Egyptian Obelisk presented by the Khedive. The cost of her purchase and refitting amounted to $94,642.58, and she is estimated to be worth $120,000.

The "City of Augusta," until the recent additions to this line, which are not yet in commission, was the largest vessel engaged in the coastwise trade, having a cargo capacity of 3000 tons, or 6000 bales of cotton. She is 323 feet over all, 40 feet beam, has three decks, and five water-tight compartments, and is built of iron. She carries compound engines, with two inverted cylinders, 42¼ and 82 inches in diameter respectively. Her screw is 16 feet in diameter, with 26 feet pitch; her working pressure, 100 pounds of steam. She has six steel tubular boilers, and steam steering-gear and capstans. With accommodations for one hundred passengers, her state-rooms are roomy, and her fitting-up is sumptuous. No steamer goes out of New York having more elegant appointments. The saloons are finished in many-colored foreign woods; polished brass dazzles the eye at every point; revolving chairs, elegantly upholstered, solicit the lazy passenger; the table equipments are tasteful and handsome. The personal administration of the company's ships leaves nothing to be desired, whether it be seamanship on deck or hospitable courtesy in the saloon.

These ships are greatly used by invalids ordered to Florida or elsewhere in the South by their physicians, and these have usually to make the winter voyage. The ships are steam-heated, and always comfortable, though twenty-four hours out of New York the weather becomes warm. The "City of Macon" and the "Dessoug" rode out the terrible cyclone of August 31, 1881, without damage, and the entire fleet is made up of thoroughly seaworthy ships. The northward-bound traffic is largely made up of cotton, of which 247,944 bales were delivered in New York in 1880–81, an increase of more than one hundred per cent. in three years. Other shipments comprise tobacco, rice, turpentine, rosin, watermelons, fruits, and vegetables, and yellow pine lumber. From New York were sent last year 130,000 tons of sundries and 6357½ tons of railroad iron.

On the retirement of Mr. Waddell (since deceased) last year from the presidency, the late Hon. Edward·C. Anderson, many years mayor of Savannah, and an ex-officer of the United States navy, and who had previously been a managing director, was elected to fill the vacancy. The wharves, docks, and warehouses of the company at Savannah are of ample capacity and excellent arrangement for the transaction of its business. Through bills of lading and tickets are given by this company over the Central Railroad of Georgia, Savannah, and Western railroads, and close connection made with the steamers and railroad to Florida.

1875.—THE MITU-BISHI STEAM NAVIGATION COMPANY.—This line of steamers, under the Japanese flag, was established in 1875, and its shares were held almost exclusively by Japanese. In 1876 it owned four steamers,—viz., the "Tokio-Murin," née "New York," the "Kunayana-Murin," née "Madras," the "Takar-Murin," née "Acanthia," and the "Zazon;" while others were in course of construction in Great Britain, which were to form a weekly line between China and the Japanese ports of Nagasaki, Hiogo, Imioscki, and Yokohama. This was a great advance from their seclusion and isolation from the rest of the world, from which they were awaked by their treaty with Commodore M. C. Perry, in 1854, only twenty-one years before. This company purchased steamers with great rapidity, and now (1882) owns considerably over thirty steamers, and they are all named for Japanese cities, as "Hiroshima Naru," City of Hiroshima, once the "Golden Age" of the Pacific Mail Company.

THE ATLAS STEAMSHIP COMPANY.—The vessels of the Atlas Line are iron screw ships constructed under the superintendence of the surveyors to English Lloyds, and in accordance with the requirements of the British Board of Trade. The company's fleet consists of the following steamships:

Name.	Gross Tonnage.	Effective Horse-power.	Name.	Gross Tonnage.	Effective Horse-power.
Albano	2350	2000	Avila	1200	900
Alene	2104	1600	Antilles	1400	1000
Alvo	2009	1500	Alpin	890	700
Athos	1948	1500	Arden	544	600
Ailsa	1950	1200	Arran	462	500
Alps	1750	1000	Aden Branch steamer	..	..
Andes	1750	1000	Etna	1250	..
Alvena	1705	950	Claribel	1100	..
Atlas	1280	900	Also the Satellite tow-boat.		

The accommodations for passengers, with a special view to their comfort, are located in the central portion of the steamer, forward of the engines, and both saloons and state-rooms are above the main-deck. This prevents any annoyance from the smell or noise proceeding from the engine-room, whilst the passengers are placed in that part where the motion is least felt and the best ventilation is secured. In the tropics these considerations are of paramount importance to the comfort of travelers. The crew and officers are all berthed in the after-portion of the vessel, so that the forepart is left clear as a promenade-deck. The steamers of this line leave New York every fourteen days for Kingston, Jamaica, Savanilla, Carthagena, and Colon, Aspinwall, from whence they return direct to New York. Their steamers also leave New York every ten days for ports in Hayti, and return *via* Kingston, Jamaica. They also leave New York for Cape Hayti and ports on the north side of Jamaica, and Greytown, Nicaraugua, returning *via* ports in Jamaica to New York. Still another line of their steamers, under the Spanish flag, sail from New York to Maracaibo, calling at Porto Rico, and returning *via* Cape Hayti to New York.

The company has also established, under a contract with the colonial government, a weekly steam-service from Kingston around the island of Jamaica, calling at all the principal ports.

The Atlas Company suddenly advertised, a short time ago, the departure of two apparently new steamers, the "Avila" and the "Antilles," and two of their well-known boats, the "Claribel" and the "Atlas," disappeared as suddenly from their list. Whence these new steamers? What had become of the old ones? It was no secret; the company wished to put two of its vessels under the Spanish flag, and had simply changed the English names to Spanish ones.

ROACH'S UNITED STATES AND BRAZIL MAIL STEAMSHIP LINE. —The steamships of the United States and Brazil Mail Steamship Line (now defunct) were built by John Roach & Son, at Chester, Pennsylvania, on the Delaware, and were fine specimens of naval architecture. They were 370 feet long over all, 39 feet beam, with a depth of hold from base line to the top of spar-deck of 31 feet 6 inches, and had a custom-house register of 3500 tons. Their mean low draught was 21 feet. They had three decks, besides the hurricane-deck, from the stern extending to the after-side of the main hatch. The deck-frames were of iron, and the deck-houses all iron braced and stiffened in the most thorough manner. They had six bulkheads dividing them into seven water-tight compartments. Connected with these compartments were bilge-pumps with separate valves, so that one or all could be simultaneously operated.

Built under the supervision of the French Bureau Veritas, and the American Shipmasters' Association of New York, they were rendered perfectly seaworthy by the use of the best of material in their construction and equipment. They were furnished with 8 metallic life-boats, having a carrying capacity of from 35 to 60 each, and with four life-rafts capable of carrying 700 persons. The hoisters, windlass, capstan, and steering apparatus were all worked by steam. The coal-bunkers carried 700 tons of coal, and the temporary and shifting bunkers would carry as many more tons. The machinery proper consisted of two compound surface condensing engines, the cylinders of which were 42 inches for the high pressure and 74 inches for the low pressure; each 60 inches stroke, 2500 horse-power, and with separate engines for working the air and circulating pumps. By this arrangement the main engines had only to turn the propeller. The six boilers were of the cylindrical return tubular type, their working pressure 90 pounds to the square inch. There was also a donkey boiler for hoisting purposes, clearing the bilge, and supplying the main boilers with water in case of fire. The propeller or screw was a four-bladed brass one, 16 feet in diameter, of the Hirsch patent. The maximum passenger capacity was 100 first-class passengers and 400 in the steerage. Commodious rooms were provided on the hurricane-deck for the captain and officers; also a large smoking-room richly furnished with lounge seats and circular tables. The accommodation for first-class passengers consisted of a saloon 130 feet long by 30 wide. It was a sumptuous and commodious apartment. It had six rows of tables parallel to each other, over 60 feet in length, sufficient to accommodate over 100 persons. Alongside of them were placed sofas with shifting backs, and in addition a range of sofas stretching almost around the saloon. The chairs and sofas were upholstered in crimson velvet.

The saloon was lighted through the day by fifty-two square sliding windows, each 26 by 20 inches, besides six large mahogany skylights fitted with ornamental glass, serving the purposes of light and ventilation. The ceiling of this spacious and beautiful saloon was over eight feet from the floor to the under edge of the deck beams, and the floors were inlaid with oak and black walnut. The saloon was richly carpeted and adorned with mirrors; its panelings were Hungarian ash and French walnut, with Honduras mahogany mouldings. The stairways were of highly-polished woods, and the newel-posts were surmounted by bronze figures supporting a lamp. The furniture and appliances were of the latest patterns and most elegant finish.

The state-rooms, or sleeping-apartments, for the first-class passengers were on the spar- and hurricane-decks aft of the saloon, and were not only commodious, well lighted, and fully ventilated, but furnished in a style of luxurious comfort. All of the berths were fitted with rich lambrequins and lace curtains. The saloon, ladies' cabin, smoking-room, and each individual berth in the first-class departments were supplied with electrical annunciators, communicating with the steward's department. The afterpart of the main saloon was the ladies' boudoir, containing a bath-room, supplied with hot, cold, and sea water, and set off with lounges, mirrors, etc. The barber-shop, amidships, on the spar-deck, had two bath-rooms complete in their appointments. The steamers were each supplied with a competent and skilled surgeon.

The rate of passage from New York to St. Thomas was $70; to Para, $130; to Pernambuco, $150; to Bakia, $160; to Rio de Janeiro, $175. Children under twelve years of age half price.

The whole project was the enterprise of one plucky man, John Roach, a deserving citizen, yet probably one of the best-abused men in the country. The founder of the line risked a million of his own private capital in starting a line of steamers to an empire six thousand miles away, from which the United States buys $60,000,000 worth of goods every year, and to which it would like to sell a similar sum annually, and could, in time, if facilities for the trade are created and maintained. Previous to the starting of the line our merchants were handicapped. It was as though Boston were trying to do business with San Francisco by means of steamers sailing to Panama, while New York was trading over a direct railroad route across the continent. We had to send a long way to reach Brazil. The English traded direct. Our mails and valuable goods to Brazil had to go by way of England, taking ten or thirteen days to cross the Atlantic, having often to wait ten days in England for a steamer, and then consuming from twenty to twenty-five days in going from the British Isles to Brazil.

When this new line from this country direct was started, facilities were created which were imperatively needed. The convenience of the line was so great that it has been frankly and cordially conceded. The steamers were well managed, and in three years never missed a trip nor failed to sail on time. By means of the line mails were sent in twenty-two days direct; and the certainty and regularity of the trips were of advantage almost to the whole American public. A wide variety of miscellaneous products were introduced, little by little, and the start of a large trade effected. In quantities of goods sold the export trade to Brazil increased constantly while the steamers ran. The line brought travelers and merchants to the country in large numbers, amounting in the three years to about 2000. Profitable orders and contracts were brought to this country by these travelers, which otherwise would not have been secured. There was a large reduction in freights also, through the operation of this American line. Instead of its costing from 70 to 85 cents a bag to get coffee to New York from Brazil, the freight was reduced to 50, and even to 30 cents a bag. This commodity was brought six thousand miles for $5 and $6 a ton, that is, at the rate of $1 a ton for a thousand miles of voyage, which is about the cheapest ocean transportation ever known.

The saving to the United States upon the immense importations of coffee was very large. The freight on measurement goods was also lowered from 35 cents a cubic foot to about 20 cents. These reductions and the more important fact of regular and quick communication were of genuine service to the public; and it was with sincere regret that business men learned of the discontinuance of the American Line. During the three years that Mr. Roach maintained the line, $1,400,000 was paid out for expenses, $92,000 for repairs in the United States, and $300,000 for expenses abroad. And it was estimated that the business men of this country saved $1,700,000 by a reduction of South American freights during that period.

Mr. Roach had very far-reaching plans. Could this line have received the support he sought to obtain for it, he would have built more steamers and started several other lines. The Brazilian fleet would have been enlarged, and direct trade would have been opened to other coasts. The Buenos Ayres project was only one of many in view.

It seems a pity that the question of mail compensation to the Brazilian Line could never have been discussed on its merits. Mr. Roach's appeal to Congress was not by any means entirely defenseless. He carried the United States mails 140,000 miles in 1879 for $1875, while three coasting lines carried them unitedly 123,400 miles and got $102,800 for the service. Mr. Roach was beaten, not by the impolicy of the subsidy system, but by an organized effort, both in the United States and in Brazil, to break him down. People went from city to city with subscription papers to raise money for use against him at Washington; and the speeches made at Washington in opposition to his line were translated into Portuguese and sent to Brazil by thousands to create a coldness in official circles there against the American steamers.

The two steamers "City of Para" and "City of Rio Janeiro" (?) were sold to the Pacific Mail Steamship Company, and are now running on the west coast of America. The history of this line is that of an unfortunate enterprise, undertaken in advance of its time, there can be little or no doubt to be revived at no very distant day with a profitable result.

THE MALLORY LINE OF STEAMSHIPS.—I have been unable to obtain the historical information I hoped for concerning this important steamship enterprise. I learn from its circular that the Mallory Line to Texas comprises the following steamships:

	Tons.		Tons.
Guadaloupe	2840	Colorado	2764
Rio Grande	2566	Carondelet	1508
San Marcos	2840	Western Texas	1210
State of Texas	1696		

These vessels stop at Key West, Florida, Galveston, Brazos, Brownsville, Corpus Christi, and Indianola, Texas. The line also has connection with Florida, Nassau, and New Providence. Steamers of the line leave New York every Friday for Florida, arriving at Fernandina on Tuesday, and from Florida there is a steamer to Nassau every week. The iron steamer "Western Texas" performs the service for Florida; and the iron steamship "City of San Antonio," 1572 tons, is now running regularly on the Mallory Line between New York and Florida. She can carry seven thousand boxes of oranges in well-ventilated spaces, has fine passenger accommodations, and is fast.

1879.—THE RED "D" LINE OF STEAMSHIPS.—This line of steamships, running to Laguayra, Puerto Cabello, Carácas, and Maracaibo, was inaugurated in November, 1879, when the company commenced to substitute them for the line of sailing vessels that had been engaged in the trade for upward of forty years. At first foreign chartered steamers were engaged in the service. Later on it was decided to replace them with steamers built in the United States specially for the trade. Accordingly contracts were entered into with the William Cramp & Son Ship-Engine Building Company of Philadelphia for the steamer "Carácas," and subsequently for the steamer "Valencia." The "Carácas" left New York on her first voyage in June, 1881, and the "Valencia" in May, 1882.

These two steamers, of about 1200 tons, new measurement (act of Congress, 1882), are built in the most substantial manner, and have the highest classification. They are well appointed for passenger as well as freight and mail service. They connect at the island of Carácas with the branch steamer "Maracaibo," running to the port of Maracaibo. The "Maracaibo" was built under contract with Messrs. Neafie & Levy, of Philadelphia, and left there in August, 1880. She is built of wood, in the most substantial manner, has ample accommodations for passengers, and is about 500 tons, old measurement. Being intended exclusively for foreign service, she carries the British flag. The steamers of the main line, the "Carácas" and "Valencia," are officered and manned by citizens of the United States, and carry the American flag.

A steamship of this line leaves New York twice a month for Laguayra, Porto Cabello, and Carácas, the round trip from and back to New York occupying about twenty-six days.

NEW YORK, HAVANA, AND MEXICAN MAIL STEAMSHIP LINE.—The company's fleet comprises the following first-class steamships: "City of Puebla," 3100 tons; "City of Alexandria;" "City of Washington," 2618 tons; "British Empire," 4000 tons, chartered; "City of Merida," 2000 tons; "City of Mexico," 1027 tons; which are appointed to leave New York every Thursday and Havana every Saturday.

Leaving New York direct for Havana, they proceed from there every Tuesday for Vera Cruz and intermediate ports. On the return trip they arrive at Havana Wednesday or Thursday, and leave direct for New York every Saturday.

Steamers of this line also run every three weeks between New Orleans and Vera Cruz, connecting with the steamers for Havana and New York.

With a view of preventing sea-sickness and of adding to the comforts of passengers, there have been placed in a number of state-rooms of the steamships "City of Washington" and "City of Alexandria" the new patent Huston self-leveling berths, which remain always and under all circumstances in a perfectly horizontal position, however great may be the rolling and pitching of the vessel.

There has also been introduced into the dining-saloons, instead of the inconvenient long tables and sofas of the old style, small tables that will accommodate from four to eight persons only, with single revolving chairs for each one, in order to avoid the usual confusion and noise incidental to the dining together of all the passengers.

The "City of Alexandria" was built by John Roach in 1880, and is 338 feet over all, 38 feet 6 inches wide, and 33 feet deep from the hurricane-deck, being 10 feet longer, 6 inches wider, and 2 feet shallower than the "City of Washington," which in all other respects she resembles. Both steamers have excellent accommodations for 150 first-class passengers.

The "City of Merida" and the "City of Mexico" are wooden ships, built at Greenpoint, Long Island. The "British Empire," chartered, was built for the New Zealand trade, and is 410 feet long, 40 feet beam, and 28 feet hold.

1882.—BOSTON AND SAVANNAH STEAMSHIP COMPANY.—Previous to the war of the Rebellion the water transportation business between the port of Savannah, Georgia, and Boston was by sailing vessels, regular lines of packets, for freighting purposes mainly, running between this and other principal Southern ports and Boston. About the close of the war a line of small steamers was put on for the Savannah business, which marked the beginning of a revolution in that trade.

These steamers were originally provided and sent out to take advantage of the call for cotton transportation between Savannah and Boston. Compared with the present facilities they were small affairs, 450 bales of cotton, without any other description of freight, being sufficient to load them completely. When the cotton-carrying season was over (September to April is the season) their business was considered nearly at a stand-still, until the autumn should again bring about the particular state of things which they were designed to fit into.

In 1869 the firm of F. W. Nickerson & Co., of Boston, established a steamer line on this route. Their first vessel, the "Oriental," was an iron screw steamer of 800 tons burden. The "Oriental" made the round trip in twenty days. The "Alhambra," a steamer of 700 tons, was added. In time other steamers took place in the line, and regular trips were made, the sailing days being the 10th, 20th, and 30th of each month. Finally weekly trips were made, and the carrying capacity of the ships had increased to 1800 bales of compressed cotton in a single cargo.

Finally, on the 7th of September, 1882, the Boston and Savannah Steamship Company was organized to take the place previously filled by F. W. Nickerson & Co., that is, this firm and connections became the company with the title just named, and a new departure has been taken in the business by the purchase from the Ocean Steamship Company of the "Gate City" and the "City of Columbus," and placing them on the line in connection with the "Seminole."

The first line of steamers established (at the close of the war) found available as freights boots and shoes, bagging for cotton-bales, furniture, fish, and the like commodities. The return cargo was exclusively cotton for the use of the New England mills. The changes which have occurred in the character of cargoes and their destination during the comparatively short time which has passed since are well worth consideration.

The bagging forming an important feature in outward cargoes was East India gunny-cloth, imported to Boston, and thence shipped by these steamers to Savannah as covering for cotton-bales. Thus it became an interesting factor in transportation both ways. The East India gunny-cloth disappeared entirely from commerce, in this direction at least, five years ago; and in its place appeared a domestic bagging, manufactured in the neighborhood of Boston. In place of the gunny-cloth once imported to Boston, now jute-butts are imported, and of these butts the domestic bagging is made, which alone is now used in covering cotton-bales.

Another change in the character of the freight carried out is in the article of fish. Formerly these were taken largely in bulk; but now the product is mostly canned, even mackerel being sent South in this form of packing. It is not unusual for one of the present steamers to take out five thousand packages of fish at a trip. Some articles of freight are so singular as to be almost unaccounted for; as, for instance, from three hundred to five hundred bedsteads are taken out at nearly every trip, and chairs and other cheap furniture in proportion.

In the present cargoes outward from Boston bacon forms an important element. The time is not long since all this supply went South from the West. Now, as many as eight hundred boxes of bacon are sent to Savannah per trip of these steamers. Immense quantities of potatoes and apples are also taken out, the first named principally for planting in Georgia and Florida, and in the spring the new potatoes produced form an important element in the return cargoes. Great numbers of pianos, organs, carriages, etc., are also taken out.

The difference in quantity of freight carried now, compared with former times, is shown by the figures, the present steamers taking about 100,000 cubic feet, or 2500 tons, of cargo, against 15,000 cubic feet, or about 400 tons each, in the early days. An ordinary freight-car will carry thirty-six bales of compressed cotton at one time. A cotton cargo for one of these steamers is, therefore, equivalent to the loading of a freight-train of 122 cars.

A peculiarity of the composition of the return cargoes is the rapid growth of the naval-stores business as an element in the transportation of this line. Eight years ago there was not perhaps a turpentine-still in Georgia, at least not one of any size. Now Savannah rivals Wilmington, North Carolina, in the production of piney products, and the shipments to Boston from Savannah average one thousand barrels of resin and three hundred barrels of spirits of turpentine per week by these steamers. Lumber, once brought in sailing-vessels by slow and laborious process, may now be telegraphed for at the mills in Georgia, and fine yellow-pine cargoes be landed in Boston within six days thereafter.

Cotton forwarded from the principal centres in Georgia reaches Boston by this means in an average of six days from starting. The preference in transportation is given to spinners' cotton,—that is, cotton to be used in the mills at this end of the route,—but usually at least one-quarter of the cargo is on through bills of lading, and goes directly across the ocean to foreign ports. The sea-island cotton, for the various thread-mills near Boston, is largely brought by these steamers, and rice, hides, and wool are also brought largely.

In the early period of the development of these transportation interests the ships were hauled off as soon as the cotton season was over, in the spring. Now the business is more profitable when cotton is "off" than during its season. This quick transportation has developed and increased to an enormous extent the truck-farming business of Georgia and Florida, it being a matter of common practice to deliver produce in Boston four days after it is harvested in Florida. Immense quantities of early vegetables are thus shipped in excellent condition to Boston, the succession taking place regularly, and anticipating the Northern crops often by many weeks. Later on, of melons alone there are often enough shipped by a single steamer to occupy the entire capacity of the upper between decks, or as many as forty thousand melons at one trip. Cotton forms a part of the cargo of every shipment, and through bills of lading for this article appear in every manifest.

The orange season for the section of the South (Florida and Georgia) continues from November to February. A few years ago only a small amount of this fruit came to Boston by water; now these steamers bring from two hundred to six hundred boxes of oranges per trip during the season.

And thus these two sections, North and South, minister to the wants of each other through the mediumship of this transportation line. Not alone this, but the system of through bills of lading, which is operated both ways, makes these ministrations far-reaching, and is already indicative of grand results in the future in the interests of Boston as a commercial centre. It will be noticed that the development already secured has touched importantly upon her export interests, and the possibilities in this direction are not limited. At least, an element worth taking into account is revealed by these transactions.

There is a large passenger business between New England and the far South during certain seasons of the year. While the heated term is on the Southerners delight in visiting our mountains, and lakes, and sea-shores,—in fact, every part of thickly-settled and open-armed New England. From November to May the New-Englander finds equal pleasure in sojourning in the mild climate of Georgia and Florida. Heretofore, transportation has been *via* New York City, involving changes of cars, hotel stoppages, and various annoying dependencies. The present steamers of the Boston and Savannah Steamship Company are fitted expressly for first-class passenger transportation, the cabins, saloons, and state-rooms being as fine as can be found anywhere afloat. Since the sea trip is direct and most delightful, and the expense of transportation less than one-half of that per rail, it is no wonder that the route is preferred.[1]

1882.—THINGVALLA LINE.—The passenger steamship "Geyser," Captain Thompson, of the new Thingvalla Line, sailed from Copenhagen in December, 1881, on her first trip to New York. The Thingvalla Company is composed of Danish capitalists, foremost among whom is C. F. Tietgen, the founder of the Great Northern Telegraph Company, whose lines extend from England through Asia to the Pacific. The steamship "Thingvalla" had for two years made

[1] The foregoing account of this company is derived from the Sunday Boston *Herald* of September 24, 1882.

irregular trips between Copenhagen and New York. The company put three new steamers on the stocks in Copenhagen and in Malmo, Sweden; of these the "Geyser" and the "Hecla" have been finished, and the "Iceland" is about to be launched. The steamers are the largest ever built in Denmark. Their engines are of 2000 tons indicated horse-power, and are designed to make twelve knots an hour. The vessels are 3000 tons burden, 312 feet long, 39 feet wide, and calculated to carry 40 cabin and 700 steerage passengers, and a crew of 50 men. Their route will be from Copenhagen around the northeast coast of Scotland, Christiansand, Norway, being their only stopping-place. By going to the north of Scotland time will be saved, and it is expected that the steamers will make the trip to New York in thirteen or fourteen days. An effort will be made to secure the carrying of the mail between the United States and the Scandinavian kingdoms as soon as all the four steamers are running. Until the summer of 1882 the steamers will make fortnightly trips; if desirable after that the company's fleet will be increased.

The "Thingvalla" brought to New York as freight forty thousand heads of cabbage that arrived in fair condition.

The "Hecla," the second of the line, made the voyage in thirteen days from Christiansand. Previous to the establishment of this line passengers and fast freight from Copenhagen and ports of Denmark had to go to Bremen, Hamburg, Havre, Liverpool, or London to take steamer for New York. Now these vessels are full of emigrant passengers, and the cabin traffic is also large. The "Hecla," on her first trip, carried 760 emigrants. She has cabin accommodations for 30 passengers. The "Hecla" was built at Malmo, Sweden; is 315 feet in length, 40 feet beam, has 30 feet depth of hold, and is of 1846 tons capacity. Her saloon and smoking-room are on the main-deck, the state-rooms and captain's room being immediately below. Electric bells communicate from the state-rooms to the steward's room, and between the bridge, wheel-house, and engine-room.

1882.—A WEST INDIA STEAMSHIP ENTERPRISE.—Senor Martinez de Campos, a lieutenant-general in the Spanish army, and a statesman of high reputation, has been elected president of a Cuban steamship company, which will confine its operations almost entirely to the West Indian islands. Of course this new enterprise will be liberally subsidized by the Spanish home government.

Seven or eight iron steamships are to be purchased or constructed in England, each to have a carrying capacity of at least 2500 tons. They will be fitted with all the modern conveniences necessary for capturing the large passenger traffic that has grown up between the islands.

Senor Campos proposes to run his ships to all the principal ports in the West Indies, to Central America, and to the northern coast of South America. They will carry cargoes of assorted goods entered in bond at Havana, and from that port will distribute these goods among all the ports embraced in the sphere of operation marked out for the new line. The return cargoes will be composed of the products of the various islands and countries at which the ships will touch; and these cargoes will enter at Havana, to be distributed by other Spanish steam lines among the markets of the world.

A marked feature of the new enterprise is the design to secure, as far as possible, the service of free Cuban negroes for firemen and coal-passers, and as sailors only those who have passed through the "vomito," or whose residence in the tropics warrants the assumption of their thorough acclimation. If a sufficient number of free negroes cannot be obtained on the island, the captains of the vessels will be empowered to employ such persons of color residing on the other islands who will fill the requirements of the company in this sanitary respect.

By the employment of none but acclimated officers and seamen the company believes it will economize both time and money. There are instances on record when ships have lost a part of their crews in one short voyage among the fever-stricken islands, and have been laid up in some out-of-the-way port until hands could be procured to work them. Passengers, also, would rather travel in vessels thus manned, for when sickness breaks out on board a ship it almost always makes its first appearance among the crew, who are more exposed to the heat of the sun than the passengers, who are protected from its rays by awnings.

Mr. De Campos's new enterprise will receive government help the moment the first ship puts to sea.

1876.—THE NEW YORK AND CUBA MAIL STEAMSHIP COMPANY.—This company forms a direct weekly mail line of American steamers between New York and Havana; it also sends a monthly steamer to Santiago de Cuba and Cienfuegos, leaving New York on Saturdays and Havana on Wednesdays. The New York and Havana Line comprises the steamships "Newport," "Saratoga," and "Niagara." The "Santiago" forms its connection between New York and Santiago, etc. The steamers of the line also connect at Havana with other lines, visiting West India and Florida ports and New Orleans.

The "Newport," built in 1880, is an iron ship of 3000 tons, 348 feet in length, 38 feet beam, and 23 feet from the spar-deck to the keelson. The "Newport" has made the fastest time on record between New York and Havana. Her engines are on the compound principle. The cylinders are 90 and 48 inches diameter respectively, with $4\frac{1}{2}$ feet stroke. The engines are capable of developing 3000 horse-power, or about one horse-power for every ton of her tonnage, which is greater in proportion than that of the "Arizona," the most powerful steamship afloat in proportion to registered tonnage. The entire engine department is said to be more roomy and better ventilated than that on any steamship afloat. All the steam pumps are so arranged that they may be connected with any part of the vessel in case of fire or leak, their united capacity being equal to 70,000 gallons, or about 1750 barrels, a minute.

The "Saratoga" takes the place of the well-known steamer bearing the same name purchased by the Russian government in 1878 and converted into a cruiser. She is 2500 tons register, 320 feet long, 38.4 feet beam, 23 feet deep to the main-deck, and 31 feet to the hurricane-deck. She has compound engines of 2000 horse-power, calculated to give her a speed of fifteen knots an hour.

The "Niagara," built in 1877, is 2300 tons, 294 feet long, and her cabin accommodations are the same as the "Niagara,"

The "Santiago" was built by John Roach & Son. She is of iron, 290 feet long, 39 feet beam, and measures 2400 tons. She has the usual water-tight compartments and all the latest improvements.

1882.—SOCIÉTÉ POSTALE FRANÇAISE DE L'ATLANTIQUE.—The Société Postale Française de l'Atlantique, established two years ago under subsidies from the governments of Canada and Brazil for carrying their mails, but sailing under the French flag, having determined to send the steamers of its line to Boston, has established two lines, one for the Brazil trade and the other for the trade between Boston, Antwerp, and Havre. The line will be a monthly one to and from each port. The line consists of the following steamships: "Ville de Para," "Ville de Ceare," "Ville de Montreal," "Ville de Quebec," and "Ville de Halifax." The "Ville de Para" left Montreal for Brazil in October, and on her return will reach Boston about November 30. The first steamer from Antwerp to Boston, the "Ville de Montreal," will leave the former city about the last of November or first of December. Mr. William D. Bentley, consul-general of the emperor of Brazil, is general agent of the company, and his connection with the Brazilian government is of great advantage to the company he represents in its relations with that country. The capital of the company is ten million francs, all paid in. The president is Monsieur Derrière, president of the Société Générale of France, and director of the Bank of France. The company began running between Canada and Brazil with chartered boats, but it now has five new steamers of 3000 tons burden. They are built in the most substantial manner, propelled by 1200 horse-power engines, and are sumptuously fitted up, with ample accommodations for forty first-class passengers each, and are said to excel anything in the way of steamers ever run from Montreal. These vessels will afford the best facilities for the direct importation of iron-ware, wire goods, wines, liquor, coffee, sugar, rubber, and, in brief, all French and Brazilian goods, and for exporting grain, meats, and breadstuffs.

1882.—STEAMERS ON LONG ISLAND.—Each of the three lines running boats on the Sound to New York—viz., the Fall River Line, so called, the Providence or Stonington Line, and the Norwich Line—have taken a new departure, as it were, within the last two years, adding a new boat to their lines. Some description of these floating palaces may not be out of place as showing, by comparison, the progress in size, construction, speed, etc., with the pioneer boats on those waters some fifty or sixty years ago.

THE "PILGRIM," OF THE FALL RIVER LINE.—The hull of this new floating palace is of iron, and both builders and owners have united to make her absolutely non-combustible and non-sinkable. The great increase in the size of the Sound steamers during the last few years had generated an intrinsic weakness which demanded radical changes in material, methods, etc., of construction. To supply the lack of natural strength, so glaring in the ancient steamers, the hull of the "Pilgrim" is cellular, or, in other words, has a double skin, inside and outside, with a system of longitudinal framing between. The system of longitudinal and transverse framing is continuous in its strength, and in a great degree is independent of the inside and outside platings, which, attached to the framework, form a hollow box or girder the whole length of the vessel's side and bottom. This hollow box or tank is 24 inches deep or wide at the sides of the vessel, and down to the turn of the bilge, whence it is increased in size (internal) to 36 inches at the centre of the hull, or across the keel. This double hull is divided into ninety-six water-tight compartments, formed by the water-tight athwartship floors and bracket frames, 27 feet apart, and the longitudinals,—keelsons running 340 feet fore and aft, and water-tight at all intersections. This tank, so to speak, was tested when building with a pressure of five pounds to the square inch, thus insuring its efficiency in practice. The outside plating being, of course, water-tight, and the inside, for a distance of 340 feet, water-tight also, it can readily be seen that a puncture or strain of the outside skin will have very little injurious effect on the vessel's buoyancy; but, in addition to the safety provided by the construction of the double hull, the interior capacity is again divided into water-tight compartments by half a dozen athwartship water-tight bulkheads, a subdivision which makes the probability of sinking by collision or a rupture of the bottom almost impossible. These bulkheads extend up to the main-deck, which is built of iron, and made water-tight to the outside of the guard-frame. The wheel batteries are of iron, and the inclosure of the engine, boilers, chimney, kitchen, smoke-pipes, and ventilators being also of iron, the probability of the vital parts of the steamer being destroyed by fire is reduced to a minimum. This non-combustible and non-sinkable hull is 384 feet long, 50 feet moulded beam,—about 87 feet wide over guards,—and 17 feet 6 inches deep at the lowest point on the sides. By reason of

HISTORY OF STEAM NAVIGATION. 407

the peculiar type of model, together with its exceedingly large dimensions, it will be observed that enormous structural strains will be generated when in service, to counteract which requires a careful and scientific adjustment of the resisting material. The longitudinal bracket plate system, which originated in the English Board of Admiralty, has been adopted, and the extent and degree of skill and care which has been exercised in proportioning the different parts of the hull to their respective strain is remarkable. The keel is double plate, the inner one 20 by $11\frac{1}{4}$ inches and the outer one 26 by $13\frac{1}{16}$ inches. The main keelson is a single plate 3 feet deep, $10\frac{1}{4}$ inches thick, and in length not less than 28 feet; the butts are double-strapped, with heavy plates. The longitudinals are six in number, each side of the centre keelson, and extend continuously, fore and aft, as far as possible, the outer ones forming breast-hooks at the ends about four feet apart. They are built of plates, 28 feet in length, with a width, according to location, of 24 to 36 inches. Two of these are secured to the outer and inner skins with single angle irons, and the other two, the heaviest ones, are secured to the outer and inner plating with double angle irons, and made water-tight.

By the peculiar construction of this hull an endurance is obtained to which the stanchest craft that ever steamed through Long Island Sound is but a basket in comparison. There are half a dozen bulkheads,—one placed 26 feet abaft of stem, of $7\frac{1}{4}$-inch plate, stiffened with angle iron; one forward of the boilers; one between the boilers and engines; one abaft the engines; and one collision bulkhead aft. All the doors fit water-tight, and are so arranged as to open and close quickly. All of the internal supports of the boat are of the best of wrought iron, and no wood whatever is employed where metallic material could be substituted.

The plating of the outer hull is of the best flange iron, $12\frac{1}{8}$ inches thick, the plates not less than 14 feet long, with all butts planed and triple riveted. The bottom plating, in alternate strokes, is $11\frac{1}{4}$ inches thick, and the side and bilge plating, extending aft from the stem and forward of the stern port, is flush far enough to compare with the in-and-out plating of the bottom. The flush plating has seam straps in long lengths, and at and about the water-line the plating is doubled as a protection against ice. No plates are less than 14 feet long, while those of the sides, for a length of 280 feet midships, are at least 28 feet in length, and everything is heavily strapped and double and triple riveted. The hull has a heavy inner as well as an outer plating; the main-deck is also laid with stringer plates, and the saloon-deck strengthened by placing six-inch T iron carlings eight feet apart, all fore and aft. The steering apparatus has a steam stearing-gear, and there is an auxiliary steering-gear, always ready for immediate use in case of accident to the other. The fitting and furnishings are costly and elaborate, and every way in keeping with the thoroughness and stability of the craft which they adorn, and all parts of the boat are illuminated by electric lights.

THE NEW "RHODE ISLAND," OF THE STONINGTON LINE.—In 1882 the Stonington Line had its fleet strengthened by the restoration, in name at least, of the renowned steamer "Rhode Island," being the third to date of the line to bear that name, her immediate predecessor having been wrecked the year previous. The engines are about all comprised in the new craft which did service in the old boats which were so popular among the Sound line travelers between New York, Providence, and Boston. The old "Rhode Island" was constructed in 1872–73, and went upon the line July 17, 1873. She was a stanch boat in every particular, and was capable of most arduous service. One season, at least, she ran day and night trips continuously. It will be remembered that on her last trip for the season of 1880 she ran ashore in a dense fog at the Bonnet, opposite Dutch Island, and in a short time went to pieces, the wreckers saving only her engine, some of her cargo, and part of her furniture. Immediately after the disaster the steamship company decided to build another steamer to take the place of the one destroyed, and on the 1st of January, or thereabouts, gave the order for its construction to Robert Palmer, ship-builder at Noank, Connecticut. The forests of Connecticut and Virginia were drawn upon for white oak. Long Island and the North River furnished locust, and Jacksonville, Florida, the live-oak; Savannah and Cedar Keys the yellow pine. About the middle of February the keel was laid. The frame is of white oak, live-oak, and locust. It is secured by immense iron straps, $\frac{1}{2}$ or $\frac{3}{4}$ inch by 4 inches, and 18 or 20 feet long, let in flush with the timbers, the ends butted together and fished with strong plates, hot riveted through and through. Her dimensions are as follows: Length of keel, 325 feet; length of 10-feet water-line, 332 feet; length over all, 344 feet; width of hull, 46 feet; width over guards, 83 feet; depth of hold (clear), 15 feet; diameter of wheels, 39 feet 4 inches; length of buckets, 12 feet; capacity (carpenter's measurement), 2800 tons. She is run by the engine that was in the old "Rhode Island," which has been entirely overhauled and put in order. As in the old "Rhode Island," she has steam steering apparatus, and, in addition, is provided with a steam windlass.

1881.—The "City of Worcester," of the Norwich Line, was built by the Harlan & Hollingsworth Company, of Wilmington, Delaware. Her hull is of iron, the plating seven-sixteenths to three-quarters of an inch thickness, and the sheer streak $1\frac{1}{2}$ inches. Her principal dimensions are: Admeasurement, 2500 tons; length on water-line, 325 feet; length over all, 340 feet; beam, moulded, 46 feet; over all, 80 feet; depth from base-line to top of beams at dead flat, 16 feet 3 inches. She has six water-tight bulkheads fitted between double frames on the

HISTORY OF STEAM NAVIGATION. 409

side. All these bulkheads are extended to the guard-deck, being thoroughly braced and stayed by both vertical and diagonal angle irons. Should two of these bulkheads be destroyed by collision, the other four would float the boat. The machinery and the steam-chambers are inclosed in iron all the way up through the hurricane-deck, to afford perfect ventilation to the fire-room and give greater protection against fire. The two smoke-pipes are also inclosed in iron casings. Her machinery consists of a surface-condensing, working-beam engine, having a cylinder 90 inches in diameter by 12 feet stroke of piston, arranged with composition valves and seats and Stevens cut-off. The wheels are 38 feet in diameter, with buckets of about 11 feet face. The steamer is fitted with iron gallows frame, iron guard logs, iron king posts, and iron batteries and bulkheads for water-wheel houses. She has three main boilers, 37 feet 6 inches long by 12 feet diameter and 13 feet face, containing about 9300 feet of fire surface and 550 feet of grate surface. They will sustain a working pressure of 50 pounds to the square inch. She also has a 40-horse-power donkey boiler, with steam pump, located on the guard-deck, and fitted with the necessary attachments and fixtures. The boat has 200 tons of boilers, and her main boilers are claimed to be the largest in the world.

The hull is extra-braced forward, where she is also extra-plated as a guard against ice, through which she can be easily propelled with the full power of her engine. The hold is ventilated by a well between the boilers and machinery space, and also through the two hollow iron masts. The bottom of the boat is covered inside with the best quality of Portland cement. The anchors, worked from the upper deck, weigh 4100 and 3000 pounds respectively. The chain cables are 1⅜ and 1¼ inches in diameter, and are each 75 fathoms long. The windlass is worked by an independent engine.

The "City of Worcester" has eight boats hung on the davits, six 22 feet long each, and two 24 feet in length. These boats are square-sterned, as it was found when the steamer "City of New York" rescued the passengers from the wrecked "Narragansett" that the double-ender boat was next to useless for that work. In addition, the steamer has a small boat 16 feet long.

The precautions against fire are: On the main-deck 9 fire-plugs, 8 in the saloon, 4 in the hold, and 4 on the hurricane-deck. These plugs are supplied by 2 pumps, always in readiness for immediate action, the steam being supplied by the donkey boiler. 1450 feet of hose are at all times attached to the plugs, and used for no other purpose.

The freight capacity of the boat will easily accommodate 90 carloads. There is a separate gangway for passengers, by which they can enter or leave the vessel, with no bales, barrels, boxes, or baggage to molest them.

The saloon on the main-deck is separated from the freight compartment by pilasters and elaborately ornamented ground glass. The joiner-work is in mahogany, bird's-eye maple, French walnut and tulip woods, marquetry and gilt, and is tastefully relieved by the white ceiling and delicately tinted cornice. The cornice and pilasters in the main saloon above are a combination of hard woods and veneer-work, finished in the Eastlake or Queen Anne style. The forward saloon has an upper tier of state-rooms, with a mahogany overhanging balustrade all around, with mahogany stairways leading thereto. These stairways, and all on the boat, are covered with stamped gold-bronze brass. Each of the stairways has a design having an elegance distinctively its own.

The dining-room is in the forward saloon of the upper-deck, away from the odors of machinery. There are 175 state-rooms in all, each having one of Jennings's closets, supplied from a tank amidships connected with a small engine, which keeps a continuous cleansing flow through them. The wash-rooms and large state-rooms are inodorous, the water coming from another tank. For two lengths abaft and forward of the wheel the state-rooms are three rows deep; elsewhere there are two rows on each side. Besides the ordinary state-rooms, having two berths in each, there are twelve large bedstead state-rooms,—four aft, two amidships, and six forward. All the rooms are ventilated by transoms over the doors, as well as by windows. Each room has an electric annunciator; the inside furnishings are in mahogany, French walnut, bird's-eye maple, and other hard woods, and are fitted with the Peerless wire mattress. There are 150 open berths in the hold, divided into forward and after gentlemen's cabins, with the ladies' cabin in the stern. These berths are well ventilated, there being several feet of space between the cabin walls and the steamer's plating.

The steamer is heated by steam; marble-top radiators are in the saloons, and each state-room has its independent heating coil. The lighting is by Edison's incandescent electric light. There are 250 of these lamps, of 16-candle power each, the electricity for which is generated by an independent 15-horse-power engine. The boat is also piped for gas, and chandeliers are fitted for burning mineral sperm oil.

The doors are furnished with "Parliament" hinges, which allows of their being unshipped and used as life-preservers. The pilot-house is finished in hard woods, with hard wood steering-wheel, chairs, sheaves, and fixtures. The steering is by steam or hand, as desired. The kitchen has its independent steam-boiler, the ice-room is near by, and in the forward hold is the officers' mess-room. There is ample room on the promenade-deck, and the roomy guards make moving about an easy and agreeable possibility.

The steamer's lines are pleasing to the eye, and her exterior ornamentation is tasteful. On each paddle-box is a seal of the City of Worcester, Massachusetts, encircled with gilt-work, from which diverge the sunset-colored rays of the lattice-work, between which one gets glimpses of the great red wheel inside. All modern improvements entering into the construction of a first-class steamer have been introduced into the "City of Worcester." She is faster than the "City of New York" of this line, that boat, the fastest on the Sound, having made the distance between docks, one hundred and twenty miles, in six hours and five minutes,—a record that has never been beaten.

The first impression on boarding the "Worcester" is the substantial character of her appointments and her capacity. Upon entering her saloons one is struck with their magnificence, and by the absence of all gaudiness, or with so little of the throbbing so disagreeable to many people. Quiet as a well or dead-house. The passenger, to the fullest sense, whichever way he turns, finds a repetition of the idea of bountiful provision or manifestation of hospitable intention.

The "City of Worcester" took her place on the Norwich Line, and began her trips in connection with the New England Railroad from Boston to New York in September, 1881.

1880.—THE "ORIENT."—The steamship "Orient," belonging to the Orient Steam Navigation Company, launched at Glasgow in 1880, was designed to sail direct for Australia. Her measurement over all was 460 feet; 455 feet 6 inches between perpendiculars; beam, 46.35 feet; depth of main-deck, 27.1 feet, and to the after-deck, 35.1 feet. She can carry 3000 tons of coal and 3600 tons of cargo of 40 feet measurement, has accommodations for one hundred and twenty first-class, one hundred and thirty second-class, and three hundred steerage or third-class passengers. Her cost was about £150,000. Her displacement 9500 tons. The crank-shaft is 20 inches in diameter; screw-shaft, 18½ inches in diameter. She is propelled by a four-bladed screw, 22 feet in diameter and having 30 feet pitch. She was expected to burn from 2500 to 2800 tons of coal on her voyage to Australia, and was steered by steam.

1882.—A new steamship, called the "Austral," has been built by John Elder & Co. for the Australian trade. Her length over all is 474 feet; her tonnage 9500 tons. She has been built throughout of mild steel, and has three steel decks. The lightness of the material of which she is constructed causes her to draw comparatively little water, and it may be said that it will be hardly possible to sink or burn her. She is divided below the inner skin and the double bottom into nineteen separate water-tight compartments; and in the hull proper within the interior skin she is divided by thirteen water-tight bulkheads, ten of which run up to the level of the main-deck. If the whole of the lower compartments were filled with water, the effect would be an additional draught to the extent of eighteen inches, and if by accident or design the sea obtained free communication with any two of the holds, the stability and surplus buoyancy of the vessel would prevent her from being endangered.

THE CASTLE LINE.—The steamships of this line carry Her Majesty's mails between London and South Africa, sailing from London every alternate Tuesday, and from Dartmouth every alternate Friday, for Cape Town, Mossel Bay, Algoa Bay, Port Alfred, East London, and Natal, calling regularly at Madeira, and touching at St. Helena and Ascension at stated intervals.

The fleet of this company comprise the

	Tons.		Tons.
Armadele, Castle of	4350	Northan Castle	2800
Antonish Castle	4350	Dunbar Castle	2800
Dunnotar Castle	4350	Taymouth Castle	1827
Garth Castle	3705	Duart Castle	1827
Drummond Castle	3705	Lapland	1269
Kinfaune Castle	3507	Dunkeld	1558
Grantuity Castle	3489	Melrose	840
Conway Castle	2966	Florence	695
Warwick Castle	2957	Venice	511
Dunrotin Castle	2857		

1854.—THE ALLAN LINE.—Previous to the inauguration of this line of steamships the trade between Great Britain and Canada had been carried on by a superior class of sailing-ships, many of which, during its early history, were commanded by their owners and their sons. Among these early merchant traders to Canada, Mr. Alexander Allan, the father of the family that gives its name to the present Allan Line of steamers, had a prominent place. He was a native of Saltcoats, North Britain, afterwards removed to Glasgow, and owned a numerous fleet of sailing-ships, one of which, in early life, he himself commanded. His eldest son, James, and his third son, Bryce Allan, of Liverpool, followed his example, while Hugh and Andrew established themselves in Montreal, and in 1851 entered into partnership as the successors of Edmonstone & Allan, where they managed the shipping business of the family, and James, when he retired from the sea, formed with Bryce and their youngest brother, Alexander, the now important branch of their business in Liverpool. When the success of screw steamers upon the Atlantic had been assured, the members of the Allan family turned their attention to the advantages to be derived from their employment of such vessels, and established a line of them to run between Liverpool, Quebec, and Montreal during the period of open navigation, and between Liverpool and Portland, Maine, when the St. Lawrence was ice-bound.

The first four steamers of this firm were built by William Denny, of Dumbarton, and the skill of this builder is evinced by the fact that one of these early steamers, the "Anglo-Saxon," of 1637 tons burden, although designed for economy of fuel and capacity for cargo and passengers rather than for speed, made the passage from Quebec to Rock Light, Liverpool, in the then altogether unprecedented short time of nine days and five hours. Built in 1856, she was wrecked on Cape Race April 27, 1863, with a sacrifice of 237 lives.

Before, however, their vessels were finished, the Canadian government, in June, 1852, advertised for the conveyance of the mails between Great Britain and Canada in summer and Portland in the winter. For this service a contract was concluded with Messrs. McKean, McCarty, and Lamont, of Liverpool, who formed a company, and opened the line in the spring of 1853 with a vessel of 500 tons register named the "Geneva." The line was continued for about eighteen months by means of the steamer "Cleopatra," of 1467 tons, two smaller vessels, the "Ottawa" and the "Charity," and the "Canadian," built in 1854, of 1764 tons, the first steamer built for the Messrs. Allan, who had chartered her to the company.

But the service, which was conducted with varying regularity, proving unprofitable, was transferred to the Allans, who undertook, with the fleet they were building specially for this trade, to carry on a fortnightly service to Quebec in summer and a monthly voyage to Portland, Maine, in winter, for the annual subsidy of £24,000. The Crimean War, however, occurring in 1854, offered more remunerative employment to the steamers of the fleet of both contractors, and consequently the regular mail service by the Allan Line, which at first was designated as the "Montreal Ocean Steamship Company," was not commenced until April, 1856. Since then it has been maintained with unbroken regularity, with the exception of various serious losses, which might almost have been anticipated in the early history of the service, considering the dangerous character of the navigation.[1] From a fortnightly line in summer and a monthly line in winter the operations of the company have expanded into a regular weekly service, supplemented by an additional fortnightly mail service between Liverpool and Halifax, extending during the summer to St. Johns, Newfoundland, and continued monthly during the winter, by means of an iceboat, between Halifax and St. Johns, when the latter port cannot be approached by ocean steamships. Steamers of the Allan fleet also trade between Liverpool and Baltimore, and a weekly line is maintained between Glasgow and Canada in the summer. There is also a line consisting of ten steamships, of between 3300 and 2500 tons each, and an aggregate tonnage of 30,100 tons, engaged in what is called the Calcutta or Indian service, and a fleet of twelve iron clipper sailing-ships, with an aggregate tonnage of 16,857 tons, also in the service of the com-

---

[1] The "Indian," built in 1855, 1764 tons, was lost February 19, 1860, on Cape Sable, with a sacrifice of 205 lives; the "Canadian," built in 1854, 1764 tons, lost June 1, 1857, near Quebec, all saved; "Canadian No. 2," sunk by ice in the Straits of Belle Isle, June 4, 1861, 30 lives lost; "Anglo-Saxon," 1673 tons, wrecked on Cape Race, April 27, 1863, 237 lives lost; "Norwegian," wrecked on St. Paul's Island, Cape Breton, June 14, 1863, all saved; "Bohemian," wrecked on Alden's Rock, off the entrance to Portland Harbor, February 22, 1864, 20 lives lost.

pany, trading to all parts of the world, but chiefly to the East Indies. The Messrs. Allan do not insure their vessels, a circumstance which of itself is the very best guarantee that great care will be exercised in the management and navigation of the ships. A rule of this company, carefully observed by the captains, requires that in case of fog the speed must be reduced to *dead slow*, safety being the chief consideration.

Their steamer, the "Hibernian," built in 1861, was the first in the Atlantic trade where deck-houses were covered in by a promenade-deck, stretching from stem to stern, which prevents a sea, when it breaks on board, from filling the passages between the deck-houses and bulwarks. So highly was the plan approved by the British government that the unproductive spaces under this deck were made, by order of the Board of Trade, the subject of a special exemption from tonnage measure by the deck-shelter clause of the Merchant Shipping Act of 1854. Other Atlantic lines adopting this protection obtained like privileges, but difficulties arising in connection with ships of somewhat different construction, which, however, claimed the same exemption, this immunity was abolished.

Some of the vessels of this line are remarkable for their speed. For instance, in October, 1872, the "Polynesian," on her first voyage, made the passage between Quebec and Londonderry in seven days, eighteen hours, and fifty-five minutes; while her sister ship, the "Sarmatian," was engaged by the government to convey the Forty-second Highlanders to the Gold Coast in the Ashantee war. The "Sarmatian" is, by the way, the favorite ship of the Princess Louise, Marchioness of Lorne, and in her she has made all her passages between England and Canada.

The "Hungarian," one of the earliest of these steamers, made the passage from Quebec to Rock Light in nine days, six hours, and thirty-five minutes, or from land to land in *six* days. Another, the "Peruvian," completed one of the fastest round voyages on record on any Atlantic line. On the 16th of December, 1864, she left Moville, the port of call, near Londonderry, at 6.24 P.M., discharged her cargo at Portland, took in her homeward cargo, and sailing, arrived back at Moville on the 10th of January, 1865, at 9.15 A.M., thus making the passage out and home, including detentions at Portland while discharging and loading her cargoes, in *twenty-four days, fifteen hours.*

As a representative ship of the Allan Line we will take the "Sardinian," which was built and had her engines constructed by Messrs. Robert Steele & Co., of Greenock. She measures 400 feet in length between perpendiculars, is 42 feet 3 inches in width of beam, and is 35 feet 8 inches in moulded depth. Her register is 2577 tons measurement, with a gross tonnage of 4376 tons. She is impelled by a pair of inverted, direct-acting, compound high- and low-pressure engines. These engines are supplied with all the most recent improvements for combining power with economy of fuel, and securing smooth and equable working. They are furnished with superheating and surface-condensing apparatus of the most improved construction; and everything which experience could dictate or science suggest to insure efficiency of working has been sedulously applied without stint or regard to first cost. Her high-pressure cylinder measures 60 inches, and her low-pressure cylinder 104 inches in diameter, and the pistons have 4 feet 6 inches of a stroke. The steam for working these powerful engines is generated in ten oblong boilers, which are heated by twenty furnaces, fired athwartship. When working at about full speed the engines make about sixty revolutions, and at that number of revolutions the ship has a regulated and sustained speed of 14 knots per hour, the indicated horse-power being calculated at 2800.

The "Sardinian" was built under special survey to take the highest classification for iron steamships. She is divided into seven water-tight compartments by six water-tight iron bulkheads. Her awning and spar-decks are both iron from stem to stern and from side to side of the ship, and firmly riveted to every deck-beam; her main-deck, also, is of iron from the after hold to the main hold, and from side to side of the ship, except that portion which is occupied by the engine space. In addition to these precautions for insuring extra strength to the hull of the ship, heavy iron stanchions have been introduced on every deck, and at every beam where they could be introduced with advantage.

While thus carefully and thoughtfully providing for the general strength of the structure, and the proportionately important power by which the stately ship is to be impelled on her ocean path, other than subsidiary, although in the aggregate scarcely less important, means for guiding, regulating, and assisting her in the management of her voyaging, in aiding her into and out of dock, and in the no less important operations of loading and stowing and unloading of cargo, together with those numerous appliances for securing comfort to all on board, which are indispensable in some degree, are provided for on the most liberal scale.

The "Sardinian" carries ten large boats, all of which are of the best life-boat construction, and as regards her passenger accommodation she necessarily stands very high, having provision for one hundred and eighty saloon, sixty intermediate, and one thousand steerage. The cabin passengers of the "Sardinian" are carried in the saloon and the state-rooms immediately connected with it. The saloon is 80 feet in length by 41 feet in breadth, and is lofty in the ceiling. It is situated on the awning-deck, and is lighted by a lantern cupola in the centre of the ceiling, augmented by an abundance of side lights, the combination producing an effulgence which, united to the gorgeous furnishings, produces an effect at once gratifying and dazzling. The ceiling is delicately paneled in French white, enriched with gold moldings. The wainscoting of the saloon is richly paneled in highly-polished walnut wood, relieved by a delicate stringing of bright rosewood, the panel-framing, rails, and mounters being of polished teakwood. This is surrounded by a rich gold carved cornice, the interspace between the panels being filled by handsome fluted columns of ebony, with rich gold capitals. The settees are upholstered in crimson velvet. As in the other steamers belonging to this line, the "Sardinian" is furnished with a hot-plate table, from which the passengers are supplied with viands served à la Russe as per carte menu. The saloon is furnished with a piano-forte and a well-selected library of books for the use of the passengers. In short, everything which can conduce to comfort has been abundantly provided, and, as a whole, the saloon, with its rich furniture and graceful surroundings, presents a coup d'œil of rare beauty and magnificence. In connection with the saloon, in two houses on deck are situated additional accommodations for the saloon passengers. Those consist of a ladies' sitting-room or boudoir, which is furnished in a style of quiet yet luxurious beauty, and a charming snuggery fitted up as a smoke-room. The dormitories or state-rooms for the saloon passengers are on the main and upper passenger-decks. They are roomy, capacious, and well-lighted, as well as fully supplied with regulated ventilation. They are elegantly furnished with bed and toilette appliances, and every means has been adopted to secure comfort and safety to all the inmates. This vessel, like others of the fleet, is supplied with electric bells in the cabin department of the ship.

The intermediate passenger berths are placed on the upper passenger-deck, the steerage passengers being located on the upper and second passenger-decks. Both these classes of passengers last referred to are supplied with cooked victuals of the best quality by the ship's stewards in unlimited quantity. The sanitary arrangements throughout the ship are of the most perfect kind. A peculiarity as to carrying steerage passengers by the ships of this line is that the company supplies passengers with the use of a suitable and ample outfit for the voyage, whereby passengers are saved the trouble, inconvenience, and loss consequent on having to supply their own outfit previous to embarking. The outfit consists of patent life-preserving pillows, mattress, pannikin to hold a pint and a half, plate, knife, nickel-plated fork, and nickel-plated spoon. The charge for the use of these articles for the voyage is only a very few shillings. Each berth in the cabin is fitted with a pair of life-saving pillows, specially adapted for fastening to the person in case of emergency.

In 1874 the head of the firm, Hugh Allan, was knighted by the Queen in London for his efforts in establishing steam communication between Canada and the mother country. During the visits of the

HISTORY OF STEAM NAVIGATION. 417

Prince of Wales, Prince Arthur, and other members of the royal family to Canada, he entertained them in princely fashion. He had the finest residence in the city of Montreal, and his hospitality was unbounded.

The Allan Line is still under contract with the governments of Canada and Newfoundland for the conveyance of the mails. Steamships of this line now leave for Portland and Liverpool, *via* Queenstown, every alternate Saturday, and for Boston and Liverpool, *via* Halifax, calling at Londonderry, every alternate Thursday, and Baltimore and Liverpool, *via* Halifax, every alternate Monday, and from Halifax for Liverpool every Saturday.

Sir Hugh Allan, the founder of this great line, died at Edinburgh, suddenly, of heart-disease, December 9, 1882. His decease caused a profound shock and the deepest regret throughout the whole city of Montreal, with which he had been connected for nearly sixty years.

Besides founding and attending to his shipping interests, he was at the head of all great enterprises for building up the city and the country as well, and when he died was president of one of the largest Canadian banks, which he founded, and of twenty-two other public companies, including railways, coal-mining, cotton, woolen, sewing-machine, telegraph, elevators, insurance, rubber, colonization, etc. In all these he had a large amount of capital invested.

His surviving brother, Andrew Allan, who resides now in Montreal, is the present head of the firm. An elder brother died a short time ago in Glasgow, and there are still two surviving in that city. They have limited interests in the firm, but the deceased and Andrew were the principal owners.[1]

---

[1] Sir Hugh Allan was born at Saltcoats, in the County of Ayr, Scotland, on the 29th of September, 1810. In the year 1824 his father removed his residence to Greenock, and in the following spring (1825), Hugh, being then fourteen years of age, was entered as a clerk in the firm of Allan, Kerr & Co. After he had been there about a year his father proposed that he should go out to Canada. He sailed from Greenock for Montreal on the 12th of April, 1826, in the brig "Favorite," and landed at Montreal for the first time on Sunday morning, the 21st of May, 1826. At that time there was only one steam-tug on the St. Lawrence, and no wharves; the city was then in its infancy, with little trade or foreign commerce. He obtained a situation as clerk with the firm of William Kerr & Co., then engaged in the dry-goods trade in St. Paul Street. He visited his home in Scotland in 1830, returning to Canada the following year. Soon afterwards he obtained a situation in the house of James Millar & Co., then engaged in building and sailing ships, and as commission merchants. He remained a clerk to the end of the year 1835, when, some changes taking place in the establishment, he was admitted a partner with Mr. Millar and Mr. Edmonstone, who had been long connected with the house. About the year 1851 the successful establishment of screw steamers on the Atlantic elicited proposals for a line to the river St. Lawrence. Mr. Allan was awarded a contract in 1853. At first the service was fortnightly, but on May 1, 1859, the weekly service was commenced, and has ever since been continued. Sir Hugh Allan was identified with a larger number of commercial and financial corporations than any other gentleman in the Dominion.

He married, September 13, 1844, Matilda, daughter of John Smith, a prominent

The company's transatlantic line is now composed of the following double-engined Clyde-built iron steamships. They are built in water-tight compartments, are unsurpassed for strength, speed, and comfort, are fitted up with all the modern improvements that practical experience can suggest, and have made the fastest time on record.

	Gross Tons.		Gross Tons.
Numidian*	6100	Scandinavian	3000
Parisian	5400	Hanoverian	4000
Sardinian	4650	Buenos Ayrean	3800
Polynesian	4100	Corean	4000
Sarmatian	3600	Grecian	3600
Circassian	4000	Manitoban	3150
Moravian	3650	Canadian 3d	2600
Peruvian	3400	Phœnician	2800
Nova Scotian	3300	Waldensian	2600
Hibernian	3440	Lucerne	2200
Caspian	3200	Newfoundland	1500
Austrian	2700	Acadian	1350
Nestorian	2700	Mersey tender	500
Prussian	3000		

* Building.

The East India Line is composed of the following steamers:

	Tons.		Tons.
City of Manchester	3300	City of London	3500
City of Edinburgh	3500	City of Oxford	2500
City of Canterbury	3500	City of Venice	3500
City of Cambridge	2500	City of Mecca	2500
City of Carthage	2800	City of Poonah	2500

The clipper sailing-ships of the Allan Company are as follows:

	Tons.		Tons.
Glendaruel	1761	Strathearn	1705
Glenmorag	1576	Strathblane	1364
Glenfinert	1530	Ravenscrag	1268
Glenbervie	800	Pomona	1200
Gleniffer	800	Chippewa	1072
Abeona	979	Medora	746
St. Patrick	992	City of Montreal	1062

TOTAL TONNAGE.

Atlantic service	59,916
India service	30,100
Sailing-ships	16,857
Grand total	106,873

Sir Hugh Allan left a fortune estimated at $15,000,000.
dry-goods merchant of Montreal. By this marriage he had thirteen children, twelve of whom survive,—eight daughters and four sons. Four of the former are married to British army officers, and live in England. Lady Allan died over a year ago. He was a life-long member of St. Andrew's Church, and one of the foremost men of the Church of Scotland in Canada. He was knighted by her Majesty in 1871. The cable announcement of his death in Edinburgh created a most profound sensation and called out universal expressions of sincerest regret throughout the Dominion of Canada.

www.ingramcontent.com/pod-product-compliance
Lightning Source LLC
Chambersburg PA
CBHW031418150426
43191CB00006B/319